LIST OF THE OFFICERS OF THE BENGAL ARMY

Printed and bound in Great Britain by Antony Rowe Ltd, Eastbourne

LIST OF THE OFFICERS
OF THE BENGAL ARMY

1758–1834

*Alphabetically Arranged and Annotated
with Biographical and Genealogical
Notices by*

MAJOR V. C. P. HODSON

INDIAN ARMY (RETIRED LIST)
AUTHOR OF 'HISTORICAL RECORDS OF THE VICEROY'S BODY-GUARD'

L - N

NOTICE

SEVENTEEN years having now elapsed since the publication of Part II of this List, some apology is needed for the delay in issuing this, the penultimate volume of the series. Due to many causes—not the least of which has naturally been the recently-concluded War in Europe—it may also be ascribed in great measure to the compiler's belated realization of the magnitude of his self-imposed task, his desire to bring the whole to a worthier conclusion, and his reluctance to take leave of a hobby that has provided for him such interest over a period that now extends to a quarter of a century.

That the intervening years have not been wasted is evidenced, it is hoped, by the many pages of Corrigenda and Addenda to be found at the end of this volume. Further delay in publication might doubtless produce a similar list, almost equally formidable in extent, for there can be no finality to a work of reference of this nature; but the time has now arrived when a bound must be set and the word FINIS inscribed.

We are told that it is better to travel hopefully than to arrive. Seldom can the truth of this aphorism be better exemplified than in cases similar to the present, where 'FINIS' may be regarded as our place of destination.

Having now reached the end of his journey, with the final instalment (S—Z), appendices and index ready for the Press, it only remains for the compiler to thank once again all those who, as formerly, have made his task easier by their generous interest and unstinted assistance in many ways.

V. C. P. H.

August 1945.

CONTENTS OF PART III

	PAGE
NOTICE	v
LACAM, WILLIAM—LYSTER, LYTTLETON	1
MABERT, RICHARD—MYLNE, WILLIAM	104
NAIL, GEORGE—NUTTALL, ADAM	368
OAKE, HENRY—OWEN, WILLIAM	409
PADMAN, SELBY—PYNE, JOHN	443
QUEIROS, JOSEPH (MARY FRANCIS)—QUIN, THOMAS	587
RABAN, GEORGE HIGGINS—RYVES, WILLIAM HENRY	589
CORRIGENDA	715
ADDENDA	731

L

N.B.—Compound names must be sought under the last element of the compound.

N.B.—An asterisk denotes that the name is omitted from *Dodwell & Miles's List*.

N.B.—The figures in brackets following the word "Artillery" refer to the serial No. as given in *Stubbs's List*.

*LACAM, William (1746-1764)., Ensign, Infantry. *b* London 25 Mar. 1746. Cadet (?) Ensign (?) *d.* Calcutta 29 July 1764.
bapt. French Chapel, London. 14th and youngest child of John Lacam and Henrietta his wife. Brother of Benjamin Lacam, free merchant in Calcutta.
Services: N.F.P.

*LACKHAM, Charles. Ensign. Engineers. (Casualty before 1 Feb. 1767.)
Services: Was Ensign and Practitioner Engr. in Aug. 1765. N.F.P.
Refs.: Broome, p. 540.

LAING, Henry (1813-1841). Lieutenant, 27th N.I. *b.* Upper Tooting, Surrey, 2 Oct. 1813. Cadet 1829. Arrived in India 6 Oct. 1830. Ensign (5 June 1830) 6 Oct. 1830. Lieut. 15 Feb. 1836. *d.* Bemaru, nr. Kabul, 23 Nov. 1841: kld. in action.
bapt. Streatham, Surrey, 2 Nov. 1813. Son of Rev. Henry Laing, of Clapham, and Jemima his wife.
Services: d.d. 53rd N.I. 23 Oct. 1830. Actg. Ensign (having been more than 2 yrs. in India) 9 Nov. 1832. Posted to 27th N.I. 20 Aug. 1833. Actg. Adjt. Left Wing 27th N.I. 29 Oct. 1838. First Afghan War 1840-1; comdg. a detachment of his Corps at Kabul Sept. 1840; Nazian Valley 1841; outbreak at Kabul; 2nd expedn. to the village of Bemaru, nr. Kabul, 23 Nov. 1841 (kld.); Lieut. 27th N.I.
Refs.: *The Times*, 14 Mar. 1842. M.I. in Afghan Memorial Church, Bombay.

*LAIRD, Charles (*d.* 1795). Lieutenant and Surgeon. Infantry. Asst. Surg. 21 Jan. 1779. Bt. Surg. 21 May 1781. Country Cadet 24 May 1781. Ensign 24 June 1781. Lieut. 21 July 1781. Surg. 21 Oct. 1783. Struck off 1793. *d.* Florence, Italy, 7 Aug. 1795.

H.B.A.—III   B

Brother of James Laird, *q.v.*, and of Surgeon John Laird, M.M.B., Bengal.

Services : Surg. of the *Stafford* 1774-7 ; of the *Gatton* 1778-9. First Mahratta War 1780-1 ; capture of Gwalior. Given brevet of full Surg. (for gallantry at Gwalior) " during his continuance with Major Popham's detachment". (M.C. 21 May 1781.) Campaign against the Rajah of Benares 1781 ; Patita. Resigned in order to go home on fur. 22 Dec. 1788 ; struck off in 1793 after 5 yrs. absence. Pensioned on Lord Clive's fund 4 July 1792.

Refs. : *Crawford,* i. 231, 232. *Roll of I.M.S.,* No. B. 226.

LAIRD, James (*d.* 1816). Lieutenant. Infantry. Afterwards Surgeon, Bengal Est. Asst. Surg. 7 Apr. 1780. Country Cadet 1781. Ensign 13 Aug. 1781. Lieut. 1 June 1783. Resigned combatant Commission 23 July 1789. Surg. 2 May 1790. Retired 27 May 1801. *d.* Baker St., London, 6 Jan. 1816. Brother of Charles Laird, *q.v. m.* Monghyr 16 May 1791, Miss Eliza Ellerker.

Services : Surg. of the *Seahorse* 1777-8 ; of the *Earl Talbot* 1778-80. Apptd. Cadet 24 May 1781. Benares insurrection 1781. Fur. 3 yrs. on full pay 5 Dec. 1785. M.D., Edin., 1803.

Refs. : *Roll of I.M.S.,* No. B. 241. *Hickey,* ii. 131. *G.M.* 1816, i. 183.

LAKE, Roby Thomas (1774-1802). Lieutenant, Marine Regt. *b.* psh. of St. George the Martyr, London, 15 Sept. 1774. Cadet 1795. Arrived in India 4 Feb. 1797. Ensign 12 Oct. 1796. Lieut. 30 Oct. 1797. *d. unm.* Berhampore, Bengal, 23 Aug. 1802. Son of James Lake, of Gloucester St., London, and Eunice his wife, dau. of William Watton. Brother of Susannah Lloyd, wife of John Farquhar, of Pitscandly, nr. Forfar.

Services : Lieut. 1/9th N.I. in Aug. 1798. Transfd. to 2nd Bengal Eur. Regt. ; to newly formed 2nd Bn. Marine Regt. May 1802. No record of active service.

Refs. : Will dated 13 Jan. 1802 ; proved 10 Sept. 1802.

LALLY, William (1761/62-1803). Lieut. Colonel, 3rd N.I. *b.* 1761/62. Cadet 1776. Admitted 21 July 1776. Ensign 24 Mar. 1777. Lieut. 18 Aug. 1778. Capt. 11 Nov. 1794. Major 31 July 1799. Lt. Col. 8 Dec. 1802. *d.* Barrackpore 20 Jan. 1803, aged 41.

Services : Apptd. Cadet 6 Dec. 1775 ; sailed for India in the *Nassau* 9 Jan. 1776. Lieut. 2/3rd Bengal Eur. Regt. in Oct. 1779.

Operations against the rebel Fateh Shah in the Chapra district, B. & O., Oct. 1781 ; capture of mud fort at Majurah 17 Oct. ; Lieut. 1/32nd N.I. Lieut. 17th Bn. Sepoys in July 1787 ; Capt. 5th N.I. in June 1798 ; transfd. to 3rd N.I. 1798.
Refs.: *India Gazette,* 3 Nov. 1781. Will dated Barrackpore, 23 Oct. 1802 ; proved in 1803. M.I. Barrackpore cemetery.

LAMB, Henry (*d.* 1770). Cadet, Infantry. Cadet 1770. *d.* 1770 : drowned in the Ganges R.
Services : N.F.P.

LAMB, Thomas (1789-1841). Captain. 12th N.I. *b.* Daventry, Northants, 10 Oct. 1789. Cadet 1808. Arrived in India 27 Oct. 1809. Ensign 13 Aug. 1810. Lieut. 16 Dec. 1814. Capt. 13 June 1825. Retired 21 June 1834. *d.* Leamington 15 Sept. 1841. Son of Edward Lamb and Catharine his wife.
Services : Barasat C.C. for 7 mos. Posted Ensign to 12th N.I. Aug. 1810. Lieut. 1/12th N.I. Actg. S.S.O. at Dinapore June 1815. Adjt. Calcutta Native Mil. 19 Jan. 1816 till 7 Aug. 1819. Transfd. to 2/12th N.I. 1817. Bk.Mr. at Fort William 10 July 1819 ; do. (title changed later to Executive Ofr.) at Berhampore 4 Dec. 1819 till Feb. 1832. Dy. Postmr. at Berhampore 3 Dec. 1819. Leave s.c. to Cape 21 Feb. 1822 till 1 Nov. 1824. Transfd. to 12th N.I. (late 1/12th) May 1824. Fur. s.c. 22 Feb. 1832 till retirement. No record of active service.
Refs.: *G.M.* 1841, ii. 556. *The Times,* 20 Sept. 1841.

LAMB, William (1779-1826). Lieut. Colonel Comdt., 51st N.I. *bapt.* St. Thomas's, Winchelsea, Sussex, 14 Mar. 1779. Cadet 1793. Arrived in India 23 Feb. 1795. Ensign 11 Oct. 1794. Lieut. 27 July 1796. Capt. 21 Sept. 1804. Major 16 Dec. 1814. Lt. Col. 1 July 1819. Lt. Col. Comdt. 1 May 1824. *d.* Jubbulpore 24 Sept. 1826, aged 47.

Elder son of Richard Lamb, jurat of Winchelsea corporation, and Sarah Gurley his wife, of Rye. Brother of Samuel Sneyd Lamb. *m.* Calcutta 10 Sept. 1805, Marcia, 2nd dau. of Rev. Patrick Sand(e)s, vicar of Selbridge and Straffan, co. Kildare, by Alicia, dau. of Rev. Jonas Burges, vicar of St. Mark's, Dublin. (*See also* G. A. P. Mee.) (She died 19 Oct. 1844, aged 63.) Father of William and Ynyr Lamb, *qq.v.,* Marcia Louisa Johnstone, wife of William Barr, *q.v.,* and Mary Arabella Burges, wife of George O'Bryen Ottley, *q.v.*
Services : Apptd. Cadet 21 May 1794 ; sailed for India in the

LIST OF THE OFFICERS OF

Royal Admiral 14 Aug. 1794. Lieut. 5th N.I. Accompanied the escort to Sir Home Popham, ambassador to the Arabian states, to Mocha in 1801; returned to Bengal July 1803. Transfd. to newly-raised 1/26th N.I. 1804. Operations in Bundelkhand 1807; Sehlehuganj; Capt. 1/26th N.I. Operations against Lachman Dawa 1809-10; Ajaigarh; Capt. 1/26th N. I. Comy. of supplies to Col. Martindell's detachment Dec. 1809 till May 1810. Apptd. to comd. 2nd Gren. Bn. Dec. 1814. Siege and capture of Hathras; Major comdg. 2nd Gren. Bn. Rejoined 1/26th N.I. Apr. 1817. Third Mahratta War; Dhamoni, Major comdg. 1/26th N.I.; Satanwara, comdg. the force. Posted Lt. Col. to 1/26th N.I. July 1819; Lt. Col. Comdt. to 51st N.I. (late 1/26th) May 1824.
Refs.: Family information. *E.I.M.C.* iii. 426. *A.J.* xxiii. 430. Will dated 1 July 1826; proved 23 Dec. 1826. M.I. at Jubbulpore.

LAMB, William (1808-1867). Colonel. 51st N.I. *b.* Tirowah, Bundelkhand, 29 Nov. 1808. Cadet 1825. Arrived in India 31 May 1826. Ensign 4 Feb. 1826. Lieut. 25 Apr. 1836. Capt. 1 July 1846. Major 11 Sept. 1858. Lt. Col. 27 Apr. 1861. Retired 31 Dec. 1861. Hon. Col. 31 Dec. 1861. *d.* at sea 10 June 1867.

3rd son of William Lamb, *q.v.*, and Marcia his wife. Brother of Ynyr Lamb, *q.v.* *m.* Fatehgarh 25 Oct. 1845, Margaret Oclanis, dau. of William George Lennox, *q.v.* (She died Littlehampton 4 Jan. 1902, aged 75.)

Services: Ensign d.d. 51st N.I. 30 June 1826. Posted to 51st N.I. 26 Sept. 1826. Fur. u.p.a., without pay, 26 Mar. 1831 till 6 Mar. 1833. d.d. 19th N.I. 6 July till 31 Dec. 1833. (? Shekhawat expedn. 1834; Ensign 51st N.I.) Intr. & Qmr. 51st N.I. 8 Apr. 1835 till 27 June 1838. Fur. s.c. 11 May 1838 till 20 July 1841. Intr. & Qmr. 51st N.I. 6 Aug. 1841. A.D.C. to C.-in-C. 1 Oct. 1842. Intr. & Qmr. 51st N.I. 29 July 1843 till Jan. 1845. Actg. 2nd in comd. Kumaon Local Bn. 11 Sept. 1843. Apptd. Postmr. to Army of Exercise 17 Nov. 1843. Gwalior campaign; Maharajpur (Bronze star). 2nd in comd. 2nd Oudh Local Inf. 22 Jan. 1845. Bde. Major Lucknow 24 Nov. 1845 till Feb. 1855. Rejoined 51st N.I. tempy. for active service 7 Oct. 1848. Second Sikh War; siege of Multan; Gujerat; Capt. 51st N.I. (Medal with clasp). D.A.A.G. Pegu Div. 2 Mar. 1855; do. Saugor 1857. A.A.G. Lahore 14 Aug. 1857. Mutiny campaign; defence of Saugor 29 June 1857 till 3 Feb. 1858; action at Zalimpur 28 Feb. 1858 (Medal).

Refs.: Howard & Crisp's Ireland, vi. 50, *s.n.* Inchiquin, B. *G.M.* 1867, ii. 397. *The Times,* 5 Aug. 1867.

LAMB, Ynyr (1807-1871). Bt. Captain. 37th N.I. *b*. Bundelkhand 2 Dec. 1807. Cadet 1824. Arrived in India 1 June 1825. Ensign 11 Dec. 1824. Lieut. 28 Nov. 1826. Bt. Capt. 11 Dec. 1839. Invalided 15 Sept. 1843. Retired 1 May 1851. *d*. 9 Dec. 1871.

2nd son of William Lamb (1779-1826), *q.v.*, and Marcia his wife. Brother of William Lamb, *q.v.*, and grand-nephew of Ynyr Burges, of East Ham, a Dir. of E.I. Co. *m*. Cawnpore 3 May 1828, Miss Mary Fitzpatrick.

Services : Ensign d.d. 31st N.I. 11 June 1825 ; do. 1st Bengal Eur. Regt. 21 June 1825. Posted Ensign to 51st N.I. 1825. Intr. & Qmr. 51st N.I. 12 Apr. 1831 till 8 Apr. 1835. Leave s.c. 1 Mar. 1833 till 15 May 1834. Intr. & Qmr. 51st N.I. 27 June 1838 till 12 Mar. 1840. Fur. s.c. 16 Apr. 1840 till 22 Mar. 1842. Actg. Intr. & Qmr. 25th N.I. 11 July 1842. (? Insurrection in Bundelkhand 1842 ; Bt. Capt. 51st N.I.) Transfd. to 37th N.I. 14 Dec. 1842. Fur. s.c. July 1848 till retirement.

Refs.: Burke's *Landed Gentry of Ireland,* p. 84, *s.n.* Burges, of Parkanaur, co. Tyrone.

LAMBERT, Anthony (1758-1800). Ensign. Infantry. Afterwards a merchant in Calcutta. *b*. Berwick-on-Tweed 5 Aug. 1758. Country Cadet 1781. Ensign 7 Sept. 1781. Resigned 24 July 1782. *d. unm*. Devonshire St., London, 17 Jan. 1800.

Of Greenses, Berwick-on-Tweed. Eldest son of Charles Lambert, of Berwick-on-Tweed, and Jane Malcolm his wife, co-heiress with her sister, Mary Strangeways, of Thomas Malcolm. Brother of Charles Lambert, of the firm of Lambert, Ross & Co., Calcutta merchants ; of Rebecca, mother of Anthony Lambert Swanston, *q.v.* ; and of Jane, wife of Thomas Gilchrist. Cousin-german of the father of Anthony Lambert, *q.v.*

Services : Went out to Bengal in the *Worcester* in 1779 ; apptd. Cadet 10 Apr. 1781. After resigning the Service he became a merchant and agent in Calcutta ; Chairman of the Gen. Bank of India ; Sheriff of Calcutta 1792. Returned to England in 1798.

Refs.: Family information. *A.A.R.* i. 77-8. *G.M.* 1800, i. 285. Will dated 7 Dec. 1799 ; proved 29 Sept. 1800.

LAMBERT, Anthony (1785-1803). Lieutenant, 15th N.I. *b*. Berwick-on-Tweed 3 Feb. 1785. Cadet 1799. Arrived in India 8 Jan. 1801. Ensign 30 Oct. 1800. Lieut. 13 July 1803. *d*. 1 Nov. 1803 : kld. in action at the battle of Laswari.

bapt. Berwick-on-Tweed 6 Feb. 1785. 3rd and youngest son of

6 LIST OF THE OFFICERS OF

Anthony Lambert, of Alnwick, atty. (who was cousin-german of Anthony Lambert, *q.v.*), and Cecily his wife, dau. of John Proctor, of Dunstan Hall. His eldest sister *m.* Charles Hutchinson (1768/69-1805), *q.v.*

Services : Posted Ensign to 2/15th N.I. 17 Apr. 1801. Operations in Jumna Doab 1803 ; Sasni ; Bijaigarh ; Kachaura ; Ensign 2/15th N.I. Second Mahratta War ; battle of Delhi ; Agra ; Laswari (kld.) ; Lieut. 2/15th N.I.

Refs. : Will (Memo. only) dated camp nr. Koil, 28 Aug. 1803.

LAMBERT, Edmund (*d.* 1808). Colonel. 2nd Bengal Eur. Regt. Cadet 1769. Arrived in India 5 Sept. 1769. Ensign 13 Sept. 1769. Lieut. 8 Mar. 1773. Capt. 22 Sept. 1780. Major (?) Lt. Col. 1 June 1796. Col. 29 May 1800. Struck off 29 May 1800. *d.* Bath 17 June 1808.

Of Lavington (of Bromham), Wilts. Elder son of Edward Lambert, of the Middle Temple, and of New Sarum, and Mary, dau. of —— Norris, of Nonsuch. *m.* Calcutta 12 Aug. 1789, Miss Sophia Hepburn. (She died 16 Nov. 1851.)

Services : First Rohilla War ; battle of St. George ; Lieut. 8th Bn. Sepoys. Fur. 19 Nov. 1779 till Nov. 1782. Capt. 3rd Bengal Eur. Regt. in Dec. 1782 ; 2nd Eur. Bn. in July 1787 ; comdg. 17th Bn. Sepoys in Dec. 1788 and Dec. 1792. Fur. 8 Jan. 1793. Transfd. from 1st N.I. to 2nd Bengal Eur. Regt. 21 Apr. 1800.

Refs. : Burke's *Commoners*, i. 67, *s.n.* Lambert, of Boyton. *G.M.* 1808, ii. 657.

LAMBERT, Peter (1761/62-1796). Bt. Captain, 31st N.I. *b.* London 1761/62. Cadet 1781. Arrived in India 23 Oct. 1781. Ensign 27 May 1781. Lieut. 10 Sept. 1782. Bt. Capt. 7 Jan. 1796. *d. unm.* Midnapore, Bengal, 17 Jan. 1796.

Brother of Thomas and William Lambert, both of Bengal, and of Jane Lambert.

Services : Apptd. Cadet 10 Jan. 1781 ; sailed for India in the *Southampton* 13 Mar. 1781, aged 19. Lieut. 31st Bn. Sepoys in July 1787 and Dec. 1792.

Refs. : Will dated 20 Oct. 1795 ; proved 3 Feb. 1796.

LAMBERT, Richard (*d.* 1805). Captain, 24th N.I. Cadet 1783. Admitted 2 Sept. 1783. Ensign 18 Jan. 1785. Lieut. 10 Mar. 1791. Capt. 1 May 1804. *d.* Berhampore, Bengal, 25 Oct. 1805.

Brother of Ann, wife of Joseph Farran, of York St., Dublin,

clerk of pleas, court of exchequer; nephew of Robert Archer; cousin of Richard Lambert, of Princess St., Bristol, merchant. *m.* 1798, Barbara, 4th dau. of John Harvey, of Killiane Castle, co. Wexford, high sheriff co. Wexford 1775. (She *re-m.* Arthur Meadows, of Hermitage, co. Wexford.)

Services: Apptd. Cadet 14 Nov. 1782; sailed for India in the *Lord Macartney* 11 Mar. 1783. Posted to 2nd Eur. Bn. Feb. 1790; to 5th do. 25 Oct. 1792; to 2nd Bn. Sepoys 1792. Fur. 27 Mar. 1797 till 5 Sept. 1799. Transfd. from 1/4th N.I. to 3rd Eur. Regt. Oct. 1798; to 13th N.I. 1798; to newly-raised 24th N.I. in 1804. Bk.Mr. at Berhampore 1803 till death.

Refs.: Burke's *Landed Gentry of Ireland*, p. 317, *s.n.* Hervey, of Killiane. Will dated 25 Jan. 1805; proved 28 Nov. 1805.

LAMBIE, John Cozens (1794-1827). Captain. 2nd L.C. *b.* Jamaica 18 Oct. 1794. Cadet 1810. Cornet 31 May 1816. Lieut. 1 Sept. 1818. Capt. 7 Oct. 1824. Retired 15 Sept. 1825. *d.* Connaught Terr., Paddington, 22 May 1827.

Posthumous son of William Lambie, of Jamaica. Nephew of George Harrison Cozens, of Jamaica, and of William Bryan. Ed. Eton 1805-8.

Services: Passed as Cadet 1 Mar. 1811. Ensign H.M. 14th Ft. 6 Nov. 1812; Lieut. do. 8 Nov. 1814 till 1816, being borne the whole time on the strength of the Bengal Army as a Cadet. Cadet d.d. 2nd N.C. 1812-13. Posted Cornet to 2nd N.C. in 1816; actg. Qmr. do. in 1818. Third Mahratta War; Lieut. 2nd N.C., in Reserve Div. Intr. & Qmr. 2nd L.C. 13 July 1821 till 28 Aug. 1823. Fur. 1823 till retirement.

Refs.: *Eton School Lists*. *A.J.* xxiii. 889. Will dated 1 Mar. 1827; proved 24 Aug. 1829.

LAMBORNE, Charles Wale (*d.* 1818). Lieut. Colonel, 4th N.I. Country Cadet 1781. Admitted 26 Nov. 1781. Ensign 7 Aug. 1782. Lieut. 27 Jan. 1785. Capt. 12 Jan. 1801. Major 24 June 1809. Lt. Col. 16 Dec. 1814. *d.* Bareilly, U.P., 2 Mar. 1818. His natural dau. *m.* Joseph Leverton Revell, *q.v.*

Services: Posted to 4th Eur. Bn. 31 Oct. 1787; transfd. to 9th Bn. Sepoys 15 Oct. 1788. Bt. Capt. 1/5th N.I. in 1798. Capt. Lt. 1/11th N.I. 22 Aug. 1800. Second Mahratta War; defence and capitulation of Shikohabad Sept. 1803 (w.); Capt. 1/11th N.I. Transfd. to newly-raised 24th N.I. in 1804. (? Capture of Gohad 1806; Capt. 2/24th N.I.) Major 2/24th N.I. Comdg. at Saharanpur in 1811. Transfd. as Lt. Col. in Jan. 1815 to comd. newly-raised 2/28th N.I., which was called after him "*Lambroon-ki-Paltan.*" Transfd. to 1/4th N. I. at the end of 1817.

Refs.: Pester, p. 161. Will dated Keitah 24 Sept. 1817; proved 4 May 1818.

LANCAKE, Lewis Robert (*d.* 1779). Lieutenant. Infantry. Cadet 1776. Ensign 7 Apr. 1777. Lieut. 2 Sept. 1778. Resigned 11 Jan. 1779. *bur.* Calcutta 25 May 1779.

Services: Apptd. Cadet 24 Nov. 1775; sailed for India, in the *Nassau* 9 Jan. 1776. N.F.P.

LAND, Sebastian (1780-1857). Colonel. 60th N.I. *b.* Tiverton, Devon, 14 July 1780. Cadet 1800. Arrived in India 17 Sept. 1801. Ensign 1 Nov. 1801. Lieut. 30 Sept. 1803. Capt. 1 Aug. 1818. Major 9 July 1825. Lt. Col. 31 May 1830. Retired 23 Apr. 1834. Hon. Col. 28 Nov. 1854. *d.* Rosamondford, Aylesbeare, Devon, 23 Aug. 1857.

bapt. Tiverton 28 Aug. 1780. Son of Rev. Henry Land and Hannah his wife. Nephew of John Walker. Ed. Blundell's 15 Aug. 1786 till 29 June 1790.

Services: Ensign d.d. 14th N.I. in 1802. Second Mahratta War; Lieut. 11th N.I. Reduction of Kalinjar 1812; Lieut. 2/11th N.I. Adjt. 2/11th N.I. 22 Apr. 1811 till 4 May 1815. Adjt. newly-raised 1/30th N.I. 4 May 1815 till Aug. 1818. Comdg. at Khurda in 1820; Capt. 1/30th N.I. Fur. s.c. 13 Dec. 1823 till 11 May 1827. Transfd. to 60th N.I. (late 2/30th) May 1824. Apptd. to tempy. comd. of troops in Rohilkhand and Kumaon 21 Jan. 1829. Posted as Lt. Col. to 60th N.I. 16 Dec. 1830. Fur. p.a. 22 Dec. 1831 till retirement. Transfd. to 72nd N.I. 4 Oct. 1834, before his retirement had been notified in India.

Refs.: Blundell's School Register. G.M. 1857, ii. 468.

LANDEG, John. Lieut. Colonel. Infantry. Country Cadet 1765. Ensign 8 Aug. 1765. Lieut. 26 Dec. 1766. Capt. 16 May 1770. Major 11 Jan. 1781. Lt. Col. 16 July 1787. Struck off 1793.

Services: Went out to India in a private capacity. Adjt. 3rd Bengal Eur. Regt. in 1766. Apptd. Bk.Mr. to Dinapore Cantt. Apr. 1772; D.Q.M.G. to Col. Champion's Bde. in June 1773. Raised 28th Bn. Sepoys for the service of the Nawab-Wazir of Oudh in 1776; A.Q.M.G. in the field at Belgram in 1777. Apptd. to comd. 22nd N.I. (late 29th Bn.), known as "*Landeg-ki-Paltan,*" 1 Jan. 1781. Fur. on h.p. 2 Oct. 1786 till struck off.

Refs.: Williams, p. 89. *Cardew*, p. 40. *Macpherson*, pp. 90, 133.

THE BENGAL ARMY, 1758-1834

Note: John Landeg, senr. and junr., were both Ensigns in Glam. Regt. of Mil. (embodied 14 Jan. 1761) in 1761.

LANDEG, Lewis (1780-1810). Captain, Pension Est. 17th N.I. *b.* Swansea, co. Glam., 27 June 1780. Cadet 1798. Arrived in India 23 Dec. 1799. Ensign 2 Sept. 1799. Lieut. 28 Oct. 1799. Capt. 4 Apr. 1807. Pensioned 15 Feb. 1808. *d.* Calcutta 2 Dec. 1810.
bapt. Swansea 25 July 1780. Son of Roger Landeg, of Swansea, banker, Major of the Swansea Legion Inf.
Services: Posted Lieut. to 1/17th N.I. 14 Apr. 1801; Capt. Lt. do. 27 Feb. 1807. No record of active service.
Refs.: *G.M.* 1812, i. 497.

*LANDER, John (*d.* 1762). Ensign, Infantry. Cadet (?) Ensign (?) *bur.* Calcutta 1 Oct. 1762.
Services: N.F.P.
Refs.: Burial register of St. John's, Calcutta.

LANDERS, John Edmondstoune (1802-1885). General. 9th N.I. *b.* Clackmannan 26 Sept. 1802. Cadet 1819. Admitted 30 May 1820. Ensign 10 Jan. 1820. Lieut. 11 July 1823. Capt. 31 Mar. 1835. Major 3 Oct. 1848. Lt. Col. 24 Dec. 1853. Bt. Col. 28 Nov. 1854. Maj. Gen. 12 Mar. 1865. Lt. Gen. 9 Dec. 1872. Gen. 1 Oct. 1877. *d.* at his residence, 7 Bryanston St., London, 6 Apr. 1885.
bapt. Clackmannan 11 Oct. 1802. Son of James Landers, of Culross, co. Fife, coal merchant (formerly factor on Clackmannan estate), and Henrietta Edmondstoune his wife. *m.* Dinapore 19 Oct. 1839, Mary Elizabeth Cordelia, only dau. of Gabriel Richard Penny, *q.v.* (She died 7 Jan. 1894.)
Services: Posted Ensign to 2/27th N.I. in 1820. Transfd. as Lieut. to 8th N.I. July 1823; to 9th N.I. (late 1/8th) May 1824. Offg. Adjt. Bareilly Provl. Bn. 13 Dec. 1825. Mily. Sec. and A.D.C. to Presdt. of Council 15 Oct. 1838. Apptd. Comdt. Bhopal Contingent 30 July 1839; received charge 22 Dec. 1839 and comdd. till 15 Dec. 1841. In charge of Bhopal Pol. Agency 14 Nov. 1841 till 12 Jan. 1842. Comdd. Bhopal Contingent 2 Feb. 1842 till 3 Mar. 1848. Comdd. this Contingent in an engagement with a party of insurgents in 1846. Fur. s.c. 5 July 1848 till 8 Oct. 1851. Posted Lt. Col. to 9th N.I. Feb. 1854. Fur. s.c. Mar. 1857 till 1860, and 11 Jan. 1862 till death.
Refs.: Boase. *The Times,* 8 Apr. 1885.

LANDON, Charles Ginkell (1803-1861). Captain. 8th N.I.
b. 18 Aug. 1803. Cadet 1824. Arrived in India 2 Feb. 1826.
Ensign 10 Sept. 1825. Lieut. 8 Jan. 1838. Capt. 30 Dec. 1844.
Retired 7 Mar. 1846. *d.* 18 Woodstock St., Bond St., London, 22 Feb. 1861.
Of Tiverton, Devon. *bapt.* Littlebury, Essex, 26 Nov. 1803. Eldest son of Rev. Charles Richard Landon, B.D., of Richmond, Surrey, rector of Vange, Essex, and Caroline Mann his wife, eldest dau. of Josiah Harrop, of George Yard, Lombard St., London. Cousin-german of John Landon Jones, *q.v. m.* Christ Church, Marylebone, 1 Aug. 1837, Louisa, 5th dau. of Benjamin Aislabie, of Lee Place, Kent. (She died Lyme Regis 29 Jan. 1887, aged 77.) Clare Coll., Camb.
Services: Posted Ensign to 8th N.I. Offg. Adjt. 8th N.I. 7 Oct. 1832. Fur. s.c. 18 Mar. 1834 till 23 Feb. 1838. Apptd. Comdt. of Khurda and Balasore Paik Coys. 9 Sept. 1842. Fur. s.c. 29 Nov. 1843 till retirement. No record of active service.
Refs.: *Howard & Crisp,* xi. 121, *s.n.* Landon. Foster's *Families of Royal Descent,* ii. 864. Burke's *Royal Families,* ped. lxxii. Burke's *Extinct Barts.,* p. 602, *s.n.* Palmer, Bart. *The Times,* 27 Feb. 1861.

LANE, Charles Richard William (1786-1872). General, C.B. 6th N.I. *b.* London 29 Oct. 1786. Cadet 1806. Arrived in India 1 Aug. 1807. Ensign 13 Aug. 1807. Lieut. 7 Mar. 1813. Capt. 30 Jan. 1824. Major 30 Apr. 1835. Lt. Col. 26 Dec. 1841. Col. 25 May 1852. Maj. Gen. 28 Nov. 1854. Lt. Gen. 12 June 1866. Gen. 25 June 1870. *d.* at his residence, Kandahar Villa, Jersey, 18 Feb. 1872.
bapt. St. Martin-in-the-Fields 23 Nov. 1786. Son of John Lane and Melissa his wife. *m.* 1st, Calcutta 18 Mar. 1829, Miss Ursula Palmer. (She died Kensington 9 Sept. 1847, aged 39.) *m.* 2nd, Camberwell, 23 Mar. 1848, Maria, elder dau. of John Gibbs, of Ballynora, co. Cork, Capt. Royal Cork City Mil.
Services: See *D.N.B.* Barasat C.C. 8 mos. Posted Ensign to 1st N.I. 1808. Nepal War 1814-15; Lieut. 2/1st N.I., in 1st Div. (India medal). Capture of Hathras; Lieut. 2/1st N.I. Third Mahratta War; Dhamoni; Mandala; Asirgarh; Lieut. 2/1st N.I. Operations against the Bhils 1823-4; Lieut. 2/1st N.I. Transfd. to 2nd N.I. (late 1/1st) May 1824. First Burma War; Arakan 1825; Capt. 2nd Gren. Bn. (clasp to India medal). Wrecked on the I. of Narguldeep 11 Dec. 1825, whilst en route from Chittagong to Arakan with Rt. Wing 2nd Gren. Bn. Actg. Intr. & Qmr. 2nd

THE BENGAL ARMY, 1758-1834　　　11

Gren. Bn. 31 May 1826. Actg. Asst. to timber agent at Natpur 5 Nov. 1828 till 12 June 1829. In charge of Comst. at Dinapore 2 May 1831. Comdd. 2nd N.I. from July 1837. Leave s.c. to Cape 19 Feb. 1839 till 16 Nov. 1840. First Afghan War 1840-2 ; comdd. the garr. of Kandahar during tempy. absence of Gen. Nott, when that place was assaulted on 10 Mar. 1842 by an Afghan detachment ; reoccupation of Kabul ; Lt. Col. 2nd N.I., with Nott's force (*Lond. Gaz.* 6 Sept. 1842) (Medal—Kandahar, Ghazni, Kabul). Posted Lt. Col. to 2nd N.I. 23 Feb. 1842. Fur. s.c. 12 Aug. 1843 till 1848. Transfd. to 20th N.I. 15 Apr. 1843 ; to 13th N.I. 11 Feb. 1844 ; to 74th N.I. 1848. Fur. p.a. 10 Sept. 1851 till death. Posted Col. to 6th N.I. June 1852. C.B. 24 Dec. 1842.

Refs.: *D.N.B.* *D.I.B.* Boase (in all of which his 2nd christian name is given incorrectly as Edward). *The Times*, 22 Feb. 1872.

Note: In 1824 he sought permission to change his name to Mattenby, but his request was refused by the Indian Govt.

LANE, George (1784-1812). Lieutenant, 8th N.I. *b.* Barningham Down, N. Eppingham, Norfolk, 23 Feb. 1784. Cadet 1800. Arrived in India 6 Feb. 1802. Ensign 27 Dec. 1801. Lieut. 27 Mar. 1804. *d.* Madras 18 July 1812.

Services: Posted Ensign to 8th N.I. in 1802. Second Mahratta War 1803-5 ; Laswari ; Rampura ; operations nr. Tonk Rampura ; assault of Dhalra 21 Mar. 1805, comdd. storming party ; Lieut. 2/8th N.I. (? Storm of Badekh 1806 ; Lieut. 2/8th N.I.) Cashiered by G.C.M. at Cawnpore 22 July 1807 ; restored to the Service in England in 1811 and reposted to 8th N.I. Returned to India and died shortly after landing at Madras.

LANE, John (1792-?). Captain. 7th L.C. *b.* London 4 Jan. 1792. Cadet 1806. Arrived in India 1 Aug. 1807. Cornet 29 July 1807. Lieut. 23 Nov. 1815. Capt. 1 May 1819. Pensioned in India 16 Sept. 1825. Struck off in England 3 June 1830.

bapt. St. James's, Westminster, 31 Jan. 1792. Eldest son of Richard Lane and Margaret his wife, *née* Cowing.

Services: Posted Cornet to 7th N.C. and served throughout with that Regt. Operations in Oudh 1808. Settlement of Hariana 1809-10. Nepal War 1814-15 ; Cornet 7th N.C., in 2nd Div. Siege and capture of Hathras 1817. Third Mahratta War ; Dhamoni ; Mandala ; Multai ; Harna. Fur. 1822 till 19 May 1825, and 1828 till struck off.

LANE, John Theophilus (1803-1895). General, C.B. Colonel Comdt. R.A. (522) b. Plymouth 3 July 1803. Cadet 1820. Arrived in India 12 Nov. 1821. 2nd Lieut. 9 June 1821. Lieut. 1 May 1824. Capt. 22 Aug. 1838. Major 10 Feb. 1849. Lt. Col. 30 Oct. 1855. Col. 18 Feb. 1861. Maj. Gen. 8 June 1856. Lt. Gen. 6 Mar. 1868. Gen. 6 Oct. 1872. Col. Comdt. 7 Oct. 1872. Retired 25 June 1881. d. Addiscombe, Surrey, 1 June 1895.

bapt. Charles, Plymouth, 21 Aug. 1803. Son of Charles Henry T. Lane, Capt. R.N., Comr. of Barbados, and Elizabeth Parmenter his wife. m. Calcutta 16 May 1826, Miss Lydia Emma Blechynden. (See also John Henry Warner.) Addiscombe Cadet 1818 till 9 June 1821.

Services : First Burma War ; Assam 1825 ; Lieut. 6th Golandaz Bn., with force under Bdr. Thomas Shuldam, q.v. Fur. s.c. 8 Jan. 1829 till 4 Aug. 1831. In charge of Agra Mag. 13 Oct. 1833. Shekhawat expedn. 1834. Adjt. & Qmr. Nimach Div. Art. 19 Jan. 1836 till 14 Feb. 1839. Reduction of Jhansi 1838-9. Apptd. Comy. of Ord. to Gen. Pollock's force 23 Feb. 1842. First Afghan War 1842 ; forcing of Khyber Pass in Apr. ; Mamu Khel (*Lond. Gaz.* 8 Nov. 1842) ; Tazin ; reoccupation of Kabul ; rearguard action under Maj.-Gen. John McCaskill Nov. 1842 ; Comy. of Ord. (Medal). Posted to 2nd Troop 3rd Bde. H.A. 7 Mar. 1843. Gwalior campaign ; Maharajpur (ib. 8 Mar. 1844) ; Bt. Major comdg. 2nd Troop 3rd Bde. (Bronze star). First Sikh War ; Aliwal ; Sobraon ; Bt. Lt. Col. comdg. 2nd Troop 3rd Bde. (Medal with clasp). Second Sikh War ; Ramnagar ; Chilianwala ; Gujerat ; Bt. Lt. Col. 2nd Troop 3rd Bde. (Medal with 2 clasps). To comd. Art. Div. at Wazirabad 21 Dec. 1849. Posted to 3rd Bn. Foot Art. 5 Sept. 1850 ; to 4th Bn. 15 Oct. 1854 ; to 6th Bn. 17 Jan. 1855 ; to 9th Bn. Jan. 1856. Bdr. 2 cl., comdg. at Thayetmyo, Burma, 22 Dec. 1854 till 1856. C.B. 27 June 1846.

Refs. : Burke's *Landed Gentry*, 15th edn., p. 1325, s.n. Lane, of Pemberton House, Chester. *The Times*, 5 June 1895 ; 6 June, p. 6. Boase.

LANE, John Thomas (1794-1825). Lieutenant, 37th N.I. b. co. Dublin 18 Nov. 1794. Cadet 1812. Ensign 30 Sept. 1814. Lieut. 5 Sept. 1817. d. Calcutta 6 May 1825.

Son of William Lane, q.v., and Margaret his wife. Nephew of Jacob Comac, q.v. Addiscombe Cadet 2 Mar. 1811 till 28 Feb. 1812, when removed to Inf.

Services : Posted Ensign to 2/18th N.I. in 1815. Nepal War

THE BENGAL ARMY, 1758-1834

1816 ; Ensign 2/18th N.I., with 8th Gren. Bn., in 2nd Bde. Left Column. Fur. 28 Mar. 1818 till 1822. Fur. s.c. 4 May 1825, but died before embarkation.

Refs. : Burke's *Landed Gentry*, 12th edn., p. 1109, *s.n.* Lane, of King's Bromley, Staffs. *Calcutta Monthly Journal*, May 1825.

*LANE, Pynsent (1789-1805). Cadet, Infantry. *b.* 27 June 1789. Cadet 1805. Never arrived in India. *d.* at sea 5 Feb. 1805 : lost in the *Earl of Abergavenny* off Portland. (See note to Charles Davis or Davies.)

bapt. Sawbridgeworth, Herts., 30 July 1789. 2nd son of Rev. John Lane, rector of Sawbridgeworth, and High Roading, Essex, and Molly Impey his wife, niece of Sir Elijah Impey, C. J. Bengal.

Refs. : Burke's *Landed Gentry*, 11th edn., p. 976, *s.n.* Lane, of Glenden, co. Dorset. *G.M.* 1805, i. 190.

LANE, Robert Cooper (1782-1804). Lieutenant, 4th N.I. *b.* Bristol 28 Aug. 1782. Cadet 1796. Arrived in India 7 Nov. 1798. Ensign 16 Oct. 1797. Lieut. 10 Sept. 1798. *d.* Agra 23 Sept. 1804.

bapt. St. Stephen's, Bristol, 28 Aug. 1782. Son of Michael Lane and Susannah his wife.

Services : Posted Lieut. to 4th N.I. Nov. 1798, and served throughout with that Regt. (? Second Mahratta War ; storm of Aligarh ; Lieut. 4th N.I.)

LANE, William (*d.* 1776). Captain, Infantry. Transfd. as Lieut. from H.M.S. Lieut. 2 Sept. 1768. Capt. 6 July 1776. *d.* Fyzabad, U.P., Dec. 1776 : kld.

Brother of Jonathan and Obadiah Lane.[1] Nephew of Ann Lane of Chelsea, and uncle of John Lane.

Services : Lieut. of Capt. Moses Lilly's Independent Coy. (4th Div., Senegal) 7 Mar. 1760 ; Lieut. newly-raised 111th Foot 25 June 1762 ; h.p. do. 1763 till death. Transfd. as Lieut. to Bengal Army, " to rank next below Lieut. Halling." (M.C. 1 Sept. 1768.)

Refs. : Will dated Rummiahpore 11 Dec. 1776 ; proved 29 Mar. 1777.

[1] *Note* : (? Obadiah Lane, of Emmanuel Coll., Camb. ; B.A. 1756 ; M.A. 1759.)

LANE, William (1753-1814). Colonel. 14th N.I. Sometime Lt. Govr. of St. Helena. *bapt.* 27 July 1753. Cadet 1767. Ensign 5 Dec. 1767. Lieut. 13 Oct. 1769. Capt. 25 Feb. 1778.

Major 21 Sept. 1781. Resigned 17 Jan. 1785. Lt. Col. St. Helena Inf. Regt. 8 Mar. 1803. *d.* Lanesville, nr. Dublin (? Apr.) 1814.

Of Lanesville. 5th son of Thomas Lane, of Bentley, Staffs., and Anne Sayer his 2nd wife. *m.* Greenmount Lodge, co. Louth, Aug. 1787, Margaret, dau. of John Camac, of Lurgan, co. Armagh, and sister of Jacob Camac, *q.v.* (*See also* Richard Scott.) Father of John Thomas Lane, *q.v.*

Services : Was A.D.C. to Col. Alexander Champion, *q.v.*, in Jan. 1770. Capt. 2/2nd Bengal Eur. Regt. in 1779; given comd. of a Sepoy Bn. 22 Mar. 1780. Operations against the Rajah of Benares 1781; Patita; capture of Bijaigarh, C.I., comdg. a Bn. of Sepoys (? 2/35th) under William Popham, *q.v.* Promoted Bt. Major by Warren Hastings in Sept. 1781, " in testimony of his merit and conduct at Patita," and given tempy. comd. of 7th N.I. in Dec. 1781; comdg. do. in Jan. 1784, when he was granted leave s.c. to C.G.H.; comdg. 14th N.I. on resignation. Lieut. Govr. of St. Helena, under Robert Patton, *q.v.*, 1802-7. Served in expedn. to Buenos Ayres under Sir Home Popham in 1806; Lt. Col. comdg. 4 Coys. St. Helena Inf. Regt. Actg. Govr. July 1807-July 1808.

Refs. : Burke's *Landed Gentry*, 12th edn., p. 1109, *s.n.* Lane, of King's Bromley, Staffs. *Genealogical Mag.*, i. 349 (Oct. 1897). *E.I.M.C.* iii. 358. *Forrest*, iii. 813. *G.M.* 1814, i. 524.

LANG, John (1808-1882). Colonel. 36th N.I. *b.* Glasgow 9 Jan. 1808. Cadet 1823. Arrived in India 19 May 1824. Ensign 16 Jan. 1824. Lieut. 9 July 1825. Capt. 25 July 1844. Bt. Major 7 June 1849. Bt. Lt. Col. 28 Nov. 1854. Retired 26 Dec. 1856. Hon. Col. 26 Dec. 1856. *d.* 56 Ladbroke Grove, Notting Hill, 10 Mar. 1882.

2nd son of Gilbert Lang, of Glasgow, merchant, and Elizabeth McFie his wife. Grand-nephew of Sir James Shaw, 1st Bart. of Kilmarnock, Chamberlain of London (*D.N.B.*). *m.* Dacca 14 Jan. 1845, Frances Catherine, 2nd dau. of Christopher Godby, *q.v.*, and widow of Charles Barwell, of Calcutta. (She died 14 May 1895, aged 72.) Glasgow Univ.; matric. 1821.

Services : Posted Ensign to 30th N.I. in 1824. Transfd. as Lieut. to 36th N.I. July 1825. Fur. s.c. 18 July 1825 till 27 Oct.. 1827. Intr. & Qmr. 36th N.I. 28 Sept. 1829 till 9 Oct. 1844. Shekhawat expedn. 1834; Lieut. 36th N.I. Offg. D.A.A.G. Dinapore Div. 22 Dec. 1843. Executive Ofr. Barisal Div., P.W.D., 30 Dec. 1844. Mily. Sec. to Presdt. of Council and Dy. Govr. of Bengal 1845-6. Offg. Supt. of Nadia rivers, P.W.D., till Oct. 1848.

THE BENGAL ARMY, 1758-1834   15

Second Sikh War; Ramnagar; Chenab; Chilianwala; Postmr. on H.Q. Staff; Gujerat; Capt. comdg. 36th N.I. (Medal with 2 clasps). Supt. Nadia rivers 10 Sept. 1849 till 12 Dec. 1856. Offg. A.G.G. at Murshidabad 29 May 1851. Fur. s.c. 6 mos. July 1855.
Refs.: *De La Ferté*, p. 46. *The Times*, 14 Mar. 1882.

LANG, Thomas. Lieutenant. Infantry. Country Cadet 1768. Ensign 22 Jan. 1769. Lieut. 21 May 1770. Resigned 1 Nov. 1776.

Services: Came out to India in a private capacity; apptd. Cadet by Govr. Verelst 2 Aug. 1768. Employed as Asst. Field Engr. 1771-6.

LANGDON, Charles (1784-1805). Lieutenant, 25th N.I. *b.* Montacute, Somerset, 19 Aug. 1784. Cadet 1803. Arrived in India 2 Dec. 1804. Ensign 15 Nov. 1804. Lieut. 15 Nov. 1804. *d.* Gwalior 14 Nov. 1805.

bapt. Montacute 10 Sept. 1784. Son of William Langdon (? Rev. William Langdon, B.D., chaplain to George III) and Elizabeth his wife.
Services: Posted Lieut. to newly-raised 25th N.I. (? Second Mahratta War; defeat of Kushal Rao at Adalatnagar; Lieut. 1/25th N.I.)

LANGLEY, William (1760-1778). Lieutenant, Infantry. *bapt.* St. George the Martyr, Middlesex, 5 Nov. 1760. Cadet 1778. Ensign 1778. Lieut. 1778. *d.* Contai, Bengal, Sept. 1778.

4th son of Arnold Langley, of Golding Hall, Salop, surgeon, and Elizabeth Lear his 1st wife. Ed. Charterhouse; admitted a Poor Scholar 25 July 1771; left 1778.
Services: Sailed for India in the *Mount Stewart* 9 Feb. 1778, aged 17. Died immediately after his arrival in Bengal whilst still unposted.
Refs.: Burke's *Family Records*, p. 372, *s.n.* Langley. *Howard & Crisp* (*Notes*), iv. 94. *Alumni Carthusiani*.

LANGSLOW, Richard (1786-1863). Captain. 22nd N.I. *bapt.* St. Lawrence's, Ludlow, Salop, 10 Mar. 1786. Cadet 1800. Arrived in India 14 Oct. 1801. Ensign 7 Oct. 1801. Lieut. 30 Sept. 1803. Capt. 1 Sept. 1815. Invalided 16 June 1816. Retired 22 Sept. 1819. *d.* at his residence, Halton, Hounslow, Middlesex, 4 Jan. 1863, aged 75.

Son of Richard Langslow and Sarah his wife. Nephew of Robert Phillips, *q.v. m.* (?) [1]

Services : Ensign d.d. 2/4th N.I. Posted Ensign to 1/7th N.I. Transfd. to newly-raised 2/22nd N.I. in 1804. Second Mahratta War ; battle and capture of Deig ; Bhurtpore ; Lieut. 2/22nd N.I. (India medal). Offg. Adjt. 2/22nd N.I. in 1805. Fur. s.c. 28 Apr. 1809 till 1815. Capt. 1st Somerset Mil. 2 Aug. 1810 till 1814. Nepal War 1816 ; Capt 2/22nd N.I., in 3rd Bde. Centre Column (clasp to India medal). Fur. s.c. 1817 till retirement.

Refs. : *E.I.M.C.* iii. 197-202. *G.M.* 1863, i. 259. *The Times*, 6 Jan. 1863.

[1] *Note :* His eldest child was born in Africa, the 2nd in Asia, the 3rd in N. America, and the 5th at Halton House, Middlesex. (*G.M.* 1821.) His youngest son d. U.S.A. 12 Nov. 1899, aged 69.

LANGTON, Richard (1800-?). Ensign. 30th N.I. *b.* London 19 Feb. 1800. Cadet 1819. Ensign 4 Mar. 1820. Resigned 17 Nov. 1821.

bapt. All Hallows, Bread St., Middlesex, 19 July 1801. Son of Zachary Langton, of London, merchant, and Elizabeth his wife, dau. of Richard Rowe, of London.

Services : Posted Ensign to 30th N.I. in 1820. No record of active service.

Refs. : Burke's *Landed Gentry*, 2nd edn., p. 692, *s.n.* Langton, of Liverpool.

LARDNER, Frederick Baratty (1802-1840). Lieutenant. 58th N.I. *b.* W. Teignmouth, Devon, 3 Nov. 1802. Cadet 1823. Arrived in India 16 Oct. 1824. Ensign 13 June 1824. Lieut. 11 Feb. 1826. Resigned 16 Apr. 1838. *d.* Calcutta 26 Sept. 1840.

bapt. W. Teignmouth 2 Dec. 1802. Son of James Lardner, of Tiverton, Capt. E. Devon Yeomanry Cav., and Harriet his wife, only child of Philip Stowey, of Kenbury, Devon. *m.* Calcutta 23 July 1829, Eliza, dau. of Isaac Beardsmore, keeper of the insane hospital at Bhowanipore, Calcutta, and widow of William Senior, *q.v.* (? She died at sea 1844.)

Services : Posted Ensign to 69th N.I. 31 Mar. 1825. Transfd. to 17th N.I. 1825 ; to 58th N.I. 15 Feb. 1830. No record of active service.

Refs. : M.I. at Bhowanipore.

LARKINS, George (1807-1857). Major, Artillery. (580) *bapt.* Lewisham, Kent, 22 Dec. 1807. Cadet 1825. Arrived in India

THE BENGAL ARMY, 1758-1834

20 May 1826. 2nd Lieut. 25 Oct. 1825. Lieut. 2 Sept. 1832. Capt. 3 July 1845. Major 30 Oct. 1855. *d.* Cawnpore 27 June 1857 : massacred by mutineers.

5th and youngest son of John Pascal Larkins, Comdr. of the *Warren Hastings* East Indiaman, and Mary Ann his wife, dau. of Capt. Henry Morse Sampson, E.I.C.N.S. Cousin-german of the mother of John Pascal Walker, *q.v. m.* 1st, Muttra 13 Jan. 1834, Elizabeth Georgina Belvidere, eldest dau. of Thomas Cade Battley, of Willbrook, and sister of Richard Edmond Battley, *q.v.* (She died Cawnpore 29 July 1837.) *m.* 2nd, Meerut 15 Mar. 1838, Emma Carnaghan. (She was massacred with him.) Addiscombe Cadet 1823-5.

Services : Transfd. from 4th Coy. 1st Bn. Foot Art. to 2nd Troop 1st Bde. H.A. 4 Mar. 1831. Leave p.a. 6 mos. to Bombay 11 Mar. 1831. Served with 3rd Troop 2nd Bde. 1835-43. First Afghan War 1842 ; forcing of Khyber ; reoccupation of Kabul ; Bt. Capt. 3rd Troop 2nd Bde., with Gen. Pollock's force (Medal). Fur. s.c. 5 Mar. 1844 till 1846. Posted as Major to 9th Bn. Foot Art. Jan. 1856 ; to 7th Bn. 19 Nov. 1856.

Refs. : Family information. *Bath Chron.* 1 Oct. 1857. M.I. All Saints Memorial Church, Cawnpore.

LA TOUCHE, Peter (1799-1849). Bt. Major, 7th N.I. *bapt.* Rathfarnham, co. Dublin, 20 Apr. 1799. Cadet 1817. Admitted 19 Sept. 1818. Ensign 26 May 1818. Lieut. 23 Oct. 1819. Capt. 12 Dec. 1831. Bt. Major 9 Nov. 1846. *d.* Almora, U.P., 16 May 1849.

4th son of David La Touche, of Marlay, Col. of the Carlow Mil., M.P. for that Co., and Lady Cecilia his wife, dau. of Joseph, 1st Earl of Milltown. 1st cousin once removed of Joseph Leeson, *q.v. m.* 1st, Kaitha, U.P., 4 Aug. 1828, Fanny, 3rd dau. of William George Maxwell, *q.v.* (*See also* Charles Henry Boisragon.) (She died Kaitha 20 July 1831.) *m.* 2nd, Cape Town 11 Sept. 1833, Ellen Maria Johanna, only dau. of Charles Bestandig, of German extraction, from Göttingen. (She died Bath 1 July 1845.)

Services : d,d. 18th N.I. 1819 ; posted Lieut. to 2/4th N.I. 1820. Fur. p.a. 17 May 1821 till 16 Jan. 1823. Transfd. to 7th N.I. (late 1/4th) May 1824. Adjt. Farrukhabad Provl. Bn. 31 May 1824 till 29 Aug. 1826. Siege and capture of Bhurtpore ; Bde. Major 5th Inf. Bde., 2nd Div. Bde. Major Bundelkhand 29 Aug. 1826 ; do. Nasirabad 5 Jan. 1832. Leave s.c. to Cape 20 Dec. 1832 till 10 Nov. 1834. Offg. Mily. Sec. to Govr. of Agra 20 Mar. 1835 till

13 Apr. 1836. Bde. Major Nasirabad 1836; do. Rajputana F.F. 1840 till death.

Refs.: Burke's *Landed Gentry of Ireland,* p. 384, *s.n.* La Touche, of Bellevue, co. Wicklow. *Mundy,* ii. 336. Will dated 14 May 1849; proved 22 July 1850. M.I. Almora.

LATTER, Barré Richard William (1777-1822). Major, 13th N.I. *b.* London 22 July 1777. Cadet 1795. Arrived in India 12 Feb. 1797. Ensign 20 Nov. 1796. Lieut. 30 Oct. 1797. Capt. 2 Nov. 1805. Major 3 Sept. 1818. *d.* Kishanganj, B. & O., 12 Sept. 1822.

bapt. Marylebone 5 Sept. 1777. 2nd son of Thomas Latter, of Harley St., London, and Elizabeth his wife. Brother of Francis Latter, *q.v. m.* Berhampore 11 Jan. 1814, Julia Ann, sister of Rev. Richard Jeffreys, rector of Cockfield, Suffolk. Ed. Rugby; admitted 1788. Admitted Lincoln's Inn 11 Nov. 1791.

Services: Lieut. 13th N.I. in 1798; Adjt. 2/13th N.I. in 1803; Adjt. & Qmr. 13th N.I. 1804-5. Operations in Bundelkhand 1805-6; Capt. 2/13th N.I. Bde. Major in Bundelkhand 1806-7; do. at Muttra 1808; do. Rewari and Delhi 31 Aug. 1809; do. at the Presdy. 1812-13. Comdd. Rangpur Local Bn. 11 Sept. 1813 till death. Nepal War 1814-15; Capt. comdg. a mixed force of 2,000 native levies, including the Rangpur Local Bn., employed in guarding the northern marches from the Kosi R., B. & O., eastward. Transfd. as Major to 1/13th N.I. 1818. Leave to Mauritius 1821-2. Collected Thibetan MSS. for a dictionary.

Refs.: *Rugby School Register.* Will dated Titalya, 22 June 1819; codicil dated 4 Apr. 1822; proved 12 Oct. 1822.

LATTER, Francis (1776-1808). Capt. Lieutenant, 2nd N.C. *b.* London 18 Jan. 1776. Cadet 1795. Arrived in India 20 Sept. 1797. Cornet 14 Oct. 1796. Lieut. 29 May 1800. Capt. Lt. 11 Mar. 1805. *d.* Monghyr, B. & O., 2 Apr. 1808.

bapt. St. John Baptist, precincts of the Savoy, London, 13 Feb. 1776. Eldest son of Thomas Latter and Elizabeth his wife. Brother of Robert James Latter, *q.v. m.* Margery. (She died 23 Aug. 1852.) Lincoln's Inn; admitted 12 May 1786.

Services: Posted Cornet to 2nd N.C. Operations in Jumna Doab 1803; Lieut. 2nd N.C. Second Mahratta War; battle of Delhi; Laswari; Lieut. 2nd N.C. Fur. 4 Mar. 1804 till 2 Aug. 1807.

Refs.: Will dated Monghyr 15 Feb. 1808; proved 9 May 1808. M.I. at Monghyr.

THE BENGAL ARMY, 1758-1834   19

LATTER, Robert James (1780-1855). General. Colonel 66th N.I. b. 17 May 1780. Cadet 1795. Arrived in India 12 Feb. 1797. Ensign 21 Oct. 1796. Lieut. 30 Oct. 1797. Capt. 21 Sept. 1804. Major 16 Dec. 1814. Lt. Col. 24 Jan. 1819. Lt. Col. Comdt. 1 May 1824. Col. 5 June 1829. Maj. Gen. 10 Jan. 1837. Lt. Gen. 9 Nov. 1846. Gen. 20 June 1854. d. 66 Oxford Terr., London, 25 Feb. 1855.

bapt. Marylebone 18 Oct. 1780. Youngest son of Thomas Latter and Elizabeth his wife. Brother of Barré Richard William Latter, *q.v. m.* Calcutta 10 May 1817, Clara, sister of James George Allerton Rice, *q.v.,* and widow of John Nathaniel Sealy, B.C.S.

Services : Midshipman R.N. 1794 ; apptd. to the *Fox* frigate (Capt. Malcolm Pulteney), and served on N. American station. Approved as Cadet 4 Mar. 1796. Adjt. 1/8th N.I. 1803-4. Operations in Jumna Doab 1803 ; Sasni ; Bijaigarh ; Lieut. 1/8th N.I. Second Mahratta War ; operations to S.W. of Delhi under Lt.-Col. G. Ball, *q.v.,* 1803 ; Narnaul ; Kanun ; battle and capture of Deig 1804 ; Bhurtpore (s.w. by musket ball in the head 9 Jan. 1805) ; Capt. 1/8th N.I. (India medal). Capt. Lt. 8th N.I. 27 Aug. 1804. Fur. s.c. 18 Feb. 1808 till 14 Nov. 1810. Nepal War 1814 ; Capt. 1/8th N.I., in 4th Div. Posted as Major to newly-raised 1/30th N.I. Jan. 1815. This Bn. (now 4th Bn. 7th Rajput Regt.) was called after him "*Latter-ki-Paltan.*" Nepal War 1816 ; Major comdg. 1/30th N.I., in 4th Bde. Centre Column (clasp to India medal). Lt. Col. 1/30th N.I. Transfd. to 2nd N.I. 1823 ; as Lt. Col. Comdt. to 66th N.I. May 1824. Fur. s.c. 23 Jan. 1823 till death. Granted a special wound pension of £90 *p.a.* 8 Nov. 1826. Col. 66th N.I. June 1829 till death.

Refs.: Memoir pub. by Mrs. E. C. Baillie in 1870 (portrait). *E.I.M.C.* ii. 346-7. *N. & Q.* 11S. ix. 215. *G.M.* 1855, i. 445. *I.M.* 3 Mar. 1855, p. 115. *Boase.*

LAUDER, James. Ensign. Infantry. Cadet 1762. Ensign 12 July 1762. Resigned May 1766.

Services : Transfd. to 3rd Bn. Sepoys 5 Dec. 1764. Resigned his Commission during the "Batta mutiny."

Note : (*Perhaps* 3rd son of Frederick Lawder, of Mough, co. Leitrim, and Rebecca his wife, dau. of Christopher Rynd. *d.s.p.* India. Cf. *Misc. Gen. et Her.* N.S. iv. 280.)

LAUDER, Richard (*d.* 1770). Capt. Lieutenant, Artillery. (48) Cadet (?) Fireworker 12 Aug. 1763. 2nd Lieut. 13 Mar. 1765.

Lieut. Jan. 1767. Capt. Lt. 6 Aug. 1768. *bur.* Calcutta 7 July 1770.

Brother of Helena Lauder.

Services: In 2nd Coy. Art. in Aug. 1765; resigned during the " Batta mutiny " in May 1766; readmitted 13 June 1766. Tried by C. M. at Allahabad June 1769.

*LAUDER, William (*d.* 1763). Ensign, Infantry.[1] Cadet (?) Ensign (?) *d.v.p.*; *bur.* Calcutta 4 Jan. 1763. Eldest son of Sir Andrew Lauder, 5th Bart., of Fountainhall, and Isobel his wife and cousin, only child of William Dick, of Grange. Grand-uncle of Sir John Dick-Lauder, 8th Bart., *q.v.*

Services: N.F.P.

Refs.: *G.E.C. Complete Baronetage,* iv. 360. *Scots Mag.* 1764, p. 55.

[1] *Note:* Although it cannot be stated definitely that he held a Commission in H.E.I.C.S., yet this would appear to be so. He has not been traced in *I.O. Rec.* nor can he be identified as belonging to H.M.S.

DICK-LAUDER, Sir John, eighth baronet (1813-1867). Lieutenant. 47th N.I. *b.* Relugas, Edinkillie, co. Moray, 21 Apr. 1813. Cadet 1834. Arrived in India 28 July 1835. Ensign (13 June 1835) 26 Oct. 1835. Lieut. 15 Dec. 1838. Retired 19 May 1847. *d.* Bournemouth 23 Mar. 1867.

8th Bart., of Fountain Hall, co. Haddington. *s.* 29 May 1848. D.L. co. Midlothian; J.P. co. Wigton. Elder son of Sir Thomas Dick Lauder, of Grange House, Edinburgh, 7th Bart., and Charles Anne his wife, only child of George Cumin, of Relugas. *m.* 22 May 1845, Lady Anne Dalrymple, 2nd dau. of North, 9th Earl of Stair. (She died 10 Aug. 1919.)

Services: " In early life served for 2 yrs. in the Portuguese Liberating Army." (*G.M.*) Ensign d.d. 5th N.I. 9 Oct. 1835; posted to 37th N.I. 28 June 1836; transfd. to 47th N.I. 28 Aug. 1838. Adjt. Cav. of Jalaun Corps (became Bundelkhand Legion) 14 Feb. 1839. Disturbances in Bundelkhand 1840-1; Jigni; Chirgaon. Actg. Capt. Comdt. of Cav., Bundelkhand Legion, 24 Jan. 1842. Leave s.c. to Singapore and China 12 Aug. 1843. Adjt. Cav. of Bundelkhand Legion 13 June 1844. Fur. s.c. 19 Nov. 1844 till retirement.

Refs.: Burke's *Peerage,* 1923, p. 1342, *s.n.* Dick-Lauder, Bart. Boase. Walford. *G.M.* 1867, i. 670, 683. *I.L.N.* 6 Apr. 1867, p. 347.

THE BENGAL ARMY, 1758-1834 21

LAUGHTON, John (1811-1861). Colonel, Engineers. *b.* Colombo, Ceylon, 5 Apr. 1811. Cadet 1828. Arrived in India 16 Feb. 1830. 2nd Lieut. 12 June 1828. Lieut. 3 Feb. 1839. Capt. 11 Nov. 1846. Local Major (in Persia) 2 June 1837. Major 10 Mar. 1857. Lt. Col. 27 Aug. 1858. Col. 18 Feb. 1861. *d.* Simla 18 Dec. 1861.

Son of George Laughton, of Fareham, Hants, and Eliza Hardinge his wife, eldest dau. of John Pieter Baumgardt, sister of Francis Robert Baumgardt, *q.v.*, and of the wife of William White Moore, *q.v.* His sister *m.* Sir Thomas Erskine May, K.C.B., afterwards 1st Baron Farnborough, of Farnborough (*D.N.B.*). *m.* during his service in Persia a dau. of Rhus Khan, a Persian. Addiscombe Cadet 1827 till 12 June 1828. Chatham 1829.

Services: Adjt. Corps of Engrs. 4 May 1830 till Apr. 1831. P.W.D., N.W.P., Apr. 1831. Asst. to Civil Architect at Calcutta 24 June 1831 till Aug. 1832. Adjt. Engrs. 25 Aug. 1832 till 21 Sept. 1833. Offg. Executive Engr. 2nd (Berhampore) Div. 2 Oct. 1832. Apptd. to serve with disciplined troops in Persia under Major Pasmore, *q.v.*, 1 Aug. 1833; sailed for Bushire 20 Nov. 1833. Remained on service in Persia till Nov. 1837, when he returned to India. Was frequently in action against the Russians, and on one occasion, in June 1835, was held prisoner for a short time. Apptd. Field Engr. 1st Div., Army of the Indus, 10 Sept. 1838. Garr. Engr., Fort Bakar, Sind, Jan.-Nov. 1839. Executive Engr. Midnapore Div. 20 Jan. 1840; do. Allahabad 15 Nov. 1844 till Dec. 1848. Fur. s.c. 14 Mar. 1849 till Nov. 1851. Supt. Grand Trunk road 2 Dec. 1851. Suptg. Engr. Punjab Circle at Lahore 3 May 1854 till May 1857. Apptd. Chief Engr. Delhi F.F. 23 May 1857. Mutiny campaign; Badli-ki-Serai; siege of Delhi till 28 June (Medal). Suptg. Engr. Lahore Aug. 1857 till Apr. 1859. Persian Order of the Lion and Sun, 2 cl. (*Lond. Gaz.* 19 Feb. 1836); 1 cl. (*ib.* 20 June 1843).

Refs.: De La Ferté. De Rhé-Philipe. *G.M.* 1862, i. 238. *The Times*, 23 Jan. 1862. M.I. in new cemetery at Simla.

LAUNDER, James and Richard. (*See* **LAUDER**.)

LAURIE or LAWRIE, Thomas (1793-1815). Lieutenant, 15th N.I. *b.* Tinwald, co. Dumfries, 27 Apr. 1793. Cadet 1811. Ensign (?) Lieut. 12 May 1815. *d.* Sitapur, U.P., 30 Nov. 1815.

3rd son of Rev. James Laurie, minister of Tinwald 1784-99, and Rachel his wife, dau. of Adam Carlyle, of Limekiln. Nephew of Thomas Herbert.

Services: Posted to 1/15th N.I. in 1814. No record of active service.

Refs.: Scott's *Fasti,* ii. 298.

LAUZUN, Kempt (*d.* 1777). Lieutenant. Infantry. Cadet (Art.) (III.-8) 2 July 1768. Ensign (Inf.) 26 Jan. 1769. Lieut. 25 May 1770. Resigned 8 Jan. 1776. *d.* Delhi 1777 : kld. in the defence of a house.¹

(*Probably* a Swiss from Bern.)

Services : Apptd. in England a Cadet for Art. ; sailed for India in the *Valentine* 2 Jan. 1768 ; transfd. to Inf. in India 19 Dec. 1768, and posted to 3rd Bde. Tried by C.M. at Berhampore June-Sept. 1775. After resigning his Commission he entered the service of Mirza Najaf Khan, of Delhi.

¹ *Note :* " Some years ago an Officer of the Name of Lazun [*sic*] on this Est. left the Army to try his fortunes in Hindustan. He was interested by Major Polier to establish his Authority over a Jagheer assigned to him by the King ; he had collected a very excellent Corps, and his success at first was great, but he lost the Fruits of it with his Life, by too great a Contempt for the Enemy." (Extract from a letter from Sir John Shore, the G.G., to Henry Dundas, undated (1793/4) pub. in " The Private Record of an Indian Governor-Generalship," by H. Furber, Harvard, 1933.)

*LAW, George John (1794-1811). Cadet, Cavalry. *b.* Kelshall, Herts., 24 Aug. 1794. Cadet 1809. *d.* Allahabad, U.P., 30 Dec. 1811.

bapt. Kelshall 4 Oct. 1794. 2nd son of Rt. Rev. George Henry Law, D.D., bishop of Bath and Wells, and Jane his wife, eldest dau. of Gen. James Whorwood Adeane, M.P. for Cambs., and sister of the wife of John Osborne, *q.v.* Nephew of Edward Law, 1st Baron Ellenborough. Ed. Charterhouse ; scholar 24 Oct. 1804 ; left 1809.

Services : Permitted to proceed to India as a passenger and to receive his appt. as Cadet on attaining 16 yrs. of age. (Cons. 5 Jan. 1810.)

Refs.: Burke's *Peerage,* 1859, p. 365, *s.n.* Ellenborough, B. Burke's *Landed Gentry,* 13th edn., p. 7, *s.n.* Adeane, of Babraham Park, Cambs. *Alumni Carthusiani. G.M.* 1812, ii. 187.

LAW, James (1746/47-1807). Major. Cavalry. *b.* 1746/47. Cadet 1767. Ensign 21 July 1767. Lieut. 20 Apr. 1769. Capt. 6 May 1777. Major 1 Dec. 1781. Resigned 23 Dec. 1782. *d.* in England 29 Jan. 1807, aged 60.

Services: Capt. 2nd N.C. in 1777 ; to comd. do. 6 Apr. 1778.

Operations against the Rajah of Benares 1781 ; (? capture of Bijaigarh) ; Capt. comdg. 2nd N.C. Fur. 23 Dec. 1782 ; granted permission to return to India with his rank in Jan. 1785; but did not do so.
Refs.: *G.M.* 1807, i. 186 (where the name is misprinted Low).

LAW, James (*d.* 1770). Cadet, Infantry. Cadet (?) *d.* in India 1770 : drowned.
Services : N.F.P.

LAW, James (1783-1805). Lieutenant, 5th N.I. *b.* Lurgan, co. Armagh, 30 Jan. 1783. Cadet 1799. Arrived in India 2 Sept. 1800. Ensign 8 Sept. 1799. Lieut. 28 Oct. 1799. *d.* Cuttack, B. & O., 7 Sept. 1805.
Son of Simon Law.
Services : Posted Lieut. to 1/5th N.I. 15 Apr. 1801. Second Mahratta War ; operations in Cuttack 1804 ; Lieut. 1/5th N.I.
Refs. : Intest. ; admon. 12 Nov. 1805.

***LAW, James Vansittart** (1805-1863). Lieutenant, Pension Est. 1st N.I. *b.* in India 11 Sept. 1805. Cadet 1824. Admitted 3 Sept. 1825. Ensign 14 Nov. 1824. Lieut. 23 Sept. 1826. Pensioned 30 Aug. 1833. *d.* 1863.
bapt. Calcutta 15 Oct. 1805. Son of Matthew Law, B.C.S., Supt. of the Western Salt Chowkies (who was son of William Law, of Londonderry), and Wilhelmina his wife, dau. of Richard Fleming, of Calcutta. Cousin-german of A. W. C. Plowden, *q.v.* Haileybury 1822-3.
Services : Was already in India when apptd. Cadet. Posted Ensign to 2nd Bengal Eur. Regt. in 1825 ; transfd. to 1st N.I. in 1826. In Nizam's service 1826 till 6 Feb. 1828. No record of active service. Permitted to reside at Cawnpore 5 Mar. 1838.

LAW, John (*d.* 1770). Ensign, Infantry. Cadet 1769. Ensign 1769. *d.* in India 1770.
Services : N.F.P.

LAW, Samuel Hamilton (*d.* 1787). Lieutenant, Infantry. Country Cadet 1780. Ensign 18 Feb. 1781. Lieut. 13 Oct. 1781. *d.* Calcutta 19 Mar. 1787.
· (*Perhaps* son of Rev. Robert Law, D.D., rector of Midleton, co. Cork, and St. Mary, Dublin, Senior Fellow T.C.D., and Eliza his 2nd wife, dau. of Alexander Hamilton, of Knock, co. Dublin.)

Services: Apptd. a Gent. Vol. in the Coy. of Art. 3 Apr. 1780. First Mahratta War 1781-4.
Refs.: (? Burke's *Landed Gentry of Ireland*, p. 385, *s.n.* Law, of Killaloe, co. Clare.)

LAWLEY, George Bateman. Lieutenant. Infantry. Country Cadet 1778. (Ensign 1778.) (Lieut. 23 Nov. 1778.) Struck off, never having claimed the appt. (? *d.* 13 May 1780.) (*Perhaps* son or grandson of George Bateman Lawley, who was son of Sir Thomas Lawley, 3rd Bart.)
Services: Enlisted in H.C.S. under the name of George Bateman and went out to India. In 2nd Bde. and employed as a draftsman in the office of the Fort Major of Ft. Wm.; deserted in July 1777. His desertion being as yet unknown to C.D. he was nominated a Cadet in Feb. 1778.
Refs.: (? Burke's *Peerage*, 1923, p. 2296, *s.n.* Wenlock, B. ? *G.M.* 1780, p. 252.)

LAWRELL, afterwards BEBB, Horatio (1805-1881). (*See* **BEBB.**)

LAWRENCE, Edward (1787-1830). Major, 22nd N.I. *b.* Bengeworth, Worcs., 18 Jan. 1787. Cadet 1805. Arrived in India 11 July 1806. Ensign 4 Aug. 1806. Lieut. 2 Oct. 1808. Capt. 15 Feb. 1824. Major 3 May 1829. *d.* Calcutta 12 Nov. 1830. *bapt.* Bengeworth 7 Mar. 1787. Son of Giles Lawrence and Margaret his wife. *m.* Lucknow 3 Mar. 1823, Miss Mary Jane Antoinette De Verinne (*probably* dau. of Jean De Verinne, of Lucknow, and niece of Joseph M.F. Queiros, *q.v.*).
Services: Barasat C.C. Posted Ensign to 2nd N.I. in 1807. Reduction of Kalinjar 1812; Lieut. 2/2nd N.I. Operations in Baghelkhand 1813; capture of Entauri; Lieut. 2/2nd N.I. Adjt. 2/2nd N.I. 4 May 1815 till Feb. 1824. Transfd. to 22nd N.I. (late 2/2nd) May 1824. Supt. of family money in Oudh 1825-8. Asst. Sec. to Govt., Mily. Dept., 5 Sept. 1828 till death.
Refs: M.I. in S. Park St. cemetery, Calcutta.

LAWRENCE, Sir George St. Patrick (1804-1884). Lieut. General, K.C.S.I., C.B. 2nd European L.C. *b.* Trincomali, Ceylon, 17 Mar. 1804. Cadet 1820. Arrived in India Sept. 1821. Cornet 5 May 1821. Lieut. 1 May 1824. Capt. 5 Jan. 1844. Major 26 Feb. 1860. Bt. Lt. Col. 7 June 1849. Bt. Col. 28 Nov. 1854. Maj. Gen. 17 Sept. 1861. Retired 29 Oct. 1866.

THE BENGAL ARMY, 1758-1834 25

Hon. Lt. Gen. 11 Jan. 1867. *d.* 20 Kensington Park Gdns., London, 16 Nov. 1884.
3rd son of Alexander Lawrence, Lt. Col. in the army and govr. of Upnor Castle, and Catherine Letitia his wife, dau. of Rev. George Knox, rector of Strabane. Brother of Sir Henry Montgomery Lawrence, *q.v. m.* Karnal 3 Apr. 1830, Charlotte Isabella, sister of C.R. Browne, *q.v.* (*See also* Thomas Hutton.) (She died 12 May 1878.) Addiscombe Cadet 1819-21.
Services: See *D.N.B.* Posted to 2nd L.C. 15 Jan. 1822. Adjt. do. 5 Sept. 1825 till 22 Mar. 1834. First Afghan War 1838-42 ; Ghazni (Medal). Awarded a gratuity of £600 for his political services in Afghanistan. Fur. s.c. 12 Aug. 1843 till Oct. 1846. Asst. P.A. Peshawar 1846 ; D.C. Peshawar 7 June 1849. Yusafzai 30 Nov. 1849 ; Kohat Pass 9 Feb. 1850 ; as D.C. Peshawar, and comdg. Mil. (India medal with clasp). P.A. Mewar 28 Dec. 1850 till 13 Mar. 1857. A.G.G. Rajputana Mar. 1857 till Dec. 1864. Bdr. Gen. in comd. of all forces in Rajputana States 8 June 1857. Posted to newly-raised 2nd Eur. L.C. May 1858. Hon. A.D.C. to G.G. 26 May. 1847 and Mar. 1856. Durani, 3 cl. C.B. (Civil) 18 May 1860. K.C.S.I. 24 May 1866. Good Service Pension 11 Jan. 1865. Author of " Forty-three years in India," 1874.
Refs.: Burke's *Peerage*, 1923, p. 1349, *s.n.* Lawrence, Bart. *D.N.B.* Boase. *D.I.B. The Times*, 18 Nov. 1884. *I.L.N.* 29 Nov. 1884, pp. 533, 542 (portrait).

LAWRENCE, Henry (1790-1887). General. Colonel 72nd N.I.
b. Beaconsfield, Bucks., 11 Nov. 1790. Cadet 1809. Arrived in India 3 Oct. 1810. Ensign 1 Nov. 1811. Lieut. 16 Dec. 1814. Capt. 19 Jan. 1828. Major 3 Aug. 1837. Lt. Col. 3 Nov. 1843. Col. 15 Apr. 1854. Maj. Gen. 5 Dec. 1855. Lt. Gen. 28 June 1868. Gen. 23 May 1874. *d.* 1 Camden Gdns., Richmond, Surrey, 23 Nov. 1887, aged 97.
bapt. Beaconsfield 15 Nov. 1790. Son of John Lawrence and Martha his wife. *m.* Westbury-on-Trym, Gloucs., 21 Apr. 1830, Honoria, youngest dau. of Samuel Hodgson, of Richmond, Surrey. (She died Richmond 10 June 1898, aged 91.)
Services: Served on board the *Astell* East Indiaman in comd. of 2 guns on her quarter-deck, in a severe action fought in the Mozambique channel on 3 July 1810 between 3 Indiamen and 4 French frigates and a corvette. Posted Ensign to 19th N.I. 1811. Nepal War 1814-15 ; Malaun ; Lieut. 2/19th N.I., in 1st Div. (India medal). Third Mahratta War 1817-19 ; Bde. Qmr to a Bde. of Irreg. Inf. with Reserve of Grand Div. 1817 ; Bde. Qmr.

4th Div.; Lieut. 2/19th N.I. Intr. & Qmr. 2/19th N.I. 17 Aug. 1819 till 1823. Leave s.c. 6 mos. to P.W.I. 21 Feb. 1822. Transfd. to newly-raised 34th N.I. 1 Oct. 1823; to 67th N.I. (late 1/34th) May 1824. Adjt. 2nd Nassiri Bn. 1 Oct. 1823 till 8 Dec. 1827. Fur. s.c. 27 Feb. 1828 till 11 Jan. 1831. 2nd in comd. Ramgarh L.I. Bn. 12 Mar. 1833; Comdt. do. 19 Dec. 1833 till Jan. 1844. Operations against the Kols; against the Chuars in Singhbhum 1835-6; against the Kols 1836-7; Ramgarh Bn., comdg. a Bde. of all arms. Leave s.c. 2 yrs. to Cape 8 Feb. 1839. Posted Lt. Col. to 35th N.I. 15 Jan. 1844; transfd. to 72nd N.I. 1846. Fur. s.c. 30 Jan. 1847 till 9 Nov. 1850. Transfd. to 2nd Bengal Eur. Regt. 1847; to 73rd N.I. Dec. 1847; to 44th N.I. 17 Sept. 1850; to 24th N.I. Jan. 1851; to 21st N.I. June 1852; to 47th N.I. July 1852; to 58th N.I. Sept. 1852. Bdr. 2 cl., comdg. at Lahore, 17 Apr. 1854 till Jan. 1856. Transfd. to 57th N.I. Apr. 1854. Posted Col. to 72nd N.I. 8 May 1854. Fur. s.c. 8 Jan. 1856 till death.

Refs.: Boase. *The Times,* 25 Nov. 1887.

LAWRENCE, Sir Henry Montgomery (1806-1857). Bdr. General, K.C.B., Artillery. (533) Chief Comr. in Oudh. *b.* Matura, Ceylon, 28 June 1806. Cadet 1821. Arrived in India 21 Feb. 1823. 2nd Lieut. 10 May 1822. Lieut. 5 Oct. 1825. Capt. 10 Feb. 1840. Major 23 Sept. 1850. Lt. Col. 18 May 1856. Bt. Col. 20 June 1854. Bdr. Gen. May 1857. *d.* Lucknow 4 July 1857, of a wound received in the defence of the Residency on 2 July.

4th son of Lt.-Col. Alexander Lawrence and Catherine Letitia his wife. Brother of Richard Charles Lawrence, *q.v.,* and of the wife of Nathaniel Dunbar Barton, *q.v. m.* Calcutta 21 Aug. 1837, Honoria, dau. of Rev. George Marshall, rector of Carndonagh, co. Donegal, and sister of James Marshall (1806-1842), *q.v.* (She died 16 Jan. 1854.) Addiscombe Cadet Aug. 1820 till 10 May 1822.

Services: See *D.N.B.* First Burma War; Chittagong; Arakan. Adjt. of Art., S.E. Div., 18 Nov. 1825. Fur. s.c. 2 Aug. 1826 till 9 Feb. 1830. Asst. to A.G.G., N.W.F., 31 Mar. 1840. First Afghan War 1842; as Pol. Ofr. (Medal). Resdt. in Nepal 1 Dec. 1843 till 1846. First Sikh War; Sobraon (Medal). Second Sikh War; Multan; Chilianwala (Medal). Resdt. at Lahore 26 Dec. 1846. Presdt. of Board of Admon. of Punjab 13 Apr. 1849. A.G.G. Rajputana 9 Feb. 1853. Chief Comr. and A.G.G. Oudh 20 Mar. 1857. C.B. 27 June 1846; K.C.B. (Civil) 27 Apr. 1848. A.D.C. to the Queen 19 June 1854. Author of " Adventures

of an Officer in the Service of Runjeet Singh," 2 vols., London, 1845 ; etc.
Refs.: Burke's *Peerage,* 1923, p. 1349, *s.n.* Lawrence, Bart., of Lucknow. *Lawrence of Lucknow,* by J. L. Morison (London, 1934). *D.N.B. Ency. Brit.* 11th edn., xvi. 305. *Boase. D.I.B.* Will dated Udaipur 2 Jan. 1856 ; proved 25 May 1858. M.I. St. Paul's cathedral, Calcutta. Litho. portrait in I.O.

LAWRENCE, Lucas (1793-1820). Lieutenant, Artillery. (431)
b. Lambeth, Surrey, 21 June 1793. Cadet 1810. Fireworker 17 Aug. 1811. Lieut. 25 Sept. 1817. *d.* Jalna, Hyderabad, 12 June 1820.
bapt. St. Mary's, Lambeth, 20 Aug. 1793. Son of Richard Lawrence and Henrietta his wife. Ed. Harrow 1807/8 till 1808/9. Addiscombe Cadet 1809-10.
Services : Siege and capture of Hathras 1817 ; Lieut. F. 4th Coy. 3rd Bn. Foot Art., d.d. from 1st Coy. 2nd Bn. Apptd. to Nizam's army in 1817, and was comdg. Nizam's Art. at Aurangabad at death.
Refs.: Harrow School Register. G.M. 1820, ii. 570. Intest. ; admon. 20 Dec. 1820. M.I. Jalna.

LAWRENCE, Morgan John (1804-1834). Lieutenant, 30th N.I.
bapt. Llanelweth, co. Radnor, 29 Nov. 1804. Cadet 1825. Arrived in India 25 June 1826. Ensign 16 Feb. 1826. Lieut. (25 Feb. 1829) 12 Aug. 1830. *d.* at sea 25 Feb. 1834, on board the *Duke of Northumberland.*
Son of Charles Lawrence, of Llanelweth Hall, Radnor, and Jane his wife.
Services : Ensign d.d. 46th N.I. 8 July 1826. Posted to 66th N.I. 26 Sept. 1826. Exchanged to 30th N.I. 27 Oct. 1826. Adjt. 30th N.I. 24 June 1829 till death. Fur. s.c. 4 Feb. 1834. No record of active service.

LAWRENCE, Richard Charles (1817-1896). General, C.B. 73rd N.I. Resident in Nepal. *b.* co. Gloucs. 26 Oct. 1817. Cadet 1833. Arrived in India 1 Dec. 1834. Ensign 13 June 1834. Lieut. 17 Sept. 1841. Capt. 7 Apr. 1851. Major 1 Jan. 1862. Lt. Col. 18 Feb. 1863. Col. 18 Feb. 1866. Maj. Gen. 1 Oct. 1877. Lt. Gen. 25 Jan. 1880. Gen. 22 Jan. 1889. *d.* Biarritz, France, 23 Jan. 1896.
7th and youngest son of Lt.-Col. Alexander Lawrence and Catherine Letitia his wife. Brother of Sir George St. Patrick

Lawrence, q.v. m. Sylhet, Assam, 30 Mar. 1839, Ellen, dau. of Col. William Youngson, Madras Est., of Bowscar, Cumberland. (*See also* Robert Delamain.) (She died 23 Jan. 1900, aged 79.) Addiscombe Cadet 1 Aug. 1832 till 13 June 1834.

Service: Ensign d.d. 11th N.I. 4 Dec. 1834; posted to 73rd N.I. 2 Mar. 1835. Adjt. 4th Inf. Levy at Cawnpore 11 Feb. 1842. Actg. Adjt. 3rd Irreg. Cav. 26 Apr. 1843. Adjt. 73rd N.I. 15 Mar. 1844 till 22 Dec. 1847. First Sikh War; Sobraon; Lieut. 73rd N.I. (Medal). Offg. 2nd in comd. Regt. of Ludhiana June 1847; permanent do. 22 Dec. 1847 till 5 Apr. 1849. Asst. Comr. in Punjab 13 Apr. 1849. Fur. p.a. Jan. 1850 till 5 Feb. 1852. Asst. Comr. in Punjab 3 Dec. 1852. Capt. of Police, Lahore Div., 5 Jan. 1853 till 1859. Mutiny campaign; as Pol. Ofr. with Kashmir Contingent; assault and capture of Delhi; comdd. 4th column of assault vice Major Reid, wounded (Medal with clasp). Granted local rank of Lt. Col. 19 Oct. 1875, whilst serving with forces of Maharajah of Jummoo and Kashmir. Fur. 1860. Transfd. to Staff Corps 18 Feb. 1861. D.C. Simla Hill States 27 Apr. 1862; offg. Resdt. in Nepal 11 Jan. 1865; permanent do. 15 Nov. 1867. Fur. m.c. 8 Apr. 1872. C.B. (Civil) 18 May 1860.

Refs.: Burke's *Peerage*, 1923, p. 1349, *s.n.* Lawrence, Bart., of Lucknow. *D.I.B. Boase. The Times*, 25 Jan. 1896, p. 6.

LAWRENCE, William Chauncy (1751/52-1783). Ensign. Infantry. Subsequently Coy.'s Junior Counsel in Calcutta. *b.* 1751/52. Cadet 1773. Ensign (?) Resigned 2 Nov. 1775. *d. unm.; bur.* St. Mary's cemetery, Madras, 7 Dec. 1783.

2nd son of Thomas Lawrence, M.D. (*D.N.B.*), and Frances his wife, dau. of Charles Chauncy, M.D., of Derby. Brother of Sir Soulden Lawrence, justice of the common pleas (*D.N.B.*). Related to Roger Elliot Roberts and Charles Herbert White, *qq.v.* Ed. St. Paul's; admitted 30 May 1761, aged 9.

Services: First Rohilla War; battle of St. George; Dy. Judge Advocate, 2nd Bde. After resigning the Service he became an advocate in Calcutta, and was apptd. Junior Counsel to the Coy. *c.* Mar. 1777.

Refs.: *Gardiner. Hickey*, iii. 149. Will undated; proved 4 Feb. 1784. M.I. on N. wall of nave of Canterbury Cathedral.

LAWRENSON, George Simson (1803-1856). Bt. Colonel, C.B. Artillery. (491) *b.* Kinnettles, co. Forfar, 18 Feb. 1803. Cadet 1818. Admitted 27 Nov. 1819. 2nd Lieut. 18 Apr. 1819. Lieut. 27 Sept. 1821. Capt. 9 July 1835. Major 5 Sept. 1845.

Lt. Col. 10 Feb. 1849. Bt. Col. 20 June 1854. *d.* Cape Town, S.A., 26 June 1856.

bapt. Kinnettles 17 Mar. 1803. 2nd son of Col. John Lawrenson, 18th Light Dgns., of Invereighty, co. Forfar, and Margaret his wife, dau. of George Simson. *m.* 1st, Port Louis, Mauritius, 2 Oct. 1822, Mary Anne, dau. of T. Mather. (She died Calcutta 30 June 1825, aged 22.) *m.* 2nd, Mhow 14 May 1838, Charlotte, dau. of Capt. Hugh Bowen, 41st Regt., and niece of Herbert Bowen, *q.v.* (*See also* Martin Hunter Hailes.) (She died Cheltenham 14 Dec. 1868, aged 50.) Addiscombe Cadet 1818 till 6 Apr. 1819.

Services: Leave s.c. to Mauritius 21 Mar. till 7 Dec. 1822. First Burma War 1824-6; with Bdr. McCreagh's detachment of Sir A. Campbell's force; offg. Adjt. Bengal detachment of Art. 8 July 1825 (India medal). Posted to newly-formed 3rd Troop 3rd Bde. H.A. 23 May 1826; to 1st Troop 3rd Bde. 1832. Adjt. & Qmr. 3rd Bde. 7 Jan. 1832; actg. Adjt. Meerut Div. Art. 9 Feb. 1832 till 9 Feb. 1833; do. Sirhind 30 Mar. 1833 till 30 Aug. 1835. Posted to 1st Coy. 5th Bn. Foot Art. 18 Nov. 1835. To comd. Art. at Lucknow 4 Dec. 1835; actg. A.A.G., Regt. of Art., 14 Dec. 1836 till 2 Oct. 1837; with 2nd Troop 1st Bde. H.A. 4 Sept. 1837 till 1844. Leave s.c. 1 yr. to Cape and Tasmania 5 Jan. 1845. First Sikh War; Aliwal; Sobraon; Major 2nd Bde. H.A. (Medal with clasp). Transfd. from 2nd to 3rd Bde. Aug. 1853. Leave to Cape Feb. 1856 till death. C.B. 27 June 1846.

Refs.: *G.M.* 1856, ii. 519.

LAWRIE, Thomas. (*See* **LAURIE, Thomas.**)

LAWSON, James George (1806-1881). Bt. Captain. 11th L.C.
b. London 5 July 1806. Cadet 1824. Arrived in India 24 Feb. 1826. Cornet 6 Sept. 1825. Lieut. 25 May 1826. Bt. Capt. 6 Sept. 1840. Retired 3 June 1844. *d.* 45 Cornwall Gdns., London, 27 May 1881.

bapt. St. Andrew's, Holborn, Aug. 1806. Son of Charles John Lawson, of Surrey Lodge, Lambeth, barr.-at-law, bencher of the Middle Temple, and Mary Ann his wife, *née* Lawson.

Services: Posted Cornet to 2nd L.C. in 1826. Leave s.c. to China and N.S.W. 16 May 1833 till 26 May 1835. Fur. p.a. 22 Feb. 1837 till 14 Feb. 1840. First Afghan War 1840; Parwandara; Bt. Capt. 2nd L.C. (Medal). d.d. 9th L.C. 6 May 1841, on disbandment of 2nd L.C. Posted to newly-raised 11th L.C. 1842. Fur. s.c. 3 Dec. 1841 till retirement.

Refs.: *The Times,* 31 May 1881.

LAWTIE, George Urquhart (1751/52-1807). Ensign. Infantry. Subsequently a merchant in Calcutta. *b.* 1751/52. Country Cadet 1782. Ensign 4 May 1783. Resigned before 1787. *d.* Calcutta 25 Nov. 1807, aged 55.

Brother of Miss Murray Lawtie, of Banff. (*Probably* brother of James Lawtie, *q.v.*) *m.* Calcutta 28 Apr. 1787, Miss Sarah Tuting. (*See also* Edward Rowland Jackson.) (She died Bath 1 May 1818.) Father of Peter Lawtie, *q.v.*

Services : Sailed for India in the *Glatton* 2 Feb. 1778. Apptd. Cadet 11 Mar. 1782 ; posted to 2nd Bengal Eur. Regt. 28 Feb. 1783. After resigning the Service he embarked on a mercantile career in Calcutta, first in the firm of Lawtie & Gould, afterwards with William Dring & Co., agents and auctioneers. Promoted Capt. from Lieut. in the Calcutta Native Mil. 3 Jan. 1802.

Refs. : Will dated Calcutta 10 Feb. 1807 ; proved 11 Dec. 1807. M.I. in S. Park St. cemetery, Calcutta.

LAWTIE, James (1755/56-1836). Lieut. Colonel. 27th N.I. *b.* 1755/56. Country Cadet 1778. Admitted 9 Mar. 1778. Ensign 4 June 1778. Lieut. 13 Nov. 1778. Capt. 1 June 1796. Major 19 May 1801. Lt. Col. 15 Jan. 1804. Retired 11 Sept. 1811. *d.* Cheltenham 28 June 1836, aged 80.

Related to Patrick Duff (1742-1803), *q.v.* (*Probably* brother of George Urquhart Lawtie, *q.v.*)

Services : Sailed for India in a private capacity in the *Greenwich* in 1775. Apptd. Cadet 27 Feb. 1778. Lieut. 19th Bn. Sepoys in July 1787. Capt. 1st Bengal Eur. Regt. 1796-8 ; transfd. to 14th N.I. 1798. Fur. 1802 till 19 Aug. 1804. Posted Lt. Col. to 1/18th N.I. 1804. Operations in Bundelkhand 1805-6 ; do. 1809 ; Rajaoli ; Ajaigarh ; Lt. Col. comdg. 1/18th N.I. Transfd. to 27th N.I. 1810. Fur. 10 Feb. 1811 till retirement.

Refs. : Bath Chron. 7 July 1836. *A.J.* N.S. xx. 275.

LAWTIE, John Urquhart. Cadet. Infantry. Cadet (?) Resigned 5 Jan. 1787.
Services : N.F.P.

LAWTIE, Peter (1792-1815). Lieutenant, Engineers. *b.* Banff 25 Feb. 1792 ; bapt. same day. Cadet 1807. Arrived in India 16 Nov. 1808. Ensign (27 Sept. 1808) 15 Dec. 1808. Lieut. 23 Dec. 1812. *d.* Ratangarh, Rajputana, 4 May 1815, " of typhus fever brought on by excessive personal fatigue and exhaustion in the Nepal War."

Son of George Urquhart Lawtie, *q.v.*, and Sarah his wife. Cousin-

german of Peter Selwood Hewett, *q.v.* Woolwich Cadet; nominated to R.M.A. 5 Apr. 1806.
Services : Sailed for India in the *Travers* 10 June 1808, which was lost in the Hooghly R. 7 Nov. 1808. Fireworker, Art. (398) 15 Dec. 1808; transfd. to Engrs. 19 Dec. 1809. Served at Cawnpore 1810-12; at Delhi 1812-14. Reduction of Kalinjar 1812. Nepal War 1814-15; Nalagarh; Ramgarh; Field Engr. and Surveyor to 1st Div.
Refs. : *G.M.* 1817, i. 278. White marble monument close to S.E. entrance of St. John's church, Calcutta.

LEACOCK, Henry William (1803-1851). Major. 74th N.I. *b.* Camberwell, Surrey, 17 Aug. 1803. Cadet 1824. Arrived in India 12 June 1825. Ensign 25 Jan. 1825. Lieut. 6 Nov. 1827. Capt. 8 July 1837. Major 1 Dec. 1848. Invalided 1 Feb. 1849. Retired 13 Sept. 1851. *d.* Anne Mount, Cork, 27 Sept. 1851.
Of Anne Mount, Cork. *bapt.* St. Giles, Camberwell, 15 Dec. 1824. Eldest son of William Leacock, of Camberwell, Madeira merchant, and Frances his wife. *m.* Glanmire 12 June 1841, Mary, eldest dau. of N. Marshall Cummins, of Woodville, co. Cork. (She died at sea 12 Aug. 1848, aged 30.)
Services : Ensign d.d. 30th N.I. 24 June 1825. Posted to newly-raised 6th Extra Regt. (became 74th N.I.) in 1825. Fur. p.a. 16 July 1835 till 4 Sept. 1838. Fur. s.c. 22 Nov. 1838 till 10 Nov. 1841, and 14 Mar. 1849 till retirement. No record of active service.
Refs. : *G.M.* 1851, ii. 557. Will dated 14 Sept. 1850; proved in London 3 Dec. 1851; admon. 21 July 1855.

LEACOCK, William Henry (1805-1832). Captain, 30th N.I. *b.* Funchal, I. of Madeira, 28 May 1805. Cadet 1820. Arrived in India Nov. 1821. Ensign 4 July 1821. Lieut. 11 Sept. 1823. Capt. 1832. *d.* Almora, U.P., 24 Apr. 1832.
Son of John Leacock, of London and Madeira, merchant, later of Westbrook, nr. Ryde, I.W., by his wife, a Portuguese native of Madeira.
Services : Posted Ensign to 1/26th N.I. in 1822. d.d. 1/29th N.I. 18 May 1822. Transfd. as Lieut. to 15th N.I. Sept. 1823; to 30th N.I. (late 1/15th) May 1824. Actg. Intr. & Qmr. 30th N.I 18 Dec. 1826. Leave s.c. 12 mos. to Mauritius 1 Mar. 1827; fur. s.c. from Mauritius 11 Mar. 1828 till 2 June 1830. Was wrecked in the *Lady Holland.* No record of active service.
Refs. : Will dated 1830; proved 8 June 1832. M.I. in Cantt. cemetery, Almora.

LEADBEATER, William Edward (1763/64-1809). Captain, 26th N.I. *b.* 1763/64. Cadet 1783. Admitted 17 Sept. 1783. Ensign 15 Feb. 1785. Lieut. 10 Mar. 1792. Capt. 13 Oct. 1803. *d.* Purnea, B. & O., 26 Apr. 1809.[1] Son of Rev. John Leadbeater, rector of Thornton, Bucks. *m.* Calcutta 24 Nov. 1786, Miss Mary Austin. (She died July 1802.) Father of William Edward Blair Leadbeater, *q.v.* Ed. St. Paul's; admitted 24 Feb. 1777, aged 13.

Services: Apptd. Cadet 13 Nov. 1782; sailed for India in the *Lord Macartney* 11 Mar. 1783. Posted to 4th Bengal Eur. Bn. 15 Feb. 1790; transfd. to 3rd do. 16 Apr. 1793. Qmr. 2nd Bengal Eur. Regt. in 1796; Adjt. & Qmr. 16th N.I.; Lieut. 8th N.I. in Jan. 1799. Transfd. to 1/18th N.I. 29 May 1800; Adjt. & Qmr. 18th N.I. 29 May 1800 till Oct. 1803. Second Mahratta War; Bundelkhand 1803; Narnaul; Kanun; Lieut. 1/18th N.I. Transfd. to newly-raised 26th N.I. 1805. Operations in Bundelkhand 1807; Sehlehuganj; Capt. 26th N.I. Comdd. Purnea Provl. Bn. 1808 till death.

Refs.: Gardiner. Cal. Monthly Journal, May 1809.

[1] *Note:* He was playing with the trigger of his fowling-piece, when the flint struck and he received a blow from the recoil which proved fatal within six hours.

LEADBEATER, William Edward Blair (1793-1853). Major, Invalid Est. 53rd N.I. *b.* Calcutta 27 Mar. 1793. Cadet 1808. Arrived in India 27 Oct. 1809. Ensign 25 Aug. 1810. Lieut. 16 Dec. 1814. Capt. 2 Sept. 1824. Major 28 June 1838. Invalided 23 June 1843. *d. unm.* Dehra Dun 23 Mar. 1853.

bapt. Calcutta 23 Jan. 1794. Son of William Edward Leadbeater, *q.v.,* and Mary his wife. Cousin-german of John Cumberlege, *q.v.*

Services: Barasat C.C. Posted Ensign to 27th N.I. Aug. 1810; Intr. & Qmr. 1/27th N.I. 22 Jan. 1817 till 2 Oct. 1824. Third Mahratta War; Madhurajpura; Lieut. 1/27th N.I. Leave s.c. Dec. 1822 till Jan. 1824. Transfd. to 53rd N.I. (late 1/27th) May 1824. Siege and capture of Bhurtpore; D.A.Q.M.G., 1st Inf. Div. (? India medal). 2nd in comd. Sirmoor Bn. 9 June 1826 till 1 June 1827. Actg. Bde. Major 5th Inf. Bde., Army of the Indus, 12 Dec. 1838. Postmaster at Ludhiana 31 Dec. 1838. Comdd. 53rd N.I. 1 June till 1 Nov. 1840. First Afghan War 1842; retreat from Ali Masjid to Jamrud in Jan.; apptd. to comd. of Ali Masjid 28 May 1842; Major 53rd N.I., with Gen. Pollock's force (Medal).

Refs.: I.M. 17 May 1853, p. 261. Will dated 22 Mar. 1853; admon. 20 Sept. 1853. M.I. Dehra Dun.

THE BENGAL ARMY, 1758-1834

LEAKE, Thomas (1752-1771). (*See* **LEEKE, Thomas.**)

MARTIN-LEAKE, Thomas (*d.* 1829). Captain. 2nd Bengal Eur. Regt. Pensioner on Lord Clive's fund. Cadet 1768. Ensign 20 Jan. 1769. Lieut. 16 May 1770. Capt. 1778. Resigned 16 Aug. 1779. *d.* in England 10 Dec. 1829.

(*Probably* one of the younger of the six sons of Stephen Martin-Leake, of Thorpe Hall, Essex, Garter King-at-Arms, and Anne his wife, dau. of Fletcher Powell.)

Services : Granted a pension of 5/- *p.d.* from Lord Clive's fund from 10 Feb. 1781 ; increased to 7/- from 10 Feb. 1782.

Refs. : (? Burke's *Landed Gentry*, 13th edn., p. 1061, *s.n.* Martin-Leake, *late* of Thorpe Hall, Essex.)

LEARMONTH, Alexander (1808-1879). Lieutenant. 54th N.I. Pensioner on Lord Clive's fund. *b.* London 4 Feb. 1808. Cadet 1823. Arrived in India 8 Oct. 1824. Ensign 16 Apr. 1824. Lieut. 18 June 1825. Pensioned 17 Jan. 1833. *d.* 15 Apr. 1879. *bapt.* St. Giles-in-the-Fields 25 Feb. 1808. Son of Walter Learmonth, of Acton, Middlesex, and afterwards of Russell Sq., London, merchant, and Helen his wife, eldest dau. of John Annand.

Services : Posted Ensign to 54th N.I. in 1824. Actg. Intr. & Qmr. 54th N.I. 30 May 1828. Fur. s.c. 18 Sept. 1830 till July 1834, when he retired with effect from 17 Jan. 1833. Granted a pension of 2/6 *p.d.* from Lord Clive's fund with effect from 16 Mar. 1834. No record of active service.

Refs. : Burke's *Landed Gentry*, 13th edn., p. 18, *s.n.* Annand, of Auchter Ellon, Surrey.

LEATHART, John (1759/60-1843). Major. 26th N.I. *b.* Northumberland 1759/60. Cadet 1782. Admitted 15 Nov. 1782. Ensign 6 Jan. 1783. Lieut. 20 Mar. 1788. Capt. 4 Feb. 1803. Major (25 Apr. 1808) 1808. Retired 1 Jan. 1811. *d.* 27 Apr. 1843.

m. Elizabeth. (She died 28 July 1851.)

Services : Lieut. Northumberland Mil. 19 June 1779. Apptd. Cadet 21 Nov. 1781 ; sailed for India in the *Nottingham* 6 Feb. 1782, aged 22. Posted to 1st Bengal Eur. Regt. 28 Feb. 1783 ; 2nd Bengal Eur. Bn in July 1787 ; 3rd do. in Dec. 1788 ; 25th Bn. Sepoys in 1792. Fur. 23 Dec. 1796 till 10 Sept. 1799. Adjt. & Qmr. 14th N.I. 29 May 1800 till 1803. Second Mahratta War ; Capt. 14th N.I. Transfd. to newly-raised 22nd N.I. in 1804 ; to 26th N.I. in 1805. Comdd. Burdwan Provl. Bn. 1804-5. Fur.

12 Dec. 1805 till 16 Oct. 1807. Suspended and ordered to Europe 30 Jan. 1809.[1] Permitted by C.D. to retire on the pay of a Capt. from 1 Jan. 1811.

[1] *Note:* He was charged with "being the author of certain papers of a seditious nature, and with an attempt to circulate those papers among the officers of the army on this (Bengal) establishment." It would appear, however, that the action of the Bengal Govt. in thus ordering him home was *ultra vires*, he not having been previously informed in writing of the charges preferred against him, nor was a reasonable time allowed him to make his defence. Hence, presumably, the grant of a reduced pension as an act of grace.

LECHMERE, Edwyn Sandys (1785-1821). Captain, 11th N.I. *b.* 1785. Cadet 1803. Arrived in India 18 Mar. 1805. Ensign 6 Apr. 1805. Lieut. 6 Apr. 1805. Capt. 27 Nov. 1817. *d. unm.* Ghazipur 22 Aug. 1821.

bapt. All Sts., Hereford, 20 Jan. 1785. Elder son of Edwyn Sandys Lechmere and Elizabeth his wife, dau. of Rev. John Jones, canon of Hereford cathedral.

Services: Posted Lieut. to 11th N.I. in 1806. Reduction of Kalinjar 1812; Lieut. 11th N.I. Adjt. 2/11th N.I. 4 May 1815 till July 1817. Siege and capture of Hathras 1817; Lieut. 2/11th N.I. 1st Ceylon Vol. Bn. 1818-19. Transfd. to 1/11th N.I. in 1820.

Refs.: Burke's *Landed Gentry*, 12th edn., p. 1126, *s.n.* Lechmere, of Fownhope Court, co. Hereford. Burke's *Peerage*, 1848, p. 596, *s.n.* Lechmere, Bart., of the Rhyd, Worcs. Will dated Benares 25 Apr. 1821; proved 15 Nov. 1821.

LECKY, Alexander Thomas (1786-1852). Lieutenant. 2nd N.I. *b.* Londonderry 12 Jan. 1786. Cadet 1804. Arrived in India 25 Mar. 1806. Ensign 17 Apr. 1806. Lieut. 30 Sept. 1808. Resigned 4 Sept. 1817. *d.* 11 Feb. 1852; *bur.* in Derry cathedral.

bapt. Templemore 26 Jan. 1786. 3rd son of William Lecky, M.P. for Londonderry 1790-7, alderman, and for 50 yrs. a mgte. for Derry, and Hannah his wife, dau. of Conolly McCausland, of Fruit Hill (now Drenagh). Cousin-german of Thomas (Kennedy) Skipton, *q.v.*

Services: Posted Ensign to 2nd N.I. A.D.C. to Maj.-Gen. Kenneth Macpherson, Bombay Eur. Regt., 1811-12. Operations in Baghelkhand 1813; capture of Entauri; Lieut. 2/2nd N.I. Fur. 10 Feb. 1815 till resignation.

Refs.: Family Information.

THE BENGAL ARMY, 1758-1834   35

LEDLIE, James (d. 1772). Lieutenant, Infantry. Cadet 1767. Ensign 15 Sept. 1767. Lieut. 2 Oct. 1769. d. Calcutta 2 Aug. 1772.
Services: N.F.P.

LEDLIE, Robert (1789-1833). Major. Bengal Eur. Regt. b. Calcutta 2 Apr. 1789. Cadet 1804. Arrived in India 10 Aug. 1805. Ensign 17 Aug. 1805. Lieut. 18 Aug. 1805. Capt. 1 Jan. 1819. Major 4 Mar. 1839. Retired 15 Dec. 1830. d. Belfast 14 July 1833.

bapt. Calcutta 21 May 1790. Son of William Ledlie, of Calcutta, atty.-at-law, and Anne his 1st wife, younger dau. of Thomas Creighton (or Crichton), Pilot of the Coy.'s investment at Dacca. Brother of William Ledlie, *q.v.*

Services: Posted Lieut. to Bengal Eur. Regt. in 1806. Served with his Regt. in Amboyna 1811-16, latterly as Adjt. of the Amboynese Corps. Fur. 1818-19. Siege and capture of Bhurtpore; Capt. 1st Bengal Eur. Regt. Fur. p.a. 11 Jan. 1830 till retirement.
Refs.: G.M. 1833, ii. 286. A.J. N.S. xi. 279.

LEDLIE, William (1787-1872). Lieut. Colonel. 38th N.I. b. Calcutta 1787. Cadet 1804. Arrived in India 10 Sept. 1803. Ensign 26 Oct. 1805. Lieut. 26 June 1806. Capt. 25 May 1821. Major 8 Mar. 1830. Retired 1 Dec. 1830. Hon. Lt. Col. 28 Nov. 1854. d. Budleigh Salterton, Devon, 13 Aug. 1872, aged 84.

Of Bristol. *bapt.* Calcutta 1 Jan. 1788. Son of William Ledlie, of Calcutta, and Anne his 1st wife. Brother of Robert Ledlie, *q.v.* m. Bombay 8 Jan. 1824, Miss Margaret F. Young. (She died 15 Jan. 1827.)

Services: Operations in Bundelkhand 1807; Sehlehuganj; Lieut. 1/19th N.I. With 4th L.I. Bn. 1810-11. Nepal War 1814-15; Lieut. 1/19th N.I., in 1st Div. Actg. Intr. & Qmr. 1/19th N.I. 1815-16. Third Mahratta War; storm and capture of Chanda; Lieut. 1/19th N.I. Served in Nizam's army 1819-30. Adjt. 1st Berar (Nizam's) Inf. Transfd. to 38th N.I. (late 1/19th) May 1824.
Refs.: The Times, 17 Aug. 1872.

LEE, Arthur Lawford Miles (1806-1830). Lieutenant, 31st N.I. b. Cawnpore 5 Aug. 1806. Cadet 1823. Arrived in India 3 Apr. 1825. Ensign 16 Sept. 1824. Lieut. 12 May 1827. d. Secrora, U.P., 8 Jan. 1830, of confluent smallpox.

bapt. Cawnpore 11 Mar. 1807. Son of Capt. A. D. Lee, H.M. 17th Regt., and Eleanor his wife. Nephew of Peppard Knight.

Services: Ensign d.d. 28th N.I. 12 Apr. 1825. Posted to 31st N.I. in 1825. Siege and capture of Bhurtpore ; Ensign 31st N.I. Operations against the Bhils 1828.
Refs. : A.J. N.S. ii. 160.

LEECH, Thomas (1791-1813). Lieutenant, 3rd N.I. *b.* Blackburn, Lancs., 26 Sept. 1791. Cadet 1808. Arrived in India 24 July 1809. Ensign 30 Aug. 1809. Lieut. 2 Sept. 1812. *d.* Mauritius 1813.
bapt. St. John's chapel, Blackburn, 6 Oct. 1791. Son of John Langton Leech and Ann his wife.
Services: Barasat C.C. Posted Ensign to 3rd N.I. No record of active service. Was *probably* on sick leave when his death occurred.

LEEKE, Ralph (1754-1829). Lieutenant. Infantry. Subsequently B.C.S. *b.* 1754. Cadet 1771. Ensign 6 Dec. 1771. Lieut. 8 Aug. 1776. Resigned Oct. 1776. *d.* Longford Hall, Salop, 30 Sept. 1829.

Of Longford and Church Aston, Salop, high sheriff 1796. 2nd son of Thomas Leeke, of the Vineyard, nr. Wellington, Salop, and Elizabeth his wife, dau. of Egerton Henshaw, of London. Brother of Thomas Leeke, *q.v. m.* 13 Dec. 1787, Honor Frances, only dau. of Walter Harvey Thursby, Capt. in the Blues. (She died 1843.)

Services: Comdd. a detachment in Sylhet against the Jaintia Rajah Feb.-Apr. 1774. Apptd. a Writer, B.C.S., 27 June 1776. 1st Asst. under Revenue Chief at Chittagong, 1778 ; Factor and Resdt. at Tipperah, 1782 ; no trace after 1782.
Refs. : Burke's *Landed Gentry,* 13th edn., p. 1070, *s.n.* Leeke, of Aston Hall, Salop. Burke's *Peerage,* 1923, p. 2178, *s.n.* Thursby, Bart. *B. :* P.P. v. 184 *et seq. G.M.* 1829, ii. 381.

LEEKE, Thomas (1752-1771). Cadet. Infantry. *b.* 1752. Cadet 1769. Resigned 23 Apr. 1770. *d.s.p.* Dinapore 9 June 1771.

Eldest son of Thomas Leeke, of the Vineyard, Salop, and Elizabeth his wife. Brother of Ralph Leeke, *q.v.*
Services : Sailed for India in the *Prince of Wales* 24 Mar. 1769.
Refs. : Burke's *Landed Gentry,* 13th edn., p. 1070, *s.n.* Leeke, of Aston Hall, Salop.

LEESON, Joseph (1796-1848). Bt. Major, 42nd N.I. *b.* 25 Mar. 1796. Cadet 1818. Was already in India when apptd. Cadet.

THE BENGAL ARMY, 1758-1834

Ensign 11 May 1819. Lieut. 18 Jan. 1822. Capt. 18 June 1833. Bt. Major 19 June 1846. *d.* Hoshiarpur, Punjab, 15 Feb. 1848.

Eldest son of Hon. John Leeson and Martha his wife, dau. of Rev. John Ryley. Cousin-german of Joseph, 4th Earl of Milltown. *m.* Calcutta 26 Nov. 1817, Anne, eldest dau. of Anthony Alexander O'Reilly, 21st Light Dgns., of the Baltrasna family. (She died Ferozepore 29 Jan. 1851, aged 49.) His dau. *m.* William Baring-Gould, *q.v.* His 3rd son, John, claimed the title on the death of the 7th Earl in Mar. 1891, and styled himself 8th Earl; but his claim was never recognized, and the succession to the Earldom has not been established. Marlow Cadet 1809-11.

Services: Cornet 21st Light Dgns. 28 Nov. 1811, and joined at the Cape. Lieut. do. 6 Jan. 1812. Accompanied his Regt. to India in 1817, and served with one Sqdn. in Cuttack during the Pindari war. Apptd. Inf. Cadet May 1819; admitted 16 Oct. 1819. h.p. 21st Light Dgns. 25 Oct. 1819 till 31 Aug. 1832, when he finally retired from the British Service, receiving a commuted allowance for his Commission. d.d. 2/4th N.I. Oct. 1819. Posted to 2/21st N.I. Jan. 1821. Sub-Asst. Stud Dept. at Hariana 21 May 1821; do. Hissar 31 Oct. 1822 till 31 Aug. 1830.[1] Transfd. as Lieut. to 1/21st N.I. 13 May 1822; to 42nd N.I. (late 2/21st) May 1824. Leave s.c. to Cape 31 Aug. 1828 till 14 Jan. 1833, when he joined 42nd N.I. for the first time. Offg. Bde. Major at Delhi 16 Apr. till 3 Nov. 1835. First Afghan War 1840-2; against the Ghilzais; skirmish at Ilmi 29 May 1841 (slight w.); operations in vicinity of Kandahar; Goaine; recapture of Ghazni; reoccupation of Kabul; capture of Istalif; Haft Kotal, comdg. rear guard (*Lond. Gaz.* 10 Jan. 1843) (Medal). Apptd. to charge of Shah Shuja's 1st Cav. Regt. (Leeson's Horse) Sept. 1840. Rejoined 42nd N.I. Apr. 1842. Hon. A.D.C. to G.G. 1 Apr. 1842. Granted a gratuity of 18 mos. full pay for his wound. Apptd. Comdt. 2nd Irreg. Cav. 12 Sept. 1842. First Sikh War; Sobraon; Capt. comdg. 2nd Irreg. Cav. (Medal). Hon. A.D.C. to Lord Dalhousie 21 Jan. 1848.

Refs.: Burke's *Peerage*, 1923, p. 1570, *s.n.* Milltown, E. De Rhé-Philipe. *I.M.* 4 Apr. 1848, p. 202. M.I. in Hoshiarpur cemetery.

[1] *Note:* His name is included in the P.R. of First Burma war, although, apparently, he did not take part in that campaign.

LE FEUVRE, James Hobbs (1804-1828). Ensign, 26th N.I. *bapt.* Millbrook, Hants, 5 Aug. 1804. Cadet 1825. Ensign 4 Feb. 1826. *d.* Nasirabad 25 Dec. 1828.

Son of Philip Le Feuvre, of Southampton, and Susan his wife.
Services: Ensign d.d. 26th N.I. 30 June 1826. Posted to 10th N.I. 26 Sept. 1826. Transfd. to 26th N.I. 14 Dec. 1826. No record of active service.
Refs.: A.J. xxvii. 755. M.I. Nasirabad.

LE FEVRE,[1] **Philip** (1784-1845). Major General. Colonel 3rd N.I. *bapt.* ptely. 22 Dec. 1784. Cadet 1799. Arrived in India 4 Jan. 1801. Ensign 15 Oct. 1800. Lieut. 13 July 1803. Capt. 13 July 1811. Major 11 July 1823. Lt. Col. 13 May 1825. Col. (18 June 1831) 18 Dec. 1834. Maj. Gen. 3 Nov. 1841. *d.* Cheltenham 7 Sept. 1845, aged 61.

bapt. St. Brelade, Jersey, 18 Jan. 1785. Son of Philip Le Fevre and Susannah his wife. *m.* Southampton 26 Apr. 1832, Eleanor, 3rd dau. of Peter Boyle De Blaquiere, and grand-dau. of John, 1st Baron De Blaquiere. (She died 15 June 1859.)

Services: Posted Ensign to 1/18th N.I. 17 Apr. 1801. Adjt. 1/18th N.I. 3 July 1804 till 1811. Second Mahratta War; operations in Bundelkhand. Operations against Lachman Dawa 1809; Rajaoli; Ajaigarh. Fur. p.a. 5 Sept. 1811 till 15 Sept. 1815. Nepal War 1816; Capt. 1/18th N.I., in 1st Bde. Rt. Column. Against the Chuars in Khurda Apr. 1817; Capt. 1/18th N.I., comdg. the force. Third Mahratta War; Jawad; Capt. 1/18th N.I. Actg. Adjt. 1/18th N.I. 22 Apr. 1820. Operations in Jodhpur; Lamba; Capt. 1/18th N.I. Transfd. to 36th N.I. (late 1/18th) May 1824. Siege and capture of Bhurtpore; Lt. Col. 36th N.I. Transfd. to 26th N.I. 1826. Fur. p.a. 20 Jan. 1829 till 20 Oct. 1833. Transfd. to 57th N.I. 26 Oct. 1832; to 3rd N.I. 17 Jan. 1833; to 15th N.I. 6 Nov. 1833. Posted as Col. to 15th N.I. 9 June 1835; to 29th N.I. 29 Nov. 1836. Fur. p.a. 3 Jan. 1837 till death. Transfd. to Left Wing Bengal Eur. Regt. 1 July 1837; to 3rd N.I. 1843.

Refs.: Burke's *Peerage*, 1905, p. 453, *s.n.* Baron De Blaquiere. *G.M.* 1845, ii. 546. *I.M.* 25 Sept. 1845, p. 572. Will dated 20 Oct. 1842; proved 19 Nov. 1846.

[1] *Note:* He signs "Le Fevre (*alias* Le Feuvre)."

LEGARD, William Barnabas (1809-1890). Lieut-Colonel. 31st N.I. *b.* Ganton, Yorks., 27 Dec. 1809. Cadet 1827. Arrived in India 21 Nov. 1828. Ensign 18 June 1828. Lieut. 1 June 1834. Capt. 2 Feb. 1845. Bt. Major 20 June 1854. Retired 31 Dec. 1861. Hon. Lt. Col. 31 Dec. 1861. *d.* Ashley House, Shalford, Guildford, 27 Jan. 1890.

THE BENGAL ARMY, 1758-1834 39

bapt. Ganton 1 Jan. 1810. 2nd son of Rev. William Legard, vicar of Ganton (who was 4th son of Sir Digby Legard, 5th Bart. of Ganton), and Cecilia Elizabeth his wife, dau. of James Oldershaw, M.D., of Stamford. *m.* St. Giles-in-the-Fields, London, 11 Dec. 1845, Ann Maria, 3rd dau. of Richard Onebye Walker.

Services: Ensign d.d. 30th N.I. 14 Jan. 1829. Posted to 30th N.I. 3 June 1829; exchanged to 31st N.I. 12 Aug. 1830. Against the Chuars 1832; Ensign 31st N.I. Against the Kols 1837-8; Lieut. 31st N.I. First Afghan War 1838-40; capture of Ghazni (Medal); capture of Kalat; Lieut. 31st N.I. Actg. S.S.O. at Aligarh 26 Nov. 1840. Fur. p.a. 18 Apr. 1843 till 1846. Second Sikh War; Sadulapur; Chilianwala; Gujerat; pursuit of Sikhs and Afghans to Peshawar; Capt. 31st N.I. (Medal with 2 clasps). Against the Kohat Pass Afridis 9 Feb. 1850; Capt. 31st N.I. (Medal). Santhal revolt 1855; Bt. Major 31st N.I. Mutiny campaign 1857-8; served with 31st N.I. (now 1st Bn. (Queen Victoria's Own L.I.) 7th Rajput Regt.) in Saugor district (Medal).

Refs.: Burke's *Peerage*, 1923, p. 1362, *s.n.* Legard, Bart., of Ganton, Yorks. *The Times*, 1 Feb. 1890.

LEGERTWOOD, Alexander (1755/56-1802). Bt. Major, Artillery. (168) *b.* 1755/56. Country Cadet 1778. Admitted 11 Aug. 1778. Fireworker 24 Sept. 1778. Lieut. 16 Apr. 1781. Capt. 6 Jan. 1792. Bt. Major 1 Jan. 1800. *d.* Cawnpore 19 Sept. 1802, aged 46.

Son of James Legertwood, of Skelmuir, and Agnes his wife, 2nd dau. of Alexander Dyce, of Raeden. Cousin-german of David Dyce, *q.v.*, and kinsman of Sir David Ochterlony, *q.v.*

Services: First Mahratta War 1780-1; Lahar; Gwalior; Lieut. 2nd Coy. 1st Bn. Art., with Popham's detachment. Leave s.c. to sea 16 July 1782. Lieut. 1st Bn. Art. in July 1787. Transfd. from 5th Coy. 2nd Bn. to 2nd Coy. 2nd Bn. 16 June 1794. On service to Madras June-Oct. 1794.

Refs.: *The Thanage of Fermartyn*, by Rev. William Temple, p. 681. Will dated Cawnpore, 17 Sept. 1802; proved in 1802.

LE HARDY, Dumaresq (1784-1807). Lieutenant, 24th N.I. *bapt.* ptely. Jersey 14 Oct. 1784. Cadet 1800. Arrived in India 26 Aug. 1801. Ensign 10 Dec. 1801. Lieut. 30 Sept. 1803. *d.* Delhi 16 Nov. 1807 : kld. by the accidental discharge of a fowling-piece.

bapt. publicly 16 Nov. 1784. 5th son of Thomas Le Hardy,

40 LIST OF THE OFFICERS OF

Major R. Jersey Mil., and Frances his wife, dau. of George Dumaresq, of Pentevrin.

Services: Posted Ensign to 10th N.I. in 1801. Transfd. to newly-raised 2/24th N.I. in 1804. Second Mahratta War 1805; Adalatnagar; Lieut. 2/24th N.I. Operations against the Rana of Gohad 1806; capture of Gohad; Lieut. 2/24th N.I.

Refs.: J. B. Payne's *Armorial of Jersey*, p. 221.

LEICESTER, Charles Byrne (1807-1831). Lieutenant, 34th N.I. *b.* Middlewich, co. Chester, 16 Mar. 1807. Cadet 1823. Arrived in India 19 May 1824. Ensign 17 Jan. 1824. Lieut. 13 May 1825. *d.* at sea 20 Sept. 1831.

2nd son of Charles Leicester (who was 3rd son of Sir Peter Byrne Leicester, 4th Bart.), of Stanthorne Hall, co. Chester, and Louisa Harriet his 2nd wife, youngest dau. of Nicholas Smythe, of N. Nibley, Gloucs., high sheriff co. Salop 1772. *m.* Calcutta 8 Sept. 1827, Emily, dau. of William Leycester, B.C.S. (She *re-m.* John Campbell (1790-1875), *q.v.*)

Services: Ensign in Mil. Nov. 1823. Posted Ensign to 34th N.I. in 1824. Adjt. 34th N.I. 11 Sept. 1826; Intr. & Qmr. do. 6 Oct. 1826 till July 1829. d.d. 28th N.I. 29 Oct. 1827 till Mar. 1828. Leave s.c. 12 mos. to N.S.W. 7 Mar. 1828. Fur. s.c. 3 July 1829; died at sea on the return voyage to India. No record of active service.

Refs.: Burke's *Peerage*, 1923, p. 1366, *s.n.* Leicester, Bart. Ruvigny's *Plantagenet Roll of the Blood Royal*, Exeter Vol., p. 231. Will dated Seacombe 5 June 1830; proved 7 Feb. 1832.

LEIGH, John Robert (1792-1827). Ensign. 24th N.I. *b.* St. Ann's, Dublin, 13 Mar. 1792. Cadet 1809. Admitted 11 Oct. 1810. Ensign 12 Oct. 1812. Pensioned in India 15 Sept. 1815. Resigned 6 Dec. 1817. *d.v.p.* 7 July 1827.

Eldest son of Francis Leigh, of Rosegarland, co. Wexford, Collector of Wexford 1794, Sovereign of New Ross 1799, and Grace his wife, dau. of Richard Baldwin. *m.* Feb. 1822, Dorothea Anne, dau. of Lt.-Col. Edward FitzGerald, and sister of Charles FitzGerald (1784-1859), *q.v.* (She *re-m.*, and died 17 June 1889, aged 95.)

Services: Barasat C.C. Cadet d.d. 13th N.I. 1811; posted Ensign to 24th N.I. 1812. No record of active service.

Refs.: Burke's *Landed Gentry of Ireland*, p. 395, *s.n.* Leigh, of Rosegarland, co. Wexford.

LEIGH, Timothy (1757/58-1814). Lieutenant. 5th Bn. Sepoys. Subsequently an indigo planter. *b.* Oxford 1757/58. Cadet

1779. Ensign 12 Feb. 1780. Lieut. 22 Mar. 1781. Resigned 28 Feb. 1795. *d. unm.* Mirzapur, U.P., 28 Mar. 1814.

4th and youngest son of Rev. Peter Leigh, rector of Lymm, co. Chester, and Mary his wife, dau. of Henry Doughty, of Broadwell, Gloucs. Ed. Manchester Grammar School; admitted 10 Nov. 1769. St. John's Coll., Camb.; admitted 14 Aug. 1775; Duchess of Somerset Scholar 7 Nov. 1775.

Services: Sailed for India in the *Walpole* 16 June 1779, aged 21. Lieut. 18th Bn. Sepoys in July 1787; transfd. to 5th Bn. Sepoys 29 Jan. 1794. After resigning the Service he became an indigo planter at Zamania, U.P.

Refs.: Burke's *Landed Gentry*, 11th edn., p. 997, *s.n.* Leigh, of West Hall, High Leigh, co. Chester. Ormerod's *Cheshire*, i. 356. *Manchester School Register*, i. 154. *G.M.* 1814, ii. 603. Will dated Mirzapur 25 Mar. 1814; proved 1814.

LEIGHTER, Timothy. Captain. Infantry. Cadet 1763. Ensign 12 Oct. 1763. Lieut. (?) Capt. 1766. Resigned 1766.

Services: Probably resigned his Commission during the "Batta mutiny." N.F.P.

LEITH, William (1759/60-1781). Lieutenant, 1st Bengal Eur. Regt. *b.* in Scotland 1759/60. Cadet 1780. Arrived in India Mar. 1781. Ensign 1780. Lieut. 28 Aug. 1781. *d.* Calcutta 1781.

Son of Margaret Leith, of co. Aberdeen. Brother of Jean Bell, Sarah, Margaret, Elizabeth and Katharine Leith.

Services: Sailed for India in the *Rochford* 3 June 1780, aged 20.

Refs.: Will dated 2 July 1781; proved 15 Oct. 1781.

FORBES-LEITH, James John (1778-1841). Lieut. Colonel. 55th N.I. *b.* Greenwich 2 Oct. 1778. Cadet 1796. Arrived in India 3 Oct. 1798. Ensign 20 Oct. 1797. Lieut. 10 Sept. 1798. Capt. 21 Oct. 1806. Major 14 Jan. 1819. Lt. Col. 1 May 1824. Retired 11 Feb. 1826. *d.* 5 Sept. 1841.

bapt. Greenwich 26 Oct. 1778. 2nd son of Theodore Forbes-Leith, M.D., of Greenwich, afterwards of Whitehaugh, and Marie d'Arboine his 1st wife. Uncle of Theodore George Forbes-Leith, *q.v. m.* 28 Nov. 1827, Williamina Helen, only child of Lt.-Col. James Stewart, 42nd Highlrs. (She *re-m.* and died 1866.)

Services: Posted Lieut. to 4th N.I. 1798. Second Mahratta War 1803-4; Aligarh; battle of Deig; Lieut. 1/4th N.I. Operations in Bundelkhand 1809; Rajaoli; Ajaigarh; Capt. 1/4th N.I.

Fur. 1814 till 3 Nov. 1815. Transfd. to newly-raised 1/28th N.I. in 1815. Third Mahratta War; Madhurajpura; Capt. 1/28th N.I. Third Ceylon Vol. Bn. 1818-19. Major 1/28th N.I. Posted Lt. Col. to 55th N.I. (late 1/28th) May 1824.

Refs.: Burke's *Landed Gentry*, 12th edn., p. 1140, *s.n.* Forbes-Leith, of Whitehaugh, co. Aberdeen. Burke's *Royal Families*, ped. xc. Anderson, iii. 709.

FORBES-LEITH, Theodore George (1813-1839). Ensign, 64th N.I. *b.* Cluny, Aberdeen, 7 Oct. 1813. Cadet 1832. Arrived in India 4 Oct. 1833. Ensign (14 Dec. 1832) 21 June 1833. *d.* Arakan 16 July 1839.

Son of George Forbes-Leith, of Knock, co. Aberdeen, surveyor of taxes. Nephew of James John Forbes-Leith, *q.v.* King's Coll., Abd. Addiscombe Cadet 4 Feb. 1831 till 14 Dec. 1832.

Services: Ensign d.d. 38th N.I. 16 Nov. 1833. Posted to 37th N.I. 24th May 1834; to 64th N.I. 28 June 1836. d.d. Arakan Local Bn. 3 Apr. 1837; actg. Adjt. do. 30 Dec. 1838; permanent do. 17 Jan. 1839 till death. No record of active service.

Refs.: Burke's *Landed Gentry*, 12th edn., p. 1140, *s.n.* Forbes-Leith, of Whitehaugh, co. Aberdeen.

LELAND, James (*d.* 1775). Lieutenant, 3rd Bengal Eur. Regt. Cadet 1767. Ensign 15 Sept. 1767. Lieut. 30 Sept. 1769. *d.* Berhampore 12 June 1775.

Services: Cashiered June 1774; restored 11 July 1774.

LE MESURIER, Henry (1811-1858). Captain. 61st N.I. *b.* Hackney, Middlesex, 13 May 1811. Cadet 1826. Arrived in India 6 Nov. 1827. Ensign (14 June 1827) 20 Feb. 1828. Lieut. 5 June 1829. Capt. 25 Jan. 1843. Invalided 1 Dec. 1846. Retired 18 Aug. 1849. *d.* Clyst Honiton, Devon, 11 Feb. 1858.

bapt. St. John at Hackney 5 June 1811. Eldest son of Frederick Le Mesurier and Martha his wife, dau. of William Brock, of Heavitree, nr. Exeter. *m.* Almora, U.P., 4 May 1840, Joanna, 4th dau. of Robert Menzies, of Dalreoch, co. Perth. (*See also* Robert Stewart (1787-1867).) Ed. Christ's Hospital.

Services: Ensign d.d. 58th N.I. 22 Jan. 1828. Posted to 61st N.I. 20 Feb. 1828. Actg. Adjt. 61st N.I. 29 Oct. 1832. Shekhawat expedn. 1834; Lieut. 61st N.I. Adjt. 61st N.I. 8 Nov. 1834 till 14 Jan. 1842. Offg. S.S.O. at Karnal 16 Feb. 1836. Fur. s.c. 29 Dec. 1841 till 15 Dec. 1844, and 18 Feb. 1847 till retirement.

THE BENGAL ARMY, 1758-1834

Refs.: Rough Index to Le Mesurier or Le Messurier Papers, by
A. Le Mesurier, 1910. *G.M.* 1858, i. 342. *The Times*, 15 Feb. 1858.

LENNON, Henry (1762/63-1812). Lieut. Colonel. 16th N.I.
b. 1762/63. Country Cadet 1780. Ensign 21 Feb. 1781. Lieut.
16 Oct. 1781. Capt. 29 May 1800. Major 22 Jan. 1804. Lt.
Col. 18 Feb. 1808. Retired 18 Apr. 1810. *d.* Cheltenham 3 Jan.
1812, aged 49.

Brother of Col. Alfred Lennon, of Bath, and of Lt.-Col. Walter
Caulfeild Lennon, Madras Engrs.

Services: Apptd. a Gent. Vol. in the Coy. of Art. 3 Apr. 1780.
First Mahratta War 1782-4. Lieut 6th Bn. Sepoys in July 1787,
and in 1792. Bt. Capt. 1/13th N.I. in Aug. 1798. Capt. Lt.
1/4th N.I.; transfd. as Capt. to 2/18th N.I. 29 May 1800. Comdd.
Sebundy Corps in the ceded district of Allahabad 1803-4; comdd.
Allahabad Provl. Bn. 1805-6: Fur. 5 Oct. 1807 till retirement.
Posted as Lt. Col. to 16th N.I. in 1808.

Refs.: Misc. Gen. et Her. N.S. ii. 440. *G.M.* 1812, i. 194. *Bath
Chron.* 22 Jan. 1812. *A.R.* liv. M.I. in psh. church, Cheltenham.

LENNON, James (*d.* 1787). Lieutenant, Infantry. Cadet 1775.
Arrived in India 2 Nov. 1777. Ensign 9 Apr. 1777. Lieut.
19 Aug. 1778. *d.* in England 24 Oct. 1787.
m. Ann.

Services: Held a Commission in Middlesex Mil. in 1773. Apptd.
Cadet 15 Feb. 1776; sailed for India in the *Sea Horse* 30 Apr. 1777.
(? Second Mysore War; Lieut. 24th N.I.) Lieut. of the Chittagong
Mil. in 1785. Fur. 24 Jan. 1786 till death.

LENNOX, William George (1798-1884). Major General. 63rd
N.I. *b.* London 19 July 1798. Cadet 1817. Admitted 15 Aug.
1818. Ensign 15 Aug. 1818. Lieut. 16 Aug. 1818. Capt.
23 Apr. 1830. Major 17 Feb. 1850. Lt. Col. 14 July 1853.
Bt. Col. 28 Nov. 1854. Retired 31 Dec. 1861. Hon. Maj. Gen.
31 Dec. 1861. *d.* Glasgow 5 May 1884.

Ward of John Innes. *m.* Cawnpore 2 Dec. 1822, Mdlle Marie
Hyacinth Oclanis de Laval, formerly of Mauritius. She lived to
celebrate their diamond wedding. His dau. m. William Lamb
(1808-1867), *q.v.*

Services: Posted Lieut. to 1/22nd N.I. in 1819. Served with
Pioneers in 1822. Transfd. to 43rd N.I. (late 1/22nd) May 1824.
Fur. u.p.a. without pay 18 Feb. 1825 till 7 Sept. 1826; fur. p.a.
3 Apr. 1835 till 29 Dec. 1836. First Afghan War 1839-40 and

1841-2 (returned to India on leave in Nov. 1840); reoccupation of Kalat; Kandahar; Ghazni; Kabul; Istalif; Capt. 43rd N.I., with Nott's force (Medal). Apptd. to charge of mily. treasure chest, Army of Exercise, 17 Nov. 1843. Gwalior campaign; Maharajpur; Capt. 43rd N.I. (Bronze star). First Sikh War; Sobraon; Capt. 43rd N.I. (Medal). Posted Lt. Col. to 43rd N.I. Aug. 1853. Transfd. to 67th N.I. in 1853; to 38th N.I. 7 Mar. 1854; to 22nd N.I. in 1856; to 34th N.I. in 1857. Fur. s.c. 15 mos. July 1857. Transfd. to 63rd N.I. in 1859.

Refs.: Boase. *The Times,* 13 May 1884.

LEONARD, Nathaniel (*d.* 1790). Lieutenant, Artillery. (230) Country Cadet 1781. Fireworker 10 Aug. 1782. Lieut. 6 Feb. 1789. *d. unm.* Midnapore 24 Dec. 1790.

Son of —— Leonard and Mary his wife. Brother of Joseph, Thomas, Mary, and Anne. Cousin of James Griffith Hoare and John Toppin, *qq.v.*

Services: Apptd. Cadet Nov. 1781. Fireworker 1st Bn. Art. in July 1787.

Refs.: Will dated 3 Apr. 1789; proved 29 Dec. 1790.

LERMIT, Alfred (1799-1829). Captain, 12th N.I. *b.* London 11 Oct. 1799. Cadet 1817. Ensign (?) Lieut. 24 Aug. 1818. Capt. 8 Sept. 1828. *d.* Bombay 3 June 1829.

Ward of George Julius, M.D., of Richmond, Surrey. *m.* St. Pancras, Middlesex, 4 July 1821, Maria Elizabeth, dau. of George Baker, of Euston Cresc., London. (She *re-m.* 19 July 1830, James Vaughan, late M.C.S.) Ed. Cambridge Grammar School.

Services: Posted Lieut. to 1/12th N.I. in 1818. Fur. 1 Jan. 1819 till 1822. With Champaran L.I. 1822-3. Raised Mandleshwar Local Bn. 1823; Adjt. do. 1823 till death. Attacked by a Sepoy of his Corps who ran amok, and severely wounded by a sword, 25 Aug. 1828. Leave p.a. 4 mos. to Bombay 9 Jan. 1829.

Refs.: A.J. xxvii. 479. Intest.; Admon. (Bombay) 26 Aug. 1830.

LESLIE, Edmund (1770-1793). Fireworker, Artillery. (292) *b.* the Vicarage, Rockfield, Dunluce, co. Antrim, 30 Sept. 1770. Cadet 1790. Fireworker 1 Dec. 1791. *d.* Chunar 2 Oct. 1793.

4th and youngest son of Ven. Edmund Leslie, archdeacon of Down 1782, and Jane his 1st wife, dau. of John Macnaghten, of Benvarden, co. Antrim.

Services: Apptd. Cadet 6 May 1791; sailed for India in the *Airly Castle* 10 May 1791. No record of active service.

THE BENGAL ARMY, 1758-1834

Refs.: Burke's *Landed Gentry of Ireland*, p. 399, *s.n.* Leslie, of Leslie Hill, co. Antrim. *S.M.* 1794, p. 373.

LESLIE, John (1765/66-1813). Major, 5th N.I. *b.* Aberdeen 1765/66. Cadet 1782. Admitted 15 Nov. 1782. Ensign 30 Jan. 1783. Lieut. 17 Dec. 1789. Capt. 30 Sept. 1803. Major 22 Feb. 1809. *d.* in camp, Rewah, C.I., 2 Dec. 1813.

3rd (eldest by 2nd wife) son of John Leslie, professor of Greek, King's Coll., Aberdeen, sometime tutor to Lord Aberdeen, and Helen Ker his 2nd wife. Half-brother of Hugh Leslie, of Powis, co. Aberdeen.

Services: Apptd. Cadet 31 Oct. 1781; sailed for India in the *Worcester* 6 Feb. 1782, aged 16. Posted to 2nd Bengal Eur. Regt. 28 Feb. 1783. Fur. p.a. 15 Dec. 1784. Ensign 3rd Eur. Bn. in July 1787; transfd. from 6th Eur. Bn. to 10th Bn. Sepoys 5 Feb. 1790. Fur. 6 Feb. 1791 till 30 Oct. 1795. Lieut. 1st Bengal Eur. Regt. in 1796. Capt. Lt. 5th N.I. Fur. 8 Feb. 1803 till 5 Apr. 1807. Operations in Bundelkhand against Gopal Singh 1810; Tirowa; Major 1/5th N.I.

Refs.: Burke's *Landed Gentry*, 13th edn., p. 244, *s.n.* Burnett, of Kemnay, co. Aberdeen. *S.M.* 1814, p. 717. Will dated 6 July 1811; proved 5 Jan. 1814.

LESLIE, John. Ensign. Infantry. Cadet 1782. Arrived in India 15 Nov. 1782. Ensign 24 Feb. 1783. Resigned 15 Dec. 1784.

Services: Apptd. Cadet 2 Jan. 1782; sailed for India in the *Norfolk* 6 Feb. 1782. Posted to 3rd Eur. Regt. 28 Feb. 1783.

*****LESLIE, Matthew** (*d.* 1778). Colonel, Infantry. Transfd. as Lt. Col. from H.M.S. Lt. Col. 1 Sept. 1768. Col. (?) *d. unm.* Rajgarh, C.I., 3 Oct. 1778, of a bilious fever.

2nd son of Rev. Matthew Leslie, rector of Kilmacrenan and vicar-gen. of the diocese of Raphoe. Uncle of William Paterson (1751-1836) and grand-uncle of the wife of Thomas Otho Travers, *qq.v.*

Services: "Mathew Leslie, Surgeon," to be " Second Surgeon's Mate of Our Garrison in Our Island of Cape Breton, N., America," 1 Sept. 1745. To be one of the 3 Surgeon's Mates to the Hospital in N. America 24 Sept. 1754; there apptd. direct to Lieut. 48th Ft. (4 Nov. 1755) without being Ensign. Capt. 48th Ft. 29 Sept. 1760; exchanged to h.p. of Capt. 76th Ft. 25 Feb. 1768 till death. Served in America during the Seven Years' War; A.Q.M.G. of Braddock's force in the expedn. to Fort du Quesne; battle of Monongahela R. 9 July 1755 (w.). A.Q.M.G. in Wolfe's attack on Quebec in

1759. Capture of Havana 1762; A.Q.M.G. of Albemarle's force. Apptd. in England Lt. Col. on Bengal Est. 24 Dec. 1767. Apptd. Q.M.G. Bengal 12 Dec. 1773. First Rohilla War; battle of St. George; Lt. Col. comdg. Rt, Wing. Comdg. 1st Bde. in 1775; assumed comd. of Tempy. Bde. at Fatehgarh 29 Oct. 1777. Comdd. the force (6 Bns. of Sepoys from 1st Bde., some Cav. and Art.) that started from Cawnpore in May 1778 in order to march to the assistance of the Bombay Govt. against the Mahrattas. Owing to his dilatoriness the Bengal Council directed his supercession and appointed Col. Goddard, *q.v.*, to comd. the expedn. Leslie died, however, before this order reached him.

Refs.: Burke's *Landed Gentry*, 15th edn., p. 1362, *s.n.* Leslie, *formerly* of Courtmacsherry. *Cardew*, pp. 40-1. *Macpherson, passim*. *E.I.M.C.* i. 114-15. Will dated London, 17 Mar. 1768; proved 18 Mar. 1779. An uninscribed tomb at Rajgarh, Chhatarpur State, C.I., is said to be his.

LESTER, John Henry (1791-1823). Bt. Captain, 16th N.I.
b. London 23 Feb. 1791. Cadet 1805. Arrived in India 13 Dec. 1806. Ensign 14 Dec. 1806. Lieut. 16 Mar. 1810. Bt. Capt. 24 May 1821. *d.* Norfolk St., London, 10 Sept. 1823.

bapt. St. Mary's, Newington, Surrey, 2 Apr. 1791. Son of John Lester and Elizabeth his wife.

Services: Barasat C.C. Posted Ensign to 16th N.I. in 1807. Operations in Bundelkhand 1809-11; Lieut. 16th N.I. (? Reduction of Kalinjar 1812; Lieut. 2/16th N.I.) Intr. & Qmr. 2/16th N.I. 1 July 1814 till 1823. Fur. 1823 till death.

Refs.: *G.M.* 1823, ii. 284.

LEVADE, Charles Isaac (1784-1823). Bt. Captain, 3rd N.I.
b. Vevey, Switzerland, 25 Aug. 1784. Cadet 1805. Arrived in India 11 Feb. 1806. Ensign 5 Aug. 1806. Lieut. 30 Mar. 1810. Bt. Capt. 27 Mar. 1821. *d.* Asirgarh, C.P., 19 May 1823.

bapt. 1 Oct. 1784. Son of Louis Levade, M.D. Leyden, of Vevey and Lausanne,[1] and Marianne Justamont his wife. *m.* (before 1816)? His dau. *m.* Samuel Gardner Johnston, *q.v.*

Services: Posted Ensign to 3rd N.I. (? Operations in Bundelkhand 1809; Rajaoli; Ajaigarh; Ensign 1/3rd N.I.) Lieut. 1/3rd N.I. With 3rd Gren. Bn. 1815-16. In garrison at Asirgarh with his Regt., 1/3rd N.I., in 1823.

Refs.: *Livre D'Or*. M.I. Upper Fort cemetery, Asirgarh.

[1] *Note:* Author of "Dictionnaire géographique, statistique et historique du canton de Vaud," Lausanne, 1824.

THE BENGAL ARMY, 1758-1834

LEVINGSTON(E), St. John Charles (*d.* 1782). Captain, 10th N.I. Cadet 1768. Ensign 16 Feb. 1769. Lieut. 14 June 1770. Capt. 24 Aug. 1779. *d.* Dinapore 12 Aug. 1782.

Son of Mrs. Frances Hull, *alias* Levingston, of Marylebone.
Services : Was Capt. 1st Bn. 3rd Bengal Eur. Regt. in Oct. 1779 ; Capt. comdg. 2/10th N.I. in Jan. 1782.
Refs. : Will dated Cawnpore 30 Jan. 1782 ; proved 12 Jan. 1784.

LEWES, Charles James (1801-1881). Colonel. 3rd Bengal Eur. Regt. *b.* Hay, co. Brecknock, 15 Mar. 1801. Cadet 1818. Admitted 17 Mar. 1820. Ensign 20 Sept. 1819. Lieut. 11 June 1822. Capt. 14 July 1835. Major 15 Nov. 1853. Bt. Lt. Col. 20 June 1854. Retired 21 Sept. 1854. Hon. Col. 28 Nov. 1854. *d.* Stanley Villa, Cheltenham, 2 Apr. 1881.

Son of Eustace Lewes and Margaret his wife. *m.* St. John's, Calcutta, 16 Apr. 1823, Miss Harriet Ann Hodges. (She died 9 Feb. 1891, aged 85.)
Services : Posted Ensign to 1/25th N.I. 1820 ; transfd. to 50th N.I. (late 2/25th) May 1824. Actg. Adjt. 50th N.I. 16 Apr. 1825. S.A.C.G. 28 May 1825. Operations against the Bhils 1827 ; S.A.C.G. D.A.C.G. 2 cl. 3 Oct. 1828 ; 1 cl. 14 Sept. 1831 ; A.C.G. 2 cl. 1 Feb. 1837 ; 1 cl. 14 Aug. 1837 till Jan. 1845. Principal Comst. Ofr. with Army of Reserve (for Afghanistan) 20 Nov. 1842 till Jan. 1843. Fur. s.c. 10 Jan. 1845 till 20 Dec. 1847. Second Sikh War ; Capt. 50th N.I., in garr. at Lahore (Medal). Fur. p.a. 21 Mar. 1852 till retirement. Posted Major to newly-raised 3rd Bengal Eur. Regt. 15 Nov. 1853.
Refs. : The Times, 5 Apr. 1881.

LEWIN, William (*d.* 1783). Lieutenant, Infantry. Cadet 1781. Ensign 16 Sept. 1781. Lieut. 24 June 1783. *d.* Gogah Nullah, B. & O., 16 Nov. 1783.

Services : Was already in India when apptd. Cadet 10 Apr. 1781. N.F.P.

LEWIN, William Charles James (1806-1846). Lieutenant, Invalid Est. Artillery. (532) *b.* Southampton 13 June 1806. Cadet 1821. Arrived in India 23 Dec. 1822. 2nd Lieut. 10 May 1822. Lieut. 11 May 1825. Invalided 30 Nov. 1833. *d.* Cherrapunji, Assam, 4 Dec. 1846.

bapt. St. Mary Extra, Southampton, 20 July 1806. 5th son of Thomas Lewin, of the Hollies, Bexley, Kent, actg. mgte. co. Kent,

late M.C.S., and Mary his wife, dau. of Maj.-Gen. John Hale, of Plantation, nr. Guisborough, Yorks. His sister was mother of Hippisley Marsh and another sister m. a brother of Frederick Grote, qq.v. m. 15 June 1827, Jane Elizabeth, only dau. of Stephen Laprimaudaye, merchant in Calcutta. (She died 15 Aug. 1877, aged 74.) Addiscombe Cadet 1820-2.
Services : First Burma War ; Arakan 1825 ; 2nd Lieut. 3rd Coy. 2nd Bn. Foot Art., with Bdr.-Gen. J. W. Morrison's force. Actg. Adjt. & Qmr. Div. Art. 15 Jan. 1827. Fur. s.c. 7 Oct. 1828 till 17 June 1832. Posted to 1st Troop 1st Bde. H.A. 1829 ; to 1st Troop 2nd Bde. 2 Mar. 1831 ; to 4th Coy. 4th Bn. 3 Aug. 1832.
Ref. : Burke's Landed Gentry, 9th edn., p. 897, s.n. Lewin, of the Hollies, Kent. Ruvigny's *Plantagenet Roll of the Blood Royal*, Mortimer-Percy Vol., p. 249. Genealogist, N.S. xxiii. 172, s.n. Laprimaudaye. Will dated Calcutta 3 Aug. 1844 ; proved 19 Dec. 1846. M:I. at Cherrapunji.

LEWIS, Alfred (1804–1889). Lieut. Colonel. 32nd N.I. b. Lambeth 26 Apr. 1804. Cadet 1819. Admitted 21 Nov. 1820. Ensign 5 June 1820. Lieut. 11 July 1823. Capt. 3 Apr. 1835. Major 9 Apr. 1849. Retired 10 Aug. 1850. Hon. Lt. Col. 28 Nov. 1854. d. at his residence, 13 Wellington Rd., Charlton, 3 Apr. 1889.
Ward of John Prince, of 2 St. Thomas's St., Borough, Middlesex, hop merchant. m. (before 1828) ?
Services : Posted Ensign to 2/20th N.I. in 1820 ; transfd. to 16th N.I. July 1823 ; to 32nd.N.I. (late 1/16th) May 1824. First Burma War ; Arakan 1825 ; Lieut. 2nd L.I. Bn. (India medal). (? Shekhawat expedn. 1834 ; Lieut. 32nd N.I.) Actg. Adjt. 32nd N.I. and S.S.O. at Aligarh 15 June 1835. Fur. s.c. 16 Jan. 1839 till 5 Mar. 1842 ; p.a. 10 Feb. 1848 till retirement.
Refs. : A.J. N.S. iii. 154. The Times, 6 Apr. 1889.

LEWIS, Francis William (1759/60-1788). Ensign, Infantry. b. London 1759/60. Cadet 1782. Ensign 18 Jan. 1783. d. Dinapore 22 Oct. 1788.
Son of Rev. John Lewis, dean of Ossory, and Charlotte his 2nd wife, dau. of Adm. Cotterell. Ed. Westminster ; admitted 12 June 1770 ; K.S. 1775, aged 15. Hertford Coll., Oxon. ; matric. 25 Mar. 1779, aged 19.
Services : Sailed for India in the Worcester 6 Feb. 1782, aged 22. Posted to 2nd Bengal Eur. Regt. 28 Feb. 1783. Was Adjt. 2nd Eur. Bn. in Mar. 1786 ; Bk.Mr. at Dinapore 3 Apr. 1786 till death.
Refs. : Alumni Westmon. Alumni Oxon. Hickey, iii. 245.

THE BENGAL ARMY, 1758-1834   49

*LEWIS, Henry (d. 1795). Fireworker, Artillery. (221) Cadet (?) Fireworker 17 Dec. 1781. d. Fort Marlbro', Sumatra, 1795.
Services: Permitted to join Lt.-Col. Camac's detachment as a Vol. 15 Feb. 1781. Transfd. from the Bencoolen Est. 6 Nov. 1786. (Appears to have been retransfd. later.)

*LEWIS, James. Bt. Major. Infantry. Country Cadet 1769. Ensign 17 Sept. 1770. Lieut. 6 July 1776. Capt. 4 Feb. 1781. Retired on invalid pension with rank of Bt. Major 22 Nov. 1781.
Services: Apptd. Cadet 28 Dec. 1769. Apptd. Adjt. 17th Bn. Sepoys 22 Mar. 1780. Leave s.c. to sea 16 Jan. 1781. Saw active service (s.w.—ball through lungs). Pensioned as Capt. on Lord Clive's fund 6 Mar. 1783.

*LEWIS, Thomas. Captain. Infantry. Lieut. 1756/7. 1st Lieut. (Art.) 7 Apr. 1757. Capt. Lt. (Art.) 1757. Capt. (Inf.) 12 Jan. 1758. Resigned 1759.
Services: A sea captain; Captain of the *Swallow* in 1756. Vol. during the siege of Calcutta 1756; apptd. Master Attendant after Drake's desertion; escaped to the Dutch when the Fort was captured. Commissioned in the Art. in 1756 and served under Clive in Bengal in Feb. 1757; in charge of mily. stores in 1757; went home in Jan. 1759.
Refs.: Hill. *Hill's Calcutta.* *Orme MSS.—India*, xiii. 3639.

LEWIS, Thomas Frye (1790-1814). Lieutenant, 23rd N.I.
b. Curry Mallet, Somerset, 20 Dec. 1790. Cadet 1806. Arrived in India 25 Nov. 1807. Ensign 18 Oct. 1807. Lieut. 4 May 1812. d. Kunch, U.P., 24 Sept. 1814.
bapt. Curry Mallet 4 Mar. 1794. 2nd son of Rev. Thomas Frye Lewis, of Curry Mallet and Martock, Somerset (of the family of Lewis, of St. Pierre, co. Monmouth), and Charlotte Georgiana his wife, née Westcote. Brother of Editha Augusta, Charlotte Georgina, Maria Sophia, and Matilda Caroline. Owned the estate of Goulds, Widcombe, Somerset.
Services: Barasat C.C. Posted Ensign to 23rd N.I. in 1808. Lieut. 1/23rd N.I. No record of active service.
Refs.: G.M. 1815, i. 645. Will dated Koonch, June 1814; proved 18 Nov. 1814.

LEWIS, William Charles. (*See* BIRD, William Charles Lewis.)

LEWIS, Wynne George (1804-1823). 2nd Lieutenant. Artillery. (514) Subsequently Lieut. Madras Art. *b.* 13 Nov. 1804. Cadet 1820. 2nd Lieut. 19 Dec. 1820. Transfd. to Madras. *d.* nr. Chok, Kathiawar, 24 Nov. 1823, on his way from Jalnah to Bombay.

bapt. Newtown, co. Montgomery, 24 Nov. 1804. Son of Rev. Edward Lewis, rector of Newtown, and Charlotte his wife. Addiscombe Cadet 1819-20.

Service: 2nd Lieut. Madras Art. 16 June 1820; Lieut. 8 June 1821.

Refs.: Leslie, No. 366. *A.J.* xvii. 566. Intest.; Admon. (Bombay) 30 Sept. 1824.

LEYS, John (1785-1826). Lieut. Colonel, 29th N.I. *bapt.* Crathie, co. Aberdeen, 17 June 1785. Cadet 1800. Arrived in India 21 Aug. 1801. Ensign 24 Nov. 1801. Lieut. 30 Sept. 1803. Capt. 19 Feb. 1812. Major 10 Nov. 1821. Lt. Col. 1 May 1824. *d.* Fatehgarh 14 Dec. 1826.

Son of Francis Leys, in Inver, and Janet his wife, sister of John Donald Michie, *q.v.* Half-brother of James Ross, of Edinburgh, solicitor, and of Mrs. Hood, of Aberdeen.

Services: Operations in Jumna Doab 1802-3; Sasni; Bijaigarh; Kachaura; Ensign 15th N.I. Second Mahratta War 1803-4; battle of Delhi; Agra; Laswari; battle of Deig; Lieut. 15th N.I. Capt. Lt. 15th N.I. 25 Apr. 1810. Capture of Java 1811; Capt. Vol. L.I. Bn. Operations against the Sultan of Mataram 1812; Capt. Vol. L.I. Bn. Transfd. to newly-raised 1/28th N.I. in 1815. Bde. Major in Kumaon 1816-19; do. in Malwa 1819-22. Dy. Postmr. at Almora 30 Sept. 1817. Transfd. as Major to 2/28th N.I. Posted Lt. Col. to 56th N.I. (late 2/28th) May 1824; transfd. to 29th N.I. in 1825.

Refs.: A.J. xxiii. 857. Will dated Camp, 12 Apr. 1825; proved 24 Feb. 1827.

LIDDELL (or LIDDLE), Henry (*d.* 1769). 2nd Lieutenant, Artillery. (74) Cadet 1765. Fireworker 4 Sept. 1765. 2nd Lieut. 3 Apr. 1769. *d.* in India 1769.

Services: Cadet in 2nd Coy. Art. on 15 Aug. 1765, when he was apptd. a Condr. of Art. stores. Lieut. F. 2nd Coy.

Resigned his Commission 6 May 1766 during the "Batta mutiny"; readmitted 13 June 1766.

Refs.: Caraccioli, iii. 198.

LIDDLE (or LIDDELL), George (*d.* 1773). Lieutenant, Infantry. Cadet (?) Ensign 10 July 1769. Lieut. 26 June 1772. *d.* Bankipore, B. & O., 16 June 1773.
Services: N.F.P.

LILLYMAN, James (1732-1774). Lieut. Colonel, Engineers. Chief Engr., Bengal. *b.* 1732. Transfd. as Major from H.M.S. Arrived in India Sept. 1768. Major 2 Sept. 1768. Lt. Col. 19 Dec. 1772. *d. unm.* Calcutta 28 Dec. 1774, aged 42.

Services: Practitioner Engr. and Ensign H.M.S. 15 Aug. 1760; Lieut. Corps of Engrs. 20 Dec. 1765. Sailed for India in the *Grenville* 7 Apr. 1768. To be Dir. of Engrs., Bengal, and to rank as Major of that Corps (M.C. 1 Sept. 1768). With the C.-in-C. at Allahabad 1768-9; architect of Ft. Wm., Calcutta, 1770; Chief Engr. 17 Dec. 1772 till death.

Refs.: Will dated Balasore 3 Nov. 1774; proved 4 Jan. 1775. M.I. in S. Park St. cemetery, Calcutta.

LIMOND, Robert (*d.* 1813). Lieut. Colonel. Infantry. Country Cadet 1769. Admitted 18 Jan. 1769. Ensign 27 Feb. 1769. Lieut. 18 Sept. 1770. Capt. 4 Sept. 1779. Major 4 Mar. 1794. Lt. Col. 1 June 1796. Retired 2 Nov. 1798. *d.* Ayr 21 Feb. 1813. *m.* (?)

Services: Capt. 2/2nd Bengal Eur. Regt. in Oct. 1779; comdg. 9th Bn. Sepoys in July 1787 and Dec. 1792. Fur. 1796 till retirement.

Refs.: *S.M.* 1813, p. 318.

LIND, Joseph. (*See* **THORNTON, Joseph.**)

LINDESAY,[1] David Bethune (1781-1806). Captain, 4th N.I. *b.* 11 Feb. 1781. Cadet 1796. Arrived in India 13 Feb. 1798. Ensign 22 Sept. 1797. Lieut. 10 Sept. 1798. Capt. 1806. *d.* Agra 20 Oct. 1806.

4th and youngest son of Henry Lind(e)say, of Kilconquhar, Collinsbury, co. Fife, formerly of Wormiston (who assumed the surname of Bethune 2 Oct. 1779), and Margaret his 2nd wife, dau. of Martin Eccles, M.D. Half-brother of Rachel, wife of James Dickson, *q.v.*, and cousin-german of George Lindesay, *q.v.*, and Gilmour Alves, *q.v.*

Services: Posted Lieut. to 4th N.I. 1798. Second Mahratta War 1803-4; Aligarh; defence of Delhi; Lieut. 2/4th N.I., comdg. bodyguard of Lt.-Col. David Ochterlony, *q.v.* Capt. Lt. 4th N.I. 19 Dec. 1805.

Refs. : Burke's *Peerage*, 1923, p. 1403, *s.n.* Lindsay, E. *S.M.* 1807, p. 317. Will dated Kumrunah, 5 Mar. 1806 ; proved 9 Feb. 1807.

[1] *Note :* Burke and other authorities omit the E in the surname throughout this family ; it is spelt as above, however, in all official records.

LINDESAY, George (1792-1821). Captain, Engineers. *b.* Newburn, co. Fife, 6 Feb. 1792. Cadet 1808. Arrived in India 7 Dec. 1809. Ensign 28 Oct. 1809. Lieut. 6 May 1815. Capt. 1 Oct. 1819. *d.* nr. Kedgeree, Bengal, 10 Oct. 1821 : drowned through the upsetting of a pinnace.

Eldest son of Patrick Lindesay, of Coats (who purchased Wormiston from his brother Henry), sometime Capt. of the Snow *Britannia* in E.I., and Mary his wife, dau. of James Ayton, of Kippo. Brother of Henry Bethune Lindesay, *q.v.* Woolwich Cadet ; nominated to R.M.A. 13 May 1807.

Services : Stationed at Benares 1811-12 ; on survey Mirzapur and district from Sept. 1812. Operations in Baghelkhand Nov. 1813 till July 1814 ; Field Engr. and Surveyor to Rewah F.F. Nepal War 1814-15, with 4th Div. Nepal War 1816 ; Makwanpur ; Lieut. Engrs., with Centre Column. Supt. of embankments in the 24-Parganas 1817 ; stationed at the Presdy. 1819 till death.

Refs. : Burke's *Peerage*, 1923, p. 1403, *s.n.* Lindsay, E. *S.M.* 1822, i. 695. M.I. in S. Park St. cemetery, Calcutta.

LINDESAY, Henry Bethune (1809-1856). Major, 3rd L.C. *b.* 27 Oct. 1809. Cadet 1826. Arrived in India 28 Sept. 1827. Cornet (4 Jan. 1828) 4 Feb. 1828. Lieut. 8 Sept. 1839. Capt. 13 Dec. 1851. Major 20 June 1854. *d.* Mussoorie, U.P., 22 June 1856.

Of Marston Lodge, Cheltenham. *bapt.* Crail 20 Nov. 1809. Youngest son of Patrick Lindesay, of Coats, and Mary his wife. Ward of Henry Cheape and brother of James Lindesay, *q.v. m.* Karnal 9 Mar. 1837, Elizabeth, 3rd dau. of Colin Campbell, M.D., Physician Gen. Bengal. (*See also* Lionel Percy Denham Eld.) (She died 1903.)

Services : Posted Cornet to 3rd L.C. 4 Feb. 1828. Operations against the Kols 1832 (w.) ; Cornet 3rd L.C. Adjt. 3rd L.C. 9 Apr. 1836 till Dec. 1842. First Afghan War 1839 ; capture of Ghazni ; Lieut. 3rd L.C. (Medal). Transfd. to 5th L.C. 3 Dec. 1842 ; retransfd. to 3rd L.C. 1844. Adjt. 3rd L.C. 1844 till 13 Feb. 1852. First Sikh War ; Badhowal ; Aliwal ; Sobraon ; Bt. Capt. 3rd L.C. (Medal with clasp).

Refs.: Burke's *Peerage*, 1923, p. 1403, *s.n.* Lindsay, E. *I.M.* 16 Aug. 1856, p. 474. Will dated 14 June 1856; proved 25 Oct. 1856.

LINDESAY, James (1793-?). Lieutenant. 8th N.I. *b.* Newburn, co. Fife, 28 June 1793. Cadet 1810. Ensign 18 Mar. 1813. Lieut. 1 Feb. 1815. Struck off 4 July 1821. (*d.* before Apr. 1858.)
2nd son of Patrick Lindesay, of Coats, and Mary his wife. Brother of George Lindesay and cousin-german of David Bethune Lindesay, *qq.v.*
Services: Cadet d.d. 4th N.I. 1811-13; posted Ensign to 2/8th N.I. in 1813. Nepal War 1816; Lieut. 5th Gren. Bn., in 2nd Bde. Left Column. Fur. 31 Dec. 1816 till struck off.
Refs.: Burke's *Peerage*, 1923, p. 1403, *s.n.* Lindesay, E.

LINDSAY, Sir Alexander (1785-1872). General, K.C.B. Artillery. (325) *b.* London 14 Jan. 1785. Cadet 1803. Arrived in India 14 Aug. 1804. Lieut. 14 Aug. 1804. Capt. Lt. 7 May 1806. Capt. 22 Mar. 1813. Major 12 Aug. 1819. Lt. Col. 1 May 1824. Col. 2 July 1835. Col. Comdt. 2 July 1835. Maj. Gen. 28 June 1838. Lt. Gen. 11 Nov. 1851. Gen. 11 Sept. 1859. *d.* Early Bank, Perth, 20 Jan. 1872, of bronchitis.
bapt. St. Botolph's, Bishopsgate, 15 Feb. 1785. 2nd son of James Smyth Lindsay and Ann his wife. *m.* Govt. House, Calcutta, 1 Jan. 1820, Flora Loudon, dau. of Capt. Donald Mackenzie, of Hartfield, Applecross, co. Ross. Woolwich Cadet 21 Jan. 1800 till 14 Feb. 1804.
Services: See *D.N.B.* Ensign Capt. Meyrick's Independent Coy. of Foot 9 Jan. 1795; Lieut. in the Army 25 Feb. 1795; do. 104th Ft. (R. Manchester Vols.) 3 Mar. 1795; h.p. do. on disbandment of that Regt. 31 Aug. 1795 till death. Capture of Gohad 1806; Lieut. 2nd Coy. 1st Bn. Art. Operations against Dhundia Khan 1807; Komona; Capt. Lt. comdg. howitzers; Ganauri; Capt. Lt. 2nd Coy. 2nd Bn. Nepal War 1814-15; Capt. comdg. 6th Coy. 2nd Bn., with 4th Div. Nepal War 1816; Harriharpur 1 Mar. 1816 (s.w.); Capt. comdg. 6th Coy. 2nd Bn., actg. Asst. Field Engr. 1st Bde. (*Lond. Gaz*, 12 Aug. 1816) (India medal). Siege and capture of Hathras; Capt. comdg. 6th Coy. 2nd Bn. Third Mahratta War; Dhamoni; Mandala (but not personally engaged); Capt. 6th Coy. 2nd Bn. (ib. 7 Dec. 1818). To comd. Art. on Chittagong frontier 24 Sept. 1824. First Burma War; Arakan 1825; comdg. Art. of Gen. Morrison's Div. (clasp to India

medal). Fur. p.a. 8 Dec. 1827 till 16 Dec. 1831. Posted as Lt. Col. to 4th Bn. Art. 18 Nov. 1835. Tempy. Bdr. and comd. troops at Barrackpore 10 May 1838. Comdg. Presdy. Div. 21 Jan.-21 Feb. 1839. Fur. p.a. 5 Dec. 1839 till death. C.B. 28 Sept. 1831. K.C.B. 10 Nov. 1862.

Refs.: D.N.B. D.I.B. E.I.M.C. iii. 110-14. *The Times*, 24 Jan. 1872. *Boase*.

LINDSAY, James Gordon Campbell (1789-1812). Ensign, 1st N.I. *b*. I. of Tobago 2 July 1789. Cadet 1807. Arrived in India 14 Aug. 1808. Ensign 31 Aug. 1808. *d*. Muttra 6 Mar. 1812, in consequence of a fall from his horse while hunting.

(? Only son of James Lindsay, of I. of Tobago, merchant.) Nephew of Thomas Porter, of William Lindsay, of Oaklands, co. Lanark (whose dau. *m*. George Palmes, of Naburn Hall, Yorks.), and of "Aunt Bidgood," his mother's sister. He was brought up under the care of Charles Hamilton, of Tobago, and his wife Henrietta Anne. Ed. Eton 1799-1805. (? Glasgow Univ.; matric. 1807.)

Services: Barasat C.C. Posted Ensign to 1/1st N.I. in 1809. No record of active service.

Refs.: Eton School Lists. S.M. 1812, p. 886. Will proved 10 June 1812.

LINDSAY, John (1778-1817). Major, 10th N.I. *b*. 3 Jan. 1778. Cadet 1794. Arrived in India 3 Oct. 1795. Ensign 10 Nov. 1795. Lieut. 8 July 1797. Capt. 28 June 1806. Major 1 Mar. 1816. *d. unm.* Buxar 29 Oct. 1817.

Son of William Lindsay, of Feddinch, and Elizabeth Balfour Cameron his wife. Brother of William and Helen, cousin of Francis Balfour, and uncle of James Moncrieff Melville, of Hanley, nr. Edinburgh, W.S. (who *m*. a sister of Henry Bethune Lindesay, *q.v.*).

Services: Apptd. Cadet 13 May 1795; sailed for India in the *Francis* 24 May 1795. Lieut. 10th N.I.; Capt. Lt. do. 21 Sept. 1804. At P.W.I. 1803-6. Operations in Baghelkhand 1813; Entauri; Capt. 2/10th N.I. Fort Adjt. at Buxar 28 Apr. 1815 till death.

Refs.: Balfour Paul's *Scots Peerage*, v. 414. Will dated Buxar 26 Oct. 1817; proved 25 June 1818. M.I. at Buxar.

LINDSAY, William (1810-1857). Bt. Major, 10th N.I. *b*. Dundee 5 Feb. 1810. Cadet 1825. Arrived in India 22 Oct. 1826. Ensign 26 Apr. 1826. Lieut. 2 Oct. 1828. Capt. 23 Nov.

THE BENGAL ARMY, 1758-1834

1841. Bt. Major 20 June 1854. *d.* Cawnpore 18 June 1857, from wounds and fever.

bapt. Dundee 23 Feb. 1810. Son of William Lindsay, of Dundee, corn merchant, and Alice McKenzie his wife. *m.* Benares 20 Apr. 1846, Lilias, dau. of William Don (? and sister of William Gilbert Don, *q.v.*). (She died Cawnpore 17 June 1857.)

Services: Posted Ensign to 10th N.I. 5 Oct. 1826. Tempy. charge of 6th Coy. Pioneers 6 Dec. 1831. (? Rising in Cuttack 1836 ; Lieut. 10th N.I.) Fur. p.a. 26 Jan. 1837 till 10 Jan. 1840. Actg. A.A.G. Meerut Div. 28 Mar. 1842 ; do. Sirhind Div. 11 Aug. 1842. Army of Reserve (for Afghanistan) Oct. 1842 till Jan. 1843 ; Capt. 10th N.I. Offg. S.A.C.G. at Sukkur, Sind, 18 Dec. 1843. D.A.A.G. Saugor 22 Dec. 1847 ; A.A.G. do. 30 Apr. 1849 ; do. Cawnpore Dec. 1849 till death. Second Burma War 1852-3 ; Capt. 10th N.I. (Medal). Apptd. A.A.G. Pegu Div. 15 Nov. 1853. Siege of Cawnpore 1857 (w.).

Refs.: The Times, 25 Sept. 1857, p. 7. *I.M.* 1 Oct. 1857, p. 637. M.I. All Saints' Memorial Church, Cawnpore.

LINSTEDT, William (*d.* 1795). Lieutenant, Bengal Eur. Regt. Country Cadet 1781. Ensign 10 July 1782. Lieut. 7 Jan. 1785. *d.* 1795 : lost at sea on his return from Fort Marlborough ; struck off with effect from 31 July 1795. *m.* (before 1788) Rosalia. (She died 1825, aged 60.)

Services: Apptd. Cadet Aug. 1781. Lieut. 3rd Bengal Eur. Bn. in July 1787. Dy. Registrar, Mily. Dept.

LIPTRAP, John (1796-1878). General. 45th N.I. *b.* London 15 Apr. 1796. Cadet 1817. Admitted 5 Sept. 1818. Ensign (21 Apr. 1818) 30 Aug. 1818. Lieut. 4 Nov. 1818. Capt. 19 June 1831. Major 17 Feb. 1850. Lt. Col. 7 May 1855. Bt. Col. 20 June 1857. Maj. Gen. 22 Aug. 1865. Lt. Gen. 8 Mar. 1873. Gen. 1 Oct. 1877. *d.* 11 Kensington Gate, London, 21 Sept. 1878.

bapt. St. Dunstan's, Stepney, 21 June 1796. Son of John Liptrap, of 6 Vansittart Terr., Greenwich, and Elizabeth his wife, dau. of James Hunt, of Union Hall, Middlesex. *m.* 1st, St. John's, Calcutta, 1 Sept. 1823, Miss Maria Perigoe. *m.* 2nd, Eliza, widow of William Cook Wallace. (She died Surbiton 26 Feb. 1850.) *m.* 3rd, Calcutta 2 Jan. 1854, Emma, dau. of William Jell, and widow of — Nash.

Services: Posted Lieut. to 2/21st N.I. 1819 ; transfd. to 42nd N.I. (late 2/21st) May 1824. First Burma War ; Arakan 1825 ; Lieut. 42nd N.I. (India medal). Adjt. Chittagong Provl. Bn.

1 Mar. 1825 till 1830. First Afghan War 1839-40; Capt. 42nd N.I. (Medal). Fur. p.a. 13 Feb. 1841 till 13 Dec. 1842. Santhal revolt 1855; Bt. Lt. Col. comdg. 42nd N.I. Posted Lt. Col. to 8th N.I. Sept. 1855. Transfd. to 45th N.I. in 1856, and was comdg. that Regt. at Ferozepore when the Mutiny broke out at that station on 12 May: he brought back the men of 45th N.I. four different times when they mutinied and marched away with the Colours—thanked in Bde. Orders for daring bravery on 13 May 1857. Comdg. at Ferozepore. Fur. 25 Apr. 1865 till death.

Refs.: Boase. *The Times,* 8 Oct. 1878.

LIPTROTT, John (1813-1890). General. 4th N.I. *b.* 29 Jan. 1813. Cadet 1828. Arrived in India 22 May 1829. Ensign 7 Feb. 1829. Lieut. 25 Feb. 1834. Capt. 30 Apr. 1846. Major 10 Aug. 1856. Lt. Col. 28 Nov. 1859. Col. 18 Feb. 1866. Maj. Gen. 20 May 1871. Lt. Gen. 1 Oct. 1877. Gen. 1 Dec. 1888. *d.* 7 Clarendon Rd., Southsea, 25 Feb. 1890.

bapt. St. Matthew's, Friday St., Middlesex, 27 Apr. 1820. Son of Rev. John Liptrott, rector of Broughton Astley, Liecs., and Frances his wife. *m.* Mussoorie 25 July 1843, Louisa Caroline Cecilia, dau. of John Angelo, *q.v.* (*See also* John Abercrombie.) (She died Southsea 30 Dec. 1899.)

Services: Ensign d.d. 19th N.I. 13 July 1829; posted to 30th N.I. 1829. Actg. Adjt. Kumaon Local Bn. 28 Jan. 1835; permanent do. 15 Feb. 1836 till 13 Aug. 1839; actg. 2nd in comd. do. 9 Apr. 1839. 2nd in comd. 3rd Local Horse 13 Aug. 1839 till 1845. Transfd. to newly-formed 2nd Bengal Eur. Regt. 8 Oct. 1839. First Afghan War 1842; action in Khyber in Jan., under Bdr. Wild; reoccupation of Kabul, with Gen. Pollock's force (Medal). Operations at Kaithal Apr. 1843; Lieut. comdg. a party of 3rd (Tait's) Irreg. Cav. First Sikh War; Aliwal (horse shot under him); Bt. Capt., with Sirmoor Bn. (Medal). Comdt. 16th (became 17th) Irreg. Cav. 24 Jan. 1846 till 1859. Transfd. as Lt. Col. to 14th N.I. 1859. To comd. 4th N.I. (now 2nd Bn. (Prince Albert Victor's) 7th Rajput Regt.) 28 Dec. 1861; Comdt. do. 1 Jan. 1864 till 1 June 1869. Fur. 4 Feb. 1871 till death. Placed on u.s.l. 1 July 1881.

Refs.: Boase. *The Times,* 28 Feb. 1890. *I.L.N.* 12 Mar. 1890, p. 325 (portrait).

LISTER, Frederick George (1790–1870). Lieut. General. Colonel 31st N.I. (now 1st Bn. 7th Rajput Regt.). *b.* London 1 Jan. 1790. Cadet 1805. Arrived in India 11 July 1806.

THE BENGAL ARMY, 1758-1834

Ensign 14 Aug. 1806. Lieut. 9 Oct. 1808. Capt. 16 Mar. 1824. Major 4 Sept. 1839. Lt. Col. 30 Sept. 1845. Col. 13 Apr. 1855. Maj. Gen. 22 Aug. 1857. Lt. Gen. 23 Aug. 1869. *d.* St. Helier, Jersey, 28 Feb. 1870.

bapt. St. George's, Hanover Sq., 17 Feb. 1790. Son of Richard Lister and Catherine his wife. *m.* Calcutta 10 Mar. 1817, Harriette Hamilton, youngest dau. of Francis Hamilton Pearson, *q.v.* (*See also* John Fleming Hyde.) (She died London 11 Dec. 1873.) His dau. *m.* Charles Seton Guthrie, *q.v.*

Services: Barasat C.C. 11 mos. Posted Ensign to 26th N.I. in 1807. Nepal War 1814-15; Lieut. L.I. Bn., in 2nd Div. (India medal). Leave to N.S.W. 1815. Third Mahratta War; Dhamoni; Satanwara, with storming party (*Lond. Gaz.* 20 Jan. 1821); Lieut. 1/26th N.I. Actg. Intr. & Qmr. 1/26th N.I. 1818; Adjt. do. 28 Jan. 1822 till 17 June 1824; transfd. to 52nd N.I. (late 2/26th) May 1824. First Burma War. Actg. 2nd in comd. Sylhet Local Bn. 26 Jan. 1825; actg. Adjt. do. 22 Mar. 1827; Comdt. do. 31 Mar. 1828 till 18 July 1854. Operations against the Khasias May 1829, 1831, 1832. P.A. in Khasi Hills, and in addition comd. Sylhet L.I. Bn. 11 Feb. 1835 till 1854. Annexed the Rajah of Jaintia's capital and palace 15 Mar. 1835. Operations against the Khasias Aug. 1835. Led an expedn. against the Lushai Hill raiders 1850. Transfd. from 70th to 53rd N.I. Nov. 1849. Fur. s.c. 12 Apr. 1854 till death. Posted Col. to 31st N.I. 1855; Col. 2nd Bengal Native (Light) Inf. (late 31st N.I.) May 1861 till 1869.

Refs.: Boase. *The Times,* 9 Mar. 1870.

LISTER, Robert (*d.* 1771). Lieutenant, Infantry. Cadet 1766. Ensign 28 May 1766. Lieut. 15 Sept. 1767. Resigned 20 May 1769. *d.* Calcutta 2 Sept. 1771.

Services: N.F.P.

***LITTLE, Archibald** (*d.* 1765). Lieutenant, Volunteer Coy. Lieut. (?) *d.* (? Bankipore, B. & O.) May 1765.

His residuary legatee was Hon. Thomas Howe (4th son of Emanuel Scrope, 2nd Visct. Howe), comdr. of the *Winchelsea* Indiaman.

Services: N.F.P.

Refs.: Will dated Bankipore 25 May 1765; filed 6 Sept. 1765; proved 20 Dec. 1765.

LITTLE, John Peter. (*See* **LITTLEJOHN, Peter.**)

LITTLE, Matthew (1762-1797). Bt. Captain, Infantry. *b.* 29 Nov. 1762. Cadet 1781. Admitted 6 Mar. 1783. Ensign

29 Mar. 1781. Lieut. 21 July 1782. Bt. Capt. 7 Jan. 1796. d. Vizagapatam, Madras, 23 Nov. 1797.

3rd son of Matthew Little, of Langholm, co. Dumfries, and Helen his wife, 2nd dau. of James Pasley, of Craig, nr. Langholm.

Services: Apptd. Cadet 11 Jan. 1781; sailed for India in H.M.S. *Monmouth*; arrived Mar. 1783. Lieut. 4th Bn. Sepoys in July 1787, and Dec. 1792.

Refs.: Burke's *Peerage*, 1848, p. 778, *s.n.* Pasley, Bart., of Craig.

LITTLE, William (1806-1841). Captain, 3rd N.I. *b.* Biddlestone, Wilts., 5 June 1806. Cadet 1822. Arrived in India 13 May 1823. Ensign 10 May 1823. Lieut. 22 Apr. 1825. Capt. 25 Jan. 1837. *d.* Meerut 18 Nov. 1841.

Son of Thomas Little, yeoman, and Mary his wife. His sister *m.* Charles Ralfe, *q.v. m.* Calcutta 10 Sept. 1840, Charlotte Fullarton, dau. of James Dunbar. (She *re-m.* James Lumsdaine Walker, *q.v.*)

Services: Posted Ensign to 6th N.I. in 1823. Transfd. to 3rd N.I. (late 1/6th) May 1824. First Burma War; Arakan 1825; Lieut. 2nd L.I. Bn. Actg. Adjt. Rt. Wing 3rd N.I. 23 June 1826. Shekhawat expedn. 1834; Lieut. 3rd N.I. Fur. p.a. 16 Feb. 1836 till 8 Dec. 1837.

LITTLEJOHN, Peter (1762/63-1834). Colonel, 57th N.I. *b.* 1762/63. Country Cadet 1782. Admitted 21 Jan. 1782. Ensign 28 Apr. 1783. Lieut. 21 Mar. 1790. Capt. 13 July 1803. Major 4 Sept. 1811. Lt. Col. 4 Mar. 1816. Lt. Col. Comdt. 1 May 1824. Col. 5 June 1829. *d.* in a shop at Devonport 13 Jan. 1834, of apoplexy, aged 71.

Sometime of Grosvenor Pl., Bath. Son of Bailie William Littlejohn, merchant burgess of Aberdeen. *m.* Calcutta 15 Dec. 1795, Jane, sister of David Thomas Richardson, *q.v.* (*See also* James Doddington Sherwood.) Father of William Douglas Littlejohn, *q.v.*, Eliza Jane, wife of Ivie Campbell, *q.v.*, and Maria, wife of Peter Young, *q.v.*

Services: Posted to 3rd Bengal Eur. Regt. 28 Feb. 1783. In consequence of the reduction of the Army, became a Supy. Ensign 1786 till 2 Feb. 1790, when posted to 3rd Eur. Bn. Transfd. to 1st do. 1 Mar. 1790; to 35th Bn. Sepoys 11 Mar. 1790. Third Mysore War 1791-2; joined the army 22 Feb. 1791, and was apptd. Adjt. 1st Bn. Bengal Vols.; capture of Bangalore; battle of Arikera. Town Major of Bangalore Jan.-May 1792; Adjt. 25th Bn. in 1793; do. 3rd Eur. Bn. Aug. 1793; Lieut. 7th N.I. in June

THE BENGAL ARMY, 1758-1834 59

1798. Qmr. 1st Bengal Eur. Regt. 1799-1801; do. Eur. Regt. 1802-3. On service in Bundelkhand 1803; Capt. Bengal Eur. Regt. A.D.C. to Maj.-Gen. Sir John Macdonald, *q.v.*, comdg. at Chunar, 1805. D.J.A.G. at Dinapore and Chunar 30 May 1805; Bk. Mr. at Berhampore 23 Jan. till 23 Oct. 1806. Comdd. Bhagulpur Hill Rangers 9 Oct. 1806 till Mar. 1816. Posted Lt. Col. to 1/16th N.I. 4 Mar. 1816; comdg. at Chittagong 1817-18. Fur. p.a. 27 Nov. 1819 till 23 Sept. 1822. Transfd. to 2/22nd N.I. 1822; to 1st N.I. 1823. Posted as Lt. Col. Comdt. to 2nd N.I. 1 May 1824; to 50th N.I. 1826. Fur. s.c. 11 Jan. 1825 till death. Posted as Col. to 50th N.I. 5 June 1829; to 44th N.I. 5 Dec. 1829; to 57th N.I. 9 Jan. 1833.

Refs.: Burke's *Landed Gentry*, 13th edn., p. 1101, *s.n.* Littlejohn, of Invercharron, co. Ross. *E.I.M.C.* ii. 347-8. *G.M.* 1834, i. 340, 662. *Bath Chron.* 16 Jan. 1834. Will dated 5 Jan. 1823; proved 30 July 1834.

LITTLEJOHN, William Douglas (1807-1891). Lieutenant. 71st N.I. Pensioner on Lord Clive's fund. Subsequently vicar of Sydenham, Oxon. *b.* Bhagulpur, B. & O., 31 Aug. 1807. Cadet 1824. Arrived in India 4 Oct. 1825. Ensign 13 May 1825. Lieut. 7 Apr. 1826. Pensioned 31 Jan. 1835. *d.* 30 Victoria Sq., Clifton, 4 June 1891.

Son of Peter Littlejohn, *q.v. m.* Amelia St. George, 5th dau. of Col. Arthur Browne, formerly 58th Regt. and govr. of Charles fort, Kinsale, and sister of Adderley Thomas Browne, *q.v.* (She died Clifton 15 Mar. 1882, aged 74.) Corpus Coll., Camb.; B.A. 1837.

Services: Posted Ensign to 3rd Extra Regt. (became 71st N.I.). Fur. s.c. 5 Jan. 1829 till 9 Jan. 1832. d.d. 33rd N.I. 3 Feb. till 9 Sept. 1832. Fur. s.c. 9 Sept. 1832 till pensioned. No record of active service. Took holy orders; deacon 1837; priest 1838; vicar of Sydenham, Oxon., 1844-79.

Refs.: *Graduati Cantab. Crockford. The Times,* 6 June 1891.

LITTLER, Sir John Hunter (1783-1856). Lieut. General, G.C.B. Colonel 36th N.I. *b.* Tarvin, co. Chester, 6 Jan. 1783. Cadet 1799. Admitted 23 Oct. 1800. Ensign 19 Aug. 1800. Lieut. 29 Nov. 1800. Capt. 16 Dec. 1814. Major 22 Sept. 1824. Lt. Col. 23 May 1828. Col. 22 Jan. 1834. Maj. Gen. 3 Nov. 1841. Lt. Gen. 11 Nov. 1851. *d.* at his seat, Bigadon, Buckfastleigh, Devon, 18 Feb. 1856.

bapt. Tarvin 26 Jan. 1783. Eldest son of Thomas Littler and

Diana his wife, dau. of John Hunter, Dir. E.I. Co. *m.* 1st (before 1808) ? *m.* 2nd, Benares 25 June 1827, Helen Olympia, only dau. of Capt. Henry Stewart, who was son of John Stewart, claimant of the Earldom of Orkney. (She *re-m.* 1858, Thomas Aston Cockayne and died 12 Jan. 1885.)

Services : See *D.N.B.* Sailed for India in the *Kent*, which was captured off the Sandheads in Oct. 1800 by the French privateer *La Confiance.* Joined 2/18th N.I. in Dec. 1800. Posted Lieut. to 2/10th N.I. 17 Apr. 1801. Second Mahratta War; operations against Holkar 1805-6 ; Lieut. 2/10th N.I. Java 1811 ; Batavia ; Weltervreden ; Cornelis ; Lieut. 6th Vol. Bn. (Medal). Served in Comst. Dept. in Java till 1816. S.A.C.G., 3 cl., 7 Apr. 1818 ; 2 cl. 30 Dec. 1820. Fur. p.a. 24 Jan. 1824 till 22 Oct. 1826. Posted Lt. Col. to 14th N.I. 10 Sept. 1828 ; to 54th N.I. 7 Jan. 1832. Assumed comd. of Rajputana F.F. 14 June 1833. Fur. s.c. 28 Jan. 1835 till 3 Nov. 1836. Comdd. 70th N.I. 3 Dec. 1836 till 15 Nov. 1837. Tempy. Bdr. 2cl. comdg. troops in Assam 15 Dec. 1837. Bdr. 2 cl. on Est., Agra Div., 13 Apr. 1843. Gwalior campaign ; Maharajpur (w.) ; Maj. Gen. comdg. 3rd Div. (Bronze star). Bdr. 1 cl. comdg. Nasirabad F.F. Mar. 1844 ; do. Ferozepore Feb. 1845. First Sikh War ; defence of Ferozepore ; Ferozshahr (2 horses kld. under him) ; Maj. Gen. comdg. 4th Div. (Medal). Comdd. in Lahore ; later comdd. Punjab Div. ; transfd. to comd. Presdy. Div. Jan. 1848. Member of the Supreme Council of India 21 Feb. 1848 till 7 Dec. 1852. Dy. Govr. of Bengal Mar. 1849 till Jan. 1852. Fur. p.a. 11 Dec. 1852 till death. K.C.B. 2 May 1844 ; G.C.B. 31 Jan. 1848.

Refs.: Burke's *Landed Gentry*, 2nd edn., p. 734, *s.n.* Littler, of Cheshire. *D.N.B. D.I.B. Boase. G.M.* 1856, i. 424. *I.L.N.* vii (1846), p. 157 (portrait). Will dated 19 Apr. 1854 ; admon. 28 Jan. 1857.

LITTON, Benjamin (*d.* 1810). Major, 3rd N.I. Country Cadet 1780. Admitted 20 Apr. 1780. Ensign 15 Feb. 1781. Lieut. 12 Oct. 1781. Capt. 29 May 1800. Major 19 Feb. 1806. *d.* Aligarh 14 May 1810.

m. (before Sept. 1805) Johanna Maria. (She *re-m.* Sir George Petre Wymer, *q.v.*)

Services : Apptd. a Gent. Vol. in the Coy. of Art. 3 Apr. 1780. First Mahratta War 1781-4. Lieut. 4th Bn. Sepoys in July 1787 and in Jan. 1796. Adjt. 1/3rd N.I. till May 1800 ; Capt. 1/3rd N.I. ; transfd. as Major to 2/3rd N.I. in 1806.

Refs.: *Royal Mily. Chron.* i. 246.

THE BENGAL ARMY, 1758-1834 61

Note: The Will of one Benjamin Litton was proved in P.C. Dublin in 1764.

LIVESAY or LIVESEY, John Pearson (1780-1804). Lieutenant, 22nd N.I. b. 2 Mar. 1780.[1] Cadet 1794. Arrived in India 30 Oct. 1795. Ensign 26 Nov. 1795. Lieut. 30 Oct. 1797. d. Fatehgarh 27 Mar. 1804.
bapt. Christ Church, Manchester, 2 Apr. 1780. Son of John Livesey and Mary his wife.
Services: Apptd. Cadet 29 Apr. 1795. Operations in Jumna Doab 1803; Sasni; Kachaura; Lieut. 2/2nd N.I. Second Mahratta War 1803; battle of Delhi; Lieut. 2/2nd N.I. Transfd. to newly-raised 22nd N.I. 9 Nov. 1803.
Refs.: Pester, passim.
[1] *Note:* There is some doubt about this. Another John Livesay, son of John and Mary, was b. London 11 Feb. 1776, and bapt. at his father's house, 13 Old Broad St., 10 Mar. 1776.

LIVINGSTON or LEVINGSTONE, James (1759/60-1783). Cadet, Infantry. b. Norfolk 1759/60. Cadet 1782. d. Madras harbour 19 Apr. 1783 : blown up in the *Duke of Athol*. (See note to James Barnes.)
Services: Apptd. Cadet 17 Apr. 1782, aged 22. Sailed for India in the *Duke of Athol* 11 Sept. 1782.

LIVINGSTON, James (1784-1809). Ensign, 11th N.I. bapt. Strathblane, co. Stirling, 4 Apr. 1784. Cadet 1807. Arrived in India 21 Mar. 1809. Ensign 6 Feb. 1809. d. Calcutta 21 Oct. 1809.
3rd son of John Livingston, of Edenhill, and Isabella Brown his wife.
Services: Posted Ensign to 11th N.I. while still at Barasat C.C., but died before joining that Regt.

LIVINGSTONE, David Charles (1784-1807). Lieutenant, 21st N.I. b. Polmont, co. Stirling, 2 Oct. 1784. Cadet 1803. Arrived in India 27 Sept. 1804. Ensign 23 Sept. 1804. Lieut. 23 Sept. 1804. d. Aligarh 22 Nov. 1807, of wounds received in the assault of Komona fort on 18 Nov.[1]
bapt. Polmont 3 Oct. 1784. 9th and youngest son of Sir Alexander Livingstone, 9th Bart. of Westquarter, co. Stirling, and Jane his 2nd wife, dau. of Capt. the Hon. William Henry Cranston. Half-brother of Adm. Sir Thomas Livingstone, 10th Bart.

Services: Posted Lieut. to 2/21st N.I. in 1805. Operations against Dhundia Khan 1807 ; Komona (s.w.) ; Lieut. Gren. Coy. 2/21st N.I.

Refs.: Burke's *Landed Gentry*, 11th edn., p. 1023, *s.n.* Fenton-Livingstone, of Westquarter. Burke's *Peerage*, 1859, p. 620, *s.n.* Livingstone, Bart., of Westquarter. *A.A.R.* x. 21. *G.M.* 1808, ii. 851.

[1] *Note:* According to the MS. journal of Capt. Charles Stuart (1776/77-1854), *q.v.*, who was present during these operations, he was mortally wounded 27 Nov. before Ganauri whilst helping another officer back to the trenches.

LLEWELLIN, John (1753/54-1808). Lieutenant, Invalid Pension Est. Infantry. *b.* 1753/54. Country Cadet 1780. Ensign 2 Mar. 1781. Lieut. 23 Oct. 1781. Invalided 16 Feb. 1787. *d. unm.* Chunar 16 Oct. 1808, aged 54.

Services: Apptd. a Gent. Vol. in the Coy. of Art. 3 Apr. 1780. First Mahratta War 1782-4.

Refs.: Will dated Mirzapur 22 July 1808 ; proved 18 Nov. 1808. M.I. at Chunar.

LLEWELLIN, Richard (or Robert.) [1] Lieutenant. Infantry. Country Cadet 1781. Ensign 24 July 1782. Lieut. 20 Jan. 1785. Resigned 28 Dec. 1788.

Services: Apptd. Cadet 5 Nov. 1781. Applied for 3 yrs. leave of absence on 2 Dec. 1785, in order to travel in Persia and Arabia. Supy. Lieut., unposted, in July 1787. Fur. on h.p. 29 Oct. 1788.

[1] *Note:* Called William Llewellyn in M.C. of 5 Aug. 1782.

LLOYD, Adolphus Thomas (1803-1828). Lieutenant. 48th N.I. *b.* Hertford June 1803. Cadet 1820. Arrived in India Sept. 1821. Ensign 17 May 1821. Lieut. 11 Sept. 1823. Cashiered by G.C.M. 30 Dec. 1826. *d.* in India 23 Mar. 1828.

bapt. All Sts., Hertford, 21 Nov. 1803, aged 5 mos. Son of Rev. Thomas Lloyd and Frances his wife.

Services: Posted Ensign to 1/4th N.I. in 1821. Transfd. to 15th N.I. 1821 ; to 24th N.I. July 1823 ; to 48th N.I. (late 2/24th) May 1824. No record of active service.

Refs.: *A.J.* xxiii. 841-2.

LLOYD, Charles Heath (1785-1849). Lieut. Colonel, Invalid Est. 15th N.I. *b.* at the Charterhouse, London, 20 Oct. 1785. Cadet 1802. Arrived in India 12 July 1803. Ensign 28 July

1803. Lieut. 21 Sept. 1804. Capt. 16 Dec. 1814. Major
1 May 1824. Lt. Col. 13 Apr. 1827. Invalided 21 Dec. 1827.
d. unm. Chunar 20 Aug. 1849.

bapt. 17 Nov. 1785. 7th son of Rev. William Lloyd, of Frogmore, Herts., preacher of the Charterhouse, and Elizabeth his wife, dau. of Rev. Edward Bourchier, rector of Bramfield. Ed. Charterhouse; admitted a Scholar 22 May 1797; left 1803.

Services: Ensign d.d. 12th N.I. 1803. Posted Lieut. to 15th N.I. 1804. Capt. Lt. 15th N.I. 15 Sept. 1814. Pindari War 1819; siege and capture of Asirgarh; Capt. 1/15th N.I. Actg. Bk. Mr. Narbada Div. 1819; do. Hoshangabad 1820-1. Transfd. as Major to 31st N.I. (late 2/15th) May 1824; to 30th N.I. 13 May 1825. Posted as Lt. Col. to 15th N.I. 20 Dec. 1827. Comdg. Eur. Invalids at Chunar 3 Dec. 1843 till death.

Refs.: Alumni Carthusiani. Will dated 14 July 1849; proved 5 Oct. 1849. M.I. new cemetery, Chunar.

LLOYD, Christopher Alderson. (*See* **ALDERSON, Christopher.**)

LLOYD, Edward Salusbury (1806-1851). Bt. Lieut. Colonel, 49th N.I. *b.* 28 Feb. 1806. Cadet 1823. Arrived in India 19 May 1824. Ensign 16 Jan. 1824. Lieut. 11 Feb. 1826. Capt. 11 Apr. 1841. Major 13 Apr. 1848. Bt. Lt. Col. 7 June 1849. *d.* Nakodar, Punjab, 24 Jan. 1851.

bapt. Llangar, co. Merioneth, 26 Mar. 1806. 3rd son of Richard Hughes Lloyd, of Plymog, co. Denbigh, Gwerclas, co. Merioneth, and Bashall, Yorks., Major R. Merioneth Mil., and Caroline his wife, dau. of Henry Thompson. Brother of Hugh Hughes Lloyd, *q.v.* *m.* Kasauli 16 Apr. 1844, Catherine Anne, only dau. of Rev. Robert Wynell-Mayow, and sister of John Harding Wynell-Mayow, *q.v.* (She *re-m.* Rev. Edward Girdlestone.)

Services: Ensign d.d. 26th N.I. 19 May 1824. Posted Ensign to 25th N.I. Aug. 1824. Served at Penang, Singapore and Malacca Dec. 1824 till Aug. 1826. Transfd. as Lieut. to 49th N.I. 11 Feb. 1826. Fur. s.c. 25 Jan. 1828 till 21 May 1831. Actg. Adjt. Nassiri Bn. 25 Feb. 1834; offg. 2nd in comd. do., and actg. Asst. to P.A. Sabathu 15 Aug. 1835 till Apr. 1836. Adjt. 49th N.I. 17 Sept. 1838 till 1 Nov. 1839. Demonstration against Jodhpur 1839. With Army of Reserve (for Afghanistan) Oct. 1842 till Feb. 1843; with 2nd L.I. Bn. Second Sikh War; both sieges of Multan; Major comdg. 49th N.I. (Medal with clasp). Comdd. 49th N.I. till death.

Refs.: Burke's *Peerage*, 1859, p. 1061, *s.n.* Williams-Bulkeley,

Bart., of Penryhn. Burke's *Landed Gentry*, 4th edn., p. 883, *s.n.* Lloyd, of Plymog; 13th edn., p. 1232, *s.n.* Wynell-Mayow, of Bray and Saltash, Cornwall. *De Rhé-Philipe*. *G.M.* 1851, ii. 216. Will dated Nakodar 20 Jan. 1851; proved 9 Feb. 1852. M.I. at Phillaur.

LLOYD, Edwin (1758/59-1804). Major, 7th N.I. *b.* Lincs. 1758/59. Cadet 1779. Admitted 1779. Ensign 24 June 1779. Lieut. 15 Feb. 1781. Capt. 30 Oct. 1797. Major 26 Dec. 1802. *d.* Cuttack 19 May 1804.

Brother of Robert Lloyd, of Dyke, nr. Bourn, Lincs. *m.* Chittagong 30 Aug. 1790, Miss Ann Speeler. (She died Chunar 3 Aug. 1797.)

Services: Apptd. Cadet 15 July 1779; sailed for India in the *Bridgwater* 12 Feb. 1780, aged 21. Lieut. 24th Bn. Sepoys in July 1787; Capt. 7th N.I. in 1798. Second Mahratta War; operations in Cuttack 1803-4; Major 2/7th N.I.

Refs.: Will dated 14 Apr. 1804; proved in 1804.

LLOYD, Frederick (1809-1856). Major, 19th N.I. *b.* Chester 12 Mar. 1809. Cadet 1826. Arrived in India 13 Oct. 1827. Ensign 8 May 1827. Lieut. 3 Sept. 1833. Capt. 29 July 1840. Major 26 Apr. 1852. *d.* Bournemouth 26 Aug. 1856.

bapt. Chester 10 Jan. 1810. Son of John Lloyd, B.C.S. Brother of Henry Lloyd and cousin-german of Sir William Lloyd, *qq.v.*[1] *m.* 1st, Meerut 13 Mar. 1830, Miss Mary Hannah Mathers. (She died Saugor 25 Mar. 1841.) *m,* 2nd, Patna 15 June 1843, Harriet Georgiana, dau. of Arthur Smelt, *q.v.*

Services: Posted Ensign to 19th N.I. 3 Jan. 1828; Intr. & Qmr. do. 10 Apr. till 1 July 1835. S.A.C.G. 1 July 1835. Operations against Jhansi 1839. First Afghan War; attached to Gen. Pollock's force 23 Feb. 1842; with force under Bdr. Monteath; operations against the Shinwaris (*Lond. Gaz.* 11 Oct. 1842); reoccupation of Kabul; S.A.C.G. (Medal). D.A.C.G. 2 cl. 24 Dec. 1842; 1 cl. 10 Jan. 1844; A.C.G. 2 cl. 24 Dec. 1847 till 1853. Second Sikh War; Multan; Gujerat; A.C.G. (Medal with clasp). Leave s.c. 1 yr. to Simla 20 Nov. 1852. Offg. A.C.G. 1 cl. Oct. 1853, for a few weeks only. Fur. s.c. 3 yrs. May 1856. till death.

Refs.: Burke's *Landed Gentry*, 2nd edn., iii. 207, *s.n.* Lloyd, of Brynestyn, co. Denbigh. *G.M.* 1856, ii. 523. Will dated 20 May 1856; admon. 14 Jan. 1857.

[1] *Note:* His dau. by Mary Hannah his 1st wife was described

on her marriage on 7 Apr. 1858 as, " niece of the late Sir William Lloyd, of Llanderden, nr. Conway."

LLOYD, George Pryce (1803-1831). Lieutenant, 2nd L.C. *b.* Llandilo, co. Carmarthen, 25 May 1803. Cadet 1823. Arrived in India 29 Dec. 1824. Cornet 11 Dec. 1824. Lieut. 13 May 1825. *d. unm.* 28 July 1831.

3rd son of Bell Lloyd, of Crogan, Merioneth (who was younger brother of Edward Pryce Lloyd, 1st Baron Mostyn), and Anne his wife, sister of Thomas, 1st Viscount Anson. Cousin-german of Frederick Walpole Anson, *q.v.*

Services : Ensign d.d. 2nd Bengal Eur. Regt. 8 Jan. 1825. Posted Ensign to 41st N.I. 31 Mar. 1825. Transfd. to Cav. 4 June 1825 ; Cornet d.d. 1st Extra Cav. Regt. 11 June 1825 ; posted to 2nd L.C. 1825 ; actg. Adjt. do. 25 Apr. 1827. Adjt. 4th Local Horse 24 Mar. 1828. Bde. Major at Cawnpore 27 Oct. 1829 till death. No record of active service.

Refs.: Burke's *Peerage*, 1923, p. 1614, *s.n.* Mostyn, B. *A.J.* N.S. vii. 104.

LLOYD, George William Aylmer (1789-1865). Lieut. General, C.B. Colonel 28th N.I. *b.* Kilbrogan, co. Cork, 4 July 1789. Cadet 1804. Arrived in India 10 Dec. 1805. Ensign 31 Oct. 1804. Lieut. 17 Sept. 1806. Capt. 11 July 1823. Major 3 June 1830. Lt. Col. 7 Jan. 1836. Col. 27 Aug. 1847. Maj. Gen. 20 June 1854. Lt. Gen. 2 June 1860. *d.* Darjeeling 4 June 1865.

Eldest son of Rev. Richard Lloyd, rector of Clonoulty, co. Tipperary, and Priscilla his wife, dau. of Rev. John Lord, rector of Clonkelly. Cousin-german of Henry Vereker Lloyd, *q.v. m.* St. John's, Calcutta, 8 Mar. 1824, Caroline Anne, 2nd dau. of Capt. William Bruce, H.E.I.C.S., Resdt. at Bushire. (She died Birkenhead 29 Jan. 1873, aged 66.)

Services: Posted Lieut. to 2nd N.I. in 1806. (? Expedn. to Macao 1808-9 ; Lieut. Vol. Bn.) Capture of Java 1811 ; Lieut. 7th (L.I.) Vol. Bn. (Medal). Returned from Java in comd. of Left Wing L.I. Vol. Bn. 15 Nov. 1816. Transfd. to newly-raised 1/28th N.I. Jan. 1815 ; Adjt. do. 28 Feb. 1817. Third Mahratta War ; Madhurajpura. Intr. & Qmr. 1/28th N.I. 9 Sept. 1818 till 1823. Transfd. to 33rd N.I. July 1823 ; to 65th N.I. (late 1/33rd) May 1824 ; to newly-raised 3rd Extra Regt. (became 71st N.I.) May 1825. Comdt. Dinajpur Local Bn. 12 July 1825 till 1826. First Burma War (India medal). To settle boundary between Nepal and Sikkim frontiers 1 Mar. 1827. Fur. p.a. 4 Dec. 1829

till 23 Dec. 1832. On special duty at Rangpur 17 Oct. 1833.
Posted as Lt. Col. to 52nd N.I. 29 Apr. 1836 ; to 43rd N.I. 19 July
1836 ; to 5th N.I. 15 Dec. 1838. First China War 1840-2 ; Chinkiang Foo (*Lond. Gaz.* 24 Nov. 1842) (Medal). Comdd. Vol. Regt.
12 Feb. 1840 till 1 June 1841 ; do. 2nd Vol. Regt. 12 Jan 1842 till
1 Mar. 1843. Transfd. from 68th to 5th N.I. 21 Jan. 1843 ; to
28th N.I. 23 Mar. 1843. Posted Col. to 28th N.I. 17 Sept. 1847.
Bdr. comdg. Rajputana F.F. 21 Jan. 1848 ; Multan F.F. Dec. 1849 ;
comdg. at Agra Dec. 1850 till Feb. 1853. To tempy. comd. of
Cawnpore Div., with rank of Bdr., Apr. 1854. Apptd. to Divl.
Staff of Army 26 Sept. 1854 ; Maj. Gen. comdg. Dinapore Div.
10 Nov. 1854. Santhal revolt 1855 ; Maj. Gen. comdg. the F.F.
Was in comd. at Dinapore on outbreak of the Mutiny and was
removed from the Divl. Staff in July 1857. C.B. 24 Dec. 1842.

Refs.: Burke's *Landed Gentry of Ireland*, p. 411, *s.n.* Lloyd,
late of Lloydsboro', co. Tipperary. *Boase. The Times*, 26 July
1865. M.I. in St. Andrew's, Darjeeling.

LLOYD, Henry (1801-1879). Major. 36th N.I. *b.* Chester
9 Feb. 1801. Cadet 1816. Admitted 9 Sept. 1817. Ensign (?)
Lieut. 1 Aug. 1818. Capt. 14 June 1833. Retired 25 July 1844.
Hon. Major 28 Nov. 1854. *d.* 29 Apr. 1879.

bapt. Holy Trinity, Chester, 28 May 1802. Son of John Lloyd,
B.C.S., and M—— his (? 2nd) wife. Brother of Frederick Lloyd,
q.v. m. Dinapore 12 July 1821, Charlotte, 3rd dau. of Bt. Capt.
William Williams, H.M. 59th Ft. (*See also* John Lewis Taylor.)
His dau. *m.* William Henry Delamain, *q.v.*

Services: d.d. 20th N.I. 1817 ; posted Lieut. to 18th N.I. in
1818. Adjt. 2/18th N.I. 3 Feb. 1821 till 1825. Transfd. to 37th
N.I. (late 2/18th) May 1824. Leave s.c. 12 mos. to N.S.W. 24 Dec.
1824. Transfd. to 36th N.I. 28 June 1825 ; Intr. & Qmr. do.
6 Jan. 1826 till 28 Sept. 1829. Fur. s.c. 15 Dec. 1828 till 9 Nov.
1831. Shekhawat expedn. 1834 ; Capt. 36th N.I. Leave s.c.
2 yrs. to Tasmania 5 Nov. 1840. Comdg. troops at Titalia, Bengal,
in Apr. 1843.

Refs.: Burke's *Landed Gentry*, 2nd edn., iii. 207, *s.n.* Lloyd, of
Brynestyn, co. Denbigh.

LLOYD, Henry Bennett (1779-1804). Lieutenant, 12th N.I.
b. St. George's, Hanover Sq., London, 2 June 1779. Cadet 1796.
Arrived in India 29 Jan. 1798. Ensign 2 Oct. 1797. Lieut.
10 Sept. 1798. *d.* Mokandra Pass 10 July 1804 : kld. in action
during Monson's retreat.

THE BENGAL ARMY, 1758-1834

bapt. 30 June 1779. Son of Richard Lloyd, of Maryland, N. America, and Joanna (or Ann) Leigh his wife, of I.W.
Services: Posted Ensign to 1st Bengal Eur. Regt. in 1798; transfd. as Lieut. to 12th N.I. 1798. Second Mahratta War 1803-4; Laswari; Monson's retreat (kld.); Lieut. 1/12th N.I.
Refs.: Pester, p. 304. Will dated Chandausi, 16 Aug. 1803; proved 26 June 1805.

LLOYD, Henry Vereker (1793-1870). Cornet. 4th N.C. Subsequently Ensign h.p. 86th Foot. *b.* St. Michael's, Limerick, 27 Jan. 1793. Cadet 1807. Arrived in India 14 Sept. 1808. Cornet 9 Dec. 1809. Resigned 31 Dec. 1812. *d.s.p.* co. Cork 16 Mar. 1870.
3rd son of Frederick Lloyd, of Ballymacrease (of Cranna), and Julia his wife, dau. of Thomas Vereker, of Roxborough, co. Limerick. *m.* Miss Elizabeth Jane Jopp. (She died Cheltenham 23 Aug. 1884.)
Services: Posted Cornet to 4th N.C. in 1809. No record of active service. Ensign 87th Foot 31 Jan. 1816; Ensign 86th Foot 1 Jan. 1819; h.p. do. 25 Oct. 1821.
Refs.: Burke's *Landed Gentry of Ireland,* p. 411, *s.n.* Lloyd, late of Lloydsboro', co. Tipperary. Burke's *Peerage,* 1923, p. 1005, *s.n.* Gort, V.

LLOYD, Herbert (1751/52-1818). Lieut. Colonel. Infantry. *b.* 1751/52. Cadet 1770. Admitted 24 Sept. 1770. Ensign 7 Dec. 1772. Lieut. 20 Aug. 1776. Capt. 9 Mar. 1781. Major 27 July 1796. Lt. Col. (?) Retired 19 June 1797. *d.* Brompton, Middlesex, 22 Feb. 1818, aged 66.
Services: First Rohilla War. Posted to Nawab-Wazir's Inf. 7 Aug. 1777. Fur. 31 Oct. 1786 till 30 Aug. 1790. Capt. 3rd Bengal Eur. Bn. Apptd. A.D.C. to Col. John Fullarton, *q.v.*, 22 Nov. 1794.
Refs.: A.J. v. 427. *G.M.* 1818, i. 468.

LLOYD, Hugh Hughes (1807-1887). Colonel. 72nd N.I. *b.* Llangar, co. Merioneth, 5 Nov. 1807. Cadet 1825. Arrived in India 25 June 1826. Ensign 5 Feb. 1826. Lieut. 20 May 1829. Capt. 7 Feb. 1838. Bt. Major 7 June 1849. Bt. Lt. Col. 28 Nov. 1854. Retired 1 July 1857. Hon. Col. 1 July 1857. *d.* Wyavon Lodge, Monmouth, 7 Apr. 1887.
bapt. Llangar 10 Nov. 1807. 4th son of Richard Hughes Lloyd and Caroline his wife. Brother of Edward Salusbury Lloyd, *q.v.*

m. St. David's 7 Apr. 1859, Caroline, 2nd dau. of Henry Braham Harris, of Bryanston Sq., London.

Services: Ensign d.d. 49th N.I. 8 July 1826. Posted to 4th Extra Regt. (became 72 nd N.I.) 26 Sept. 1826. Fur. p.a. 13 Dec. 1837 till 10 Aug. 1840. Actg. Dy. Paymr. Sirhind Div. 26 Nov. 1843. Second Sikh War; 1st Siege of Multan, comdg. 72nd N.I. till 30 Nov. 1848 ; comdd. Rt. Centre Column in attack on suburbs of that fortress 27 Dec. ; Gujerat ; Capt. comdg. 72nd N.I. (Medal with clasps). Fur. 1853 till Nov. 1854 ; fur. s.c. 18 mos. Mar. 1857.

Refs.: Burke's *Landed Gentry*, 4th edn., p. 883, *s.n.* Lloyd, of Plymog, Gwerclas and Bashall. Burke's *Peerage*, 1859, p. 1061, *s.n.* Williams-Bulkeley, Bart., of Penryhn, co. Carnarvon. *The Times*, 14 Apr. 1887.

LLOYD, John. Ensign. Infantry. Cadet 1761. Ensign 11 Oct. 1761. Dismissed 12 Jan. 1762.

Services: N.F.P.

LLOYD, John (*d.* 1778). Lieutenant, Cavalry. Cadet 1771. Ensign 15 Feb. 1773. Lieut. 11 Mar. 1778. *d.* 1778, on active service with the Bombay detachment.

Services: Transfd. from Inf. to Cav. 6 Apr. 1778. First Mahratta War 1778 ; Lieut. Cav.

LLOYD, John (1787-1819). Lieutenant, Invalid Est. 15th N.I. *bapt.* St. Peter's, Worcester, 20 Feb. 1787. Cadet 1804. Arrived in India 21 June 1806. Ensign 7 Oct. 1805. Lieut. 15 Nov. 1805. Invalided 12 May 1815. *d.* 1819.

Son of James Lloyd and Elizabeth his wife.

Services: Posted Lieut. to 15th N.I. in 1806. With Rangpur Bn. 1813-15. No record of active service.

LLOYD, Randall Walne (1789-1808). Ensign, 16th N.I. *b.* and *bapt.* N. Walsham, Norfolk, 13 Mar. 1789. Cadet 1804. Arrived in India 25 Feb. 1806. Ensign 3 May 1806. *d.* Kunch, U.P., 22 May 1808.

Son of Rev. Thomas Lloyd and Susannah his wife, *née* Walne. (*Probably* cousin-german of James Wright (*b.* 1784), *q.v.*)

Services: Barasat C.C. Posted Ensign to 1/16th N.I. in 1807. (? Operations in Bundelkhand 1807 ; Sehlehuganj ; Ensign 1/16th N.I.)

LLOYD, Sir William (1782-1857). Lieut. Colonel, Kt. Bach. 3rd Extra Regt. N.I. *b.* Wrexham Regis 29 Dec. 1782. Cadet

THE BENGAL ARMY, 1758-1834

1799. Admitted 18 Dec. 1800. Ensign 6 Nov. 1800. Lieut. 16 Nov. 1802. Capt. 16 Dec. 1814. Major 22 Oct. 1824. Retired 14 July 1825. Hon. Lt. Col. 28 Nov. 1854. *d.* Llandudno 16 May 1857.

Of Brynestyn, nr. Wrexham, co. Denbigh. J.P.; high sheriff 1829. *bapt.* Wrexham 26 Jan. 1783. Eldest son of Richard Middleton Massie Lloyd, of Plas Madoc and Brynestyn, and Mary his wife, dau. and co-heir of William Bowey, of Chester. Cousin-german of Christopher Alderson, *q.v.*, and of Thomas Evans (1776-1812), *q.v. m.* (?)

Services: Posted Ensign to 2/5th N.I. 17 Apr. 1801. Comdd. the Marines in the *Bombay* frigate in the expedn. under Commodore John Hayes, Bombay Marine, against the seaport of Muckee, on the W. coast of Sumatra, in July 1804. Comdd. Resdt.'s escort at Nagpur 1807 till Aug. 1820, when it was disbanded. Third Mahratta War; Sitabaldi (w. 4 times); battle of Nagpur; siege of Nagpur; Capt. comdg. Resdt.'s escort (India medal). Travelled in Upper India 1821-2. Fur. 1823 till retirement. Transfd. to 11th N.I. (late 1/5th) May 1824; to newly-raised 3rd Extra Regt. May 1825. Pub. 1840 "Narrative of a Journey from Cawnpore to the Borendo Pass in the Himalayas, via Gwalior, Agra, Delhi and Sirhind," 2 vols. 8vo, London. Kt. Bach. 18 July 1838. Major Comdt. Denbigh Yeomanry Cav.; Lt. Col. do. 9 Apr. 1856.

Refs.: Burke's *Landed Gentry*, 2nd edn., iii. 207, *s.n.* Lloyd, of Brynestyn, co. Denbigh. *D.N.B., s.n.* Alexander Gerard, *q.v. E.I.M.C.* iii. 146-67. Lodge's *Peerage, etc.* 1851. *Boase.*

LLOYD, William Christopher (1815-1841). Lieutenant. 53rd N.I. *b.* 26 Aug. 1815. Cadet 1832. Arrived in India 10 June 1834. Ensign 10 June 1834. Lieut. 21 Apr. 1837. Struck off 29 Feb. 1840. *d. unm.* Llangadock (or Llangennech), co. Carmarthen, 14 June 1841.

bapt. Woolwich 20 Sept. 1815. 5th son of John William Lloyd, of Dan-yr-Allt, co. Carmarthen, and of South Park, Kent, J.P. cos. Carmarthen and Kent, sometime clerk of the survey, Woolwich dockyard, and Anna Maria his wife, 6th dau. of John Longley, recorder of Rochester. Ed. Westminster; admitted 9 Apr. 1828.

Services: Ensign d.d. 43rd N.I. 21 June 1834. Posted to 53rd N.I. 5 Nov. 1834. Fur. s.c. 14 Aug. 1837 till struck off with effect from 29 Feb. 1840 (G.O. 26 Aug. 1842.). No record of active service.

Refs.: Burke's *Landed Gentry*, 13th edn., p. 1106, *s.n.* Lloyd, late of Dan-yr-Allt. *Westminster School Register. The Times,* 25 June 1841.

*LOCK, Henry (1798-1824). Lieutenant, 52nd N.I. *bapt.* Newchurch, I.W., 10 June 1798. Cadet 1819. Ensign 7 Jan. 1820. Lieut. 16 Apr. 1822. *d.* Mominabad, Hyderabad, 16 May 1824, of cholera.

Son of Walter Lock, of Haylands, I.W., Adm. R.N., by his wife, sister of Michael Head, Capt. R.N. *m.* Barrackpore 28 Sept. 1820, Louisa Sophia Raynsford, 2nd dau. of Nicolls Raynsford. (She *re-m.* Fred Alston.)

Services: Ensign 51st Ft. 13 Oct. 1814; battle of Waterloo (Medal); h.p. 60th Ft. 30 Sept. 1819. Posted Ensign to 2/24th N.I. 1820. d.d. Nizam's army 1820 till death; with Russell Cav. 1820-2; with Reformed Horse 1822 till death; Bde. Major. Transfd. to 26th N.I. Sept. 1823; to 52nd N.I. (late 2/26th) May 1824.

Refs.: Misc. Gen. et Her. 3S. ii. 162, *s.n.* Raynsford. Intest.; admon. (Bombay) 7 Dec. 1825. M.I. Mominabad.

LOCK, John Bascombe (1807-1842). Bt. Captain, 5th N.I. *b.* Dorchester 25 Mar. 1807. Cadet 1825. Arrived in India 28 June 1826. Ensign 13 Feb. 1826. Lieut. 13 Mar. 1834. Bt. Capt. 13 Feb. 1841. *d.* 24 Jan. 1842: kld. in action in the Khyber Pass.

bapt. St. Peter's, Dorchester, 12 Jan. 1808. 3rd son of William Lock, of North St., Dorchester, coal merchant, and Ann his wife. *m.* Calcutta 12 Dec. 1840, Jane, eldest dau. of William May, of Bridgwater, Somerset. (She died 30 July 1870.)

Services: Ensign d.d. 6th Extra Regt. 8 July 1826. Posted to 1st Bengal Eur. Regt. 26 Sept. 1826; exchanged to 1st Extra Regt. 12 Mar. 1827; to 5th N.I. 10 May 1827. Fur. s.c. 15 Jan. 1836 till 10 Dec. 1838. First Afghan War; action in Khyber Pass 24 Jan. 1842 (kld.); Bt. Capt. 5th N.I., d.d. 60th N.I.[1]

Refs.: G.M. 1842, i. 677. *A.J.* N.S. xxxviii. 80. M.I. in St. Peter's, Ft. Wm., and in St. Peter's, Dorchester.

[1] *Note:* Being on leave, he escaped massacre in the retreat from Kabul with his Regt. He was on his way to rejoin, and was attached to 60th N.I. under Bdr. Charles Frederick Wild, *q.v.*, when he met his death.

LOCKE, John (1808-1886). Lieutenant. 22nd N.I. *b.* Bromham, Wilts., 11 July 1808. Cadet 1824. Arrived in India 2 Feb. 1826. Ensign 10 Sept. 1825. Lieut. 9 Oct. 1826. Resigned in England 20 July 1839. *d.* 1886.

Of Rowdeford, Wilts. (of Cricklade House, Wilts.); J.P. and D.L.

bapt. Bromham 25 Sept. 1810. 3rd son of Wadham Locke, of Rowdeford House, J.P. and D.L., high sheriff of Wilts. 1804, M.P. for Devizes 1832, and Anna Maria Selina his wife, dau. of Francis Powell, of Hurdcott House, Wilts. *m.* 1839, Frances Augusta, dau. of Thomas Moore Wayne, of S. Wanborough, Hants. Ed. Harrow 1820-4.

Services: Posted Ensign to 22nd N.I.; actg. Adjt. do. 10 Nov. 1829; permanent do. 1 Mar. 1830 till 23 June 1836. Shekhawat expedn. 1834. Actg. Bde. Major to troops in Shekhawat 2 Mar. till 1 Apr. 1835; tempy. Detachment Staff do. 20 Apr. 1835. Fur. p.a. 20 Jan. 1837 till Sept. 1841, when he resigned with effect from 20 July 1839. Promoted Bt. Capt. 10 Sept. 1840, but this was cancelled on his resignation.

Refs.: Burke's *Landed Gentry*, 13th edn., p. 1113, *s.n.* Locke, of Melksham. *Walford. Harrow School Register.*

LOCKETT, Abraham (1781-1834). Lieut. Colonel, 58th N.I. *b.* Clonfeade, co. Tyrone, 21 June 1781. Cadet 1800. Arrived in India 23 Aug. 1801. Ensign 19 Nov. 1801. Lieut. 30 Sept. 1803. Capt. 26 Aug. 1815. Major 12 Jan. 1825. Lt. Col. 21 Jan. 1829. *d.* Cape Town 10 May 1834.

Son of John Lockett. *m.* Trincomali, Ceylon, 14 Mar. 1817, Miss Mary (Bailey) Barnett (*probably* sister of Hugh Laird Barnett, *q.v.*).

Services: Ensign d.d. 13th N.I. in 1802; transfd. as Lieut. to 14th N.I. Second Mahratta War; defence of Delhi Oct. 1804; action at Deoband; Lieut. 2/14th N.I.; Bhurtpore (w. in 3rd assault 20 Feb. 1805); Lieut. Pioneers. Apptd. Asst. Comy. of Supplies to Grand Army 29 Nov. 1805. Apptd. Examiner to Coll. of Ft. Wm. 1808; Examiner and Asst. Sec. do. Nov. 1811. On leave in Iraq and Arabia 24 Dec. 1810 till 22 June 1812. Fur. s.c. 26 Dec. 1814 till 27 Sept. 1816. Third Mahratta War; Dhamoni; Mandala; Garhakota; Capt. 1/14th N.I. Served with 1/14th N.I. in Saugor F.F. 1819-20. Sec. to Council, Coll. of Ft. Wm., 1821-4. Transfd. to newly-formed 2/32nd N.I. July 1823; to 63rd N.I. (late 1/32nd) May 1824. Asst. to Resdt. at Lucknow 1 Mar. 1824. Asst. Sec. to Govt., Mily. Dept., 22 Apr. 1825; Dy. do. 17 June 1825. Siege and capture of Bhurtpore; Major 63rd N.I., extra A.D.C. to C.-in-C. A.G.G. Bhurtpore 1827. Posted Lt. Col. to 19th N.I. 1829; to 69th N.I. 13 Jan. 1830. P. A. Ajmer 9 Sept. 1831. Transfd. to 33rd N.I. 10 Aug. 1832; to 16th N.I. 14 Sept. 1833; to 58th N.I. 6 Nov. 1833. A. G. G. States of Rajputana, and Comr. for Ajmer, 16 Apr. 1832 till 29 Nov. 1833.

Leave s.c. 18 mos. to Cape 6 Feb. 1834. Nominated Resdt. at Nagpur 24 May 1834.
Refs.: B.: P.P. No. 48, p. 134. A.J. iv. 530.

LOCKHART, Richard Dickson (1807-1826). Ensign, 68th N.I. *b.* Glasgow 31 Mar. 1807. Cadet 1824. Ensign 10 Sept. 1825. *d.* Sandoway, Arakan, 27 Dec. 1826: drowned.

8th son of Rev. John Lockhart, D.D., minister of Glasgow, and Elizabeth his 2nd wife, dau. of Rev. John Gibson. Half-brother of William Lockhart, *q.v.* Glasgow Univ.; matric. 1821.

Services: Recommended for a Cadetship by Sir Walter Scott. Posted Ensign to 68th N.I. No record of active service.

Refs.: Burke's *Landed Gentry*, 13th edn., p. 1114, *s.n.* Lockhart, of Milton Lockhart and Germiston, co. Lanark. Scott's *Fasti*, iii. 400.

LOCKHART, William (1787-1856). Bt. Captain. 17th N.I. *b.* Cambusnethan, co. Lanark, 28 Sept. 1787. Cadet 1803. Arrived in India 29 Apr. 1805. Ensign 20 Apr. 1805. Lieut. 21 Apr. 1805. Bt. Capt. 1 Jan. 1818. Resigned 22 May 1819. *d.s.p.* Milton Lockhart 25 Nov. 1856.

Of Milton Lockhart, co. Lanark, D.L. M.P. co. Lanark 1841 till death. Eldest son of Rev. John Lockhart, D.D., sometime minister of Cambusnethan, later of Glasgow, and Elizabeth his 1st wife, dau. of Robert Dinwiddie, Germiston. Half-brother of Richard Dickson Lockhart, *q.v.* *m.* Walcot, Somerset, 16 Apr. 1822, Mary Jane, younger dau. of Sir Hugh Palliser, 2nd Bart. (She *re-m.* John, 3rd and last Baron Keane, and died 29 Oct. 1881.) Glasgow Univ.; matric. 1800.

Services: Posted Lieut. to 17th N.I. in 1806. Nepal War 1814-15; Lieut. 1/17th N.I., in 2nd Div. (India medal). Fur. 1817 till resignation. Lt. Col. Comdt. Lanarkshire Yeomanry Cav.

Refs.: Burke's *Landed Gentry*, 13th edn., p. 1114, *s.n.* Lockhart, of Milton Lockhart and Germiston, co. Lanark. Scott's *Fasti*, iii. 400. *Anderson*, ii. 682. A.J. xiii. 629.

LOCKWOOD, Joseph (1791-1813). Ensign, Engineers. *bapt.* Huddersfield 15 Oct. 1791. Cadet 1808. Arrived in India 6 Nov. 1809. Ensign 30 Oct. 1809. *d.* Banca I. 14 May (? Mar.) 1813.

Son of Joseph Lockwood. Brother of Elizabeth Lockwood.

Services: Asst. to Supt. of public bldgs. at Dum-Dum 1810-11. Capture of Java 1811; Ensign Engrs.

Refs.: Will dated 18 Feb. 1813; proved 16 Apr. 1816.

THE BENGAL ARMY, 1758-1834   73

LODER, Joseph William (1788–1829). Major, 32nd N.I. *b.* Whitechapel, London, 2 Apr. 1788. Cadet 1803. Arrived in India 14 Aug. 1804. Ensign 11 Sept. 1804. Lieut. 21 Sept. 1804. Capt. 1 Jan. 1818. Major 13 May 1825. *d.* 30 May 1829.

bapt. St. Mary's Whitechapel (*alias* Matfelon), 5 May 1788. Son of Joseph Sutton Loder, of Mansel St., and Jane his wife. Brother of James, Henry, Edward, Sarah, and Jane. *m.* St. John's, Calcutta, 10 June 1824, Harriet Mary, sister of George Taylor Seton Sandby, *q.v.* (*See also* George Arthur Brownlow.) (She died Gt. Marlow 1 June 1859.)

Services: Posted Lieut. to 16th N.I. in 1805. Operations in Bundelkhand 1809-11 ; Lieut. 2/16th N.I. Capture of Java 1811 ; Lieut. 5th Bengal Vol. Bn. Capt. 2/16th N.I. Fur. 27 Dec. 1820 till 1823. Transfd. to 32nd N.I. (late 1/16th) May 1824. Executive Ofr. 17th Div., P.W.D., 1824-5. Siege and capture of Bhurtpore ; Major 32nd N.I.

Refs.: Will dated 7 Aug. 1824 ; proved 19 June 1829.

LODGE, John Edward (1794-1817). Lieutenant, 6th N.I. *bapt.* St. Mary's, Newington, Surrey, 25 Aug. 1794. Cadet 1810, Ensign 26 Apr. 1813. Lieut. 1 Oct. 1815. *d.* at sea 27 June 1817, on board the pilot schooner *Hastings.*

Son of John Lodge, of London, merchant, and Catherine his wife. Ward of C. Robertson.

Services: Cadet d.d. 15th N.I. 1811-13. Posted Ensign to 6th N.I. in 1813. (? Nepal War 1814-15 ; Ensign 1/6th N.I., in 2nd Div.) Lieut. 1/6th N.I. Fur. s.c. June 1817.

LOFFT, Robert Emlyn (1783-1847). Bt. Captain. 14th N.I. *bapt.* Troston, Suffolk, 9 Nov. 1783. Cadet 1803. Arrived in India 18 Mar. 1805. Ensign 9 Apr. 1805. Lieut. 10 Apr. 1805. Bt. Capt. 1 Jan. 1818. Retired 14 July 1820. *d.* 20 Sept. 1847 ; *bur.* Troston.

Of Troston Hall, nr. Bury St. Edmunds. 2nd son of Capel Lofft, of Troston Hall and Stanton, Suffolk, and Anne his 1st wife, dau. of Henry Emlyn, F.S.A., of Windsor. *m.* 1826, Letitia Niel, dau. of Francis Richardson, Col. 1st Regt. of Foot Gds. (She died Ghent 1832.) Ed. Bury Grammar School ; Trin. Coll., Camb., 1802.

Services: Posted Lieut. to 14th N.I. in 1806. Intr. & Qmr. 2/14th N.I. 1 July 1814 till 4 Nov. 1816. (? Nepal War 1814-15 ; with Left Wing 2/14th N.I., in 3rd Div.) Fur. 1817 till retirement.

Refs.: Burke's *Landed Gentry*, 13th edn., p. 1116, *s.n.* Lofft (*now*

Bevan), of Troston Hall, Suffolk. *Bury Grammar School List. Patrician*, iv. 499.

LOFTIE, Malcolm Edward (1808-1859). Bt. Colonel, Invalid Pension Est. 30th N.I. *b.* Surinam, W.I., 8 Mar. 1808. Cadet 1824. Arrived in India 21 Dec. 1825. Ensign 21 Oct. 1824. Lieut. 12 May 1827. Capt. 1 Dec. 1839. Major 11 May 1857. Bt. Lt. Col. 20 June 1854. Bt. Col. 23 Sept. 1857. Invalided 8 June 1858. *d.* Agra 11 July 1859.

Son of William Loftie, Major H.M. 55th Regt. Sandhurst Cadet.

Services: Posted Ensign to 7th N.I. in 1825. Transfd. to 30th N.I. 1826. Intr. & Qmr. 30th N.I. 28 Sept. 1829 till 14 July 1830, and 23 Dec. 1832 till 10 Jan. 1840. Actg. Bde. Major to Bdr. Wild's force 1 Dec. 1841; Bde. Major 2nd Inf. Bde. 5 Jan. 1842; do. 3rd Bde. of Gen. Pollock's force 23 Feb. 1842. First Afghan War 1842; action in Khyber Pass 19 Jan. 1842 (s.w.); forcing of Khyber 5 Apr. 1842 (*Lond. Gaz.* 17 Mar. 1843); Bde. Major (Medal). Granted a gratuity of 6 mos. pay for wound. Offg. Bde. Major to troops in Oudh Feb. 1845. First Sikh War; Aliwal; Bde. Major 10th Inf. Bde. (Medal). Second Sikh War; passage of Chenab (w.); Chilianwala (w.); Bt. Major 30th N.I. (Medal with clasp). Offg. Executive Ofr. 16th (Dum-Dum) Div., P.W.D., 15 Oct. 1852. Leave s.c. 1855-6, and 22 Feb. 1857 till invalided.

Refs.: I.M. 22 Aug. 1859, p. 697.

LOGAN, James (1761/62-1780). Lieutenant, Infantry. *b.* in Scotland 1761/62. Cadet 1778. Ensign Oct. 1778. Lieut. 1 Nov. 1778. *d.* 20 Apr. 1780: kld. in action at the capture of Lahar fort, U.P.

Services: Apptd. Cadet 1 Jan. 1778. Sailed for India in the *Southampton* 7 Mar. 1778, aged 16. First Mahratta War.

LOGIE, William (1781-1828). Lieut. Colonel Comdt., 34th N.I. *b.* Speymouth, co. Elgin, 10 Aug. 1781. Cadet 1795. Arrived in India 2 Feb. 1798. Ensign 12 Aug. 1797. Lieut. 9 Aug. 1798. Capt. 25 Dec. 1807. Major 14 July 1815. Lt. Col. 25 May 1821. Lt. Col. Comdt. 22 Oct. 1824. *d.* Saugor 13 Jan. 1828.

Son of James Logie, at Boat of Bog, psh. of Speymouth, and Elizabeth Gordon his wife. *m.* Cawnpore 29 Aug. 1807, Elizabeth Sophia, dau. of Sir John Arnold, *q.v.* (*See also* Charles Jackson Doveton.) (She died 12 Apr. 1824.) His daus. *m.* George William Hamilton, *q.v.*, and Samuel Athill Lyons, *q.v.*

Services: Posted Lieut. to 19th N.I. 1798. Expedn. to Egypt 1801-2; Lieut. Bengal Vol. Bn. Capt. Lt. 19th N.I. 28 Oct. 1806. Operations in Bundelkhand 1806-9; Sehlehuganj; Capt. 1/19th N.I. Served in Alwar 1813. Nepal War 1814-15; Capt. 1/19th N.I., in 1st Div. Comdg. at Hansi in 1816. Served with Nagpur Subsdy. Force 1817. Third Mahratta War; storm of Chanda; Major comdg. 1/19th N.I. Posted as Lt. Col. to 1/19th N.I. in 1821. Transfd. to 14th N.I. 1823; to 29th N.I. (late 2/14th) May 1824; as Lt. Col. Comdt. to 3rd N.I. Oct. 1824. Fur. s.c. 4 Feb. 1825 till 1826. Transfd. to 34th N.I. 7 July 1826.

Refs.: *E.I.M.C.* ii. 305-6. *A.J.* xxvi. 76. Will dated 5 Jan. 1828; proved 1 Mar. 1828. M.I. at Saugor.

LOMAS, Anthony (1786-1831). Captain, Pension Est. 1st N.I. *b.* Deptford 25 Aug. 1786. Cadet 1805. Arrived in India 11 July 1806. Ensign 3 Sept. 1806. Lieut. 26 Oct. 1808. Capt. (27 Mar. 1821) 28 May 1823. Pensioned 2 Aug. 1829. *d.* Calcutta 22 Jan. 1831.

bapt. St. Paul's, Deptford, 3 Oct. 1786. Son of Joshua Lomas, of Red House Row, Deptford, cooper, and Martha his wife. *m.* (before 1812)?

Services: Barasat C.C. Posted Ensign to 12th N.I. in 1807. Operations in Oudh 1808; Ensign 12th N.I. Lieut. 1/12th N.I. Adjt. Chittagong Provl. Bn. 2 Jan. 1816 till 1819. Fur. 1819-21. Transfd. to 2/12th N.I. in 1821; d.d. with Hill Bildars in 1822; transfd. to 1st N.I. (late 2/12th) May 1824.

LOMER, Owen (1804-1844). Captain, 21st N.I. *bapt.* All Sts., Southampton, 2 Aug. 1804. Cadet 1819. Arrived in India Feb. 1821. Ensign 3 Sept. 1820. Lieut. 11 July 1823. Capt. 18 June 1834. *d.* Allahabad 28 June 1844.

2nd son of Joseph Lomer, of Southampton, tea dealer, sometime mayor of Southampton, and Sarah his wife. Brother of William Humphrey Lomer, *q.v.* *m.* Salisbury 8 Sept. 1828, Eliza, youngest sister of Mrs. Col. Kemp, of the Polygon. (She died London 26 Sept. 1879, aged 71.)

Services: Posted Ensign to 26th N.I. in 1821; transfd. to Bengal Eur. Regt. 1821; as Lieut. to 9th N.I. July 1823; to 21st N.I. (late 2/9th) May 1824. Siege and capture of Bhurtpore; Lieut. 21st N.I. Intr. & Qmr. 21st N.I. 29 July 1825 till May 1828. Fur. s.c. 10 Sept. 1827 till 1 June 1829. Offg. 2nd in comd. Mhairwara Local Bn. 7 Feb. till 29 Apr. 1831.

Refs.: *G.M.* 1828, ii. 270. *I.M.* 12 Sept. 1844, p. 528.

LOMER, William Humphrey (1810-1877). Lieut. Colonel. 21st N.I. *b.* London 1 Jan. 1810. Cadet 1825. Arrived in India 22 Oct. 1826. Ensign 27 June 1826. Lieut. 19 Mar. 1833. Capt. 1 July 1844. Major 13 Apr. 1855. Retired 27 Feb. 1856. Hon. Lt. Col. 27 Feb. 1856. *d.* 25 Mar. 1877.

bapt. St. Leonard Foster, London, 24 Jan. 1812. Son of Joseph Lomer, of Southampton, tea dealer. Brother of Owen Lomer, *q.v.* *m.* All Sts., Southampton, Mar. 1833, Harriet, 3rd dau. of William Bishop, of Gray's Wood, Haslemere, and North Bank, Regent's Pk., London. (*See also* Thomas Bradridge Studdy, Sir Francis Wheler, Bart., and David Wilkie.) (She died London 26 Oct. 1883, aged 73.)

Services: Ensign d.d. 67th N.I. 9 Nov. 1826; posted to 43rd N.I. 8 Jan. 1827; to 21st N.I. 11 Apr. 1827. Fur. s.c. 9 Sept. 1832 till 18 Nov. 1833. Adjt. Recruit Depot at Karnal 8 Sept. 1838 till 18 Jan. 1839; do. 2nd Recruit Bn. at Fatehgarh 7 Sept. 1839. Actg. Adjt. 21st N.I. 10 Nov. 1840; permanent do. 7 Oct. 1841 till 8 Oct. 1844. Fur. s.c. 2 July 1845 till 7 Dec. 1847, and 28 Jan. 1849 till 8 Oct. 1851. No record of active service.

LONG, Charles (*d.* 1786). Major. Infantry. Subsequently Lt. Col. H.M.S. Transfd. as Major from H.M.S. Major 20 Oct. 1763. Resigned 24 Feb. 1764. *d.* Jersey 22 Apr. 1786.[1]

Of Tubney, Berks. *m.* Margaret. (She died Apr. 1829.) Grandfather of Richard and Samuel Long, *qq.v.*

Services: Ensign 34th Ft. 4 Apr. 1755; Lieut. do. 8 Apr. 1755; Capt. Lt. do. 25 Aug. 1756; Capt. 2/34th Ft. 1 Mar. 1758; do. 73rd Ft. (late 2/34th) 30 Apr. 1758, with his old date of Capt. Capt. 84th Ft. 30 Dec. 1758; Third Major do. 15 Jan. 1764. Wounded in different engagements against Mir Muhammad Kasim 1763; battle of Katwa. h.p. Capt. 84th Ft. 25 June 1765 till 1785. Bt. Lt. Col. 84th Ft. 25 May 1772. Pensioned as Major on Lord Clive's fund 25 Dec. 1784. Capt. of one of the Independent Coys. of Invalids in Jersey 9 Sept. 1785 till death.

Refs.: *Caraccioli,* i. 91. *Broome,* p. 361.

[1] *Note:* Overtaken by the tide and drowned when returning from St. Helier to Elizabeth Castle.

LONG, Michael (*d.* 1782). Lieutenant, Infantry. Country Cadet 1779. Ensign 5 Oct. 1779. Lieut. 16 May 1781. *d.* Lucknow 1782.

Services: Apptd. Cadet 19 Aug. 1779. N.F.P.

THE BENGAL ARMY, 1758-1834

*LONG, Richard. 2nd Lieutenant. Artillery. (43) Cadet 1762. Fireworker 1763. 2nd Lieut. 17 Sept. 1763.
Services: Out of the Service before 1 Feb. 1767. N.F.P.
Refs.: Stubb's List.

LONG, Richard. Captain. Comdg. Burdwan Militia Corps. Cadet 1769. Ensign Sept. 1769. Lieut. 10 Feb. 1773. Capt. 6 Oct. 1780. Resigned 6 Jan. 1783.
Services: Was comdg. 2 Coys. Mil. Sepoys at Burdwan in Sept. 1777; comdg. 1,200 men as a bodyguard to the Rajah of Burdwan in Aug. 1781; resigned comd. of Mil. Corps at Burdwan 6 Jan. 1783.

LONG, Richard (1809-1837). Lieutenant, 25th N.I. *b.* Lee, Kent, 13 Apr. 1809. Cadet 1825. Arrived in India 5 Sept. 1826. Ensign 15 Apr. 1826. Lieut. 23 Dec. 1828. *d.* Kyaukpyu, Arakan, 25 Feb. 1837, of Arakan fever.
bapt. Lee 7 July 1822. Son of Samuel Richard Long and Jane his wife. Grandson of Charles Long and brother of Samuel Long, *qq.v.* (? and of Jane, 2nd wife of John Hoggan, *q.v.*).
Services: Posted Ensign to 25th N.I. 5 Oct. 1826. Comdd. escort of Resdt. at Ava Oct. 1832 till Dec. 1834. d.d. Sylhet L.I. Bn. 6 Aug. 1835; do. Arakan Local Bn. 29 Oct. 1835 till death; actg. Adjt. do. 28 Dec. 1836. No record of active service.
Refs.: A.J. N.S. xxiii. 317. M.I. at Arakan.

LONG, Samuel (1804-1845). Captain, Invalid Est. 40th N.I. *b.* London 28 Mar. 1804. Cadet 1820. Arrived in India May 1821. Ensign 16 Jan. 1821. Lieut. 11 July 1823. Capt. 9 Nov. 1835. Invalided 2 June 1845. *d. unm.* Meerut 7 Oct. 1845.
bapt. St. Pancras, Middlesex, 15 June 1806. Son of Samuel Richard Long and Jane his wife. Brother of Richard Long (1809-1837), *q.v.* Ward of Sir William Wynn, Kt., govr. of Sandown fort (who *m.* 29 Dec. 1801, Mary, eldest dau. of Charles Long, *q.v.*).
Services: Posted Ensign to 1/20th N.I. in 1821, and served with his Regt. in Singapore, Sumatra and Malacca July 1823 till June 1827. Transfd. to 25th N.I. (late 1/20th) May 1824; to 40th N.I. (late 2/20th) 1 Jan. 1828; actg. Adjt. Rt. Wing 40th N.I. 18 Nov. 1829. Attached to 1st Vol. Regt. for China 15 Feb. 1840 till May 1841. First China War 1840-1; Capt. 1st Vol. Regt. (Medal). Comdd. 40th N.I. Sept.-Oct. 1841. Insurrection in Bundelkhand 1842; Capt. 40th N.I., comdg. a detachment.

Refs.: *G.M.* 1846, i. 110. Will dated 23 June 1841 ; proved 13 Mar. 1846. *M.I.* in Barrackpore church.

LONG, Stephen (1776-?). Captain. Bengal Eur. Regt. *bapt.* Trinity psh. church, Waterford, 20 Feb. 1776. Cadet 1795. Arrived in India 3 Apr. 1797. Ensign 1 Nov. 1796. Lieut. 30 Oct. 1797. Capt. 21 Sept. 1804. Struck off 29 Dec. 1804. Son of Peter Long, of Waterford, and Anne his wife, eldest dau. of Stephen Roche, of Limerick.
Services : Lieut. 1st Bengal Eur. Regt. in June 1798. Fur. 29 Dec. 1799 till struck off from 29 Dec. 1804, being 5 yrs. from the date of his quitting India. (Gen. Letter of 19 Aug. 1808.)
Refs. : Burke's *Landed Gentry of Ireland*, p. 600, *s.n.* Roche, of Granagh Castle, co. Kilkenny.

LONG, Thomas (1752/53-1819). Captain, Invalid Est. Infantry. *b.* in Ireland 1752-53. Cadet 1779. Admitted 12 Feb. 1780. Ensign 19 June 1779. Lieut. 12 Feb. 1781. Capt. 30 Oct. 1779. Invalided 24 Aug. 1800. *d. unm.* Dinapore 11 Oct. 1819, aged 74 (*sic*).
Son of Mrs. Phoebe Long, of Limerick.
Services : Sailed for India in the *Ceres* 16 June 1779, aged 26. Lieut. 2nd Bengal Eur. Bn. in July 1787 ; 1st Bengal Eur. Regt. in 1796. Capt. 1st Bengal Eur. Regt. ; 5th N.I. in Jan. 1799.
Refs. : *A.J.* ix. 626. Will dated 4 June 1795 ; proved 4 Oct. 1819.

LONG, Timothy. Ensign. Infantry. Cadet 1783. Ensign 21 Mar. 1785. Dismissed by C.M. Dec. 1792.
Services : Apptd. Cadet 14 Oct. 1783 ; sailed for India in the *Valentine* 6 Jan. 1784. Posted to 6th Bengal Eur. Bn. 15 Feb. 1790. After dismissal he resided in Calcutta till 1813, first as a merchant, latterly as a mariner.
Note : One of this name was reported to the Council by the Town Adjt. in Feb. 1796 as, " a very disorderly person, who was in a miserable condition and had become a pest to the Settlement."

LOUGHNAN, John Michael (1806-1875). Lieutenant. 10th L.C. *b.* London 11 Jan. 1806. Cadet 1826. Arrived in India 13 Oct. 1827. Cornet (4 Jan. 1828) 6 Feb. 1828. Lieut. 6 June 1835. Invalided 2 June 1841. Retired 13 July 1842. *d.* at his residence, Kelso House, Richmond, nr. Melbourne, Aust., 20 Sept. 1875.
bapt. Spanish Ambassador's chapel, London, 17 Jan. 1806. Son

of Andrew Loughnan, of 18 Wimpole St., London, merchant, and Mary Ann his wife, née Hamilton, of I. of Grenada. m. Calcutta 26 Jan. 1836, Marion, relict of Lieut. Robertson, Bengal Est.[1]
Services: Posted Cornet to 10th L.C. 6 Feb. 1828. Fort Adjt. at Ft. Wm. 20 Feb. till 4 June 1833. Leave s.c. 18 mos. to Mauritius and Tasmania 30 Mar. 1833. Fort Adjt. at Ft. Wm. 4 Feb. 1835. Fur. s.c. 2 yrs. to N.S.W. 2 Apr. 1838 till 4 Mar. 1840. Fort Adjt. at Ft. Wm. 4 Mar. 1840, and in addition from 1 July 1840, Supt. of Cadets. Fur. p.a. via N.S.W. 11 June 1841 till retirement. No record of active service.
Refs.: The Times, 15 Oct. 1875.
[1] Note: Probably John Robertson (1804-1833), q.v.

LOVEDAY, Lambert Richard (1762/63-1843). Lieut. General. Colonel 32nd N.I. b. 1762/63. Country Cadet 1778. Admitted 11 Aug. 1778. Ensign 11 Aug. 1778. Lieut. 9 Jan. 1781. Capt. 25 Apr. 1797. Major 21 Jan. 1803. Lt. Col. 21 Sept. 1804. Col. 4 June 1813. Maj. Gen. 12 Aug. 1819. Lt. Gen. 10 Jan. 1837. d. at his residence, Grosvenor Pl., Bath, 20 Dec. 1843, aged 80.
2nd son of Richard Loveday, of Hammersmith, apothecary, and Maria Bainbridge his wife. Brother of William Loveday, of Brixham. m. St. Helena 30 July 1804, Anne Louise, sister of Henry Martin D'Esterre, q.v. Father of William Loveday, Mary, wife of Francis Spencer Hawkins, Eliza Anne, wife of John Herring, Louisa Maria, wife of John Inglis, and Jessy Eliza, wife of Arthur Cole Spottiswood, qq.v.
Services: Sailed for India as a passenger in the Nassau 7 Mar. 1778. On arrival at Madras volunteered as a Midshipman for the siege of Pondicherry, which place, however, capitulated 17 Oct. 1778, before he could join the operations. In 1779 [1] joined as Cornet 3rd Cav., which crossed the Jumna in 1781 to reinforce Camac's detachment during First Mahratta War; apptd. to act as Qmr. to Corps of Cav.; apptd. A.D.C. to Maj. Gen. G. B. Eyres, q.v., comdg. the Corps, till the Independent Troops were reduced. Retransfd. to 2nd Ressalah Cav. 1783; Lieut. 2nd Eur. Bn. in July 1787; transfd. from 29th Bn. Sepoys to 3rd Eur. Bn. 25 Jan. 1794; Major 9th N.I. Fur. p.a. 7 Feb. 1803 till 24 Jan. 1805. Transfd. as Lt. Col. to 25th N.I. Sept. 1804; to 15th N.I. 1805; to 8th N.I. 1806; to 1/20th N.I. 1810. Comdt. at P.W.I. from 31 Jan. 1811. Capture of Java 1811; Lt. Col. comdg. 1/20th N.I. (Gold Medal). Returned to Bengal in comd. of 1/20th N.I. 16 Apr. 1814. Posted as Col. to 20th N.I. 15 Nov. 1817. Comdt. at

P.W.I. in 1818; to comd. troops at Agra and Muttra, with tempy. rank of Bdr., 21 Aug. 1819. Apptd. to Gen. Staff 11 Jan. 1821; comdd. Benares Div. 30 Jan. 1821 till Dec. 1824. Transfd. to 32nd N.I. May 1824. Fur. s.c. 24 Dec. 1824 till death.
Refs.: *G.M.* 1844, ii. 91. *Bath Chron.* 28 Dec. 1843.
[1] *Note*: Cornet 3 May 1779.

LOVEDAY, William (1809-1840). Lieutenant, 37th N.I. *b.* Calcutta 26 Sept. 1809. Cadet 1827. Arrived in India 4 Sept. 1828. Ensign 16 Apr. 1828. Lieut. 22 Aug. 1833. *d.* Dadar, Baluchistan, 2 Nov. 1840: murdered in camp by Nasir Khan, of Kalat, whilst a prisoner of war.

Eldest son of Lambert Richard Loveday, *q.v.*

Services: Ensign d.d. 37th N.I. 5 Nov. 1828. Posted to 37th N.I. 4 Mar. 1829. Offg. Intr. & Qmr. 37th N.I. 12 Mar. 1832; permanent do. 3 Dec. 1833. Adjt. 37th N.I. 14 Dec. 1833 till 18 Mar. 1840. First Afghan War 1838-40; apptd. to Shah Shuja's army 9 Apr. 1839; Asst. to P.A. at Shawal 17 May 1839. Left at Kalat as P.A. with the new chief Shah Nawaz; defence of Kalat July 1840. Kalat capitulated 29 July, and on 20 Aug. he was taken prisoner by Nasir Khan. His corpse, with the head nearly severed from the trunk, was found chained to a camel *khajawah*.

Refs.: *Fortescue*, xii. 127-8, 131-2. *I.N.* viii. 170, 172; ix. 194. Bdr. L. R. Stacey's *Narrative*, p. 64. M.I. Afghan Memorial Church, Bombay.

LOVELACE, Henry Philip (1789-1865). Cadet. Cavalry. Subsequently Lieut. 16th Light Dgns. *b.* 23 Oct. 1789. Cadet 1804. Never arrived in India. Resigned in England 11 July 1806. *d.* 14 Dec. 1865.

bapt. Godalming, Surrey, 25 Nov. 1789. Son of Robert Lovelace and Elizabeth his wife. *m.* St. John's, Calcutta, 8 Apr. 1823, Miss Louisa Cleveland Garnett.

Services: Cornet 25th Light Dgns. 25 Aug. 1809; Lieut. do. 24 May 1811; h.p. 25 Jan. 1820. Lieut. 16th Light Dgns. 26 May 1822; h.p. unattached 23 Aug. 1827 till death.

***LOVELL, Edwin** (1808-1877). Cadet. Infantry. *b.* Brislington, Somerset, 17 May 1808. Cadet 1825. Never arrived in India. Withdrawn from the Service. *d.* Dinder, Wells, 21 May 1877.

Of Chilcote Manor, Wells, and Dinder, Somerset. Clerk of the Peace, Somerset. 3rd and youngest son of Joseph Lovell Lovell,

THE BENGAL ARMY, 1758-1834   81

of Wells, solicitor, and Margaret his wife, eldest dau. of Edmund Broderip, of Wells. *m.* 14 Sept. 1836, Elizabeth Charlotte, eldest dau. of Edmund Broderip, of Cossington, Somerset. (*See also* George Dennistoun Scott.) Ed. Eton; in 5th Form in 1823.
Refs.: Burke's *Landed Gentry*, 9th edn., p. 930, *s.n.* Lovell, late of Chilcote Manor and Dinder, Somerset. *Eton School Lists.*

LOW, John Handcock (1805-1849). Major, 39th N.I. *b.* 2 May 1805. Cadet 1823. Arrived in India 6 Oct. 1824. Ensign 16 Apr. 1824. Lieut. 13 May 1825. Capt. 27 Sept. 1837. Major 28 Nov. 1849. *d.* Rajmahal, B. & O., 28 Nov. 1849.

bapt. Ballymacward, co. Galway, 19 May 1805. Youngest son of William John Low, of Lowville, co. Galway, and of 76th Regt., and Hon. Sophia Hamilton his wife, 4th dau. of Richard, 4th Viscount Boyne. *m.* 1st, Agra 8 Oct. 1830, Emily, 4th dau. of Henry Revell, of Round Oak, Surrey, and sister of John Raithby Revell, *q.v.* (*See also* Reymond Hervey De Montmorency.) (She died Dehra Dun, U.P., 21 Oct. 1847.) *m.* 2nd, Lucknow 9 Dec. 1848, Clementina Clara Jane, dau. of Joseph Hockley.

Services: Posted Ensign to 39th N.I. (? Siege and capture of Bhurtpore.[1]) Actg. Adjt. 39th N.I. 14 Dec. 1827. Offg. Comdt. Delhi Palace Gds. 28 Oct. 1833 till Apr. 1834. Junior Asst. to A.G.G., Saugor & Narbada, at Jubbulpore 19 June 1834. Fur. s.c. 3 Feb. 1836 till 31 Dec. 1838. Actg. D.J.A.G. Sirhind Div. 11 June 1841. Leave s.c. 2 yrs. to N.S.W. 26 Dec. 1842. D.J.A.G. at Cawnpore 2 Mar. 1847 till Mar. 1848.

Refs.: Burke's *Peerage*, 1923, p. 326, *s.n.* Boyne, V. Foster's *Families of Royal Descent*, ii. 793.

[1] *Note:* This on the authority of *I.O. Rec.* His name does not appear in the Bhurtpore P.R., and 39th N.I. did not participate in the siege, but he may have been attached to some other Corps.

*LOW, Joseph (*d.* 1768). Cadet. Cadet (?) *bur.* Madras ("Cadet for Bengal") 14 Sept. 1768.
Services: N.F.P.

LOW, Robert (1791-1863). Colonel. 42nd N.I. *b.* Langton, co. Berwick, 23 Feb. 1791. Cadet 1808. Admitted 24 July 1809. Ensign 23 Jan. 1810. Lieut. 16 Dec. 1814. Capt. 18 Feb. 1825. Major 6 Aug. 1835. Lt. Col. 23 June 1842. Retired 1 July 1842. Hon. Col. 28 Nov. 1854. *d.* Mayfield, Edinburgh, 20 Sept. 1863.

Of Laws, co. Berwick. *bapt.* Langton 12 Mar. 1791. Son of Alexander Low, in Woodend, and Susan Anderson his wife.

Services : Barasat C.C. Posted Ensign to 1/17th N.I. in 1810. Nepal War 1814-15 ; Lieut. 1/17th N.I., in 2nd Div. (India medal). Operations against the Bhattis of Hariana 1818 ; actg. Intr. & Qmr. 1/17th N.I. Asst. to A.G.G., Saugor & Narbada territories, 25 Jan. 1823 till Dec. 1839. Transfd. to 35th N.I. (late 2/17th) May 1824 ; to 34th N.I. 15 May 1825. Offg. Resdt. at Jaipur 1826-7. Principal Asst. at Narsinghpur Apr. 1834. Fur. p.a. 1 Jan. 1840 till retirement. Posted as Lt. Col. to 42nd N.I. June 1842.
Refs. : *G.M.* 1863, ii. 522.

LOWDER, William (1786-1820). Bt. Captain, 13th N.I. *bapt.* Walcot, Bath, 21 Oct. 1786. Cadet 1804. Arrived in India 6 Apr. 1806. Ensign 13 Oct. 1805. Lieut. 12 Jan. 1806. Bt. Capt. 1 Jan. 1818. *d.* at sea 20 May 1820, on board the *Princess Charlotte*, on the voyage home.
Son of John Lowder and Anne his wife.
Services : Posted Lieut. to 13th N.I. in 1806. Pindari War 1819 ; siege of Asirgarh ; Bt. Capt. 2/13th N.I. Fur. 1820.
Refs. : *Bath Chron.* 24 Aug. 1820.

LOWE, John (*d.* 1789). Lieutenant, Invalid Est. 30th Bn. Sepoys. Cadet 1779. Ensign 12 Feb. 1780. Lieut. 3 Mar. 1781. Invalided Nov. 1788. *d.* Chunar 12 Oct. 1789.
Services : Was abroad when apptd. Cadet in Dec. 1778. First Mahratta War 1781-4.

LOWE, John Thomas (1801-1825). Lieutenant, 65th N.I. *b.* London 20 Mar. 1801. Cadet 1820. Arrived in India May 1821. Ensign 16 Jan. 1821. Lieut. 11 July 1823. *d.* Penang 13 Oct. 1825.
bapt. Islington 10 Jan. 1802. Son of John Lowe and Matilda Deborah Jepson his wife. Ward of Frances, widow of Sir Robert Chambers, Kt., C. J. Bengal. Ed. Exeter Grammar School.
Services : Posted Ensign to 1/28th N.I. in 1821 ; transfd. to 33rd N.I. July 1823 ; to 65th N.I. (late 1/33rd) May 1824. A.D.C. to (? his stepfather) Maj.-Gen. Robert Bourke Gregory, *q.v.*, comdg. Dinapore Div. No record of active service.
Refs. : *Cal. Monthly Journal,* Jan. 1825, pp. 85-6.

LOWIS, John Thornton (1793-1858). Lieut. Colonel. 28th N.I. *b.* in India 25 Jan. 1793. Cadet 1807. Arrived in India 1 Nov. 1808. Ensign 29 Sept. 1808. Lieut. 20 Nov. 1814. Capt.

THE BENGAL ARMY, 1758-1834   83

13 May 1825. Major 6 Nov. 1832. Retired 26 June 1833. Hon. Lt. Col. 28 Nov. 1854. d. Newport, Barnstaple, 6 May 1858.
bapt. Calcutta 14 Oct. 1793. Son of John Lowis, of Calcutta, and Mary his wife, widow of Samuel Skardon, *q.v.* Stepson of Lawrence O'Hara. *m.* Calcutta 19 Oct. 1818, Miss Mary Vincent.
Services: Barasat C.C. Posted Ensign to 14th N.I. in 1809. Nepal War 1814-15; Jitgarh; Lieut. 1/14th N.I., in 3rd Div. (India Medal). Third Mahratta War; Dhamoni; Mandala [1]; (Garhakota); Lieut. 1/14th N.I. Adjt. 2/14th N.I. 1819; Intr. & Qmr. do. 24 Feb. 1821 till 15 June 1822; Adjt. Saharanpur Provl. Bn. 12 June 1822 till 12 July 1825. Transfd. to 28th N.I. (late 1/14th) May 1824. Actg. Regulating Ofr. of Invalid Tannah Ests. at Shahabad 30 Dec. 1826 till 1 Feb. 1830; in charge of Burdwan Provl. Bn. 18 Jan. 1830. Fur. s.c. 14 Dec. 1831 till retirement.
Refs.: *G.M.* 1858, i. 686. *The Times,* 13 May 1858.
[1] *Note:* He led the advance party at the assault of Mandala on 26 Apr. 1818, and in ascending the breach fell near the stump of a tree, injuring himself severely. He continued however to lead his party (*Lond. Gaz.* 7 Dec. 1818). In June 1820 he met with a bad riding accident at Dinapore. Paralysis eventually supervened, and he lost the use of both legs. He was in consequence permitted to retire on his full pay as a Major, and was granted an additional allowance of £60 *p.a.*

LOWIS, Ninian (1802-1838). Captain, 63rd N.I. *b.* Edinburgh 17 Oct. 1802. Cadet 1818. Admitted 17 July 1819. Ensign 7 Feb. 1819. Lieut. 3 Sept. 1820. Capt. 10 May 1831. *d.* at sea 10 Sept. 1838: lost in the *Haidee.*[1]
bapt. Edinburgh 4 Dec. 1802. Son of Capt. Ninian Lowis, E.I.C.N.S., sometime Comdr. of the *Woodcot* East Indiaman, and Isabella his wife, youngest dau. of John Monro, of Auchinbowie, co. Stirling, advocate. *m.* Mullye, B. & O., 21 Apr. 1834, Eliza Mary Anne, eldest dau. of Thomas Reynolds (1788-1873), *q.v.* (She died Singapore 20 Aug. 1838, aged 26.) Ed. Edinburgh Coll.
Services: Ensign d.d. 19th N.I. 1819. Posted Lieut. to 1/27th N.I. 1820; transfd. to newly-raised 32nd N.I. 11 July 1823; to 64th N.I. (late 2/32nd) May 1824; exchanged to 63rd N.I. (late 1/32nd) 24 Aug. 1824. Leave s.c. 18 mos. to New Holland and Tasmania 17 Dec. 1829. Asst. to Gen. Supt. for suppression of *Thagi* 20 Jan. 1836 till 3 Apr. 1838. Leave s.c. 6 mos. to Singapore 7 July 1838. No record of active service.

Refs. : *Munro of Fowlis*, pp. 318-19, *s.n.* Monro of Auchinbowie.
N. & Q. 12S. viii. 367. Family information.

¹ *Note :* He and his three children embarked for England at Singapore after the death of his wife, but were never heard of again. Promotions in his room were made from 10 Sept., the date the vessel left Singapore.

LOWNDS, Lawrence. Ensign. Infantry. Country Cadet 1782. Ensign 3 May 1783. Resigned 1783.

Services : Was 1st Ofr. of the packet *Fly* ketch when apptd. Cadet 10 Mar. 1782, and was then allowed to proceed on an expedn. with Capt. Forrest. Returned to Europe in 1783 as 1st Ofr. of the *Fly*.

LOWRY, Richard (1808-1842). Lieutenant, 21st N.I. *bapt.* St. Mary's, Carlisle, 20 Dec. 1808. Cadet 1827. Arrived in India 4 Sept. 1828. Ensign 16 Apr. 1828. Lieut. 27 Feb. 1834. *d.* Malda 23 Dec. 1842.

Son (twin with Catherine) of Richard Lowry, of Carlisle, atty., and Jane Wilson his wife.

Services : Ensign d.d. 70th N.I. 5 Nov. 1828. Posted to 21st N.I. 4 Mar. 1829. Actg. S.S.O. at Hansi 4 Dec. 1837. (? First Afghan War 1839; Lieut. 21st N.I.) Fur. s.c. 28 Feb. 1840 till 30 Mar. 1842.

LOWRY, Thomas (1780-1819). Major, C.B., 7th N.I. *bapt.* Donaghadee, co. Down, 11 Feb. 1780. Cadet 1795. Arrived in India 26 Sept. 1796. Ensign 12 Nov. 1796. Lieut. 30 Oct. 1797. Capt. 22 Sept. 1808. Major 16 Dec. 1814. *d. unm.* Berhampore, Bengal, 2 Dec. 1819.

Son of Murray Lowry and Eleanor his wife, dau. of Hugh Casement. Brother of James and Casement William Lowry. Cousin-german of William Gowdy and of Sir William Casement, *q.v.*

Services : Posted Ensign to 3rd Bengal Eur. Regt. in 1796; Lieut. 7th N.I. in 1798; Adjt. 1/7th N.I. 1803-8. Capt. Lt. 7th N.I. 21 Oct. 1807. Reduction of Kalinjar 1812; Capt. 1/7th N.I. Nepal War 1814-15; Major 7th N.I. Third Mahratta War 1817-19; Major 2/7th N.I. C.B. 8 Dec. 1815.

Refs. : Will dated Karnal 2 Oct. 1817; proved 22 Dec. 1819. M.I. in Donaghadee churchyard (where he is incorrectly styled "Sir Thomas Lowry, C.B.").

LOWTH, Charles (1805-1873). Major. 4th L.C. *b.* Hinton-Ampner, Hants, 28 Aug. 1805. Cadet 1823. Arrived in India

12 June 1824. Cornet 7 Jan. 1824. Lieut. 13 May 1825. Capt. 13 Jan. 1842. Retired 1 Jan. 1848. Hon. Major 28 Nov. 1854. *d.* at his residence, Freelands, Winchester, 5 Feb. 1873.

4th son of Rev. Robert Lowth, preby. of St Paul's, and Frances his wife, 4th dau. of Rev. John Harington, D.D., preby. of Salisbury. Grandson of Rt. Rev. Robert Lowth, D.D., bishop of London, and cousin-german of Thomas Lowth Harington, *q.v. m.* Westend, S. Stoneham, Hants, 24 Oct. 1850, Susan Eliza, youngest dau. of Maj. George Groves, H.M. 28th Regt. (She died 12 Jan. 1889, aged 81.) Ed. Eton 1820-2.

Services: Posted Cornet to 4th L.C. in 1824. Siege and capture of Bhurtpore; Lieut. 4th L.C. (India medal). Intr. & Qmr. 4th L.C. 19 Oct. 1830 till Aug. 1835. Shekhawat expedn. 1834; Lieut. 4th L.C. Fur. p.a. 5 Aug. 1835 till 9 Feb. 1839. Bde. Major 4th Cav. Bde., Army of Exercise, 17 Nov. till 11 Dec. 1843. (? Gwalior campaign; Maharajpur; Capt. 4th L.C.—Bronze star.) First Sikh War; Mudki; Ferozshahr; Sobraon; Capt. 4th L.C. (Medal with 2 clasps).

Refs.: Howard & Crisp (Notes), ix. 128. *Eton School Lists. The Times,* 7 Feb. 1873.

LUARD, Peter William (1817-1876). Colonel. Comdt. 25th N.I. (now 1st Bn. 15th Punjab Regt.). *b.* Warwick 11 July 1817. Cadet 1832. Arrived in India 17 July 1834. Ensign (12 Dec. 1833) 1 June 1834. Lieut. 1 Dec. 1836. Capt. 8 May 1845. Major 27 Aug. 1858. Lt. Col. 27 Nov. 1859. Col. 18 Feb. 1866. *d.* Machynlleth, co. Montgomery, 21 Dec. 1876.

bapt. St. Mary's, Warwick, 23 Aug. 1817. Eldest son of Peter Francis Luard, M.D., of N. Gate St., Warwick, and Mary Magdalen his wife, dau. of William Morgan. *m.* 1st, Lucknow 27 Apr. 1839, Emma Anne, only dau. of William Hodgson (1790-1828), *q.v.* (She died Dacca 25 May 1841, aged 19.) *m.* 2nd, Meerut 13 Feb. 1845, Emilia Frederica, dau. of George Russell Crommelin, *q.v.* Addiscombe Cadet 3 Feb. 1832 till 13 Dec. 1833.

Services: d.d. 50th N.I. 2 Aug. 1834; posted to 55th N.I. 5 Nov. 1834. Adjt. Lower Assam Sebundy Corps 9 July 1839. Adjt. 1st Assam Sebundy Corps 21 Feb. 1840 till 8 Mar. 1841; attached to 2nd L.I. Bn. 4 Aug. 1841; Adjt. 3rd Depot Bn. at Aligarh 4 Mar. 1842 till 1 Mar. 1843; Adjt. 55th N.I. 18 Aug. 1843 till 16 July 1845. First Sikh War; no actions; Capt. 55th N.I. Postmr. at Jhansi Dec. 1852. Mutiny campaign; comdg. 17th Punjab Inf. (Lahore Punjab Bn.—became 25th N.I.) with the Saugor Field Bde. in 1859. Comdt. 25th N.I. 27 Nov. 1859 till

5 Feb. 1868. A.A.G. Meerut Div. 5 Feb. 1868. Fur. p.a. 10 Feb. 1873 till death.
Refs.: Burke's *Landed Gentry*, 13th edn., p. 1135, *s.n.* Luard, of Blyborough, Lincs.

LUCADON, James Lewis. (*See* **WEST, James Louis.**)

LUCADOU, James Louis. (*See* **WEST, James Louis.**)

LUCAS, John (*d.* 1792). Captain. Comdt. 7th Bn. Sepoys. Cadet 1770. Ensign 4 Apr. 1771. Lieut. 16 July 1776. Capt. 12 Feb. 1781. Resigned 15 Dec. 1784. *d.* Teignmouth, Devon, 10 Jan. 1792.
(*Possibly* father of John Moore Adolphus Lucas, *q.v.*)
Services: First Mahratta War; Capt. comdg. 7th Bn. Sepoys, with Goddard's detachment. Apptd. by Goddard in July 1781 to comd. 7th Bn. Sepoys.
Refs.: *Eur. Mag.* 1792, i. 159.

LUCAS, John Moore Adolphus (1788-1833). Captain. 24th N.I. *bapt.* Walcot, Bath, 30 June 1788. Cadet 1806. Arrived in India 14 Oct. 1807. Ensign 15 Oct. 1807. Lieut. 18 Mar. 1813. Capt. 1 May 1824. Retired 12 May 1830. *d.* at his residence, 18 Green Pk. Bldgs., Bath, 2 Jan. 1833.
Son of John Lucas and Jenny Hodges his wife. *m.* Charlotte. (She *re-m.* Mossom Boyd, *q.v.*)
Services: Barasat C.C. Posted Ensign to 8th N.I. in 1808. Adjt. Purnea Provl. Bn. 18 Sept. 1810 till 1817. Lieut. 2/8th N.I. Intr. & Qmr. 1/8th N.I. 14 Aug. 1817. (? Third Mahratta War; Lieut. 1/8th N.I.) Asst. in office of Mily. Board in 1818. Bk.Mr. (title changed later to Executive Ofr.) 5th, Sikraul, Div. 1820-8. Transfd. to 24th N.I. (late 2/8th) May 1824. Fur. 1828 till retirement.
Refs.: *G.M.* 1833, i. 93. *Bath Chron.* 10 Jan. 1833. Will dated 23 Nov. 1832; proved 6 Aug. 1833.

LUCAS, Richard (*d.* 1804). Major General. Colonel 16th N.I. *b.* Dublin. Lieut. 8 Sept. 1768. Capt. 9 July 1776. Major 3 Feb. 1781. Lt. Col. 7 Dec. 1793. Col. 30 Oct. 1797. Maj. Gen. 25 Sept. 1803. *d. unm.* Sultanpur, U.P., 26 Mar. 1804, in consequence of a fall from his horse, "leaving about 3 lacs of rupees."
Services: 2nd Lieut. 85th Ft. 11 Aug. 1759; 1st Lieut. do. 16 Dec. 1761; h.p. 1763. Transfd. as Lieut. to Bengal Army (M.C. 1 Sept. 1768); sailed for India in the *Ponsborne* 21 Mar. 1768.

Lieut. 22nd Bn. Sepoys in May 1770. To comd. 36th Bn. Sepoys 17 Aug. 1779; to comd. 23rd Bn. 22 June 1781; Major comdg. 32nd N.I. in Aug. 1781. Operations against the rebel Fateh Shah in the Chapra district, B. & O., Oct. 1781; capture of mud fort at Majurah 17 Oct.; Major comdg. the force (1/32nd N.I.). To comd. 12th Sepoys 4 Apr. 1785; Major in 3rd Sepoy Bde. in July 1787 and in Dec. 1788. Transfd. from 4th Sepoy Bde. to 5th Eur. Bn. 13 Dec. 1793. Apptd. Col. of newly-raised 16th N.I. Nov. 1798.

Refs.: *India Gazette*, 3 Nov. 1781. *G.M.* 1804, ii. 1168. Will dated Sultanpore, 20 Mar. 1804; proved 20 Apr. 1804.

LUCAS, Robert St. John (1809-1842). Lieutenant, Pension Est. 9th N.I. *b.* Lyndhurst, Hants, 11 June 1809. Cadet 1825. Arrived in India 25 Oct. 1826. Ensign 23 May 1826. Lieut. 25 Sept. 1833. Pensioned 20 Apr. 1835. *d.* Calcutta 28 Nov. 1842.

bapt. Lyndhurst 13 Aug. 1809. Son of Robert Hayward Lucas, M.D., of Teignmouth, and Mary his wife.

Services: Posted Ensign to 9th N.I. 9 Nov. 1826, and served throughout with that Regt. No record of active service. Permitted to reside at Monghyr from 1 Oct. 1835.

LUCAS, William Edwards (1810-?). Ensign. Infantry. Unposted. *bapt.* Little Wymondley, Herts., 7 Jan. 1810. Cadet 1828. Arrived in India 5 Sept. 1829. Ensign (7 May 1829). Resigned in India 8 Oct. 1830.

Son of William Edwards Lucas and Ann his wife. Nephew of Philip Monoux Lucas, of 29 Nottingham Pl., Marylebone.

Services: Unposted Ensign; really only a Cadet. No record of active service. Ensign d.d. 30th N.I. 1830.

LUDLOW, Edmund Emilius (1804-1882). Captain. 20th N.I. *b.* London 29 Apr. 1804. Cadet 1820. Arrived in India May 1821. Ensign 16 Jan. 1821. Lieut. 11 July 1823. Capt. 18 June 1833. Retired 23 July 1837. *d.* 129 Inverness Terr., Bayswater, London, 6 Oct. 1882.

bapt. Allhallows, Barking, 3 June 1804. Son of Samuel Ludlow, Surgeon Bengal Est., and Mary his wife. Ward (*probably* nephew) of Edmund Ludlow. *m.* Kensington 3 Aug. 1847, Elizabeth Catherine, widow of H. Houston. Ed. Merchant Taylors' Oct. 1813 till Mar. 1816.

Services: Posted Ensign to 2/6th N.I. in 1821. Transfd. as Lieut. to 5th N.I. July 1823; to 20th N.I. (late 2/5th) May 1824.

Actg. Intr. & Qmr. 20th N.I. 3 Mar. 1828 ; permanent do. 12 Aug. 1828 till 1 Oct. 1833. Fur. p.a. 23 Jan. 1835 till retirement. Retired on h.p., *viz.* 7/– *p.d.* No record of active service.
Refs.: Robinson. *The Times,* 10 Oct. 1882.

LUDLOW, Edward Henry (1805-1850). Bt. Lieut. Colonel. Artillery. (526) *b.* Walcot Pl., Lambeth, Surrey, 13 July 1805. Cadet 1820. Arrived in India 16 Jan. 1822. 2nd Lieut. 9 June 1821. Lieut. 11 Aug. 1824. Capt. 20 Oct. 1839. Major 5 May 1849. Bt. Lt. Col. 7 June 1849. Retired 23 Sept. 1850. *d.* Dum-Dum 26 Sept. 1850.

bapt. Cheshunt, Herts., 22 May 1806. Youngest son of Edmund Ludlow, of Cuckfield, and of Cowley St., Westminster, hop merchant, and Anne Elizabeth his wife. Brother of John Ludlow (1801-1882), *q.v.* Ed. Merchant Taylors' Mar. 1814-Mar. 1818. Ed. Westminster School 31 Mar. 1818-Whitsun 1819. Addiscombe Cadet 1819-21.

Services: Actg. Adjt. Art. Div. in Rajputana 1 Dec. 1827. Adjt. 7th Bn. Foot Art. 19 Sept. 1828. Leave s.c. 8 mos. to Cape 23 Oct. 1830. Fur. s.c. 18 Dec. 1833 till 19 Feb. 1838. Comdd. detachment of 4th Bn. Art. 28 Mar. till 25 Aug. 1838. Dy. Comy. Ord. at Chunar 22 Apr. 1840 ; posted to Expense Mag. at Dum-Dum 26 June 1840 ; Comy. Ord. 5 Aug. 1840 ; offg. Dy. Principal Comy. Ord. at Ft. Wm. 1 June 1844. Fur. s.c. 1846-8. Second Sikh War ; Chilianwala ; Bt. Major 2nd Coy. 4th Bn. (Heavy Battery) ; Gujerat ; 3rd Coy. 7th Bn. (Medal with 2 clasps). Leave s.c. 6 mos. to Singapore and China Mar. 1850. Admitted Lincoln's Inn 3 July 1834.

Refs.: Robinson. *Westminster School Register.* *G.M.* 1851, i. 110. *I.M.* 20 Nov. 1850, p. 673.

LUDLOW, John (1777/78-1821). Lieut. Colonel, C.B., 6th N.I. Comdg. Nimach F.F. *b.* 1777/78. Cadet 1793. Arrived in India 16 Feb. 1795. Ensign 10 Oct. 1794. Lieut. 27 July 1796. Capt. 15 Aug. 1803. Major 31 May 1813. Lt. Col. 15 Nov. 1817. *d.* in camp at Barode, Kotah State, 22 Sept. 1821, aged 43.

Late of Romsey, Hants. Of the Hill Deverell branch of the Wiltshire Ludlows. Uncle of John Ludlow, *q.v. m.* Bombay 18 Jan. 1810, Maria Jane, dau. of Murdoch Brown, of Tellicherry, Madras.

Services: Apptd. Cadet 21 May 1794 ; sailed for India in the *Lascelles* 14 Aug. 1794. Ensign 6th Eur. Bn. in Feb. 1796 ; Lieut. 7th N.I. in 1798. Expedn. to Egypt 1801 ; Lieut. Bengal Vols. Capt. 1/6th N.I. Comdd. Benares Provl. Bn. Sept. 1803 till 1807 ;

THE BENGAL ARMY, 1758-1834

do. Burdwan Provl. Bn. July 1808 till May 1813. Leave s.c. 6 mos. to sea 18 May 1809. Nepal War 1814-15 ; Kalanga ; Major 1/6th N.I., in 2nd Div. Third Mahratta War ; Lt. Col. 6th N.I. Comdg. Advance Corps in Mewar in 1818 ; comdd. Nimach F.F. 1819 till death. C.B. 8 Dec. 1815.
Refs.: Edin. Mag. x. 695. Will dated Nimach 14 June 1821 ; proved 29 Nov. 1821. M.I. in St. John's church, Calcutta, and at Barode.

LUDLOW, John (1801-1882). Major General. 36th N.I. *b.* Llantillio-Pertholey, co. Monmouth, 13 May 1801. Cadet 1818. Admitted 26 June 1819. Ensign 21 June 1819. Lieut. 15 Aug. 1820. Capt. 1 Apr. 1829. Major 20 Dec. 1843. Lt. Col. 6 Apr. 1850. Retired 9 Aug. 1854. Bt. Col. 28 Nov. 1854. Hon. Maj. Gen. 1857. *d.* at his residence, Yotes Court, Maidstone, Kent, 30 Nov. 1882.
bapt. 10 June 1801. Eldest son of Edmund Ludlow, of Westminster, hop merchant, and Anne Elizabeth his wife. Brother of William Andrew Ludlow, *q.v. m.* Brightling, Sussex, 1 Oct. 1859, Isabella Leigh, 2nd dau. of Benjamin Smith, of Blandford Sq., and of Gottenham, Sussex, M.P., and niece of Frederick Coape Smith, *q.v.* Ed. Merchant Taylors' Oct. 1813-Mar. 1816.
Services: d.d. 19th N.I. 1819 ; posted Lieut. to 2/3rd N.I. 1820. Mily. student at Coll. of Ft. Wm. 4 Jan. till 7 July 1821. Attached to Pioneers 28 Dec. 1822 ; Adjt. do. 28 Sept. 1825 till 27 July 1829. Transfd. to 6th N.I. (late 1/3rd) May 1824. Operations against the Bhils 1824 ; comdg. a Coy. of Pioneers under Bdr. J. R. Lumsden, *q.v.* First Burma War ; Sylhet and Cachar 1824 ; Arakan 1825 ; Lieut. Pioneers (India medal). Fur. s.c. 2 Jan. 1830 till 14 Dec. 1833. Asst. to A.G.G. Rajputana 21 Feb. 1835 ; offg. P.A. at Kotah 11 Oct. 1837 ; P.A. Jodhpur 19 Sept. 1839 ; do. Jaipur 8 Jan. 1844 till 25 Dec. 1847. Occupation of Jodhpur Nov. 1839 (s.w.—sabre cut on head and hands). Fur. s.c. 10 Feb. 1848 till 5 Dec. 1851. Posted Lt. Col. to 12th N.I. July 1850. Fur. s.c. 6 Feb. 1852 till retirement. Transfd. to 14th N.I. 21 Mar. 1853 ; to 9th N.I. Aug. 1853 ; to 36th N.I. 2 Feb. 1854. The suppression of female infanticide and *Suttee* in Rajputana was in great measure due to his efforts.
Refs.: D.I.B. Boase. The Smith Family, by C. Reade, p. 174. Robinson. *The Times,* 2 Dec. 1882. *Guardian,* xxxvii. 1709b.

LUDLOW, William Andrew (1803-1853). Major, 12th N.I. *b.* Llangenny, co. Brecon, 23 June 1803. Cadet 1819. Admitted

1 July 1820. Ensign 31 Dec. 1819. Lieut. 11 July 1823. Capt. 19 Oct. 1833. Major 10 Oct. 1849. d. Hants 28 Aug. 1853.

bapt. 17 July 1803. Son of Edmund Ludlow, of Cowley St., Westminster, hop merchant, and Anne Elizabeth his wife. Brother of Edward Henry Ludlow, q.v. m. Allahabad 8 Nov. 1836, Mary Anne, youngest dau. of James Ferris, q.v. (She re-m. John Halliday, of Lloyd's, and died his widow at Coblentz 11 Nov. 1873.) Ed. Merchant Taylors' Oct. 1813 till Mar. 1818.

Services: Posted Ensign to 2/29th N.I. in 1820. Transfd. as Lieut. to 12th N.I. July 1823; to 12th N.I. (late 1/12th) May 1824. Adjt. 12th N.I. 17 June 1824 till 14 Oct. 1833. Fur. p.a. 18 Dec. 1833 till 19 Feb. 1836. Offg. A.A.G. Presdy. Div. 20 Oct. 1837. Second in comd. newly-raised 1st Inf., Oudh Auxy. Force, 27 Dec. 1837. Comdd. Narbada Sebundy Corps 1 Jan. 1840 till 30 Apr. 1843, when it was broken up. Served at Gorakhpur in Dept. for suppression of *Thagi* 1 May 1843 till Oct. 1849. Fur. 1853 till death. No record of active service. Pub. in May 1835 a litho. representation of " Bengal Troops on the line of March."

Refs.: Robinson. G.M. 1853, ii. 429. Will dated Multan 1 June 1852; proved 9 Jan. 1855.

LUMLEY, Sir James Rutherford (1773-1846). Major General, K.C.B. Colonel 9th N.I. A.G. Bengal. b. Parsonage house, Longford, nr. Newport, Salop, 21 Oct. 1773. Cadet 1794. Arrived in India 25 Feb. 1796. Ensign 17 Oct. 1794. Lieut. 15 Mar. 1797. Capt. 24 May 1804. Major 22 Aug. 1812. Lt. Col. 20 Sept. 1816. Lt. Col. Comdt. 1 May 1824. Col. 5 June 1829. Maj. Gen. 10 Jan. 1837. d. Ferozepore 1 Mar. 1846.

bapt. 22 Dec. 1773. Son of Rev. James Lumley, rector of Barnwell St. Andrews, Northampton, and Alice his wife, youngest dau. of David Rutherfurd of Capehope. m. Calcutta 25 Nov. 1809, Miss Caroline Wilkinson. Father of James Rutherford Lumley and William Brownrigg Lumley, qq.v.

Services: Posted Ensign to 2nd Bengal Eur. Regt.; transfd. to 1/2nd N.I. Oct. 1796; to newly-formed 1/15th N.I. Sept. 1798; to 8th N.I. Nov. 1798; posted to 1/8th N.I. 20 Jan. 1799. Operations in Jumna Doab 1803; Sasni; Lieut. 1/8th N.I. Second Mahratta War; Narnaul; Kanun; on Shekhawat frontier under Col. George Ball, q.v.; relief of Delhi; battle and capture of Deig; Bhurtpore; Capt. comdg. 1/8th N.I. Expedn. to Mauritius 1 Sept. 1810 till Oct. 1811; Capt. comdg. 2nd Bengal Vol. Bn. Comdd. 2nd Vol. Bn. till its disbandment 31 July 1812. Posted Major to

2/8th N.I. Feb. 1813; transfd. to 1/8th N.I. 1 May 1813. Nepal War 1814-15; Major comdg. 1/8th N.I., in 4th Div. Nepal War 1816; Major comdg. 1/8th N.I., in 2nd Bde. Centre Column. Third Mahratta War; Lt. Col. comdg. 1/8th N.I., in 2nd Bde. Centre Div. Transfd. to Bengal Eur. Regt. Jan. 1819. Comdt. fort of Asirgarh 3 July 1819 till 12 Oct. 1821. Transfd. to 2/16th N.I. Jan. 1820; to 1/28th N.I. June 1821. Comdd. Nimach F.F. (became Mewar F.F.) 13 Oct. 1821 till 9 Jan. 1833. Posted as Lt. Col. Comdt. to 62nd N.I. 11 June 1824. Bdr. 9 June 1826. Col. 62nd N.I. June 1829. Comy. Gen. 1 Jan. 1833. A.G. of the Army 28 Nov. 1833 till 28 Feb. 1846. Col. 9th N.I. 1 July 1837. Gwalior campaign; Maharajpur; A.G. (Bronze star). K.C.B. 2 May 1844. Served continuously for 50 yrs. in India.

Refs.: *D.I.B.* *De Rhé-Philipe.* *G.M.* 1847, ii. 558. M.I. at Ferozepore.

LUMLEY, James Rutherford (1810-1885). Major. 9th N.I. *b.* Calcutta 27 Oct. 1810. Cadet 1826. Arrived in India 2 June 1827. Ensign 3 Feb. 1827. Lieut. 24 Apr. 1829. Capt. 14 Dec. 1844. Retired 4 Mar. 1848. Hon. Major 28 Nov. 1854. *d.* at his residence, Sutton, Surrey, 24 Jan. 1885.

bapt. Calcutta 24 Dec. 1810. Eldest son of Sir James Rutherford Lumley, *q.v.* Brother of William Brownrigg Lumley, *q.v.* *m.* 1st, Chapel Royal, Tower of London, 24 Apr. 1838, his cousin Arabella, youngest dau. of Rev. Thomas Chambers Wilkinson, rector of All Saints, Stamford, Lincs. *m.* 2nd, Calcutta 1 May, 1843, Clara Letitia, 8th dau. of William Conrad Faithful, *q.v.* (*See also* J. D. D. Bean.) (She died Bexhill-on-Sea 23 Oct. 1905, aged 80.)

Services: Posted Ensign to 64th N.I. 19 June 1827; exchanged to 9th N.I. 2 Dec. 1829. Actg. Adjt. 9th N.I. 5 Oct. 1833. Adjt. Ramgarh Local Bn. 5 Jan. till 9 Sept. 1835. Asst. in *Thagi* Dept. 16 Dec. 1835 till 5 June 1838. Fur. u.p.a. 5 Dec. 1838 till 6 Sept. 1839. A.D.C. to his father 4 Mar. 1841. Actg. D.J.A.G. at Cawnpore 4 Feb. 1842. 2nd A.A.G. of the Army of Reserve (for Afghanistan) 9 Nov. 1842. To conduct duties of A.G.'s office in Calcutta 9 Sept. 1843; 1st A.A.G. of the Army 27 Oct. 1843 till 28 Mar. 1846. First Sikh War; Mudki; Ferozshahr; Capt. 9th N.I., A.A.G. of the Army (Medal with clasp).

Refs.: *I.M.* 22 June 1848, p. 359. *The Times*, 27 Jan. 1885.

LUMLEY, William Brownrigg (1812-1889). Captain. 2nd Bengal Eur. Regt. *b.* Calcutta 3 Sept. 1812. Cadet 1828. Arrived in India 1 June 1829. Ensign 6 Jan. 1829. Lieut.

8 Oct. 1839. Capt. (6 Jan. 1844) 1847. Retired 12 June 1847. *d.* 20 Aug. 1889.

Son of Sir James Rutherford Lumley, *q.v.* Brother of James Rutherford Lumley, *q.v. m.* Hampstead July 1847, Elizabeth, dau. of Thomas Haines, late R.N.

Services : Ensign d.d. 9th N.I. 13 July 1829 ; posted to 64th N.I. 1829 ; exchanged to 9th N.I. 2 Dec. 1829 ; to 57th N.I. 13 Apr. 1830 ; d.d. 9th N.I. 13 Apr. 1830 till 16 July 1831. Actg. Adjt. & Qmr. Inv. Bn. at Chunar 5 Nov. 1837. Adjt. 2nd Local Horse 25 Aug. 1838 ; 2nd in comd. do. 9 Sept. 1839. Leave s.c. to Mussoorie 7 Mar. 1840 till 25 Mar. 1842. Actg. 2nd in comd. Kumaon Local Bn. 18 Mar. 1842. Adjt. Sirmoor Bn. 1 June 1842 ; actg. 2nd in comd. do. 12 Oct. 1842 ; permanent do. 4 Jan. 1843 till 10 Jan. 1845. Fur. s.c. 10 Jan. 1845 till retirement. No record of active service.

LUMSDAINE, James (1785-1816). Bt. Captain (officially Major), 4th N.C. Dy. Comy. Gen. Bengal. *b.* Canongate, Edinburgh, 1 July 1785. Cadet 1800. Arrived in India 17 Oct. 1801. Cornet 3 Jan. 1802. Lieut. 11 Mar. 1805. Bt. Capt. 8 Jan. 1816. (Major 26 June 1812.) *d.* Meerut 14 Sept. 1816.

bapt. Canongate 6 Aug. 1785. Eldest son of William Lumsdaine (who was 4th son of James, of Rannyhill), of Edinburgh, W.S., and Ann his wife, dau. of Sir Alexander Gordon of Lesmoir, Bart. Brother of William Lumsdaine and cousin-german of Alexander Irvine, *qq.v. m.* Cawnpore 12 Feb. 1813, Selina, dau. of Robert Patton, *q.v.* (*See also* James Henry Brooke.)

Services : Expedn. to Egypt 1801-2. Posted Cornet to 4th N.C. 1802. Second Mahratta War ; Lieut. 4th N.C. A.D.C. to G.G. 1805-6. Operations against Dhundia Khan 1807 ; Komona ; Ganauri ; Agent for camels and gram. A.C.G. 1809 ; Dy. Comy. Gen. (with official rank of Major) 26 June 1812 till death.

Refs. : E.I.M.C. i. 421-2. *G.M.* 1817, i. 476. *S.M.* 1817, i. 584. M.I. St. John's churchyard, Meerut.

LUMSDAINE, John (*d.* 1823). Major. Infantry. Country Cadet 1766. Ensign 22 Sept. 1766. Lieut. 7 Dec. 1767. Capt. 3 Apr. 1773. Major 27 Jan. 1781. Resigned 21 Dec. 1784. *d.* 4 Oct. (? Dec.) 1823.

Of Lathallan, co. Fife, which estate he purchased in 1787. 3rd son of Robert Lumsdaine, of Innergellie, co. Fife. *m.* Elizabeth Home. Father of John Lumsdaine and cousin of William Lumsdaine, *qq.v.*

THE BENGAL ARMY, 1758-1834

Services: Permitted to proceed to India as a Free Merchant 30 Jan. 1765. Actg. 4th Mate of the *Falmouth* Indiaman, which was wrecked on Saugor Bank at the mouth of the Ganges R. 13 June 1766. First Rohilla War; battle of St. George 23 Apr. 1774 (w.); Capt. comdg. Grenadiers. Apptd. to comd. one of the three Sepoy Bns. of the Nawab-Wazir of Oudh Sept. 1777; to comd. 29th N.I. 1 Jan. 1781.

Refs.: Burke's *Landed Gentry*, 8th edn., p. 1255, *s.n.* Lumsdaine, of Lathallan, co. Fife. *Anderson*, ii. 702. *B.M. Addl. MSS.* 23, 679.

LUMSDAINE, John (1782–1805). Lieutenant, 9th N.I. *b.* Duns, co. Berwick, 18 Nov. 1782. Cadet 1798. Arrived in India 23 Nov. 1799. Ensign 18 Jan. 1800. Lieut. 29 May 1800. *d.* 20 Feb. 1805: kld. in action in the trenches before Bhurtpore.

Son of John Lumsdaine, *q.v.*, and Elizabeth his wife. First cousin once removed of William Lumsdaine, *q.v. m.* Fatehgarh 10 July 1804, Harriott, dau. of St. George Ashe, *q.v.* (*See also* Peter Bearsley Hume.) (She *re-m.* Howe Daniel Showers, *q.v.*) Father of John Charles Lumsdaine, *q.v.*

Services: Posted Lieut. to 2/9th N.I. 15 Apr. 1801. Second Mahratta War 1803-5; Agra; Laswari; Gwalior; Monson's retreat; Bhurtpore (kld.); Lieut. 2/9th N.I. " Lumsdaine was a gallant officer, and has distinguished himself on many occasions, and particularly in re-taking our trenches the morning on which he fell." (*Pester*).

Refs.: Burke's *Landed Gentry*, 13th edn., p. 1139, *s.n.* Sandys-Lumsdaine, of Lumsdaine, co. Berwick. *Pester*, p. 414. Will dated camp nr. Agra 29 July 1804; proved 15 May 1805.

LUMSDAINE, John Charles (1805-1845). Captain, 58th N.I. *b.* Agra 27 Mar. 1805. Cadet 1821. Arrived in India 10 Aug. 1822. Ensign 10 Mar. 1822. Lieut. 13 May 1825. Capt. 1 Jan. 1837. *d.* Agra 6 Dec. 1845.

bapt. Agra 23 June 1805. Son of John Lumsdaine (1782-1805), *q.v. m.* Agra 19 Nov. 1828, Henrietta Eliza, eldest dau. of Sir William Richards, K.C.B., *q.v.* (*See also* Hyder John Hearsey, Appendix A.) (She died Cawnpore 8 Nov. 1891, aged 93.)

Services: Posted Ensign to 29th N.I. Transfd. to 58th N.I. (late 2/29th) May 1824. Siege and capture of Bhurtpore (w.); Lieut. 58th N.I. (*Lond. Gaz.* 4 July 1826). Intr. & Qmr. 58th N.I. 2 Oct. 1827; Adjt. do. 11 June 1828 till 13 Mar. 1834. A.D.C. to his father-in-law, comdg. Dinapore Div., 29 Jan. 1834 till 2 Mar.

1836. Placed under orders of Resdt. at Gwalior 2 Mar. 1836. Postmr. at Sipri 29 May 1839. Capt. 2nd in comd. Cav., Gwalior Contingent. Operations in S. Mahal 1840. Leave s.c. 12 mos. 20 Dec. 1840. Comdt. 2nd Cav., Gwalior Contingent, 13 Jan. 1844. Postmr. at Gwalior 23 Nov. 1844.

Refs.: Will dated 26 Feb. 1837; proved 10 Feb. 1846. M.I. Cantt. cemetery, Agra.

LUMSDAINE, William (1792-1830). Captain, 9th L.C. Dy. Comy. Gen. Bengal. *b.* Canongate, Edinburgh, 27 Feb. 1792. Cadet 1806. Arrived in India 25 Nov. 1807. Cornet 31 July 1807. Lieut. 16 Sept. 1815. Capt. 14 Apr. 1822. *d. unm.* Calcutta 6 Jan. 1830.

Of Lumsdaine, Blanerne, and Innergellie, to which estates he *s.* on the death of his cousin John, the father of John Lumsdaine (1782-1805), *q.v.* Third son of William Lumsdaine, of Edinburgh, W. S., and Ann Gordon his wife. Brother of James Lumsdaine, *q.v.*

Services: Posted Cornet to 5th N.C. Served in Comst. Dept. 1811 till death. A.C.G., and Supervisor of horses, bullocks and camels at Hissar, 4 Oct. 1816 till 1824. Dy. Comy. Gen. 1824 till death. Transfd. to newly-raised 1st Extra Regt. (became 9th L.C.) 17 June 1825. Siege and capture of Bhurtpore; Dy. Comy. Gen.

Refs.: Burke's *Landed Gentry*, 13th edn., p. 1139, *s.n.* Sandys-Lumsdaine, of Lumsdaine, co. Berwick. Will dated Cawnpore 25 June 1829; proved 25 Feb. 1830. M.I. in S. Park St. cemetery, Calcutta.

LUMSDEN, David (1765-1823). Lieut. Colonel. 16th N.I. *b.* in Scotland 1765. Cadet 1781. Admitted 4 June 1782. Ensign 3 May 1781. Lieut. 20 Aug. 1782. Capt. 31 July 1799. Major 22 Sept. 1808. Lt. Col. 15 June 1814. Retired 1 June 1818. *d. unm.* London 10 Apr. 1823.

Of Margaret St., Cavendish Sq., London. 4th son of John Lumsden, of Cushnie, and Anne his wife, dau. of Capt. John Forbes, of Newe. Brother of John, Dir. E.I. Co., James, Lt. Col. 55th Ft., and of Matthew, LL.D. (D.N.B.). Uncle of David Lumsden, *q.v.*, and cousin of Alexander McVeagh, *q.v.* Ed. King's Coll., Aberdeen.

Services: Apptd. Cadet 6 Apr. 1781, aged 16; sailed for India in the *Deptford* 26 June 1781. Lieut. 34th Bn. Sepoys in July 1787 and in Jan. 1796. Comdg. Kandahar Horse in 1798. Capt. 7th N.I., comdg. Resdt.'s guard at Lucknow in 1802. Fur. 19 Jan. 1803 till 19 June 1806. Regulating Ofr. of Invalid Tannah Ests. at Bhagulpur 1807-8; comdd. Calcutta Native Mil. 19 Dec. 1808

till 1814. Apptd. Mily. Sec. to V. P. Aug. 1809. Posted Lt. Col. to 2/16th N.I. in 1815. Fur. 11 Jan. 1816 till retirement.
Refs.: *Memorials of the Families of Lumsdaine, Lumisden, or Lumsden*, by Lt.-Col. H. W. Lumsden, p. 97. Anderson, ii. 703. Temple's *Thanage of Fermartyn*, p. 627 (where date of birth is given as 1768). *A.A.R.* i. 150. *S.M.* 1823, i. 648. Will dated 22 Apr. 1822; proved 22 Sept. 1823.

LUMSDEN, David (1812-1842). Lieutenant, 27th N.I. *b.* Briton Ferry, co. Glam., 6 Oct. 1812. Cadet 1828. Arrived in India 14 Jan. 1830. Ensign (12 June 1829) 7 Nov. 1829. Lieut. 22 May 1834. *d.* Afghanistan 9 Mar. 1842: kld. in the retreat from Ghazni.
bapt. Briton Ferry 11 Oct. 1812. 3rd son of Lt.-Col. James Lumsden, 55th Ft., and Lydia his wife, formerly Miss Hitchins, of Penzance. Brother of John Richard Lumsden and nephew of David Lumsden, *qq.v.* *m.* Kabul 1 June 1841, Rosamond Harriet, 3rd dau. of Rev. George Henry Deane, of Leamington. (She was kld. with him during the retreat.) Addiscombe Cadet 1827-9.
Services: Ensign d.d. 63rd N.I. 25 Jan. 1830. Fur. s.c. 11 Jan. 1831 till 25 Jan. 1833. Posted to 36th N.I. 26 Jan. 1833; to 27th N.I. 9 Apr. 1833; d.d. Arakan Local Bn. 20 July till 28 Sept. 1835. Leave p.a. to Mussoorie 15 Sept. 1838 till 31 Dec. 1839. First Afghan War 1840-2; Nazian Valley 1841; defence of Ghazni 1841-2 (kld.); Lieut. 27th N.I.[1]
Refs.: *Memorials of the Families of . . . Lumsden*, p. 96. Anderson, ii. 703. *G.M.* 1842, ii. 334. *The Times*, 15 July 1842. M.I. Afghan Memorial Church, Bombay.
[1] *Note*: On the capitulation of Ghazni he remained behind with the Rear Guard, and was in a house with his wife awaiting the moment to march, when the mob burst in and murdered the whole party.

LUMSDEN, John Richard (1808-1841). Bt. Captain, 63rd N.I. *b.* Briton Ferry, co. Glam., 25 Nov. 1808. Cadet 1824. Arrived in India 12 May 1825. Ensign 9 Jan. 1825. Lieut. 4 Apr. 1828. Bt. Capt. 9 Jan. 1840. *d.* Kyaukpyu, Arakan, 29 Sept. 1841: his leg was bitten off by a crocodile (? shark) whilst bathing.
bapt. Briton Ferry 27 Nov. 1808. 2nd son of Lt.-Col. James Lumsden and Lydia his wife. Brother of David Lumsden (1812-1842), *q.v.* *m.* Calcutta 21 Dec. 1835, Sarah Swaine, only dau. of Rev. George Henry Hough, of New Bedford, Mass., U.S.A. (She *re-m.* George Borlase Tremenheere, *q.v.*)

Services: Ensign d.d. 28th N.I. 23 May 1825 ; posted to 63rd N.I. 1825. Siege and capture of Bhurtpore ; Ensign 63rd N.I. Apptd. to d.d. Arakan Local Bn. 29 Jan. 1835 ; Adjt. do. 14 Mar. 1835 till 28 Aug. 1837. Placed at disposal of Civil Comr. in Arakan 16 June 1835. Operations against dacoits July 1835. Offg. Junior Asst. in Arakan 22 Dec. 1835 ; tempy. charge of district of Ramri 20 Sept. 1836 till 1 Feb. 1837 ; Junior Asst. to Comr. of Arakan 19 May 1837 ; Senior do. 21 Sept. 1839.

Refs.: *Memorials of the Families of* . . . *Lumsden,* p. 96. *A.J.* N.S. xxxvi. 342. *I.N.* i. 454.

LUMSDEN, Thomas (1789-1874). Colonel, C.B. Artillery. (392) *b.* Aberdeen 12 June 1789. Cadet 1807. Arrived in India 16 Nov. 1808. Fireworker 21 Sept. 1808. Lieut. 11 Dec. 1810. Capt. 21 Nov. 1821. Major 5 Apr. 1837. Lt. Col. 16 Dec. 1843. Retired 14 Jan. 1844. Hon. Col. 28 Nov. 1854. *d.* Belhelvie Lodge, co. Aberdeen, 8 Dec. 1874.

Of Belhelvie. *bapt.* 25 June 1789. 5th son of Harry Lumsden, of Belhelvie and Pitcaple, advocate, J.P. and D.L. co. Aberdeen, and Catherine his wife, dau. of Hugh McVeagh. Cousin-german of Hugh Gordon and nephew of Alexander McVeagh, *qq.v.* *m.* Aberdeen 8 Feb. 1821, Hay, youngest dau. of John Burnett, of Elrick. (She died 11 Oct. 1873, aged 74.) Father of Lt.-Gen. Sir Harry Burnett Lumsden, K.C.S.I., " Lumsden of the Guides." (*D.N.B.*)

Woolwich Cadet ; nominated for R.M.A. 13 Feb. 1805.

Services: 2nd Troop H.A. 4 Oct. 1809 till 1813. Apptd. Adjt. & Qmr. 2nd Troop 27 June 1816. Siege and capture of Hathras ; Lieut. 1st Troop, Adjt. H.A. Third Mahratta War ; Lieut. 2nd Troop, Adjt. & Bde. Qmr. to H.A., Rocket Troop, and Dromedary Corps, with Centre Div. of Grand Army. Transfd. to 4th Troop 1820. Fur. p.a. via Persia and the Caucasus 13 Jan. 1820 till 17 Nov. 1821. Capt. comdg. 1st Troop 1821-7. First Burma War 1824-6 ; Donabyu ; action of 2 Dec. 1825 (s.w.) ; capture of Minhla 19 Jan. 1826 (*Lond. Gaz.* 25 Oct. 1825, 26 Apr. and 4 July 1826) ; Capt. comdg. 1st Troop H.A. and Rocket Troop, with Sir A. Campbell's force (India medal). Agent for gun carriages at Fatehgarh 25 June 1832 till 1 Jan. 1843. Posted as Lt. Col. to 3rd Bn. Foot. Art. 10 Feb. 1844. C.B. 20 July 1838. Author of " A Journey from Meerut in India to London during the years 1819-20," London, 1822.

Refs.: Burke's *Landed Gentry,* 13th edn., p. 1140, *s.n.* Lumsden, of Pitcaple Castle, co. Aberdeen. *A.J.* xi. 313. *The Times,* 11 Dec. 1874. M.I. Belhelvie churchyard.

LUSHINGTON, Matthew (1808-1839). Cornet. 7th L.C. *b.* London 5 Oct. 1808. Cadet 1826. Arrived in India 6 Dec. 1827. Cornet (4 Jan. 1828) 7 Aug. 1828. Dismissed by G.C.M. 1 July 1836. *d.* Cornwall estate, Jamaica, 16 May 1839.

4th son of Sir Henry Lushington, 2nd Bart., of South Hill Park, Berks., sometime H.B.M. Consul Gen. at Naples, and Fanny Maria his wife, eldest dau. of Matthew Lewis, Under Sec. at War. Uncle of Laura, wife of Hon. Sir Henry Ramsay, K.C.S.I., *q.v.*

Services: Ensign H.M. 43rd Foot 11 Mar. 1824. Cornet d.d. 6th L.C. 22 Jan. 1828. Posted to 1st L.C. 25 Nov. 1828. Extra A.D.C. to Govr. of Madras 24 Mar. 1829. Transfd. to 7th L.C. 2 Sept. 1831. d.d. 3rd L.C. 1 June till 1 Nov. 1833. Shekhawat expedn. 1834; Cornet 7th L.C. Four times tried by G.C.M.

Refs.: Burke's *Peerage*, 1923, p. 1455, *s.n.* Lushington, Bart., of Hill Park, Berks. *A.J.* N.S. ix. 37; xvii. 126; xxi. 250.

LUTTRELL, John (*d.* 1773). Lieutenant, Infantry. Cadet 1768. Ensign 4 Jan. 1769. Lieut. 19 Dec. 1769. *d.* on the river 24 Sept. 1773.

Services: N.F.P.

LUXFORD, John Bellamy Bowes (1791-1814). Fireworker, Artillery. (407) *b.* Ewell, Surrey, 14 Nov. 1791. Cadet 1807. Arrived in India 16 Nov. 1808. Fireworker 3 Apr. 1809. *d.* 29 Nov. 1814, of wounds received in the 2nd assault on Kalanga fort on 27 Nov.

bapt. Ewell 23 Feb. 1792. Only son of John Luxford, of Salisbury, printer, and Caroline his wife, dau. of Mrs. Parsloe, of St. James's St. Ed. St. Paul's School; admitted 13 Sept. 1802.

Services: Posted Lieut.F. to 3rd Troop H.A. 4 Oct. 1809. Nepal War 1814; Kalanga (kld.); Lieut. 3rd Troop H.A., in 2nd Div.

Refs.: Gardiner. G.M. 1815, i. 645. Name on cenotaph in St. John's churchyard, Meerut.

LYALL, Andrew (1783-1807). Lieutenant, 8th N.I. *b.* Montrose 12 July 1783. Cadet 1801. Arrived in India 17 July 1802. Ensign 8 July 1802. Lieut. 1 May 1804. *d.* Saugor roads, Bengal, 16 Oct. 1807, on board the *Lord Duncan.*

Son of James Lyall and Helen Pyott his wife. Cousin of Andrew Millar, of 33 Lombard St., London.

Services: Barasat C.C. 1802-3. Posted Ensign to 8th N.I. in 1803. Second Mahratta War; Lieut. 8th N.I. Fur. s.c. 1807.

*LYDIARD, William (1805-1896). Colonel. 11th N.I. *b.* 27 Jan. 1805. Cadet 1825. Admitted 11 Nov. 1826. Ensign (15 Mar. 1826) 10 Nov. 1826. Lieut. 1 Dec. 1836. Capt. 27 Mar. 1846. Major 13 Apr. 1860. Lt. Col. (?) Retired 31 Dec. 1861. Hon Col. 31 Dec. 1861. *d.* 5 St. James's Sq., Bath, 28 Aug. 1896.

Son of Charles Lydiard, Capt. R.N. *m.* Simla 26 Oct. 1843, Victoria Hannah, youngest dau. of Major Henry White, of Portsmouth. Ed. Westminster 22 Oct. 1819 till 27 Mar. 1823. Admitted to Lincoln's Inn 17 Nov. 1823.

Services: Was at the Cape when nominated Cadet in Mar. 1826. Posted Ensign to 2nd Bengal Eur. Regt. 26 Sept. 1826. Transfd. to 11th N.I. 1827. Leave s.c. 6 mos. to Mauritius 21 Sept. 1831 till 15 Jan. 1832. Adjt. 11th N.I. 14 Nov. 1833 till 18 Nov. 1840. A.D.C. to C.-in-C. 20 Oct. 1840. Bde. Major to troops assembled for service in Bundelkhand 4 Nov. 1842. Disturbances in Bundelkhand 1842-3; Bde. Major. To continue to act as A.D.C. to C.-in-C. 21 June 1843. D.A.A.G. Benares Div. 21 June 1843; A.A.G. do. 1845; do. Dinapore Div. 1846-59. Served in latter part of Second Sikh War, after the general actions. Fur. s.c. Mar. 1855 till 1 Aug. 1856.

Refs.: Westminster School Register. The Times, 1 Sept. 1896.

LYELL, Henry (1804-1875). Lieut. Colonel. 43rd N.I. *b.* Eling, Hants, 1 Dec. 1804. Cadet 1821. Arrived in India 19 Aug. 1822. Ensign 25 Apr. 1822. Lieut. 1 May 1824. Capt. 10 Oct. 1839. Bt. Major 11 Nov. 1851. Retired 6 Mar. 1854. Hon. Lt. Col. 28 Nov. 1854. *d.* 42 Regent's Pk. Rd., London, 5 Feb. 1875.

bapt. Eling 7 Jan. 1805. 3rd son of Charles Lyell, of Kinnordy, J.P., vice-lieut. of Forfarshire, and Frances his wife, only dau. of Thomas Smith, of Maker Hall, Swaledale, Yorks. Younger brother of Sir Charles Lyell, 1st Bart. *m.* Hamptonwick, Middlesex, 25 Jan. 1848, Katherine Murray, 4th dau. of Leonard Horner, of Montagu Sq. (She died 18 Feb. 1915.) Father of Sir Leonard Lyell, 1st Baron Lyell, of Kinnordy, and a baronet. Sandhurst Cadet.

Services: Posted Ensign to 29th N.I. in 1823. Transfd. to 22nd N.I. 1823; to 44th N.I. (late 2/22nd) May 1824; to 43rd N.I. (late 1/22nd) May 1825. Fur. p.a. 21 Jan. 1833 till 28 Dec. 1836. First Afghan War 1839-42; Ghazni; Capt. 43rd N.I. (Medal). Gwalior campaign; Maharajpur; Capt. 43rd N.I. (Bronze star). First Sikh War; Sobraon (s.w.); Capt. 43rd N.I. (Medal). Fur. s.c. 10 Apr. 1847 till 5 Nov. 1851.

THE BENGAL ARMY, 1758-1834

Refs.: Burke's *Peerage*, 1923, p. 1456, *s.n.* Lyell, B. *The Times*, 10 Feb. 1875.

LYELL, Richard. Fireworker. Artillery. (16) Cadet (?) Fireworker 6 June 1758. Resigned 11 Dec. 1760.
Services: N.F.P.
Refs.: Orme MSS.—India, xiii. 3639.

LYFORD, William (1803-1836). Lieutenant, 3rd N.I. *bapt.* St. Thomas's, Winchester, 4 Apr. 1803. Cadet 1823. Arrived in India 8 Oct. 1824. Ensign 11 May 1824. Lieut. 13 May 1825. *d.* Mainpuri, U.P., 25 Aug. 1836.
Son of Giles King Lyford, of Winchester, surgeon, and Eliza his wife, 2nd dau. of Rev. (? Henry) Binfield, of Dunmer, Hants. (*Probably* of the family of Lyford, of Hurley.)
Services: Posted Ensign to 3rd N.I. 31 Mar. 1825. Actg. Adjt. to a small detached force of all arms 29 Jan. 1834. Shekhawat expedn. 1834 ; actg. Adjt. to a detachment of 4 Coys. 39th N.I.
Refs.: (? *The Genealogist*, v. 286.) *A.J.* N.S. xxii. 130.

LYNCH, Robert Blosse (1806-1836). Lieutenant, 26th N.I. *b.* Rochester 9 May 1806. Cadet 1823. Arrived in India 3 May 1824. Ensign (?) Lieut. 11 Nov. 1824. *d.* on the Euphrates R. 21 May 1836 : lost in the *Tigris* in a tornado.
bapt. St. Nicholas, Rochester, 5 June 1806. 2nd son of Henry Blosse Lynch, of Partry, co. Mayo, Major 73rd Ft., and Elizabeth his wife, dau. of Robert Finnis, of Hythe. Nephew of John Finnis, *q.v.*
Services: Posted Lieut. to 26th N.I. in 1824. First Burma War ; Arakan 1825 ; Lieut. 26th N.I. Adjt. 26th N.I. 2 Nov. 1825 till 3 May 1832. Fur. s.c. 19 Mar. 1832 till 1834, when he returned overland. Volunteered in Dec. 1834 to accompany the expedn. led by Col. F. R. Chesney (*D.N.B.*) to explore the Euphrates and Tigris with a view to steam navigation on those rivers.
Refs.: Burke's *Landed Gentry of Ireland*, p. 424, *s.n.* Lynch, of Partry, co. Mayo. *Lond. Gaz.* 29 July 1836. *The Times*, 29 July 1836. *A.J.* N.S. xxi. 48-9. M.I. on Lynch monument in private cemetery at Partry.

LYON, Edward (1806-1825). Ensign, 49th N.I. *b.* Templeogue, co. Dublin, 29 Mar. 1806. Cadet 1823. Ensign 21 Feb. 1824. *d.* Arakan 10 Dec. 1825.
Son of Edward Lyon, Lieut. R.N., of Prince's Pl., Pimlico, Westminster. Ed. Westminster 26 Mar. 1821 till Dec. 1823.

Services: Posted Ensign to 49th N.I. in 1824. First Burma War; Arakan 1825; Ensign 49th N.I.
Refs.: Westminster School Register.

LYON, Hugh (1748-1797). Capt. Lieutenant. Artillery. (131) *b.* 29 Jan. 1748. Cadet 1771. Fireworker 22 Feb. 1773. Capt. Lt. 17 Apr. 1781. Resigned 27 Jan. 1784. *d.* Dundee 12 Oct. 1797.

Of Wester Ogil. 2nd son of Rev. George Lyon, of Wester Ogil, minister of Longforgan 1738-93, and Margaret his wife, dau. of Hugh Rodger, merchant and provost of Glasgow. Uncle of Sir Hugh Lyon Playfair, *q.v. m.* (?)

Services: Removed as Cadet from Inf. to Art. 24 Nov. 1772. First Rohilla War; battle of St. George; Lieut. F. Art. Granted leave s.c. on full pay 29 Mar. 1782.

Refs.: Burke's *Landed Gentry*, 11th edn., p. 1068, *s.n.* Lyon, of Kirkmichael, co. Dumfries. *Family of Playfair*, by Rev. A. G. Playfair, 3rd edn., 1913. Scott's *Fasti*, v. 353. *G.M.* 1797, ii. 897. *S.M.* 1797, p. 782.

LYONS, Daniel (1761/62-1819). Lieut. Colonel, 12th N.I. *b.* in Ireland 1761/62. Cadet 1781. Admitted 29 May 1782. Ensign 4 July 1781. Lieut. 6 Oct. 1782. Capt. 29 May 1800. Major 13 Sept. 1807. Lt. Col. 25 Feb. 1813. *d.* Bareilly 13 Nov. 1819.

Owned an estate at Listaff. Brother of Martin, Joseph, Honora and Mary. Brother-in-law of Thomas Bell.

Services: Apptd. Cadet 31 Jan. 1781, aged 19; sailed for India in the *Hinchinbrooke* 13 Mar. 1781. Lieut. 34th Bn. Sepoys in July 1787 and in Jan. 1796. Bt. Capt. 1/9th N.I. in Aug. 1798; Capt. Lt. 10th N.I. 21 Apr. 1800. Second Mahratta War; operations against Holkar 1805; Capt. 1/10th N.I. Comdg. Resdt.'s escort with Sindhia 1805-6; comdg. Resdt.'s escort at Lucknow 1806-7. Fur. 22 Jan. 1810 till 1812. Posted Lt. Col. to 7th N.I. in 1813. Nepal War 1814-15; Lt. Col. 2/7th N.I., in 1st Div. Transfd. to newly-raised 2/29th N.I. in 1815; to 1/4th N.I. in 1816; to 8th N.I. in 1817; to 2/12th N.I. in 1818. Comdg. troops in Kumaon 1816 till death.

Refs.: A.J. xxiv. 392. Will dated 5 Nov. 1819; codicil dated 12 Nov. 1819; proved 4 Dec. 1819.

LYONS, David (*d.* 1807). Captain, 25th N.I. Cadet 1782. Admitted 22 Jan. 1783. Ensign 15 Mar. 1783. Lieut. 25 Feb. 1790. Capt. 30 Sept. 1803. *d.* Gaya, B. & O., 17 Oct. 1807.

m. Calcutta 16 Mar. 1793, Elizabeth, dau. of Edward Clayton,

THE BENGAL ARMY, 1758-1834

q.v. (She *re-m.* Asst. Surg. John Marshall, afterwards Physician Gen., Bengal.)

Services : Apptd. Cadet 24 Oct. 1781 ; sailed for India in the *Ganges* 6 Feb. 1782. Posted to 3rd Bengal Eur. Regt. 28 Feb. 1783. Ensign 5th Eur. Bn. in Dec. 1788 ; transfd. to 5th Bn. Sepoys Feb. 1790 ; to 34th Bn. 16 Apr. 1793. Lieut. 7th N.I. in Jan. 1799 ; transfd. to 19th N.I. ; to newly-raised 25th N.I. in 1805. (? Second Mahratta War 1805 ; Adalatnagar ; Capt. 1/25th N.I.) Operations against the Rana of Gohad 1806 ; capture of Gohad ; Capt. 25th N.I.

Refs. : Will dated Calcutta 7 Aug. 1807 ; filed 22 Dec. 1807.

LYONS, Edward Robbins (1810-1849). Captain, 37th N.I. *b.* Boldre, Hants, 2 Feb. 1810. Cadet 1825. Arrived in India 4 Sept. 1826. Ensign 15 Apr. 1826. Lieut. 22 Nov. 1828. Capt. 24 Dec. 1841. *d. unm.* Cachar 23 Apr. 1849.

bapt. Boldre 10 Mar. 1810. 12th (younger by 2nd wife) son of John Lyons, of Lyons, Antigua, and of St. Austins, Hants, Capt. R.N., and Elizabeth his 2nd wife, dau. of William Robbins, Brother of Samuel Athill Lyons, *q.v.*, and half-brother of Sir Edmund, 1st Baron Lyons, and of Theodore Lyons, *q.v.*

Services : Posted Ensign to 37th N.I. 5 Oct. 1826. Actg. Intr. & Qmr. 37th N.I. 21 Dec. 1834. d.d. Assam L.I. 16 June 1835 ; do. Sylhet L.I. 30 Oct. 1835 ; 2nd in comd. do. 1 Mar. 1836. Tempy. Offg. Supt. of Cachar 8 July 1839 ; Supt. of Upper and Lower Cachar 2 Sept. 1839 till death. Leave s.c. to Straits 15 Apr. till 20 Sept. 1842 ; s.c. 2 yrs. to Cape 13 Aug. 1847. No record of active service.

Refs. : Foster's *Peerage*, p. 434, *s.n.* Lyons, B. Will dated Sylhet, 14 July 1847 ; proved 5 Feb. 1850.

LYONS, Samuel Athill (1805-1881). Lieut. Colonel. 34th N.I. *b.* Boldre, Hants, 14 Apr. 1805. Cadet 1822. Arrived in India 22 Sept. 1823. Ensign 17 May 1823. Lieut. 18 Feb. 1825. Capt. 1 Aug. 1841. Major 11 Nov. 1851. Retired 29 June 1853. Hon. Lt. Col. 28 Nov. 1854. *d.* Middlesex House, Batheaston, Somerset, 19 Sept. 1881.

11th (elder by 2nd wife) son of John Lyons, Capt. R.N., and Elizabeth his 2nd wife. Brother of Edward Robbins Lyons, *q.v. m.* 1st, Cawnpore 22 June 1827, Sophia, eldest dau. of William Logie, *q.v.* (*See also* George William Hamilton.) (She died 18 Feb. 1840.) *m.* 2nd, Moradabad 5 July 1842, Mary, dau. of Thomas Wall, of Hereford. (She died 22 Nov. 1893.)

Services: Posted Ensign to 17th N.I. Transfd. to 35th N.I. (late 2/17th) May 1824; to 34th N.I. 13 May 1825. Actg. Intr. & Qmr. 34th N.I. 13 July 1827; Adjt. do. 30 June 1828 till 6 Sept. 1841. Detachment Staff Ofr., Chota Nagpur F.F., 1831-2. Operations against the Kols and Chuars in Chota Nagpur 1832. d.d. 74th N.I. at Mirzapur 15 Apr. till 20 Oct. 1833. Actg. A.A.G. Meerut Div. 25 Oct. 1842; actg. Bde. Major Barrackpore 28 Nov. 1842. On disbandment of 34th N.I. for mutiny, transfd. to 2nd N.I. 18 Apr. 1844; retransfd. to new 34th N.I. (late Bundelkhand Legion) July 1846. Fort Adjt. at Allahabad 31 Oct. 1845 till July 1846. Fur. p.a. 22 Jan. 1852 till retirement.

Refs.: Foster's *Peerage*, p. 434, *s.n.* Lyons, B. *The Times*, 23 Sept. 1881.

LYONS, Theodore (1788-1825). Captain, Pension Est. Artillery. (367) *b.* Lyndhurst, Hants, 5 Oct. 1788. Cadet 1805. Arrived in India 11 July 1806. Lieut. 7 Apr. 1806. Capt. Lt. 25 Sept. 1817. Capt. 1 Sept. 1818. Pensioned 18 Oct. 1822. *d. unm.* Intally, Calcutta, 5 Sept. 1825.

bapt. Lyndhurst 22 Nov. 1788. 2nd son of John Lyons, of Lyons, Antigua, and St. Austins, Hants, and Catherine his 1st wife, dau. of Maine Swete Walrond, of Antigua. Half-brother of Edward Robbins Lyons, *q.v.*, and cousin-german of Thomas Charles Torriano Fluker, *q.v.*, and of William George Walcott, *q.v.* Nominated to R.M.A., Woolwich, 20 Apr. 1803, but went to Marlow as Art. Cadet.

Services: Served throughout with Foot Art. No record of active service. Found guilty by a G.C.M. at Ft. Wm. 3 Sept. 1822, and sentenced to be discharged. The C.-in-C. commuted the sentence to being placed on the pension list.

Refs.: Foster's *Peerage*, p. 434, *s.n.* Lyons, B. Oliver's *History of Antigua*, ii. 214.

LYSAGHT, Thomas Vallencey (1804-1849). Bt. Major, 1st Bengal Eur. Fus. *b.* Dublin 8 Mar. 1804. Cadet 1819. Admitted 23 Oct. 1820. Ensign 3 June 1820. Lieut. 11 July 1823. Capt. 27 Sept. 1837. Bt. Major 9 Nov. 1846. *d.* Hingoli, Hyderabad, 29 June 1849, of wounds received in action at Gaori on 6 May.

bapt. Dublin 12 Mar. 1804. Son of Thomas Lysaght, solicitor, and Catherine his wife. *m.* 1st, Dacca 3 Apr. 1829, Fanny Sophia, eldest dau. of Charles William Hamilton, *q.v.* (*See also* Charles Prior and Richard Salisbury Simpson.) (She died 29 Oct. 1830.) *m.* 2nd, Dinapore 22 Jan. 1833, Maria Nugent, 7th daughter of Sir

Joseph O'Halloran, G.C.B., *q.v.* (*See also* George Cuninghame.) (She died Hingoli 25 Apr. 1843.)
Services : Posted Ensign to 6th N.I. in 1820 ; transfd. to 2/7th N.I. 1821 ; as Lieut. to Bengal Eur. Regt. July 1823 ; to newly-formed 2nd Bengal Eur. Regt. May 1824. Actg. Adjt. 2nd Bengal Eur. Regt. 2 Aug. 1824 ; permanent do. 14 Oct. 1824 till 13 Nov. 1829, on the amalgamation of the two Regts. First Burma War ; Lieut. 2nd Bengal Eur. Regt. Joined the detachment under Capt. George Bolton, *q.v.*, Dec. 1826 ; actg. Adjt. & Qmr. do. 15 Jan. 1827. Adjt. Dacca Provl. Bn. 5 Feb. 1830. Adjt. Left Wing, Bengal Eur. Regt. 15 July 1831 till 16 Apr. 1836. Placed under orders of Resdt. at Hyderabad 17 Mar. 1836. Served with Nizam's army 11 Sept. 1836 till death ; sometime with 4th Inf., latterly Bde. Major and Paymr. at Hingoli. Insurrection of the impostor Appa Sahib 1849 ; action at Gaori 6 May (s.w.) ; Bde. Major to Bdr. George Hampton, comdg. the force.
Refs. : Burke's *Colonial Gentry*, i. 83, *s.n.* O'Halloran. *Burton*, p. 132. Will dated Hingoli 22 July 1844 ; proved 5 Oct. 1849. M.I. Hingoli.

LYSTER, Lyttleton (1789-1850). Lieutenant. 3rd N.I. Subsequently Capt. 1st R. Surrey Mil. *b.* St. George's, Dublin, 2 Nov. 1789. Cadet 1806. Arrived in India 21 July 1807. Ensign 28 July 1807. Lieut. 1811. Resigned 11 Mar. 1812. *d.* Richmond Hill, Dublin, 20 Feb. 1850, after an operation.
Of Union Hall, and of Lysterfield, Skibbereen, co. Cork (which he built), J.P. co. Cork. 2nd son of Rev. John Lyster, D.D., of Dublin and Bath, rector of Clonpriest, co. Cork, and Mary Aleyne his wife, dau. of Thomas Cameron, M.D., of Worcester, and cousin of George, 1st Marquis of Buckingham. *m.* St. Peter's, Cork, 15 Aug. 1811, Charlotte Cameron, eldest dau. of Rev. Paul Limerick, D.D., sometime Chaplain of Calcutta.[1] (She died 14 May 1849.)
Services : Ensign Bucks. Mil. 2 Jan. 1806 ; Lieut. do. 24 Oct. 1806. Sailed for India in the *Adm. Gardiner* Feb. 1807. Posted Ensign to 3rd N.I. in 1807 whilst still at Barasat C.C., but never joined his Regt. Fur. 5 Oct. 1807 till resignation. Capt. 1st R. Surrey Mil. 23 Dec. 1812, in which he was for over 20 yrs. a Capt.
Refs. : Burke's *Landed Gentry of Ireland*, p. 426, *s.n.* Lyster, of Rocksavage. *A Hist. of family of Lyster or Lister*, by Rev. Sir H. L. L. Denny, Bt., p. 88. *John Cameron, non-Juror*, pt. iii. p. 115 (portrait).
[1] *Note :* He was nephew of Judith, the mother of William Neville Cameron, *q.v.*

M

MABERT, Richard (*d.* 1818). Colonel, 27th N.I. Country Cadet 1779. Ensign 9 Sept. 1779. Lieut. 26 Apr. 1781. Capt. 9 Aug. 1798. Major 18 Mar. 1803. Lt. Col. 21 Sept. 1804. Bt. Col. 4 June 1813. *d.* Mazagon, Bombay, 2 Sept. 1818.

m. 1st, 15 Sept. 1779, Miss Helen Leslie. *m.* 2nd, Maria. (She died Bandel 7 Feb. 1798.) His dau. *m.* William Turner (1791-1871), *q.v.*

Services: Apptd. Cadet 19 Aug. 1779. Adjt. 30th Bn. Sepoys 1786-95. Major 9th N.I. Posted Lt. Col. to newly-raised 2/27th N.I. in 1805. This Bn. was called after him "*Mapert-ki-Paltan.*" Operations against Dhundia Khan 1807; Komona; Ganauri; Lt. Col. 2/27th N.I. Operations in Oudh 1810; Lt. Col. 2/27th N.I. Comdg. at Bareilly 1815-16. Fur. 1818.

Refs.: Will dated 17 Jan. 1818; proved 5 Oct. 1818.

MACADAM, James (1809-1888). Lieut. Colonel. 33rd N.I. *b.* Maybole, co. Ayr, 20 Apr. 1809. Cadet 1828. Arrived in India 24 Oct. 1828. Ensign 10 May 1828. Lieut. 9 Jan. 1833. Capt. 23 Mar. 1840. Major 17 Nov. 1852. Retired 30 Dec. 1852. Hon. Lt. Col. 28 Nov. 1854. *d.* East Villa, Leamington Spa, 13 Mar. 1888.

Son of John Macadam, writer in Maybole, and Janet Blane his wife.

Services: Ensign d.d. 7th N.I. 20 Nov. 1828; d.d. 63rd N.I. 21 Jan. 1829; posted to 33rd N.I. 4 Mar. 1829. Adjt. 33rd N.I. 2 Dec. 1837 till 30 Apr. 1840. Actg. D.J.A.G. Meerut Div. 16 June 1840 and 22 May 1841; do. Cawnpore Div. 29 Oct. 1841 till Jan. 1842. Apptd. D.J.A.G. to Gen. Pollock's force 23 Feb. 1842. First Afghan War 1842; forcing of Khyber (*Lond. Gaz.* 7 June 1842); Mamu Khel (ib. 8 Nov. 1842); Tazin; Kabul; Capt. 33rd N.I., D.J.A.G. (Medal). D.C. 1 cl., Saugor & Narbada territories, at Jubbulpore, 31 Mar. 1843 till retirement. In addition comdd. 1st Bn. Saugor Mily. Police for some years.

Refs.: The Times, 16 Mar. 1888.

MACALISTER, Donald (1790-1828). Captain. Artillery. (387) *b.* Clachaig, co. Argyll, 16 Feb. 1790. Cadet 1807. Arrived in India 17 Mar. 1808. Fireworker 16 June 1807. Lieut. 15 Sept. 1809. Capt. 15 Jan. 1821. Retired 21 Apr. 1824. *d.s.p.* 1828.

LIST OF OFFICERS OF THE BENGAL ARMY 105

4th and youngest son of Alexander Macalister, of Strathaird, Skye, and Janet McLeod, of Grishernish, his 2nd wife.
Services : Lieut. 5th Coy. 1st Bn. Foot Art. Served with 3rd Troop H.A. 1817-18; 1st Troop 1818-19; 6th (Native) Troop 1819 till retirement. Siege and capture of Hathras. Third Mahratta War. Fur. 16 July 1821 till retirement.
Refs. : *Clan Donald*, iii. 197.

MACALISTER, Matthew (*d.* 1796). Ensign, Infantry. Cadet 1794. Arrived in India 24 Feb. 1796. Ensign 30 Nov. 1795. *d.* Dinapore 15 Aug. 1796.

Of Strath, I. of Skye. (*Possibly* son of Col. Matthew Macalister, of Glenbarr and Cour, late a Capt. on Madras Est., and nephew of Norman Macalister, *q.v.*)
Services : Apptd. Cadet 10 June 1795 ; sailed for India in the *Rodney* 9 July 1795.
Refs. : (? Burke's *Landed Gentry*, 13th edn., p. 1152, *s.n.* Macalister, of Glenbarr, co. Argyll.) *G.M.* 1797, i. 356.

MACALISTER, Norman (*d.* 1810). Bt. Major, Artillery. (274) (Local Col. at P.W.I.) Cadet 1783. Ensign (Inf.) 31 Jan. 1785. Fireworker 6 June 1785. Lieut. 28 Oct. 1794. Capt. Lt. 18 June 1802. Capt. 25 July 1805. Bt. Major 25 July 1810. Local Col. 1806. *d.* at sea (? Sept.) 1810 : lost in the ship *Ocean* in the China seas.

b. Skerrinish, I. of Skye. 8th son of Ranald Macalister and Anne his wife, dau. of Alexander Macdonald of Kingsburgh. Brother of Col. Matthew Macalister, of Glenbarr and Cour, and of Keith Macalister. Cousin of John Macalister, of Cour, and uncle of Lt.-Col. John Macdonald and Lieut. James Ranald Macdonald, Madras Est. Father of Frances Macalister, *alias* Johnstone, and of Flora Macalister, *alias* Scott.[1]
Services : 2/Lt. in a Corps of Vols. under Col. Charles Campbell raised for defence of Campbeltown, 1780-1. Apptd. Inf. Cadet 25 Mar. 1783 ; sailed for India in the *Orpheus* frigate ; arrived Sept. 1784. Transfd. from Inf. to Art. 1785. Apptd. Asst. in the Secret Dept. 9 Aug. 1786. To comd. Art. at P.W.I. 10 Oct. 1793. Fur. 19 Apr. 1802 till 11 Jan. 1806. Apptd. in 1805 Comdt. of the forces at P.W.I. and 4th in Council ; Govr. and C.-in-C. 1807. Sailed from P.W.I. to China in the *Ocean* 16 Aug. 1810.
Refs. : Burke's *Landed Gentry*, 11th edn., p. 1071, *s.n.* Macalister, of Glenbarr and Cour, co. Argyll. *MacInnes* (portrait). *Clan*

Donald, iii. 196. *Cal. Gaz.* 17 Oct. 1805. Will dated 23 Nov. 1808; codicil dated 10 Mar. 1809; proved 29 May 1811.

[1] *Note:* "Said to be illegitimate." (*Clan Donald*.)

MACALLY or McCALLY, Andrew (1763-1819). Ensign. Infantry. Subsequently Bt. Col. 18th Madras N.I. *b.* 1763. Cadet 1780. Ensign 9 Feb. 1781. Transfd. to Madras Est. 1781. *d.* Madras 26 Jan. 1819, aged 55.

Brother of Arthur Macally, *q.v. m.* Christina Paulina. (She died Pondicherry 21 May 1822.)

Refs.: Will dated 7 Mar. 1818; proved (Madras) 13 Mar. 1819. M.I. St. Mary's cemetery, Madras.

MACALLY, Arthur [1] (*d.* 1804). Ensign. Infantry. Subsequently Major 12th Madras N.I. Cadet 1780. Ensign 8 Feb. 1781. Transfd. to Madras Est. 1781. *d.* Ajanta, Hyderabad, 10 Mar. 1804, of wounds received at the battle of Assaye, 23 Sept. 1803.

Brother of Andrew Macally, *q.v.*

Services: Served as a Vol. with Bengal Detachment during 2nd Mysore War.

Refs.: Intest.; Admon. (Madras) 25 June 1804.

[1] *Note:* His christian name is given as Thomas in *Dodwell & Miles* in the Bengal list, but correctly in the Madras list.

MACAN, Clements Gillespie (1803-1867). Lieut. Colonel. 16th N.I. *b.* Newry, co. Down, 5 Mar. 1803. Cadet 1819. Admitted 21 Aug. 1820. Ensign 9 Jan. 1820. Lieut. 11 July 1823. Capt. 13 Sept. 1829. Major 23 Dec. 1845. Retired 1 Nov. 1849. Hon. Lt. Col. 28 Nov. 1854. *d.* 22 Feb. 1867.

bapt. Jonesborough, co. Armagh, 16 Mar. 1803. Son of Robert Macan, of Newry, banker, later of Paris, and Margaret Gillespie his wife. Brother of John Macan, *q.v. m.* 1st, Barrackpore 2 Mar. 1826, Miss Harriet Augusta Williams. (She died Gorakhpur 7 Feb. 1828, aged 26.) *m.* 2nd, Sikraul, B. & O., 1 Nov. 1830, Mary, sister of James Coutts Crawford Gray, *q.v.* (*See also* Henry Carter (1793-1844).)

Services: Posted Ensign to 2/8th N.I. Transfd. as Lieut. to 10th N.I. July 1823; to 16th N.I. (late 2/10th) May 1824. Adjt. 16th N.I. 7 Apr. 1825 till 3 May 1830. Offg. 2nd in comd. 4th Local Horse 9 Dec. 1831. Apptd. Comdt. Shah Shuja's 2nd Inf. 17 Aug. 1838. First Afghan War 1839-42; Ghazni (Medal); recapture of Kalat (*Lond. Gaz.* 12 Feb. 1841); action under Col. G. P. Wymer, *q.v.*, at Baba Wali against Durani Horse 25 Mar. 1842

THE BENGAL ARMY, 1758-1834 107

(ib. 6 Sept. 1842); Capt. comdg. Shah's 2nd Inf. (Medal). (? Gwalior campaign ; Maharajpur ; Capt. 16th N.I.—Bronze star.) Fur. s.c. 2 Mar. 1845 till 4 Feb. 1848, and 23 June 1849 till retirement.

MACAN, John (1800-1851 ?). Captain. 52nd N.I. *b*. Newry, co. Down, 9 Sept. 1800. Cadet 1817. Ensign (?) Lieut. 1 Aug. 1818. Capt. 14 June 1828. Retired 4 June 1828. *d*. 1851 ?[1] *bapt*. Armagh 4 Oct. 1800. Eldest son of Robert Macan, of Ballynow, Armagh, banker. Brother of Clements Gillespie Macan, *q.v. m*. 1st, Berhampore 20 Sept. 1821, Charlotte Maria, eldest dau. of William Towers Smith, B.C.S., judge at Murshidabad. (She died 2 Feb. 1825.) *m*. 2nd, Lurgyvallen, co. Armagh, 14 Jan. 1828, Jessie, only dau. of William Campbell, of Edinburgh. Addiscombe Cadet 1817-18.

Services : Posted Lieut. to 2/26th N.I. in 1818. Fur. 1822-3. Transfd. to 52nd N.I. (late 2/26th) May 1824. (? First Burma War ; Cachar 1825 ; Lieut. 52nd N.I.) Fur. 1826 till retirement.

Refs. : A.J. xiii. 407 ; xxv. 413.

[1] *Note :* His name appears for the last time in E.I.R. for Jan. 1851, but he did not draw his pension after 31 Jan. 1842.

MACAN, Richard (*d*. 1812). Major General, Cavalry. Comdg. at the Presdy. Cadet 1772. Admitted 3 Feb. 1772. Ensign 20 Jan. 1773. Lieut. 13 May 1777. Capt. 4 Apr. 1781. Major 25 Apr. 1797. Lt. Col. 1 Nov. 1798. Col. 21 Feb. 1801. Col. Comdt. 17 July 1801. Maj. Gen. 25 Apr. 1808. *d*. at sea 26 Feb. 1812, on board the *Gen. Hewett* between Calcutta and St. Helena, of fever.

Son of Thomas MacCann, of Cariff, co. Armagh. Brother of Turner Macan, of Greenmount, B.C.S., of Thomas Macan, *q.v.*, of Samuel Macan, B.C.S., and of Arthur Jacob Macan, Lieut. 24th Light Dgns. Uncle of Thomas Richard Macqueen, *q.v.*

Services : Apptd. Qmr. 1st Bengal Eur. Regt. 11 Jan. 1779 ; transfd. to Sepoy Corps Sept. 1781 ; posted to a Regt. of L.I. 30 Nov. 1781. Supy. Capt., unposted, in July 1787 ; 3rd Eur. Bn. in Dec. 1788. Raised in 1795 the Ramgarh Provl. Bn. for duty on the Ramgarh frontier. Lt. Col. 4th N.C. in 1798 ; apptd. Col. Comdt. of Cav. 17 July 1801. Second Mahratta War 1803-4 ; Agra ; Laswari ; battle of Deig ; comdg. 3rd Cav. Bde.[1] Comdg. at Fatehgarh in 1805. Fur. 12 Feb. 1806 till 10 Nov. 1809, and 1811 till death. "Took part in all the campaigns of Lords Cornwallis and Lake." (*G.M.*)

Refs.: Burke's *Landed Gentry of Ireland*, p. 429, *s.n.* Macan, of Drumcashel, co. Louth. *A.R.* liv. *G.M.* 1812, ii. 404. Will dated 3 Nov. 1811; proved 21 Sept. 1812.

[1] *Note:* "H.E. in Council is pleased to determine, in consequence of the recommendation of H.E. the C.-in-C., founded on the zeal, gallantry, and distinguished conduct of Col. Richard Macan, that the appt. of 'Col. Comdt. of Native Cav.' shall be revived as an honorary distinction for Col. Macan." (*Cal. Gaz.* 2 Aug. 1804.)

MACAN, Thomas (*d.* 1848). Major. 27th N.I. Cadet 1783. Admitted 25 Nov. 1784. Ensign 20 Feb. 1785. Lieut. 15 Mar. 1793. Capt. 21 Sept. 1804. Major 25 June 1810. Retired 29 Aug. 1810. *d.* 8 Mar. 1848.

Of Greenmount, co. Louth. Son of Thomas MacCann, of Cariff, co. Armagh. Brother of Richard Macan and uncle of Thomas Macan, *qq.v. m.* Bathwick, Somerset, May 1814, Mary Joanna, sister of Edmond Morris, *q.v.*, and widow of Christopher Oldfield B.C.S. (She died Castle Hacket 26 Nov. 1854.) Stepfather of Charles James Oldfield, *q.v.*

Services: Apptd. Cadet 13 Mar. 1783; sailed for India in the *Earl Cornwallis* 31 Mar. 1784. Posted to 3rd Bn. Sepoys 15 Feb. 1790. Third Mysore War 1790-2; Ensign 3rd Bn. Transfd. from 5th Eur. Bn. to 3rd do. 18 Dec. 1792; to 15th Bn. Sepoys 22 Mar. 1793. Fur. 14 Mar. 1794 till 1 Jan. 1797. Adjt. & Qmr. 9th N.I. in 1803. Second Mahratta War; A.D.C. to his brother. Transfd. as Adjt. & Qmr. to newly-raised 21st N.I. in 1804; as Capt. to newly-raised 27th N.I. in 1805. Fur. 12 Feb. 1806 till retirement.

Refs.: Burke's *Landed Gentry of Ireland*, p. 429, *s.n.* Macan, of Drumcashel, co. Louth. Burke's *Family Records*, p. 448, *s.n.* Oldfield. *M.M.* 1814, i. 483.

MACAN, Thomas (1790-1809). Lieutenant, 8th N.I. *b.* Kilbroggan, co. Cork, 20 May 1790. Cadet 1805. Arrived in India 25 Mar. 1806. Ensign 13 Apr. 1806. Lieut. 17 July 1807. *d. unm.* Nilganj, nr. Barasat, 14 June 1809: kld. in a duel; *bur.* at Barrackpore.

Eldest son of Robert Macan, of Cariff, co. Armagh, and Hanna Bagwed his wife. Nephew of Richard Macan, *q.v.* His sisters *m.* William Henry Rainey and John Richardson, *qq.v.*

Services: Barasat C.C. Posted Ensign to 1/8th N.I. in 1807; Lieut. 2/8th N.I. Apptd. a Cav. Cadet in 1808, but remained with 8th N.I. No record of active service.

THE BENGAL ARMY, 1758-1834

Refs.: Burke's *Landed Gentry of Ireland*, p. 429, *s.n.* Macan, of Drumcashel, co. Louth. M.I. in Barrackpore cemetery.

MACARTNEY, John (1781-1811). Lieutenant, 5th N.C. *b.* Antrim 6 Aug. 1781. Cadet 1798. Arrived in India 22 Dec. 1799. Cornet 30 Dec. 1800. Lieut. 11 Mar. 1805. *d.* Meerut 29 Apr. 1811.

Son of Rev. Dr. George Macartney, LL.D., J.P., vicar of Antrim, and Mildred Brown his wife.

Services: 2/Lt. Antrim Mil. 31 Oct. 1798. Second Mahratta War 1803-4 ; Cornet 5th N.C. Qmr. 5th N.C. 22 Jan. 1803 till death. A prisoner of war in the I. of Bourbon ; released and left the island 6 May 1807. Accompanied Elphinstone's mission to Kabul in 1809, and submitted on his return a " Memoir of a Map of Caubul and the adjacent Countries.' Employed on survey of Delhi canals 1810-11.

Refs.: Burke's *Landed Gentry of Ireland*, p. 431, *s.n.* Ellison-Macartney, of Mountjoy Grange, co. Tyrone. M.I. Meerut.

MACARTNEY, John (1785-1813). Lieutenant, 11th N.I. *b.* St. Peter's, Dublin, 12 Aug. 1785. Cadet 1804. Arrived in India 30 Sept. 1805. Ensign 12 Aug. 1805. Lieut. 13 Aug. 1805. *d.* Java 19 Aug. 1813.

3rd son of Sir John Macartney, 1st Bart., of Lish, co. Armagh, M.P., and Anne his 1st wife, dau. of Edward Scriven. T.C.D. ; Fellow Commoner 27 Oct. 1802.

Services: Posted Lieut. to 11th N.I. in 1806. Capture of Java 1811 ; Lieut. 4th Bengal Vol. Bn. Lieut. 1/11th N.I.

Refs.: Burke's *Peerage*, 1923, p. 1460, *s.n.* Macartney, Bart., of Lish, co. Armagh. Burke's *Colonial Gentry*, ii. 473, *s.n.* Macartney. *Alumni Dub.* Will dated 22 June 1812 ; proved 1 Mar. 1817.

MACBARNET, James William (1814-1832). Cadet, Infantry. *b.* Kingussie, co. Inverness, 23 May 1814. Cadet 1829. Arrived in India 22 Oct. 1830. *d.* Rangamati, nr. Berhampore, Bengal, 16 May 1832 : drowned in attempting to cross a nullah whilst pig-sticking.

Son of Donald Macbarnet, of Chiry, Strathspey, Capt. H.M. 92nd Regt., and Helen McPherson his wife.

Services: Cadet d.d. 63rd N.I. 24 Nov. 1830 ; d.d. 72nd N.I. at Berhampore 7 Jan. 1832. No record of active service.

Refs.: *A.J.* N.S. ix. 142.

LIST OF THE OFFICERS OF

MacBEAN, John Gordon (1797-1828). Captain, 52nd N.I. *b.* Inverness 20 Nov. 1797. Cadet 1813. Ensign 16 Dec. 1814. Lieut. 6 Apr. 1818. Capt. 8 Feb. 1828. *d.* Chittagong 14 June 1828, of cholera.

Son of Robert MacBean, of Nairnside, and Margaret his wife, dau. of Donald MacIntosh, of Dalmigary. Brother of German Margaret MacBean. Ed. R. Acad., Inverness. King's Coll., Aberdeen; M.A. 26 Apr. 1813.

Services: Posted Ensign to 2/26th N.I. in 1815. Operations against the Bhattis of Hariana 1818; Lieut. 2/26th N.I. Fur. 1823-5. Transfd. to 52nd N.I. (late 2/26th) May 1824. Intr. & Qmr. 52nd N.I. 14 Nov. 1825 till death.

Refs.: *A.J.* xxvi. 740. Will dated Chittagong 26 July 1827; proved 27 June 1828. M.I. at Chittagong.

McCALLY, Andrew. (*See* **MACALLY.**)

MacCARTHY, Patrick (1781-?). Lieutenant. 1st N.I. *b.* Dublin 14 Sept. 1781. Cadet 1805. Arrived in India 11 July 1806. Ensign 14 July 1806. Lieut. 10 Aug. 1808. Resigned in India 9 Dec. 1814.

His parents were prisoners in France when he obtained his Cadetship.

Services: Posted Ensign to 1st N.I. in 1807, and served throughout with that Regt.

McCAUSLAND, John Kennedy (1803–1879). Lieut. General, C.B. 29th N.I. *b.* Dublin 1 June 1803. Cadet 1819. Admitted 27 Mar. 1820. Ensign 20 Sept. 1819. Lieut. 5 Oct. 1821. Capt. 1 July 1836. Major 18 Mar. 1847. Lt. Col. 31 Mar. 1853. Bt. Col. 28 Nov. 1854. Maj. Gen. 29 Aug. 1861. Retired 31 Dec. 1861. Hon. Lt. Gen. 31 Dec. 1861. *d.* at his residence, Melrose Villa, Cheltenham, 23 July 1879.

Of The Park, Cheltenham. 2nd son of Marcus Langford McCausland and Maria his wife, 2nd dau. of John Kennedy, of Cultra. Nephew of Charles Pratt Kennedy, *q.v. m.* Simla 26 July 1834, Emma, 5th dau. of William Conrad Faithful, *q.v.* (*See also* John Dickson Dyke Bean.) (She died 28 July 1889.)

Services: Posted to 1/16th N.I. in 1820. d.d. 1st Nassiri Bn. 1821 till 30 Aug. 1824. Transfd. to 4th N.I. July 1823; to 7th N.I. (late 1/4th) May 1824. First Burma War; Cachar 1825; Lieut. 7th N.I. (India Medal). Transfd. to 2nd Extra Regt. (became 70th N.I.) 13 May 1825. Adjt. 1st Nassiri Bn. 28 Dec. 1826; 2nd in comd. do. 3 May 1832 ; Asst. to P.A. Sabathu 19 Mar. 1833 ; Supt. of public bldgs. in Sabathu, 1 May 1833. To take charge of office of P.A. Sabathu, and comd. Nassiri Bn., 15 Aug. 1835 ; received charge 2 Nov. 1835 till 1838. Employed in quelling disturbances in Bilaspur district Mar. 1840 ; Capt. 70th N.I. Tempy. Comdt. Nassiri Bn. 14 May till 24 Sept. 1841. Comdt. Arakan Local Bn. 12 Sept. 1842 till 19 Jan. 1846. Fur. Jan. 1846 till 15 Nov. 1847. Second Sikh War ; Ramnagar ; passage of Chenab ; Chilianwala ; Gujerat (s.w.) ; Major 70th N.I. (Medal with clasp). Fur. p.a. 19 Jan. 1852 till July 1853. Posted as Lt. Col. to 2nd N.I. June 1853 ; to 50th N.I. 4 Aug. 1853 ; to 45th N.I. 1 Dec. 1854 ; to 66th N.I. (or Gurkha Regt., late Nassiri Bn.) 2 Nov. 1855. To assume comd. of Kumaon district Oct. 1857. Bdr. 2 cl., comdg. at Fatehgarh, 14 May 1858 ; do. 1 cl., comdg. Gwalior 20 Jan. 1860. Transfd. to 29th N.I. in 1860. C.B. 21 Mar. 1859.

Refs.: Burke's *Landed Gentry of Ireland*, p. 434, *s.n.* McCausland, of Drenagh, co. Londonderry. *Boase. The Times*, 26 July 1879.

MacCLARY, William (1745-1817). Major. Infantry. *bapt.* Ramsbury, Wilts., 6 May 1745. Country Cadet 1766. Ensign 30 Dec. 1766. Lieut. 9 Apr. 1768. Capt. 3 July 1776. Major 31 Jan. 1781. Struck off 1793. *d.* Somerset Pl., Bath, June 1817, aged 72.

Of Manoravon, co. Carmarthen. Youngest son of William MacClary and Margaret his wife. Brother of Capt. John McClary, of the privateer *Dodalay.* *m.* Claines, Worcs., 7 Jan. 1792, Miss Alicia Cookes, of Bourbourne House, nr. Worcester, only dau. of Rev. Thomas Cookes, of Notgrove, Gloucs. (She died Somerset Pl., Bath, 2 Jan. 1821.)

Services : Permitted to proceed to India as a Free Merchant 9 Jan. 1765. *Probably* commissioned owing to the " Batta mutiny." Apptd. to comd. a vacant Sepoy Bn. 19 Aug. 1779 ; to comd. newly-raised 41st Bn. Sepoys 13 Nov. 1780. First Mahratta War 1780-1 ; Lahar ; Gwalior ; Major comdg. 34th N.I. (late 41st Bn.). Fur. 31 Aug. 1785 till struck off. Was junior Major in Carmarthenshire Mil. in 1798 and 1802.

Refs. : Burke's *Landed Gentry*, 10th edn., p. 339, *s.n.* Cookes, late of Bentley, Worcs. *G.M.* 1792, i. 88 ; 1817, i. 645. *Bath Chron.* 4 June 1817.

McCLINTOCK, Alexander. Captain. 2nd Bengal Eur. Regt. Cadet 1767. Ensign 19 July 1767. Lieut. 18 Apr. 1769. Capt.

8 Apr. 1777. Resigned 16 Feb. 1778. Pensioned on Lord Clive's fund 28 Apr. 1784. (Living in 1790.)

Services: Dangerously wounded (left leg shattered and musket shot through body) nr. Cawnpore in Jan. 1771. Adjt. & Qmr. Chunargarh fort till Apr. 1777.

Refs.: *Macpherson*, p. 62.

McCLINTOCK, Alexander (1763/64-1784). Lieutenant, Infantry. *b.* in Ireland 1763/64. Cadet 1781. Ensign 31 Mar. 1781. Lieut. 23 July 1782. *d. unm.* Jilda (?), 24 Aug. 1784.

Younger son of William McClintock (who was eldest son of John McClintock, of Trinta) and Francelina his wife, 3rd dau. of James Nesbitt, of Greenhills. (*Probably* brother of John McClintock,* *q.v.*)

Services: Apptd. Cadet 15 Dec. 1780, aged 16; sailed for India in the *Chapman* 13 Mar. 1781, aged 17. N.F.P.

Refs.: Burke's *Landed Gentry*, 4th edn., p. 929, *s.n.* McClintock, of Drumcar, co. Louth.

McCLINTOCK, George Frederick (1808-1848). Lieutenant. 4th L.C. Subsequently B.C.S. *b.* Calcutta 15 Aug. 1808. Cadet 1825. Arrived in India 18 Mar. 1826. Cornet 28 Sept. 1825. Lieut. 29 Dec. 1826. Struck off 21 Nov. 1828. *d.* Brighton 11 Oct. 1848.

bapt. Calcutta 15 Sept. 1808. Son of Robert McClintock, of Calcutta, merchant and agent,[1] and Marianne Hardyman his wife. His sister *m.* Moring Agnew Bignell, *q.v.* *m.* Calcutta 12 Jan. 1839, Elizabeth Catherine, eldest dau. of W. Graham, M.D., of Calcutta. Ed. Charterhouse Sept. 1821-July 1822; Harrow 1822-5.

Services: Posted Cornet to 4th L.C. Fur. u.p.a. 1 yr. 21 Nov. 1827. No record of active service. Apptd. Writer, B.C.S., 30 Apr. 1829. Arrived in India 4 May 1829. Apptd. 3rd Govt. Agent and *ex-officio* Sec. to Govt. Savings Bank, 4 Mar. 1840.

Refs.: *Charterhouse School List. Harrow School Register.*

[1] *Note*: "The aged merchant prince, who presented the great chandelier and brass sconces at a cost of Rs. 10,000 to the old cathedral."

McCLINTOCK, John. Lieutenant. Infantry. Cadet 1767. Ensign 15 Sept. 1767. Lieut. 21 Apr. 1769. Resigned 1769.

Services: N.F.P.

***McCLINTOCK, John** (1763/64-1786). Lieutenant, Infantry. *b.* in Ireland 1763/64. Cadet 1781. Ensign 5 July 1781. Lieut. 7 Oct. 1782. *d.* Dinapore 2 Sept. 1786.

THE BENGAL ARMY, 1758-1834   113

N.B.—The following is conjectural only : (? Elder son of William McClintock and Francelina his wife, 3rd dau. of James Nesbitt, of Greenhills. Brother of Alexander McClintock (1763/64-1784), *q.v.* *m.* Grace, dau. of Rev. Ralph Mansfield, of Killygordon, co. Donegal.)
Services : Apptd. Cadet 20 Dec. 1780 ; sailed for India in the *Chapman* 13 Mar. 1781, aged 17. N.F.P.
Refs. : (? Burke's *Landed Gentry*, 4th edn., p. 929, *s.n.* McClintock, of Drumcar, co. Louth.)

McCONNELL, William George (1810-1834). Lieutenant, 16th N.I. *b.* Reading 12 Apr. 1810. Cadet 1825. Arrived in India 2 Jan. 1827. Ensign 14 Aug. 1826. Lieut. 3 May 1833. *d.* Mhow 4 June 1834.
bapt. St. Mary's, Reading, 15 June 1810. Son of John McConnell, residing in France, and Sophia his wife.
Services : Ensign d.d. 67th N.I. 13 Jan. 1827. Posted to 16th N.I. 10 May 1827. No record of active service.
Refs. : *A.J.* N.S. xv. 227. M.I. Mhow old cemetery.

M'CORKILL, James (*d.* 1793). Lieutenant, Infantry. Cadet 1778. Ensign 1778. Lieut. 18 Sept. 1780. *d.* 16 May 1793 : drowned in the Ganges R.
Son of Anne McCorkill, of the city of Dublin. (*Perhaps* son of Archibald McCorquodale and Anne MacCallum his wife.)
Services : Transfd. from Inf. to Cav. 30 Nov. 1778. Lieut. 14th Bn. Sepoys in July 1787. Third Mysore War ; battle of Arikera ; operations before Savandrug ; Seringapatam ; Lieut. 14th Bn.
Refs. : Will undated ; admon. 10 Oct. 1793.

McCRAE, John Morison (1804–1822). Ensign, 17th N.I. *b.* Edinburgh 8 May 1804. Cadet 1819. Arrived in India Nov. 1820. Ensign 5 June 1820. *d.* Ludhiana 15 June 1822.
Son of William Gordon McCrae, controller of customs at Lerwick, Shetland, and Margaret his wife, dau. of Andrew Morison, writer. Ed. Edin. High School.
Services : Ensign d.d. Bengal Eur. Regt. Dec. 1820 till May 1821. Posted as Ensign to 2/17th N.I. in Jan. 1821, and joined in the autumn of that year. No record of active service.
Refs. : De Rhé-Philipe. M.I. at Ludhiana.

McCRAKEN, James (1785-1816). Lieutenant, 14th N.I. *b.* Treqhair, co. Kirkcudbright, 29 June 1785. Cadet 1805. Arrived in India 13 Nov. 1806. Ensign 31 Dec. 1806. Lieut. 6 July 1811. *d.* Cawnpore 1 Aug. 1816.

Son of John McCraken and Mary Anderson his wife. *m.* Calcutta 14 May 1812, Elizabeth, dau. of Bennet Marley, *q.v.* (*See also* William Burroughs.) (She *re-m.* John Tanzia Savary, *q.v.*)

Services : Barasat C.C. Posted Ensign to 14th N.I. in 1807 ; Adjt. 1/14th N.I. 1812 ; A.D.C. to Maj.-Gen. Bennet Marley, *q.v.*, comdg. Dinapore Div., 1813-15. Nepal War 1814-15 ; A.D.C. to Maj.-Gen. Marley, comdg. 4th Div. Nepal War 1816 ; Lieut. 5th Gren. Bn., in 2nd Bde., Left Column.

McCULLOCH, Edward (*d.* 1796). Lieutenant. Infantry. Cadet 1783. Arrived in India Feb. 1784. Ensign 11 Feb. 1785. Lieut. 16 Dec. 1791. Resigned 21 Feb. 1795. *d.s.p.* in Scotland 22 June 1796.

VIII of Ardwall and III of Hills, co. Kirkcudbright. Eldest son of David McCulloch, VII of Ardwall and II of Hills, and Janet his wife, dau. of Robert Rae Corsane, of Meikleknox, co. Kirkcudbright.

Services : Apptd. Cadet 11 Mar. 1783 ; sailed for India in the *Sulivan* 16 Mar. 1783. Posted to 4th Bengal Eur. Bn. 15 Feb. 1790 ; transfd. to 1st do. 1 Mar. 1790 ; to 2nd do. ; to 5th do. 25 Oct. 1792 ; to 3rd do. 9 Nov. 1792.

Refs. : Burke's *Landed Gentry*, 15th edn., p. 1236, *s.n.* McCulloch Jameson, of Ardwall.

McCULLOCH, Patrick (or Peter) (1764/65-1795). Lieutenant, 27th Bn. Sepoys. *b.* in Scotland 1764/65. Cadet 1781. Arrived in India 1 June 1782. Ensign 16 May 1781. Lieut. 30 Aug. 1782. *d.* Dinapore 1 Jan. 1795.

Services : Apptd. Cadet 9 May 1781, aged 16 ; sailed for India in the *Deptford* 26 June 1781. Lieut. 9th Bn. Sepoys in July 1787 ; Adjt. 27th Bn. 1788 till death.

Refs. : S.M. 1795, p. 612.

*McCULLOCH, William (1753/54-1817). Major General. Colonel 3rd N.I. *b.* in Ireland 1753/54. Cadet 1777. Arrived in India 2 Nov. 1777. Ensign 14 Feb. 1778. Lieut. 24 Sept. 1778. Capt. 7 Jan. 1796. Major 8 Feb. 1800. Lt. Col. 12 Jan. 1803. Col. (1 Jan. 1812) 11 Apr. 1814. Maj. Gen. 4 June 1814. *d.* Devonshire Pl., London, 15 Nov. 1817, in his 67th year (*sic*).

Brother of James, Henry, Elizabeth, and Rebecca, wife of John Orr, of Strabane.

Services : Apptd. Cadet 7 Feb. 1777 ; sailed for India in the *Sea Horse* 30 Apr. 1777, aged 23. Lieut. 2/1st Bengal Eur. Regt.

THE BENGAL ARMY, 1758-1834   115

in Oct. 1779 ; 32nd Bn. Sepoys in July 1787 ; Adjt. 22nd Bn. in Mar. 1790. Capt. 14th N.I. in 1798. Posted Lt. Col. to 1/14th N.I. Feb. 1803. Second Mahratta War ; battle of Delhi ; action before Agra ; siege of Gwalior ; Monson's retreat (w. 28 Aug. 1804) ; Lt. Col. comdg. 1/14th N.I. Transfd. to 5th N.I. in 1812. Fur. 12 Jan. 1813 till death. Col. 3rd N.I. 1815 till death.
Refs.: Hickey, ii. 103. *S.M.* 1817, ii. 501. *G.M.* 1817, ii. 568. Will dated 12 Nov. 1817 ; proved 8 Dec. 1817.

McCULLOCH, William (1816-1885). Lieut. Colonel. 13th N.I. P.A. at Manipur. *b.* St. Cuthbert's, Edinburgh, 28 Feb. 1816. Cadet 1834. Arrived in India 21 July 1835. Ensign 12 Dec. 1834. Lieut. 18 Feb. 1839. Capt. 30 June 1848. Major 4 Sept. 1857. Retired 31 Dec. 1861. Hon. Lt. Col. 31 Dec. 1861. *d.* Shillong, Assam, 4 Apr. 1885.

Eldest son of John Ramsay McCulloch, comptroller of H.M. stationery office (*D.N.B.*), and Isabella Stewart his wife. *m.* Mary. (She died Shillong 1888.) Ed. Edinburgh High School. Addiscombe Cadet 15 Feb. 1833 till 12 Dec. 1834.

Services : See *D.N.B.* Ensign d.d. 56th N.I. 28 July 1835 ; d.d. 38th N.I. 12 Aug. 1835 ; posted to 13th N.I. 24 Sept. 1835. Operations against the Nagas of Jaipur 1837 ; Ensign 13th N.I. Intr. & Qmr. 13th N.I. 5 July 1839. Asst. to P.A. Manipur Apr. 1840 ; P.A. Manipur 7 Mar. 1845 till retirement. Offg. Supt. Cachar 2 Feb. till 7 Nov. 1842. He rejoined at Manipur as P.A., owing to the failure of his successor, late in 1864, retiring finally in 1867. Pub. Calcutta, 1859, " Account of the Valley of Munnipore and the Hill Tribes."

Refs. : *D.N.B.* Boase. *D.I.B.* The Times, 14 May 1885. M.I. at Shillong.

*****McCUTCHAN, John** (*d.* 1792). Bt. Ensign, Infantry. Invalids. Bt. Ensign 4 Nov. 1782. Invalided (?) *d.* Berhampore Aug. 1792 ; *bur.* there 8 Aug. 1792.

Services : Enlisted in 1767 ; Corporal 1770 ; Pay Sergt. in Corps of Art. ; Sergt. G.G.B.G. in 1782.
Refs. : *V.B.G.* p. 304.

McDERMOTT, Hugh (*d.* 1787). Captain, Infantry. Cadet 1769. Ensign 2 Aug. 1769. Lieut. 28 Nov. 1772. Capt. 23 Sept. 1779. *d.* Calcutta 2 Feb. 1787.

Brother of Terence McDermott, of Mount Talbot, Galway, Dr. of Physick.

Services: On fur. s.c. in July 1777 ; returned from fur. Mar. 1783 ; granted fur. on h.p. 30 Oct. 1786.
Refs.: Will dated 1 Jan. 1787 ; proved 12 Feb. 1787.

McDERMOT(T), Matthew. Lieutenant. Artillery. (222) Country Cadet 1781. Fireworker 2 July 1782. Lieut. 24 June 1788. Resigned 8 Mar. 1791.

Services: Apptd. a Vol. by Sir Eyre Coote 17 Aug. 1781, to serve with the Bengal Detachment. Second Mysore War 1781-5; Lieut. F. 5th Coy. 2nd Bn. Adjt. 1st Bn. Art. 24 Aug. 1786 till 1790.

McDERMOT, Owen St. George Eyre (1789-1806). Lieutenant, 4th N.I. *b.* Foxborough, Elphin, co. Roscommon, 4 Nov. 1789. Cadet 1804. Arrived in India 10 Sept. 1805. Ensign 27 Oct. 1805. Lieut. 1 July 1806. *d.* Cawnpore 29 July 1806.

bapt. Elphin 10 Nov. 1789. Son of Christopher French McDermot and Elizabeth F. Atkinson his wife.
Services: Posted Ensign to 4th N.I. in 1805. No record of active service.

McDONAGH, Eugene (1756/57-1787). Lieutenant, Infantry. *b.* in Ireland 1756/57. Cadet 1781. Ensign 1 Apr. 1781. Lieut. 24 July 1782. *d.* Calcutta 30 June 1787.

Services: Apptd. Cadet 30 May 1781, aged 24 ; sailed for India in the *Norfolk* 6 Feb. 1782. Sometime Surgeon, Somerset Mil. ; Ensign do. 2 Sept. 1778.

McDONAGH, James (1783-1818). Captain, 19th N.I. *b.* Banagher, co. Londonderry, Nov. 1783. Cadet 1803. Arrived in India 29 Apr. 1805. Ensign 22 Mar. 1805. Lieut. 23 Mar. 1805. Capt. 8 Jan. 1818. *d.* Cawnpore 3 Oct. 1818.

Son of Mary McDonagh, of Eden, psh. of Banagher. Owned the lands of Eden, Moneyhanger and Kilkreen, Banagher. Nephew of George McDonagh, and ward of John Claudius Beresford (who was nephew of George, 1st Marquess of Waterford), sometime lord mayor of Dublin.
Services: Posted Lieut. to 19th N.I. in 1806. Operations in Bundelkhand 1807 ; Sehlehuganj ; Lieut. 1/19th N.I. Nepal War 1814-15 ; Lieut. 1/19th N.I., in 1st Div. Adjt. 1/19th N.I. 21 July 1815 till May 1818.
Refs.: Will dated 3 Nov. 1814 ; proved 31 Oct. 1818.

THE BENGAL ARMY, 1758-1834   117

MACDONALD, Alexander (*d*. 1773). Ensign. Infantry. Cadet 1769. Ensign 28 Aug. 1769. Resigned 28 Mar. 1771. *d*. Calcutta 20 June 1773.
Services: N.F.P.

MACDONALD, Alexander. Lieutenant. Infantry. Country Cadet 1778. Cornet 30 Apr. 1779. Lieut. 8 Jan. 1781. Struck off 1793.
Services: Was Adjt. of Nawab of the Carnatic's Cav. for several years prior to 1778. Apptd. Cadet for Cav. 11 Aug. 1778 ; removed to Inf. 18 Oct. 1778 ; posted Cornet to 1st Regt. Cav. 18 July 1779. First Mahratta War ; Cornet 1st Cav., with Bombay detachment under Col. Thomas Goddard, *q.v.* Adjt. & Qmr. of Sepoy Corps in 6th Bde. in July 1787. On fur. in 1788.

MACDONALD, Alexander (*d*. 1833/34). Lieut. Fireworker. Artillery. (259) Subsequently Lt. Col. 2nd I. of Skye Regt. of Vols. Cadet 1783. Fireworker 28 Mar. 1785. Struck off 1793. *d*. 1833/34.
IX (or IV) of Balranald, N. Uist ; II of Lyndale, Skye. Eldest son of Donald Macdonald, VIII (or III) of Balranald, and Catherine his wife, dau. of Capt. James Macdonald, of Aird. Cousin of John Macdonald (*d*. 1791), *q.v. m.* Jane Craigdallie, of an ancient Perthshire family of clan MacGregor. Father of Alexander Macdonald (1804-1833), *q.v.*
Services: Apptd. Cadet 20 Dec. 1782 ; sailed for India in the *Fox* 11 Mar. 1783. Second Mysore War ; Cadet d.d. 4th Coy. 2nd Bn. Art. Apptd. Asst. in Secret and Mily. Dept. 9 Aug. 1786. Fireworker 1st Bn. Art. in July 1787. On fur. s.c. in 1790. Pensioned on Lord Clive's fund 1 Aug. 1792. Raised and comdd. 2nd I. of Skye Regt. of Vols.
Refs.: Burke's *Landed Gentry*, 15th edn., p. 1452, *s.n.* Macdonald, of Balranald. Mackenzie's *Macdonalds, s.n.* Balranald. *MacInnes. Clan Donald*, p. 491.

MACDONALD, Alexander (1789-1825). Captain, 10th N.I. b. 25 Nov. 1789. Cadet 1804. Arrived in India 13 May 1806. Ensign 30 Mar. 1806. Lieut. 21 Oct. 1807. Capt. 11 July 1823. *d*. Partabgarh, Rajputana, 4 Sept. 1825.
5th son of John Macdonald, of Sanda, comptroller of customs at Bo'ness, and Cecilia Maria Douglas Kinneir, of Kinneir, his wife, only child of William Douglas, of the Tilwhilly family. Younger brother of Sir John Macdonald Kinneir, of Sanda (*D.N.B.*). *m.*

Bombay 23 July 1824, Maria, dau. of John Elphinston, Bo. C.S., late Member of Council, Bombay.

Services: Barasat C.C. Posted Ensign to 7th N.I. 1807. Reduction of Kalinjar 1812 ; Lieut. 1/7th N.I. Actg. Adjt. 1/7th N.I. 1813 ; Intr. & Qmr. do. 1 July 1814 till July 1821. Nepal War 1814-15 ; Lieut. 1/7th N.I., in 2nd Div. Third Mahratta War ; Lieut. 1/7th N.N., Bde. Major 6th Inf. Bde., Left Div. of Grand Army. On pol. duty with Sir John Malcolm in 1819. Asst. to Resdt. in Malwa 1822 ; P.A. and Supt. of Partabgarh at death. Transfd. to 10th N.I. (late 2/7th) May 1824.

Refs.: Burke's *Landed Gentry*, 7th edn., p. 1037, *s.n.* Kinnear, of Kinnear and Kinloch, co. Fife. Mackenzie's *Macdonalds*, *s.n.* Sanda. *Genealogist*, v. 208. *S.M.* 1825, i. 127. Will dated 15 Aug. 1818 ; proved 14 Dec. 1825.

MACDONALD, Alexander (1804-1833). Captain, 16th N.I. *b.* Lyndale, Snizort, I. of Skye, 4 Aug. 1804. Cadet 1820. Arrived in India Oct. 1821. Ensign 21 Mar. 1821. Lieut. 4 Aug. 1823. Capt. 19 Dec. 1831. *d. unm.* Mhow 18 Sept. 1833. 3rd son of Lt.-Col. Alexander Macdonald, of Lyndale, *q.v.*, and Jane his wife.

Services: Posted Ensign to 1/10th N.I. in 1821. Transfd. to 16th N.I. (late 2/10th) May 1824. Fur. s.c. 22 Feb. 1823 till 30 June 1825 ; was wrecked in the *City of Rochester*. No record of active service.

Refs.: Burke's *Landed Gentry*, 15th edn., p. 1452, *s.n.* Macdonald of Balranald. Mackenzie's *Macdonalds*, *s.n.* Balranald. *G.M.* 1834, ii. 558. M.I. Mhow old cemetery.

MACDONALD, Alexander (1808-?). Lieutenant. 62nd N.I. *b.* London 11 June 1808. Cadet 1824. Ensign 13 May 1825. Lieut. 16 May 1828. Resigned 28 Aug. 1828.

bapt. St. Botolph, Bishopsgate, 1 July 1808. Son of Alexander Macdonald, of 42 Bedford Sq., merchant, and Louisa his wife. Ed. St. Andrews Univ. ; matric. 16 Dec. 1823.

Services: Posted Ensign to 62nd N.I. No record of active service.

MACDONALD, Allan Ronald (1800-1842). Captain, 4th N.I. *b.* Flodigarry 22 Jan. 1800. Cadet 1817. Admitted 11 Aug. 1818. Ensign 29 Mar. 1818. Lieut. 9 Oct. 1818. Capt. 23 Aug. 1831. *d.* Lucknow 2 Jan. 1842.

2nd son of Capt. James Macdonald, of Flodigarry (who was 4th

THE BENGAL ARMY, 1758-1834

son of Allan Macdonald, VII of Kingsburgh, by Flora Macdonald), and Emily his wife, dau. of James Macdonald, of Skaebost. Cousin-german of Robert Collins Macdonald, *q.v.* m. Saugor 7 Oct. 1835, Anne Eliza, eldest dau. of John Nicholas Smith, *q.v.* (*See also* Mathew Smith.) (His widow, Leila, died Clarence House, Windsor, 2 Feb. 1896, aged 77.) Ed. Elgin Acad.

Services : Posted Lieut. to 2/1st N.I. in 1819 ; Intr. & Qmr. do. 3 May 1822. Transfd. to 4th N.I. (late 2/1st) May 1824. Operations against the Bhils 1824 ; Lieut. 4th N.I. Intr. & Qmr. 4th N.I. May 1824 ; Adjt. do. 11 Mar. 1825 till 20 Nov. 1828. Actg. Intr. & Qmr. 4th N.I. 18 May 1829. Offg. A.A.G. Saugor Div. 1 Dec. 1833. Actg. A.D.C. to Bdr.-Gen. J. N. Smith, *q.v.*, comdg. Saugor Div., 25 Sept. 1834 ; permanent do. 17 Feb. 1835. Offg. D.J.A.G. Saugor Div. 25 Apr. 1835 till 25 Dec. 1837. Bde. Major of newly-raised Oudh Auxy. Force 29 Jan. 1838 till 31 Dec. 1840. Actg. Comdt. Bundelkhand Legion 4 Dec. 1840. Comdt. 2nd Regt. Oudh Local Inf. 15 May 1841.

Refs. : Mackenzie's *Macdonalds, s.n.* Kingsburgh. *MacInnes.* *G.M.* 1842, i. 567. *The Times,* 11 Mar. 1842.

MACDONALD, Archibald (1810-1842). Lieutenant, 40th N.I. *b.* Strath, Inverness, 16 Dec. 1810. Cadet 1828. Arrived in India 10 Jan. 1829. Ensign 19 July 1828. Lieut. 1 Apr. 1835. *d.* Landour, U.P., 9 July 1842 : kld. by a fall from his horse down a *khud.*

bapt. Strath 16 Jan. 1811. 2nd son of Lt.-Col. Archibald Macdonald, K.H., A.G. of H.M. forces in India, and Maria his wife, dau. of Rev. —— King. Brother of Norman (William) Macdonald, *q.v.,* and nephew of Lt.-Gen. Sir John Macdonald, G.C.B. (*D.N.B.*).

Services : Ensign d.d. 7th N.I. 26 Jan. 1829 ; posted to 40th N.I. 3 June 1829. Fur. s.c. 13 Dec. 1835 till 23 Nov. 1838. On sick leave at Landour, nr. Mussoorie, 1839 till death. No record of active service.

Refs. : Clan Donald, iii. 529. *G.M.* 1843, i. 554.

MACDONALD, Charles (1751-1795). Cadet. Infantry. *b.* 22 Oct. 1751. Cadet 1772. Resigned Feb. 1775. *d.* Scotland 2 Mar. 1795.

VIII of Kingsburgh. Eldest son of Allan Macdonald, VII of Kingsburgh, Capt. 84th Ft., and Flora Macdonald (*D.N.B.*) his wife. Brother of John Macdonald (1759-1831) and uncle of Donald Kenneth Macdonald, *qq.v.* m. 1787, Isabella, 2nd dau. of Capt. James Macdonald, Aird.

LIST OF THE OFFICERS OF

Services: Lieut. H.M. 2/84th (R. Highland Emigrant) Regt. 18 May 1776 till 24 Nov. 1779. Afterwards comdd. a troop of horse in Tarleton's Brit. Legion during the campaign in S. Carolina. Returned to Scotland in 1784.
Refs.: MacInnes, pp. 24-8 (portrait). *Clan Donald,* iii. 508.

MACDONALD, Colin (1789-1818). Lieutenant, 18th N.I. *b.* Kilmallie, co. Argyll, 12 Aug. 1789. Cadet 1804. Arrived in India 16 May 1806. Ensign 19 Apr. 1806. Lieut. 22 Apr. 1809. *d.* Cuttack 29 Apr. 1818.

3rd son of Alexander Macdonald, of Glenco, and Mary his wife, eldest dau. of Sir Ewen Cameron, of Fassifern, 1st Bart. Cousin-german of Archibald Fraser Macpherson, *q.v.*

Services: Barasat C.C. Posted Ensign to 18th N.I. in 1807. Operations in Hariana 1809; Bhawani (w.); Lieut. 2/18th N.I. Capture of Java 1811; Lieut. 5th Vol. Bn. Fur. 5 June 1814 till 1818.

Refs.: Burke's *Peerage,* 1848, p. 167, *s.n.* Cameron, Bart., of Fassifern, co. Argyll. Will dated Calcutta, 20 Mar. 1818; proved 8 May 1818. M.I. at Puri.

*MACDONALD, Cosmo (1791-1823). Lieutenant, 16th N.I. *b.* Laggan, Inverness, 25 July 1791. Cadet 1808. Admitted 16 Apr. 1810. Ensign 22 Apr. 1811. Lieut. 16 Dec. 1814. *d.* Nagpur, C.P., 27 Oct. 1823.

Son of Alexander Macdonald, II of Tullochrom, by his 2nd wife, sister of John Read, of Aberdeen. *m.* Dacca 6 Sept. 1819, Miss Lucy Gibbs (? dau. of John Gibbs, *q.v.*). (She *re-m.* William Frederick Steer, *q.v.*)

Services: Was abroad as a Midshipman in the *Retreat* when apptd. Cadet in July 1809. Posted Ensign to 16th N.I. in 1811. Intr. & Qmr. 1/16th N.I. 10 June 1820 till death. No record of active service.

Refs.: Will dated Kishengunge, 13 Oct. 1820; proved 5 Feb. 1824. M.I. Tiger Gap cemetery, Nagpur.

MACDONALD, Donald Kenneth (1793-1813). Cadet, Infantry. *b.* Kingsburgh, Snizort, I. of Skye, 15 Feb. 1793. Cadet 1810. *d.* Benares 19 Aug. 1813.

Son of Lieut. Donald Macdonald, VI of Cuidreach, Skye, and Frances his wife, younger sister of Charles Macdonald, *q.v.*

Services: Cadet d.d. 16th N.I. 1811; transfd. to 4th N.I.
Refs.: *Clan Donald,* iii. 513. M.I. Benares.

THE BENGAL ARMY, 1758-1834

MACDONALD, James (1803-?). Ensign. 29th N.I. *b.* Forres 30 May 1803. Cadet 1820. Ensign 21 Mar. 1821. Resigned in India 19 July 1822. *d. unm.*

bapt. Forres 29 June 1803. Only son of Capt. John Macdonald, of Springfield, and Ann Dewar his wife, younger dau. of Alexander Fraser, VIII of Torbreck. Ed. Edin. Coll.

Services: Posted Ensign to 1/29th N.I. in 1821. No record of active service.

Refs.: Frasers of Lovat, p. 734.

McDONALD, James Horsbrugh (1806-1872). Lieut. Colonel. Artillery. (534) Comdt. 1st Surrey Rifle Vols. *b.* Elie, co. Fife, 2 Feb. 1806. Cadet 1821. Arrived in India 3 Jan. 1823. 2nd Lieut. 10 May 1822. Lieut. 30 Dec. 1825. Capt. 18 Mar. 1840. Bt. Major 30 Apr. 1844. Retired 1 May 1846. Hon. Lt. Col. 28 Nov. 1854. *d.* at his residence, Herne Hill, London, 7 May 1872.

J.P. co. Surrey. *bapt.* Elie 16 Feb. 1806. Eldest son of Duncan McDonald, sailor in Elie, and Anne his wife. Addiscombe Cadet 1821-2.

Services: First Burma War 1824-6; 2nd Lieut. 4th Coy. 5th Bn. Foot Art., with Sir A. Campbell's force in Burma (India medal). Offg. Adjt. Art. details at Rangoon 12 Feb. 1825. Returned to Bengal on 3 mos. s.c. 4 Feb. 1826. Leave s.c. 6 mos. to Mauritius 8 Mar. 1828. Wahabi rising; Barasat 19 Nov. 1831; Lieut. in charge of the guns. Fur. s.c. 14 Feb. 1832 till 24 July 1835. Adjt. 6th Bn. Art. 10 June 1836 till 13 Apr. 1840. Apptd. D.A.A.G. of Art. on Divl. Staff, Army of Exercise, 18 Nov. 1843. Gwalior campaign; Maharajpur (*Lond. Gaz.* 8 Mar. 1844); D.A.A.G. of Art. (Bronze star).

Refs.: The Times, 8 May 1872.

MACDONALD, Sir John (1747/48-1824). Lieut. General, K.C.B. 15th N.I. *b.* 1747/48. Cadet 1766. Admitted 14 June 1767. Ensign 23 July 1767. Lieut. 22 Apr. 1769. Capt. 7 May 1777. Major 27 July 1781. Lt. Col. 1 Mar. 1794. Col. 1 Jan. 1798. Maj. Gen. 1 Jan. 1805. Lt. Gen. 4 June 1813. *d.* Calcutta 30 May 1824, aged 76.

Brother of Jane Christie (? and of Col. Allan Macdonald, of Kinlochmoidart, co. Inverness), uncle of Richard Alexander Mackenzie, and cousin of Clementina, wife of Charles Vaughan Schnell, *q.v.*

Services: To comd. a corps in the Gorakhpur district in the service of the Nawab-Wazir of Oudh 21 Jan. 1779; to comd. 8th Regt. Sepoys 29 Mar. 1782. Major 15th Bn. Sepoys in Apr. 1786 ; 2nd Eur. Bn. in Dec. 1788. Resdt. at the Court of Sindhia. Transfd. from 2nd Sepoy Bde. to 2nd Eur. Bn. 7 Nov. 1793. Second Rohilla War; battle of Bitaurah; Lt. Col. comdg. 2nd Bengal Eur. Regt. Apptd. in 1798 to comd. the newly-raised 15th N.I., the 1st Bn. of which was called after him " *Macdoon-ki-Paltan.*" (? Operations in Jumna Doab 1803 ; Sasni; Bijaigarh ; Kachaura ; Col. comdg. 15th N.I.) Second Mahratta War 1803-4 ; battle of Delhi ; Agra ; Laswari (w.) ; battle of Deig ; Col. 15th N.I., Bdr. comdg. 3rd Bde. Maj. Gen. comdg. at Chunar 1805-9 ; do. Benares Div. 1809-11. Col. 15th N.I. till 1818. Was unemployed in India 1812 till death, but was latterly for a short while Presdt. of the Clothing Board. K.C.B. 7 Apr. 1815.

Refs. : *E.I.M.C.* i. 398-401. *S.M.* 1824, ii. 639. Will dated 17 May 1824 ; proved 7 June 1824. M.I. in S. Park St. cemetery, Calcutta.

McDONALD, John (*d*. 1791). Lieutenant, Infantry. Country Cadet 1772. Ensign 9 Aug. 1776. Lieut. 26 July 1778. *d.* Bangalore 9 Mar. 1791.

Brother of Janet and Margaret. Nephew of Donald McDonald, of Balranald, N. Uist, and cousin-german of Alexander McDonald, IX of Balranald, *q.v.*

Services : Apptd. Cadet 29 Aug. 1772. First Rohilla War ; battle of St. George ; Cadet in the Select Picket. Lieut. 33rd Bn. Sepoys in July 1787. Third Mysore War ; siege of Bangalore.

Refs. : Will dated Barrackpore 1 Apr. 1790 ; codicil dated Barrackpore 8 Nov. 1790 ; proved 17 Dec. 1791.

MACDONALD, John (1759-1831). Captain. Engineers. *b.* Flodigarry, I. of Skye, 30 Oct. 1759. Cadet (Bo. Inf.) 1780. Ensign (Bo. Engrs.) 6 Apr. 1781. Country Cadet (Bengal) 1782. Ensign (Engrs.) (Sept. 1782) 25 Apr. 1783. Lieut. 16 Dec. 1794. Bt. Capt. 13 June 1784. Capt. 8 Jan. 1798. Retired 30 July 1800. *d.* Summerland Pl., Exeter, 16 Aug. 1831.

5th and youngest son of Allan Macdonald, VII of Kingsburgh, Capt. 84th Foot, and Flora Macdonald (*D.N.B.*) his wife. Brother of Charles Macdonald, *q.v.* Uncle of John Macleod (1788-1807) and cousin of Alexander Murray (1746-1822), *qq.v. m.* 1st (*c*. 1784), Nancy Scott, dau. of George Salmon, and widow of Lawrence Bogle, Sec. at Ft. Marlbro'. (She died Bencoolen 28 Oct. 1786, aged 25.) *m.* 2nd, 24 Oct. 1799, Frances Maria, eldest dau. of Sir Robert

Chambers, Kt., C.J. of Bengal. (She died 28 July 1860, aged 85.) Father of Robert Collins Macdonald *q.v.*
Ed. Edinburgh High School and Univ.
Services: See *D.N.B.* Went out to India in 1780 as a Cadet for the Bombay Inf.; transfd. to Engrs. (Ensign 6 Apr. 1781). Leave to Calcutta in 1782. Apptd. Ensign in Bengal Engrs. Sept. 1782; sent to Bencoolen on duty; apptd. Asst. Engr. Bencoolen 1783, and employed on a survey of northern parts of Sumatra. Went to Penang 1786; returned to Sumatra 1788 as Mily. and Civil Engr., with local rank of Capt., and comd. of Art. Was at Fort Marlbro' in 1794 when the place was unsuccessfully attacked by the French. Remained in Sumatra till 1796, when he went home on fur. s.c. till retirement on h.p. Capt. in R. Edin. Vol. Art.; Major in Lord Macdonald's Western Fenc. 1799; Col. R. Clan Alpine Fenc. Inf. June 1800 till 1801, when disbanded. Afterwards Field Ofr. in the Corps of Cinque Port Vols. at Dover. Author of several mily. and technical engineering works, and translations from French and German. F.R.S. 1800.
Refs.: *D.N.B. Clan Donald*, iii. 509. *MacInnes* (portrait). *Memoir*, printed by J. L. Cox & Sons, Gt. Queen St., 1831. *Anderson*, ii. 727. Burke's *Colonial Gentry*, ii. 766. *D.I.B. Stubbs*, i. 246. *A.J.* N.S. vi. 135-8. *G.M.* 1832, i. 85, 650. M.I. in Exeter cathedral.

*McDONALD, John (1736-1791). Ensign, Invalid Est. Infantry. *b.* 1736. Bt. Ensign 4 Mar. 1782. Ensign 12 Apr. 1783. Invalided (?) *d. unm.* Chunar 24 Dec. 1791, aged 55.
Services: Commissioned as Bt. Ensign from Sergt. Major; promoted Ensign Feb. 1787, to rank from 12 Apr. 1783.
Refs.: Will dated Chunargarh, 1 Sept. 1791; proved 27 Dec. 1791. M.I. Chunar old cemetery.

*McDONALD, John (*d.* 1790). Bt. Ensign, Infantry. Bt. Ensign 1 Aug. 1782. *d. unm.* Monghyr 2 Jan. 1790.
Services: Sergt. Major 8th Bn. Sepoys; apptd. Condr. of Ord. 22 Aug. 1778.
Refs.: Will dated Monghyr, 18 Oct. 1789; proved 1 Mar. 1790.

MACDONALD, John (1802-1895). General. Colonel 74th N.I. *b.* Tanera 9 June 1802. Cadet 1820. Arrived in India Oct. 1821. Ensign 4 Apr. 1821. Lieut. 27 Aug. 1823. Capt. 26 Sept. 1833. Major 11 Apr. 1845. Lt. Col. 11 Apr. 1851. Bt. Col. 28 Nov. 1854. Maj. Gen. 12 Dec. 1862. Lt. Gen.

26 Sept. 1871. Gen. 1 Oct. 1877. *d.* Palmer's Cross, Elgin, 16 Mar. 1895.

Son of Donald Macdonald, of Snizort, I. of Skye, tacksman of Tanera, IV of Heisker and Skeabost, and Margaret his wife, dau. of Donald MacDonald, V of Rigg. *m.* Inverness 16 Dec. 1834, Catherine, elder dau. of John Matheson, of Attadale, and sister of Sir Alexander Matheson, 1st Bart. (She died Elgin 28 Dec. 1883.) Addiscombe Cadet 1819-20.

Services: Posted Ensign to 1/9th N.I. 3 Jan. 1822; transfd. to 24th N.I. Aug. 1823; to 47th N.I. (late 1/24th) May 1824; to 69th N.I. Nov. 1824; to 61st N.I. 8 Mar. 1825. Actg. S.A.C.G., and in charge of mily. chest at Akyab, 8 May 1826; S.A.C.G. 9 Dec. 1831. Fur. s.c. 2 May 1832 till 20 Sept. 1835. Actg. Bde. Major at Agra 30 Apr. 1841; permanent do. 1 Sept. 1841 till 24 Feb. 1843. On service in Bundelkhand 1843-5; Major 61st N.I. Second Sikh War; Major 61st N.I., in Reserve Div. (Medal). Posted Lt. Col. to 61st N.I. in 1851; transfd. to 19th N.I. Oct. 1852; to 39th N.I. 15 Nov. 1854, and was in comd. when the Mutiny broke out. The Regt. was disarmed at Dera Ismail Khan, was marched to Siakot and subsequently disbanded. Transfd. to 73rd N.I. 2 Nov. 1859. Apptd. Bdr. on the Est., to comd. at Barrackpore, 18 Sept. 1860. Col. 74th N.I. 23 July 1861 till July 1869.

Refs.: Clan Donald, iii. 497. Burke's *Peerage*, 1923, p. 1528, *s.n.* Matheson, Bart., of Lochalsh, co. Ross. Boase. *The Times*, 19 Mar. 1895.

MACDONALD, John (1807-1872). Major (? Lt. Col.[1]). 50th N.I. *b.* Plymouth 24 June 1807. Cadet 1824. Arrived in India 21 Dec. 1825. Ensign 26 Mar. 1825. Lieut. 27 June 1828. Capt. 24 Jan. 1845. Retired 22 Oct. 1849. Hon. Major 28 Nov. 1854. (? Hon. Lt. Col. 1859.) *d.* Canada 9 Jan. 1872.

bapt. St. Mary-le-Bow, Durham, 11 Sept. 1809. Eldest son of Archibald Macdonald, Comdr. R.N., and Harriet Cox his wife, a native of St. John's, Newfoundland. (*Perhaps* related to George Hamilton Cox, *q.v.*) *m.* 1st, Gorakhpur 16 May 1831, Ann Christiana, only dau. of Robert Tytler, M.D., Surg. Bengal, and sister of Robert Christopher Tytler, *q.v.* (She died Barrackpore 7 Sept. 1834, aged 18.) *m.* 2nd, Dacca 29 Dec. 1835, Anne, dau. of Gardner Boyd, *q.v.*, and niece of Robert Blackall, *q.v.*

Services: Posted Ensign to 50th N.I. in 1826. Operations against Kols and Chuars 1832; Lieut. 50th N.I. Adjt. 50th N.I. 29 Feb. 1842 till 25 Feb. 1845. Insurrection in Bundelkhand

THE BENGAL ARMY, 1758-1834

1842-3. Gwalior campaign ; Paniar ; Bt. Capt. 50th N.I. (Bronze star). Fur. p.a. 22 Apr. 1847 till retirement.
Refs.: Clan Donald, p. 393, *s.n.* Macdonald, of Sanda. *Genealogist*, v. 208. *A.J.* N.S. vi. 138 ; N.S. xx. 106.
[1] *Note :* He is shown as Major on the retired list till 1859, afterwards as Lt. Col. : the higher rank is probably a misprint.

MACDONALD, John (1808-1892). Lieut. Colonel. 66th N.I.
b. Borrodale, Ardnamurchan, 8 June 1808. Cadet 1828. Arrived in India 11 Oct. 1828. Ensign (10 May 1828) 4 Mar. 1829. Lieut. 5 May 1834. Capt. 24 Jan. 1845. Major 31 May 1857. Retired 1 Apr. 1859. Hon. Lt. Col. 1 Apr. 1859. *d.* Aberdeen 16 Feb. 1892.

3rd son of John Macdonald, of Borrodale, and Jane his wife, 2nd dau. of Alexander McNab, of Inishewen, co. Perth. *m.* 1848, Helen Morgan. (She died Sialkot 1 Sept. 1855.)

Services : Ensign d.d. 13th N.I. 5 Nov. 1828. Posted to 36th N.I. 4 Mar. 1829. Transfd. to 47th N.I. 27 Aug. 1831 ; to 36th N.I. 16 Sept. 1831 ; to 66th N.I. 12 Oct. 1832. Adjt. 66th N.I. 19 Jan. 1843 till 2 Apr. 1845. Fur. p.a. 10 Aug. 1845 till 1848. On disbandment of 66th N.I. for mutiny in Feb. 1850, transfd. to new 66th (or Gurkha) Regt. (late 1st Nassiri Bn.). Offg. Bde. Major at Meerut 22 Aug. 1850. Comdt. 5th Irreg. Cav. 24 Sept. 1850 till Aug. 1857, when the Regt. deserted *en masse*.[1] Fur. p.a. 18 mos. 2 Aug. 1858 till retirement.

Refs. : Burke's *Landed Gentry*, 12th edn., p. 1227, *s.n.* Macdonald, of Glenaladale, co. Inverness. Mackenzie's *Macdonalds*. *I.M.* 17 Sept. 1857, p. 591.

[1] *Note :* In June 1857 this Regt. was stationed in the Santhal district, with headquarters at Rohni. On 12 June three sowars of the Regt. made a murderous attack on Major Macdonald, the Adjt., and the medical ofr. Sir Norman Leslie, the Adjt., was kld., and Macdonald was scalped and otherwise severely wounded. The assassins were caught and hanged.

MACDONALD, Michael (*d.* 1773). Cadet, Infantry. Cadet 1772. *d.* Sultanpur, Benares, 30 Aug. 1773.
Services : Was Qmr. to the Select Picket at date of death.

MACDONALD, Norman (William) (1807-1893). Lieutenant. 9th L.C. Subsequently Govr. of Sierra Leone. *bapt.* Mallow, co. Cork, 30 May 1807. Cadet 1825. Cornet 12 Jan. 1826. Lieut. 28 Dec. 1827. Cashiered 3 Dec. 1828. *d.* Priory Field House, Taunton, 13 May 1893, aged 85.

Eldest son of Lt.-Col. Archibald Macdonald, K.H., and Maria King his wife. Brother of Archibald Macdonald, *q.v.* Haileybury 1825.
Services: Cornet d.d. 9th L.C. 26 Sept. 1826. Posted Cornet to 9th L.C. and served throughout with the Regt. No record of active service. Govr. of Sierra Leone 7 Apr. 1846 till 13 Sept. 1852.
Refs.: Clan Donald, iii. 529. *Boase. A.J.* xxvii. 736. *The Times,* 17 May 1893.

MACDONALD, Ranald Dugald Harcourt (1800-1848). Major, 8th L.C. *bapt.* Madras 8 Aug. 1800. Cadet 1817. Arrived in India Jan. 1819. Cornet 24 May 1818. Lieut. 27 July 1819. Capt. 17 May 1829. Major 21 Jan. 1839. *d.* Anarkalli, Lahore, 21 Nov. 1848.
Son of James Macdonald, Lt. Col. H.M.S., and Margaret his wife. *m.* Calcutta 28 Nov. 1836, Mary, eldest dau. of James Henry Crawford, Bo. C.S. (She died London 18 May 1887, aged 70.) Ed. Edin. High School.
Services: Cornet d.d. 4th N.C. Jan. 1819; posted Cornet to 4th N.C. Feb. 1819; transfd. as Lieut. to 8th L.C. 26 Feb. 1820. Apptd. to comd. escort to Envoy to Court of Persia 12 Apr. till 20 Aug. 1824, when the Mission was countermanded. Adjt. 8th L.C. 26 Jan. 1825 till 14 Feb. 1826. Siege and capture of Bhurtpore; Lieut. 8th L.C. Apptd. to comd. Escort to British Envoy in Persia Feb. 1826, and comdd. till 1831. Attached to the British Embassy and employed with troops under British officers in that country till 18 Jan. 1835, when he was sent home with a despatch from the Envoy. Returned to India Oct. 1836. Disturbances in Bundelkhand 1842-3; action at Bhagaura 7 Dec. 1842; comdg. H.Q. and 2 Sqdns. 8th L.C. Gwalior campaign; Paniar; Major comdg. 8th L.C. (Bronze star). Apptd. Supt. Muttra Remount Depot Sept. 1845. Rejoined 8th L.C. Jan. 1846. His death occurred whilst on his way down to Calcutta on sick leave, preparatory to applying for leave to sea. Persian Order of Lion and Sun, 2 cl., Oct. 1835.
Refs.: De Rhé-Philipe. M.I. at Lahore.

McDONALD, Robert (1793-1812). Ensign, 9th N.I. *b.* Durham 27 Jan. 1793. Cadet 1808. Admitted 19 July 1809. Ensign 5 Jan. 1810. *d.* St. Helena 5 Aug. 1812.
Son of Mary Coyley, late McDonald.
Services: Barasat C.C. Posted Ensign to 9th N.I. in 1810. Capture of Java 1811; Ensign 3rd Bengal Vol. Bn. Fur. s.c. 1812. Ensign 1/9 N.I.

THE BENGAL ARMY, 1758-1834

MACDONALD, Robert Collins (1800-1841). Major, 49th N.I. b. London 2 Oct. 1800. Cadet 1816. Admitted 9 Sept. 1817. Ensign (?) Lieut. 1 Aug. 1818. Capt. 28 Dec. 1825. Major 16 Nov. 1835. d. Calcutta 11 Apr. 1841.

bapt. Marylebone 13 Dec. 1801. Eldest son of John Macdonald (1759-1831), *q.v.*, and Frances Maria his 2nd wife. Cousin-german of Allan Ronald Macdonald, *q.v. m.* Salcombe, Devon, 11 Feb. 1836, Susanna Hawley, eldest dau. of James Clarke, of Sid Abbey, Sidmouth. Addiscombe Cadet 1816-17.

Services : " Permitted to proceed to his duty and to take rank of all other Cadets apptd. in the same season who may not have been at the Institution, nor held H.M. Commission for 1 yr.". (Mily. Letter to Bengal, 9 Apr. 1817.) Ensign d.d. 1st N.I. 1817. Posted Lieut. to 1/25th N.I. Aug. 1818. Transfd. to 49th N.I. (late 1/25th) May 1824. Intr. & Qmr. 49th N.I. 30 Aug. 1824 till 25 Sept. 1826. First Burma War; Arakan 1825 ; Lieut. 49th N.I. Capt. d.d 4th N.I. 4 Nov. 1829 till 1 Nov. 1831, when he rejoined 49th N.I. Fur. p.a. 24 Apr. 1833 till 9 Oct. 1836. Comdd. 49th N.I. 13 Oct. 1838 till 12 Dec. 1840.

Refs.: Mackenzie's *Macdonalds, s.n.* Kingsburgh. M.I. in Circular Rd. cemetery, Calcutta.

MACDONALD, Roderick (1804-1837). Bt. Captain, 69th N.I. *b.* Snizort, I. of Skye, 12 Apr. 1804. Cadet 1821. Arrived in India 3 Aug. 1822. Ensign 23 Feb. 1822. Lieut. 22 Mar. 1824. Bt. Capt. 23 Feb. 1837. d. Edinburgh 3 Mar. 1837.

bapt. Snizort 22 Apr. 1804. Son of Alexander Macdonald, Lieut. H.M. 34th Foot, and Christian Macleod his wife. Sandhurst Cadet.

Services : Posted Ensign to 17th N.I. in 1822. Transfd. to 1st N.I. in 1823 ; to 2nd N.I. (late 1/1st) May 1824 ; to 4th N.I. (late 2/1st) 21 July 1824. Operations against the Bhils 1824 ; Lieut. 4th N.I. Transfd. to newly-raised 1st Extra Regt. (became 69th N.I.) May 1825. Adjt. 69th N.I. 5 Aug. 1825 till 20 Feb. 1828. S.S.O. at Fatehgarh 18 Oct. 1826 till 15 Jan. 1827. Operations against the Bhils 1827. Apptd. Asst. Revenue Surveyor 18 Jan. 1828 ; posted to Gt. Trig. Survey 12 Mar. 1832 ; 1st Asst. do. 1 Oct. 1833. Fur. s.c. 5 Jan. 1836 till death.

Refs. : Will dated Edinburgh, 27 Feb. 1837 ; admon. 1 Feb. 1838. M.I. St. Cuthbert's psh. churchyard, Edin.

McDONALD, Thomas (*d.* 1768). 2nd Lieutenant, Artillery. (56) Cadet (?) Fireworker 4 Dec. 1763. 2nd Lieut. Feb. 1767. *d.* Patna 5 July 1768.

Son of James McDonald.
Services: Apptd. Dy. Comy. of Art. at Patna 17 Feb. 1765. Fireworker 4th Coy. Art.; resigned his Commission 1 May 1766, during the "Batta mutiny"; readmitted later.
Refs.: Will dated Patna 2 July 1768; proved 23 Jan. 1770.

MACDONELL, George (1787-1818). Lieutenant, 23rd N.I. *b.* Glenelg, co. Inverness, 20 Mar. 1787. Cadet 1805. Arrived in India 20 July 1807. Ensign 29 June 1807. Lieut. 28 Sept. 1810. *d.* Calcutta 8 Sept. 1818.
Son of John Macdonell, of Finiskaig, psh. of Glenelg.
Services: Barasat C.C. Posted Ensign to 23rd N.I. in 1808. (? Operations in Hariana 1809; Bhawani; Ensign 2/23rd N.I.) Lieut. 2/23rd N.I. Leave to N.S.W. 1815-18.

MACDONELL, Ronald (1809-1897). Colonel. 4th Bengal Eur. L.C. *b.* Kilmonivaig, co. Inverness, 1 Mar. 1809. Cadet 1825. Arrived in India 21 Sept. 1826. Cornet 2 Mar. 1826. Lieut. 3 May 1829. Capt. 10 June 1842. Major 27 Nov. 1853. Lt. Col. 23 July 1858. Retired 31 Dec. 1861. Hon. Col. 31 Dec. 1861. *d.* 19 June 1897.
Son of Alexander Macdonell, Capt. Lt. h.p. 92nd Foot, and Mary Fraser his wife. Ward of Anthony Macdonell, of Lochgarry. *m.* Ludhiana 12 Oct. 1844, Mary M., dau. of Alexander Johnston. (She died Kartarpur 9 July 1852, aged 33.) Sandhurst Cadet.
Services: Cornet d.d. 10th L.C. 26 Sept. 1826. Posted to 10th L.C. 1826. Actg. Intr. & Qmr. 10th L.C. 31 May 1833. First Afghan War 1842; Capt. 10th L.C., with Gen. Pollock's force (Medal). Gwalior campaign; Maharajpur; Capt. 10th L.C. (Bronze star). Second Sikh War; operations in Jullundur Doab; Capt. 10th L.C. Fur. s.c. Jan. 1853 till Jan. 1855. Transfd. as Lt. Col. to newly-raised 4th Bengal Eur. L.C. in 1859.

MACDOUGALL, Andrew (1808-1900). Lieut-Colonel. 73rd N.I. *b.* Abbots Langley, Herts., 24 July 1808. Cadet 1825. Arrived in India 25 June 1826. Ensign 5 Feb. 1826. Lieut. 13 Nov. 1827. Capt. 29 May 1844. Bt. Major 3 Apr. 1846. Retired 19 July 1853. Hon. Lt. Col. 28 Nov. 1854. *d.* at his residence, Halebank, Torquay, 24 Oct. 1900.
Son of Alexander Macdougall, of Parliament St., London, solicitor, and Elizabeth his wife. *m.* Brighton 2 July 1839, Myra Sophia, eldest dau. of John Nuthall, *q.v.* (She died Garhmukhtesar, U.P., 15 Sept. 1844, aged 23.)

Services: Ensign d.d. 42nd N.I. 8 July 1826. Posted to 5th Extra Regt. (became 73rd N.I.) 26 Sept. 1826, and served throughout with that Regt. Fur. p.a. 8 Dec. 1836 till 1 Jan. 1840. First Sikh War; Capt. 73rd N.I. (Medal). Second Sikh War; in garr. at Lahore; Bt. Major 73rd N.I. (Medal).
Refs.: *A.J.* N.S. xxix. 341. *The Times,* 27 Oct. 1900.

*McDOUGAL, James (*d.* 1783). Cadet, Infantry. Cadet 1783. Never arrived in India. *d.* at sea 20 Aug. 1783 : drowned in the loss of the *Duke of Kingston* by fire off Ceylon.
Services: Apptd. Cadet 22 Jan. 1783 ; sailed for India in the *Duke of Kingston* 11 Mar. 1783.

MacDOUGALL, James Patrick (1800-1867). Captain. 21st N.I. (now 4th Bn. 1st Punjab Regt.). *b.* Kilbride 21 July 1800. Cadet 1818. Admitted 6 Nov. 1819. Ensign 29 May 1819. Lieut. 1 July 1821. Capt. 16 May 1829. Retired 12 June 1833. *d.* Fir Grove, N. Brixton, 15 July 1867.

J.P. and D.L. co. Surrey. 4th son of Capt. Duncan MacDougall, of Ardentrive, and Jean his wife, 2nd dau. of Capt. Neil Campbell, of Duntroon. Cousin-german of G.W.A.T. Grant, *q.v.* *m.* St. John's, Calcutta, 14 Jan. 1825, Eliza, elder dau. of John Jackson, B.C.S., and sister of Randle Jackson, *q.v.*

Services: Ensign H.M. 91st Ft. 21 Mar. 1816. Ensign d.d. Bengal Eur. Regt. 1819-20 ; posted Ensign to 2/9th N.I. 1820. (? Operations in Oudh ; capture of Bardgaon Feb. 1822 ; Lieut. 2/9th N.I.) d.d. Left Wing 2/19th N.I. May till Oct. 1823 ; transfd. to 1/9th N.I. Oct. 1823 ; to 21st N.I. (late 2/9th) May 1824. Supy. S.A.C.G. 22 July 1824 ; S.A.C.G. 14 May 1825 ; D.A.C.G. 2 cl. 7 Mar. 1828. Fur. p.a. 24 Jan. 1831 till retirement. Retired on h.p., *viz.* 7/- *p.d.* Became chairman of the Church of England Assurance Office.
Refs.: Burke's *Landed Gentry,* 12th edn., p. 1230, *s.n.* MacDougall, of MacDougall and Dunollie. *The Times,* 17 July 1867.

MACDOUGALL, Patrick (1751/52-1798). Bt. Lieut. Colonel, 13th N.I. *b.* 1751/52. Cadet 1770. Admitted 16 July 1770. Ensign 23 Nov. 1771. Lieut. 6 Aug. 1776. Capt. 27 Feb. 1781. Major 1 Mar. 1794. Bt. Lt. Col. (?) *d.* Chunar 9 Sept. 1798, aged 46.

Son of Margaret Hathorn, of Belfast. Brother of Capt. John Macdougall, R.N.

Services: Capt. comdg. 2/6th Sepoys in Aug. 1781 ; 1st Bengal

130 LIST OF THE OFFICERS OF

Eur. Bn. in July 1787 and Dec. 1788 ; 6th do. in 1792. Major 1/13th N.I.
Refs. : A.A.R. i. 179. Will dated 16 June 1791 ; codicil dated Chunar 9 Nov. 1794 ; proved 1 Nov. 1798. M.I. Chunar.

MACDOUGALL, William (1776-1807). Lieutenant, Engineers. Professor at Coll. of Fort Wm. *b.* Edinburgh 6 July 1776. Cadet 1796. Arrived in India 18 Feb. 1798. Ensign 15 Jan. 1799. Lieut. 15 Apr. 1806. *d.* Calcutta 16 Sept. 1807.
bapt. Edinburgh 26 July 1776. Son of Allan Macdougall, of Gallanach, Hayfield, and Dunach, and of Edinburgh, W.S., and Margaret his wife, dau. of John Hay, of Newhall, and sister of George, 7th Marquess of Tweedale.
Services : Served at the Presdy. 1800-2 ; at Cawnpore 1803. Operations in the Jumna Doab 1803 ; Sasni. Asst. Hindustani Professor at Coll. of Ft. Wm. 1803-7 ; apptd. Sec. to the Council of the Coll. May 1807.
Refs. : Burke's *Landed Gentry*, 13th edn., p. 1160, *s.n.* Macdougall, of Gallanach, co. Argyll. *S.M.* 1808, p. 398. M.I. in S. Park St. cemetery, Calcutta.

MACDOWALL, Hay (1803-1820). Ensign, Infantry. Unposted. *b.* Walkinshaw, co. Renfrew, 7 Feb. 1803. Cadet 1818. Ensign (?) *d.* Banda 23 Aug. 1820.
3rd and youngest son of Day Hort Macdowall, of Walkinshaw, formerly B.C.S., Collector of Rangpur, and Wilhelmina his wife, dau. of William Graham, of Airth, co. Stirling. Nephew of Lt.-Gen. Hay Macdowall, C.-in-C., Madras.
Services : Ensign d.d. Bengal Eur. Regt.
Refs. : Burke's *Landed Gentry*, 13th edn., p. 1163, *s.n.* Macdowall, of Garthland, co. Renfrew. *Edin. Mag.* viii. 398.

MACDOWALL, John (*d.* 1760). Lieutenant, Infantry. Cadet (?) Ensign 14 May 1758. Lieut. 27 July 1759. *d.* 16 June 1760 : kld. in action at the battle of Birpur, nr. Patna.[1]
Services : Was in Calcutta during the siege, 1756.
Refs.: Hill's Calcutta, p. 61. Broome, p. 301.
[1] *Note :* This is the date given by *Dodwell & Miles* and *Broome* : his name, however, is given in a MS. list at India Office as having been kld. in the assault of Patna 25 June 1763.

MACDOWELL, John (1787-1826). Major. Artillery. (342) *b.* Magherafelt, co. Londonderry, Aug. 1787. Cadet 1804.

Admitted 7 Nov. 1805. Lieut. 2 May 1805. Capt. Lt. 21 Feb. 1810. Capt. 25 Sept. 1817. Major 30 May 1824. Struck off 25 Mar. 1826. *d.* Belfast 18 July 1826.

Son of Dr. Thomas Macdowell, of Magherafelt, and Mary his wife. *m.* Cawnpore 23 May 1811, Miss Eliza Douglas Cooke. (She died Calcutta 30 Oct. 1820, aged 30.)

Woolwich Cadet; nominated for R.M.A. 7 Apr. 1802; obtained his certificate 21 Nov. 1804.

Services: Nepal War 1814-15; Jitpur 3 Jan. 1815 (w.); Capt. Lt. comdg. 5th Coy. 2nd Bn., with 3rd Div. Nepal War 1816; Capt. Lt. 5th Coy. 2nd Bn. Third Mahratta War; storm and capture of Chanda; Capt. 5th Coy. 2nd Bn. Comy. Ord. at P.W.I. 11 Jan. 1822; do. at Saugor 1823. Fur. Mar. 1824; struck off after 2 yrs. absence from India.

MACEWEN, William (*d.* 1779). Cadet, Infantry. Country Cadet 1778. *d.* in India Feb. 1779.

Services: Apptd. Cadet 11 Aug. 1778.

MACFARLANE, Hugh Falconer (1788-1817). Lieutenant, Pension Est. 3rd N.I. *b.* Inverness 15 Jan. 1788. Cadet 1804. Ensign 13 July 1806. Lieut. 24 Jan. 1809. Pensioned 19 June 1816. *d.* Serampore, Bengal, 13 Feb. 1817.

bapt. Inverness 22 Jan. 1788. Son of Rt. Rev. Andrew Macfarlane, bishop of Moray, senior bishop of the Scottish Episcopal Church, and Magdalen Duff his wife.

Services: Captured by the enemy on board the *Belle* packet on his voyage to India, and was detained a prisoner of war in France till 1811. Posted Lieut. to 3rd N.I. in 1812; Intr. & Qmr. 1/3rd N.I. 1815. No record of active service.

Refs.: *G.M.* 1817, ii. 637. *S.M.* 1817, ii. 100.

MACFARLANE, James (1774-1849). Captain. 1st N.I. Subsequently Adjt. H.E.I.C. Depot at Chatham. *b.* Edinburgh 19 Apr. 1774. Cadet 1798. Admitted 24 Oct. 1799. Ensign 16 Oct. 1799. Lieut. 28 Oct. 1799. Capt. 1 July 1810. Retired 22 Mar. 1814. *d.* 25 Oct. 1849.

bapt. Edinburgh 30 Apr. 1774. Son of Duncan Macfarlane, of S. Leith, and Janet Alston his wife. *m.* Anne. (She died 29 Apr. 1857, aged 74.)

Services: Posted Lieut. to 1/1st N.I. 15 Apr. 1801. Second Mahratta War 1804-6; operations in Bundelkhand; Lieut. 1/1st N.I. Adjt. 1/1st N.I. 1804-9; Adjt. & Qmr. 1st N.I. 4 Mar. 1809 till July 1810. Fur. 1811 till retirement. Adjt. H.E.I.C. Depot at Chatham 1821-31.

MACFARQUHAR, Hugh (1791-1849). Major. 40th N.I. *b.* Jamaica Jan. 1791. Cadet 1808. Admitted 6 Nov. 1809. Ensign 12 May 1811. Lieut. 3 June 1816. Capt. 1 May 1824. Major 1 Sept. 1841. Retired 1 Jan. 1844. *d.* Tavoy, Tenasserim, Jan. 1849.

Grandson of Hugh Macfarquhar, of Edinburgh.

Services: Twice captured in the *Wyndham* on the voyage out, and was in consequence permitted to draw pay and allowances from 3 Dec. 1810, the date of surrender of Mauritius. Posted Ensign to 2/13th N.I. in 1811. Nepal War 1816; actg. Intr. & Qmr., Gren. Bn., with Sir D. Ochterlony's Div. Transfd. as Lieut. to 2/20th N.I. June 1816; d.d. Sirmoor Bn. 1816-18. With 1st Ceylon Vol. Bn. Oct. 1818 till 1 Mar. 1820, when he rejoined 2/20th N.I. at P.W.I. Adjt. 2/20th N.I. 26 Feb. 1820 till 17 June 1824. To proceed to S. frontier of Chittagong against the Burmese Oct. 1823. Leave s.c. 6 mos. to Mauritius 24 Mar. 1824 till Aug. 1825. Transfd. to 25th N.I. (late 1/20th) May 1824; to 40th N.I. (late 2/20th) in 1827. Asst. to Comr. of Tenasserim Prov. Aug. 1831; offg. Resdt. at Ava Oct. 1832; Asst. to do. 16 Mar. 1833. Senior Asst. in Judicial and Revenue Dept., Tavoy, 1 Nov. 1834 till retirement. Offg. Comr. of Tenasserim Prov. July 1835 and 12 Jan. till 30 Mar. 1841.

MACFIE or MACPHEE, Thomas (1760-1794). Lieutenant, Infantry. *b.* in Scotland 1760. Cadet 1778. Ensign Oct. 1778. Lieut. 19 Nov. 1778. *d.* Fatehgarh 6 July 1794, aged 34.

Brother of John Macfie.

Services: Sailed for India in the *Southampton* 7 Mar. 1778, aged 17. Lieut. 2/2nd Bengal Eur. Bn. in Oct. 1779; Lieut. 21st Bn. Sepoys in July 1787, and in 1792.

Refs.: Will dated Fatehgarh, 24 June 1794; proved 20 May 1795. M.I. Fatehgarh fort cemetery.

MACGEORGE, Henry John (1803-1865). Lieut. Colonel. 7th N.I. *bapt.* St. Luke's, Chelsea, 21 May 1803. Cadet 1823. Was already in India when apptd. Cadet. Ensign 21 Feb. 1824. Lieut. 27 Jan. 1826. Capt. 1 June 1843. Bt. Major 11 Nov. 1851. Retired 9 Jan. 1855. Hon. Lt. Col. 16 Mar. 1855. *d.* 2 Dec. 1865.

Younger son of William MacGeorge and Bridget his wife, dau. of —— Brown, of Grassington, Yorks. Brother of William MacGeorge, *q.v. m.* Dacca 25 July 1831, Eliza Ann, dau. of Henry Williams, B.C.S. (*See also* Frederick Knyvett.)

Services : Recommended for a Cadetship by Rt. Rev. Reginald Heber, bishop of Calcutta (*D.N.B.*). Admitted 10 June 1824. Posted Ensign to 7th N.I. Actg. Intr. & Qmr. 1 Dec. 1827 ; do. 64th N.I. 19 Aug. 1830 ; do. 7th N.I. 27 Aug. 1834 ; do. 4th L.C. 28 Nov. 1837. Intr. & Qmr. 7th N.I. 8 Mar. 1839 till 16 Sept. 1843. Fur. s.c. 12 Feb. 1844 till 1846. D.J.A.G. Saugor Div. 21 Jan. 1847 ; do. Cawnpore Div. 21 Dec. 1849 till Dec. 1854.

Refs. : Burke's *Landed Gentry*, 7th edn., p. 1181, *s.n.* MacGeorge, of Hames Hall, Cumberland.

MACGEORGE, William (1799-1873). Lieut. Colonel. 71st N.I. *b.* London 28 June 1799. Cadet 1820. Admitted 29 Nov. 1821. Ensign 23 June 1821. Lieut. 11 Sept. 1823. Capt. 1 Jan. 1838. Bt. Major 9 Nov. 1846. Retired 21 Aug. 1849. Hon. Lt. Col. 28 Nov. 1854. *d.* 27 Green St., Grosvenor Sq., London, 28 Mar. 1873.

bapt. Fulham 25 July 1799. Elder son of William MacGeorge and Bridget his wife. Brother of Henry John MacGeorge, *q.v. m.* 1st, St. Mary's, Marylebone, 18 Oct. 1825, Theophila Louisa, only dau. of Richard Turner, B.C.S. (She died Mar. 1828.) *m.* 2nd, Mhow 22 Sept. 1832, Olivia Lockhart, widow of Charles Duffin (1791-1831), *q.v. m.* 3rd, Bridekirk, Cumberland, 1 Jan. 1850, Dora Fagan, eldest dau. of James Steel, *q.v.* (She died 30 Jan. 1893, aged 69.)

Services : Ensign d.d. 1/10th N.I. 27 Apr. 1822. Posted Ensign to 12th N.I. 1822. Fur. s.c. 12 Dec. 1822 till 7 May 1826. Transfd. as Lieut. to 3rd N.I. July 1823 ; to 6th N.I. (late 1/3rd) May 1824 ; to newly-raised 3rd Extra Regt. (became 71st N.I.) 13 May 1825 ; Adjt. Bareilly Provl. Bn. 14 Mar. 1827. Served with Pioneers 26 Aug. 1828 till 1834. Offg. D.J.A.G. 20 May 1835 ; apptd. D.J.A.G. on the Est. 11 Jan. 1836 ; posted to Saugor 21 Mar. 1836 ; do. at Meerut 1840-7. Fur. s.c. 21 Feb. 1847 till retirement. No record of active service.

Refs. : Burke's *Landed Gentry*, 7th edn., p. 1181, *s.n.* MacGeorge, of Hames Hall, Cumberland ; 4th edn., p. 1427, *s.n.* Steel, of Derwent Bank, Cumberland. *A.J.* xx. 608. *The Times*, 1 Apr. 1873.

MACGEOUGH,[1] **Samuel** (*d.* 1792). Lieutenant, Infantry. Cadet 1776. Ensign 26 Mar. 1777. Lieut. 20 Aug. 1778. *d.s.p. ; bur.* Bombay 1 July 1792.

Younger son of Samuel MacGeough, of Derrycaw, co. Armagh,

high sheriff 1776, and Elizabeth his wife, dau. of William Smyth. Brother of Joshua MacGeough, of Greenwood Park, co. Tyrone.

Services: Apptd. Cadet 28 Feb. 1776; sailed for India in the *Hector* 10 Apr. 1776. Apptd. Adjt. 10th Bn. Sepoys 22 Mar. 1780; Qmr. of Sepoy Corps in 1st Bde. 18 Apr. 1782 till death.

Refs.: Burke's *Landed Gentry of Ireland*, p. 61, *s.n.* MacGeough-Bond, of Drumsill, co. Armagh. Will dated 18 Sept. 1791; proved 6 Aug. 1792.

[1] *Note:* The name also appears in contemporary documents as Mageogh and M'Geaugh.

MACGLASHAN, Alexander (*d.* 1822). Bt. Major. Infantry. Cadet 1771. Ensign 19 June 1771. Lieut. 17 July 1776. Capt. 13 Feb. 1781. Bt. Major 17 Dec. 1781. Resigned on pension 22 Feb. 1782. *d.* Eastertyre 19 June 1822.

Of Eastertyre, co. Perth. *m.* Perth 2 July 1792, Miss Margaret Campbell.

Services: Apptd. Adjt. 21st Bn. Sepoys 22 Mar. 1780. Comdt. at Buxar Feb.-May 1781. Pensioned as Capt. on Lord Clive's fund 6 Feb. 1783.

Refs.: *G.M.* 1792, ii. 672. *S.M.* 1822, ii. 270.

McGOWAN, John (*d.* 1798). Colonel, Infantry. Ensign 1 June 1766. Lieut. 29 Aug. 1767. Capt. 3 Nov. 1771. Major 23 Jan. 1781. Lt. Col. 3 Feb. 1788. Col. 26 Feb. 1795. *d.* Cawnpore 30 June 1798.

m. Ft. St. George, Madras, 12 Jan. 1765, Maria de Cruz. Father of Suetonius McGowan, *q.v.*

Services: Commissioned from the ranks after the " Batta Mutiny." Apptd. Baggage Mr. to Col. Champion's Bde. 8 Mar. 1773. First Rohilla War. Dy. Judge Advocate. Apptd. to comd. newly-raised 36th Sepoy Bn. 11 Aug. 1778; to survey Ganges and Kasim Bazar rivers 31 May 1780. Second Mysore War 1781-3; Major with Col. Pearse's force. Fur. 1 Apr. 1783 till 2 Sept. 1784. Resigned comd. of 11th Sepoys 2 Apr. 1786; Major in 5th Bde. in July 1787; Lt. Col. comdg. 6th Eur. Bn. in Dec. 1788. Second Rohilla War; battle of Bitaurah; Lt. Col. comdg. Left Bde. Was comdg. at Anupshahr, U.P., in 1795. " By the dint of his own abilities, he rose himself from the ranks to the honourable situation which he filled at the time of his death. He was an intrepid and gallant soldier, . . ."

Refs.: *A.A.R.* i. 178. Will dated Cawnpore 13 May 1798; proved 16 Aug. 1798.

THE BENGAL ARMY, 1758-1834   135

McGOWAN, Suetonius (c. 1775-1798). Ensign, Engineers.
b. Bengal c. 1775. Cadet 1793. Arrived in India 7 Feb. 1794.
Ensign 11 Feb. 1794. d. Chunar 27 May 1798.
   Son of John McGowan, q.v., and Mary his wife.
   Services: Apptd. Cadet 11 Apr. 1792; sailed for India in the *Winterton* 2 May 1792.¹ N.F.P.
   Refs.: A.A.R. i. 177. M.I. old cemetery below Chunar fort.
   ¹ *Note:* She was lost off Madagascar 20 Aug. 1792.

McGRATH, Frederick Vaughan (1804-1851). Bt. Major, Invalid Est. 62nd N.I. b. in India June 1804. Cadet 1821. Arrived in India 29 May 1822. Ensign 9 Dec. 1821. Lieut. 11 Sept. 1823. Capt. 9 Mar. 1837. Bt. Major 9 Nov. 1846. Invalided 1 May 1848. d. Calcutta 26 Sept. 1851.
   bapt. Calcutta 24 Aug. 1806, " aged about 2 yrs. and 2 mos." Son of John McGrath (d. 1811), q.v., and Mary his wife. Brother of John O'Driscol McGrath, q.v., and nephew of John Stevens, of Castle Horneck, Penzance.
   Services: Posted Ensign to 20th N.I. in 1822. Transfd. as Lieut. to 30th N.I. in 1823; d.d. 2/31st N.I. 10 Mar. till 1 June 1824. Transfd. to 60th N.I. (late 2/30th) May 1824; exchanged to 62nd N.I. (late 2/31st) 21 Aug. 1824. First Burma War; Arakan 1825; Lieut. 62nd N.I. (India medal, awarded posthumously). d.d. Arakan Local Bn. 13 Feb. 1835; joined 24 Jan. 1836. Operations against dacoits in Arakan Apr. 1836. Actg. Adjt. Arakan Local Bn. 13 July 1836; 2nd in comd. do. 28 Aug. 1837; actg. Comdt. do. May 1838; permanent do. 10 July 1838 till 12 Sept. 1842. (? Gwalior campaign; Maharajpur; Capt. 62nd N.I.—Bronze star.)
   Refs.: A.J. N.S. ii. 95; N.S. xv. 29. I.M. 5 Dec. 1848, p. 711. G.M. 1852, i. 105.

McGRATH, John (d. 1811). Lieut. Colonel, 9th N.I. Country Cadet 1779. Admitted 20 Mar. 1779. Ensign 10 Sept. 1779. Lieut. 27 Apr. 1781. Capt. 9 Aug. 1798. Major 5 Nov. 1803. Lt. Col. 13 Sept. 1807. d. at sea, off Java, 2 Aug. 1811.
   m. Dinapore 22 June 1791, Mary, dau. of John McCabe, Dy. Comy. of Ord. Father of Frederick Vaughan McGrath, q.v., and of John O'Driscol McGrath, q.v. (She died Lucknow 5 Aug. 1805.)
   Services: Lieut. 2/10th Sepoys in June 1782, when he was tried and acquitted by G.C.M. at Cawnpore for the murder of John Edgar, q.v. Lieut. 4th Eur. Bn. in July 1787. Transfd. to 20th Bn. Sepoys 15 Dec. 1787, and was still serving in this Bn. in 1794.

Third Mysore War; Lieut. Bengal Vols. Capt. 10th N.I. in 1798. Second Mahratta War; operations against Holkar 1805-6; Major 10th N.I. Transfd. as Lt. Col. to 1/9th N.I. in 1808. Operations in Hariana 1809; Bhawani; Lt. Col. 1/9th N.I. Operations in Oudh 1809-10; Pragpur; Lt. Col. 1/9th N.I. Sailed with the expedn. against Java (? as Lt. Col. comdg. 3rd Bengal Vol. Bn.), but died shortly before landing.

MACGRATH, John (*d.* 1804). Captain, 18th N.I. Cadet 1783. Admitted 2 Sept. 1783. Ensign 10 Jan. 1785. Lieut. 28 Nov. 1790. Capt. 30 Sept. 1803. *d.* Dinapore 3 Nov. 1804.

Brother of Lucinda, wife of Capt. Richard Warburton (who was son of Rev. Richard Warburton, formerly of Britannia, nr. Banagher, King's Co.). He bequeathed his estate on Castor I., N. America, to Josette, dau. of Joseph Précoure, of the psh. of Barthier, Canada.

Services: Ensign H.M. Regt. of R. Highland Emigrants 10 May 1779. Apptd. Cadet 14 Jan. 1783; sailed for India in the *Bellmont* 11 Mar. 1783. Posted to 5th Eur. Bn. 25 Feb. 1790. Transfd. from 2nd Eur. Bn. to 1st do. 20 Sept. 1792; from 5th do. to 4th do. 22 Oct. 1794. Lieut. 3rd Bengal Eur. Regt. in 1796. Transfd. from 7th to 2/18th N.I. 29 May 1800. Second Mahratta War; operations in Bundelkhand 1803; Kapsa; Kalpi; Gwalior; defeat of Rajah Ram Singh 2 July 1804; capture of Jaitpur; Capt. 2/18th N.I.

Refs.: Will dated Cawnpore, 3 Oct. 1804; proved 20 Dec. 1804.

McGRATH, John O'Driscol (1794-1825). Captain, 40th N.I. *b.* Cawnpore 6 Aug. 1794. Cadet 1809. Ensign 1 Sept. 1812. Lieut. 28 July 1817. Capt. 1 Oct. 1824. *d.* Ramree, Burma, 18 Aug. 1825.

bapt. Cawnpore 28 Apr. 1795. Son of John McGrath, *q.v.*, and Mary his wife. Brother of Frederick Vaughan McGrath, *q.v.*, and nephew of Michael McGrath, Surgeon Bengal Est.

Services: Barasat C.C. Cadet d.d. 21st N.I. 1811-12. Capture of Java 1811; with 5th Bengal Vol. Bn. Posted Ensign to 2/10th N.I. in 1812. Operations in Rewah 1813-14; Entauri; Ensign 2/10th N.I. Adjt. Farrukhabad Provl. Bn. 11 Jan. 1816 till 1818. S.S.O. at Fatehgarh in 1817. Transfd. as Lieut. to 1/20th N.I. in 1817. Adjt. 1st Ceylon Vol. Bn. 1818-19; Adjt. 1/20th N.I. 27 Sept. 1820 till May 1824. Offg. in Q.M.G.'s Dept. 1821-2. Transfd. to 40th N.I. (late 2/20th) May 1824. Adjt. 40th N.I. 17 June till 30 Dec. 1824. First Burma War 1824; Chittagong; Ramu; Capt. 40th N.I.

MacGREGOR, Alexander Nugent Murray (1811-1845). Captain, 66th N.I. *b.* Kinsale barracks 19 Feb. 1811. Cadet 1828. Arrived in India 25 Nov. 1829. Ensign 7 Nov. 1829. Lieut. 2 Apr. 1835. Capt. 5 Aug. 1845. *d.* Hansi 13 Nov. 1845.

Eldest son of Maj.-Gen. Alexander MacGregor Murray (who resumed his paternal surname by R. L. 23 Dec. 1822), formerly 1/6th Foot, and Lady Charlotte Sinclair his wife, dau. of James, 12th Earl of Caithness. Grandson of Alexander Murray (1746-1822), *q.v.*, and nephew of Hon. Patrick Campbell Sinclair, *q.v.* *m.* Chunar 10 Aug. 1835, Eleanor, dau. of Capt. Henry Hudson Hopper. (*See also* Robert Stein.) (She *re-m.* Richard Francis Macvitie, *q.v.*) Ed. Harrow 1825-6. Addiscombe Cadet 1827-9.

Services: Ensign d.d. 11th N.I. 18 Dec. 1829; d.d. 57th N.I. 17 July 1830; d.d. 54th N.I. 12 Nov. 1831. Actg. Ensign (having been 2 years in India) 3 May 1832. Posted to Left Wing, Bengal Eur. Regt., 23 Dec. 1832; transfd. to 66th N.I. 26 Jan. 1833. Actg. Adjt. Inf., Bundelkhand Legion, 24 Sept. 1839; tempy. actg. Adjt. 3rd L.I. Bn. 10 Dec. 1840; Adjt. Hariana L.I. 8 Jan. 1845 till death. No record of active service.

Refs.: Foster's *Baronetage*, p. 401, *s.n.* Macgregor of Macgregor, Bart. Foster's *Families of Royal Descent*, i. 65. *Harrow School Register*.

MACGREGOR, formerly DRUMMOND, Alpin (1746/47-1781). Captain, Infantry. *b.* 1746/47. Cadet 1770. Ensign 31 Mar. 1771. Lieut. 13 July 1776. Capt. 9 Feb. 1781. *d.* Calcutta 26 Aug. 1781, aged 34.

Permitted to resume his original surname of MacGregor (Mily. Cons. 19 Feb. 1777). (*Probably* brother of Daniel Macgregor, *q.v.*)

Services: Capture of French prizes in July 1778; Lieut. 3rd Bengal Eur. Regt. Apptd. Adjt. 20th Bn. Sepoys 22 Mar. 1780.

Refs.: M.I. in S. Park St. cemetery, Calcutta.

MACGREGOR, formerly DRUMMOND, Daniel. Captain. Infantry. Cadet 1770. Ensign 1 Apr. 1771. Lieut. 14 July 1776. Capt. 10 Feb. 1781. Resigned 8 Jan. 1785.

Of Inverarderan. Permitted to resume his original surname of MacGregor (Mily. Cons. 19 Feb. 1777). Son of Gregor MacGregor ("Gregor *Boach*"), of Inverarderan, of the family of MacGregor of Glengyle, Capt. Middlesex Mil. (*Probably* brother of Alpin Macgregor, *q.v.*, and related to Hugh Drummond, *q.v.*) *m.* Edinburgh 3 Mar. 1786, Anne, dau. of Adam Austin, of Edinburgh, physician, and niece of Lord Sempill and of Hon. George Sempill, *q.v.* (She

died his widow, Edinburgh 24 Aug. 1809.) Father of Sir Gregor Macgregor (*D.N.B.*).
Services : Apptd. to comd. Burdwan Mil. Nov. 1780, and was still comdg. in Aug. 1781.
Refs. : Burke's *Landed Gentry*, 2nd edn., iii. 214*n*, *s.n.* Macgregor, of Glengyle, co. Perth. *S.M.* 1786, p. 154.

MACGREGOR, Sir George Hall (1810-1883). Major General, K.C.B. Artillery (584) *b.* Cuttack 1 May 1810. Cadet 1825. Arrived in India 1 May 1827. 2nd Lieut. 16 June 1826. Lieut. 24 June 1833. Capt. 3 July 1845. Major 18 May 1856. Lt. Col. 4 July 1858. Bt. Col. 13 July 1858. Retired 22 Dec. 1858. Hon. Maj. Gen. 18 Mar. 1859. *d.* Glencarnock, Torquay, 2 Jan. 1883.

Son of John Alexander Paul Macgregor, *q.v. m.* 1st, Preston 14 Oct. 1845, Harriet, dau. of Sir Thomas Whitehead, *q.v.* (*See also* Sir Andrew Scott Waugh.) (She died 24 July 1873.) *m.* 2nd, 17 Apr. 1879, Flora Elizabeth, youngest dau. of Rev. Montagu Oxenden, rector of Eastwell and Luddenham, Kent, and granddau. of Sir Henry Oxenden, 7th Bart. (She died 25 May 1915.) Addiscombe Cadet 1824-6.
Services : With 3rd Troop 2nd Bde. H.A. 1829-32. Leave s.c. 5 mos. to Singapore 13 Feb. 1829. A.D.C. to G.G. 7 Mar. 1836 till 4 Jan. 1839. P.A. Jalalabad Aug. 1838. Asst. to Envoy to Shah Shuja 1 Jan. 1839. First Afghan War 1839-42, in Pol. Dept. ; capture of Ghazni (Medal) ; Zurmat Valley Oct. 1841 ; defence of Jalalabad (Medal) ; reoccupation of Kabul 1842, A.D.C. to Gen. Pollock ; Pol. Agent (Medal). Fur. p.a. 1 Mar. 1843 till 1846. Principal Asst. to Resdt. at Lahore 26 Dec. 1846 ; A.G.G. Benares, and Supt. of ex-Rajahs of Coorg and Satara 11 Feb. 1848 ; D.C. Punjab, at Lahore, 29 Oct. 1849 ; A.G.G. Murshidabad 18 Sept. 1852 till retirement. Posted as Lt. Col. to 3rd Bde. H.A. Oct. 1856. Mily. Comr. and A.G.G. with Gurkha auxy. force under Sir Jang Bahadur in the Mutiny. Mutiny campaign ; capture of Lucknow ; operations in E. Oudh 1858 (Medal with clasp). Durani 2 cl. 7 Sept. 1841. Bright Star of the Punjab 1842. C.B. 4 Oct. 1842. K.C.B. (Civil) 25 June 1861.
Refs. : Burke's *Peerage*, 1923, p. 1728, *s.n.* Dixwell-Oxenden, Bart., of Dene, Kent. *D.I.B. Fortescue*, xii. *passim. The Times*, 5 Jan. 1883. *Boase*.

MacGREGOR, James Melville (1808-?). Lieutenant. 16th N.I. *b.* Chittagong 23 Jan. 1808. Cadet 1823. Arrived in

India 7 June 1824. Ensign 21 Feb. 1824. Lieut. 1 July 1825. Dismissed by G.C.M. 30 Dec. 1833. (Living in Oct. 1843.)
bapt. Calcutta 23 Jan. 1809. 2nd son of James Murray MacGregor, *q.v.* Brother of Robert Guthrie MacGregor, *q.v.*, and cousin-german of John Graham MacGregor and Charles Seton Guthrie, *qq.v.*

Services : Posted Ensign to 16th N.I. Suspended from rank, pay and allowances for 3 mos. by G.C.M. 9 July 1828. No record of active service.

Refs. : Burke's *Landed Gentry*, 2nd edn., iii. 216, *s.n.* Rob Roy MacGregor, of Craigrostan and Inversnaid. *A.J.* xxvii. 205-6; N.S. xiv. 126.

MacGREGOR, James Murray (1759/60-1818). Major General, Cavalry. Colonel 4th N.C. *b.* 1759/60. Country Cadet 1778. Admitted 11 Aug. 1778. Cornet (11 Aug. 1778) 11 May 1779. Lieut. 9 Jan. 1781. Capt. 8 Jan. 1796. Major 29 May 1800. Lt. Col. 21 Feb. 1801. Col. 25 July 1810. Invalided 27 Feb. 1812. Maj. Gen. 4 June 1813. *d.* Monghyr 7 Dec. 1818, aged 58.

Elder son of John MacGregor, Capt. 60th Foot, by his wife, dau. of John MacAlpine, of Edinburgh. Brother of Robert MacGregor, *q.v.*, cousin of Lt.-Col. E. J. MacGregor Murray, 8th (K.R.I.) Light Dgns., and 2nd cousin of Thomas MacGregor, *q.v. m.* Edinburgh 26 Feb. 1801, Catherine Wedderburn, dau. of Thomas Dunbar, of Westfield, Caithness. (*See also* John Robeson.) (She died 17 Nov. 1856.) Father of James Melville MacGregor, Robert Guthrie MacGregor, Thomas Alexander Knox MacGregor, *qq.v.*, of Margaret, wife of John Graham (1777-1816), *q.v.*, Isabella Dunbar, wife of Hon. Patrick Campbell Sinclair, *q.v.*, and Sarah, wife of John Samuel Henry Weston, *q.v.*

Services : Apptd. Cadet for Engrs. 11 Aug. 1778. Lieut. 33rd Bn. Sepoys in July 1787 and in Dec. 1788. Third Mysore War; capture of Seringapatam ; Lieut. 14th Bn. Sepoys. Transfd. from 14th Bn. and apptd. Adjt. 6th Bn. Sepoys 6 Nov. 1794. Posted to newly-raised 4th N.C. in 1797; Capt. 4th N.C. Fur. 9 Mar. 1800 till 26 Aug. 1802. Comdd. 4th N.C. 1801-10. Operations in Jumna Doab 1803 ; Sasni ; Bijaigarh ; Kachaura. Second Mahratta War ; Laswari. Invalided in 1812, but appears to have returned to the active list in 1817. Comdg. at Monghyr 1813-16. "Was present at the taking of Seringapatam, and various sieges and battles, where his gallant conduct was repeatedly mentioned in G.O." (*Burke.*)

Refs. : Burke's *Landed Gentry*, 2nd edn., iii. 216, *s.n.* Rob Roy

Macgregor, of Craigrostan and Inversnaid. *A.A.R.* i. 162. Will proved 31 Dec. 1818. M.I. at Monghyr.

McGREGOR, John (1758/59-1781). Ensign, Infantry. *b.* in Ireland 1758/59. Cadet 1781. Never arrived in India. Ensign 9 May 1781. *bur.* St. Helena 5 Dec. 1781 : drowned on the voyage out.

Services : Apptd. Cadet 1 May 1781, aged 22 ; sailed for India in the *Lord Mulgrave* 26 June 1781.

MACGREGOR, John (1783-1822). Captain, 29th N.I. *b.* Edinburgh 19 Apr. 1783. Country Cadet 1804. Admitted 9 Aug. 1804. Ensign 14 Aug. 1804. Lieut. 21 Sept. 1804. Capt. 1 Jan. 1819. *d. unm.* Calcutta 29 Oct. 1822.

bapt. St. Giles's, Edinburgh, 23 Apr. 1783. Son of Daniel Macgregor and Margaret Scott his wife.

Services : Went out to India as a Free Mariner in 1800. Posted Lieut. to 4th N.I. in 1805 ; transfd. to newly-raised 1/29th N.I. in 1815. Siege and capture of Hathras 1817 ; Lieut. 1/29th N.I. Third Mahratta War 1817-18 ; Lieut. 1/29th N.I. Fur. 5 Feb. 1820 till 1822.

Refs. : Will dated London, 17 Jan. 1822 ; proved 31 Oct. 1822.

MACGREGOR, John Alexander Paul (1780-1868). General. Colonel 54th N.I. *b.* 1780. Cadet 1795. Arrived in India 4 Feb. 1797. Ensign (4 Feb. 1797) 15 Oct. 1797. Lieut. 30 Oct. 1797. Capt. 1 May 1805. Major 12 July 1814. Lt. Col. 1 Aug. 1818. Lt. Col. Comdt. 1 May 1824. Col. 5 June 1829. Maj. Gen. 10 Jan. 1837. Lt. Gen. 9 Nov. 1846. Gen. 20 June 1854. *d.* 7 Sussex Pl., Hyde Pk. Gdns., London, 5 Mar. 1868, aged 88.

Son of Lachlan Paul, *q.v.*, and Drummond Mary his wife. He assumed the surname of MacGregor in compliance with the Will of his uncle, John MacGregor, Commodore, Bombay Marine (*d.* 23 Mar. 1784), who was a cousin of Alexander Murray (1746-1822), *q.v. m.* London May 1807, Jane, dau. of James Ness, of Osgodby, Yorks. (She died 30 Jan. 1858.) Father of George Hall Macgregor, *q.v.*, and of Thomas Paul Macgregor (*see* Appendix A.).

Services : Apptd. a Minor Cadet 22 Nov. 1781. Lieut. 1st Bengal Eur. Regt. in June 1798. Fourth Mysore War 1799 ; Malavelli ; Seringapatam ; Lieut. 2nd Vol. Bn. (Medal). Operations in N. Circars 1800 ; Adjt. 2nd Vol. Bn. Adjt. 1/2nd N.I. 1801-4. Operations in Jumna Doab 1803 ; Sasni ; Kachaura. Second Mahratta War ; battle of Delhi ; Agra ; battle and capture of

THE BENGAL ARMY, 1758-1834

Deig (horse shot under him); Lieut. and Adjt. 1/2nd N.I.; Bhurtpore; Bde. Major (India Medal). Fur. p.a. 5 Dec. 1805 till 19 Sept. 1808. A.D.C. to G.G. 24 July 1810 till Nov. 1813; Fort Adjt. at Ft. Wm. 11 July 1812 till Mar. 1813; Dy. Mily. Auditor Gen. 13 Mar. 1813 till Mar. 1830. Major 2/2nd N.I. Posted Lt. Col. to 25th N.I. 1818; to 23rd N.I. 1820; to 11th N.I. July 1823; to 22nd N.I. May 1824. Posted Col. to 22nd N.I. 1829. Mily. Auditor Gen. 26 Mar. 1830 till Mar. 1846. Transfd. to 37th N.I. 18 Nov. 1830; to 61st N.I. 29 July 1833; to 28th N.I. 1 Mar. 1836. Leave s.c. to Cape 20 Jan. 1839 till 23 Dec. 1840; fur. s.c. 10 Mar. 1846 till death. Col. 54th N.I. 17 Sept. 1847 till death.

Refs.: *Hist. of Clan Gregor*, by Miss A. G. Murray of MacGregor, ii. 393. *Boase. E.I.M.C.* iii. 295-6. *M.M.* xxiii. 495. *S.M.* 1824, ii. 510. *The Times*, 7 Mar. 1868.

MacGREGOR, John Graham (1803-1825). Lieutenant, 49th N.I. *b.* Cawnpore 3 Jan. 1803. Cadet 1818. Ensign (?) Lieut. 26 Aug. 1820. *d. unm.* Chittagong 30 Nov. 1825.

Younger son of Robert MacGregor, *q.v.* Brother of Robert Stuart MacGregor, *q.v.*, cousin-german of Thomas Alexander Knox MacGregor, *q.v.*, and related to Sir John Murray MacGregor, Bart., *q.v.*

Services: Ensign d.d. 14th N.I. 1819. Posted Lieut. to 2/25th N.I. 1820; transfd. to 49th N.I. (late 1/25th) May 1824. First Burma War; Arakan 1825; Lieut. 49th N.I.

Refs.: Burke's *Landed Gentry*, 2nd edn., iii. 216, *s.n.* Rob Roy Macgregor, of Craigrostan and Inversnaid. *Calcutta Monthly Journal*, Jan. 1825. Will undated; proved 1 Feb. 1826.

MACGREGOR, Sir John Murray, first baronet (1745-1822). Lieut. Colonel. 15th N.I. Mily. Auditor Gen. *b.* 10 Apr. 1745. Cadet 1770. Admitted 17 Oct. 1770. Ensign 13 Nov. 1771. Lieut. 28 July 1776. Capt. 21 Feb. 1781. Major 1 Mar. 1794. Lt. Col. 31 Aug. 1798. Retired 12 Feb. 1799. *d.* Portobello, Edinburgh, 29 June 1822.

1st Bart., of Lanrick and Balquhidder. *cr.* 3 July 1795. J.P. and D.L. co. Perth. Eldest son of Evan Murray and Janet his wife, youngest dau. of John MacDonald, of Balcony. Resumed the original surname of the family by R.L. in 1822. Brother of Peter Murray, *q.v. m.* Murshidabad 10 Apr. 1775, Anne, dau. of Roderick Macleod (of Bernera), of Edinburgh, W.S. (She died 5 Feb. 1830, aged 81.)

Services: " Bred to the law." Posted to 2nd Bengal Eur. Regt.

and apptd. Dy. Judge Advocate to 2nd Bde. at Berhampore in Nov. 1771. Apptd. Mily. Sec. and A.D.C. to Col. A. Champion, *q.v.*, 19 Jan. 1774. First Rohilla War; battle of St. George; Ensign 2nd Eur. Regt., Mily. Sec. Sec. to the Board of Ordnance in Calcutta 1776-80; Comy. Gen. 1780-5. Fur. 21 Feb. 1786 till 27 Aug. 1788. Mily. Auditor Gen. (with official rank of Col.) 1789-96. Senior M.M.B. Major 3rd Bengal Eur. Regt. in 1796; Lt. Col. 15th N.I. in 1798. Fur. 18 Jan. 1797 till retirement.

Refs.: Burke's *Peerage*, 1923, p. 1467, *s.n.* Macgregor, Bart., of Lanrick and Balquhidder, Chief of Clan Gregor. *E.I.M.C.* ii. 461-3. *Macpherson. S.M.* 1822, ii. 270. *G.M.* 1803, ii. 884; 1822, ii. 277.

McGREGOR, Malcolm (*d.* 1804). Fireworker. Artillery. (191) Subsequently Major 10th Madras N.I. Country Cadet 1778. Fireworker 10 Dec. 1778. Transfd. to Madras Est. 3 Feb. 1780. *d.* Masulipatam 4 Nov. 1804.

(*Perhaps* eldest son of Patrick McGregor by Margaret McGregor his wife.)

Services: Apptd. Cadet 10 Sept. 1778. Ensign (Madras) 12 Aug. 1778; Lieut. 1 Apr. 1783; Capt. 1 June 1796; Major 10 Dec. 1799. Invalided 10 July 1802.

Refs.: Intest.; admon. 21 Mar. 1806. M.I. at Masulipatam.

MacGREGOR, Robert (*d.* 1803). Captain, 15th N.I. Cadet 1779. Arrived in India 1779. Ensign 23 July 1779. Lieut. 14 Mar. 1781. Capt. 30 Oct. 1797. *d.* Patparanj 11 Sept. 1803: kld. in action at the battle of Delhi.[1]

Younger son of John MacGregor, Capt. 60th Foot. Brother of James Murray MacGregor, *q.v. m.* Calcutta 19 Apr. 1799, Sarah, dau. of John Graham, of Brednock House and Duchray Castle, co. Perth, and sister of John Graham (1777-1816), *q.v.* (She died Edinburgh 13 July 1833.) Father of John Graham MacGregor, *q.v.*, and of Robert Stuart MacGregor, *q.v.*

Services: Lieut. in an Invalid Coy. in Guernsey in Oct. 1778. Apptd. Cornet 1st Regt. Cav. 19 Aug. 1779. First Mahratta War; Cornet 1st Cav., with Bombay detachment under Col. Thomas Goddard, *q.v.* Lieut. 1st Bn. Sepoys in 1781; Adjt. & Qmr. at Midnapore 1784-5; Lieut. 14th Bn. in July 1787. Third Mysore War; Seringapatam; Lieut. 14th Bn. Expdn. to Assam 1793-4; actg. Adjt. to the force under Capt. Thomas Welsh, *q.v.* Transfd. to 15th N.I. Persian translator and Sec. in the field to Lord Lake 1803. Second Mahratta War; Koil; Aligarh; battle of Delhi

(kld.); Persian Intr. to C.-in-C. " Served with distinction at Seringapatam and was present at many actions and storming of forts, both in Madras and Bengal Presidencies, . . ." (*Burke.*)
Refs.: Burke's *Landed Gentry*, 2nd Edn., iii. 216, *s.n.* Rob Roy Macgregor, of Craigrostan and Inversnaid. *A.A.R.* i. 162. Will dated Cawnpore 19 Jan. 1803; proved 17 Dec. 1803.

[1] *Note*: Each of his sons was granted a pension of £50 *p.a.* until he attained the age of 16.

MacGREGOR, Robert Guthrie (1805-1869). Major. Artillery. (528) 1st Asst. Mily. Auditor Gen. *b.* in India 17 Oct. 1805. Cadet 1821. Arrived in India 16 Jan. 1823. 2nd Lieut. 10 May 1822. Lieut. 24 Oct. 1824. Capt. 31 Dec. 1839. Invalided 29 Apr. 1840. Retired 10 Sept. 1852. Hon. Major 28 Nov. 1854. *d.* at his residence, Hallsannery, Bideford, 27 Aug. 1869.

Eldest son of James Murray MacGregor, *q.v.* Brother of Thomas Alexander Knox MacGregor, *q.v.*, and cousin-german of Robert Stuart MacGregor, *q.v.* *m.* Calcutta 6 Jan. 1838, Alexina, 2nd dau. of Archibald Watson, *q.v.* (*See also* Murray Mackenzie and James Remington.) (She died 1 Feb. 1889.) Father of Maj.-Gen. Sir Charles Metcalfe MacGregor (*D.N.B.*). Addiscombe Cadet 1821-2.

Services: First Burma War 1824-5; capture of Rangoon; capture of Martaban 30 Oct. 1824 (*Lond. Gaz.* 19 Apr. 1825); Donabyu (s.w.); Lieut. 3rd Coy. 5th Bn. Art., with Sir A. Campbell's force (India medal). Returned to Bengal July 1825. Adjt. 1st Bn. Art. 22 July 1825. Siege and capture of Bhurtpore (s.w. in leg) (*Lond. Gaz.* 4 July 1826); Adjt. 1st Bn. (clasp to India medal). Granted wound pension and donation of 1 yr's pay. Fur. s.c. 4 Feb. 1827 till 29 May 1830. Offg. 2nd Asst. Mily Auditor Gen. 1 Oct. 1831. D.J.A.G. Saugor Div. 21 Mar. 1835. 2nd Asst. Mily. Auditor Gen. 8 Dec. 1835; 1st do. 31 Dec. 1835; offg. Dy. Mily. Auditor Gen. 1 July 1839. Engaged from Dec. 1832 till July 1835 in compiling a " Digest of the Pay and Audit Regulations," for which work he was awarded a donation of Rs. 1,000. Sec. to the Agra Bank 1841-50. Pub. London 1828, a translation of Voltaire's " Henriad."

Refs.: Burke's *Landed Gentry*, 2nd edn., iii. 216, *s.n.* Rob Roy MacGregor, of Craigrostan and Inversnaid. *A.J.* xxvi. 592. *The Times*, 31 Aug. 1869.

MACGREGOR, Robert Murray (*d.* 1831). Captain. 8th N.I. Afterwards Lt. Col. Royal Clan Alpine Fenc. Country Cadet 1778. Admitted 11 Aug. 1778. Cornet 29 July 1779. Lieut.

144   LIST OF THE OFFICERS OF

8 Jan. 1781. Capt. 25 Apr. 1797. Retired 22 Jan. 1800. d. London 11 Apr. 1831.

4th and youngest son of Evan Murray. Resumed his patronymic by R.L. 21 Dec. 1822. Brother of Sir John Murray Macgregor, Bart., q.v., and of Alexander Murray (1746-1822), q.v. m. 1st, (?) (She was bur. Calcutta 29 Jan. 1783.) m. 2nd, Edinburgh 11 June 1798, Barbara, sister of Sir Alexander Mackenzie, Bart., of Fairburn, and widow of Kenneth Murchison, of Tarradale, the father of Kenneth Archibald John Murchison, q.v. (She died Clifton 9 Sept. 1836, aged 66.)

Services: Was Qmr. of Nawab of the Carnatic's Cav. for several years prior to 1778. Apptd. Cadet for Cav. 11 Aug. 1778; removed to Inf. 18 Oct. 1778; retransfd. to Cav. 1779. Lieut. in Cav. in Jan. 1783; 3rd Bengal Eur. Bn. in July 1787. Posted to 1st Regt. Cav. 14 Dec. 1787; Qmr. do. in Jan. 1791; 2nd Regt. Cav. in 1792. Fur. 27 Mar. 1797 till retirement.

Refs.: Burke's *Peerage*, 1923, p. 1467, s.n. Macgregor, Bart., of Lanrick. *G.M.* 1831, i. 379.

MacGREGOR, Robert Stuart (1800-?). Lieutenant. 17th N.I. Afterwards Capt. Stirling Mil. b. Cawnpore 8 Feb. 1800. Cadet 1816. Ensign (?) Lieut. 1 Aug. 1818. Cashiered 4 Feb. 1823. (Living in 1866.)

bapt. Cawnpore 8 Mar. 1800. Elder son of Robert MacGregor, q.v., and Sarah his wife. Brother of John Graham MacGregor, q.v., and nephew of John Graham (1777-1816), q.v. m. 18 June 1835, Helen Kea, dau. of Adam Bissett, of Leith, merchant. (She died his widow at Portobello 1 Mar. 1886, aged 74.) Ed. Edinburgh High School.

Services: Served in R.N. 1812-17, in which he was engaged against French batteries, Danish gunboats, and cutting out (w. in body and head by splinters, ball through rt. thigh); blockade of Norway 1814-15; passed exam. for Lieut. at Portsmouth Coll. 1817 (*Hart's A.L.*). Posted Lieut. to 2/17th N.I. in 1818. "Comdd. a large detachment of Inf., Cav. and Art. for several mos. in C.I." (*Hart.*) Capt. Stirlingshire Regt. of Mil. 26 Oct. 1844.

Refs.: Burke's *Landed Gentry*, 2nd edn., iii. 216, s.n. Rob Roy Macgregor, of Craigrostan and Inversnaid.

MACGREGOR, Thomas (1781-1805). Lieutenant, 15th N.I. b. Edinburgh 28 Nov. 1781. Cadet 1798. Admitted 12 May 1800. Ensign 15 Dec. 1799. Lieut. 29 May 1800. d. Bhurtpore 21 Jan. 1805 : kld. in action during the 2nd assault of the fortress.

THE BENGAL ARMY, 1758-1834 145

bapt. Edinburgh 7 Dec. 1781. Son of Deacon Gregor Drummond (*alias* Macgregor), of New Kirk psh., Edinburgh, flesher, and Margaret his wife, dau. of Thomas Tibbets, maltmill maker. 2nd cousin of Robert MacGregor, *q.v.* *m.* Calcutta 14 Aug. 1804, Miss Eliza Grand.

Services: Posted Lieut. to 1/15th N.I. 15 Apr. 1801. Operations in Jumna Doab 1803; Sasni; Bijaigarh; Kachaura; Lieut. 1/15th N.I. Transfd. to 2/15th N.I.; Adjt. do. 1804 till death. Second Mahratta War; battle of Delhi; Agra; Laswari; battle of Deig; Bhurtpore (kld.); Lieut. 2/15th N.I.

Refs.: *Hist. of the Clan Gregor*, ii. 338. Will dated Muttra, 15 Dec. 1804; proved 8 May 1805.

MacGREGOR, Thomas Alexander Knox (1809-1835). Lieutenant, Pension Est. Bengal Eur. Regt. *b.* Calcutta 7 June 1809. Cadet 1827. Arrived in India 1 June 1828. Ensign (3 Dec. 1827) 4 Nov. 1828. Lieut. 19 June 1831. Pensioned 13 Mar. 1835. *d.* Calcutta 27 Mar. 1835.

Youngest son of James Murray MacGregor, *q.v.* Brother of James Melville MacGregor, *q.v.*

Services: Posted Ensign to 2nd Bengal Eur. Regt. 4 Nov. 1828. Fur. s.c. 11 Sept. 1832 till 11 Dec. 1834. No record of active service.

Refs.: Burke's *Landed Gentry*, 2nd edn., iii. 216, *s.n.* Rob Roy Macgregor, of Craigrostan and Inversnaid. *A.J.* N.S. xviii. 33.

MACGUIRE, John (1761/62-1792). Lieutenant. 35th Bn. Sepoys. *b.* 1761/62. Country Cadet 1781. Ensign 28 Sept. 1781. Lieut. 3 July 1783. Resigned 3 Mar. 1790. *d.* 8 Feb. 1792, aged 30.[1]

Services: First Mahratta War; apptd. by Gen. Goddard to act as Ensign. Lieut. 35th Bn. Sepoys in July 1787. *Probably* became an indigo planter after resigning the Service.

[1] *Note:* Two separate tombstones, both stating that his remains lie beneath, are, or were 50 years ago, in existence. One is at English Bazar, Malda, B. & O., and the other at Gunwanti, a small village in the Raniganj thana, B. & O., some 50 miles distant. Both give the same inscription.

MACHARG, James (*d.* 1773). Ensign, Sepoys. Cadet 1771. Ensign 10 Mar. 1773. *d.* Dinapore 23 June 1773.

Son of Anthony Macharg, M.D., of Edinburgh.
Services: N.F.P.

MACHARG, James (*d.* 1794). Ensign. Infantry. Cadet 1783. Never arrived in India. Ensign 7 May 1785. Struck off 1788. *d.* 1794.

Son of Archibald Macharg, writer in Edinburgh.

Services: Apptd. Cadet 4 Dec. 1782; should have sailed for India in the *Pigot* 11 Mar. 1783. Admitted W.S. 7 Mar. 1788. Sometime Lieut. H.M. 99th Regt.

MACHARG, James (1786-1822). Captain, 6th N.I. *b.* St. Dunstan-in-the-East, London, 4 Dec. 1786. Cadet 1803. Arrived in India 14 Aug. 1804. Ensign 29 Aug. 1804. Lieut. 21 Sept. 1804. Capt. 15 Nov. 1817. *d. unm.* Benares 29 Aug. 1822.

Son of James Macharg, of Keirs, co. Ayr, and Cecilia his wife. Brother of Elizabeth, wife of Archibald Kelso (who was uncle of Fleming Kelso, *q.v.*), Cecilia, wife of Archibald Tod, and Mary, wife of John Macalister. Ed. Merchant Taylor's 1795.

Services: Posted Lieut. to 6th N.I. in 1805. Operations in Bundelkhand 1805-6; Lieut. 6th N.I. Adjt. & Qmr. 6th N.I. 25 Jan. 1810; Adjt. 2/6th N.I. 1 July 1814. Nepal War 1814-15; Lieut. 2/6th N.I., in 1st Div. Raised 2nd Nassiri Bn. at Sabathu (G.O. 24 Apr. 1815), and comdd. Aug. 1815 till death. Capt. Lt. 2/6th N.I. 9 Sept. 1817. Transfd. as Capt. to 1/6th N.I.

Refs.: Burke's *Landed Gentry*, 11th edn., p. 938, *s.n.* Kelso, of Sauchrie. *Robinson*. *S.M.* 1823, i. 519. Will dated 8 May 1822; proved 16 Sept. 1822.

MacINNES, John (1779-1859). General. Colonel 1st Eur. Bengal Fus. *b.* Camuscross, Sleat, I. of Skye, 1 Aug. 1779. Cadet 1798. Arrived in India 23 Nov. 1799. Ensign 5 Nov. 1799. Lieut. 4 Mar. 1800. Capt. 3 Aug. 1811. Major 3 June 1816. Lt. Col. 26 Aug. 1822. Lt. Col. Comdt. 13 May 1825. Col. 5 June 1829. Maj. Gen. 28 June 1838. Lt. Gen. 11 Nov. 1851. Gen. 4 July 1856. *d.* Hale End, Woodford, Essex, 12 Mar. 1859.

Of Fern Lodge, Hampstead, Middlesex. Eldest son of Miles MacInnes and Grizel his wife, eldest dau. of Rev. William Grant, minister of Kilmonivaig 1750-75. *m.* 1st, Clifton 1 Nov. 1820, Mary Elizabeth, youngest dau. of Bedingfield Pogson, of I. of St. Kitts, and sister of Wredenhall Robert Pogson, *q.v.* (She died Fort Marlbro' 27 Mar. 1823.) *m.* 2nd, Dorking 6 Sept. 1828, Anna Sophia, 2nd dau. of Jacob Foster Reynolds, of S. Lambeth, and of Carshalton, Surrey. (She died 16 Nov. 1877.)

Services: Ensign Strathspey Fenc. Inf. 13 Sept. 1798. Posted

Lieut. to 2nd Bengal Eur. Regt. 15 Apr. 1801. Transfd. to Marine Regt. (became 1/20th N.I.) 1803. Persian Intr. to C.O., and Asst. to Comr. for affairs of Cuttack, 21 June 1804. Bde. Major at P.W.I. 1806-16. Capt. Lt. 1/20th N.I. 19 May 1808. A.D.C. to Govr. of P.W.I. 1 May 1812. Major 1/20th N.I. Fur. p.a. 26 Aug. 1818 till 6 July 1822. To tempy. comd. of troops and local corps at Fort Marlbro' 7 Oct. 1822. Posted Lt. Col. to 30th N.I. 1822; to 31st N.I. 1823; to 61st N.I. (late 1/31st) May 1824. To comd. Light Bde. (2 Bns. L.I. and Magh Levy), S.E. Div., 4 June 1825. First Burma War; Arakan 1825; Lt. Col. comdg. Light Bde. (India medal). Tempy. comd. S.E. Div. of Army 16 Dec. 1825; permanent do. 9 Jan. 1826. Fur. s.c. 18 Aug. 1826 till death. Posted as Col. to 61st N.I. June 1829; to 73rd N.I. 30 Nov. 1830; to 40th N.I. 1842; to 59th N.I. 1843; to 24th N.I. 1846; to 64th N.I. 1851; to 1st Eur. Fus. (Rt. Wing) Sept. 1855 till death.

Refs.: Burke's *Landed Gentry*, 12th edn., p. 1236, *s.n.* MacInnes, of Rickerby, Cumberland. *MacInnes* (portrait). *Boase. S.M.* N.S. vii. 574. *I.M.* 16 Mar. 1859, p. 231.

MACINTYRE, John. (*d.* 1828). Lieut. General. Artillery. (130) Cadet 1771. Arrived in India 23 Oct. 1771. Fireworker 2 Mar. 1773. Lieut. 28 Sept. 1777. Capt. Lt. 16 Apr. 1781. Capt. 1 Feb. 1785. Major 8 Jan. 1796. Lt. Col. 21 Apr. 1800. Lt. Col. Comdt. 1 May 1804. Col. 25 Apr. 1808. Maj. Gen. 4 June 1811. Lt. Gen. 19 July 1821. Transfd. to Senior List 29 Aug. 1824. *d.* Bognor, Sussex, 6 July 1828.

Son of Dr. Donald Macintyre, 42nd Black Watch, and Isobel his wife, sister of James Macpherson, of Belleville, editor of Ossian's Poems (*D.N.B.*), and grand-aunt of David Edward Brewster-Macpherson, *q.v.* Cousin-german of James Macpherson, *q.v.*, and 1st cousin once removed of John Macpherson, *q.v.* *m.* 1806, Harriet, dau. of Allan Macpherson, *q.v.* (She *re-m.* 1829, Col. E. B. Craigie, of Ferry Bank, Fife.[1])

Services: Apptd. Cadet for Inf.; transfd. to Art. June 1772. Asst. Sec. to Board of Ord. 1777-80; Sec. do. 1780-5. Fur. 21 Nov. 1785 till 15 Dec. 1789. Second Rohilla War; battle of Bitaurah; Capt. comdg. 3rd Coy. 3rd Bn. Art. Fur. 5 Nov. 1804 till death.

Refs.: *A.J.* xxvi. 239. *G.M.* 1828, ii. 284. *M.I.* in St. Columba's, Kingussie. Portrait at Blairgowrie.

[1] *Note:* (? Edmund Buchan Craigie, *q.v.*)

MACINTYRE, John (1766-1793). Lieutenant, 13th Bn. Sepoys. *b.* 12 Aug. 1766. Cadet (Art.) (III.-12) 1781. Was already in

India when apptd. Ensign (Inf.) 13 Aug. 1782. Lieut. 30 Jan. 1785. d. Benares 6 Oct. 1793.

Eldest son of Rev. Joseph Macintyre, minister of Glenorchy 1765-1823, and Christian his wife, dau. of Rev. John M'Vean, minister of Glenorchy.

Services: Apptd. Art. Cadet in India 26 Nov. 1781. Transfd. to Inf. Aug. 1782. Posted to 13th Bn. Sepoys 15 Dec. 1787. Third Mysore War; Arikera; Seringapatam; Lieut. 13th Bn.

Refs.: Scott's Fasti, iv. 87. S.M. 1794, p. 373.

MacINTYRE, John Duncan (1789-1808). Ensign, 25th N.I. b. St. Pancras, Middlesex, 27 Sept. 1789. Cadet 1806. Arrived in India 3 Oct. 1807. Ensign 31 July 1807. d. Barasat 10 Dec. 1808.

Son of John MacIntyre.

Services: Died whilst under instruction at Barasat C.C.

MACKAY, Æneas John (1808-1865). Lieut. Colonel. 16th N.I. b. Edinburgh 20 Jan. 1808. Cadet 1825. Arrived in India 22 Oct. 1826. Ensign 21 June 1826. Lieut. 31 Jan. 1829. Capt. 24 Jan. 1845. Bt. Major 3 Apr. 1846. Retired 2 Nov. 1848. Hon. Lt. Col. 28 Nov. 1854. d. Gale Cottage, Keswick, 8 Feb. 1865.

5th child of Æneas Mackay, of Scotstoun, sometime Capt. Madras Est., and Helen Mylne, of Mylnefield, his 2nd wife. Brother of Donald Æneas Mackay, q.v. m. 1849, Eleanor, dau. of William Roberts, banker. (She died Kippen, co. Perth, 16 Oct. 1855.) Ed. Edin. High School and Coll.

Services: Posted Ensign to 16th N.I. 8 Jan. 1827. d.d. 27th N.I. 1 Aug. till 5 Oct. 1831. Actg. Adjt. Left Wing 16th N.I. 30 Jan. 1839; Actg. Adjt. 16th N.I. 1 Nov. 1839. First Afghan War 1838-42; capture of Ghazni 1839 (Medal); against Ghilzais 1841; advance on Kabul 1842; Bt. Capt. 16th N.I., with Nott's ,force (Medal). Gwalior campaign; Maharajpur; Bt. Capt. 16th N.I. (Bronze star). Adjt. 16th N.I. 31 Oct. 1844 till Feb. 1845. Fur. p.a. 18 Dec. 1846 till retirement.

Refs.: Mackay, p. 337. G.M. 1865, i. 397. The Times, 11 Feb. 1865.

MACKAY, Donald Æneas (1796-1831). Lieutenant, Artillery. (469) b. Newlands, Tweedale, 27 Nov. 1796. Cadet 1816. Admitted 4 Nov. 1817. Fireworker 25 Sept. 1817. Lieut. 1 Sept. 1818. d. Agra 22 Nov. 1831.

bapt. Newlands 13 Dec. 1796. Eldest son of Æneas Mackay, of Scotstoun, and Helen Mylne his 2nd wife. Brother of James Mackay, *q.v. m.* Koil, U.P., 24 Nov. 1825, Agnes Anne, 4th dau. of William Spottiswoode, of Clayquhat, co. Perth. (She was pensd. Lord Clive's fund 8 Jan. 1834, till her *re-m.* in 1843.) Addiscombe Cadet 1814-16.

Services : 6th Troop H. A. in 1819 ; 3rd Troop 1820-5. Siege and capture of Bhurtpore ; Adjt. 1st Bde. H. A. Posted to 3rd Troop 1st Bde. in 1830. Offg. Bde. Major at Agra 4 Mar. 1831 ; permanent do. 18 Mar. 1831. Transfd. to 7th Coy. 6th Bn. in 1831.

Refs. : *Mackay*, p. 337. *S.M.* 1826, i. 639. Will dated Agra 6 Nov. 1831 ; proved 27 Jan. 1832. M.I. Cantt. cemetery, Agra.

MACKAY, Hugh (1713/14-1762). Captain, Infantry. *b.* in Scotland 1713/14. Capt. 6 Jan. 1759. *d.* 1762.

Services : Sailed for India as a Capt. of Inf. in the *Bombay Castle* in 1758, aged 44. *Probably* transfd. as Capt. from H.M.S. N.F.P.

MACKAY,[1] **Hugh** (*d.* 1763). Ensign, Bengal Eur. Regt. Cadet (?) Ensign 18 Sept. 1761. *d.* 5th, 6th or 11th Oct. 1763 : massacred at or near Patna by order of Nawab Mir Muhammad Kasim.

Note : " . . . on the nights of the 5th or 6th and 11th of October 1763, brutally massacred near this spot by the troops of Mir Kasim, Nawab Subahdar of Bengal, under command of Walter Reinhardt *alias* Samru, a base renegade." (M.I. in Patna city.)

Services : N.F.P.

Refs. : MS. " List of Persons kld. in the Massacre at Patna, and at other places during the Troubles, 1763," in I.O. *Broome*, p. 365. *Innes*, p. 169. His diary pub. in *Swinton of Kimmerghame Records*, pp. 48-57.

[1] *Note :* His name also appears as M'Kay and Mackie.

MACKAY, Jacob (*d.* 1787). Ensign, Infantry. Country Cadet 1782. Admitted 24 Sept. 1782. Ensign (24 Feb. 1783) 11 May, 1783. *d.* Barrackpore 9 Sept. 1787.

Services : Apptd. Vol. by Sir Eyre Coote 25 July 1782, to serve with Bengal Detachment during 2nd Mysore War. Posted Ensign to 1st Bengal Eur. Regt. 28 Feb. 1783, whilst still in Madras.

MACKAY, James (1806-1831). Lieutenant, 27th N.I. *b.* Newlands, Tweedale, 6 June 1806. Cadet 1825. Arrived in India 7 July 1826. Ensign 15 Mar. 1826. Lieut. 23 Dec. 1827. *d.s.p.* Gadarwara, C.P., 25 Nov. 1831.

LIST OF THE OFFICERS OF

4th child of Æneas Mackay, of Scotstoun, Newlands, and Helen Mylne his 2nd wife. Brother of Æneas John Mackay, *q.v. m.* Saugor 20 Oct. 1830, Emma Jane, dau. of Samuel Pidding Bishop, *q.v.* (*See also* William Alston.) (She *re-m.* Charles Marshall, *q.v.*) Ed. Edinburgh High School.

Services: Ensign d.d. 39th N.I. 2 Aug. 1826. Posted to 27th N.I. 26 Sept. 1826. Adjt. 27th N.I. 24 Feb. 1829 till death. No record of active service.

Refs.: Mackay, p. 337. M.I. Narsinghpur.

MACKAY, Walter (1806-1827). Lieutenant, 52nd N.I. *b.* Edinburgh 17 June 1806. Cadet 1823. Ensign 10 Feb. 1824. Lieut. 24 Oct. 1825. *d.* Calcutta 17 Jan. 1827.

2nd son of John Mackay, of Clyde St., Edinburgh, and Janet Dunlop his wife. Ed. Edin. Univ.

Services: Posted Ensign to 52nd N.I. in 1824. (? First Burma War; Cachar 1825; Ensign 52nd N.I.)

Refs.: Mackay, *s.n.* Strathy Mackays. *A.J.* xxiii. 857.

McKEAN, Alexander (1803-1822). Ensign, 14th N.I. *b.* E. Barnet 25 May 1803. Cadet 1819. Ensign 3 June 1820. *d.* in India 18 Dec. 1822: murdered.

bapt. 23 July 1803. Son of Archibald McKean, W.I. merchant, and Elizabeth his wife. Brother of Archibald McKean, *q.v.*

Services: Posted Ensign to 1/14th N.I. in 1820. No record of active service.

McKEAN, Archibald (1801–1844). Captain, 42nd N.I. *b.* London 6 May 1801. Cadet 1819. Admitted 14 June 1820. Ensign 2 Feb. 1820. Lieut. 7 Aug. 1822. Capt. 24 July 1837. *d.* Mainpuri, U.P., 18 July 1844.

bapt. St. Luke's, Middlesex, 22 May 1801. Son of Archibald McKean, W.I. merchant, and Elizabeth his wife. Brother of Robert McKean, *q.v. m.* Cawnpore 19 July 1827, Miss Harriet Anderson (aged 15). (She died 20 Jan. 1858.)

Services: Posted Ensign to 1/21st N.I. in 1820. Transfd. to 42nd N.I. (late 2/21st) May 1824. First Burma War; Arakan 1825; s.w. whilst leading Light Coy. against the position of Mahattu on 27 Mar. 1825 (*Lond. Gaz.* 1 Oct. 1825); Lieut. 42nd N.I., with Bdr. J. W. Morrison's force. Granted a wound pension from 28 Mar. 1826, and a donation of 1 yr.'s pay. Placed in charge of young officers 2 Oct. 1826. Adjt. Delhi Provl. Bn. 15 Jan. 1828 till Jan. 1832. Adjt. & Qmr. Eur. Invalids 14 Feb.

1832 till 11 Nov. 1837. Fur. s.c. 22 June 1839 till 14 Jan. 1842. Rejoined 42nd N.I. in 1842.

Refs.: *A.J.* xxv. 265. *I.M.* 4 Oct. 1844, p. 564. Will dated 8 June 1844; proved 5 Nov. 1844.

MACKEAN, Robert (1811-1853). Captain, 17th N.I. Comdt. Regt. of Kalat-i-Ghilzai. *b.* Holborn, Middlesex, 11 June 1811. Cadet 1828. Arrived in India 3 June 1828. Ensign 3 Feb. 1828. Lieut. 15 Oct. 1832. Capt. 24 Jan. 1845. *d.* Rawal Pindi 17 Mar. 1853.

Son of Archibald McKean, of John St., London, W.I. merchant, and Elizabeth his wife. Brother of Alexander McKean, *q.v.* *m.* Calcutta 3 Aug. 1846, Matilda Fanny, dau. of A. Chalmers.

Services: Posted Ensign to 17th N.I. 4 Nov. 1828. Apptd. Adjt. 3rd Inf., Shah Shuja's Contingent, 17 Aug. 1838. First Afghan War; Pashut; operations in Nazian Valley Feb. 1841; defence of Kalat-i-Ghilzai (Medal); Kandahar; Ghazni; Kabul; Lieut. Shah's 3rd Inf. (Medal). Second in comd. Regt. of Kalat-i-Ghilzai (late Shah's 3rd Inf.) 4 Oct. 1842; Comdt. do. 13 Jan. 1852 till death. Black Mountain expedn. Dec. 1852; Capt. comdg. Regt. of Kalat-i-Ghilzai.

Refs.: *I.M.* 17 May 1853, p. 261. M.I. Rawal Pindi.

MACKELCAN,[1] **John** (1727/28-1762). Lieutenant, Infantry. *b.* London 1727/28. Cadet 1758. Ensign 2 Mar. 1760. Lieut. 9 July 1762. *d.* Calcutta 9 Dec. 1762.

Services: Sailed for India in the *Calcutta* in 1758, aged 30. N.F.P.

[1] *Note:* Mackelcan in burial register; Macklecan in embarkation roll; MacKellan in Letter from Court, dated London, 23 Jan. 1759; Mackleton in *Dodwell & Miles.*

McKENLY,[1] **Clements Brown** (1791-1833). Captain, 60th N.I. *b.* Calcutta 10 Oct. 1791. Cadet 1809. Arrived in India 3 Oct. 1810. Ensign 7 Jan. 1812. Lieut. 25 Apr. 1816. Capt. 9 July 1825. *d.* Cawnpore 12 July 1833.

bapt. Calcutta 1 Feb. 1797. Son of Henry McKenly, *q.v.*, and Edith his wife. Brother of Henry Christopher McKenly, *q.v.*

Services: Cadet d.d. 15th N.I. 1811. Posted Ensign to 11th N.I. Jan. 1812. (? Operations in Baghelkhand 1813; Entauri; Ensign 11th N.I.) Transfd. to newly-raised 2/30th N.I. 1815. Third Mahratta War; in action with the enemy on 29 Jan. 1818 (services noted by Maj.-Gen. Clements Brown—*Lond. Gaz.* 25 Feb. 1819). Actg. Adjt. 2/30th N.I. 1818. A.D.C. to Maj.-Gen. Clements

Brown (? his uncle), *q.v.*, 1819-20. Actg. Bde. Major Dinapore Div. 24 Jan. 1820. d.d. 2/21st N.I. 3 Apr. 1822. Actg. Intr. & Qmr. 2/30th N.I. 17 Oct. 1823. Transfd. to 60th N.I. (late 2/30th) May 1824. Adjt. 60th N.I. 17 June 1824 till 6 Dec. 1825. Siege and capture of Bhurtpore; Capt. 60th N.I. Actg. Bde. Major at Meerut 8 Jan. 1827.

Refs.: *G.M.* 1833, ii. 556. *A.J.* N.S. xiii. 39.

[1] *Note*: The name also appears as McKenley, McKinly, M'Kenly, and M'Kinlay.

McKENLY, Henry (*d.* 1800). Lieutenant, Invalid Est. 3rd Bengal Eur. Bn. Cadet 1782. Admitted 2 June 1782. Ensign 18 Aug. 1782. Lieut. 31 Jan. 1785. Invalided 1790. *d.* Calcutta 2 May 1800.

m. Calcutta 28 Mar. 1789, Miss Edith Brown (*perhaps* related to Clements Brown, *q.v.*). Father of Clements Brown McKenly, *q.v.*, and Henry Christopher McKenly, *q.v.*

Services: Apptd. Asst. Sec. in Mily. Dept. of Inspection 2 Aug. 1786. After transfer to the Invalid Est. he became proprietor of the " Telegraphic Press " in Calcutta, and edited the *Telegraph* and the annual *Bengal Directory*.

Refs.: *A.A.R.* iii. 103.

McKENLY, Henry Christopher (Smyth) (1793-1842). Captain, Invalid Est. 41st N.I. *b.* Calcutta 31 Mar. 1793. Cadet 1810. Admitted 21 Jan. 1812. Ensign 2 Dec. 1813. Lieut. 6 July 1816. Capt. 18 June 1833. Invalided 6 Apr. 1835. *d. unm.* Almora, U.P., 16 July 1842.

bapt. Calcutta 1 Feb. 1797. Son of Henry McKenly, *q.v.*, and Edith his wife. Brother of Clements Brown McKenly, *q.v.*

Services: Admitted as one of the first mily. students at Coll. of Ft. Wm. in May 1812, and in 1814 was awarded diplomas and a medal for proficiency in Oriental languages; posted Ensign to 1/21st N.I. in 1814. Nepal War 1816; Harriharpur; Ensign 1/21st N.I., with Left Wing of that Regt. under Major James Cock, *q.v.* Third Mahratta War 1817-18; actg. A.D.C. to (? his uncle) Maj.-Gen. Thomas Brown, *q.v.* Actg. Adjt. Mainpuri Levy 15 Oct. 1821; Intr. & Qmr. 1/21st N.I. 12 June 1823 till 18 Feb. 1831; transfd. to 41st N.I. (late 1/21st) May 1824. Siege and capture of Bhurtpore; Lieut. 41st N.I. Was absent on s.c. for considerable periods between Oct. 1831 and Feb. 1835.

Refs.: Will dated Almora 13 July 1842; proved 21 Nov. 1842.

THE BENGAL ARMY, 1758-1834

MACKENZIE, Sir Alexander, sixth baronet (*d.* 1796). Major General. Infantry. Provincial C.-in-C. Bengal. Capt. 28 July 1764. Major 2 Apr. 1768. Lt. Col. 12 Sept. 1779. Col. 27 May 1786. Maj. Gen. 1793. Resigned 1793. *d.* Coul, co. Ross, 14 Sept. 1796.

6th Bart. of Coul. *s.* 21 May 1792. Eldest son of Sir Alexander Mackenzie, 5th Bart., and Janet his wife, youngest dau. of Sir James Macdonald, of Sleat, 6th Bart. *m.* Leith 30 Apr. 1778, Katharine, dau. of Robert Ramsay, of Camno. Grandfather of Sir Alexander Mackenzie, 8th Bart., *q.v.*

Services : Probably transfd. as Capt. from H.M.S. Apptd. to tempy. comd. of 10th Bn. Sepoys 3 Mar. 1765; d.d. Eur. Bn. 12 June 1765; posted to 3rd Bengal Eur. Bn. 5 Aug. 1765. Sailed for India on return from fur. s.c. in the *Earl of Lincoln* 29 Dec. 1771. First Rohilla War; battle of St. George; Major Sepoy Corps. Returned from fur. Oct. 1784. To comd. 2nd Eur. Bn. 31 May 1786. Comdg. at Chunar in July 1787; at Barrackpore in 1789; at Berhampore in 1791. Provincial C.-in-C. in Bengal during the absence of Lord Cornwallis in Madras, 6 Dec. 1790 till Aug. 1793.

Refs. : Burke's *Peerage,* 1923, p. 1471, *s.n.* Mackenzie, Bart., of Coul, co. Ross. *S.M.* 1796, p. 792. *G.M.* 1796, ii 798.

MACKENZIE, Sir Alexander, sixth baronet (1802-1841). Captain, 48th N.I. *b.* Edinburgh 16 May 1802. Cadet 1823. Arrived in India 10 Aug. 1824. Ensign 10 Feb. 1824. Lieut. 13 May 1825. Capt. 1 Mar. 1840. *d. unm.* Calcutta 28 Apr. 1841.

6th Bart. of Tarbat. Served heir male to his great-great-granduncle George, 1st Earl of Cromarty, 17 Aug. 1826; assumed the dormant baronetcies of Tarbat, of Grandvale and Cromarty, and of Royston 20 Oct. 1826. Elder son of Robert Mackenzie, of Milnmount, *q.v.,* and Katharine his 2nd wife. Ed. Edin. High School.

Services : Posted Ensign to 48th N.I. Dy. Paymr. at Benares 12 Feb. 1829 till 7 July 1830. Fur. p.a. 21 Oct. 1830 till 14 Sept. 1832. First Afghan War 1839-40; capture of Ghazni 1839; Lieut. 48th N.I. Apptd. to Comst. Dept. in Afghanistan 26 Nov. 1840. Leave s.c. to Calcutta 1 Mar. 1841.

Refs. : Burke's *Peerage,* 1923, p. 1472, *s.n.* Mackenzie, Bart., of Scatwell, co. Ross. *A.J.* N.S. xxix. 132. *G.M.* 1841, ii. 334. M.I. Circular Rd. cemetery, Calcutta.

MACKENZIE, Sir Alexander, eighth baronet (1805-1856). Major. 11th N.I. *b.* Contin, co. Ross, 10 Jan. 1805. Cadet

1824. Arrived in India 12 June 1825. Ensign 25 Jan. 1825. Lieut. 9 Nov. 1826. Capt. 24 Jan. 1845. Retired 1 Aug. 1851. Hon. Major 28 Nov. 1854. *d. unm.* Kinellan Lodge, Coul, co. Ross, 3 Jan. 1856.

8th Bart. of Coul. *s.* Oct. 1848. Eldest son of Sir George Steuart Mackenzie, 7th Bart., and Mary his 1st wife, 5th dau. of Donald MacLeod, of Geanies. Grandson of Sir Alexander Mackenzie, 6th Bart., *q.v.*, and nephew of Duncan Macleod (1780-1856), *q.v.* Ed. Edin. High School.

Services : Ensign d.d. 16th N.I. 21 June 1825. Posted Ensign to 11th N.I. Siege and capture of Bhurtpore; Ensign 11th N.I. (India medal). Actg. D.A.Q.M.G. Saugor Div. 12 Dec. 1838 till 11 Feb. 1839. Occupation of Jhansi 1838-9 under Sir T. Anbury, *q.v.*; D.A.Q.M.G. Offg. D.J.A.G., Army of Exercise, 26 Dec. 1843. Gwalior campaign; Maharajpur (horse kld. under him); D.J.A.G. (Bronze star). First Sikh War; no actions; Capt. 11th N.I. (Medal). Fort Adjt. at Chunar 31 Dec. 1847 till 25 Feb. 1851.

Refs. : Burke's *Peerage*, 1923, p. 1471, *s.n.* Mackenzie, Bart., of Coul, co. Ross. *Boase. G.M.* 1856, i. 301. *Inverness Courier*, 10 Jan. 1856.

MACKENZIE, Bernard (*d.* 1765). Ensign, Infantry. Cadet (?) Ensign 7 Apr. 1764. *d.* 1765.
Services : N.F.P.

MACKENZIE, Cunningham (1777-1799). Lieutenant, Bengal Eur. Regt. *bapt.* Belfast 27 Jan. 1777. Cadet 1797. Arrived in India 27 Apr. 1797. Ensign 19 Oct. 1797. Lieut. 30 Oct. 1797. *d.* Dinapore 4 Aug. 1799.
Son of Charles Mackenzie, of Belfast.
Services : Lieut. 6th N.I. in 1798.

MACKENZIE, David. Captain. Infantry. Cadet (?) Ensign 10 Jan. 1764. Lieut. 27 Feb. 1765. Capt. 5 June 1767. Resigned Dec. 1772. (Was living in July 1786.)

m. 1771, Ann, youngest sister of Henry Grant, *q.v.* (She is believed to have died in Lisbon.)

Services : Posted to 19th Bn. Sepoys 13 Aug. 1765. Was comdg. 27th Provl. Bn. in May 1769. Permitted to return to India with his rank 12 May 1780, but it does not appear that he ever did so.

Refs. : Family information. *B. : P.P.*, Vol. lv, p. 86 *n.*

MACKENZIE, Frederick (1791-1829). Captain, 64th N.I. *b.* Hendon, Middlesex, 13 Jan. 1791. Cadet 1807. Arrived in

India 16 Nov. 1808. Ensign 29 Nov. 1808. Lieut. 16 Dec. 1814. Capt. 13 May 1825. *d.* Noakhali, Bengal, 24 Apr. 1829. Youngest son of Kenneth Mackenzie, of Taunton. Brother of Kenneth Mackenzie (1788-1816), *q.v.*, and of Elizabeth, wife of James Pugh, of Severn Fields, Shrewsbury. *m.* St. Helena 18 Apr. 1825, Sarah, dau. of John Nelley, *q.v.*, and widow of Roderick Peregrine Ochterlony. (She died at sea on board the *Thalia* 10 Feb. 1832.) Stepfather of Sir Charles Metcalfe Ochterlony, 2nd Bart.

Services: Barasat C.C. Posted Ensign to 13th N.I. in 1809; transfd. to newly-raised 1/28th N.I. in 1815; Intr. & Qmr. do. 4 May 1815; Adjt. do. 9 Sept. 1818 till July 1823. Third Mahratta War; Madhurajpura; Lieut. 1/28th N.I. Transfd. to newly-formed 31st N.I. July 1823; to 62nd N.I. (late 2/31st) May 1824. Fur. u.p.a. 30 Dec. 1824 till 6 July 1828.

Refs.: *A.J.* xxi. 314; xxviii. 604. *G.M.* 1829, ii. 477. Will dated 1 June 1826; proved 2 June 1829.

MACKENZIE, Frederick George (1809-1840). Lieutenant, Artillery. (573) *b.* London 22 Jan. 1809. Cadet 1825. Arrived in India 2 Feb. 1826. 2nd Lieut. 16 June 1825. Lieut. 19 May 1832. *d.* Dum-Dum 11 Apr. 1840.

bapt. Marylebone 23 Feb. 1809. Son of George Mackenzie, of Wandsworth, late Asst. I.G. of Barracks (who later received young gentlemen for instruction), and Elizabeth his wife, only dau. of Isaac King, of High Wycombe. Addiscombe Cadet 1824-5.

Services: With 2nd Troop 1st Bde. H.A. 1829-31; transfd. to 4th Coy. 1st Bn. Foot Art. 4 Mar. 1831; Adjt. & Qmr. 1st Bn. 8 Feb. 1831 till 1839. Granted fur. s.c. 1 Apr. 1840. No record of active service.

Refs.: M.I. Dum-Dum cemetery.

MACKENZIE, Hector (1801-1838). Major, 74th N.I. *bapt.* Urquhart, co. Ross, 5 Apr. 1801. Cadet 1816. Admitted 9 Sept. 1817. Ensign (?) Lieut. 1 Aug. 1818. Capt. 4 Nov. 1829. Major 30 Jan. 1837. *d.s.p.* Nasirabad 1 Mar. 1838.

3rd son of Sir Hector Mackenzie, 4th Bart. of Gairloch, of Conan House, co. Ross, and Christian his 2nd wife, dau. of William Henderson. *m.* Inverness 8 Jan. 1835, Mary Lydia, eldest dau. of Gen. Sir Hugh Fraser, of Braelangwell. (She *re-m.* 10 Apr. 1839, Fleetwood Williams, B.C.S.)

Services: Ensign d.d. 1/11th N.I. 1818. Posted Lieut. to 1/11th N.I. Aug. 1818. Transfd. to 17th N.I. (late 2/11th) May

LIST OF THE OFFICERS OF

1824; to 6th Extra Regt. (became 74th N.I.) May 1825. Offg. Adjt. Mandleshwar Local Bn. 24 Dec. 1823; 2nd in comd. do. 24 Mar. 1826 till its disbandment on 17 Feb. 1831. Leave s.c. to Singapore and China 22 Apr. 1831; fur. p.a. 10 Jan. 1832 till 19 Sept. 1835. No record of active service.

Refs.: Burke's *Peerage*, 1923, p. 1469, *s.n.* Mackenzie, Bart., of Gairloch, co. Ross. *A.J.* N.S. xxvi. 105. Will dated Bareilly 8 Oct. 1836; proved 29 May 1838. M.I. Nasirabad.

MACKENZIE, Hugh (1805-1885). Lieut. Colonel. 2nd Eur. Bengal Fus. *b.* Roskeen, Invergordon, 14 Sept. 1805. Cadet 1825. Arrived in India 7 July 1826. Ensign 15 Mar. 1826. Lieut. 28 June 1827. Capt. 4 Feb. 1845. Major 28 Nov. 1859. Retired 15 Dec. 1859. Hon. Lt. Col. 15 Dec. 1859. *d.* Forres 3 Apr. 1885.

6th son of Capt. John Mackenzie, VI of Kincraig, co. Ross, 73rd Regt., and Mary his wife, dau. of Rev. Colin Mackenzie, minister of Fodderty. Brother of Kenneth Francis Mackenzie, and of Mary, wife of Sir Donald Macleod, K.C.B., *qq.v. m.* 1st, Clova 15 Apr. 1840, Anne Walker, 4th and youngest dau. of Thomas Duncan, advocate in Aberdeen. (She died 26 Feb. 1857.) *m.* 2nd, Edith S. Hastings, of co. Oxford.

Services: Ensign d.d. 6th Extra Regt. 2 Aug. 1826; posted to 56th N.I. 26 Sept. 1826. Fur. s.c. 19 Dec. 1836 till 27 Oct. 1840. Transfd. to newly-raised 2nd Eur. Regt. 8 Oct. 1839; comdg. Depot 2nd Eur. Regt. 25 Nov. 1842. Fur. p.a. 2 Mar. 1845 till 1846. Second Sikh War; Ramnagar; passage of Chenab; Chilianwala; Gujerat; Capt. 2nd Eur. Regt. (Medal with 2 clasps). Second Burma War 1852-3; Pegu; Capt. 2nd Eur. Fus. (Medal with clasp). Fur. s.c. 3 yrs. 26 Jan. 1855 till Oct. 1858.

Refs.: Mackenzie, p. 546. *I.M.* 22 Jan. 1850, p. 37. *The Times*, 7 Apr. 1885.

MACKENZIE, Jabez (1750/51-1833). Lieut. Colonel. 5th N.I. *b.* 1750/51. Cadet 1769. Admitted 28 June 1770. Ensign 27 Sept. 1769. Lieut. 21 Mar. 1773. Capt. 26 Jan. 1781. Major 1 Mar. 1794. Lt. Col. 30 Oct. 1797. Retired 17 June 1801. *d.* at his residence, 12 Belmont, Bath, 5 Mar. 1833, aged 82.

m. Chunar 10 Aug. 1789, Judith Margaretta, eldest dau. of Sir William Gordon, of Embo, Bart., and sister of Sir John Gordon, Bart., *q.v.* (*See also* William Neville Cameron.) (She died Bath 22 Sept. 1839.)

Services: Apptd. to the staff as Adjt. of N.I. in 1778. First

Mahratta War 1778-84; Bde. Major with the Bengal detachment under Col. Goddard. Apptd. to comd. 2/36th N.I. 1784. Fur. 1 Oct. 1785 till 20 Sept. 1787. To comd. 3rd Bengal Eur. Bn. 31 Oct. 1787; comdg. 1st do. in Dec. 1788; comdg. 27th Bn. Sepoys in 1792; Lt. Col. comdg. 2/5th N.I. in 1797. Fur. 29 Dec. 1799 till retirement.

Refs.: Burke's *Peerage*, 1923, p. 994, *s.n.* Gordon, Bart., of Embo. *E.I.M.C.* i. 77-8. *G.M.* 1833, i. 477. Will dated 8 May 1830; proved 6 June 1835.

MACKENZIE, James (*d.* 1792). Lieutenant, 22nd Bn. Sepoys. Cadet 1778. Ensign 4 June 1778. Lieut. 20 Nov. 1780. *d. unm.* in the Carnatic 5 Apr. 1792.

2nd son of Thomas McKenzie, IV of Highfield and VI of Applecross, co. Ross, and Elizabeth his wife, dau. of Donald McKenzie, of Kilcoy.

Services: Ensign 1/2nd Bengal Eur. Regt. in Oct. 1779; Lieut. 22nd Bn. Sepoys in July 1787. Third Mysore War; Lieut. Bengal Vols.

Refs.: Burke's *Landed Gentry*, 2nd edn., p. 804, *s.n.* Mackenzie, of Applecross. *Mackenzie. S.M.* 1792, p. 570.

MACKENZIE, James (1804-1859). Bt. Colonel, 8th L.C. *b.* Edinburgh 31 Aug. 1804. Cadet 1820. Arrived in India 25 May 1821. Cornet 13 Jan. 1821. Lieut. 13 May 1825. Capt. 5 Oct. 1836. Major 10 Aug. 1850. Lt. Col. 1 Apr. 1854. Bt. Col. 28 Nov. 1854. *d.* Simla 15 Aug. 1859.

Eldest son of Kincaid Mackenzie, of Edinburgh, merchant, sometime lord provost of Edinburgh, and Charlotte Hall his wife, dau. of William Hall, merchant in Edinburgh. *m.* Nasirabad 6 Sept. 1830, Napier Louisa, youngest dau. of Francis James Thomas Johnston, *q.v.* (*See also* John Nicolson.) Ed. Edin. High School and Univ.

Services: Posted Cornet to 8th L.C. Intr. & Qmr. 8th L.C. 14 July 1825. Siege and capture of Bhurtpore; capture of the usurper Durjan Sal; Lieut. 8th L.C. (India medal). Adjt. 8th L.C. 14 Feb. 1826 till 21 Jan. 1836. Leave s.c. in India Apr. 1828 till Dec. 1829. Fur. s.c. 16 Dec. 1835 till 1 Jan. 1839. To take charge of 1st Regt. Cav., Oudh Auxy. Force, 18 Jan. 1840; Comdt. do. (became 6th Irreg. Cav. on 23 Dec. 1840) 2 Sept. 1840 till Jan. 1846. With Army of Reserve (for Afghanistan) Dec. 1842 till Feb. 1843. Against Hill Tribes in Sind 1844; action nr. Mubarikpur 23 Aug. 1844. Rejoined 8th L.C. Jan. 1846. First Sikh War (no actions); Capt. 8th L.C. Comdd. 6th Irreg. Cav. Apr. 1846 till 13 Oct. 1848. Rejoined 8th L.C. 7 Dec. 1848. Second Sikh War; Chilianwala; Gujerat; Bt. Major comdg. 8th L.C. (Medal with 2 clasps). Comdd. 6th Irreg. Cav. Apr. 1849 till 26 Feb. 1853. Rejoined 8th L.C. Nov. 1854. Posted Lt. Col. to 8th L.C. Apr. 1855. Leave s.c. to Simla Apr.-Oct. 1857. Comdd. troops at Ferozepore, with rank of Bdr., Oct. 1857 till Apr. 1859. Was on sick leave in Simla when his death occurred.

Refs.: *De Rhé-Philipe*. *I.M.* 6 Nov. 1844, p. 578. *Boase*. *G.M.* 1859, ii. 541. *The Times*, 13 Oct. 1859. M.I. in new cemetery, Simla.

MACKENZIE, John (1788-1856). Bt. Colonel, 6th L.C. *b.* Hanover, Jamaica, 28 Feb. 1788. Cadet 1805. Arrived in India 19 Sept. 1806. Cornet 19 Sept. 1806. Lieut. 25 May 1816. Capt. 16 July 1823. Major 1 Nov. 1838. Lt. Col 30 Oct. 1848. Bt. Col. 28 Nov. 1854. *d.* Simla 5 May 1856. Of Hilton. Eldest son of Alexander Mackenzie, XI of Hilton and Brae, and Mary his wife, dau. of James Walker. *m.* 1813, his cousin Elizabeth, dau. of Kenneth Mackenzie, W.S., of Inverinate. (She died Babugarh, nr. Meerut, 7 Aug. 1833.) His dau. *m.* Arthur Hall, *q.v.*

Services: Capt. 2nd Bn. Ross-shire Vols. Barasat C.C. till 1 Feb. 1807. Posted Cornet to 3rd N.C. Feb. 1807. (? Operations against Dhundia Khan 1807; Cornet 3rd N.C.) Operations in Bundelkhand against insurgents 1808-9; Cornet 3rd N.C. Leave s.c. 6 mos. to sea 14 July 1810; fur. s.c. 15 Jan. 1811 till 12 June 1813. Operations in Alwar Nov. 1813. Third Mahratta War; Rampur; Jawad; Lieut. 3rd N.C., in Centre Div. Did duty with G.G.B.G. Aug. 1818 till May 1819. Sub-Asst. in Stud Dept. at Buxar 7 May 1819; 2nd Asst. to Supt. Stud at Buxar 1825 till May 1829. Supt. Stud N.W.P. at Hapur May 1829; do. C.P. Jan. 1834 till 28 Oct. 1842. Leave s.c. to Cape Nov. 1845 till Dec. 1847. Posted Lt. Col. to 9th L.C. 1 Jan. 1849. Leave s.c. 14 Feb. 1849; fur. s.c. Feb. 1850 till 2 Apr. 1852. Transfd. to 7th L.C. 14 Apr. 1852. Leave s.c. to Simla May 1855 till death. Transfd. to 6th L.C. 16 Oct. 1855.

Refs.: Burke's *Landed Gentry*, 13th edn., p. 1169, s.n. Mackenzie, of Glack, co. Aberdeen. *Mackenzie*. *Boase*. *V.B.G. De Rhé-Philipe*. *I.M.* 1 July 1856, p. 378. Will dated 5 Sept. 1855; proved 6 Jan. 1857. M.I. new cemetery, Simla.

MACKENZIE, Kenneth (1787-1811). Lieutenant, 5th N.I. *b.* Todderty, co. Ross, 10 June 1787. Cadet 1804. Arrived in

THE BENGAL ARMY, 1758-1834

India 29 Apr. 1805. Ensign 10 May 1805. Lieut. 11 May 1805. *d. unm.* Java Sept. 1811, of wounds received in action in Aug.

3rd son of George McKenzie, III of Pitlundie and Culbo, and Anne his wife, dau. of Alexander McKenzie, VIII of Davochmoluag.

Services: Posted Lieut. to 5th N.I. in 1806. With escort to Resdt. at Hyderabad in 1810. Capture of Java 1811; Cornelis (s.w.); Lieut. 5th N.I., Asst. Dy. Comy. Gen.

Refs.: Mackenzie. S.M. 1812, p. 78. Will dated 2 Aug. 1811; proved 25 Oct. 1811.

MACKENZIE, Kenneth (1788-1816). Lieutenant, Engineers. *bapt.* St. Giles-in-the-Fields, London, 13 May 1788. Cadet 1804. Arrived in India 12 Sept. 1805. Ensign 10 Sept. 1805. Lieut. 15 Nov. 1807. *d.* I.W. 28 Sept. 1816.

Son of Kenneth Mackenzie and Mary his wife. Brother of Frederick Mackenzie, *q.v.*

Woolwich Cadet; nominated for R.M.A. 16 Nov. 1803; obtained his certificate 6 Jan. 1805.

Services: Stationed at Allahabad 1807; at Cuttack 1808-11. Capture of Java 1811. Fur. from Java 1815 till death.

MACKENZIE, Kenneth Francis (1801-1856). Bt. Colonel, 64th N.I. *b.* Rosskeen, co. Ross, 18 Sept. 1801. Cadet 1819. Arrived in India 11 Dec. 1820. Ensign 8 July 1820. Lieut. 11 July 1823. Capt. 10 May 1834. Major 24 Apr. 1842. Lt. Col. 26 Oct. 1848. Bt. Col. 28 Nov. 1854. *d.* at sea 14 Jan. 1856, on board the *Hindostan*, in the Red Sea.

Of Chanory, co. Ross. 4th son of John Mackenzie, VI of Kincraig, and Mary his wife. Brother of Roderick Mackenzie, *q.v.*, and nephew of Lt.-Gen. Colin Mackenzie. *m.* Edinburgh 6 Jan. 1832, Margaret, 2nd dau. of Rev. Thomas Taylor, D.D., of Tibbermore. (She died 1893, aged 89.) His dau. *m.* Charles Brown-Constable, *q.v.* Ed. Aberdeen Coll.

Services: Posted Ensign to 1/25th N.I. Operations in Jodhpur 1823; capture of Lamba; Lieut. 1/25th N.I. Transfd. as Lieut. to newly-formed 32nd N.I. July 1823, but continued to d.d. with 1/25th N.I. for some months. Transfd. to 64th N.I. (late 2/32nd) May 1824. Fur. s.c. 21 Jan. 1829 till 11 June 1832. Comdd. C.-in-C.'s escort 15 Dec. 1838 till 14 Jan. 1839. First Afghan War 1842; retreat from Ali Masjid to Jamrud in Jan.; Pollock's advance on Kabul; in comd. of garr. at Ali Masjid in Nov. 1842; Major 64th N.I. (Medal). Operations against Hill tribes in Sind

1845 ; Major 64th N.I. Fur. 1846-8. Posted Lt. Col. to 18th N.I. in 1848. Second Sikh War; in garr. at Lahore; Lt. Col. 18th N.I. (Medal). Transfd. to 52nd N.I. Dec. 1849 ; to 22nd, 39th, 45th, 55th, 44th, 22nd ; to 35th N.I. Jan. 1855 ; to 64th N.I. Dec. 1855. Fur. s.c. 3 yrs. Nov. 1855.

Refs.: Mackenzie, *s.n.* Redcastle and Kincraig.

MACKENZIE, Murray (1812-1857). Bt. Lieut. Colonel, Artillery. (623) *b.* Finchley, Middlesex, 29 July 1812. Cadet 1828. Arrived in India 23 May 1829. 2nd Lieut. 12 Dec. 1828. Lieut. 11 Oct. 1837. Capt. 29 Dec. 1846. Bt. Major 30 Dec. 1846. Bt. Lt. Col. 20 June 1854. *d.* Simla 5 Oct. 1857, of wounds received at the siege of Delhi on 2 July.

Son of Andrew John Mackenzie, of Walthamstow, merchant, and Helen his wife. *m.* Agra 27 Nov. 1847, Emily Gershoma, youngest dau. of Archibald Watson, *q.v.* (*See also* Robert Guthrie MacGregor.) Addiscombe Cadet 1827-8.

Services : Posted to 3rd Coy. 2nd Bn. Foot Art. 14 Mar. 1833. Transfd. to 2nd Troop 1st Bde. H.A. 6 Sept. 1833 ; to 4th Troop 3rd Bde. 15 Feb. 1836. First Afghan War 1838-40 ; Bamian (*Lond. Gaz.* 9 Jan. 1841) ; Lieut. 4th Troop 3rd Bde. Fur. 1 Apr. 1841 till Jan. 1844. Transfd. to 4th Troop 2nd Bde., and apptd. Adjt. & Qmr. Nimach Div. Art. Feb. 1844. Transfd. to 1st Bde. H.A. and apptd. Adjt. & Qmr., and Adjt. Sirhind Div. Art., 24 July 1845. Apptd. Bde. Major of Art. in the field Dec. 1845. First Sikh War ; Mudki ; Ferozshahr (w.) ; Sobraon (Medal with 2 clasps). Adjt. & Qmr. 1st Bde. H.A. till Jan. 1847. Posted to 2nd Coy. 6th Bn. Jan. 1847, and to comd. new No. 9 Light Field Battery. To comd. 4th Troop 1st Bde. H.A. Jan. 1848. Second Sikh War ; both sieges of Multan ; Gujerat ; Capt. comdg. 4th Troop 1st Bde. (Medal with 2 clasps). Leave s.c. to Simla May 1854 till Nov. 1855. To comd. Meerut Bde. Art. Oct. 1856. Mutiny campaign ; action on Hindan R. 30 and 31 May 1857 ; Badli-ki-Serai. To comd. H.A. of Delhi F.F. 28 June 1857. Siege of Delhi (s.w. 2 July 1857) ; comdg. Art. of Bdr. Wilson's force.

Refs.: De Rhé-Philipe. *G.M.* 1858, i. 336. Will dated 2 May 1855 ; proved 4 June 1858. M.I. in new cemetery, Simla.

MACKENZIE, Robert (1743-1809). Lieut. Colonel. Infantry. *b.* 1743. Country Cadet 1767. Admitted 21 Nov. 1767. Ensign 8 Dec. 1767. Lieut. 16 Oct. 1769. Capt. 24 Mar. 1778. Major 21 Feb. 1782. Lt. Col. 1 Mar. 1794. Retired 25 Nov. 1798. *d.* Milnmount, co. Ross, 26 Apr. 1809.

THE BENGAL ARMY, 1758-1834

Of Milnmount. 2nd son of Alexander Mackenzie, of Ardloch, and Margaret his wife, dau. of Robert Sutherland, of Langwell, Caithness. *m.* 1st, Edinburgh 1 May 1780, Harriot Anne, 2nd dau. of Dr. Alexander Mackenzie, of Bayfield, physician in Ross. *m.* 2nd, 15 Aug. 1801, Katharine, dau. of Lt.-Col. James Sutherland, of Uppat. Father of Sir Alexander Mackenzie, 6th Bart., of Tarbat, *q.v.*

Services: Posted to Cav. 7 Aug. 1778. Fur. 15 Nov. 1778 till 17 May 1783. Major 30th Bn. Sepoys in July 1787; 3rd Bde. N.I. in 1792. Apptd. 2nd in comd. of 2nd Bde. of Army on service in Rohilkhand 17 Oct. 1794.

Refs.: Burke's *Peerage*, 1923, p. 1472, *s.n.* Mackenzie, Bart., of Scatwell, co. Ross. *G.E.C. Complete Baronetage*, Appendix, p. 80. *Mackenzie, s.n.* Ardloch. *S.M.* 1780, p. 279; 1801, p. 587; 1809, p. 399.

MACKENZIE, Roderick (1788-1863). Major. 15th N.I. *b.* Kincraig, co. Ross, 28 Feb. 1788. Cadet 1805. Arrived in India 19 Sept. 1806. Ensign 20 Sept. 1806. Lieut. 16 Aug. 1808. Capt. 22 Aug. 1821. Major 3 May 1832. Retired 26 Feb. 1835. *d.* Kincraig 6 Apr. 1863.

VII of Kincraig. Eldest son of John Mackenzie, VI of Kincraig, Capt. 73rd (? 71st) Regt., and Mary his wife. Brother of Hugh Mackenzie, *q.v. m.* Dingwall May 1836, Katherine, dau. of Alexander Mackenzie, of Burton Cresc., and grand-dau. of Hector Mackenzie, bailie of Dingwall.

Services: Capt. Ross-shire Mil. Posted Ensign to 11th N.I. in 1807. Reduction of Kalinjar 1812; Lieut. 11th N.I. Adjt. 1/11th N.I. 1 July 1814 till 7 Sept. 1821. Capt. 1/11th N.I. Transfd. to 15th N.I. (late 1/11th) May 1824. Fur. s.c. 19 June 1824 till 29 Nov. 1827; p.a. 10 Mar. 1828 till 8 Mar. 1831. Tempy. Bde. Major at Mhow 26 Dec. 1833.

Refs.: Mackenzie, s.n. Redcastle and Kincraig. *S. N. & Q.* 3S. vi. 44. *A.J.* N.S. xx. 131.

MACKENZIE, William Boyd (1788-1809). Cadet, Infantry. *b.* Edinburgh 22 Dec. 1788. Cadet 1808. Never arrived in India. *d.* at sea 18 Nov. 1809: kld. on board the *Windham*, in action with the French frigate *La Manche*.

Son of John Mackenzie, of Richmond Pl., Edinburgh, and Jean Thomson his wife.

MACKENZIE, William Gordon (1785-1842). Lieut. Colonel. 24th N.I. *b.* Edinburgh 9 May 1785. Cadet 1801. Arrived in India 6 July 1802. Ensign 15 July 1802. Lieut. 25 Aug. 1804. Capt. 1 Aug. 1818. Major 25 Apr. 1826. Lt. Col. 23 May 1831. Retired 19 Sept. 1840. *d.* 20 July 1842.

bapt. Edinburgh 21 Aug. 1786. Son of Henry Mackenzie, atty. in the Exchequer, miscellaneous writer (*D.N.B.*), and Penuel his wife, dau. of Sir Lodovick Grant, Bart. Brother of Rt. Hon. Holt Mackenzie, sometime B.C.S. *m.* (before 1828) Sarah.

Services : Fur. s.c. 24 Apr. 1803 till 19 June 1806. Present at capture of the Cape in Jan. 1806. Posted Lieut. to 2/2nd N.I. in 1805. Leave s.c. 6 mos. to sea 6 Mar. 1809. At Amboyna in 1810; 3rd Asst. to Resdt. at Amboyna 1812-17; 2nd Asst. to Resdt. at Fort Marlbro' 10 Oct. 1817. Capt. Lt. 2/2nd N.I. 30 May 1816. Transfd. to 5th N.I. May 1824. Resdt. at Malacca 22 Aug. 1825. Agent for army clothing 2nd Div. 23 Feb. 1827; P.A., S.W. frontier, and comd. Ramgarh Local Bn. 10 Mar. 1828. Leave s.c. to Cape 15 Apr. 1830 till 19 Mar. 1832. Posted Lt. Col. to 59th N.I. in 1831; to 31st N.I. 7 Jan. 1832. Fur. s.c. to Cape and Europe 14 Jan. 1833 till 19 Dec. 1835; s.c. 2 yrs. to Cape 14 Apr. 1836; p.a. Cape and Europe 23 June 1839 till retirement. Transfd. from 32nd to 15th N.I. 9 June 1835; to 6th N.I. 29 Nov. 1836; to 36th N.I. 30 May 1838; to 24th N.I. in 1840.

McKERRELL, Robert (1787-1812). Lieutenant, Bengal Eur. Regt. *b.* Paisley 7 Nov. 1787. Cadet 1803. Arrived in India 17 Mar. 1805. Ensign 7 May 1805. Lieut. 8 May 1805. *d.* Banda 9 Mar. 1812.

bapt. Abbey of Paisley 15 Nov. 1787. 2nd son of William McKerrell, of Hillhouse, 9th Laird, and Ann his 2nd wife, dau. of Robert Govane, of Anderstone, co. Lanark. Nephew by marriage of Moses Crawford, *q.v.*, and of John Reid, *q.v.*, and cousin-german of John Fulton (1807-1887), *q.v.*

Services : Posted Lieut. to Bengal Eur. Regt. in 1806, and served throughout with that Regt. At Amboyna in 1801-11; at Banda in 1812.

Refs. : Burke's *Landed Gentry*, 13th edn., p. 1174, *s.n.* McKerrell, late of Hillhouse, co. Ayr.

MACKESON, Frederick (1807-1853). Captain and Bt. Lieut. Colonel, C.B., 14th N.I. Comr. at Peshawar. *b.* Woodbridge 2 Sept. 1807. Cadet 1825. Arrived in India 10 Aug. 1826. Ensign 4 Dec. 1825. Lieut. 22 July 1828. Capt. 24 Jan. 1845. Bt. Lt. Col. 7 June 1849. *d.* Peshawar 14 Sept. 1853, of wounds inflicted by a *ghazi* on 10 Sept.

THE BENGAL ARMY, 1758-1834

bapt. Hythe, Kent, 24 Sept. 1807. Son of William Mackeson, of Woodbridge, and Harriet his wife. Ed. King's School, Canterbury.

Services : See *D.N.B.* Posted Ensign to 14th N.I. May 1826. British Agent for navigation of Indus, in Pol. Dept., 16 Jan. 1835 till 1837. Accompanied the Mission of Sir Alexander Burnes to Kabul 1837-Mar. 1838. First Afghan War 1839, 1841-2 ; in Pol. Dept. (Medal). P.A. at Peshawar 1 Sept. 1839. Offg. Supt. of Bhatiana, and Asst. to A.G.G. Rajputana 21 Nov. 1843 till Jan. 1846. First Sikh War ; Aliwal ; Pol. Ofr. with Sir Harry Smith's Div. (Medal). Supt. Cis-Sutlej territories 16 Mar. 1846. Second Sikh War ; Chilianwala ; Gujerat ; pursuit of Sikhs to Peshawar ; as A.G.G. at H.Q. (Medal with 2 clasps). Fur. Apr. 1850 (took home with him the Koh-i-noor diamond for presentation to the Queen) till 3 Nov. 1851. Comr. and Supt. of Peshawar 20 Dec. 1851 till death. Operations on N.W.F. ; against Ranizais Mar. 1852, as Pol. Ofr. ; against Utman Khel May 1852, as Civil and Pol. Ofr. ; comdd. expedn. against Hassanzais of Black Mountain Dec. 1852 and Jan. 1853 ; and against Hindustani Fanatics Jan. 1853. C.B. 24 Dec. 1842. Durani 3cl.

Refs. : *D.N.B.* Boase. *D.I.B.* De Rhé-Philipe. *G.M.* 1854, i. 200. *I.M.* 1853, p. 688. Will dated 13 Sept. 1853 ; admon. 10 Jan. 1854. Memorial at Peshawar and in Canterbury cathedral (*I.L.N.* 12 July 1856).

MACKIE, William (1782-1846). Major. 59th N.I. *b.* 14 Apr. 1782. Cadet 1800. Arrived in India 22 Aug. 1801. Ensign 7 Dec. 1801. Lieut. 30 Sept. 1803. Capt. 1 Jan. 1819. Major 15 Dec. 1824. Retired 3 Apr. 1826. *d.* 25 June 1848.

bapt. Balmaclellan, co. Kirkcudbright, 15 Apr. 1782. Elder son of Rev. Nathaniel Mackie (M'Kie), minister of Balmaclellan 1780-90, and Mary his wife, elder dau. of Alexander Gordon, of Carleton.

Services : Ensign d.d. 18th N.I. in 1802. Operations in Jumna Doab 1803 ; Sasni ; Ensign 8th N.I. Transfd. as Lieut. to 11th N.I. Jan. 1804 ; retransfd. to 8th N.I. Sept. 1804. Second Mahratta War ; Lieut. 8th N.I. Transfd. to newly-raised 2/30th N.I. in 1815 ; to 59th N.I. (late 1/30th) May 1824. Fur. 1824 till retirement.

Refs. : Scott's *Fasti,* ii. 390.

MACKINLAY, James Houston (1790-1856). Colonel. 68th N.I. *b.* Greenock 10 May 1790. Cadet 1808. Admitted 19 July

1809. Ensign 8 Jan. 1810. Lieut. 12 July 1814. Capt. 12 Dec. 1825. Major 14 Oct. 1841. Lt. Col. 10 Dec. 1847. Retired 10 Oct. 1849. Hon. Col. 28 Nov. 1854. *d.* Edinburgh 25 Mar. 1856.

Son of Alexander Mackinlay, landwaiter, and Elizabeth Campbell his wife.

Services : Barasat C.C. 6 mos. Posted Ensign to 7th N.I. in 1810. ˙ (? Reduction of Kalinjar 1812 ; Ensign 1/7th N.I.) Nepal War 1814-15 ; Lieut. 1/7th N.I., in 2nd Div. (India medal). Adjt. 1/7th N.I. 4 May 1815 till July 1823. Third Mahratta War 1817-19 ; Lieut. 1/7th N.I. Bk. Mr. 8th (Rohilkhand) Div. 1822-3. Transfd. to 1/32nd N.I. July 1823. Adjt. 1/32nd N.I. 1 Oct. 1823 till 17 Jan. 1826. Transfd. to 63rd N.I. (late 1/32nd) May 1824. Siege and capture of Bhurtpore ; comdg. C.-in-C.'s escort (clasp to India medal). Apptd. D.A.A.G. on the Est. 27 Feb. 1826 ; posted to Presdy. Div. 22 Mar. 1826 ; Cawnpore 30 Aug. 1826. Dy. Postmr. Cawnpore 1 Nov. 1826. A.A.G. Cawnpore Div. 29 Dec. 1829 ; transfd. to Meerut 3 Dec. 1834 ; removed from the Staff 18 Mar. 1835 for remonstrating against this transfer, but permitted to retain civil office of Dy. Postmr. at Cawnpore 18 May 1835 till Jan. 1840. Fur. p.a. 11 Jan. 1840 till 14 Feb. 1843. Offg. as M.M.B. at Calcutta 1845-6. Fur. s.c. 10 Apr. 1847 till retirement. ˙ Posted Lt. Col. to 74th N.I. 24 Apr. 1848 ; transfd. to 13th N.I. and to 68th N.I. in 1848.

Refs. : *A.J.* N.S. xvii. 239. *I.M.* 3 Apr. 1856, p. 188. Will dated Calcutta 7 Apr. 1847 ; codicil dated 21 Mar. 1854 ; admon. 6 Dec. 1860.

MACKINNON, Alexander (1788-1849). Captain. 42nd N.I. *b.* Strath, Inverness, 20 Mar. 1788. Cadet 1808. Arrived in India 6 Nov. 1809. Ensign 21 Nov. 1809. Lieut. 16 Dec. 1814. Capt. 7 Oct. 1824. Retired 6 July 1838. *d.* Edinburgh 17 Apr. 1849, as the result of an accident.

4th and youngest son of John Mackinnon, VI of Kyle, Skye, and Jane his wife, dau. of Capt. John MacDonald of Kyles, Kirkibost, N. Uist.

Services : Posted Ensign to 21st N.I. in 1810. Nepal War 1816 ; Harriharpur ; Lieut. 2/21st N.I. Intr. & Qmr. 1/21st N.I. 12 June 1818 till 12 June 1823. Actg. Adjt. and Paymr. of Invalids at Allahabad 1821-3. Apptd. 2nd Ofr. in a *ressalah* of Nagpur Auxy. Horse 7 June 1823 till Sept. 1824. Transfd. to 42nd N.I. (late 1/21st) May 1824. First Burma War ; Arakan 1825 ; Capt. 42nd N.I. Transfd. to 39th N.I. 13 May 1825 ; retransfd. to 42nd

THE BENGAL ARMY, 1758-1834

N.I. 1825. Restored to Nagpur Horse on the return of his Regt. from Arakan. Granted a donation of 6 mos. pay on breaking up of the Nagpur Auxy. Force June 1830. Fur. p.a. 15 Jan. 1833 till 8 Feb. 1837. Bt. Major 28 June 1838; cancelled on retirement.
Refs.: Family information. *MacInnes,* p. 214.

MACKINTOSH, Æneas (1784-1864). Lieutenant. 21st N.I. Subsequently a Calcutta merchant. *b.* Raigmore, Inverness, 23 Oct. 1784. Cadet 1800. Arrived in India 17 Sept. 1801. Ensign 17 Dec. 1801. Lieut. 30 Sept. 1803. Resigned 24 Nov. 1803. *d. unm.* at his residence, 17 Montagu Sq., London, 27 Feb. 1864; *bur.* Kensal Green 5 Mar. 1864.

4th and youngest son of Æneas Mackintosh, of Raigmore, Lieut. in the army, and Ann his wife, dau. of Lachlan McPherson, of Strathnoon.
Services: Posted Ensign to Bengal Eur. Regt.; transfd. as Lieut. to newly-raised 21st N.I. in 1803. No record of active service. Joined the firm of Mackintosh, Fulton & McClintock, Calcutta merchants, of which his eldest brother Lachlan was head.
Refs.: Family information. *The Mackintoshes and Clan Chattan,* by A. M. Mackintosh (Edin., 1903), p. 368. *The Times,* 2 Mar. 1864.

MACKINTOSH, Æneas (1790-1832). Lieutenant, Invalid Est. 14th N.I. *b.* Inverness 14 Oct. 1790. Cadet 1809. Ensign 20 Aug. 1811. Lieut. 16 Dec. 1814. Invalided 26 Aug. 1820. *d.* Monghyr 19 May 1832.

Son of John Mackintosh, of Dores, co. Inverness, and Isobel McKillican his wife. *m.* 1st, Cawnpore 9 Jan. 1817, Miss Elizabeth Wilson. *m.* 2nd, Calcutta 20 Nov. 1823, Henrietta Louisa, youngest dau. of Charles Child, of Calcutta, merchant. (*See also* Alexander Fraser (1786-1822) and Steele Hawthorne.) *m.* 3rd, Bhagulpur 19 Apr. 1827, Eliza Baithe.
Services: Barasat C.C. Posted Ensign to 14th N.I. in 1811. (? Nepal War 1814-15; Jitgarh; Lieut. 1/14th N.I.) Third Mahratta War; Dhamoni; Mandala; Garhakota; Lieut. 1/14th N.I. Resided at Monghyr 1820 till death.
Refs.: M.I. at Monghyr.

MACKINTOSH, Alexander. Lieutenant. Infantry. Cadet 1770. Ensign 24 Sept. 1770. Lieut. 9 July 1776. Dismissed by C.M. 3 Aug. 1778.[1]
Services: Comdg. 3rd Sqdn., 2nd Regt. Cav. in June 1777.

After dismissal from the Service he appears to have become a mariner and captain of his own ship.

Refs.: *Hickey,* ii. 271.

¹ *Note:* Dismissed for maltreating a native revenue official, "and for a sum of money delivering him into the hands of his enemies who put him to death." (*See also* Ebenezer Nunn.)

MACKINTOSH, Alexander (1809-1853). Captain, 52nd N.I.
b. Kinchyle, co. Nairn, 1 Jan. 1809. Cadet 1826. Ensign 7 Feb. 1827. Lieut. 14 June 1828. Capt. 8 Apr. 1842. *d.* Nimach 20 May 1853.

Son of James Mackintosh, of Kinchyle, gentleman farmer, and Anne Macbean his wife. Brother of William Mackintosh (1803-1841), *q.v. m.* Ninach 21 Aug. 1845, Flora Anna, dau. of Adam Gilmour. Ed. Inverness Acad.

Services: Posted Ensign to 6th Extra Regt. 19 June 1827; transfd. to 52nd N.I. 23 June 1827. Actg. Intr. & Qmr. 52nd N.I. 24 Mar. 1828, 16 Feb. 1830, 24 Sept. 1831; permanent do. 18 Feb. 1832 till 11 Aug. 1842. Asst. to Comr. for States of Rajputana 11 Sept. 1842; Supt. of Jawad Nimach 26 June 1844 till death. Leave s.c. 6 mos. to China 5 June 1852. No record of active service.

Refs.: *I.M.* 19 July 1853, p. 411. Will dated 12 June 1852; proved 19 July 1853. M.I. Nimach.

MACKINTOSH, Henry (1804-1834). Lieutenant, 43rd N.I.
b. Poonamallee, Madras, 27 Sept. 1804. Cadet 1820. Admitted 16 Apr. 1821. Ensign 9 Oct. 1820. Lieut. 11 July 1823. *d. unm.* Akyab, Burma, 3 Apr. 1834, of jungle fever.

3rd son of William Mackintosh, II of Geddes, Surg. Madras Est., and Jessie (Janet) his 1st wife, dau. of Lachlan Mackintosh, of Balnespick. Nephew of Lt.-Col. Alexander Mackintosh, 15th Madras N.I., and cousin-german of William Lachlan Mackintosh, *q.v.* Ed. Edin. High School.

Services: Posted Ensign to 1/2nd N.I. Transfd. as Lieut. to 22nd N.I. July 1823; to 44th N.I. (late 2/22nd) May 1824. Adjt. Left Wing 44th N.I. 22 June 1824. First Burma War; Cachar 1825; Lieut. 44th N.I. Transfd. to 43rd N.I. 13 May 1825; Adjt. do. 12 July 1825 till 12 May 1828. Fur. s.c. 10 Mar. 1828 till 29 Nov. 1830. Junior Asst. to Comr. of Arakan 12 Mar. 1832. Operations against dacoits and marauders from Ava territory 1833-4.

Refs.: Family information. *G.M.* 1835, i. 221. *A.J.* N.S. xv. 172. Will dated 7 Apr. 1830; proved 26 July 1834.

MACKINTOSH, John. Lieutenant. Infantry. Country Cadet 1777. Ensign 24 Sept. 1777. Lieut. 4 Oct. 1778.
Brother of Mrs. Margaret Symmers.
Services: Went out to Bengal as a Sergt. in 1774; given a cadetship by C.D. 31 July 1777, " being a Person of Family who has received a liberal education." N.F.P.
Refs.: Will dated 24 May 1780; proved 6 Mar. 1783. (Exor. and residuary legatee was William Mackintosh (*d.* 1799), *q.v.*)

MACKINTOSH, John (1791-1825). Captain, 49th N.I. *b.* Inverness 23 Sept. 1791. Cadet 1808. Arrived in India 27 Oct. 1809. Ensign 20 Mar. 1810. Lieut. 16 Dec. 1814. Capt. (24 Apr. 1824) 1825. *d.* Arakan 28 Dec. 1825.
bapt. Inverness 12 Oct. 1791. Son of Bailie John Mackintosh, of Inverness, and Catherine Chisholm his wife. Brother of William Mackintosh, of 1 Surrey St., Strand, London. Woolwich Cadet.
Services: Posted Ensign to 25th N.I. in 1810. Siege and capture of Hathras 1817; Lieut. 1/25th N.I. Third Mahratta War 1817-18; Lieut. 1/25th N.I. With 3rd Ceylon Vol. Bn. 1818-19. Adjt. 1/25th N.I. 3 Sept. 1821 till death. Transfd. to 49th N.I. (late 1/25th) May 1824. First Burma War; Arakan 1825; Capt. 49th N.I.

MACKINTOSH, Thomas (1802-1850). Major, 24th N.I. *b.* St. Catherine's, Jamaica, 16 Sept. 1802. Cadet 1823. Arrived in India 10 Oct. 1824. Ensign (?) Lieut. 5 Apr. 1825. Capt. 18 July 1840. Major 12 Sept. 1846. *d.* Gorakhpur, U.P., 6 Oct. 1850.
Brother of Lachlan Mackintosh.
Services: Posted Ensign to 24th N.I. 31 Mar. 1825, and served throughout with that Regt. Operations against the Kols and Chuars 1832-3. Rising in Cuttack 1836. Adjt. 24th N.I. 24 Aug. till 10 Oct. 1836. Insurrection in Bundelkhand 1842-3. First Sikh War; Mudki; Ferozshahr (Medal with clasp). Fur. 1847-8.
Refs.: *I.M.* 3 Dec. 1850, p. 707. Will dated Jubbulpore, 18 Aug. 1842; proved 2 Dec. 1850.

MACKINTOSH, William (*d.* 1799). Lieut. Colonel. 13th N.I. Country Cadet 1769. Admitted 8 Dec. 1769. Ensign 18 June 1770. Lieut. 2 July 1776. Capt. 31 Jan. 1781. Major 1 Mar. 1794. Lt. Col. 30 Oct. 1797. Retired 1 Aug. 1798. *d.* London (*c.* Apr.) 1799.
Brother of Edward Mackintosh.

Services : Siege and capture of Ahmedabad 15 Feb. 1780 (w.); Lieut. 1st Bn. Sepoys. Capt. 4th Bengal Eur. Bn. in July 1787. Fur. 26 Sept. 1788 till 1790. 5th Bengal Eur. Bn. in 1792; apptd. to comd. 10th Bn. Sepoys 18 Mar. 1793. Second Rohilla War; battle of Bitaurah; Capt. comdg. 10th Bn. Fur. 18 Jan. 1797 till retirement.

Refs.: Williams, p. 146. *S.M.* 1799, p. 351. Will dated Osborn's Hotel, Adelphi, 25 Apr. 1798; proved 3 May 1799.

MACKINTOSH, William (1803-1841). Captain, 5th N.I. *b.* Dores, co. Inverness, 25 Nov. 1803. Cadet 1819. Admitted 14 June 1820. Ensign 10 Jan. 1820. Lieut. 17 May 1822. Capt. 25 Dec. 1834. *d.* 23 Nov. 1841 : kld. in action nr. Kabul.

Son of James Mackintosh, farmer in Kinchyle, and Anne McBean his wife. Brother of Alexander Mackintosh and cousin-german of Henry Mackintosh, *qq.v.* Ed. Inverness R. Acad.

Services : Posted Ensign to 1/19th N.I. in 1820; transfd. to 2nd N.I. 11 July 1823; to 5th N.I. (late 1/2nd) May 1824. To take charge of 7th Coy. Pioneers 4 Nov. 1824. Adjt. 5th N.I. 25 Aug. 1826 till 9 Feb. 1835. Fur. s.c. 20 Jan 1837 till 27 July 1839. Actg. tempy. Bde. Major at Ferozepore 28 Oct. 1840. First Afghan War 1840-1; actg. Bde. Major 3rd Inf. Bde. till 22 Oct. 1841; outbreak at Kabul; kld. in 2nd expedn. against village of Bemaru, nr. Kabul.

Refs.: M.I. in St. Peter's, Fort William, Bengal.

MACKINTOSH, William Lachlan (1814-1844). Lieutenant, 43rd N.I. *b.* Kincraig 8 Sept. 1814. Cadet 1833. Arrived in India 11 Aug. 1834. Ensign 12 Oct. 1834. Lieut. 3 Oct. 1840. *d. unm.* Alipore, Calcutta, 8 Sept. 1844.

4th son of William Mackintosh, of Balnespick, co. Inverness, and Emilia Colina his wife, dau. of Dr. William Chisholm, provost of Inverness. Cousin-german of Henry Mackintosh and Francis Sherriff, *qq.v.*

Services : Ensign d.d. 43rd N.I. 20 Aug. 1834; posted to 43rd N.I. 2 Mar. 1835. A.D.C. on personal staff of Lord Auckland, the G.G., 16 Oct. 1837 till 18 Jan. 1840. First Afghan War 1839; Ghazni; Ensign 43rd N.I. (Medal). Asst. to P.A. in Upper Sind 18 Jan. 1840. A.D.C. to Lord Auckland 20 May 1840. Fort Adjt. at Ft. Wm., and Supt. of Gentlemen Cadets, 8 Feb. 1843; Supt. of Mysore Princes 17 Mar. 1844 till death.

Refs.: Burke's *Landed Gentry*, 13th edn., p. 1176, *s.n.* Mackintosh. M.I. in Circular Rd. cemetery, Calcutta.

THE BENGAL ARMY, 1758-1834

MACKLECAN, John. (*See* **MACKELCAN.**)

MACKLETON, John. (*See* **MACKELCAN.**)

MACKLEWAINE, Ezekiel. Major. Artillery. (76) Cadet 1765. Fireworker 20 June 1766. 2nd Lieut. 8 July 1769. Lieut. 6 Mar. 1770. Capt. Lt. 10 Jan. 1773. Capt. 16 June 1774. Major 20 Feb. 1782. Resigned 26 Jan. 1784.
Services: Apptd. Lieut. Fireworker in England, to be employed under the Engrs., 28 Dec. 1764; sailed in the *Falmouth* 10 May 1765; wrecked on Saugor Bank 13 June 1766. First Mahratta War 1781; capture of Sipri fort in Jan.; action at Mahatpur.

McLACHLAN, Lachlan (William) (1790-1813). Ensign, 17th N.I. *b.* Dunoon, co. Argyll, 25 Jan. 1790. Cadet 1807. Arrived in India 21 Mar. 1809. Ensign 16 Feb. 1809. *d.* Saharanpur, U.P., 31 Aug. 1813.
bapt. Dunoon 30 Jan. 1790. Son of James McLachlan, of Stronchullin, tacksman, and Violet Campbell his wife. Cousin of Alexander Livingstone Campbell, *q.v.*
Services: Posted Ensign to 17th N.I. and served throughout with that Regt. No record of active service. Ensign 1/17th N.I.

MACLAREN, James (1793-1846). Lieut. Colonel, C.B., 16th N.I. *b.* Nairn 23 May 1793. Cadet 1808. Arrived in India 27 Oct. 1809. Ensign 25 Aug. 1810. Lieut. 16 Dec. 1814. Capt. 9 Aug. 1824. Major 3 May 1833. Lt. Col. 28 Nov. 1839. *d. unm.* Ferozepore 26 Feb. 1846, of wounds received at the battle of Sobraon on 10 Feb.
bapt. Nairn 31 May 1793. Son of Thomas Maclaren and Susannah Stewart his wife. Brother of Major Alexander Maclaren.
Services: Barasat C.C. till July 1810. Ensign d.d. Bengal Eur. Regt. Posted to 2/10th N.I. 21 Oct. 1810. Operations in Rewah 1813-14; Ensign 2/10th N.I. Posted to 4th Gren. Bn. 1815; actg. Adjt. do. 1815. Nepal War 1816; with 4th Gren. Bn. Third Mahratta War; Chanda; Lieut. 2/10th N.I. Adjt. 1/10th N.I. 20 Nov. 1818 till May 1824. First Burma War; Cachar 1824; Dudhpatli; Lieut. 1/10th N.I., and Staff Ofr. to Col. Bowen's detachment. Transfd. to 16th N.I. (late 2/10th) May 1824. Adjt. 16th N.I. 17 June 1824 till 7 Apr. 1825. First Afghan War 1838-42; Kandahar; capture of Ghazni 1839 (Medal); operations in Ghilzai country; comdd. fortress of Ghazni for 2 yrs. till June 1841; with Kandahar force under Nott; relief of Kalat-i-

Ghilzai; Goaine; recapture of Ghazni; reoccupation of Kabul; Lt. Col. comdg. 16th N.I. (Medal). Gwalior campaign; Maharajpur (w.); Lt. Col. comdg. 16th N.I. (Bronze star). Apptd. Bdr. comdg. 3rd Bde. 30 Dec. 1843 till Jan. 1844. First Sikh War; Mudki; Ferozshahr; Sobraon (s.w.—leg amputated); Bdr. comdg. 4th Bde. C.B. 24 Dec. 1842. Durani, 3 cl., 14 Dec. 1843. (Intimation was received after his death that he had been apptd. A.D.C. to the Queen, with the rank of Col. in the Army.)

Refs.: *De Rhé-Philipe.* Will dated 20 Dec. 1845; proved 12 May 1846.

McLARKIN, Thomas (*d.* 1791). Lieutenant, 7th Bn. Sepoys. Cadet 1772. Ensign 11 July 1776. Lieut. 1 July 1778. *d.* Rayakota, Madras, 12 Nov. 1791.

Services: First Rohilla War; battle of St. George; Cadet in the Select Picket. Lieut. 7th Bn. Sepoys in July 1787. Third Mysore War; battle of Arikera; storm of Penagra; assault of Krishnagiri; Lieut. 7th Bn.

MACLARY, William. (*See* **MacCLARY, William.**)

*McLAUGHLIN, William (1787-?). Cadet. Infantry. *b.* Templemore 1 Apr. 1787. Cadet 1809.

Son of Daniel McLaughlin, merchant. Brother of Daniel McLaughlin, and nephew of Mr. Hunter, of co. Londonderry. Ed. Mr. Knox's Free School, Londonderry.

Services: Lieut. Mil. of Foot, co. Londonderry, 4 Apr. 1809. Not traced later; *probably* never proceeded to India.

MACLEAN, Alexander (*d.* 1772). Lieutenant, Infantry. Cadet 1769. Ensign 9 Mar. 1769. Lieut. 16 Sept. 1770. *d.* Chittagong 25 Sept. 1772.

Services: N.F.P.

MACLEAN, Alexander Macdonald Lockhart (1804-1840). Captain, 67th N.I. *b.* Berwick 1 Sept. 1804. Cadet 1820. Arrived in India May 1821. Ensign 16 Jan. 1821. Lieut. 11 July 1823. Capt. 25 Feb. 1833. *d.* in the Punjab 9 Nov. 1840.

bapt. Low Meeting House, Berwick, 20 Sept. 1804. Son of Lachlan Maclean (of the Grishipoll, Coll, co. Argyll family), Lt. Col. in H.M. Barrack Dept., and Hannah Barbara Cottnam his wife. *m.* Louisa Maria. (She died Kyaukpyu, Arakan, 15 Dec. 1837, aged 23.)

THE BENGAL ARMY, 1758-1834

Services: Posted Ensign to 2/5th N.I. in 1821; transfd. as Lieut. to 34th N.I. July 1823; to 67th N.I. (late 1/34th) May 1824. First Burma War; Arakan 1825; Lieut. 67th N.I. Actg. Intr. & Qmr. 67th N.I. 3 Jan. 1827. Fur. s.c. 15 Apr. 1831 till 13 Sept. 1834. In charge of office of Executive Engr., Arakan, 1 Apr. till 31 July 1837. Comdg. his Regt. at Kyaukpyu in Apr. 1838; to comd. Recruit Bn. at Meerut Sept. 1838; do. at Aligarh Feb. 1839.
Refs.: *A.J.* N.S. xvii. 241.

MACLEAN, Daniel (*d.* 1812). Major. Artillery. (239) Lieut. (from the Bencoolen Est.[1]) 25 Nov. 1790. Capt. Lt. 8 Jan. 1798. Capt. 10 Mar. 1803. Major 30 Sept. 1808. Retired 15 Sept. 1809. *d.* Largs, co. Ayr, 11 Sept. 1812.
Services: Comdt. at Bencoolen 1805-7. Fur. May 1807 till retirement.
Refs.: *S.M.* 1813, p. 80.
[1] *Note:* Was a Lieut. of Art. on the Bencoolen Est. in Nov. 1786.

MACLEAN, George (1802-1833). Lieutenant. Artillery. (485) *b.* St. Mary's, Newington, Surrey, 9 May 1802. Cadet 1818. Admitted 13 Nov. 1819. 2nd Lieut. 12 Apr. 1819. Lieut. 9 Oct. 1820. Retired 28 May 1831. *d.* Pembroke House, Hackney, 25 July 1833.
bapt. 28 June 1802. Son of David Maclean, of Clapham, and Sally his wife. Addiscombe Cadet 1817-19.
Services: Served with 4th Troop H.A. 1823-5. Siege and capture of Bhurtpore; Lieut. 4th Troop 3rd Bde., from 4th Troop 1st Bde. Transfd. to 3rd Troop 3rd Bde. in 1829. Fur. s.c. 15 Jan. 1829 till retirement. Placed on the retired list with an allowance of £100 *p.a.* with effect from 28 May 1831 (*M.C.* 28 Dec. 1832).

MACLEAN, James (1760/61-1792). Lieutenant, 19th Bn. Sepoys. *b.* London 1760/61. Cadet 1778. Arrived in India 2 Oct. 1778. Ensign Oct. 1778. Lieut. 21 Nov. 1778. *d.* Monghyr Mar. 1792.
Services: Sailed for India in the *Nassau* 7 Mar. 1778, aged 17. Lieut. 19th Bn. Sepoy in July 1787.

MACLEAN, James (*d.* 1811). Lieut. Colonel, 11th N.I. Cadet 1782. Ensign 29 Apr. 1783. Lieut. 22 Mar. 1790. Capt. 7 Jan. 1796. Major 21 Oct. 1801. Lt. Col. 10 May 1804. *d.* at sea 3 July 1811, on board the *Castle Eden,* on his passage to India.

Son of James Maclean, of the Criel St. coffee house, Strand, London. Brother of Allan, Hector, and Alexander.
Services: Posted to 3rd Bengal Eur. Regt. 28 Feb. 1783; to 2nd do. 5 Feb. 1790. Comdd. 2nd Bengal Vol. Bn. 1801-2; posted to newly-formed Marine Regt. June 1802. Posted Lt. Col. to newly-raised 27th N.I. in 1804; transfd. to 11th N.I. in 1805. Fur. 21 Sept. 1806 till death.
Refs.: Will dated Berhampore, 1 Jan. 1802; proved 20 Aug. 1811.

MACLEAN, James (1802-1843). Captain, Invalid Est. 11th N.I. *b.* Sudbury, Suffolk, 5 Sept. 1802. Cadet 1820. Admitted 5 June 1821. Ensign 16 Jan. 1821. Lieut. 11 July 1823. Capt. 30 July 1839. Invalided 16 Dec. 1839. *d.* Allahabad 16 June 1843.
bapt. St. Gregory's, Sudbury, 22 Jan. 1803. Son of Lachlan Maclean, M.D., of Sudbury, and Mary his wife, youngest dau. of James Young, of Clare, Suffolk. Sandhurst Cadet.
Services: Posted Ensign to 2/2nd N.I. Transfd. as Lieut. to 5th N.I. July 1823, but remained for some months with 2/2nd N.I. on Sylhet and Cachar borders. Transfd. to 11th N.I. (late 1/5th) May 1824. First Burma War; Arakan 1825; attached to 2nd L.I. Bn. till 28 Mar., when he rejoined 11th N.I. Siege and capture of Bhurtpore; Lieut. 11th N.I. Leave s.c. 6 mos. to Mauritius 21 Apr. 1828. Fur. s.c. 13 Jan. 1832 till 19 Sept. 1834.
Refs.: *I.M.* 10 Oct. 1843, p. 145.

MACLEAN, James Charles (1801-1830.) Lieutenant, 17th N.I. *b.* Humbie, co. Haddington, 25 June 1801. Cadet 1817. Ensign (?) Lieut. 27 Oct. 1819. *d.* Calcutta 27 Oct. 1830.
6th son of Alexander Maclean, of Ardgour, 13th Laird, Col. of the Argyllshire Mil., D.L., and Lady Margaret Hope his wife, dau. of John, 2nd Earl of Hopetoun. *m.* Bareilly 9 Apr. 1823, Jane, dau. of Thomas Hall, *q.v.* (*See also* J. H. Hampton.) Ed. Harrow 1812-16. Addiscombe Cadet 1817-18.
Services: Ensign d.d. Cawnpore Levy 1819. Posted Lieut. to 2/11th N.I. Transfd. to 17th N.I. (late 2/11th) May 1824. Adjt. 2nd (Gardner's) Local Horse 1824-5. First Burma War; Arakan 1825; Lieut. 2nd Local Horse. Bk.Mr. at Fort William 1826 till death.
Refs.: Burke's *Landed Gentry*, 13th edn., p. 1180, *s.n:* Maclean, of Ardgour, co. Argyll. *Clan Maclean,* p. 273. *Harrow School Register.* M.I. Bhowanipore cemetery, Calcutta.

THE BENGAL ARMY, 1758-1834

MACLEAN, John. Lieutenant, Pension Est. Artillery. (178) Country Cadet 1778. Fireworker 4 Oct. 1778. Lieut. 5 July 1782. Resigned on pension 24 Aug. 1785 (? 1786).
m. Edinburgh 28 May 1789, Frances, dau. of Colin M'Donald, of Boisdale.
Services : Apptd. Cadet from Condr. of Ord. 11 Aug. 1778. First Mahratta War ; joined the force in Mar. 1781 (thrice w.). Arrived in England 18 Aug. 1788, and pensioned on Lord Clive's fund from 3 Sept. 1788.

MACLEAN, Lachlan (1729/30-?). Captain. 2nd N.I. *b.* Coll, co. Argyll, 1729/30. Lieut. (Madras) 11 Nov. 1757. Capt. (Bengal) Apr. 1759. Resigned Jan. 1766. *d.* Coll, after 1790.
Elder son of Roderick Maclean, of Coll. 2nd cousin of ' Secretary ' Lachlan Maclean(e), *q.v. m.* 1st, Florence, elder dau. of his uncle, Rev. Hector Maclean, minister of Coll 1733-1775. *m.* 2nd (before 1781), Isabel, dau. of Alexander Maclean, of Sollose.
Services : Transfd. from Madras Eur. Bn. to Bengal Est. in 1758. Expedn. to N. Circars 1758 ; storm of Masulipatam 8 Apr. 1759 ; promoted Capt. for his gallantry in the assault. Went home in 1759 ; returned to India in the *Chesterfield* 1761, aged 31, as the senior Lieut. on the Bengal Est. and to succeed to the first vacant Coy. after his arrival. Campaign against the Nawabs of Bengal and Oudh 1764 ; battle of Patna ; Capt. comdg. 2nd N.I. (Burdwan Bn.).[1] Was removed from his comd. in consequence of a representation from the Native Ofrs.
Refs. : Clan *Maclean,* p. 319. Scott's *Fasti,* iv. 108. *Wilson,* i. 483. *Williams,* p. 74.
[1] Note : Raised by him at Burdwan in 1762 as 8th Bn., became 2nd Bn. in 1764.

MACLEAN, Roderick Norman (1808-1844). Captain, 2nd N.I. *b.* N. Uist 2 July 1808. Cadet 1825. Arrived in India 6 Dec. 1826. Ensign 12 July 1826. Lieut. 28 May 1829. Capt. 26 Dec. 1841. *d.* at sea 8 Nov. 1844, on board the *Enterprise* off Cape Cormorin.
Son of John Maclean, of Borreray and Drimmin, and Jessie his wife, youngest dau. of Donald MacLeod, of Bernara. His sister *m.* Duncan Macpherson (1778-1853), *q.v. m.* Calcutta 20 June 1844, Flora Anne, elder dau. of Sir Walter Raleigh Gilbert, Bart., G.C.B., *q.v.* (She *re-m.* 8 Feb. 1849, Capt. Richard Shubrick, 5th Madras N.I., and died 2 Oct. 1894.)
Services : Ensign d.d. 2nd N.I. 13 Jan. 1827 ; posted Ensign

to 2nd N.I. 10 May 1827; actg. Adjt. do. 12 Dec. 1838. First Afghan War 1840-2; against the Ghilzais 1840; action under Capt. H. W. Farrington, q.v., at Sharack 3 Jan. 1841; action of 17 Aug. 1841; operations in vicinity of Kandahar; Ghazni; Kabul 1842; Capt. 2nd N.I., with Nott's force (Medal). Comdd. escort with the gates of temple of Somnath 23 Dec. 1842 till 18 Mar. 1843. A.D.C. to Lord Ellenborough 1 June 1843. Gwalior campaign; Maharajpur (w.); Capt. 2nd N.I. A.D.C. to Lord Hardinge 23 July 1844 till death. Supt. of Mysore Princes 17 Sept. 1844.

Refs.: Burke's Peerage, 1859, p. 432, s.n. Gilbert, Bart. MacInnes.

*MACLEAN(E), Lachlan (Lauchlan) (d. 1778). Lieut. Colonel. Comy. Gen., Bengal. Lt. Col. 1773. d. 1778: lost at sea on the voyage home in the wreck of H.M.S. Swallow, between the Cape and England.

Eldest son of Rev. John Maclean, minister of Clogher, co. Tyrone, and Elizabeth his wife, dau. of Rev. Philip Mathews, rector of Ballymoney. Brother-in-law of Cuthbert Wilson, and 2nd cousin of Lachlan Maclean, q.v. m. Elizabeth.

Services: Said to have been bred to the medical profession and to have practised in Philadelphia for some years; M.P. for Arundel 1786; Under Sec. to Lord Shelburne, whence he was known as 'Secretary Maclean.' Apptd. in England, 9 Dec. 1772, by the influence of Sir George Colebrooke, Chairman of C.D., Comptroller of the Army and Fortification Accounts in Bengal, which title was altered to Comy. Gen., 25 Mar. 1773. Arrived Calcutta 1773; resigned 17 Dec. 1774, and returned to England in the Dutton. Selected to act as Hastings's agent in England, 1775, and as agent for the Nawab of Arcot. Went out overland to India in 1777, and sailed for England the following year. One of the reputed authors of the Letters of Junius.

Refs.: Clan Maclean, pp. 320-1. Hist MSS. Commn., No. lxxiv. Holzman. B.: P.P. vii (1911), pp. 223-4.

MACLEISH, Robert (d. 1792). Ensign. Infantry. Cadet 1783. Ensign 8 Jan. 1785. Dismissed by C.M. 7 Apr. 1788. d. in goal at Calcutta 17 Mar. 1792.

Services: Cornet 4th Dgns. 19 Sept. 1771. Apptd. Cadet 30 Dec. 1782; sailed for India in the Fox 11 Mar. 1783; arrived in India 17 Sept. 1783. N.F.P.

Refs.: C.G. 7 June 1789.

MACLEOD, Alexander (*d.* 1793). Lieutenant, 3rd Bn. Sepoys. Country Cadet 1778. Ensign 5 June 1778. Lieut. 8 Sept. 1779. *d.* Calcutta 30 Mar. 1793.
(*Perhaps* brother of Norman Macleod, *q.v.*)
Services: Lieut. 1/2nd Bengal Eur. Regt. in Oct. 1779. Benares insurrection Aug. 1781. Lieut. 3rd Bn. Sepoys in July 1787; unposted in Dec. 1788. Third Mysore War; Lieut. 3rd Bn. Sepoys.

MACLEOD, Alexander (*d.* 1821). Lieutenant. 13th Bn. Sepoys. Country Cadet 1779. Ensign 1 Oct. 1779. Lieut. 12 May 1781. Resigned 14 Dec. 1789. *d.* 3 Feb. 1821.
Services: Apptd. Cadet for Cav. 19 Aug. 1779. Persian Intr. and Sec. to Col. Norman Macleod of Macleod, H.M. 73rd Regt., Comdt. at Cawnpore, in Dec. 1788. Pensioned on Lord Clive's fund 9 July 1794.

MACLEOD, Sir Alexander (1766-1831). Colonel, Kt. and C.B. Comdt. Bengal Artillery. (262) *b.* 9 Jan. 1766. Cadet 1783. Admitted 27 Sept. 1783. Fireworker 18 Apr. 1785. Lieut. 7 Apr. 1793. Capt. Lt. 21 Feb. 1802. Capt. 21 Sept. 1804. Major 1 Mar. 1812. Lt. Col. 15 Feb. 1818. Lt. Col. Comdt. 1 May 1824. Col. 5 June 1829. *d. unm.* Dum-Dum 20 Aug. 1831.

Youngest son (of 19 children) of Alexander Macleod, II of Luskentyre, and Margaret Morrison his wife. Grand-uncle of Isabella, wife of Harry Burrard Dalzell, 11th Earl of Carnwath, *q.v.* His natural dau. *m.* Charles Stewart (1813-1842), *q.v.*

Services: Apptd. Cadet 12 Feb. 1783. Fireworker 3rd Bn. Art. in July 1787. Third Mysore War 1790-2; Bangalore; Lieut. 5th Coy. 2nd Bn. Adjt. & Qmr. 3rd Bn. 1799-1800; Adjt. do. 1801-5. To join 5th Coy. 3rd Bn. in the field Dec. 1805. Apptd. Bde. Major to Col. John Horsford, *q.v.*, comdg. Reserve in the field, 26 Oct. 1807. Operations against Dhundia Khan 1807; Komona; Ganauri; Capt. comdg. 2nd Coy. 2nd Bn. Capture of Bhawani 1809. To comd. Art. at Karnal 16 May 1812. Nepal War 1814-15; Nalagarh (*Lond. Gaz.* 17 June and 16 Nov. 1815); Major 3rd Bn., comdg. Art. with Ochterlony's Div. Siege and capture of Hathras. Third Mahratta War; in action with Rajah of Berar's troops under Doveton 19 Dec. 1817 (*Lond. Gaz.* 6 May 1818); Major comdg. Art. of Rt. Div. Lt. Col. comdg. Art. in the field 1819-20. Apptd. Comdt. of Art. 12 Dec. 1823. M.M.B. 2 Jan. 1824. Siege and capture of Bhurtpore; comdg. Art., as Bdr. 1cl., from 3 Dec. 1825. Bdr. 12 Jan. 1828. C.B. 3 Feb. 1817. Kt. 29 Aug. 1827.

Refs.: Mackenzie's *Macleods, s.n.* Bernera. *D.I.B. Stubbs,* ii. 243-4. *MacInnes. A.J.* N.S. vii. 83. Will dated 6 June 1828; proved 6 Feb. 1832. M.I. in St. Stephen's, Dum-Dum.

MACLEOD, Alexander (1788-1828). Major, 12th N.I. *b.* co. Inverness 14 Jan. 1788. Cadet 1803. Arrived in India 29 Apr. 1805. Ensign 19 Mar. 1805. Lieut. 20 Mar. 1805. Capt. 24 Apr. 1816. Major 9 July 1825. *d.* Edgefield, nr. Forres, Oct. 1828.

3rd son of Norman Macleod, VII of Drynoch, I. of Skye, and last of Islandreoch (Ellanriach), Glenelg, co. Inverness, and Alexandrina his wife, eldest dau. of Donald Macleod, of Bernera. *m.* Bengal 20 Apr. 1818, Miss Louisa Brown, " dau. of Henry Brown, B.C.S., a cadet of the family of Oranmore and Browne." (She was pensd. Lord Clive's fund 21 Apr. 1829; living in 1860.)

Services: Posted Lieut. to 1/12th N.I. in 1806. Operations in Oudh 1807-8; reduction of Forts Bhadri, Samanpur, Gurha; Lieut. 1/12th N.I. Operations in Bundelkhand against Lachman Dawa; Rajaoli; Ajaigarh; Lieut. 12th N.I., with Light Bn. under Lt. Col. G. Martindell, *q.v.* Transfd. to 2/12th N.I. Apptd. to 7th (or L.I.) Vol. Bn. in 1812. Capture of Sambas, Borneo, 1813; operations against Rajah of Boni, in Celebes, 1816; Lieut. Vol. L.I. Bn. For some time Resdt. at Sourabaya and Banjuwangi in Java. Returned to Bengal in Aug. 1816. 2nd in comd. Cuttack Legion 19 May 1817 till 1822; Comdt. do. 1822-3. Operations against the Larka Kols in Singhbhum district 1821; Capt. comdg. mounted Sqdn. of Cuttack Legion. Comdt. Rangpur L.I. Bn. (formed from Cuttack Legion, Sylhet Frontier Bn. and Dinajpur Local Bn.) 1823-8. Transfd. to 12th N.I. (late 1/12th) May 1824. First Burma War; Assam 1824-5; occupation of Rangpur; Major comdg. Rangpur L.I. Bn. Fur. 1828 till death.

Refs.: Mackenzie's *Macleods,* p. 221. *E.I.M.C.* iii. 523-5. *A.J.* xxvi. 645. *G.M.* 1829, i. 182. M.I. at Drynoch.

MACLEOD, Alexander Francis Peter (1787-1829). Captain, 22nd N.I. *b.* Spanish Town, Jamaica, 5 Oct. 1787. Cadet 1805. Arrived in India 13 Nov. 1806. Ensign 8 Jan. 1807. Lieut. 1 Apr. 1812. Capt. 1 May 1824. *d.* Kaitha 4 June 1829.

Son of Alexander Macleod, of Sloane St., Chelsea.

Services: Barasat C.C. Posted Ensign to 2nd N.I. in 1807. With 3rd Bengal Vol. Bn. 1811-16. Capture of Java; Ensign 3rd Vol. Bn. Capture of Sambas; Lieut. 3rd Vol. Bn. Lieut. 1/2nd N.I.; transfd. to 2/2nd N.I. in 1817; to 22nd N.I. (late 2/2nd

May 1824. With Gorakhpur L.I. Bn. 1821-3 ; with Ramgarh Bn. 1823-8.

Refs. : M.I. Kaitha cemetery.

MACLEOD, Donald (*d.* 1772). Ensign, Infantry. Cadet (?) Ensign 1769. *d.* Calcutta 6 Dec. 1772.

Services : N.F.P.

MACLEOD, Sir Donald (*d.* 1843). Major General, K.C.B. Colonel 38th N.I. Country Cadet 1781. Admitted 10 Apr. 1781. Ensign 5 Sept. 1781. Lieut. 23 June 1783. Capt. 22 Aug. 1800. Major 22 May 1810. Lt. Col. 15 May 1815. Lt. Col. Comdt. 1 May 1824. Col. 5 June 1829. Maj. Gen. 10 Jan. 1837. *d.* Montagu Sq., London, 9 Aug. 1843.

Son of Donald Macleod, of Bernara, co. Inverness (of Bharkasaig, nr. Orbost, I. of Skye), who was grandson of Donald, 6th son of Sir Roderick Macleod, of Macleod. *m.* Melville Pl., Stirling, 28 Jan. 1813, Mary, eldest dau. of John Mackenzie, of Kincraig, and sister of Hugh Mackenzie, *q.v.* (She died Leamington 21 Aug. 1841.)

Services : Cadet d.d. 1st Bengal Eur. Regt. ; posted Ensign to 3rd Bengal Eur. Regt. in 1781. Transfd. to 29th N.I. 1785 ; to 6th Eur. Bn. 1786 ; to 13th Sepoy Bn. 1790. Third Mysore War 1790-2 ; Seringapatam ; Lieut. 13th Bn. Second Rohilla War ; battle of Bitaurah (w.) ; Lieut. 13th Bn. Adjt. 25th Bn. 1796 ; do. 2/11th N.I. 22 Apr. 1799. Second Mahratta War 1803-5 ; Kapsa ; Kalpi (w.) ; Gwalior ; Capt. 2/11th N.I. Capture of Gohad 1806 ; Capt. 2/11th N.I. Fur. p.a. 7 July 1810 till 1813. Capture of Hathras ; Lt. Col. 2/11th N.I. Third Mahratta War ; Lt. Col. 2/11th N.I. Comdt. of fortress of Agra 3 July 1819 till Jan. 1826. Transfd. to 2/4th N.I. 26 Oct. 1822 ; as Lt. Col. Comdt. to 17th N.I. May 1824. Fur. s.c. 24 Jan. 1826 till death. Transfd. to 1st Bengal Eur. Regt. 28 Dec. 1826 ; to 38th N.I. 1839. C.B. 14 Oct. 1818. K.C.B. 16 Feb. 1838.

Refs. : *MacInnes*. *E.I.M.C.* i. 116-21. *G.M.* 1813, i. 282 ; 1843, ii. 434. *The Times*, 10 Aug. 1843.

MACLEOD, Donald (1787-1818). Capt. Lieutenant, Artillery. (353) *bapt.* St. Paul's, Aberdeen, 17 Dec. 1787. Cadet 1804. Arrived in India 11 July 1805. Lieut. 13 May 1805. Capt. Lt. 1 Aug. 1814. *d. unm.* at sea off Mauritius, 13 July 1818, on his passage from India.

2nd son of Rev. Roderick Macleod, D.D., Principal of King's Coll., Aberdeen (who held College office for 67 yrs.), and Isobel his

wife, dau. of Dr. Christie, of Baberton. Kinsman of Wemyss Macleod, *q.v.* King's Coll., Aberdeen; M.A. 28 Mar. 1803.
Services: Served throughout with Foot Art. Operations in Bundelkhand against Lachman Dawa 1809; Rajaoli; Ajaigarh. Reduction of Kalinjar 1812. Capt. Lt. 2nd Coy. 3rd Bn. Fur. 1818.
Refs.: Burke's *Landed Gentry*, 15th edn., p. 1496, *s.n.* Macleod, of Talisker. Mackenzie's *Macleods*, p. 232, *s.n.* Talisker. Scott's *Fasti*, vii. 367. *S.M.* 1819, i. 584. Will dated 10 June 1818; proved 30 Dec. 1818.

MACLEOD, Duncan (*d.* 1763). Ensign, Bengal Eur. Regt. Cadet 1760. Ensign 1761. *d.* 5th, 6th or 11th Oct. 1763: massacred at or near Patna by order of Nawab Mir Muhammad Kasim. (See note to Hugh Mackay.)
Services: N.F.P.
Refs.: Innes, p. 169. Firminger, p. 71.

MACLEOD, Duncan (1780-1856). Lieut. General, Engineers. *b.* Tarbat, co. Ross, 20 Feb. 1780. Cadet 1794. Arrived in India 17 Feb. 1797. Ensign 28 Nov. 1795. Lieut. 13 Nov. 1803. Capt. 9 Feb. 1810. Major 1 Dec. 1826. Lt. Col. 28 Sept. 1827. Col. 18 June 1831. Maj. Gen. 23 Nov. 1841. Lt. Gen. 11 Nov. 1851. *d.* at his residence, 3 Clifton Pl., Hyde Pk., London, 8 June 1856.
XVII of Assynt, and V of Geanies. Youngest son of Sheriff Donald Macleod, III of Geanies, advocate at the Scottish Bar, and Margaret his 1st wife, dau. of James Craufurd, of Rotterdam. Uncle of Sir Alexander Mackenzie, 8th Bart. of Coul, *q.v. m.* Calcutta 28 Apr. 1804, Miss Henrietta Caroline Lestock Friell, sister of Simeon Philip Friell, *q.v.* (She died Calcutta 29 Nov. 1830, aged 48.) Father of Sir Donald Friell Macleod, K.C.S.I., Lt. Govr. of the Punjab 1865-70 (*D.N.B.*), and of Henrietta Peach, wife of Robert Boileau Pemberton, *q.v.*
Services: See *D.N.B.* Transfd. from Inf. to Engrs. 28 Apr. 1797. Bk.Mr. at Fort William 1807-10; Supt. of mily. roads 1810-14. In charge of gunpowder agency, Ichapur, 12 Jan. 1816 till 1820. Fur. 1822 till 8 June 1825. Supt. of Nizamat bldgs.[1] 1825-6. A.G.G. Murshidabad 9 Mar. 1836. Chief Engr., with a seat at Mily. Board, 24 Nov. 1836 till Feb. 1841. Fur. p.a. 27 Feb. 1841 till death. Afterwards Presdt. of the board of directors of the London agency of the Agra bank. A.C.I.E. 1842.
Refs.: Mackenzie's *Macleods*, *s.n.* Geanies. *D.N.B.* Boase.

G.M. 1856, ii. 126. *I.M.* 16 June 1856, p. 368. *Inverness Courier*, 12 June 1856. Will dated 1 June 1855 ; proved 11 Sept. 1856.
¹ *Note :* *i.e.* the palace of the Nawab Nazim at Murshidabad, and the other houses and mosques belonging to the dignity.
Note : The *Quarterly Bengal A.L.* credits him with service during the 2nd Mahratta war, including battle of Delhi, Deig and Bhurtpore. He appears, however, to have been employed at Ft. Wm. during the years 1803-5, and his name is not included in the roll of recipients of the India medal.

MACLEOD, Evan (1794-1820). Lieutenant, 18th N.I. *b.* 5 Apr. 1794. Cadet 1810. Ensign 4 May 1813. Lieut. 25 Dec. 1817. *d.* Malda 25 Aug. 1820.

5th son of William Macleod, VIII of Meidle and Glendale, surgeon in Luskentyre, Harris, J.P. co. Inverness, and sometime Capt. in a Coy. of Vols., and Isabella his wife, eldest dau. of Alexander Macleod, of Luskentyre.
Services : Barasat C.C. Cadet d.d. 21st N.I. 1812-13. Posted Ensign to 1/25th N.I. in 1813. Leave to Cape 1815-16. Siege and capture of Hathras ; Ensign 1/25th N.I. Transfd. as Lieut. to 1/18th N.I. Dec. 1817. Third Mahratta War ; Baggage Mr. to Rt. Div. of Grand Army. Executive Ofr. 16th (Purnea) Div. Bk. Dept. 1819.
Refs. : Mackenzie's *Macleods.*

MACLEOD, John (1788-1807). Lieutenant, 27th N.I. *b.* Dunvegan, co. Inverness, 24 Sept. 1788. Cadet 1803. Arrived in India 3 Dec. 1804. Ensign 21 Oct. 1804. Lieut. 21 Oct. 1804. *d.* 18 Nov. 1807 ; kld. in action at the assault of Komona.

4th and youngest son of Major Alexander Macleod, of Lochbay, Skye, and of Glendale, Moore Co., U.S.A., and Annie his wife, elder sister of John Macdonald (1759-1831), *q.v.*
Services : Posted Lieut. to newly-raised 2/27th N.I. in 1805. Operations against Dhundia Khan 1807 ; Komona (kld.) ; Lieut. 2/27th N.I.
Refs. : *Clan Donald,* iii. 516. *A.A.R.* x. 21.

MACLEOD, John Charles (1807-1830). Lieutenant, 2nd N.I. *b.* Dalvey ; *bapt.* Dyke, co. Elgin, 30 July 1807. Cadet 1824. Arrived in India 12 June 1825. Ensign 25 Jan. 1825. Lieut. 29 Sept. 1827. *d. unm.* at sea 19 May 1830 ; lost in the *Blossom.*¹

4th son of Alexander Macleod, 1st of Dalvey, Major in the army, and Marion his wife, 4th dau. of Donald Macleod, of Bernera, by his 3rd wife.

Services : Ensign d.d. 16th N.I. 21 June 1825. Posted Ensign to 2nd N.I. in 1825. Leave p.a. 4 mos. to Madras 27 June 1828; leave s.c. 7 mos. to P.W.I. 6 Mar. 1830. No record of active service.

Refs. : Mackenzie's *Macleods*.

¹ *Note :* He embarked at Penang in the *Blossom* on 19 May 1830, " since which period he has not been heard of, and is supposed to have perished with the other passengers." (Cons. 4 Mar. 1831.)

MACLEOD, Malcolm (*d.* 1823). Major. 9th N.I. Cadet 1783. Admitted 24 Sept. 1783. Ensign 31 Mar. 1785. Lieut. 9 Aug. 1793. Capt. 21 Sept. 1804. Bt. Major 25 July 1810. Retired 5 June 1811. *d. unm.* London 27 Mar. 1823.

Of Attadale, co. Ross. 3rd son of John Macleod, IX of Raasay, and Jane his wife, 3rd dau. of Angus Macqueen, of Rigg, Skye. Uncle of Isabella Rose, wife of Sir Walter Raleigh Gilbert, Bart., *q.v.*, and of Jane, wife of John James Farrington, *q.v.*

Services : Apptd. Cadet 15 Jan. 1783 ; sailed for India in the *Fox* 11 Mar. 1783. Apptd. A.D.C. to Sir John Macpherson, Bart., actg. G.G., 31 July 1786. Adjt. 10th Bn. Sepoys 31 Oct. 1787. Second Rohilla War 1794 ; Bitaurah ; actg. Qmr. 1st Bde. Fur. 18 Jan. 1797 till 14 Mar. 1801. Lieut. 9th N.I. in 1798. Comdd. Sebundy Corps in ceded district of Gorakhpur 1803-7. Comdt. Barasat C.C. July 1807 till Aug. 1809. Fur. 22 Jan. 1810 till retirement.

Refs. : Burke's *Landed Gentry*, 15th edn., p. 1496, *s.n.* Macleod, of Raasay. *MacInnes*, p. 170.

*MACLEOD, Norman (*d.* 1794). Captain, comdg. 13th Bn. Sepoys. Cadet 1769. Ensign 6 Dec. 1769. Lieut. 1772. Capt. 19 Sept. 1780. *d. unm.* 26 Oct. 1794 : kld. in action at the battle of Bitaurah.

2nd son of Alexander Macleod, of Ulinish, sheriff of Skye. Brother of Lieut. Alexander Macleod and kinsman (? cousin-german) of Sir John Macpherson, Bart.

Services : Apptd. Adjt. 26th Bn. Sepoys 22 Mar. 1780. Was A.D.C. to Provl. C.-in-C. in 1782. Comdd. Nawab-Wazir of Oudh's bodyguard 30 Sept. 1782 till 1784. Apptd. Mily. Sec. to Sir John Macpherson, actg. G.G., 14 Feb. 1785. Was comdg. the Nawab-Wazir's bodyguard in 1787 ; Capt. comdg. 13th Bn. Sepoys in Dec. 1788. Third Mysore War ; Seringapatam ; comdg. 13th Bn. Second Rohilla War ; Bitaurah (kld.) ; Capt. comdg. 13th Bn.

THE BENGAL ARMY, 1758-1834 181

Refs.: Mackenzie's *Macleods*, *s.n.* Dalvey. *MacInnes. List of Mily. Secs. to the G.G.* Hickey, iv. 122. Will dated 5 Feb. 1790; codicil dated 30 Sept. 1794; proved 26 Jan. 1795. M.I. in St. John's churchyard, Calcutta.

MACLEOD, Norman Chester (1813-1875). Colonel. Engineers. *b.* Calcutta 15 June 1813. Cadet 1831. Arrived in India 17 Aug. 1833. 2nd Lieut. 8 Dec. 1831. Lieut. 20 May 1839. Capt. 28 Feb. 1851. Bt. Major 25 Apr. 1856. Lt. Col. 1 Jan. 1859. Retired 1 July 1860. Hon. Col. 1 July 1860. *d.* Brighton 23 Jan. 1875.

bapt. Calcutta 19 July 1813. Son of Norman Macleod, B.C.S., offg. judge of the provincial court at Murshidabad (who was grandson of Norman Macleod, IV of Drynoch), and Eleanora Sophia his wife, sister of George Gladwin Denniss, *q.v. m.* 20 May 1846, Maria Isabella, youngest dau. of J. Uniacke, of Broughton House, co. Chester, and 8 Belmont, Bath.

Addiscombe Cadet 2 Feb. 1830 till 8 Dec. 1831. Chatham 2 Feb. 1832 till 14 Feb. 1833.

Services: d.d. S. & M. at Delhi 4 Oct. 1833. Actg. Asst. Engr. Delhi Div. 14 Mar. 1834 till Jan. 1836. Constructed bridge over Hindaun R. May 1834 till 15 Jan. 1835. Rejoined S. & M. 19 Jan. 1836. 2nd Asst. Supt. Canals W. of Jumna 13 Mar. 1837. To comd. Coy. of S. & M. with Army of Indus 21 Oct. 1838. First Afghan War 1839; capture of Ghazni, when he assisted Sir H. M. Durand, *q.v.*, in blowing in the Kabul gate (*Lond. Gaz.* 30 Oct. 1839) (Medal). Executive Engr. Ramgarh Div., P.W.D., 3 June 1840. Actg. Asst. Sec., Mily. Board, 3 Mar. 1841. Fur. s.c. 9 Jan. 1844 till 1848. Executive Engr. Midnapore Div. 1 Mar. 1850; do. Agra 19 Apr. 1850 till 1857. Leave s.c. 2 yrs. to Nilgiris Dec. 1850. Executive Engr. 1 cl. Agra Div. 15 May 1857. Mily. Sec. to Lt. Govr. N.W.P. 18 May 1857. Suptg. Engr. Allahabad 20 Aug. 1858 till retirement.

Refs.: Mackenzie's *Macleods. The Times*, 26 Jan. 1875.

MACLEOD, Thomas Harrison Scott (1810-1832). Ensign, 34th N.I. *b.* Greenwich 12 Jan. 1810. Cadet 1828. Arrived in India 4 Sept. 1828. Ensign 16 Apr. 1828. *d.* Tomar, Chota Nagpur, 10 Mar. 1832, of an arrow wound received in action at Arkee on 8 Mar.

Son of Thomas Harrison Macleod and Jane his wife.

Services: Ensign d.d. 51st N.I. 5 Nov. 1828; do. 24th N.I. 16 Feb. 1829; posted Ensign to 34th N.I. 4 Mar. 1829.

Operations against the Kols and Chuars in Chota Nagpur 1832 (kld.); Ensign 34th N.I.
Refs.: *A.J.* N.S. ix. 35. M.I. in Barrackpore church.

MACLEOD, Wemyss (1793-1817). Lieutenant, 21st N.I. *b.* Rogart, co. Sutherland, 2 Apr. 1793. Cadet 1810. Ensign 18 Aug. 1813. Lieut. 17 May 1815. *d.* Barrackpore 23 June 1817.

5th and youngest son of Rev. Angus Macleod, minister of Rogart 1774-94, and Jane his wife, dau. of William Mackay at Morvich. Ward of his kinsman Rev. Roderick Macleod, the father of Donald Macleod (1787-1818), *q.v.*
Services: Cadet d.d. 12th N.I. 1811-13; posted Ensign to 21st N.I. 1813. Nepal War 1816; Harriharpur; Lieut. 2/21st N.I.
Refs.: Scott's *Fasti*, vii. 98. M.I. Barrackpore old cemetery.

McMAHON, Alexander (1791-1887). Captain. 67th N.I. *b.* Lisnagrot, Kilrea, co. Londonderry, 1 Aug. 1791. Cadet 1806. Arrived in India 1 Aug. 1807. Ensign 28 Aug. 1807. Lieut. 1 Oct. 1812. Capt. 13 May 1825. Retired 19 Jan. 1828. *d.* 6 June 1887.

Son of Arthur McMahon, latterly of the French army, and Anna Maria Ashbourne his wife. *m.* Calcutta 10 June 1817, Anne, eldest dau. of William Mansell, Paymr. H.M. 84th and 66th Regts., Mily. Kt. of Windsor.
Services: Barasat C.C. Posted Ensign to 24th N.I. 1808; Intr. & Qmr. 1/24th N.I. 1 July 1814 till July 1823. Third Mahratta War; Lieut. 1/24th N.I., with Centre Div. of Grand Army. Transfd. to newly-raised 1/34th N.I. July 1823; Intr. & Qmr. do. 1 Oct. 1823 till July 1825. Transfd. to 67th N.I. (late 1/34th) May 1824. Fur. 19 July 1825 till retirement.
Refs.: *The Family of Fasken*, by Bdr.-Gen. W. H. Fasken, C.B. (Stroud, 1931), p. 18.

McMAHON, Henry (1812-1836). Ensign, 1st N.I. *b.* Limerick 15 Oct. 1812. Cadet 1828. Arrived in India 23 May 1829. Ensign 12 Dec. 1828. *d.* Bulandshahr, U.P., 29 May 1836.

Son of Matthew McMahon, of Dublin, and Frances his wife, dau. of John Tierney, of Ballyscandlend, co. Limerick. Brother of Thomas McMahon, *q.v.*, nephew of Sir Matthew John Tierney, 1st Bart. (*D.N.B.*), and cousin-german of John Tierney, *q.v.* Addiscombe Cadet 1827-8.

THE BENGAL ARMY, 1758-1834

Services : Ensign d.d. 59th N.I. 13 July 1829 ; d.d. 38th N.I. 18 July 1829 ; posted to 11th N.I. 7 Jan. 1830. Wahabi rising 1831 ; Ensign 11th N.I. Exchanged to 7th N.I. 24 Jan. 1834 ; to 1st N.I. 2 Mar. 1835. Leave s.c. to Bulandshahr 12 Mar. 1836.
Refs. : Burke's *Peerage,* 1859, p. 995, *s.n.* Tierney, Bart., of Brighton.

McMAHON, Thomas (1809-1894). Ensign. 41st N.I. Pensioner on Lord Clive's fund. *b.* St. Michael's, Limerick, 1 Oct. 1809. Cadet 1825. Ensign 26 Dec. 1825. Pensioned 19 Feb. 1830. *d.* 17 Jan. 1894.
Son of Matthew MacMahon, of Dublin. Brother of Henry McMahon, *q.v. m.* (before 1831) ?
Services : Posted Ensign to 41st N.I. in 1826. Fur. 1827 till pensioned. No record of active service.
Refs. : Burke's *Peerage,* 1859, p. 995, *s.n.* Tierney, Bart.

McMILLAN, Alexander (1761/62-1782). Lieutenant, Infantry. *b.* in Scotland 1761/62. Cadet 1780. Ensign 1780. Lieut. 21 Aug. 1781. *d.* 11 May 1782, on active service with the Bombay detachment.
Services : Sailed for India in the *Neptune* 3 June 1780, aged 18. First Mahratta War 1781-2 ; with the detachment under Lt.-Col. Grainger Muir, *q.v.*

*McMILLAN, John (*d.* 1781). Lieutenant, Infantry. Cadet (?) Ensign (?) Lieut. (?) *bur.* Cawnpore 27 Nov. 1781.
Services : N.F.P.

McMILLAN, John Porter (1791-1826). Lieutenant, 18th N.I. *b.* Campbeltown, co. Argyll, 21 Jan. 1791. Cadet 1809. Ensign 10 July 1812. Lieut. 1 Sept. 1815. *d. unm.* Nimach 4 July 1826.
bapt. Campbeltown 25 Jan. 1791. Son of Rev. William McMillan, of Campbeltown, schoolmaster, and Anne Porter his wife. Brother of Anne and Betsey.
Services : Barasat C.C. Cadet d.d. 25th N.I. 1811-12 ; posted Ensign to 1/6th N.I. in 1812. Nepal War 1814-15 ; Ensign 1/6th N.I., in 2nd Div. Third Mahratta War ; Lieut. 1/6th N.I., in Reserve Div. Intr. & Qmr. 1/6th N.I. 1823-4 ; transfd. to 18th N.I. (late 2/6th) May 1824 ; Intr. & Qmr. do. 17 June 1824 till death. Siege and capture of Bhurtpore ; Lieut. 18th N.I.
Refs. : Will dated Nimach 28 Oct. 1825 ; proved 16 Nov. 1826.

McMORINE, Charles (1801-1843). Captain, Artillery. (493)
b. Nipburton (?), N. Carolina, 14 July 1801 (? Apr. 1802).[1]
Cadet 1818. Arrived in India Sept. 1819. 2nd Lieut. 20 Apr.
1819. Lieut. 10 Dec. 1821. Capt. 23 Nov. 1835. *d. unm.*
Delhi 20 Feb. 1843.

Son of —— McMorine, of Caerlaverock, co. Dumfries. Brother
of John McMorine, and ward of John Hyslop. (*Probably* nephew of
George Macmorine, *q.v.*) Addiscombe Cadet 1818-19.

Services : Posted to 4th Coy. 3rd Bn. Foot Art. Oct. 1819.
Transfd. to 5th Troop H.A. Feb. 1822 ; to newly-formed 2nd Troop
3rd Bde. 1 Aug. 1825. Siege and capture of Bhurtpore ; Lieut.
2nd Troop 3rd Bde. Offg. Adjt. 3rd Bde. and Meerut Div. H.A.
14 May till Oct. 1830. Transfd. to 3rd Troop 3rd Bde. Aug. 1832.
Shekhawat expedn. 1834. Transfd. as Capt. to comd. 1st Coy.
5th Bn. Foot Art. 15 Feb. 1836. A.D.C. to Maj.-Gen. Clements
Brown, *q.v.*, comdg. Benares Div., 22 Nov. 1836 till 26 Jan. 1838.
Comdd. 2nd Troop 3rd Bde. H.A. 26 Jan. 1838 till death. With
Army of Reserve (for Afghanistan) Oct. 1842 till Jan. 1843.

Refs. : De Rhé-Philipe. I.M. No. 1, p. 19. Will dated Delhi
19 Feb. 1843 ; proved 8 Apr. 1843. M.I. in Rajpura cemetery, Delhi.

[1] *Note :* The inscription on his tomb states that he was " aged
41 Years 7 Months and 6 Days." In an affidavit sworn 2 Sept. 1818
he states that he was *b.* Apr. 1802.

MACMORINE, George (1763-1824). Lieut. Colonel Comdt.
(Bdr. Gen.), 21st N.I. *b.* 15 May 1763. Country Cadet 1781.
Admitted 29 Oct 1781. Ensign 23 July 1782. Lieut 20 Jan.
1785. Capt. 3 Jan. 1802. Major 13 Sept. 1809. Lt. Col. 16 Dec.
1814. Lt. Col. Comdt. 1 May 1824. *d. unm.* Gauhauti, Assam,
30 May 1824, of cholera.

5th son of Rev. Robert MacMorine, of Nether Macartney (now
Walton Park), minister of Kirkpatrick-Durham 1744-74, and
Elizabeth his wife, dau. of John Maxwell, of Breconside. Brother
of Rev. Dr. William MacMorine, of Caerlaverock.

Services : Supy. Lieut. unposted in July 1787 ; 1st Eur. Bn. in
Dec. 1788 ; transfd. to 22nd Bn. Sepoys in 1790. Bt. Capt. and
Adjt. of a Gren. Bn. on service in Rohilkhand in 1799. Transfd.
as Adjt. to 1/10th N.I. June 1800. Capt. Lt. 1/10th N.I. 21 Feb.
1801. Second Mahratta War ; operations against Holkar 1805-6 ;
Comy. of Supplies to Maj.-Gen. W. Dowdeswell's Div. Bde. Major
at Saharanpur 1807 till Jan. 1809. Lt. Col. comdg. 1/10th N.I.
Apptd. to comd. 1st Bde., Nagpur Subsdy. Force, 1816. Pindari
War 1817-18 ; capture of Serinagur 6 Jan. 1818 ; Lt. Col. comdg.

THE BENGAL ARMY, 1758-1834

1st Inf. Bde. 5th Div., Army of the Deccan, under Bdr. J. W. Adams, *q.v.* Fur. 5 Feb. 1820 till 1823. Transfd. to 21st N.I. 1823. First Burma War; operations in Assam Mar.-May 1824; Lt. Col. Comdt. comdg. the force.

Refs.: Scott's *Fasti*, ii. 285. *E.I.M.C.* i. 141-7. *S.M.* 1824, ii. 767. Will dated 13 Oct. 1819; proved 19 June 1824. M.I. at Gauhauti, Assam.

MACMULLEN, Frederick Summers (1817-1842). Lieutenant, 1st Bengal Eur. L.I. *b.* Wellington, Somerset, 11 Feb. 1817. Cadet 1834. Arrived in India 24 July 1835. Ensign (12 Dec. 1834) 5 Feb. 1835. Lieut. 18 Dec. 1837. *d.* Karnal 1 Nov. 1842.

bapt. Wellington 12 Mar. 1817. 3rd son of Stephen Macmullen, M.D., of Wells, and Anne his wife. Brother of Stephen Francis Macmullen, *q.v. m.* Agra 16 May 1837, Mary Anne,[1] eldest dau. of W. Bristow, of Calcutta. Addiscombe Cadet 12 Apr. 1833 till 12 Dec. 1834.

Services: Ensign d.d. 51st N.I. 8 Aug. 1835. Posted to Rt. Wing Bengal Eur. Regt. 24 Sept. 1835. First Afghan War 1838-9; capture of Ghazni (medal); occupation of Kabul; action in Khyber pass 19 Nov. 1839 (w.); Lieut. Bengal Eur. Regt. Granted gratuity of 18 mos. pay for wound. Fort Adjt. at Ft. Wm. and Supt. of Gentlemen Cadets 9 June 1841 till July 1842, when he was ordered to rejoin his Regt. warned for service. Rejoined 1st Eur. L.I. at Karnal, with Army of Reserve (for Afghanistan), 1 Oct. 1842.

Refs.: De Rhé-Philipe. *G.M.* 1843, i. 557. *The Times*, 16 Jan. 1843. M.I. in new cemetery at Karnal.

[1] *Note:* Author of a "History of Taunton," 1858, and other works.

MACMULLEN, Stephen Francis (1812-1896). General. 3rd Bengal Eur. L.C. *b.* 11 Oct. 1812. Cadet 1828. Arrived in India 27 Aug. 1829. Cornet (28 Mar. 1829) 27 Aug. 1829. Lieut. 20 Nov. 1841. Capt. 31 Dec. 1851. Bt. Major 28 Nov. 1854. Lt. Col. 18 Feb. 1861. Col. 18 Feb. 1866. Maj. Gen. 31 Dec. 1872. Lt. Gen. 18 July 1879. Gen. 1 Dec. 1888. *d.* The Hermitage, Brentwood, Essex, 8 June 1896.

bapt. St. Mary the Virgin, Dover, 22 Jan. 1813. Son of Stephen Macmullen, M.D., of Bridgwater, Somerset, Surg. H.M. 59th Regt., and Anne his wife. Brother of Frederick Summers Macmullen, *q.v. m.* Mirzapur, U.P., 26 Mar. 1840, Louisa Anne, eldest dau. of Robert Wood Smith, *q.v.* (She died 18 Jan. 1900, aged 79.)

Services: Actg. Cornet (having been 2 yrs. in India) 14 Oct. 1831. Served (? with 44th N.I.) in operations under Lt.-Col. J. Holbrow, *q.v.*, in Jhabua, C.I., Feb.-Mar. 1836. Posted Cornet to 9th L.C. 9 June 1836. Transfd. to 6th L.C. 13 Oct. 1836. Adjt. 6th L.C. 8 July 1840 till Oct. 1851. Transfd. to 5th L.C. 14 Dec. 1842; retransfd. to 6th L.C. 1844. Bde. Major 2nd Cav. Bde., Army of the Punjab, 13 Oct. 1848. Second Sikh War; passage of the Chenab; Chilianwala; Gujerat; Bt. Capt. 6th L.C., Bde. Major (Medal with 2 clasps). Fur. s.c. Feb. 1854 till Dec. 1856. Was senior ofr. with 6th L.C. at Jullundur when that Regt. mutinied on 7 June 1857; was fired at by a sowar with a pistol, and w. in the hand. Transfd. to newly-raised 3rd Eur. L.C. in 1858. Transfd. to u.s.l.

Refs.: The Times, 11 June 1896; 12 June, p. 5.

McMULLIN, Robert (1786-1865). Major. 44th N.I. *b.* St. John's, Sligo, 13 Dec. 1786. Cadet 1806. Arrived in India 17 Mar. 1808. Ensign 1 Apr. 1808. Lieut. 29 July 1813. Capt. 1 May 1824. Retired 21 July 1835. Hon. Major 28 Nov 1854. *d.* Boulogne-sur-Mer 2 Sept. 1865.

Brother of John McMullin, M.D. *m.* (before 1817) Marie Louise Antoinette Lenferna de Lareste. (She died 20 Feb. 1885, aged 87.)

Services: Barasat C.C. 7½ mos. Expedn. against Mauritius 1810; Ensign 2nd Vol. Bn. Posted Ensign to 22nd N.I. in 1812. Lieut. 2/22nd N.I. Fur. s.c. to sea 1 Dec. 1814 till 16 July 1816. Adjt. 2/22nd N.I. 6 Nov. 1818 till 22 June 1824. Leave u.p.a. to Mauritius 2 Oct. 1820 till 31 Aug. 1821. Transfd. to 44th N.I. (late 2/22nd) May 1824. Served in P.W.D., 11th (Meerut) Div., 1823-31. Leave p.a. to Mauritius 2 June 1831 till 14 Nov. 1832; fur. p.a. 21 Jan. 1833 till retirement. Retired on a pension of 10/6 *p.d.*

Refs.: Howard & Crisp, xvi. 86, *s.n.* Leigh. *G.M.* 1865, ii. 531. *The Times*, 14 Sept. 1865.

McMURDO, Alured Charles (1793-1864). Ensign. 21st N.I. Subsequently Major 10th Light Dgns. *b.* New York 3 Dec. 1793. Cadet 1808. Arrived in India 29 Oct. 1809. Ensign 20 Mar. 1810. Resigned 29 Jan. 1814. *d.* N. Berwick, co. Haddington, 30 Apr. 1864.

Son of Charles McMurdo, Col. H.M. 31st Foot. Brother of Aston Edward McMurdo, *q.v.* Marlow Cadet.

Services: Posted Ensign to 21st N.I. in 1810. Cornet 8th Light Dgns. (1 Jan. 1814) 30 Dec. 1814; h.p. Cornet 21st Light Dgns. 3 July 1823. Lieut. 29 June 1826; Capt. 22 Mar. 1831; h.p.,

unattached, 22 Mar. 1831. Retired as Capt. 10th Dgns. 9 Nov. 1846; promoted Major in the Army 24 Mar. 1854. Served with 8th Light Dgns. at siege of Hathras in 1817, and afterwards in Pindari War.
Refs.: *G.M.* 1864, i. 810.

McMURDO, Aston Edward (1804-1829). Lieutenant, 33rd N.I.
b. Edinburgh 27 Nov. 1804. Cadet 1820. Ensign 13 Jan. 1821. Lieut. 11 July 1823. *d.* Cawnpore 25 Jan. 1829.
Son of Charles McMurdo, of Lotus, Col. 31st Foot, and Catherine Sweetman his wife. Brother of Robert McMurdo (1806-1891), *q.v.* Ed. Edinburgh High School.
Services: Posted Ensign to 1/23rd N.I. in 1821; transfd. as Lieut. to 16th N.I. July 1823; to 33rd N.I. (late 2/16th) May 1824. Siege and capture of Bhurtpore; Lieut. 33rd N.I. Actg. Intr. & Qmr. 33rd N.I. in 1827.
Refs.: *A.J.* xxviii. 92. Will dated 20 Jan. 1828; proved 28 Apr. 1829. M.I. at Cawnpore.

MACMURDO, Robert (*d.* 1781). Captain, 2/1st Bengal Eur. Regt. Cadet 1770. Ensign 21 Sept. 1770. Lieut. 8 July 1776. Capt. 5 Feb. 1781. *d. unm.* Madras Presdy. Feb. 1781.
Brother of Philadelphia, 1st wife of William Campbell, of Crawfordton, W.S.; nephew of Barbara Douglas.
Services: Was Qmr. 2nd Bengal Eur. Regt. in Oct. 1773. First Rohilla War 1774. Apptd. Qmr. 1st Eur. Regt. 16 Oct. 1777; Lieut. 1/1st Eur. Regt. in Oct. 1779; Qmr. do. 22 Mar. 1780. Second Mysore War 1781; Capt. 2/1st Eur. Regt., with Coote's detachment.
Refs.: *India Gazette,* 31 Mar. 1781. Will dated Calcutta 10 Oct. 1780; codicils dated Madras 15 Dec. 1780 and 15 Feb. 1781; proved 10 May 1781.

McMURDO, Robert (1806-1891). Lieutenant. 13th N.I. Pensioner on Lord Clive's fund. *b.* Weir Bank, Melrose, 10 July 1806. Cadet 1821. Ensign 6 Jan. 1823. Lieut. 13 May 1825. Pensioned 6 May 1829. *d.* 23 June 1891.
bapt. 3 Sept. 1806. Son of Charles McMurdo, Col. 31st Foot, and Isabella his wife, dau. of John Coffin, of Quebec. Brother of Alured Charles McMurdo, *q.v.* *m.* St. Paul's, Covent Gdn., London, 24 Aug. 1829, Sarah Anne, only dau. of Henry Robert Whitcombe, Bo.C.S., of Whittern House, co. Hereford.
Services: Posted Ensign to Bengal Eur. Regt. in 1823; transfd.

to 13th N.I. May 1824. Fur. s.c. 29 Nov. 1826 till pensioned. No record of active service.
Refs. : *A.J.* xxviii. 509.

MACNAB, Duncan (*d.* 1782). Lieutenant, Infantry. Country Cadet 1779. Ensign 6 Oct. 1779. Lieut. 17 May 1781. *d.* Buxar 11 May 1782.
Services: Apptd. Cadet 19 Aug. 1779; Ensign 30th Bn. Sepoys in 1780.

MACNAB, Robert (*d.* 1770). Lieutenant, Infantry. Lieut. 11 Sept. 1768. *d.* Patna 2 Apr. 1770.
m. (before 1768) Josepha Louisa (? Maria).
Services: Ensign 79th Ft. 15 July 1761; Lieut. (?); h.p. 1763; transfd. as Lieut. from H.M.S. (M.C. 1 Sept. 1768).
Refs.: Macpherson, p. 28.

McNAGHTEN, James (*d.* 1807). Lieutenant, 20th N.I. Cadet 1798. Admitted 5 Dec. 1799. Ensign 15 Oct. 1799. Lieut. 28 Oct. 1799. *d.* Bencoolen 13 Oct. 1807.
Services: Posted Lieut. to 2nd Bengal Eur. Regt. 15 Apr. 1801; transfd. to Marine Regt. (became 20th N.I. in 1803).

MACNAGHTEN, John Dunkin (1810-1861). Captain, Invalid Est. 5th L.C. *b.* Madras 12 May 1810. Cadet 1825. Arrived in India 22 Oct. 1826. Cornet (13 June 1826) 13 Jan. 1829. Lieut. 14 Dec. 1835. Capt. 13 Jan. 1842. Invalided 6 Mar. 1846. *d.* Dacca 19 Nov. 1861.
5th son of Sir Francis Workman Macnaghten, 1st Bart., of Dundarave, co. Antrim, and Letitia his wife, eldest dau. of Sir William Dunkin, of Clogher, and sister of Edward Dunkin, *q.v.* His sister *m.* Thomas Robarts Thellusson, *q.v.* Ed. Rugby; admitted 1822. Addiscombe Cadet 1825.
Services: Cornet d.d. 9th L.C. 9 Nov. 1826; posted Cornet to 6th L.C. 8 Jan. 1827; exchanged to 5th L.C. 13 Jan. 1829. A.D.C. to Bdr.-Gen. George Carpenter, *q.v.*, comdg. Benares Div., 7 Nov. 1829. 3rd Asst. to A.G.G. Rajputana 14 May 1832; offg. P.A. Kotah 12 Feb. 1834; 2nd Asst. to A.G.G. Rajputana 28 Feb. 1835; 1st do., and Supt. Ajmer, 30 Jan. 1839. Leave s.c. to Cape 4 Aug. 1842 till 4 June 1843. No record of active service.
Refs.: Burke's *Peerage*, 1923, p. 1482, *s.n.* Workman-Macnaghten, Bart., of Dundarave, Bushmills, co. Antrim. *Rugby School Register.* *G.M.* 1862, i. 237. *The Times*, 31 Dec. 1861.

THE BENGAL ARMY, 1758-1884

McNAGHTEN, Robert Adair (1796-1845). Captain. 61st N.I. Editor and proprietor of the Calcutta *Englishman*. *b.* Ballysillan, co. Antrim, 24 Mar. 1796. Cadet 1813. Admitted 5 Aug. 1814. Ensign 16 Dec. 1814. Lieut. 13 July 1818. Capt. 2 May 1826. Retired 16 July 1839. *d.* Calcutta 18 May 1845. Son of Samuel Alexander McNaghten, of Beardville, nr. Coleraine, M.P. for Orford, Suffolk. *m.* 1st, Chelsea 3 Nov. 1827, Laura Henrietta, elder dau. of Capt. William Roberts, sister of Miss Emma Roberts, the authoress (*D.N.B.*), and widow of Arthur Newport. (She died Etawah 20 Oct. 1830.) *m.* 2nd, Lyndhurst, Hants, 21 Nov. 1832, Susanna Ann, eldest dau. of George Halford, of Lyndhurst. (She died 8 Feb. 1861, aged 54.)

Services: Posted Ensign to 10th N.I. Dec. 1814; transfd. to 1/19th N.I. 1 July 1815. Third Mahratta War 1818; storm and capture of Chanda; Ensign 1/19th N.I. Adjt. 1/19th N.I. 19 May 1818 till 28 Oct. 1822. Actg. D.J.A.G. 1st Div. of Field Army at Cawnpore 14 Dec. 1821; permanent do. 4 Oct. 1822; do Presdy. Div. 17 Feb. till 2 June 1825, when removed from his appt. Transfd. to 31st N.I. July 1823; to 61st N.I. (late 1/31st) May 1824. Fur. u.p.a. 6 June 1826 till 3 June 1828; fur. s.c. 2 Nov. 1831 till 1 Nov. 1834. Editor of the Calcutta *Hurkaru* for a short time till 7 Apr. 1825, when he resigned by order of Govt., and joint editor of the *Englishman* 1829-31. After retirement he resided in Calcutta and became part proprietor and occasional editor of the *Englishman* and *Mily. Chron.* Author of "Memoir of the Military Operations of the Nagpore Subsidiary Force, 1816-19," Calcutta, 1820.

Refs.: A.J. xxiv. 798; N.S. ix. 197; N.S. xx. 42. *Calcutta Monthly Journal*, June 1825, pp. 533-4, 546-52. *G.M.* 1845, ii. 318. Will dated 22 Apr. 1845; proved 20 May 1845. M.I. in Circular Rd. cemetery, Calcutta; tablet in St. John's church, Calcutta. Portrait in C. Grant's *Outline Portraits of Calcutta Celebrities*.

McNAIR, Robert (1803-1857). Lieut. Colonel, 17th N.I. *b.* Glasgow 25 Dec. 1803. Cadet 1820. Admitted 31 May 1821. Ensign 13 Jan. 1821. Lieut. 11 May 1823. Capt. 2 Aug. 1839. Major 7 Apr. 1851. Lt. Col. 18 July 1856. *d.* Coonoor, Madras, 20 July 1857, "of fatigue."

Son of Robert McNair, of Janefield and Belvidere, sometime sugar refiner in Glasgow, afterwards collector of customs at Leith, and Helen McCall his wife. *m.* 1st, Edinburgh 12 June 1834, Catharine, 2nd dau. of J. S. More, advocate. (She died Calcutta 10 Nov. 1835, aged 21.) *m.* 2nd, St. Andrew's, Calcutta 2 Aug. 1837, Harriet

Caroline, 2nd dau. of Capt. Jonathan Hayter ("John") Garstin, H.M. 88th Regt. (*See also* Augustus Abbott.) Ed. Edin. High School.

Services : Posted Ensign to 1/21st N.I.; transfd. as Lieut. to 11th N.I. July 1823; to 15th N.I. (late 1/11th) May 1824. Attack on and capture of Maharaj Bulwant Singh at Patan, nr. Kotah, 7 Nov. 1824; Lieut. 15th N.I., under Capt. Charles Kiernander, *q.v.* Transfd. to 5th Extra Regt. (became 73rd N.I.) May 1825. Intr. & Qmr. 73rd N.I. 29 July 1825 till 15 Feb. 1832. Fur. p.a. 30 Mar. 1832 till 30 Jan. 1835. d.d. Assam L.I. 21 Feb. till 8 Apr. 1835. Intr. & Qmr. 73rd N.I. 8 Feb. 1836 till 2 Sept. 1839. Leave s.c. 6 mos. to China 14 Sept. 1836. Offg. tempy. Bde. Major to Bdr. J. H. Littler's force on E. frontier 5 Jan. 1838 and 27 May 1839; permanent do. 22 Oct. 1839 till 30 Dec. 1840. Actg. A.A.G. Meerut Div. 21 May 1842. Tempy. comdg. 1st Inf. Levy 11 Oct. 1842. Asst. Executive Engr. 12th (Ambala) Div., P.W.D., 17 Apr. 1844 till Apr. 1847. Second Sikh War; in garr. at Lahore; Bt. Major 73rd N.I. (Medal). Fur. s.c. Jan. 1850 till Nov. 1851. With F.F. for annexation of Oudh 1856; Bt. Lt. Col. 73rd N.I. Posted Lt. Col. to 73rd N.I. Sept. 1856; transfd. to 17th N.I. in 1857.

Refs. : *I.M.* 17 Sept. 1857, p. 605. Will dated 8 Jan. 1856; admon. 10 Nov. 1858.

McNAMARA, Edward Comerford William (*d.* 1796). Captain, Infantry. Cadet 1774. Admitted 2 Nov. 1774. Ensign 17 Aug. 1776. Lieut. 31 July 1778. Capt. 10 Dec. 1793. *d.* Chittagong 15 Dec. 1796.

m. Patna 15 Aug. 1781, Miss Sally Parkinson.

Services : Was Adjt. 28th Bn. Sepoys in Mar. 1786 and in 1793. Third Mysore War; Lieut. 28th Bn. Transfd. as Capt. to 3rd Eur. Bn. 19 Dec. 1793; to 4th do. 28 Nov. 1794.

Refs. : Will dated 13 Nov. 1796; proved 10 Feb. 1798.

McNAMARA, Matthew (1761/62-1824). Lieut. Colonel, Pension Est. 17th N.I. *b.* 1761/62. Cadet 1783. Admitted 20 Apr. 1784. Ensign 11 Jan. 1785. Lieut. 26 Dec. 1790. Capt. 25 Aug. 1804. Major 5 Dec. 1812. Lt. Col. 4 June 1817. Pensioned 1 Jan. 1820. *d.* Monghyr 31 Jan. 1824, aged 62.

Services : Ensign H.M. 77th Ft. 24 Jan. 1783. Apptd. Cadet 2 Apr. 1783; sailed for India in H.M.S. *Euridyce*. Posted to 4th Bengal Eur. Bn. 5 Feb. 1790; transfd. to 6th do. 1791. Apptd. Adjt. 6th Eur. Bn. 25 Jan. 1794; Adjt. 2nd Bengal Eur. Regt. 1796; do. 1/9th N.I. in 1803-4. Second Mahratta War; pursuit

THE BENGAL ARMY, 1758-1834 191

of Holkar 1805-6 ; Capt. 1/9th N.I. Fur. 24 Feb. 1807 till 1810. Nepal War 1816 ; Makwanpur ; Major 2/9th N.I., in 4th Bde. Centre Column. Posted Lt. Col. to 1/23rd N.I. in 1817. (? Third Mahratta War ; Nagpur ; Lt. Col. 1/23rd N.I.) Transfd. to 17th N.I. in 1818.
Refs.: M.I. in Monghyr old cemetery.

McNAMARA, William (1759-1781). Lieutenant. 3rd Bengal Eur. Regt. *b.* in Ireland 1759. Cadet 1778. Ensign 2 Oct. 1778. Lieut. 19 Nov. 1778. Resigned 20 Dec. 1779. *d.* 28 May 1781, aged 22.
Services: Sailed for India in the *Mount Stewart* 9 Feb. 1778, aged 17. Leave s.c. to coast of Coromandel 17 Aug. 1779. Lieut. 1/3rd Bengal Eur. Regt. in Oct. 1779.
Refs.: G.M. 1781, p. 294.

McNEIL, William (*d.* 1786). Lieutenant, Infantry. Country Cadet 1780. Ensign 27 Feb. 1781. Lieut. 21 Oct. 1781. *d.* 2 Sept. 1786.
Services: A Vol. in 1780. N.F.P.

McNEILLY, Arthur (1784-1807). Lieutenant, 23rd N.I. *b.* 23 Apr. 1784. Cadet 1805. Arrived in India 11 July 1806. Ensign 22 July 1806. Lieut. 19 Nov. 1807. *d.* Ganauri, U.P., 24 Nov. 1807.
bapt. Mourne, co. Down, 29 Apr. 1784. Son of Henry McNeilly.
Services: Posted Ensign to 23rd N.I. Operations against Dhundia Khan 1807 ; Komona ; siege of Ganauri (? kld. in action) ; Lieut. 1/23rd N.I.

MACPHEE, Alexander ; Ferdinand ; Joseph. (*See* **McVEAGH.**)

MACPHEE, Thomas. (*See* **MACFIE.**)

MACPHERSON, Æneas (*d.* 1784). Lieutenant, Infantry. Cadet 1772. Ensign 30 July 1776. Lieut. 16 July 1778. *d. unm.* Calcutta 19 June 1784.
Brother of Murdoch and Annabel Macpherson ; nephew of Lachlan Macpherson ; and kinsman of Allan Macpherson, *q.v.* ; and of John Macpherson, *alias* Samuelson, in Pitgown in Badenoch.
Services: Lieut. 14th Bn. Sepoys in Aug. 1778.
Refs.: Will dated 21 May 1784 ; proved 23 Sept. 1784.

MACPHERSON, Allan (1740-1816). Lieut.-Colonel. Infantry. Q.M.G. Bengal. *b.* Badenoch, co. Inverness, 7 June 1740. Cadet 1763. Arrived in India 1764. Ensign 28 Sept. 1764. Lieut. 18 Oct. 1765. Capt. 1 Apr. 1769. Major 1 Jan. 1781. Lt. Col. 10 Dec. 1783. Resigned 5 Jan. 1787. *d.* Blairgowrie, co. Perth, 30 May 1816.

Of Blairgowrie, which estate he purchased in 1788. Son of William Macpherson, Purser of his Clan, and Anna his wife, sister of Donald Macpherson, of Kinloch (Laggan), and relict of Grant of Laggan. Brother of John Macpherson, *q.v.*, and related to John Macintyre (*d.* 1828), Æneas Macpherson, Duncan Macpherson (1762-1804), and James Macpherson *qq.v. m.* Calcutta 3 Jan. 1782, Eliza Dell, eldest dau. of Alexander Fraser of Fairfield, and sister of Andrew Fraser (*d.* 1812), *q.v.* (*See also* Hiram Cox.) (She died Blairgowrie 1836.) His dau. *m.* John Macintyre (*d.* 1828), *q.v.*

Services : Enlisted in 42nd (Black Watch) 1756 or 1757. Served in N. America; Ticonderoga 1758 and 1759; campaign of 1760 on the St. Lawrence; capture of Havana 1762; took his discharge and returned to Scotland in 1762. Joined Bengal Eur. Regt. Oct. 1764. Reduction of Chunar 1765. Adjt. 1st Regt. 1st Bde. 1765-7. A.D.C. to Sir Robert Fletcher, *q.v.* Resigned during the " Batta mutiny "; reinstated later. First Mysore War 1767-9. A.D.C. to Col. A. Champion, comdg. 3rd Bde., *q.v.*, 1769-74. First Rohilla War; battle of St. George. Accompanied Col. John Upton, *q.v.*, on a mission to the Mahratta Govt. 1775-7, as Sec. and Intr. Apptd. to comd. 15th Bn. Sepoys Oct. 1776; exchanged to 3rd Bn. Jan. 1778; to 1st Bn. Aug. 1780 till Mar. 1781. Q.M.G., Bengal, Dec. 1781 till Jan. 1787. Pte. Sec. and Persian Intr. to his kinsman John Macpherson, the G.G., Jan. 1785 till Sept. 1786. Left India 29 Jan. 1787. Raised and comdd. 1st, or Strathmore and Stormont, Bn. of Perth Vols. July 1798 till May 1802; comdd. 2nd, or Belmont and N. Strathmore, Bn. 1803-5.

Refs. : Burke's *Landed Gentry*, 15th edn., p. 1501, *s.n.* Macpherson, of Blairgowrie. *Macpherson* (portrait). *Frasers of Lovat*, p. 687, *s.n.* Fraser of Fairfield. *Williams*, p. 91. Portrait, painted Calcutta 1782, by Thomas J. Seton.

MACPHERSON, Andrew (*d.* 1784). Bt. Ensign, Infantry. Bt. Ensign 11 May 1780. *d.* Luckipore (Lakshmipur, Bengal) 29 Aug. 1784.

Services : Commissioned as Bt. Ensign of Mil. Sepoys from Sergt., " as a reward for his diligence at the late fire at the Old Fort."

Apptd. to comd. the Sepoy guards at Luckipore and Colinda Dec. 1783.

MACPHERSON, Andrew (1784-1804). Cadet, Infantry. *b.* Laggan, co. Inverness, 3 Apr. 1784. Cadet 1803. Arrived in India 14 Aug. 1804. *d. unm.* Barrackpore 1 Sept. 1804.

Younger son of Lachlan Macpherson, XXI of Ralia, and Grace his wife, eldest dau. of Andrew Macpherson, of Banchor, and sister of Robert Macpherson, *q.v.*

Refs.: Burke's *Landed Gentry*, 13th edn., p. 1187, *s.n.* Macpherson, of Glentruim, co. Inverness. Family information.

MACPHERSON, Archibald Fraser (1807-1877). Colonel. 43rd N.I. *b.* Laggan, co. Inverness, 13 Dec. 1807. Cadet 1824. Arrived in India 19 Jan. 1826. Ensign 9 Aug. 1825. Lieut. 23 Feb. 1827. Capt. 24 Jan. 1845. Major 26 Apr. 1859. Bt. Lt. Col. 30 May 1859. Retired 24 Mar. 1860. Hon. Col. 24 Mar. 1860. *d. unm.* Waverley Hotel, Inverness, 26 May 1877.

3rd son of Duncan Macpherson, of Cluny, Lt. Col. 3rd Scots Fus. Gds., and Catherine his wife, youngest dau. of Sir Ewen Cameron, Bart., of Fassifern. Brother of Ewen Cameron Macpherson, *q.v.*, and cousin-german of Colin Macdonald, *q.v.* Ed. Edin. High School; Edin. Acad. 1824-5.

Services: Posted Ensign to 43rd N.I. in 1826. Fur. s.c. 8 Sept. 1836 till 27 July 1839. First Afghan War 1839-42; defence of Dadar Oct. 1840 (s.w.), comdg. Dadar post [1]; operations in vicinity of Kandahar; advance on Kabul; capture of Istalif (*Lond. Gaz.* 6 Dec. 1842, 7 Feb. 1843); Bt. Capt. 43rd N.I., with Nott's force (Medal). Gwalior campaign; Maharajpur; Bt. Capt. 43rd N.I. (Bronze star). Second in comd. 3rd Inf., Gwalior Contingent, 13 Jan. 1844; Comdt. do. 13 June 1850 till 1857. Fur. p.a. 25 May 1858 till retirement.

Refs.: Burke's *Landed Gentry*, 13th edn., p. 1187, *s.n.* Macpherson, of Cluny Macpherson, co. Inverness. *Cardew*, p. 176. *The Times*, 2 June 1877.

[1] *Note:* "On 29 Oct. 1840 Nasir Khan attacked Dadar but was beaten off by a headlong charge of 120 sowars of Skinner's Horse, a fine feat of arms, in which the leader, Capt. Macpherson, and all his native officers were wounded." (*Fortescue*, xii. 132.)

MACPHERSON, Charles James (1784-1808). Lieutenant, 20th N.I. *b.* London 15 May 1784. Cadet 1799. Arrived in India 12 Jan. 1801. Ensign 9 Aug. 1800. Lieut. 4 Sept. 1800. *d.* at sea 13 May 1808, on board the *Thomas Henchman*.

bapt. St. Martin-in-the-Fields, London, 11 June 1784. Son of James Macpherson and Monica his wife.

Services : Posted Lieut. to 2nd Bengal Eur. Regt. 17 Apr. 1801 ; transfd. to newly-raised 2nd Bn. Marine Regt. (became 2/20th N.I.) in 1803 ; Adjt. 2/20th N.I. 1805 till death.

MACPHERSON, Duncan (1764/65-1791). Lieutenant, Artillery. (214) *b.* in Scotland 1764/65. Cadet 1781. Arrived in India 15 Nov. 1782. Fireworker 13 Sept. 1781. Lieut. 3 Feb. 1788. *d.* 21 (or 23) May 1791, of wounds received in action at the battle of Arikera on 15 May.

Services : Sailed for India in the *Worcester* 6 Feb. 1782, aged 17. Fireworker 3rd Bn. Art. in July 1787. Third Mysore War 1790-1 ; Bangalore ; Arikera (s.w.) ; Lieut. 1st Coy. 2nd Bn.

MACPHERSON, Duncan (1762-1804). Captain, 1st N.I. *b.* 1762. Country Cadet 1781. Admitted 10 Apr. 1781. Ensign 28 Feb. 1783. Lieut. 15 Feb. 1790. Capt. 30 Sept. 1803. *d. unm.* on board his *budgerow* nr. Mirzapur 14 Dec. 1804.

Son of Lachlan Macpherson, of Dalchully, in Badenoch, and Catherine his wife, dau. of Campbell, of Achtyre. Brother of Evan, John, James, Mrs. Allan Stewart, of Kirkmichael, and Mrs. Alexander Stewart, of Moulin. Cousin of Col. Duncan Macpherson, of Cluny, and 2nd cousin of Allan Macpherson, *q.v.*

Services : Posted Ensign to 1st Bengal Eur. Regt. 28 Feb. 1783 ; apptd. Examiner, Mily. Dept. of Inspection, 2 Aug. 1786. Ensign 3rd Eur. Bn. ; transfd. as Lieut. to 25th Bn. Sepoys in 1790. Bt. Capt. 1/9th N.I. in Aug. 1798 ; transfd. to 1st N.I. Operations in Bundelkhand 1804 ; Capt. 1/1st N.I.

Refs. : Family information. Will dated Camp nr. Eckpayah Pass, 17 Mar. 1804 ; proved 14 Jan. 1805.

MACPHERSON, Duncan (1778-1853). Lieut. General. Colonel 16th N.I. *b.* Laggan, Inverness, 11 Nov. 1778. Cadet 1794. Arrived in India 25 Feb. 1796. Ensign 3 Oct. 1795. Lieut. 3 Oct. 1796. Capt. 21 Sept. 1804. Major 1 Oct. 1815. Lt. Col. 1 Aug. 1819. Lt. Col. Comdt. 1 May 1824. Col. 5 June 1829. Maj. Gen. 10 Jan. 1837. Lt. Gen. 9 Nov. 1846. *d.* Lansdown Cresc., Cheltenham, 24 Nov. 1853.

Son of Rev. Robert Macpherson, chaplain 78th Foot. Brother of William Macpherson (1783-1819), *q.v.*, of John, writing factor to Lord Macdonald, of Skye, and of Eliza, wife of Donald Macnabb. (*Probably* cousin of Robert Macpherson, *q.v.*) *m.* Drimmin House

25 July 1827, Alexandrina, eldest dau. of John Maclean, of Boreray and Drimmin, and sister of Roderick Norman Maclean, *q.v.* (She died 15 Nov. 1870, aged 73.)

Services: Lieut. 1st Bn. Breadalbane Fenc. Regt. Approved as Cadet 7 Apr. 1795. Fourth Mysore War; Seringapatam; Lieut. Vol. Bn. (Medal). Lieut. 1/10th N.I. Second Mahratta War 1805-6; escort duty; Capt. 1/10th N.I. (? Operations against Dhundia Khan 1807; with 27th N.I.) Settlement of Hariana 1809; Bhawani; Capt. 1/10th N.I. Operations in Rewah 1813-14; Capt. 1/10th N.I. To rank as Major from 16 Dec. 1814. Major comdg. 4th Gren. Bn. 1816. Transfd. to 2/10th N.I. in 1816. Third Mahratta War 1817-19; capture of fort Seoni 21 Jan. 1818 (*Lond. Gaz.* 25 Feb. 1819); Major comdg. 2/10th N.I., and the force. Apptd. to a civil situation in 1819. Fur. s.c. 26 Jan. 1821 till death. Transfd. as Lt. Col. Comdt. to 67th N.I. May 1824. Posted Col. to 67th N.I. June 1829; to 16th N.I. 8 Oct. 1836 till death.

Refs.: Boase. *A.J.* xxiv. 402. *I.M.* 30 Nov. 1853, p. 721.

MACPHERSON, Ewen Cameron (1806-1832). Lieutenant, 48th N.I. *b.* Inverness 21 June 1806. Cadet 1822. Arrived in India 6 July 1823. Ensign 11 July 1823. Lieut. 13 May 1825. *d.* Barrackpore 15 Apr. 1832.

2nd son of Duncan Macpherson, of Cluny, and Catherine his wife. Brother of Archibald Fraser Macpherson, *q.v.*

Services: d.d. 1/10th N.I. 28 Aug. 1823; posted Ensign to 48th N.I. and served throughout with that Regt. Leave p.a. 12 mos. 14 Oct. 1829. No record of active service.

Refs.: Burke's *Landed Gentry*, 13th edn., p. 1187, *s.n.* Macpherson, of Cluny Macpherson, co. Inverness. *A.J.* N.S. ix 142.

MACPHERSON, James (*d.* 1824). Captain. 4th N.I. Cadet 1782. Admitted 27 July 1783. Ensign 9 Mar. 1783. Lieut. 20 Feb. 1790. Capt. 20 Dec. 1801. Struck off 31 Aug. 1804. *d.s.p.* Apr. 1824.

II of Belleville (*now* Balavil). Elder natural son of James Macpherson, of Belleville, M.P. (*D.N.B.*). Uncle of David Edward Brewster-Macpherson, cousin-german of John Macintyre (*d.* 1828), and 1st cousin once removed of Allan Macpherson, *qq.v.* *m.* Maria Sophia Craigie, sister of Edmund Buchan Craigie, *q.v.*

Services: Apptd. Cadet 5 June 1782; sailed for India in the *Gen. Coote* 11 Sept. 1782. Apptd. A.D.C. to his kinsman, Sir John Macpherson, Bart., actg. G.G., 14 Feb. 1785. Apptd. Asst. to

James Anderson, *q.v.*, Resdt. with Sindhia, 16 May 1786, and was still holding this post in 1792. Fur. 18 Jan. 1797 till struck off. Capt. Lt. 4th N.I. 6 Aug. 1801.

Refs. : *The Mackintoshes and Clan Chattan*, by A. M. Mackintosh (Edin., 1903), pp. 470-1. *Macpherson*, pp. 345-8. *Scottish N. & Q.* 3S. iii. 124.

MACPHERSON, Sir James Duncan (1811-1874). Major General, K.C.B. 6th Bengal Eur. Inf. Comy. Gen. *b.* Ardclach, Nairn, 24 Jan. 1811. Cadet 1828. Arrived in India 5 May 1829. Ensign 4 Dec. 1828. Lieut. 26 Nov. 1836. Capt. 1 Nov. 1848. Major 1 Dec. 1855. Lt. Col. 4 Aug. 1859. Bt. Col. 5 Apr. 1858. Maj. Gen. 24 Jan. 1867. *d.* 31 Belsize Pk. Gdns., London, 29 May 1874, of pneumonia.

Of Ardersier. *bapt.* Ardclach 24 Feb. 1811. Son of Lt.-Col. Duncan Macpherson, Fornighty, 78th Highrs., and Anne Campbell his wife. Brother of Maj.-Gen. Sir Herbert Taylor Macpherson, K.C.B. (*D.N.B.*). *m.* Nasirabad 25 Aug. 1840, Mary, 8th dau. of James Kennedy, *q.v.* (*See also* William Alexander.) (She died Oct. 1903, aged 82.) Ed. King's Coll., Aberdeen.

Services : Ensign d.d. 52nd N.I. 10 June 1829. Posted to 22nd N.I. 18 Nov. 1829. Intr. & Qmr. 22nd N.I. 20 Sept. 1833 till Sept. 1845 ; Adjt. do. 12 Sept. 1845 till Feb. 1848. Shekhawat expedn. 1834. Apptd. Bde. Major 7th Inf. Bde., Army of the Punjab, 13 Oct. 1848. Second Sikh War ; Chilianwala ; Gujerat ; Bde. Major (Medal with clasp). Mily. Sec. to Punjab Govt. 1852-8. Operations against the Bori Afridis 29 Nov. 1853 (Medal). Leave s.c. 1 yr. to Mauritius Apr. 1856. Offg. Q.M.G. of the Army 27 Feb. 1858. Mutiny campaign ; Lucknow Mar. 1858 ; offg. Q.M.G. Oudh (Medal with clasp). Mily. Sec. to Chief Comr. Punjab 19 Jan. 1859. Posted Lt. Col. to newly-raised 6th Eur. Regt. 21 Oct. 1859. Fur. p.a. 18 mos. 26 Mar. 1860. Bdr. Gen. 1cl., comdg. Agra Bde., 20 Aug. 1862. Comy. Gen. Bengal 5 Mar. 1864 till 22 July 1869. Fur. 10 Feb. 1868 till death. C.B. 26 July 1858 ; K.C.B. 24 May 1873.

Refs. : D.I.B. Boase. I.L.N., lxiv. 547. *The Times*, 1 June 1874.

MACPHERSON, John (*c.* 1742-1784). Bt. Lieut. Colonel. 8th N.I. *b.* Badenoch, co. Inverness, *c.* 1742. Transfd. as Ensign from H.M.S. Ensign 27 Dec. 1764. Lieut. 8 Dec. 1766. Capt. 17 Apr. 1769. Major 7 Jan. 1781. Bt. Lt. Col. 24 Dec. 1781. Resigned on pension 4 Jan. 1782. *d.* at his house, nr. Edinburgh, 23 Aug. 1784.

THE BENGAL ARMY, 1758-1834

Son of William Macpherson and Anna his wife. Brother of Allan Macpherson, *q.v. m.* 1783, Grace, dau. of James Hay, of co. Banff. (She *re-m.* Alexander Murray (1746-1822), *q.v.*)

Services: Went to India in 1760 in the ranks of H.M. 89th Highland Regt. (Gordons). Capture of French Settlements on Malabar coast 1761. Went to Bengal in 1764 with a detachment of the Regt. under Sir Hector Munro. Battle of Buxar; assault of Chunar Dec. 1764 (w.); Sergt. 89th Regt. Transfd. to Bengal Army Dec. 1764 [1]; posted to 1st Bengal Eur. Regt. 13 Aug. 1765; resigned his Commission during the " Batta mutiny " in May 1766; readmitted later. Adjt. & Bde. Major under Carnac. First Rohilla War. Apptd. to comd. 14th Bn. Sepoys (became 8th N.I. in 1781, and was disbanded for mutiny in 1795) 22 Apr. 1777. First Mahratta War 1779; Capt. comdg. 14th Bn., with Camac's detachment. Sailed from India Apr. 1782. Pensd. as Major on Lord Clive's fund 26 Mar. 1783.

Refs.: Macpherson (portrait, painted Calcutta 1782, by Thos. J. Seton). *G.M.* 1784, ii. 716. *S.M.* 1784, p. 448.

[1] *Note:* " Mr. John MacPherson, late Sergt. in H.M. 89th Regt., on account of his good behaviour at Chunar, is now promoted to the rank of Ensign on the Bengal Est. until the Govr.'s pleasure is known." (Major Munro's Orders, 11 Dec. 1764.)

MACPHERSON, Robert (1774-1823). Major,• 17th N.I. *b.* Kingussie 1774. Cadet 1794. Arrived in India 5 Jan. 1796. Ensign 27 Oct. 1795. Lieut. 25 Apr. 1797. Capt. 27 Feb. 1805. Major 22 Jan. 1817. *d.* Delhi 5 Jan. 1823.

Of Benchar.[1] 3rd son of Andrew Macpherson, of Banchor, and Isabel his wife, eldest dau. of George Macpherson, of Invershie. Uncle of Andrew Macpherson (1784-1804), *q.v.*, and of Lieut. Evan Macpherson, 21st M.N.I., cousin-german of Sir George Macpherson-Grant, 1st Bart., and related to Duncan Macpherson (1778-1853), *q.v.*

Services: Operations in Jumna Doab 1803; Lieut. 17th N.I. (? Second Mahratta War; Aligarh; battle of Delhi; defence of Delhi; pursuit of Holkar 1805-6; Capt. 2/17th N.I.) Nepal War 1814-15; Jitpur; Bt. Major 2/17th N.I., in 3rd Div. Comdd. Delhi Palace Gds. 1815 till death.

Refs.: Burke's *Landed Gentry*, 13th edn., p. 1187, *s.n.* Macpherson, of Glentruim, co. Inverness. Burke's *Peerage*, 1923, p. 1025, *s.n.* Macpherson-Grant, Bart., of Ballindalloch. Family information. *S.M.* 1823, ii. 255. Will dated Delhi, 11 Apr. 1822; proved 16 July 1823.

[1] *Note:* Sometimes spelt Banchor, Bencher or Binchar.

*MACPHERSON, Samuel (d. 1767/69). Ensign, Infantry. Cadet 1765. Arrived in India 26 June 1766. Ensign 5 Aug. 1766. d. 1767/69 whilst on active service with Col. Joseph Peach's detachment in the N. Circars.
Services: Lieut. in one of H.M. Regts. disbanded after the Seven Years' War (but not traced). Sailed for India in the *Lord Camden* 21 Feb. 1766. First Mysore War.
Refs.: Narrative of the Life of a Gentleman long resident in India, by G. F. Grand, q.v. (1910 edn.), pp. 8-10. *B.M. Add. MS.* 6050, p. 90.

*MACPHERSON, William (d. 1765). Captain, 5th Bn. Sepoys. Capt. 20 Oct. 1763. d. 1765.
Son of James Macpherson, of Killiehuntly, and Barbara his wife, youngest dau. of Rev. William Moncrieff, minister of Largo.
Services: Lieut. H.M. 89th Ft. 28 Oct. 1759. (? Raised a Coy. from 89th for the Bombay Regt. and was made a Capt. on that Est. for doing so.) Battle of Buxar; Capt. Bo. Transfd. in Feb. 1765 as Capt. from the Bo. Est., when he took over comd. of 5th Bn. from George Witchcot q.v. (Orders of 17 Feb. 1765). This transfer caused much dissatisfaction amongst the Bengal Officers.
Refs.: Williams, p. 93. Broome, pp. 472, 518-9, 537, lxii.

MACPHERSON, William (1780-1813). Captain, 1st N.I. bapt. 22 Dec. 1780. Cadet 1797. Arrived in India 29 Oct. 1798. Ensign 9 Oct. 1798. Lieut. 1 Nov. 1798. Capt. 4 Aug. 1806. d. unm. Fort Nugent, Java, 6 Mar. 1813.
Son of Kenneth Macpherson and Barbara McIntosh his wife. Stepson of Donald Macpherson.
Services: Expedn. to Egypt 1801; Lieut. Vol. Bn. Lieut. 1st N.I. Operations in Bundelkhand 1805-6; Lieut. 1st N.I. Capt. Lt. 1st N.I. 19 Feb. 1806. Capture of Java 1811; Cornelis (w.); Capt. 6th Bengal Vol. Bn. Capture of Palembang 1812; Capt. comdg. 6th Vol. Bn.
Refs.: Will dated 8 Dec. 1809; proved 6 Sept. 1813.

MACPHERSON, William (1783-1819). Captain, 24th N.I. b. Laggan, co. Inverness, 19 Nov. 1783. Cadet 1798. Arrived in India 24 Feb. 1800. Ensign 3 Dec. 1799. Lieut. 29 May 1800. Capt. 28 Apr. 1812. d. Purnea, B. & O., 14 Sept. 1819.
Youngest son of Rev. Robert Macpherson, chaplain, 78th Foot. Brother of Duncan Macpherson (1778-1853), q.v.
Services: Posted Lieut. to 2/5th N.I. 15 Apr. 1801; transfd. to newly-raised 1/24th N.I. in 1805. Capt. Lt. 24th N.I. 24 June

THE BENGAL ARMY, 1758-1834

1809. Suptg. construction of bldgs. at Sikraul 1815-17. (? Third Mahratta War; Capt. 1/24th N.I.)

Refs.: *S.M.* 1820, i. 583. Will dated Jaunpur, 8 May 1817; codicil dated 13 Sept. 1819; proved 18 Dec. 1819. M.I. Purnea.

BREWSTER-MACPHERSON, David Edward (1815-1878). Lieut. Colonel. 62nd N.I. *b*. Edinburgh 17 Aug. 1815. Cadet 1834. Arrived in India 11 Feb. 1835. Ensign (13 June 1834) 9 Oct. 1834. Lieut. 9 Mar. 1837. Capt. 24 Jan. 1845. Major 11 May 1855. Retired 11 May 1855. Hon. Lt. Col. 1856. *d*. 29 Jan. 1878.

Of Belleville, Kingussie, co. Inverness. J.P. and D.L. 3rd son of Sir David Brewster, Kt., K. H. (*D.N.B.*), and Juliet his wife, natural dau. of James Macpherson, of Belleville, M.P. (*D.N.B.*). Nephew of James Macpherson, *q.v.* Assumed the additional surname of Macpherson in 1862. *m*. Mussoorie 6 Oct. 1849, Lydia Julia, eldest dau. of Henry James Blunt, *q.v.* Addiscombe Cadet 17 Aug. 1832 till 13 June 1834. Edin. Univ.

Services: Posted to 62nd N.I. 2 Mar. 1835; actg. Adjt. do. 19 Oct. 1840; Intr. & Qmr. do. 15 Dec. 1840 till 10 Nov. 1843; Adjt. do. 10 Nov. 1843 till 28 Feb. 1845. Gwalior campaign; Maharajpur; Lieut. 62nd N.I. (Bronze star). Comdt. Bhagulpur Hill Rangers 7 Feb. 1852 till Dec. 1854.

Refs.: Family information.

MACQUARIE (MacQUARRIE), John.[1] Ensign. 20th Bn. Sepoys. Country Cadet 1773. Ensign (?) Discharged 10 Mar. 1775. *d.s.p.* in India before June 1790.[2]

Eldest son of Lachlan Macquarie, XVI of Ulva, Chief of the Clan (*d*. 1818, aged 103), and Alice his 1st wife, dau. of Donald Maclean, of Torloisk. Cousin of Maj.-Gen. Lachlan Macquarie, govr. of N.S.W. (*D.N.B.*).

Services: Lieut. H.M. 114th Regt. (R. Highland Vols.) 1761; h.p. do. (Regt. disbanded) 1763. Was already in India when apptd. Cadet in G.O. of 26 Oct. 1773. First Rohilla War; battle of St. George; Ensign 20th Bn.

Refs.: Burke's *Landed Gentry*, 2nd edn., p. 816, *s.n.* Macquarie, of Ormaig, co. Argyll. Douglas's *Baronage*, p. 509, *s.n.* Macguarie of Macquarie. *Lachlan MacQuarrie, XVI of Ulva*, by Capt. R. W. Munro, Karachi, p.p., 1944.

[1] *Note*: Incorrectly given as James in *Dodwell & Miles*.

[2] *Note*: Living in India in Mar. 1777; probably *d*. before 1781, as his name is not in h.p. list of 114th Regt. for that year.

MACQUEEN, Alexander (1778-1807). Lieutenant, 1st N.I. *b.* Strath, I. of Skye, 15 June 1778. Cadet 1798. Arrived in India 23 Nov. 1799. Ensign 20 Dec. 1799. Lieut. 29 May 1800. *d. unm.* 29 Jan. 1807 : kld. in action at the assault of Chamir fort. *bapt.* 22 June 1778. Son of John Macqueen and Mary Grant his wife. Brother of Kenneth, John, Archibald, and Mrs. Margaret Irvine.
Services: Posted Lieut. to 2/1st N.I. 15 Apr. 1801. Operations in Bundelkhand 1806-7 ; capture of Chamir (kld.) ; Lieut. 2/1st N.I.
Refs.: Will dated 26 Mar. 1806 ; proved 20 Apr. 1807.

MACQUEEN, John (or James, or Joseph) [1] (1755/56-1784). Ensign, Infantry. *b.* in Scotland 1755/56. Cadet 1782. Ensign 9 Apr. 1783. *d.* Calcutta 7 Nov. 1784 ; *bur.* there 9 Nov.
Services: Apptd. Cadet 31 Oct. 1781 ; sailed for India in the *Worcester* 6 Feb. 1782, aged 26. Posted to 2nd Bengal Eur. Regt. 28 Feb. 1783.
[1] *Note:* His christian name is given as John in Embarkation Roll and *Dodwell & Miles*, as James in the burial register, as Joseph in G.O. of 28 Feb. 1783.

MACQUEEN, Thomas Richard (1792-1840). Major, 45th N.I. *bapt.* Cariff, co. Armagh, 20 Sept. 1792. Cadet 1807. Arrived in India 19 Aug. 1808. Ensign 5 Sept. 1808. Lieut. 20 July 1812. Capt. 17 May 1824. Major 27 Jan. 1839. *d.* on the river nr. Bhagulpur 10 Nov. 1840.
2nd son of John McQueen, of Braxfield, co. Lanark, Capt. 18th Ft., and Anne his 1st wife, dau. of Thomas Macan, of Cariff, and sister of Richard Macan, *q.v. m.* Lucknow 1 Oct. 1819, Charlotte Anne, dau. of John Baillie, of Leys, *q.v.* (*See also* Henry Francis Caley.) (She died 28 Jan. 1892, aged 90.)
Services: Barasat C.C. Posted Ensign to 23rd N.I. in 1809. Third Mahratta War ; capture of fort Seoni 21 Jan. 1818 ; assault of Bainsudder 22 Jan. 1818 (*Lond. Gaz.* 25 Feb. 1819) ; Lieut. 2/23rd N.I. Transfd. to 1/23rd N.I. Adjt. Baddeley's Horse 12 June 1822 till 29 June 1824. Transfd. as Capt. to 45th N.I. (late 1/23rd) May 1824. (? First Burma War ; Chittagong 1824 ; Cachar 1825 ; Capt. 45th N.I.)
Refs.: Burke's *Landed Gentry*, 7th edn., p. 1205, *s.n.* McQueen, of Braxfield. Burke's *Landed Gentry of Ireland*, p. 429, *s.n.* Macan, of Drumcashel, co. Louth. Buchan & Paton's *Peebles-shire*, iii. 261. *E.I.M.C.* iii. 432. M.I. at Bhagulpur.

McQUHAE, William (1787-1824). Major, Artillery. (340) *b.*
St. Quivox, co. Ayr, 15 June 1787. Cadet 1803. Arrived in
India 11 Dec. 1804. Lieut. 29 Aug. 1804. Capt. Lt. 15 Sept.
1809. Capt. 25 Sept. 1817. Major 1 May 1824. *d.* Calcutta
23 Oct. 1824.
bapt. St. Quivox 25 June 1787. 3rd son of Rev. Dr. William
McQuhae, minister of St. Quivox 1764-1823, Father of the Synod,
and Mary Laurie his 2nd wife. *m.* Meerut 8 Oct. 1812, Rose,
dau. of Joseph Barnard Smith, B.C.S., and aunt of Charles Corfield,
q.v. (*See also* James Richard Mockler.) (She died 3 Mar. 1851.)
His daus. *m.* James Tobin Bush, John William Collin Chalmers,
William Richard Maidman, and Peter Arnold Torckler, *qq.v.*
Glasgow Univ.; matric. 1800.
Services: Operations against Dhundia Khan 1807; Komona
(w.); Ganauri; Lieut. 3rd Coy. 1st Bn. Foot. Art. Posted to
1st Troop augmented H.A. 4 Oct. 1809. Nepal War 1814-15;
Capt. Lt. 1st Troop, Qmr. to Reserve with 2nd Div. Comy. of Ord.
at Allahabad 16 June 1815; Principal Dy. Comy. do. 27 May 1824.
Refs.: Scott's *Fasti*, iii. 66. Will dated 23 Dec. 1822; proved
3 Nov. 1824. M.I. in S. Park St. cemetery, Calcutta.

MACRAE, Farquhar (1805-1847). Lieutenant. 67th N.I. *b.*
Chittagong 8 July 1805. Cadet 1821. Ensign 18 Jan. 1822.
Lieut. 27 Apr. 1824. Retired 8 Dec. 1828. *d.* 1847.
bapt. Chittagong 6 Oct. 1805. 2nd son of John Macrae, M.D.,
Bengal Medical Est., of the Inverinate family, and Margaret his
wife, dau. of Col. Erskine.
Services: Posted Ensign to 13th N.I. in 1822; transfd. to 34th
N.I. 11 July 1823; to 67th N.I. (late 1/34th) May 1824. First
Burma War; Arakan 1825; Lieut. 67th N.I. Fur. 1826 till
retirement.
Refs.: History of Clan Macrae.

MACREDIE, Archibald (1777-1799). Lieutenant, 16th N.I. *b.*
Dreghorn, co. Ayr, 29 May 1777. Cadet 1793. Ensign 30 Sept.
1794. Lieut. 1 June 1796. *d.* Krishnagiri, Madras, 10 May
1799.
5th son of William Macredie, of Perceton, co. Ayr, and Barbara
his wife, only child of Robert Wilson, of Glasgow, merchant.
Services: Apptd. Cadet 9 Apr. 1794; sailed for India in the
Busbridge 2 May 1794. Fourth Mysore War; Lieut. Bengal Vols.
Refs.: Burke's *Landed Gentry*, 7th edn., p. 1205, *s.n.* Macredie,
of Perceton, co. Ayr. *S.M.* 1799, p. 908.

202 LIST OF THE OFFICERS OF

McROBERTS, James (*d.* 1793). Lieutenant, Invalid Est. Infantry. Country Cadet 1780. Ensign 27 Feb. 1781. Lieut. 20 Oct. 1781. Invalided 12 Apr. 1787. *d.* Berhampore 16 May 1793.

Of co. Carlow. Brother of Anne, wife of John Russell, and of Elizabeth Cole. Cousin of William Higginbotham. *m.* Maria Wemyss.

Services : Apptd. a Gent. Vol. in the Coy of Art. 3 Apr. 1780. Granted fur. on h.p. 6 Nov. 1786.

Refs. : Will dated 14 May 1793 ; proved 1 Aug. 1793.

McSHERRY, Thomas (1801-1856). Colonel, C.B., 23rd N.I. *b.* Dromiskin, co. Louth, 17 May 1801. Cadet 1816. Admitted 16 Dec. 1817. Ensign (?) Lieut. 1 Aug. 1818. Capt. 11 Mar. 1826. Major 1 Dec. 1839. Lt. Col. 19 Jan. 1846. Col. (20 June 1854) 1856. *d.* Condette, nr. Boulogne-sur-Mer, 17 Apr. 1856.

bapt. Dromiskin 18 May 1801. Son of Hugh McSherry and Eleanor Connely his wife.

Services : Posted Lieut. to 1/15th N.I. in 1818. Pindari War 1819 ; Asirgarh ; Lieut. 1/15th N.I. Actg. Intr. & Qmr. 1/15th N.I. 20 Aug. 1821. Transfd. to 30th N.I. (late 1/15th) May 1824. Actg. Intr. & Qmr. 30th N.I. 20 Aug. 1824 ; permanent do. 7 Feb. 1825 till 1828. Actg. Bde. Major in Cuttack 30 Nov. 1826. Bde. Major to Shah Shuja's force 3 Sept. 1838 till 1841. First Afghan War 1839-42 ; Ghazni (Medal) ; raised Gurkha levies ; rejoined 30th N.I. Mar. 1841 ; Kandahar ; Kabul (Medal). Fur. s.c. 1 Apr. 1843 till 1846. Posted as Lt. Col. to 30th N.I. 1846. Transfd. to 73rd N.I. 1847 ; to 1st N.I. 17 Sept. 1847. Second Sikh War ; in garr. at Fort Govindgarh ; Lt. Col. 1st N.I. (Medal). Fur. p.a. 4 Mar. 1852 till death. Transfd. as Bt. Col. to 2nd Bengal Eur. Fus. Feb. 1855 ; as Col. to 23rd N.I. Mar. 1856. Durani 3cl. 22 Oct. 1841. C.B. 9 June 1849.

Refs. : Boase. Will dated 16 Apr. 1853 ; admon. 25 Oct. 1856.

MACTIER, William (1793-1855). Bt. Colonel, C.B., 2nd L.C. Bdr. comdg. Benares Div. *b.* Wigton 16 July 1793. Cadet 1809. Admitted 17 Nov. 1810. Cornet (28 Mar. 1810) 13 Nov. 1813. Lieut. 1 Sept. 1818. Capt. 1 May 1824. Major 13 Jan. 1842. Lt. Col. 2 Oct. 1851. Bt. Col. 20 June 1854. *d.* Jaunpur, U.P., 16 Sept. 1855.

Son of Alexander Mactier and Rosanna his wife. Brother of Anthony Mactier, Head Comr., Court of Bequests, Bengal, and of Durris House, co. Kincardine. *m.* Muttra 10 June 1821, Miss Harriet Armstrong.

Services: Barasat C.C. 8½ mos. Cadet d.d. 4th N.C. 1811. Posted Cornet to 4th N.C. 1813. Leave s.c. 6 mos. to sea 4 July 1817. Third Mahratta War 1818; Cornet 4th N.C. Intr. & Qmr. 4th L.C. 10 Apr. 1819 till 29 June 1824. Operations in Kotah 1821; Mangrol (? w.); Lieut. 4th L.C.[1] Leave u.p.a. to Calcutta 19 Apr. till 14 Dec. 1822. Leave s.c. 12 mos. to N.S.W. 3 May 1823 till 16 Apr. 1826. Fur. s.c. 4 June 1826 till 14 May 1831. (? Shekhawat expedn. 1834; Capt. 4th L.C.) Offg. D.J.A.G. Sirhind Div. 23 Feb. 1838; D.J.A.G. Dinapore and Benares 6 Mar. 1839; do. Presdy. Div. 25 June 1839 till 21 Dec. 1842. Gwalior campaign; Maharajpur (*Lond. Gaz.* 8 Mar. and 30 Apr. 1844); Major comdg. 4th L.C. (Bronze star). First Sikh War; Mudki (s.w.), comdg. 3rd Cav. Bde.; Ferozshahr; Bt. Lt. Col. comdg. 4th L.C. (Medal with clasp). Offg. M.M.B. 1849-50; stipendiary M.M.B. 8 Nov. 1850. Posted Lt. Col. to 1st L.C. Dec. 1851; to 2nd L.C. Nov. 1852. Bdr. 2 cl. comdg. Delhi 22 Sept. 1854; do. Benares Jan. 1855 till death. C.B. 3 Apr. 1846.

Refs.: Boase. *G.M.* 1856, i. 96. *I.M.* 5 Nov. 1855, p. 613. M.I. in St. Andrew's, Calcutta.

[1] *Note:* In a footnote to p. 84 of "A Record of the Redes," by Compton Rede (Hereford, 1899), it is stated that, "When within fifty yards of the enemy, an Officer in the rear rank, Lieut. Mactier, suddenly gave the order to retire, with the result that the two Officers at the front (Edward Jervoise Ridge and Henry Jonathan Reade, *qq.v.*), deserted by their men, rode alone to meet inevitable death. Mactier's interest with the E.I.C. being strong, he escaped with a reprimand." The C.-in-C., however, published his sentiments in regard to what he characterized as 'these base insinuations' in G.O. of 6 Jan. 1823. A Court of Enquiry which was ordered by the C.D. in June 1825, was not held owing to the absence in England of many witnesses.

McVEAGH, Alexander (1763/64-1786). Lieutenant, Infantry. *b.* 1763/64. Country Cadet 1781. Ensign 18 July 1782. Lieut. 15 Jan. 1785. *d.s.p.* Purnea, B. & O., 10 May 1786, aged 22.

Son of Hugh McVeagh and Margaret his wife, dau. of Henry Lumsden, of Cushnie. Uncle of Thomas Lumsden, of Belhelvie, *q.v.*, and cousin-german of David Lumsden (1764/65-1823) and Joseph McVeagh, *qq.v.* (*Probably* brother of Ferdinand McVeagh, *q.v.*)

Services: Apptd. Cadet Oct. 1781. N.F.P.

LIST OF THE OFFICERS OF

Refs.: Burke's *Landed Gentry of Ireland*, p. 446, *s.n.* McVeagh, of Drewstown, co. Meath. Will dated Purnea 4 May 1786; proved 5 June 1786. M.I. Purnea.

McVEAGH, Ferdinand (1758/59-1781). Fireworker, Artillery. (201) *b.* Scotland 1758/59. Cadet 1778. Fireworker 19 Jan. 1779. *d.* 28 July 1781, on active service with the Madras detachment; *bur.* St. Mary's, Madras, 30 July.

Brother of Henry McVeagh, Lieut. 89th Foot. (*Probably* brother of Alexander McVeagh, *q.v.*)

Services: Apptd. Cadet for Bombay; sailed for India in the *Colebrooke* 27 Apr. 1778, aged 19. She was lost entering False Bay 24 Aug. 1778, and he was obliged to proceed to Bengal and was transfd. as Cadet to that Est. Second Mysore War; Lieut. F. 5th Coy. 2nd Bn. Art.

McVEAGH, Joseph (*d.* 1794). Captain. Infantry. Country Cadet 1767. Ensign 7 Dec. 1767. Lieut. 15 Oct. 1769. Capt. 24 Mar. 1778. Resigned 4 Jan. 1779. *d.* Aug. 1794.

Of Drewstown, co. Meath; high sheriff 1790. Younger son of Simon McVeagh and Alice his wife, dau. of Joseph Wilson. Maternal uncle of Thomas Shaw (1761-1841) and Ezekiel Davys Wilson, *qq.v.*, and cousin-german of Alexander McVeagh, *q.v. m.* 13 Mar. 1787, Margery, dau. of Alexander Wynch, Govr. of Madras. (She died Apr. 1794.)

Services: Apptd. (probably from the ranks) Adjt. 101st Ft. 1 July 1762. This Regt. was disbanded in 1763, and he remained on h.p. of Adjt. for the rest of his life. Allowed to proceed to India as a surgeon 24 Feb. 1767; sailed in the *Adm. Pocock* 3 Apr. 1767. Dy. Judge Advocate to the New Bde.; posted to 1st Regt. Nawab-Wazir's Cav. 7 Aug. 1777.

Refs.: Burke's *Landed Gentry of Ireland*, p. 466, *s.n.* McVeagh, of Drewstown, co. Meath. Will proved P.C. Dublin, 1795.

MACVICAR, George (*d.* 1775). Lieutenant, Infantry. Cadet (?) Ensign 23 Jan. 1769. Lieut. 22 May 1770. *d.* Chunar 5 Apr. 1775.

Services: Lieut. in 3rd Bde.
Refs.: *S.M.* 1776, p. 395.

MACVITIE, Richard Francis (1806-1877). Captain. 49th N.I. *b.* Calcutta 14 Aug. 1806. Cadet 1823. Arrived in India 3 May 1824. Ensign 9 Jan. 1824. Lieut. 13 May 1825. Capt. 26 Apr.

THE BENGAL ARMY, 1758-1834   205

1833. Invalided 14 Mar. 1845. Retired 12 Nov. 1863. *d.* nr. Dumfries 7 Feb. 1877, of heart disease.

bapt. Calcutta 27 Aug. 1806. Posthumous son of William Bushby Macvitie, q.v., and Margaret his wife. Brother of William John Macvitie, *q.v. m.* 1st, Delhi 10 Feb. 1833, Mary, eldest dau. of Edward Henry Simpson, *q.v. m.* 2nd, St. John's, Calcutta, 6 Aug. 1849, Eleanor, dau. of Capt. Henry Hudson Hopper, and widow of Alexander Nugent Murray MacGregor, *q.v.*

Services: Posted Ensign to 49th N.I. in 1824. First Burma War; Arakan 1825; Lieut. 49th N.I. Actg. Intr. & Qmr. 49th N.I. 19 Sept. 1825. Actg. Adjt. Magh Levy 7 Nov. 1825. Fur. s.c. 18 Mar. 1826 till 2 Jan. 1829. Actg. Adjt. 49th N.I. 6 Mar. 1832. After being invalided he resided in Calcutta till retirement.

Refs.: The Times, 20 Feb. 1877.

MACVITIE, William Bushby (1779-1806). Lieutenant, 11th N.I. *bapt.* Episcopal chapel, Dumfries, 15 Aug. 1779. Cadet 1795. Arrived in India 6 Mar. 1797. Ensign 10 Dec. 1796. Lieut. 30 Dec. 1797. *d.* 22 Feb. 1806: kld. in action at the capture of Gohad.

m. Penang Nov. 1801, Miss Margaret Jolliffe. (She *re-m.* the Adjt. of H.M. 91st Ft.) Father of Richard Francis Macvitie, *q.v.*, and of William John Macvitie, *q.v.*

Services: Lieut. 1/1st N.I. in July 1798. Transfd. to 2/11th N.I. Served at P.W.I. 1801-3. Second Mahratta War; Lieut. 2/11th N.I. Operations against the Rana of Gohad 1806; capture of Gohad (kld.); Lieut. 2/11th N.I.

MACVITIE, William John (1802-1847). Major, Invalid Est. Artillery. (479) *b.* P.W.I. 6 Oct. 1802. Cadet 1818. Admitted 11 Sept. 1819. 2nd Lieut. 6 Apr. 1819. Lieut. 2 Feb. 1820. Capt. 21 Oct. 1833. Major 3 July 1845. Invalided 5 Sept. 1845. *d.* Barrackpore 24 Sept. 1847.

bapt. P.W.I. 26 Feb. 1803. Son of William Bushby Macvitie, *q.v.*, and Margaret his wife. Brother of Richard Francis Macvitie, *q.v. m.* Cawnpore 3 May 1824, Catherine, dau. of Alexander Campbell (1780-1825), *q.v.* Addiscombe Cadet 1817-19.

Services: Actg. Adjt. & Qmr. 3rd Coy. 3rd Bn. Foot Art. 6 Aug. 1824. To comd. Art. details at P.W.I. 8 Dec. 1824. Posted to 2nd Coy. 3rd Bn. 8 Oct. 1834. Comdg. Art. Div. at Sultanpur in Jan. 1839. To comd. No. 11 Light Field Battery 30 Oct. 1844. Posted Major to 3rd Bn. 24 July 1845. No record of active service.

Refs.: I.M. 22 Dec. 1847, p. 743.

MADDEN, Edward (1805-1856). Lieut. Colonel. Artillery. (525) *b.* Birr, King's Co., 24 July 1805. Cadet 1821. Arrived in India 23 Mar. 1822. 2nd Lieut. 9 June 1821. Lieut. 30 May 1824. Capt. 12 Sept. 1839. Major 5 May 1849. Retired 1 Oct. 1849. Hon. Lt. Col. 28 Nov. 1854. *d.* Edinburgh 24 June 1856.

2nd son of Samuel Madden, of Kellsgrange, co. Kilkenny, Major 15th Regt., J.P., alderman and mayor of the city of Kilkenny, and Margaret Grace Cumming his wife, eldest dau. of Sir Alexander Penrose Cumming Gordon, Bart. *m.* Charlotte. (She *re-m.* 29 Apr. 1859, Rt. Rev. Charles Hugh Terrot, D.D., bishop of Edinburgh.) Addiscombe Cadet 1819-21.

Services : Actg. Adjt. Saugor Div. Art. 27 Oct. 1828. Shekhawat expedn. 1834 ; comdg. a Battery of guns and howitzers, and a party of Golandaz. Adjt. & Qmr. 2nd Bn. Foot Art. 29 June 1837 till 12 Nov. 1839. Fur. p.a. 27 Feb. 1841 till 11 Dec. 1843. Capt. comdg. 1st Coy. 7th Bn. Art. Author of " Observations on Himalayan Coniferæ," Calcutta, 1850.

Refs. : Burke's *Landed Gentry*, 5th edn., p. 868, *s.n.* Madden, of Inch House, co. Dublin. *G.M.* 1856, ii. 258.

MADDOCK, John (1783-1808). Lieutenant, 26th N.I. *b.* London 27 July 1783. Cadet 1803. Arrived in India 17 Mar. 1805. Ensign 19 Apr. 1805. Lieut. 20 Apr. 1805. *d.* Banda 19 Oct. 1808.

bapt. St. Clement Danes, London, 24 Aug. 1783. Son of Henry Maddock and Jane his wife. Brother of Henry, Maria Stevenson, and Matilda Leeson. Nephew of John Ford, Adm. R.N.

Services : Posted Lieut. to 26th N.I. Operations in Bundelkhand 1807 ; Sehlehuganj ; Lieut. 27th N.I.

Refs. : Will undated ; proved 16 Nov. 1808.

MADDOCK, Thomas (1788-1841). Lieut. Colonel, 10th N.I. *bapt.* St. Michael's, Macclesfield, co. Chester, 13 Aug. 1788. Cadet 1803. Arrived in India 27 Sept. 1804. Ensign 21 Sept. 1804. Lieut. 21 Sept. 1804. Capt. 1 Jan. 1819. Major 18 June 1828. Lt. Col. 10 Jan. 1833. *d.* Mussoorie 14 Oct. 1841, aged 58.

Son of Edward Maddock, of Edge, co. Chester, of an old Cheshire family descended from Owen Gwynedd, and Fanny his wife. *m.* 1st, Calcutta 3 June 1815, Harriet, eldest dau. of Benjamin Comberbach, atty.-at-law. *m.* 2nd, Bengal 6 Nov. 1820, Miss Louisa Comberbach.

Services : Barasat C.C. Posted Lieut. to 1/7th N.I. in 1805. 1st Asst. Sec. Mily. Board 11 Mar. 1808 till 1824 ; Sec. Clothing

THE BENGAL ARMY, 1758-1834 207

Board 17 Apr. 1820 till 2 July 1828. Capt. 1/7th N.I. ; transfd. to 2/7th N.I. ; to 10th N.I. (late 2/7th) May 1824. Posted Lt. Col. to 10th N.I. 14th Sept. 1833. Cuttack insurrection 1836 ; Lt. Col. comdg. 10th N.I.
Refs. : Will dated Calcutta 15 Nov. 1828 ; proved 9 Feb. 1842. M.I. in Landour cemetery.

MAGINNIS, Andrew Ferguson (1807-1830). Lieutenant, Bengal Eur. Regt. *b.* Templemore, co. Londonderry, 7 Jan. 1807. Cadet 1824. Arrived in India 5 June 1825. Ensign 23 Jan. 1825. Lieut. 7 Aug. 1826. *d.* Aligarh 29 Sept. 1830, of fever. *bapt.* Londonderry cathedral 21 Jan. 1807. Son of Robert Maginnis, mayor of Londonderry, and Jane Ferguson his wife.
Services : Ensign d.d. 1st Bengal Eur. Regt. 11 June 1825. Posted Ensign to 1st Bengal Eur. Regt. in 1825. Siege and capture of Bhurtpore ; Ensign Bengal Eur. Regt. On the amalgamation of the 1st and 2nd Eur. Regt. in Jan. 1830, was posted to Rt. Wing of the Bengal Eur. Regt.
Refs. : *A.J.* N.S. iv. 145.

MAGNAY, Edward (1812-1862). Major. 1st Bengal Eur. Fus. *b.* Lambeth 17 Jan. 1812. Cadet 1828. Arrived in India 16 Feb. 1830. Ensign 16 Feb. 1830. Lieut. 15 Nov. 1836. Capt. 31 Mar. 1846. Invalided 1 Apr. 1849. Retired 1 June 1859. Hon. Major 1 June 1859. *d. unm.* Tunbridge Wells 13 June 1862. *bapt.* St. Mary's, Lambeth, 14 Dec. 1813. 7th son of Christopher Magnay, of Clapham Rd., stationer, and of the Manor House, Wandsworth, sheriff of London 1813, lord mayor 1821, by Harriet his 2nd wife, dau. of John Burdon, of Winchester. Younger brother of Sir William Magnay, 1st Bart. Ed. Winchester ; scholar 1823.
Services : Ensign d.d. 11th N.I. 31 Mar. 1830. Actg. Ensign (having been 2 yrs. in India) 12 Mar. 1832. Posted to Left Wing Bengal Eur. Regt. 14 Mar. 1833. First Afghan War 1839 ; capture of Ghazni (w.) (*Lond. Gaz.* 30 Oct. 1839) ; Lieut. Bengal Eur. Regt. (Medal). First Sikh War ; Ferozshahr ; Sobraon (s.w.) ; Bt. Capt. Left Wing 1st Eur. L.I. (Medal with clasp). Postmr. at Naini Tal 1853. Fur. 3 yrs. 20 Jan. 1859.
Refs. : Burke's *Peerage*, 1923, p. 1486, *s.n.* Magnay, Bart., of Postford House, Surrey. *Kirby. G.M.* 1862, ii. 117. *The Times*, 17 June 1862.

MAIDMAN, William Richard (1802-1841). Captain, Artillery. (480) *b.* Ingeram, Madras, 6 July 1802. Cadet 1818. Admitted

1 Jan. 1820. 2nd Lieut. 7 Apr. 1819. Lieut. 4 May 1820. Capt. 10 Feb. 1834. d. Cawnpore 12 Aug. 1841, of cholera. *bapt.* Ingeram 2 Oct. 1803. Son of George Maidman, M.C.S., Dy. Commercial Resdt. at Ingeram, and Elizabeth his wife, 3rd dau. of Edward Watts. *m.* Calcutta 2 Dec. 1834, Charlotte Elizabeth, 3rd dau. of William McQuhae, *q.v.* (*See also* James Tobin Bush.) (She died Chelsea 5 Sept. 1850, aged 31.) Addiscombe Cadet 1817-19.

Services: With Rocket Troop in 1823. Siege and capture of Bhurtpore; Lieut. 1st Troop 3rd Bde. H.A. Transfd. from 4th Troop 3rd Bde. to 1st Troop 2nd Bde. 10 Nov. 1830. Actg. Adjt. 2nd Bde. H.A. 20 Apr. 1831. Posted Capt. to 2nd Coy. 4th Bn. Foot Art. 8 Nov. 1834; transfd. to 3rd Troop 3rd Bde. H.A. 21 Mar. 1837.

Refs.: G.M. 1841, ii. 668; 1842, i. 117.

MAILLARD, Andrew Richard (1784-1804). Lieutenant, 9th N.I. *bapt.* Allhallows, London Wall, 25 Feb. 1784. Cadet 1798. Arrived in India 22 Dec. 1799. Ensign 28 Dec. 1799. Lieut. 29 May 1800. *d.* Sikandra 24 Aug. 1804: kld. in action on the banks of the Banas R. during Monson's retreat.

(*Probably* son of James Nicholas Maillard and Sarah his wife.)

Services: Posted Lieut. to 1/9th N.I. 15 Apr. 1801. Second Mahratta War; Monson's retreat (kld.); Lieut. 2/9th N.I.

MAINWARING, Boulton (1772-1816). Lieut. Colonel, 16th N.I. *bapt.* Dunston, Lincs., 8 Mar. 1772. Cadet 1791. Admitted 27 Aug. 1791. Ensign 2 Jan. 1792. Lieut. 21 Oct. 1794. Capt. 30 Sept. 1803. Major 3 Aug. 1811. Lt. Col. 1 Oct. 1815. *d.* Rewari, Punjab, 18 Sept. 1816.

Son of William Mainwaring, a Bencher of Lincoln's Inn, M.P. for Middlesex 1784-1802, and Ann his wife. Ed. Tonbridge School 1789-90.

Services: Apptd. Cadet 4 Mar. 1791; sailed for India in the *Kent* 27 Mar. 1791. Posted Cadet to 4th Bengal Eur. Bn. 7 Sept. 1791; posted Lieut. do. 19 Nov. 1794; Lieut. 6th Eur. Bn. in Feb. 1796. Fur. 3 Mar. 1796 till 11 Sept. 1800. Adjt. newly-raised 2nd Bn. Marine Regt. (became 2/20th N.I.) 1802-3. Fur. 22 Sept. 1806 till 1810. Capture of Java 1811; Major 1/20th N.I. Posted Lt. Col. to 1/16th N.I., but was tempy. comdg. 2/16th at date of death.

Refs.: Tonbridge School Register, 1553-1820 (1935).

THE BENGAL ARMY, 1758-1834

MAINWARING, Charles John (1809-1848). Captain, 1st N.I. *b.* Dacca 2 June 1809. Cadet 1825. Arrived in India 4 Sept. 1826. Ensign 15 Apr. 1826. Lieut. 30 Aug. 1833. Capt. 16 May 1846. *d.* Ludhiana 16 Aug. 1848.

2nd son of Thomas Mainwaring, B.C.S., actg. salt agent at Tamluk, and Sophia his wife, dau. of Thomas Walker, of Wendlebury, Oxon. Brother of Edward Rowland Mainwaring, *q.v.*, and cousin-german of Gordon Mainwaring, *q.v.*, and of Anna Maria, wife of Cuthbert Davidson, *q.v.*

Services: Posted Ensign to 1st N.I. 5 Oct. 1826. Actg. Intr. & Qmr. 19th N.I. 19 Aug. 1830 till Feb. 1831. Intr. & Qmr. 1st N.I. 7 Feb. till Oct. 1835. Fur. s.c. 30 Oct. 1835 till 20 Oct. 1838. Actg. Intr. & Qmr. 11th N.I. 21 Aug. 1839 till Dec. 1840; do. 31st N.I. 5 Feb. 1841 till 12 Nov. 1842. S.S.O. at Mainpuri 13 Mar. till 10 Nov. 1841. Apptd. to Comst. Dept. with troops for Bundelkhand 12 Nov. 1842. Insurrection in Bundelkhand 1842-3; offg. in Comst. Dept. Offg. D.A.C.G. at Nowgong Mar. 1843 till Jan. 1844; permanent do. 1 Jan. 1844. Gwalior campaign; Paniar (*Lond. Gaz.* 8 Mar. 1844); S.A.C.G. (Bronze star). First Sikh War; Ferozshahr; Aliwal; actg. as Chief of Comst. Dept. with Sir Harry Smith's force (Medal with clasp).

Refs.: Burke's *Landed Gentry*, 12th edn., p. 1262, *s.n.* Cavenagh-Mainwaring, of Whitmore and Biddulph, Staffs. Burke's *Family Records*, p. 415. *De Rhé-Philipe.* M.I. at Ludhiana.

MAINWARING, Edward Henry (1781-1807). Lieutenant, 3rd N.I. *bapt.* St. Mary's, Lichfield, 7 Nov. 1781. Cadet 1796. Arrived in India 23 Sept. 1797. Ensign 23 Sept. 1797. Lieut. 10 Sept. 1798. *d. unm.* Dacca 22 July 1807: "while out at exercise he complained of a sudden attack in the head, and died in a few minutes in consequence of the rupture of a blood vessel in his brain." (*G.M.*)

Eldest son of Major Rowland Mainwaring, of Four Oaks, co. Warwick (of Northampton), and Jane his 2nd wife, dau. of Capt. Latham, R.N. Uncle of Edward Rowland Mainwaring, *q.v.*, and of Gordon Mainwaring, *q.v.* Ed. Rugby; adm. Jan. 1791.

Services: Ensign 1st Bengal Eur. Regt. in June 1798. Lieut. 1/3rd N.I. A.D.C. to Maj.-Gen. Edward Clarke, *q.v.*, comdg. at Dinapore, 1805-6. Adjt. 1/3rd N.I. 1806. No record of active service.

Refs.: Burke's *Landed Gentry*, 12th edn., p. 1262, *s.n.* Cavenagh-Mainwaring, of Whitmore and Biddulph, Staffs. Burke's *Family Records*, p. 415. Will dated 18 Mar. 1807; proved 10 Aug. 1807. M.I. at Dacca.

LIST OF THE OFFICERS OF

MAINWARING, Edward Rowland (1807-1868). Major General. 28th N.I. *b.* Dacca 20 Nov. 1807. Cadet 1823. Arrived in India 4 May 1824. Ensign 9 Jan. 1824. Lieut. 13 May 1825. Capt. 20 Feb. 1838. Major 13 Dec. 1854. Lt. Col. 24 Nov. 1858. Bt. Col. 7 May 1855. Maj. Gen. 28 Mar. 1865. *d.* Madras 8 Apr. 1868.

Eldest son of Thomas Mainwaring, B.C.S., and Sophia his wife. Brother of Henry George Mainwaring, *q.v. m.* Delhi 25 June 1838, Georgina Caroline Barbara, widow of George Byron, *q.v.* (She died 23 July 1881, aged 67.)

Services: Posted Ensign to 16th N.I. Actg. Intr. & Qmr. 16th N.I. 14 July 1829; permanent do. 18 Feb. 1831 till 13 Sept. 1838. In charge of Comst. duties with Art. Div., Army of the Indus, 2 May 1839. First Afghan War 1839-42; capture of Ghazni 1839 (Medal); offg. S.A.C.G., in charge of 4th Bde., Army of the Indus; defence of Jalalabad (*Lond. Gaz.* 7 and 10 June, and 9 Aug. 1842) (Medal); reoccupation of Kabul (Medal). S.A.C.G. 27 May 1842. Insurrection in Bundelkhand 1843. Gwalior campaign; Paniar; S.A.C.G. (Bronze star). First Sikh War; Sobraon; S.A.C.G. (Medal). D.A.C.G. 2cl. 24 Dec. 1847; 1cl. 29 May 1851 till 1854. Second Sikh War; Ramnagar; Sadulapur; Chilianwala; Gujerat; D.A.C.G. (Medal with 2 clasps). Fur. Feb. 1858 till 30 Jan. 1860. Transfd. to 28th N.I. 14 Jan. 1860.

Refs.: Burke's *Landed Gentry*, 13th edn., p. 1192, *s.n.* Cavenagh-Mainwaring, of Whitmore and Biddulph, Staffs. Burke's *Family Records*, p. 415. M.I. St. Mary's cemetery, Madras.

MAINWARING, Gordon (1817-1872). Lieutenant. 53rd N.I. *bapt.* Walcot, Somerset, 5 Mar. 1817. Cadet 1833. Arrived in India 1 Dec. 1834. Ensign 25 Sept. 1834. Lieut. 4 Mar. 1839. Resigned 20 May 1839. *d.* 21 Dec. 1872.

Of Whitmore Hall and Biddulph, Staffs. 3rd son of Rear-Adm. Rowland Mainwaring, R.N., of Whitmore Hall and Biddulph, J.P. and D.L., and Sophia Henrietta his 1st wife, only child of Major Duff, 26th Regt. Nephew of Edward Henry Mainwaring, *q.v.*, and cousin-german of Henry George Mainwaring, *q.v. m.* 5 July 1843, Mary, dau. of Michael Hickey. (She died Dec. 1890.) Addiscombe Cadet 3 Aug. 1832 till 13 June 1834.

Services: Ensign d.d. 4th N.I. 4 Dec. 1834; posted to 53rd N.I. 2 Mar. 1835. No record of active service.

Refs.: Burke's *Landed Gentry*, 13th edn., p. 1192, *s.n.* Cavenagh-Mainwaring, of Whitmore, Staffs. Burke's *Family Records*, p. 416, *s.n.* Mainwaring.

MAINWARING, Henry George (1812-1868). Major. 1st N.I. *b.* Calcutta 29 June 1812. Cadet 1828. Arrived in India 11 Jan. 1829. Ensign 19 July 1828. Lieut. 3 Jan. 1835. Capt. 16 Aug. 1848. Invalided 31 Oct. 1848. Retired 7 Nov. 1854. Hon. Major 28 Nov. 1854. *d.* Château d'Oex, canton Vaud, Switzerland, 8 June 1868.

bapt. Calcutta 26 Oct. 1812. 3rd son of Thomas Mainwaring, B.C.S., and Sophia his wife. Brother of Charles John Mainwaring, *q.v. m.* All Saints, St. John's Wood, London, 15 Jan. 1850, Frances Sanders, eldest dau. of John Kelk, of St. John's Wood. (She died 29 Dec. 1890, aged 82.)

Services: Ensign d.d. 7th N.I. 11 Feb. 1829. Posted to 13th N.I. 3 June 1829. d.d. 16th N.I. 15 July till 15 Oct. 1831. Transfd. to 1st N.I. 11 Oct. 1833. Fur. s.c. 27 Oct. 1839 till 10 Feb. 1842; s.c. 2 yrs. to Cape 21 Oct. 1844. Second Sikh War; in garr. at Fort Govindgarh, Amritsar; Capt. 1st N.I. (Medal). Fur. p.a. 10 Dec. 1848 till 6 Apr. 1850.

Refs.: Burke's *Family Records*, p. 416, *s.n.* Mainwaring. *The Times*, 23 June 1868.

MAINWARING, Philip (1811-1847). Major, 33rd N.I. *b.* Weybridge, Surrey, 8 Jan. 1811. Cadet 1826. Arrived in India 8 June 1827. Ensign 16 Feb. 1827. Lieut. 9 Sept. 1831. Capt. 11 Dec. 1837. Major 29 Jan. 1846. *d.* Kherwara, Mewar, 4 Jan. 1847.

bapt. Weybridge 15 Feb. 1811. Son of George Boulton Mainwaring, barr.-at-law, residing at Metz, and Letitia his wife. His sister *m.* George Carr, *q.v.*

Services: Posted Ensign to 33rd N.I. in 1827. Offg. Intr. & Qmr. 33rd N.I. 28 Apr. 1832. Attached to Sylhet L.I. 5 Sept. 1832; actg. Adjt. do. 1 Nov. 1834; offg. 2nd in comd. do. 5 May 1837. In charge of Supt.'s office in Cachar 21 Dec. 1835 till 13 Apr. 1836. Rejoined 33rd N.I. 2 Feb. 1838. Offg. D.A.Q.M.G. to troops assembled for service against Jhansi 25 Dec. 1838 till Jan. 1839. Comdt. Upper Assam Sebundy Corps (later 2nd Assam Sebundy Corps) 9 Sept. 1839 till 1843. Fur. s.c. 17 Mar. 1844 till 1846.

Refs.: M.I. Kherwara.

MAIR, John (*c.* 1743-1827?). Captain. Cavalry. *b. c.* 1743. Cornet 14 Mar. 1762. Lieut. 23 July 1763. Capt. 8 July 1766. Dismissed 1 Nov. 1766. (? *d.* Upper Kensington Gore, London, 8 Sept. 1827, aged 83.)

A native of Kent. (? Of the Lodge, Iron Acton, Gloucs.)
Services : Apptd. in England 1 May 1761, a Cornet for the Troop of Light Horse being raised for Madras ; sailed as Cornet in the *Chesterfield* 1761, aged 18. Lieut. in one of the Troops of Eur. Dgns. till their disbandment in July 1764 ; subsequently comdd. 3rd Troop of Moghal Horse. Battle of Buxar. Petitioned C.D. in Feb. 1770 and Jan. 1775 to be restored to the Service.
Refs. : Caraccioli, ii. 54. (? *G.M.* 1827, ii 283.)

MAITLAND, Charles (1752-1822). Lieut. Colonel. Infantry. *b.* 9 Apr. 1752. Country Cadet 1768. Ensign 10 May 1768. Lieut. 20 Dec. 1769. Capt. 8 July 1778. Major 26 Jan. 1784. Lt. Col. 1 Mar. 1794. Retired 1 June 1796. *d.* 3 Apr. 1822.
Of Craigieburn, Dumfries, and Maitlandfield, Haddington. Only son of Thomas Maitland, of Woodcot, and Mary, dau. of James Martin, of Clermont. *m.* Edinburgh 28 Apr. 1797, Isabel, eldest dau. of Maj.-Gen. Hon. Mark Napier, and sister of John George Napier, *q.v.* (She died 11 Dec. 1805, aged 33.)
Services : Apptd. Cadet 8 Feb. 1768. Capt. 1/2nd Bengal Eur. Regt. in Oct. 1779 ; to comd. 39th Bn. Sepoys 3 Sept. 1780. First Mahratta War 1778-84 ; succeeded Solomon Earle, *q.v.*, in comd. of 2nd N.I. in 1781, whilst serving with Col. Goddard's detachment, and brought it back to Bengal in 1784. Major comdg. 10th Bn. Sepoys in July 1787 and Dec. 1792. Fur. 5 Mar. 1793.
Refs. : Scottish Antiquary, viii. 93. Burke's *Peerage*, 1923, p. 1644, *s.n.* Napier and Ettrick, B.

*MAITLAND, Frederick Colthurst (1808-1876). Major General. 5th Bengal Eur. Inf. *b.* Calcutta 1 Jan. 1808. Cadet 1825. Was already in Calcutta when apptd. Cadet. Ensign (17 Aug. 1826) 10 May 1827. Lieut. 21 Jan. 1838. Capt. 15 Feb. 1851. Major 31 Dec. 1856. Lt. Col. 18 Nov. 1860. Col. 18 Feb. 1866. Maj. Gen. 3 Sept. 1871. *d.* 5 Shardeloes Rd., New Cross, 3 Aug. 1876.
bapt. Calcutta 26 Dec. 1809. Elder son of Patrick Maitland, a partner in the bank of John Palmer & Co., Calcutta, afterwards of Kilmaron Castle, co. Fife, and Anne his wife, 2nd dau. of Colthurst Bateman, and sister of John Bateman (1790-1819), *q.v.* Gt.-grandson of Charles, 6th Earl of Lauderdale. *m.* St. Mary's, Marylebone, 29 Aug. 1837, Anne Dering, eldest dau. of Stephen Williams, barr.-at-law. (She died 24 Mar. 1887.) Father of Frederick Henry, 13th Earl of Lauderdale. Ed. Charterhouse ; admitted 1821, left Oct. 1822.

THE BENGAL ARMY, 1758-1834

Services: Posted Ensign to 4th N.I. 10 May 1827. Actg. Adjt. 4th N.I. 20 Nov. 1829. Leave s.c. to Simla 17 Feb. 1830 till 20 Dec. 1831. Fur. s.c. 23 Oct. 1835 till 19 Feb. 1838. Actg. Intr. & Qmr. 50th N.I. 7 May 1838; do. 67th N.I. 5 June 1839. Intr. & Qmr. 4th N.I. 25 Oct. 1839 till 26 June 1843. Transfd. to 5th N.I. 14 Dec. 1842. Intr. & Qmr. 5th N.I. 26 June 1843 till Mar. 1845. Second in comd. 6th Inf., Gwalior Contingent, 31 Mar. 1845; do. 7th Inf. 10 Jan. 1846; Comdt. do. 14 Aug. 1851 till 1 Jan. 1857. Transfd. to newly-raised 5th Eur. Inf. in 1858. Did general duty at Meerut for several years. Fur. 10 Mar. 1870 till death.

Refs.: Burke's *Peerage*, 1923, p. 1344, *s.n.* Lauderdale, E. *G.E.C.* (1929 edn.) vii. 497. *Charterhouse School List*. *A.J.* N.S. xxiv. 123. *The Times*, 5 Aug. 1876.

MAITLAND, Henry Daniel (1809-1895). Lieut. Colonel. 72nd N.I. *b.* 15 Aug. 1809. Cadet 1825. Arrived in India 24 Sept. 1826. Ensign 15 May 1826. Lieut. 11 June 1832. Capt. 29 Oct. 1838. Bt. Major 11 Nov. 1851. Retired 1 Jan. 1857. Hon. Lt. Col. 1 Jan. 1857. *d.* Edinburgh 21 Apr. 1895.

bapt. Pyrford, Surrey, 5 July 1812. Son of Maitland Maitland, of Bruges, physician, and Amelia his wife. *m.* Kensington 30 Sept. 1845, Anne, eldest dau. of Thomas Montgomery Hunter, of Eastwood, Portishead, and grand-dau. of Saul Solomon, of St. Helena. (She died Sialkot 4 July 1855, aged 30.) Ed. Bruges Coll.

Services: Posted Ensign to 4th Extra Regt. (became 72nd N.I.) in 1826. Intr. & Qmr. 72nd N.I. 4 Mar. 1830; Adjt. do. 23 Sept. 1835 till 9 Jan. 1839. Bde. Major at Meerut 15 Apr. till 13 Oct. 1842. Bde. Major 3rd Inf. Bde., Army of Reserve (for Afghanistan), 26 Oct. 1842. Fur. p.a. 18 June 1843 till 1846. Second Sikh War; Multan (s.w. 6 Nov. 1848); Capt. 72nd N.I. (Medal). Bde. Major Nasirabad 31 Mar. 1849; do. Wazirabad 1849; do. Sialkot 1852; do. Pegu Jan. 1856. Fur. p.a. Feb. 1856 till retirement.

MAJOR, William (*b.* 1786). Lieutenant, Infantry. Country Cadet 1781. Ensign 9 Aug. 1782. Lieut. 29 Jan. 1785. *d.* Dinajpur, Bengal, 12 Apr. 1786.

m. (?) His dau. *m.* Samuel Pidding Bishop, *q.v.*
Services: Apptd. Cadet Nov. 1781. N.F.P.

MALCOLM, John (1758-1822). Major. 22nd N.I. *b.* 1758. County Cadet 1777. Admitted 20 Mar. 1778. Ensign 4 June 1778. Lieut. 21 Nov. 1780. Capt. 16 Apr. 1797. Major 30 Sept. 1803. Retired 4 Mar. 1804. *d.* Haughton-le-Skerne, co. Durham, 16 Oct. 1822.

Eldest son of Dr. John McColme or Malcolm, of Ayr, Surg. 1st Royals, and Anne Gould his wife. Uncle of Gen. Sir John Low, K.C.B., K.C.S.I. (*D.N.B.*), and grand-uncle of A. F. C. Deas, *q.v.* *m.* London 19 Aug. 1806, Miss Eleanor Todd, of Darlington, sister of Capt. William D'Arcy Todd, K.H., H.M.S.

Services : Ensign 2/2nd Bengal Eur. Regt. in Oct. 1779. Campaign against the Rajah of Benares 1781. Lieut. 11th Bn. Sepoys in July 1787 and Dec. 1788; apptd. Adjt. 29th Bn. 26 Oct. 1793. Fourth Mysore War 1798-1800; Seringapatam; service on N. frontier of Mysore; Capt. comdg. 1st Vol. Bn. (Medal). Second Mahratta War; Aligarh; Capt. 2/4th N.I. Posted to newly-raised 22nd N.I. 9 Nov. 1803.

Refs. : Fifty Years with John Company, ed. Ursula Low (London, 1936). *M.M.* 1806, p. 297. *A.J.* xiv. 521.

MALDEN, Thomas Barlow (1793-1824). Lieutenant, 21st N.I. *b.* 22 Feb. 1793. Cadet 1809. Ensign 21 Sept. 1812. Lieut. 27 Jan. 1815. *d.* Saugor 14 Oct. 1824.

bapt. Putney, Surrey, 22 Mar. 1793. Son of Jonas Malden, of Putney, surgeon and apothecary, and Mary his wife, dau. of Thomas Barlow. Brother of Charles Robert Malden, Lieut. R.N.[1] *m.* Calcutta 4 Jan. 1817, Miss Catherine White Williams. (She died 6 Dec. 1871, aged 73.) Ed. Eton; K.S. 1805.

Services : Barasat C.C. Posted Ensign to 9th N.I. in 1812. Lieut. 1/9th N.I. 25 Mar. 1820. Transfd. to 21st N.I. (late 2/9th) May 1824. Adjt. 21st, N.I. 17 June 1824 till death. No record of active service.

Refs. : Eton School Lists.

[1] *Note :* He afterwards founded and conducted a preparatory school for boys at Brighton, which is still (1928) carried on by the family.

MALING, Christopher Simpson (1808-1860). Bt. Colonel, 18th N.I. *b.* Gorakhpur, U.P., 11 Jan. 1808. Cadet 1823. Arrived in India 3 May 1824. Ensign 9 Jan. 1824. Lieut. 13 May 1825. Capt. 23 May 1834. Major 1 Nov. 1849. Lt. Col. 16 Dec. 1854. Bt. Col. 20 June 1857. *d.* on board the river steamer *Benares,* off Mirzapur, 16 Mar. 1860, of cholera.

bapt. Gorakhpur 13 Apr. 1808. Son of Irwin Maling, *q.v.,* and Jane his 1st wife. *m.* 1st, St. Mary's, Marylebone, 17 May 1836, Jane Wemyss, widow of Charles Hay Campbell, *q.v.* (She died Mirzapur 28 Mar. 1844.) *m.* 2nd, Ambala 24 Sept. 1849, Eliza Caroline, 2nd dau. of Sir Francis Ford, 2nd Bart. (She *re-m.* 12 Feb. 1866, Lt.-Col. William Charles Newhouse, late 5th Fus., and died 5 Jan. 1879, aged 56.) Addiscombe Cadet 1822-4.

THE BENGAL ARMY, 1758-1834 215

Services : Posted Ensign to 68th N.I. in 1824. First Burma War ; Arakan 1825 ; Lieut. 68th N.I. (India medal). Adjt. 68th N.I. 28 Dec. 1826 till 21 Nov. 1833. Leave s.c. 6 mos. to Singapore 8 Aug. 1828 ; do. 8 mos. to Penang 14 July 1830. Fur. s.c. 4 July 1835 till 28 July 1838. Tempy. comdg. Jodhpur Legion 23 Jan. 1839 till 7 Dec. 1840. First Sikh War ; Sobraon ; Capt. 68th N.I. (Medal). Bde. Major at Ambala 24 July 1846 till 1849. Second Burma War 1852-3 ; Major 68th N.I. (Medal with clasp). Posted Lt. Col. to 68th N.I. ; transfd. to 18th N.I. May 1855. Fur. s.c. 27 Feb. 1855 till Oct. 1859.

Refs. : The Times, 27 Apr. 1860. *I.M.* 5 May 1860, p. 345. M.I. Mirzapur cemetery.

MALING, Irwin (1781-1831). Major, Invalid Est. 64th N.I. Presdy. Paymr. *b.* 24 Nov. 1781. Cadet 1799. Arrived in India 6 Dec. 1800. Ensign 20 Oct. 1800. Lieut. 4 Apr. 1802. Capt. 15 Jan. 1815. Major 13 May 1825. Invalided 18 Apr. 1829. *d.* Calcutta 17 Nov. 1831.

4th son of Christopher Thompson Maling, of Hendon Lodge, West Herrington, co. Durham, J.P., and Martha his 2nd wife, only dau. of John Sheeles, of Queen's Sq., Bloomsbury. Brother of Thomas James Maling, Vice Adm. of the Red, of Martha Sophia, 1st Countess of Mulgrave, and of the wife of Thomas Welsh, *q.v.* *m.* 1st, Calcutta 27 Dec. 1806, Miss Jane Mabel Allenby Fletcher. (She died 7 May 1816.) Father of Christopher Simpson Maling, *q.v.* *m.* 2nd, Calcutta 3 Nov. 1817, Miss Henrietta Augusta Murray.

Services : Posted Ensign to 1/9th N.I. 17 Apr. 1801 ; Adjt. & Qmr. 9th N.I. 1804 till 1 June 1809. (? Second Mahratta War.) Supy. A.D.C. to Lord Minto, the G.G., 13 Jan. 1809. Comdd. Purnea Provl. Bn. 6 May 1809 till 1813 ; Dy. Paymr. at Cawnpore 21 May 1813 till 1823. Transfd. to newly-formed 32nd N.I. July 1823 ; to 64th N.I. (late 2/32nd) May 1824. Supy. A.D.C. to G.G. 15 Aug. 1823. Agent for army clothing, 2nd Div., 1824 till Feb. 1827. Paymr. at Presdy. and to King's troops 23 Feb. 1827 till invalided. Supy. A.D.C. to G.G. 13 Mar. 1828.

Refs. : Foster's *Yorks. W.R. Peds.*, iii. *Pester*, p. 88. *A.J.* N.S. viii. 41. Will dated Calcutta 3 Oct. 1831 ; proved 14 Nov. 1831. M.I. in S. Park St. cemetery, Calcutta.

MALLETT, John Charles (1791-1825). Lieutenant, Pension Est. 18th N.I. *bapt.* Petrockstow, Devon, 20 Mar. 1791. Cadet 1805. Arrived in India 19 Sept. 1806. Ensign 27 Sept. 1806. Lieut. 25 Oct. 1809. Pensioned 15 Nov. 1813. *d.* Serampore 20 Aug. 1825.

Son of John Mallett, of Sheepwash, Lieut. N. Devon Yeomanry, and Honoria his wife.

Services: Barasat C.C. Posted Ensign to 18th N.I. in 1807. Operations in Bundelkhand 1809; Rajaoli; Ajaigarh; Lieut. 1/18th N.I.

MALLOCK, Samuel (1806-1833). Lieutenant, Engineers. Asst. Sec. Mily. Board. *b.* Cockington, Devon, 1 Nov. 1806. Cadet 1823. Arrived in India 7 May 1825. 2nd Lieut. 18 Dec. 1823. Lieut. 28 Feb. 1825. *d. unm.* at sea 24 Dec. 1833, on board the *Mary Ann Webb* on his passage to England.

bapt. Cockington 15 Nov. 1806. 5th son of Rev. Roger Mallock, of Cockington Court, nr. Newton Abbot, and Mary his wife, dau. of John Mudge, and sister of Zachary Mudge, Adm. R.N. Brother of Zachary Mudge Mallock, *q,v.*, and cousin of John Mudge, *q.v.* Addiscombe Cadet 1822-3.

Services: Offg. Adjt. Engrs., and Visiting Ofr. of Works in Ft. Wm., 14 June 1825. Surveyor to Sundarbans Comrs. 18 Nov. 1826. Executive Engr. Purnea Div., P.W.D., 24 Oct. 1827. Asst. Sec. to Mily. Board 29 Dec. 1830 till 13 Sept. 1833. Leave s.c. 4 mos. to Singapore 6 Sept. 1832. Fur. s.c. 24 Oct. 1833. No record of active service.

Refs.: Burke's *Landed Gentry*, 13th edn., p. 1196, *s.n.* Mallock, of Cockington Court, Devon. Vivian's *Visitation of Devon*, p. 549. *A.J.* N.S. xiii. 222.

MALLOCK, Zachary Mudge (1808-1866). Colonel. Artillery. (590) *b.* Cockington, Devon, 2 Oct. 1808. Cadet 1826. Arrived in India 13 Aug. 1827. 2nd Lieut. 23 Sept. 1827. Lieut. 21 Oct. 1833. Capt. 3 July 1845. Major 17 Nov. 1856. Lt. Col. 27 Aug. 1858. Retired 1 Jan. 1859. Hon. Col. 18 Mar. 1859. *d.* Paignton, Devon, 28 June 1866, suddenly, whilst bathing.

bapt. Cockington 22 Jan. 1809. 6th son of Rev. Roger Mallock and Mary his wife. Brother of Samuel Mallock, *q.v. m.* Chunar 30 Nov. 1842, Laura, 4th dau. of Rev. James Lynn, vicar of Crosthwaite and rector of Caldbeck, Cumberland. (*See also* William Murray (1801-1842).) Addiscombe Cadet 1824-6.

Services: Operations against the Kols 1832-3. Posted to 3rd Coy. 7th Bn. 16 Sept. 1834; to 1st Coy. 5th Bn. 20 Dec. 1837. Fur. p.a. 8 Mar. 1838 till 8 Nov. 1841. Offg. Dy. Comy. Ord. at Chunar 9 Mar. 1842. Second Burma War 1852-3; capture of Rangoon and Pegu, comdg. Art.; relief of Pegu 1852; defence of Pegu Jan. 1853; Capt. 3rd Coy. 5th Bn., comdg. the Art. (Medal

THE BENGAL ARMY, 1758-1834 217

with clasp). Fur. s.c. May 1853 till 30 Aug. 1856. Posted Major to 6th Bn. Foot Art. 10 Mar. 1857.
Refs.: Burke's *Landed Gentry*, 13th edn., p. 1196, *s.n.* Mallock, of Cockington, Devon. Vivian's *Visitation of Devon*, p. 549. *G.M.* 1866, ii. 275.

MALONE, Edward (1792-1829). Captain, 9th L.C. *b.* The Residency, Malda, Bengal, 23 Oct. 1792. Cadet 1809. Cornet 29 July 1814. Lieut. 27 Oct. 1818. Capt. 1828. *d.* Margate 9 Jan. 1829.
bapt. Malda Residency Nov. 1800. Son of Edward Malone, of Hampton, formerly of Calcutta, steward to George Udny, B.C.S., Commercial Resdt. at Malda, and Ann Batley his wife.
Services: Barasat C.C. Cadet d.d. 3rd N.C. 1811-13; posted Cornet to 1st N.C. in 1814; actg. Intr. & Qmr. do. 1817. Third Mahratta War; Cornet 1st N.C. Transfd. as Lieut. to 6th N.C. in 1818; to newly-raised 9th L.C. 17 June 1825. Siege and capture of Bhurtpore; Lieut. 9th L.C. Actg. Intr. & Qmr. 9th L.C. 1826-7. Fur. 1828.
Refs.: *A.J.* xxvii. 253.

MALTBY, Brough (1791-1829). Captain, Invalid Est. 61st N.I. *b.* Southwell, Notts., 1791. Cadet 1807. Arrived in India 16 Nov. 1808. Ensign 24 Nov. 1808. Lieut. 1 Oct. 1814. Capt. 13 May 1825. Invalided 4 Nov. 1825. *d.* Chunar 2 Nov. 1829, aged 37.
bapt. Southwell 15 Nov. 1791. 6th and youngest son of Brough Maltby, formerly of Shelton Manor, Notts., and Mary Ince his wife. Brother of Samuel Maltby, *q.v.*
Services: Barasat C.C. Posted Ensign to 9th N.I. in 1809. (? Operations in Oudh 1810; Pragpur; Ensign 1/9 N.I.) Lieut. 1/9th N.I. Transfd. to newly-formed 31st N.I. July 1823; to 61st N.I. (late 1/31st) May 1824.
Refs.: Family information. M.I. at Chunar.

MALTBY, Samuel (1787-1877). Lieut. Colonel. 2nd N.I. *b.* Shelton, Notts., 28 Oct. 1787. Cadet 1805. Arrived in India 11 July 1806. Ensign 9 Sept. 1806. Lieut. 1 July 1810. Capt. 7 Nov. 1821. Major 11 Feb. 1835. Retired 30 Apr. 1835. Hon. Lt. Col. 28 Nov. 1854. *d.* at his residence in Southwell 16 Mar. 1877.
4th son of Brough Maltby and Mary his wife. Brother of Brough Maltby, *q.v.*, and of the wife of Sir George Nicholls, K.C.B. (*D.N.B.*).

Services: Barasat C.C. 10 mos. Posted Ensign to 1st N.I. in 1807. Lieut. 1/1st N.I. Nepal War 1814-15; Lieut. L.I. Bn., in 2nd Div. (India medal). Third Mahratta War 1817-18; Rampur; Jawad; Lieut. 1/1st N.I. Actg. Adjt. 1/1st N.I. 1819. Transfd. to 2nd N.I. (late 1/1st) May 1824. First Burma War; Arakan 1825; Capt. 2nd L.I. Bn. (clasp to India medal). Fur. p.a. 15 Dec. 1828 till 10 Nov. 1831. Detached with a Coy. of 2nd N.I. to aid in suppressing an insurrection amongst the Kols in Chota Nagpur; joined Capt. Wilkins early in Feb. 1832; to comd. Left Column of troops in Chota Nagpur Mar. 1832.

Refs.: Family information. *The Times,* 20 Mar. 1877.

MANCLARK, Thomas. Ensign. Infantry. Cadet 1782. Never arrived in India. Ensign 26 Mar. 1783. Struck off 1788.

Services: Apptd. Cadet 18 June 1782; should have sailed for India in the *Rodney* 11 Sept. 1782.

MANDALL, Joseph (1784-1812). Lieutenant, 20th N.I. *b.* 14 Sept. 1784. Cadet 1805. Arrived in India 11 July 1806. Ensign 31 Aug. 1806. Lieut 19 May 1808. *d.* Chittagong 31 May 1812.

bapt. Doncaster 14 Nov. 1784. Son of Thomas Mandall, plumber and glazier.

Services: Barasat C.C. Posted Ensign to 20th N.I. in 1807. Served at Fort Marlbro' 1810-12. No record of active service.

MANFIELD, John Callard (1791-1825). Captain, 12th N.I. *bapt.* ptely. Dorchester 17 Sept. 1791; *bapt.* Holy Trinity Dorchester, 14 June 1792. Cadet 1810. Ensign 1 June 1813. Lieut. 29 June 1815. Capt. 4 Sept. 1825. *d.* Dacca 12 Sept. 1825.

Son of John Callard Manfield, atty., and Catherine his wife. Ed. Blundell's 21 Aug. 1805 till 29 June 1808.

Services: Barasat C.C. Cadet d.d. 15th N.I. 1811-13. Posted Ensign to 1/12th N.I. in 1813. Nepal War 1816; Lieut. 5th Gren. Bn. Transfd. to 12th N.I. (late 1/12th) May 1824. First Burma War; Arakan 1825; Capt. 1st, afterwards 2nd, Gren. Bn.

Refs.: Blundell's School Register. M.I. Dacca cemetery.

MANIFFE, Bartholomew. (*See* **MINIFIE, Barnett or Burnet.**)

MANLEY, George. Cadet. Artillery. (III.-17) Cadet 1783. Declined coming out.

THE BENGAL ARMY, 1758-1834

MANLEY, Henry (1778-1820). Major, 8th N.I. *bapt.* ptely. St. Mary Magdalene, Taunton, 12 July 1778. Cadet 1794. Arrived in India 5 Mar. 1797. Ensign 15 Nov. 1796. Lieut. 30 Oct. 1797. Capt. 27 Oct. 1804. Major 16 Dec. 1814. *d.* Berhampore 2 Jan. 1820.

4th son of James Manley, Lt. Col. Somerset Mil., and Leonora Langley his wife. Brother of Mrs. Hennessy and 2nd cousin of Nicholas Manley, *q.v. m.* Calcutta 19 Mar. 1813, Thomasin Sophia, dau. of George Fleming (1760/61-1818), *q.v.* (She *re-m.* James Alexander Ayton, *q.v.*)

Services: Lieut. 8th N.I. in 1798. Operations in Jumna Doab 1803; Sasni; Lieut. 8th N.I. Second Mahratta War 1804-5; assault and capture of Rampura; Lieut. & Adjt. 2/8th N.I., Bde. Qmr. 2nd Bde. (? Storm of Badekh Oct. 1806; Capt. 2/8th N.I.) Expedn. to Mauritius 1810; Capt. 2nd Vol. Bn. Nepal War 1816; Major comdg. 5th Gren. Bn., in 2nd Bde. Left Column. Third Mahratta War; Major 2/8th N.I.

Refs.: Burke's *Landed Gentry of Ireland*, p. 454, *s.n.* Manley, of Whitehouse, co. Antrim. Will dated Jubbulpore, 15 Mar. 1818; proved 10 Feb. 1820.

MANLEY, Nicholas (1784-1823). Major, 20th N.I. *bapt.* Cullompton, Devon, 3 Mar. 1784. Cadet 1798. Arrived in India 22 Nov. 1799. Ensign 19 Dec. 1799. Lieut. 29 May 1800. Capt. 12 Apr. 1814. Major 26 Aug. 1822. *d. unm.* P.W.I. 23 May 1823, aged 37.

7th son of Rev. Henry Chorley Manley, incumbent of Bradford, Somerset, and Dulcibella his wife, dau. of —— Maddox. 2nd cousin of Henry Manley, *q.v.*

Services: Posted Lieut. to 2nd Bengal Eur. Regt. 15 Apr. 1801. Transfd. to 1st Bn. Marine Regt. (became 1/20th N.I.) in 1803. Adjt. 1/20th N.I. 12 July 1805 till 1815. Actg. Adjt. & Qmr. 20th N.I. 1810-11. Nepal War 1816; Capt. 8th Gren. Bn., in 2nd Bde. Left Column. Comdt. Bencoolen Local Bn. 1822-3.

Refs.: Burke's *Landed Gentry of Ireland*, p. 455, *s.n.* Manley, of Whitehouse, co. Antrim. *Bath Chron.* 18 Dec. 1823. Will dated Ramnagar 7 Feb. 1816; proved 29 May 1823.

MANNERS, Arthur (1780-1821). Major, 16th N.I. *b.* Goadby Marwood, Leics., 28 May 1780. Cadet 1798. Arrived in India 19 Sept. 1799. Ensign 1 Nov. 1799. Lieut. 17 Nov. 1799. Capt. 16 Aug. 1810. Major 5 May 1821. *d. unm.* Hoshangabad, C.P., 5 Oct. 1821.

Owned an estate at Goadby Marwood and the perpetual advowson of Goadby Marwood Rectory, also Kirby Bellart, Leics., left to his father by John, Duke of Rutland. Son of Edward Manners and Ann his wife, dau. of Edward Stafford, late of Knipton, Leics. Brother of Laura, Susan, Alethea, Mary Ann, Roger, Emma, Walter and Otho Manners.

Services: Posted Lieut. to 1/16th N.I. 15 Apr. 1801, and served throughout with that Bn. Operations in Jumna Doab 1803; attack on Thathia fort. Operations in Bundelkhand 1807; Chamir; Sehlehuganj. Operations in Bundelkhand 1810-11.

Refs.: *N. & Q.* 2S. iv. 171, 217. Will dated 4 Sept. 1820; proved 8 Nov. 1821.

MANNING, Charles (1802-?). Lieutenant. 30th N.I. *b.* Peasenhall, Suffolk, 24 July 1802. Cadet 1819. Ensign 10 Jan. 1820. Lieut. 11 July 1823. Cashiered by G.C.M. 25 May 1829.

bapt. Peasenhall 30 Aug. 1802. Son of Alderman [1] Manning and Henrietta Margaret his wife, of Dedham.

Services: Posted Ensign to 1/18th N.I. in 1820. Operations in Jodhpur 1823; Lamba; Ensign 1/18th N.I. Transfd. as Lieut. to 15th N.I. July 1823; to 30th N.I. (late 1/15th) May 1824. Sub-Asst. in Stud Dept. at Hissar 1825 till cashiered.

Refs.: *A.J.* xxviii. 723-5.

[1] *Note:* Alderman would appear to be his christian name.

MANNING, Francis Edward (1803-1844). Bt. Major, 16th N.I. *b.* 25 Mar. 1803. Cadet 1818. Admitted 4 Sept. 1819. Ensign (?) Lieut. 1 Jan. 1821. Capt. 31 Jan. 1829. Bt. Major 30 Apr. 1844. *d.* Etawah, U.P., 8 Oct. 1844.

bapt. Sidmouth, Devon, 19 May 1803. Son of Henry Manning, of Wonford House, a freeholder of Devon, and Harriet his wife. *m.* 1st, Barrackpore 2 May 1825, Frances Maria, eldest dau. of Lewis Wiggins or Wiggens, *q.v.* (*See also* Anthony Highmore Jellicoe.) (She died Mhow 1 Jan. 1834, aged 28.) *m.* 2nd, Exeter 12 June 1838, Susanna, dau. of Robert Kekewich, and widow (4th wife) of Lt.-Col. Sir Henry Maturin Farrington, 3rd Bart.

Services: Ensign d.d. Bengal Eur. Regt. 1819-20. Posted Lieut. to 2/10th N.I. in 1821. Intr. & Qmr. 1/10th N.I. 1 Oct. 1823. Transfd. to 16th N.I. (late 2/10th) May 1824; Intr. & Qmr. do. 17 June 1824 till Jan. 1829. Actg. Bde. Major at Mhow 24 Oct. 1834. Fur. p.a. 6 Feb. 1836 till 14 Jan. 1839. First Afghan War 1839-42; Ghazni 1839 (Medal); comdg. a convoy proceeding to Kabul 23 July 1841; Nott's advance on Kabul

THE BENGAL ARMY, 1758-1834 221

1842; Capt. 16th N.I. (Medal). Gwalior campaign; Maharajpur
(*Lond. Gaz.* 8 Mar. 1844); Capt. 16th N.I. (Bronze star).
Refs.: Burke's *Peerage*, 1923, p. 887, *s.n.* Farrington, Bart.
Burke's *Family Records*, p. 140, *s.n.* Carlyon. *I.M.* 4 Jan. 1845,
p. 13. *G.M.* 1845, i. 222.

MANNINGFORD, Frederick Shapland (1810-1832). Ensign,
38th N.I. *b.* Marshfield, Gloucs., 18 May 1810. Cadet 1828.
Arrived in India 4 May 1829. Ensign 8 Jan. 1829. *d.* nr.
Midnapore 28 May 1832, of fever.[1]
Youngest son of John Manningford, of Bristol, banker, and
Elizabeth his wife.
Services: Ensign d.d. 44th N.I. 10 June 1829. Posted to 38th
N.I. 14 Sept. 1829.
Refs.: *Bristol Mirror*, 20 Oct. 1832. *A.J.* N.S. ix. 186. M.I.
at Midnapore.

[1] *Note*. He died at camp Bunterra on the march from Bamanghati
to Midnapore. The surgeon and four junior officers of 38th N.I.
all succumbed to fever in the space of a few days, while engaged
in operations against a rebellious zemindar.

MANSFIELD, James (1795-1827). Lieutenant, 1st N.I. *b.*
Edinburgh 27 Nov. 1795. Cadet 1812. Ensign 11 Nov. 1814.
Lieut. 13 July 1815. *d.* Muttra 24 Nov. 1827.
Son of James Mansfield, of Midmar, banker, and Marion Dalrymple
his wife, 3rd dau. of Gen. Robert Dalrymple-Horn-Elphinstone,
of Horn and Westhall, co. Aberdeen.
Services: Posted Ensign to 2/12th N.I. in 1814, and served
throughout with that Bn. Nepal War 1816; in 3rd Bde. Centre
Column. Siege and capture of Hathras 1817. Third Mahratta
War; Dhamoni. Operations against the Bhattis of Hariana
1818. Intr. & Qmr. 2/12th N.I. 17 Aug. 1820 till 16 Oct. 1826.
Transfd. to 1st N.I. (late 2/12th) May 1824.
Refs.: Burke's *Peerage*, 1923, p. 656, *s.n.* Elphinstone-Dalrymple,
Bart. *A.J.* xxv. 683. M.I. in Muttra Cantt. cemetery.

MANSON, James (1791-1862). Major General. Colonel 44th
N.I. *b.* St. Mary's, Lambeth, 16 July 1791. Cadet 1807.
Arrived in India 14 Aug. 1808. Ensign (1 Mar. 1808) 14 Sept.
1808. Lieut. 16 Dec. 1814. Capt. 13 May 1825. Major 11 July
1841. Lt. Col. 24 Apr. 1847. Col. 29 May 1857. Maj. Gen.
15 May 1859. *d.* 14 Westbourne Sq., London, 15 July 1862.
Son of Thomas Manson and Susan Blake his wife. *m.* (before
1820) Henrietta. His dau. *m.* Samuel Cross-Starkey, *q.v.*

Services: Barasat C.C. 7½ mos. Posted Ensign to 8th N.I. in 1809. Expedn. against Mauritius 1810; Ensign 2nd Vol. Bn. Nepal War 1814-15; Lieut. 2/8th N.I., 1st Coy. Pioneers, in 4th Div. d.d. Gardner's Irreg. Cav. 1815. Nepal War 1816; Lieut. 2/8th N.I., in 4th Bde. Centre Column. (India medal). Suptg. construction of bldgs. at Mirzapur 21 Feb. 1817. Fur. s.c. 19 Nov. 1818 till 6 July 1822. Adjt. Burdwan Provl. Bn. 21 Aug. 1822 till 1 Oct. 1823. Asst. to Supt. geological survey of Himalayas 24 June 1823 till 3 Oct. 1828. Transfd. to 9th N.I. (late 1/8th) May 1824; to 4th Extra Regt. (became 72nd N.I.) in 1825. Actg. Comdt. Kumaon Local Bn. 8 Nov. 1828. 2nd Asst. Mily. Auditor Gen. 26 Oct. 1829; offg. tempy. 1st do. 5 Aug. 1830. Comr. with Baji Rao, the ex-Peishwa, at Bithur 1 Nov. 1831 till Sept. 1851. Posted Lt. Col. to 28th N.I. Sept. 1847; to 42nd N.I. 5 Feb. 1848; to 48th N.I. 27 Mar. 1850; to 70th N.I. 6 Nov. 1851; from 20th to 21st N.I. May 1854; to 28th N.I. Nov. 1854; to 53rd N.I. 1855. Fur. s.c. 21 Feb. 1852 till Dec. 1854; p.a. 2 Mar. 1857 till death. Posted Col. to 44th N.I. 1857.

Refs.: Boase. *G.M.* 1862, ii. 237. *The Times*, 18 July 1862.

MANSON, John (1786-1818). Lieutenant, 15th N.I. Pioneers. *b.* Lambeth 23 Aug. 1786. Cadet 1807. Arrived in India 14 Aug. 1808. Ensign 26 Sept. 1808. Struck off 12 May 1809. Cadet 1810. Ensign 20 Sept. 1812. Lieut. 2 Jan. 1815. *d.* 9 June 1818: kld. in action at the assault of Satanwara, C.I.

bapt. Bermondsey 21 Sept. 1786. Son of Alexander Manson, shipbuilder, and Jane (Jean) his wife, sister of Robert Bowie, *q.v.* Brother of Robert Manson, *q.v.*

Services: Barasat C.C. 1808-9. Struck off the list of the Army by order of the C.D., having obtained his appt. by improper means. Reapptd. Cadet Mar. 1810. Cadet d.d. 25th N.I. 1811. Posted Ensign to 2/15th N.I. in 1812. Nepal War 1814-15; Lieut. 2/15th N.I., in 4th Div. Served with Pioneers 1815 till death. Third Mahratta War; Satanwara (kld.).

Refs.: Caithness Family History, p. 313. Will dated Dinapore, 8 Aug. 1814; proved 12 Sept. 1818.

MANSON, Robert (1788-1818). Lieutenant, 23rd N.I. *b.* Bermondsey, Surrey, 29 Aug. 1788. Cadet 1807. Arrived in India 14 Aug. 1808. Ensign 8 Sept. 1808. Struck off 12 May 1809. Cadet 1810. Ensign 21 Sept. 1812. Lieut. 15 Sept. 1816. *d.* Gadarwara, C.P., 3 Nov. 1818.

bapt. Bermondsey 25 Sept. 1788. Son of Alexander Manson,

shipbuilder, and Jane (Jean) his wife. Brother of John Manson, q.v.
Services: Barasat C.C. 1808-9. Struck off the list of the Army by order of the C.D., having obtained his appt. by improper means. Reapptd. Cadet Mar. 1810. Cadet d.d. 25th N.I. 1811. Posted Ensign to 2/23rd N.I. in 1812. Third Mahratta War; Lieut. 2/23rd N.I.
Refs.: Caithness Family History, p. 313. M.I. Narsinghpur.

*MARCH, Richard (1727/28-?). Cadet. Infantry. *b.* London 1727/28. Cadet 1759.
Services: Apptd. Cadet Jan. 1759; sailed for India in the *Royal George* in 1759, aged 31. N.F.P.

MARGRAVE, Robert Rush (1804-1834). Captain, 25th N.I. *b.* Gillingham, Norfolk, 22 May 1804. Cadet 1819. Admitted 21 Nov. 1820. Ensign 5 May 1820. Lieut. 11 July 1823. Capt. 23 Dec. 1828. *d.* 6 Sept. 1834: drowned by the grounding of the *Jean* at George's River (? George Rocks), Tasmania.[1]
Son of Thomas Margrave, of New Broad St., London, merchant.
Services: Posted Ensign to Bengal Eur. Regt. in 1820. Transfd. to 2/22nd N.I. in 1821; as Lieut. to 2/20th N.I. July 1823. Actg. Intr. & Qmr. 2/20th N.I. 6 Apr. 1824. Transfd. to 40th N.I. (late 2/20th) May 1824. First Burma War; occupation of Cheduba I. May 1824 (s.w.); actg. Adjt. 40th N.I.; Ramri Oct. 1824; unsuccessful expedn. against Ramri I. Feb. 1825; Lieut. 40th N.I. (*Lond. Gaz.* 23 Nov. 1824, 22 Mar. and 9 Aug. 1825). Intr. & Qmr. 40th N.I. 24 Sept. 1825; do. 25th N.I. (late 1/20th) 21 May 1827 till 3 Mar. 1829. Fur. s.c. 10 Jan. 1830 till 5 Mar. 1833. Leave s.c. 2 yrs. to Tasmania and the Cape 14 Mar. 1834.
Refs.: G.M. 1835, i. 335. A.J. N.S. xvi. 202.
[1] *Note:* He had gone there with the view of collecting indigenous seeds and plants for the Botanic Gdns., Calcutta.

MARISCHALL, Thomas (1779-1804). Lieutenant, 14th N.I. *bapt.* St. John the Baptist's, Peterborough, 1 Oct. 1779. Cadet 1795. Arrived in India 2 Feb. 1797. Ensign 21 Nov. 1796. Lieut. 30 Oct. 1797. *d.* Balchari I., Sundarbans, Bengal, 31 Mar. 1804.
Son of Robert Marischall and Elizabeth his wife.
Services: Lieut. 1st Bengal Eur. Regt. in June 1798. Second Mahratta War 1803-4; battle of Delhi; action before Agra; siege and capture of Gwalior; Lieut. 1/14th N.I.

Refs.: Will dated Balcheree camp, 24 Mar. 1804 ; proved 16 June 1804.

MARJORAM or MARGROVE,[1] **John.** Lieutenant. Infantry. Cadet (?) Ensign 5 Apr. 1764. Lieut. 14 Aug. 1765. Resigned 1766.

Services: N.F.P. *Probably* resigned his Commission during the " Batta mutiny " in May 1766.

[1] *Note*: The name is given as Marjoram in *Dodwell & Miles*, as Margrove in *B.M. Addl. MSS.* 6050.

*MARKHAM, Timothy (1754/55-?). Lieutenant. Infantry. *b. co.* Hereford 1754/55. Cadet 1780. Never arrived in India. Ensign (?) Lieut. 28 Aug. 1782. Struck off (?)

Services: Apptd. Cadet 8 Dec. 1780 ; should have sailed for India in the *Latham* 13 Mar. 1781, aged 26. N.F.P.

MARLEY, Bennet (1753/54-1842). General. Colonel 6th N.I. *b.* 1753/54. Cadet 1771. Admitted 10 Dec. 1771. Ensign 27 Jan. 1773. Lieut. 1 Jan. 1778. Capt. 3 June 1781. Major 6 Aug. 1797. Lt. Col. 31 July 1799. Lt. Col. Comdt. 21 Sept. 1804. Col. 25 Apr. 1808. Maj. Gen. 4 June 1811. Lt. Gen. 19 July 1821. Gen. 28 June 1838. *d.* Barrackpore 14 June 1842, aged 88.

Son of Robert Marley. Brother of Margaret, wife of Rev. John Barnet, and nephew of John Marley, of Dunston. *m.* Mary. (She died Barrackpore 7 Sept. 1846.) Father of Charles Hyde Marley, *q.v.*, Elizabeth, wife of James McCraken, *q.v.*, and Charlotte Mary, wife of William Burroughs, *q.v.*

Services: Lieut. 3rd Bengal Eur. Regt. ; transfd. to 13th Bn. Sepoys 1 Jan. 1779. Capt. 2nd Eur. Regt. in 1782 ; transfd. to 6th Eur. Bn. ; with 25th Bn. Sepoys in July 1787. Fur. 14 Jan. 1789 till 3 Mar. 1792. With 6th Eur. Bn. in Feb. 1796. Transfd. as Major to 1/9th N.I. ; as Lt. Col. to 6th N.I. Disturbances in Gumsur, N. Circars, 1801 ; Lt. Col. comdg. 6th N.I. Returned to Bengal Mar. 1802. Posted Col. to 6th N.I. Apr. 1808. Apptd. to comd. troops in Rohilkhand 14 Nov. 1808. Transfd. to 8th N.I. in 1809. Maj. Gen. comdg. Dinapore Div. 1813. To comd. 4th (Dinapore) Div. for service against Nepal 15 Nov. 1814. Nepal War 1814-15 ; Maj. Gen. comdg. 4th Div. (*Lond. Gaz.* 19 Aug. 1815). Superseded by Maj.-Gen. George Wood, and removed from the Gen. Staff 10 Feb. 1815 (G.O. 17 Mar. 1815).[1] Comdt. of fortress and garr. of Allahabad 4 July 1817 till 22 July 1840. Col. 6th N.I. May 1824 till death.

THE BENGAL ARMY, 1758-1834

Refs.: Fortescue, xi. 145-6. *The Marleys of Langton, co. Durham*, pp. 11-12. Will dated 13 June 1842; proved 20 June 1842. M.I. in Barrackpore cemetery.

[1] *Note:* The disasters which had overtaken portions of his Div. at Samanpur and Pursa on 1 Jan. 1815 upset him to such a degree that on 10 Feb., " without publishing a word of warning to the troops or delegating his authority to any subordinate, he rode out of camp before daylight and vanished from the scene." (*Fortescue, op. cit.*)

MARLEY, Charles Hyde (1793-1849). Captain, Invalid Est. 29th N.I. *bapt.* Dinapore 28 July 1793. Cadet 1810. Ensign 20 Feb. 1813. Lieut. 10 Oct. 1815. Capt. 13 May 1825. Invalided 15 Jan. 1830. *d.* Buxar 23 Feb. 1849.

Son of Bennet Marley, *q.v.*, and Mary his wife. Nephew of Frances Hollings. *m.* 1st, Caroline. (She died Buxar 10 Jan. 1837.) *m.* 2nd, Ghazipur 30 July 1838, Miss Sarah Varley. (She died Buxar 5 Oct. 1846, aged 24.) Ed. E.I.C. Coll. at Hertford.

Services: Cadet d.d. 8th N.I. 1811-13. Posted Ensign to 1/14th N.I. in 1813. With 2nd Ceylon Vol. Bn. 1818-19. Adjt. 1/14th N.I. Sept. 1822. Transfd. to 29th N.I. (late 2/14th) May 1824. Adjt. 29th N.I. 17 June 1824 till 10 Aug. 1825. Posted to 1st Bn. Native Invalids 23 Jan. 1830. Fort Adjt. at Buxar 21 May 1830 till death, and Comdt. of the garr. at Buxar 1841 till death.

Refs.: Will dated Buxar 4 Dec. 1845; admon. 10 May 1850. M.I. at Buxar.

MARLEY, George (*d.* 1779). Lieutenant, Infantry. Cadet 1769. Ensign 27 July 1769. Lieut. 23 Nov. 1772. *d.* 1779, on active service with the Bombay detachment.

Services: First Mahratta War.

MARLEY, Joseph (*d.* 1799). Captain, 15th N.I. Country Cadet 1778. Admitted 9 Mar. 1778. Ensign 4 June 1778. Lieut. 7 Sept. 1779. Capt. 16 Dec. 1796. *d.* Cawnpore 5 Feb. 1799.

Services: Lieut. 1/1st Bengal Eur. Regt. in Oct. 1779; 6th Eur. Bn. in July 1787; 1st Bn. Sepoys in 1792. Capt. 7th N.I. in June 1798.

MARLEY, Thomas (*d.* 1790). Lieutenant, 25th Bn. Sepoys. Cadet 1782. Arrived in India 22 Jan. 1783. Ensign 31 Mar. 1783. Lieut. 6 Mar. 1790. *d.* Fatehgarh 3 June 1790.

Services: Apptd. Cadet 10 Oct. 1781; sailed for India in the

Warren Hastings 6 Feb. 1782. Posted Ensign to 2nd Bengal Eur. Regt. 28 Feb. 1783. Posted to 25th Bn. Sepoys Mar. 1790.

MARRIOTT, Charles (Seymour) (1788-1825). Lieutenant, Pension Est. 7th N.I. *b.* London 10 July 1788. Cadet 1808. Admitted 25 Jan. 1810. Ensign 13 May 1811. Lieut. 30 June 1815. Pensioned 10 July 1823. *d.* Calcutta 28 June 1825.

bapt. St. Bene't Finck, London, 6 Aug. 1788. Son of Thomas Marriott, of Broad St., and Lucy his wife.

Services: Barasat C.C. Posted Ensign to 7th N.I. in 1811. Third Mahratta War; Lieut. 2/7th N.I.

MARRIOTT, Edwin (1805-1870). Colonel. 57th N.I. *b.* Enfield 16 July 1805. Cadet 1825. Arrived in India 14 July 1826. Ensign 26 Dec. 1825. Lieut. 21 Sept. 1828. Capt. 21 July 1841. Major 17 Nov. 1857. Bt. Lt. Col. 28 Nov. 1859. Retired 31 Dec. 1861. Hon. Col. 31 Dec. 1861. *d.* St. Helier, Jersey, 23 Aug. 1870.

bapt. Enfield 4 Dec. 1805. Son of John William Marriott, of Taunton, printer, and Anne his wife. *m.* Calcutta 18 Sept. 1838, Miss Sarah Leslie. (She died 9 Feb. 1884.)

Services: Posted Ensign to 57th N.I. Actg. Adjt. 57th N.I. 6 Jan. 1841. Tempy. charge of Abkari Dept. and Sudder bazar at Cawnpore 11 Nov. 1842 till Jan. 1843. Fur. s.c. 13 Nov. 1844 till 1847. Paymr. and Supt. of native pensioners in Oudh, at Lucknow, 6 Dec. 1851 till 1858. Mutiny campaign; defence of Lucknow Residency (? Medal & clasp [1]). Fur. s.c. Mar. 1858 till 2 Nov. 1859.

Refs.: The *Times*, 31 Aug. 1870.

[1] *Note:* His name is not in the Mutiny medal roll.

*MARRIOTT, William (1744-1803). Ensign. Infantry. Subsequently Senior Merchant, B.C.S. *b.* 23 Sept. 1744. Ensign May 1766. Resigned (?) *d.* Pershore, Worcs., 16 Dec. 1803.

bapt. Darfield, Yorks., 24 Oct. 1744. 6th son of Rev. Randolph Marriott, D.D., rector of Darfield, and Lady Diana Feilding his wife, 3rd dau. of Basil, 4th Earl of Denbigh. *m.* Jan. 1774, Jane, dau. of Peter Capper, of Redland, nr. Bristol. (She died 20 Aug. 1825.)

Services: Went out to India as a Bengal Writer 1764; Asst. under his brother, Randolph, at Benares 1765. Served as a Vol. with the force under Major Giles Stibbert, *q.v.*, to whom he was apptd. A.D.C. 14 Jan. 1765. Given a Commission as Ensign in

May 1766, when he was described as a " Free Merchant," in order to fill one of the vacancies caused by the " Batta mutiny." Zemindar of the 24-Parganas in 1769 ; Factor at Burdwan in 1770 ; Collector of Dinajpur 1771-2. Fur. s.c. 1773-5. Second in council at Burdwan 1777 ; Chief at Burdwan 1779 ; returned to Europe 1781 ; out of the Service 1782.

Refs.: Burke's *Landed Gentry*, 13th edn., p. 1203, *s.n.* Wynne-Marriott, of Avonbank, Worcs. *Holzman.*

MARSACK or MARSAC, Charles (1736-1820). Captain. Infantry. *b.* 1736. Cadet 1765. Ensign 3 Nov. 1765. Lieut. 29 Mar. 1767. Capt. 26 June 1771. Resigned 27 Jan. 1779. *bur.* Caversham, Reading, 15 Nov. 1820, aged 84.

Of Caversham Park, Oxon., which he purchased from the 1st Earl Cadogan ; J.P. and D.L. ; high sheriff, Oxon., 1787. Natural son of Frederick Louis, Prince of Wales (the father of George III), by Marguerite de Marsac, Comtesse de Marsac.[1] *m.* (before 1784) Charlotte, dau. of Richard Becher, B.C.S., of Calcutta, by Ann Hasleby his 2nd wife, sister of Charles Becher and cousin-german of Henry John Pattle, *qq.v.* (She died Brighton 20 Jan. 1837, aged 69.) Father of Robert Marsack, *q.v.*

Services : With 1st Bde. at Monghyr in May 1766, when he resigned his Commission during the " Batta mutiny " ; readmitted 11 Nov. 1766. Raised one of the two Cav. Regts. for the service of the Nawab-Wazir of Oudh in 1776, and comdd. till its transfer to the Coy. in Aug. 1777 ; raised 31st Bn. Sepoys at Cawnpore in July 1778, but refused the comd. on 12th of that month.

Refs. : Family information. Burke's *Landed Gentry*, 15th edn., p. 1530, *s.n.* Marsack, *formerly* of Caversham Park. *Holzman.* *V.B.G.* p. 12. *N. & Q.* 11S. x. 11, 386 ; xi. 115. *M.M.* 1820, ii. 484.

[1] *Note :* It is said that the Comte de Marsac, a Frenchman, was attached to the Court at Hanover and came over to England with it.

*****MARSACK, Robert** (1788-1805). Cadet. *bapt.* Caversham 11 Sept. 1788. Cadet 1804. Never arrived in India. *d.* at sea 5 Feb. 1805 ; lost in the wreck of the *Earl of Abergavenny.* (See note to Charles Davis or Davies.)

Eldest son of Charles Marsack, *q.v.*, and Charlotte his wife. *Refs. :* Family information.

MARSDEN, Frederick (1757-1834). Lieut. Colonel. 19th N.I. *bapt.* St. Michan's, Dublin, 3 Dec. 1757. Country Cadet 1778.

Admitted 26 Aug. 1778. Ensign 25 May 1779. Lieut. 28 Jan. 1781. Capt. 25 Oct. 1797. Major 30 Sept. 1803. Lt. Col. 8 June 1806. Retired 17 Feb. 1808. *d.s.p.* Brook Lodge, Youghal, 6 June 1834.

8th and youngest son of John Marsden, of Vervale, co. Wicklow, Dir. of the Bank of Ireland, and Eleanor his 2nd wife, dau. of Alexander Bagnell, of Edinburgh. *m.* 1802, ——, dau. of Rev. —— Henry, of Waterford. His dau. *m.* Thomas Samuel Oliver, *q.v.*

Services: Lieut. Bombay Marine 26 Aug. 1778. Apptd. Cadet 10 Sept. 1778. Served on detachment at Bencoolen Feb. 1780 till July 1781. Leave s.c. to sea 20 Mar. 1783; fur. 30 July 1785 till July 1787. Posted to 1st Bengal Eur. Bn. 31 Oct. 1787. Fur. on h.p. 22 Oct. 1788 till 1 Sept. 1790. Posted to 3rd Eur. Bn. 9 Feb. 1791; transfd. to 28th Bn. Sepoys 26 Mar. 1793. Capt. 16th N.I. Fur. 29 Jan. 1800. Transfd. to 19th N.I. 29 May 1800. Posted Lt. Col. to 2/19th N.I. in 1806.

Refs.: Genealogical Memoirs of Family of Marsden, by Rev. B. A. Marsden (Birkenhead, 1914), p. 107. Burke's *Landed Gentry*, 12th edn., p. 1275, *s.n.* Marsden, of Chelmorton. Burke's *Family Records*, p. 422. *A.J.* N.S. xiv. 226.

MARSDEN, Frederick Carleton (1803-1889). Lieut. Colonel, C.B. 29th N.I. *b.* 15 Dec. 1803. Cadet 1824. Arrived in India 15 Sept. 1825. Ensign 18 Mar. 1825. Lieut. 4 Sept. 1826. Capt. 22 Dec. 1844. Major 9 Mar. 1855. Retired 15 June 1857. Hon. Lt. Col. 15 June 1857. *d.* Earl's Colne, Essex, 13 Oct. 1889.

Of Colne House; J.P. Essex. *bapt.* Upton-on-Severn 8 Aug. 1806. Eldest son of James Marsden, Capt. 7th D.G., and Harriette his wife, dau. of Wakeman Long, of Pershore, Worcs. *m.* St. Mary de Crypt, Gloucester, 14 June 1838, Sydney Jane, 5th and youngest dau. of Sir William Bulkeley Hughes, Kt., of Plas Coch, co. Anglesey. (She died Colne House 16 May 1866, aged 59.)

Services: Posted Ensign to 29th N.I. Intr. & Qmr. 29th N.I. 3 Sept. 1829 till 6 Jan. 1836. Fur. p.a. 13 Dec. 1835 till 22 Jan. 1840. Adjt. 29th N.I. 23 Oct. 1841 till 21 Nov. 1843. D.C. 3cl., Saugor & Narbada territories, 23 Oct. 1843; D.C. 2cl., Saugor Div., 7 Mar. 1845; D.C. Punjab 13 Apr. 1849; D.C. Multan Div. 1851; do. Jhelum Div. 1855. Leave p.a. June-Dec. 1854; fur s.c. May 1855 till Aug. 1856. Reapptd. D.C. 1cl., Jhelum Div., 26 Sept. 1856. No record of active service. C.B. (Civil) 18 May 1860.

Refs.: Genealogical Memoirs of Family of Marsden, p. 114. Burke's *Landed Gentry*, 12th edn., p. 996, *s.n.* Hughes, of Coedhelen, co. Carnarvon. *A.J.* N.S. xxvi. 284. *The Times*, 15 Oct. 1889.

MARSH, Hippisley (1808-1884). Lieut. Colonel. 3rd L.C. *b.* Madras 1 Dec. 1808. Cadet 1824. Arrived in India 16 Nov. 1825. Cornet 22 June 1825. Lieut. 13 Mar. 1826. Capt. 29 May 1847. Bt. Major 11 Nov. 1851. Retired 20 Sept. 1854. Hon. Lt. Col. 28 Nov. 1854. *d.* 3 Laurel Grove, Penge, London, S.E., 1 Mar. 1884. *bapt.* Madras 13 Mar. 1809. Only son of Charles Marsh, sometime offg. J.A.G. at Madras, and Mary Hale his wife, eldest sister of W. C. J. Lewin, *q.v. m.* Etawah 21 Oct. 1835, Louisa Harriot, eldest dau. of Sir Robert Henry Cuncliffe, 4th Bart., *q.v.* (She died Tonbridge 10 Feb. 1899, aged 89.) Addiscombe Cadet 1824-5.
Services: Posted to 3rd L.C. in 1826. Operations against the Kols 1832; Lieut. 3rd L.C. Shekhawat expedn. 1834; Lieut. 3rd L.C. Intr. & Qmr. 3rd L.C. 27 Mar. 1837 till 15 June 1838. Asst. in *Thagi* Dept. 15 June till 25 Sept. 1838. Rejoined his Regt. for service in Afghanistan 30 Oct. 1838. First Afghan War 1839-41; in charge of the depot of his Regt. at Kandahar till 28 Aug. 1839; Lieut. 3rd L.C. (Medal). Placed at the disposal of the Envoy and Minister at the Court of Shah Shuja 25 Jan. 1840 till 15 Feb. 1841. Intr. & Qmr. 3rd L.C. 14 July till 3 Nov. 1841. Asst. in *Thagi* Dept. 3 Nov. 1841 till 1 Oct. 1842. With Army of Reserve (for Afghanistan) Oct. 1842 till Jan. 1843; Lieut. 3rd L.C. Asst. in *Thagi* Dept. 23 Mar. 1843 till 1845. Intr. & Qmr. 3rd L.C. 2 June 1845 till 13 May 1846. First Sikh War; Badhowal; Aliwal; Sobraon; Bt. Capt. 3rd L.C. (Medal with clasp).
Refs.: Howard & Crisp, xvi. 73, *s.n.* Cunliffe. *The Times,* 4 Mar. 1884. Burke's *Landed Gentry,* 9th edn., p. 897.

MARSHALL, Bristow (1805-1842). Captain. 25th N.I. *b.* Killala, co. Mayo, 6 May 1805. Cadet 1824. Arrived in India 4 Oct. 1825. Ensign 13 May 1825. Lieut. 9 Sept. 1826. Capt. 5 Sept. 1834. Resigned 5 Jan. 1837. *d.* Burma Feb. 1842.
5th son of Rev. George Marshall, rector of Carndonagh, co. Donegal, and Elizabeth Sophia his 1st wife, dau. of James Willson, M.P. Stepson of Isabella, dau. of William Paterson (1751-1836), *q.v.*, and brother of James Marshall (1806-1842), *q.v.*, and of Honoria, wife of Sir Henry Montgomery Lawrence, K.C.B., *q.v.*
Services: Posted Ensign to 25th N.I. and served throughout with that Regt. No record of active service.
Refs.: Family information. *Marshall of Manor Cunningham,* by Maj.-Gen. Marshall (privately printed).

MARSHALL, Charles (1795-1874). Colonel. 68th N.I. *b.* Calcutta 28 Oct. 1795. Cadet 1811. Admitted 22 Aug. 1812.

Ensign 15 Sept. 1814. Lieut. 1 Dec. 1815. Capt. 7 Apr. 1826. Major 10 Mar. 1849. Bt. Lt. Col. 19 June 1846. Retired 1 Nov. 1849. Hon. Col. 28 Nov. 1854. d. 6 Westbourne Sq., London, 8 Dec. 1874.

bapt. Calcutta 9 Feb. 1800. 3rd son of William Hodney Marshall, of Calcutta, atty., sometime with Messrs. Forbes & Co., later in the Accountant Gen.'s office, and Catherine Clark his 1st wife. Brother of John Samuel Marshall, *q.v.*, and half-brother of George Turnbull Marshall, *q.v. m.* Cawnpore 5 Jan. 1835, Emma Jane, dau. of Samuel Pidding Bishop, *q.v.*, and widow of James Mackay, *q.v.* (*See also* William Alston.) (She died 8 June 1887, aged 75.)

Services: Posted Ensign to 2/15th N.I. in 1814. Nepal War 1814-15; Ensign 2/15th N.I., in 4th Div. Nepal War 1816; Lieut. 2/15th N.I., with Champaran L.I. (India medal). Siege and capture of Hathras 1817; Lieut. 2/15th N.I. Adjt. Cawnpore Inf. Levy 1819-22. Transfd. to newly-raised 1/34th N.I. July 1823; to 68th N.I. (late 2/34th) May 1824. Adjt. 68th N.I. 17 June 1824 till 28 Dec. 1826. First Burma War; Arakan 1825; Lieut. 68th N.I. In charge of Comst. Dept. at Dinapore 22 Jan. 1830. Actg. 2nd in comd. Ramgarh Local Bn. Apr. 1831. Offg. A.A.G. Cawnpore Div. 16 Oct. 1838; D.A.A.G. do. 10 Feb. 1840; A.A.G. do. 9 Feb. 1843 till 1844. First Sikh War; Sobraon; Bt. Major 68th N.I. (Medal).

Refs.: *The Times,* 10 Dec. 1874.

MARSHALL, Sir Dyson (1752 ?-1823). Lieut. General, K.C.B. Colonel 10th N.I. *b.* 1752 ? Cadet 1771. Admitted 19 Sept. 1771. Ensign 8 Feb. 1773. Lieut. 6 Mar. 1778. Capt. 4 Oct. 1781. Major 30 Oct. 1797. Lt. Col. 31 Oct. 1799. Lt. Col. Comdt. 20 Oct. 1805. Col. 25 Apr. 1808. Maj. Gen. 4 June 1811. Lt. Gen. 19 July 1821. *d.* Cawnpore 20 July 1823.

Son of Capt. William Marshall, 81st Ft. (Invalids), and Charlotte his wife, dau. of Capt. Robert Jennings. His daus. *m.* Christopher D'Oyly Aplin, Charles William Brooke, William James (1785-1855), William Larkins Watson, and John Winston, *qq.v.*

Services: First Rohilla War; battle of St. George. First Mahratta War 1778-81, under Cols. Jacob Camac and Grainger Muir, *qq.v.* (w. 12 May 1781); Lieut. comdg. a Bn. of 34th N.I. Capt. 2nd Bengal Eur. Regt. in 1782; 24th Bn. Sepoys in July 1787; 2nd Eur. Bn. in Dec. 1788. Second Rohilla War 1794. Comdt. Ramgarh Local Bn. Posted Major to 1/9th N.I.; Lt. Col. to 1/15th N.I. 15 Nov. 1799; transfd. to 10th N.I. 21 Apr. 1800. Maj. Gen. comdg. at Karnal 1810-13; do. 3rd Div. 1813; do.

Cawnpore Div. and Field Army 1 May 1814. Operations against
Dyaram, taluqdar of Hathras, 1817 ; siege and capture of Hathras ;
Maj. Gen. comdg. the force. Third Mahratta War 1817-18 ; Maj.
Gen. comdg. 3rd (Left) Div. of the Grand Army. K.C.B. 14 Oct.
1818.
Refs.: *India Gazette*, 9 June 1781. *N. & Q.* clxv. 122-3.
E.I.M.C. i. 395-7. Will dated Cawnpore 21 Aug. 1822 ; proved
22 Aug. 1823.

MARSHALL, Ebenezer (1795-1843). Captain, Invalid Est.
71st N.I. *b.* Perth 30 Mar. 1795. Cadet 1813. Admitted
5 Aug. 1814. Ensign 1 Dec. 1814. Lieut. 28 Dec. 1814. Capt.
7 Apr. 1826. Invalided 5 Feb. 1835. *d.* Perth 8 Nov. 1843.
bapt. 20 Apr. 1795. Son of William Marshall, Bank of Scotland's
agent at Perth, and Margaret Wingate his wife. Brother of James
Marshall (1791-1848), *q.v.*
Services : Posted Lieut. to 2/1st N.I. in 1815. Siege and capture
of Hathras 1817 ; Lieut. 2/1st N.I. Third Mahratta War 1818-19 ;
Dhamoni ; Asirgarh ; Lieut. 2/1st N.I. Fur. s.c. 15 Nov. 1819 till
31 Oct. 1823. Transfd. to 31st N.I. July 1823 ; to 62nd N.I. (late
2/31st) May 1824 ; to newly-raised 3rd Extra Regt. (became
71st N.I.) in 1825. Fur. s.c. 19 June 1824 till 24 May 1828, and
27 Feb. 1841 till death.
Refs. : *A.J.* 3S ii. 220.

MARSHALL, George Turnbull (1803-1854). Lieut. Colonel,
59th N.I. *b.* Calcutta 13 Dec. 1803. Cadet 1821. Arrived in
India 17 May 1822. Ensign 1 Dec. 1821. Lieut. 11 Sept. 1823.
Capt. 21 Aug. 1831. Major 11 Mar. 1847. Lt. Col. 17 Nov.
1852. *d.* at sea 10 Dec. 1854, on board the *Nile*.
Son of William Hodney Marshall, of Calcutta, and Frances
Turnbull his 2nd wife. Half-brother of John Samuel Marshall, *q.v.*
m. Calcutta 12 Mar. 1834, Margaret Louisa, youngest dau. of Mrs.
E. Turner, of Intally, Calcutta. (She died Omeath, co. Louth,
16 Aug. 1880, aged 60.)
Services : Posted Ensign to 1/17th N.I. ; transfd. to 35th N.I.
(late 2/17th) May 1824. Siege and capture of Bhurtpore ; Lieut.
35th N.I. (India medal). Actg. Intr. & Qmr. 11th N.I. 24 Mar.
1828 ; do. 53rd N.I. 12 Aug. 1828 ; Intr. & Qmr. 35th N.I. 3 Feb.
1829 till 22 Sept. 1831. Passed the Degree of Honour in Persian ;
apptd. actg. Examiner at Coll. of Ft. Wm. 22 May 1832 ; permanent do. 16 Oct. 1832 till July 1838 ; Examiner and Sec. do.
14 July 1838 till Mar. 1853 ; Sec. of Sanskrit Coll. 20 Mar. 1839 till

17 Mar. 1841. Posted Lt. Col. to 14th N.I. Feb. 1853; transfd. to 12th N.I. 21 Mar. 1853; to 59th N.I. Mar. 1854. Fur. s.c. 18 mos. Dec. 1854.

Refs.: I.M. 29 Jan. 1855, p. 27. Will dated 24 Sept. 1847; proved 20 Apr. 1855.

MARSHALL, James (1791-1848). Captain. Bengal Eur. Regt. *b.* Perth 31 July 1791. Cadet 1807. Arrived in India 25 Oct. 1808. Ensign 10 Nov. 1808. Lieut. 16 Dec. 1814. Capt. 21 Sept. 1824. Retired 15 Nov. 1836. *d.* 21 June 1848.

bapt. Perth 11 Aug. 1791. Son of William Marshall and Margaret his wife. Brother of Ebenezer Marshall, *q.v.*

Services: Barasat C.C. 8 mos. Posted Ensign to Bengal Eur. Regt. in 1809; to Amboyna May 1812. Fur. p.a. 2 Jan. 1820 till 10 Dec. 1822. Transfd. to newly-formed 2nd Bengal Eur. Regt. May 1824; Adjt. do. 17 June till 14 Oct. 1824. First Burma War; Capt. 2nd Bengal Eur. Regt. Posted to Left Wing, Bengal Eur. Regt., Jan. 1830.

MARSHALL, James (1806-1842). Bt. Captain, 61st N.I. *b.* Killala 15 July 1806. Cadet 1824. Arrived in India 4 Oct. 1825. Ensign 13 May 1825. Lieut. 23 Nov. 1827. Bt. Capt. 13 May 1840. *d.* Jagdalak, Afghanistan, 12 Jan. 1842: kld. in action during the retreat from Kabul.

6th son of Rev. George Marshall, rector of Carndonagh, co. Donegal, by his 1st wife. Brother of Bristow Marshall, *q.v.*

Services: Posted Ensign to 61st N.I. Actg. Adjt. Left Wing 61st N.I. 7 Jan. 1832 and 3 Jan. 1838. Apptd. 2nd in comd. Shah Shuja's 6th L.I. May 1840, and assumed charge 5 Dec. 1840. Employed in training Gurkha recruits at Hawalbagh July 1840. First Afghan War 1840-2; outbreak at Kabul; action at village of Bemaru, nr. Kabul, 13 Nov. 1841; retreat from Kabul, mortally w. whilst leading a party to clear the heights above Jagdalak; Bt. Capt. 61st N.I., with Shah Shuja's force.

Refs.: G.M. 1842, i. 677. M.I. Afghan Memorial Church, Bombay.

MARSHALL, James Nasmyth (1811-1843). Bt. Captain, 73rd N.I. *b.* London 16 Jan. 1811. Cadet 1826. Arrived in India 31 Oct. 1827. Ensign 26 May 1827. Lieut. 29 Nov. 1834. Bt. Capt. 25 May 1842. *d.* at sea 14 Jan. 1843: wrecked on board the *Conqueror* off the coast of France.

bapt. St. Martin-in-the-Fields 7 Mar. 1811. Son of George Marshall, Col. R.M., and Mary his wife. *m.* Delhi 20 June 1842,

Elizabeth, 3rd dau. of William Butt, of Corneybury, Herts. (She perished with him in the *Conqueror*.)

Services: Posted Ensign to 5th Extra Regt. (became 73rd N.I.) 3 Jan. 1828. d.d. Assam L.I. 7 Mar. 1837; actg. Adjt. do. 2 Feb. 1839; actg. 2nd in comd. do. 28 Feb. 1839; Adjt. do. 19 July 1839. Operations against rebel chief Pechee Gaum Mar. 1838; attack on Sadiya 28 Jan. 1839; against the Singphos and Kumptees May 1839. Removed from Assam L.I. and rejoined 73rd N.I. 13 Oct. 1839. Fur. s.c. 12 Sept. 1842.

Refs.: *G.M.* 1843, i. 557. *The Times*, 1 Feb. 1843, p. 8.

MARSHALL, Jasper (*d.* 1777). Lieutenant, comdg. a Bn. of the Nawab-Wazir of Oudh's Inf. Cadet 1769. Ensign 14 Aug. 1769. Lieut. 26 Jan. 1773. *d. unm.* in Oudh Mar. 1777.

Brother of Jean and Sophia.

Services: Was D.J.A.G. at Berhampore in Nov. 1775.

Refs.: Will dated Daranaghur, Rohilkhand 27 Nov. 1776; proved 5 Nov. 1778.

MARSHALL, John Samuel (1793-1853). Lieut. Colonel. 71st N.I. *b.* Calcutta 16 Feb. 1793. Cadet 1807. Arrived in India 21 Mar. 1809. Ensign 13 Feb. 1809. Lieut. 16 Dec. 1814. Capt. 14 July 1825. Major 6 Aug. 1839. Lt. Col. 7 Sept. 1845. Retired 13 Aug. 1850.[1] *d.* 7 Oct. 1853.

bapt. Calcutta 9 Feb. 1800. Son of William Hodney Marshall, of Calcutta, and Catherine Clark his 1st wife. Brother of William Henry Marshall, *q.v. m.* Meerut 29 June 1847, Ty Moti (spinster, aged 35), dau. of a *Gosain* [2] of Assam. (She died Meerut 2 Aug. 1847.)

Services: Barasat C.C. Posted Ensign to 1/20th N.I. Capture of Java 1811; Ensign 1/20th N.I. Returned to Bengal from P.W.I. 16 Apr. 1814. Transfd. to newly-raised 1/29th N.I. in 1815. Siege and capture of Hathras 1817; Lieut. 1/29th N.I. Third Mahratta War; Lieut. 1/29th N.I. Leave s.c. to sea 10 mos. 16 Oct. 1819. Intr. & Qmr. 1/29th N.I. 16 Oct. 1823 till July 1825. (? First Burma War; Assam 1824; Lieut. 1/29th N.I.) Transfd. to 57th N.I. (late 1/29th) May 1824; to newly-raised 3rd Extra Regt. (became 71st N.I.) July 1825. Intr. & Qmr. 3rd Extra Regt. 12 July 1825 till 25 Aug. 1826. Suspended by G.C.M. from rank, pay and allowances for 6 mos. 14 Mar. 1835. Posted Lt. Col. to 54th N.I. 1846; to 1st N.I. 1846; to 1st Bengal Eur. Fus. Sept. 1847; to 2nd Bengal Eur. Regt. Dec. 1847. Leave s.c. to Cape and N.S.W. 29 Jan. 1848. Transfd. to 60th N.I. 1849; to 48th N.I.

Nov. 1849; to 71st N.I. Jan. 1850. Removed from the Service of E.I.Co. by order of the C.D. from 13 Aug. 1850, but without prejudice to the pension to which he was entitled on that date, viz. that of a Col.

Refs.: *A.J.* N.S. xi. 129; xiv. 289; xvii. 240-1. *I.M.* 5 Oct. 1850, p. 571.

¹ Note: "Removed from the Service by the C.D. for reasons which have not been made public." (*I.M.*)

² *Note*: "A religious mendicant, 'Lord of Passions' (lit. 'Lord of Cows')"—*Hobson-Jobson*.

MARSHALL, Thomas (1789-1833). Captain, Artillery. (380) *b.* London 15 Sept. 1789. Cadet 1805. Arrived in India 19 Sept. 1806. Fireworker 6 May 1807. Lieut. 16 Sept. 1807. Capt. 8 Nov. 1818. *d.* Allahabad 29 July 1833.

bapt. St. James's, Westminster, 11 Oct. 1789. Son of Thomas Marshall and Mary his wife. *m.* 1st, Fatehgarh 8 Feb. 1813, Sarah, 3rd dau. of Robert Blake, Assay Master of the Fatehgarh Mint. (She died 2 Jan. 1829.) *m.* 2nd, Saugor 24 July 1830, Miss Sarah Susannah Martin. (She *re-m.* 15 Jan. 1838, William Budd.)

Services: A survivor from the wreck of the *Lady Burges* on 20 Apr. 1806. Served throughout with Foot Art. Operations in Bundelkhand against Lachman Dawa 1809; Rajaoli; Ajaigarh. Nepal War 1814-15; Lieut. 3rd Coy. 3rd Bn., with detachment under Lt.-Col. Robert Bourke Gregory, *q.v.* Apptd. to officiate as Supt. of timber yard at Kasipur 7 Oct. 1817.

Refs.: *A.J.* N.S. xiii. 205.

MARSHALL, William Henry (1794-1868). Lieut. General. Colonel 3rd N.I. *b.* Calcutta 12 May 1794. Cadet 1810. Admitted 27 Aug. 1811. Ensign 12 June 1813., Lieut. 1 Sept. 1816. Capt. 10 Oct. 1825. Major 2 Apr. 1834. Lt. Col. 4 Jan. 1841. Col. 15 Mar. 1851. Maj. Gen. 28 Nov. 1854. Lt. Gen. 23 July 1865. *d.* Southport 29 Jan. 1868.

2nd son of William Hodney Marshall, of Calcutta, and Catherine his 1st wife. Brother of Charles Marshall, *q.v.*

Services: Cadet d.d. 9th N.I. 1811-13. Posted Ensign to 1/17th N.I. June 1813. Nepal War 1814-15; Ensign 1/17th N.I., in 2nd Div. (India medal). Actg. Adjt. 1/17th N.I. 21 May 1820; do. to 5 Coys. 17th N.I. on service in Rajputana Dec. 1820. Transfd. to 34th N.I. (late 1/17th) May 1824. Intr. & Qmr. 34th N.I. 29 June 1824. Transfd. to 35th N.I. 28 June 1825. Siege and capture of Bhurtpore; Capt. 35th N.I. (clasp to India medal). Fur. p.a.

THE BENGAL ARMY, 1758-1834   235

3 Jan. 1830 till 21 Jan. 1833. Operations against the Garos in Singmari, Assam, Mar. 1834. Leave s.c. to Cape 12 Mar. 1839 till 31 Dec. 1840. Posted Lt. Col. to 26th N.I. 19 Feb. 1841 ; to 17th N.I. 19 Mar. 1841 ; to 34th N.I. 19 Jan. 1842. Leave s.c. 2 yrs. to Cape and N.S.W. 30 Dec. 1843. Transfd. to 73rd N.I. 1846 ; retransfd. to new 34th N.I.[1] July 1846 ; to 32nd N.I. Aug. 1850. Col. 32nd N.I. (became 3rd B.N.I. in May 1861, and 3rd Brahmins in 1893) May 1851 till death. Fur. s.c. 21 Feb. 1852 till death.
Refs. : *Boase. I.M.* 1850, pp. 316, 571, 575. *The Times*, 3 Apr. 1868.
[1] *Note :* This Regt., late Inf. of the Bundelkhand Legion, took the number of the original 34th disbanded in 1844.

MARSON John (1754/55-1794). Lieutenant, Invalid Est. 1st Bengal Eur. Bn. *b.* 1754/55. Cadet 1776. Ensign 27 Dec. 1777. Lieut. 7 Sept. 1778. Invalided 20 Sept. 1792. *d.* Chunar 26 Jan. 1794.
A native of Middlesex. Ed. Merchant Taylors' Mar. 1763-Apr. 1764.
Services : Sailed for India in the *Duke of Kingston* 24 Mar. 1777, aged 22. Posted to Cav. 6 Apr. 1778. Lieut. 1st Eur. Bn. in July 1787.
Refs. : Robinson.

MARSTON, Thomas (1779-1802). Ensign, 2nd N.I. *bapt.* Dublin 16 June 1779. Cadet 1800. Arrived in India 24 Aug. 1801. Ensign 12 Nov. 1801. *d.* Fatehgarh, U.P., 22 Oct. 1802.
3rd son of Daniel Marston, of Dublin, merchant, and of Leixlip Park, co. Dublin, and Dorothea his wife, sister of Rt. Hon. Isaac Corry, chancellor of the Irish exchequer (*D.N.B.*). Cousin-german of William Molyneux Marston, *q.v.*
Services : Posted Ensign to 1/2nd N.I. Attack on the village of Camney, nr. Shikohabad, U.P., 29 Aug. 1802 ; Ensign 1/2nd N.I. " Poor Marsden [*sic*] never recovered this fatigue, and died soon afterwards. He was shot through the jacket on this occasion." (*Pester.*)
Refs. : Burke's *Landed Gentry*, 2nd edn., iii. 226, *s.n.* Marston, late of Willenhall, Staffs. *Pester*, pp. 13, 15, 18.

MARSTON, William Molyneux (1760/61-1817). Lieutenant. 15th Bn. Sepoys. *b.* 1760/61. Cadet 1780. Ensign 1780. Lieut. 23 July 1781. Resigned 16 Jan. 1790. *d.s.p.* The Grove, Ashbourne, co. Derby, June 1817.

Of Willenhall, Staffs. Eldest son of Richard Marston, of Willenhall, and Barbara his wife, of Doveridge Hall, co. Derby, dau. of Thomas Kirby, of Lutterworth, Leics. Cousin-german of Thomas Marston, q.v. m. 1st, Cawnpore 12 Mar. 1789, Eliza Douce, dau. of William Hancock, M.D., of the Close, Salisbury, and widow of —— Phillips. m. 2nd, his cousin Rosamond, dau. of John Sneyd, of Belmont and Bishton, and widow of William Mills, of Barlaston, Staffs.

Services : Sailed for India in the *Earl of Dartmouth* 3 June 1780, aged 19. Posted to 2nd Bengal Eur. Regt. May 1781 ; Lieut. 15th Bn. Sepoys in July 1787.

Refs. : Burke's *Landed Gentry,* 2nd edn., iii. 227, *s.n.* Marston, late of Willenhall, Staffs. *Misc. Gen. et Her.* N.S. iv. 425. *G.M.* 817, i. 643.

MARTIN, Anthony Peter (1811-1898). Lieut. Colonel. 33rd N.I. b. Lisbon, Portugal, Feb. 1811. Cadet 1829. Arrived in India 15 May 1830. Ensign 23 Apr. 1830. Lieut. 14 Nov. 1837. Capt. 11 May 1846. Major 21 July 1857. Retired 31 Dec. 1861. Hon. Lt. Col. 31 Dec. 1861. d. Fleetlands, nr. Fareham, Hants, 28 Dec. 1898.

Son of Thomas Ladford Martin. m. Benares 9 Apr. 1847, Mary Anne, dau. of Capt. Andrew Henderson Donaldson, 92nd Highlrs. Ward and godson of James Evan Baillie, J.P. co. Glam.

Services : Cadet d.d. 33rd N.I. 7 June 1830 ; Actg. Ensign (having been 2 yrs. in India) 16 July 1832. Operations against the Kols 1832. Posted to 47th N.I. 20 Aug. 1833 ; transfd. to 33rd N.I. 4 Oct. 1833 ; Adjt. 33rd N.I. 30 Apr. 1840 till Feb. 1846. First Afghan War 1842 ; forcing of Khyber ; Haft Kotal ; re-occupation of Kabul ; Lieut. 33rd N.I., with Gen. Pollock's force (Medal). First Sikh War ; Sobraon ; Bt. Capt. 33rd N.I. (Medal). Capture of Kot Kangra Apr. 1846. Second in comd. 4th Irreg. Cav. 28 Feb. 1846 till Nov. 1850 ; Comdt. do. 23 Nov. 1850, and was comdg. when part of that Regt. mutinied in May 1857. Mutiny campaign ; siege and capture of Delhi (Medal with clasp). Fur. Feb. 1858 till 1861.

Refs. : *G.M.* 1847, ii. 198. *The Times,* 30 Dec. 1898.

MARTIN, Charles (1779-1824). Major, 61st N.I. b. London 26 June 1779. Cadet 1798. Arrived in India 14 May 1800. Ensign 13 Dec. 1799. Lieut. 29 May 1800. Capt. 13 Dec. 1809. Major 11 July 1823. d. Barrackpore 9 Oct. 1824.

bapt. Allhallows, Lombard St., London, 12 July 1779. Eldest son of Peter Martin, of Ely Pl., Holborn, and Mary his wife. Ed. Rugby; admitted midsummer 1789.

Services : " Was for a few years in a mercantile House in Amsterdam, where he was distinguished for his powers as a linguist. The House having failed, he entered the Mily. Service of E.I.C." Posted Lieut. to 2/6th N.I. 15 Apr. 1801. Operations in Baghelkhand 1803; Chaukandi; Lieut. 2/6th N.I. Nepal War 1814-15; Capt. 2/6th N.I., in 1st Div. Operations against Maharao Kishor Singh of Kotah; Mangrol; Capt. 2/6th N.I. Transfd. as Major to newly-formed 31st N.I. July 1823; to 61st N.I. (late 1/31st) May 1824. *Refs.* : *Rugby School Register*. Will dated Barrackpore 14 Aug. 1824; proved 8 Oct. 1824. M.I. Barrackpore cemetery.

MARTIN, Claud [1] (1735-1800). Major General. Infantry. *b.* Lyons, France, 5 Jan. 1735. Country Cadet 1762. Ensign 17 Sept. 1763. Lieut. 18 Apr. 1764. Capt. 30 July 1766. Major 11 Sept. 1779.[2] Lt. Col. 21 Feb. 1782. Col. 30 Jan. 1793. Maj. Gen. 3 May 1796. *d.* Lucknow 13 Sept. 1800.

Son of Fleury Martin, of Lyons, cooper, and Ann Vaginay his wife. Brother of Louis Martin and uncle of Pierre Martin.

Services : Arrived in India as a private in the French Army in 1752; served in the Cavaliers d'Aumont at Porto Novo; as a dragoon under Bussy. Joined the Lorraine Regt. in 1758, and served with it at Wandewash in Jan. 1760 under Lally and Bussy; at siege of Pondicherry Sept. 1760 till its surrender to Coote 15 Jan. 1761. Was given comd., with the rank of Ensign, of a Coy. of Chasseurs which he raised from among the French prisoners at Madras, with which he reached Bengal in Jan. 1762. Served with the force under Major W. Jennings, *q.v.*, in Jan. and Feb. 1764, in comd. of this Coy. of Frenchmen. (*Possibly* served at battle of Buxar.) Posted to 3rd Troop Moghal Horse 5 Dec. 1764. In 1765 was engaged in collecting revenue in Oudh, and later in surveying in Bihar and N.E. Bengal. Dismissed in Jan. 1767 for his mutinous support of Sir Robert Fletcher, *q.v.*; restored in 1769. Passed over for comd. of a Bn. in 1773, on the grounds that, " he has ever been employed in the surveying branch and is a foreigner, although in general esteem as a brave and experienced officer and a man of strict honour." (Cons. 16 Dec. 1773.) Allowed to enter the service of the Nawab-Wazir of Oudh *c.* 1779, as Supt. of his Art. and arsenal, and spent the last 25 yrs. or so of his life at Lucknow, where he built a large residence which he called Constantia, now the La Martinière Coll., which is principally supported by an endowment left by him. He was placed on h.p., but rose regularly in the Service to the rank of Maj. Gen. At the commencement of the third Mysore War he presented the Coy. with a number of horses, and himself served in the Carnatic as a Vol., and acted as A.D.C. to Lord Cornwallis at siege of Seringapatam. Nearly one half of his large fortune of 33 lacs of rupees he left in legacies to the women of his zenana and his principal servants. The remainder he bequeathed to the poor of Lucknow, Calcutta, Chandernagore, and his native city Lyons. The Martinière Coll. at Calcutta was constructed 1833-5 from his legacy for the purpose.

Refs.: Maj.-Gen. Claud Martin, by S. C. Hill. Biog. by M. Octave Sachot. *D.I.B. E.I.M.C.* ii. 455-9. *Wilson,* i. 174. *Broome,* p. 355. *B.: P.P.* ii. 277-87; iii. 102-9. *G.M.* 1801, i. 275. Will dated 1 Jan. 1800. M.I. in St. John's church and La Martinière, Calcutta. Portrait in Zoffany's 'Col. Mordaunt's Cock Match.' [3] Engraved portrait by Legoux, from a portrait painted at Lucknow by F. Renaldi, is in India Office. Bust in Victoria Memorial Hall, Calcutta.

[1] *Note:* He signs himself both Claud and Claude: although his surname frequently appears with a final 'e' in contemporary documents, he himself always wrote it 'Martin.'

[2] *Note:* ? 20 Sept. 1778—" Capt. Claude Martin to be promoted Major and apptd. to the vacancy in the Cavalry Corps." (*Mily. Cons.* 20 Sept. 1778.)

[3] *Note:* Zoffany's picture, 'The Artist with Col. Claude Martin and friends,' was sold at Christie's for 1,100 guineas on 28 June 1929.

MARTIN, Fleming (*d.* 1799). Lieut. Colonel. Comdt. Bengal Art. (29) Capt. (Engrs.) 26 July 1764. Capt. (Art.) 21 May 1766. Major 13 May 1767. Lt. Col. 21 Feb. 1768. Resigned 7 Nov. 1768. *d.* Belvidere, Bath, 17 July 1799.

Of Staplake Mount, Devon. *m.* (in England before 1763) Jane. (She died Calcutta 29 Aug. 1766,[1] aged 35.) His dau. *m.* Thomas Brisbane, *q.v.*[2]

Services: Fireworker R.A. 1 Mar. 1755; 2nd Lieut. 12 May 1756; 1st Lieut. 2 Apr. 1757; Capt. Lt. 1 Jan. 1759; resigned Dec. 1763. Apptd. in England 12 Oct. 1763, Principal Engr. at Ft. Wm.; sailed for India in the *Vansittart* 4 Mar. 1764. Employed in building the new fort in Calcutta; took charge of the fortifications 8 Oct. 1764. Comdd. 3rd Coy. Art. in garr. at Ft. Wm. 1765-6; Agent for army clothing in 1766; Chief Engr. 20 Sept. 1766. " Capt. Fleming Martin, of the Engr. Corps, is apptd. a Lt. Col. and Comdt. of the Art. Bn. He is to take rank in the Army agreeably to the

THE BENGAL ARMY, 1758-1834   289

Commission sent out by the C.D., which is from 21 Feb. 1768."
(M.C. 1 Sept. 1768.)
Refs.: Kane, No. 195. Stubbs, iii. 490n. M.M. 1799, p. 585.
G.M. 1799, ii. 718.
¹ Note : This date from the burial register : M.I. gives the date as 15 Sept. 1766.
² Note : See Addenda at end of this vol.

MARTIN, George (d. 1785). Captain, Infantry. Cadet 1769. Ensign 5 Aug. 1769. Lieut. 29 Nov. 1772. Capt. 14 Sept. 1779. d. Buxar 10 June 1785.
m. Margaret, only dau. of Rev. Alexander Jacob, one of the royal chaplains in ordy. (She re-m. James Dunn, q.v.)
Services: Comdg. 2nd Sqdn., 2nd Regt. Cav. in June 1777 ; serving with Nawab-Wazir's troops in Nov. 1777 ; Capt. 1/3rd Bengal Eur. Regt. in Oct. 1779.
Refs.: Betham's Baronetage, ii. (1802) 267.

MARTIN, George Brackstone (1781-1830). Captain. 8th N.I. bapt. St. Michael's, Southampton, 23 Mar. 1781. Cadet 1798. Arrived in India 22 Dec. 1799. Ensign 13 Nov. 1799. Lieut. 17 May 1800. Capt. 9 July 1812. Retired 2 June 1814. d. Bath 16 Feb. 1830.
Son of John Martin and Mary his wife.
Services: Posted Lieut. to 1/8th N.I. 15 Apr. 1801. Operations in Jumna Doab 1803 ; Sasni ; Lieut. 1/8th N.I. Second Mahratta War 1804-5 ; capture of Deig ; siege of Bhurtpore ; Lieut. 1/8th N.I. Capt. Lt. 8th N.I. 18 Apr. 1810. Fur. 1812 till retirement.

MARTIN, James (1792-1827). Lieutenant, 3rd N.I. bapt. Aberdeen 24 June 1792. Cadet 1809. Arrived in India 3 Oct. 1810. Ensign 1 June 1812. Lieut. 1 Sept. 1815. d. Lucknow 6 Jan. 1827.
Son of James Martin, of Aberdeen. Brother of William Martin (1789-1882), q.v., and cousin-german of Jane Amelia, wife of Robert Delamain, q.v. Ed. Aberdeen Coll.
Services: Barasat C.C. Cadet d.d. 10th N.I. 1811. Posted Ensign to 2/6th N.I. in 1812. Nepal War 1814-15 ; Ensign 2/6th N.I., in 1st Div. With 2nd Ceylon Vol. Bn. 1818-19 ; at Coll. of Ft. Wm. 1820. Leave to Bombay and Persian Gulf 1821-2. Transfd. to 3rd N.I. (late 1/6th) May 1824 ; Intr. & Qmr. do. 17 June 1824 till death.
Refs.: A.J. xxiii. 857. Will dated Lucknow, 5 Mar. 1826 ; proved 18 Mar. 1827.

LIST OF THE OFFICERS OF

MARTIN, John (1801-1838). Captain, 41st N.I. *bapt.* Tavistock, Devon, 10 Nov. 1801. Cadet 1817. Admitted 3 Oct. 1818. Ensign 3 May 1818. Lieut. 1 Jan. 1819. Capt. 18 Nov. 1834. *d.* at sea 19 Oct. 1838 : drowned on board the *Protector* in a gale off the Sandheads, Bengal, aged 38.

Son of William Martin, of Tavistock, builder and carpenter, and Joan his wife.

Services : Posted Supy. Lieut. to 1/21st N.I. in 1819. Offg. Adjt. Left Wing 1/21st N.I. 20 Jan. 1824. Transfd. to 41st N.I. (late 1/21st) May 1824. Siege and capture of Bhurtpore ; Lieut. 41st N.I. Actg. Intr. & Qmr. 41st N.I. 9 Nov. 1826. Was absent from his Regt. on sick leave for considerable periods 1827-35. Fur. s.c. 15 Jan. 1836 ; permitted to return to India (M.C. 16 May 1838).

Refs. : The *Times*, 23 Jan. 1839, p. 5. M.I. in St. John's, Calcutta.

MARTIN, Peter (1811-1831). Ensign, 44th N.I. *b.* Edinburgh 4 Sept. 1811. Cadet 1828. Arrived in India 24 Oct. 1828. Ensign 10 May 1828. *d.* Muzaffarnagar, U.P., 17 Oct. 1831, " of a short but severe attack of brainfever, caught on the journey from Simla." (*A.J.*)

Son of William Alexander Martin, of 45 Melville St., Edinburgh, W.S., and Margaret his wife, dau. of John Davie, of Gavieside. Edin. Acad. 1824-7 ; Edin. Univ.

Services : Ensign d.d. 47th N.I. 20 Nov. 1828 ; d.d. 59th N.I. 17 Jan. 1829 ; posted to 44th N.I. 4 Mar. 1829. No record of active service.

Refs. : A.J. N.S. viii. 41.

MARTIN, Richard (1774-1804). Lieutenant, 2nd N.I. *bapt.* Elton, Hunts., 29 Nov. 1774. Cadet 1794. Admitted 23 Feb. 1796. Ensign 31 Oct. 1795. Lieut. 25 Apr. 1797. *d.* Agra 10 June 1804.

Son of Henry Martin and Elizabeth his wife.

Services : Apptd. Cadet 22 Apr. 1795 ; sailed for India in the *Rodney* 9 July 1795. Operations in Jumna Doab 1803 ; Sasni ; Lieut. 2nd N.I. Second Mahratta War ; battle of Delhi ; Lieut. 2nd N.I.

MARTIN, Robert (1810-1842). Lieutenant, Engineers. *bapt.* Keston, Kent, 13 June 1810. Cadet 1828. Arrived in India 27 Aug. 1829. 2nd Lieut. (?) Lieut. 9 May 1829. *d.* Akyab, Arakan, 1 July 1842.

Son of Rev. Joseph William Martin, rector of Keston, and Anne

THE BENGAL ARMY, 1758-1834   241

his wife. Brother of William Joseph Martin, *q.v.* Addiscombe Cadet 1826-7.
Services: Actg. Adjt. 4 Coys. S. & M. at Allahabad 22 Aug. 1832. On survey duty in Shekhawat 9 Feb. till 29 Mar. 1835. Asst. to Supt. of new road to Benares 9 Oct. 1835 till 1 Aug. 1836. Executive Engr. Arakan 1 Aug. 1836. Employed in building lighthouse at Kyaukpyu.
Refs.: The Times, 15 Oct. 1842. M.I. in Akyab cemetery.

MARTIN, Russel (1781-1839). Lieut. Colonel. 2nd Bengal Eur. Regt. *b.* 21 Nov. 1781. Cadet 1800. Arrived in India 15 Oct. 1801. Ensign 6 Dec. 1801. Lieut. 4 Nov. 1803. Capt. 1 Jan. 1818. Major 1 May 1824. Lt. Col. 18 Jan. 1828. Retired 2 June 1830. *d.* Jordan Bank, Morningside, 10 July 1839.
bapt. Pittenweem, co. Fife, 25 Nov. 1785. Son of Thomas Martin and Elizabeth Bridges his wife. Brother of Thomas Martin, writer in Edinburgh.
Services: Ensign d.d. 18th N.I. in 1802; transfd. as Ensign to 7th N.I. Second Mahratta War; Ensign 7th N.I. Transfd. to 18th N.I. Jan. 1804; retransfd. to 2/7th N.I. 1804. Professor and Asst. Adjt. at Barasat C.C. 1806-11. Asst. Professor of Hindustani at Coll. of Ft. Wm. 18 Dec. 1813 till 23 Dec. 1816. Fur. s.c. 30 Jan. 1817 till 1819. Capt. Lt. 7th N.I. 25 July 1817. Comdd. Gorakhpur L.I. Bn. 1821-7. Transfd. as Major to 10th N.I. (late 2/7th) May 1824. Posted Lt. Col. to 11th N.I. 3 June 1828; to 2nd Bengal Eur. Regt. 18 Dec. 1828. Fur. 1828 till retirement.
Refs.: A.J. N.S. xxix. 341.

MARTIN, Thomas (1761/62-1847). Captain. 24th N.I. *b.* London 1761/62. Cadet 1781. Admitted 12 Apr. 1782. Ensign 22 Mar. 1781. Lieut. 18 July 1782. Capt. 29 May 1800. Retired 21 Feb. 1806. *d.* 27 Nov. 1847.
m. Norton, nr. Stockton, Durham, Dec. 1807, a dau. of George Wardell, of Sedgefield, Durham. [1]
Services: Apptd. Cadet 14 May 1781, aged 19; sailed for India in the *Northumberland* 26 June 1781. Apptd. D.J.A.G. 27 May 1782; J.A.G. 8 Jan. 1783 till Mar. 1786. Lieut. 2nd Eur. Bn. in July 1787; transfd. to 12th Bn. Sepoys 5 Feb. 1790; 14th N.I. in 1798. Second Mahratta War; battle of Delhi; Agra; Gwalior; Monson's retreat; Capt. 1/14th N.I. Transfd. to newly-raised 24th N.I. in 1805.
[1] *Note:* This may possibly refer to the following.

MARTIN, Thomas. Captain. 14th N.I. *b.* Orleans. Cadet 1794. Arrived in India 6 Feb. 1797. Ensign 14 Nov. 1795. Lieut. 13 Sept. 1797. Capt. 6 June 1806. Invalided 17 July 1806. Retired May 1807. (? *d.* 1838.) [1]
Services: Apptd. Cadet 11 Nov. 1795; sailed for India in the *Lord Camden* 12 Apr. 1796. On the voyage out volunteered at the Cape against the Dutch fleet, which was captured in Saldanha Bay in Aug. 1796. Posted Ensign to 1st Bengal Eur. Regt.; as Lieut. to 2/14th N.I. in 1799. d.d. Marine Bn. 1800-1. Operations in Jumna Doab 1803; against Rajah Chatter Sal of Thathia fort Sept. 1803; Lieut. 2/14th N.I. Second Mahratta War; defence of Delhi Oct. 1804; action with Holkar at Shamli 30 Oct. 1804; defence of Shamli fort (s.w. 2 Nov.—shot through both eyes and blinded for life [2]); Lieut. 2/14th N.I. Posted to 2nd Coy. Eur. Invalids 22 July 1806. Fur. s.c. Aug. 1806 till retirement.
Refs.: E.I.M.C. iii. 91-6. *M.M.* 1807, p. 602.
[1] *Note:* His name appears in E.I.R. for Jan. 1838 for the last time.
[2] *Note:* His pension augmented as a special case to £300 p.a., 17 Sept. 1808.

MARTIN, Thomas (1781-?). Lieutenant. 3rd N.C. *b.* 15 Dec. 1781. Cadet 1798. Arrived in India 22 Nov. 1799. Cornet 5 June 1800. Lieut. 6 Aug. 1803. Resigned 28 Mar. 1805.
bapt. Rathcony 30 Dec. 1781. 2nd son of Thomas Martin, of Springmount.
Services: Operations in Jumna Doab 1803; Sasni; Bijaigarh; Kachaura; Lieut. 3rd N.C. (? Second Mahratta War 1803-4; battle of Delhi; Laswari; Rampura; battle of Deig; Lieut. 3rd N.C.)

MARTIN, Thomas (1805-1866). Lieut. Colonel. 20th N.I. *b.* E. Moulsey, Surrey, 11 Jan. 1805. Cadet 1825. Arrived in India 10 May 1826. Ensign 18 Dec. 1825. Lieut. 8 Apr. 1828. Capt. 14 Mar. 1843. Major 28 Nov. 1854. Lt. Col. 27 Aug. 1858. Retired 11 Dec. 1859. *d.* 35 Sackville St., London, 13 Oct. 1866.
bapt. E. Moulsey 15 Aug. 1805. Son of William Greening Martin, of E. Moulsey, and Elizabeth his wife.
Services: Posted Ensign to 20th N.I.; Adjt. do. 12 Mar. 1836 till 26 July 1843. 2nd Asst. Mily. Auditor Gen. 2 June 1846 till Feb. 1854. Rejoined his Regt. for service 13 Oct. 1848. Second Sikh War; Chilianwala; Gujerat; Capt. 20th N.I. (Medal with

THE BENGAL ARMY, 1758-1834   243

clasp). Offg. 1st Asst. Mily. Auditor Gen. Jan. 1850; actg. Presdy. Paymr., and to Queen's troops, 18 Oct. 1850; permanent do. 10 Feb. 1854 till Aug. 1858.
Refs. : *G.M.* 1866, ii. 705. *The Times,* 19 Oct. 1866.

MARTIN, Thomas Derisley (1806-1868). Major. 28th N.I. *bapt.* Saltash, Cornwall, 25 June 1806. Cadet 1825. Arrived in India 27 June 1826. Ensign 13 Feb. 1826. Lieut. 24 Mar. 1833. Capt. 17 Sept. 1846. Retired 1 May 1852. Hon. Major 28 Nov. 1854. *d.* 22 Jan. 1868.
Son of Joseph Martin, of Saltash, surgeon, and Catherine Harriett his wife. *m.* 1st, Calcutta 5 Apr. 1828, Miss Hannah Simpson. (She died Jaunpur 7 Aug. 1829, aged 21.) *m.* 2nd, Nimach 8 May 1837, Miss Caroline Russell. (She died at sea on board the *Blenheim* 7 June 1852, aged 34.)
Services : Ensign d.d. 4th Extra Regt. 8 July 1826; posted to 28th N.I. 26 Sept. 1826. Adjt. 28th N.I. 17 Feb. 1841 till 11 Feb. 1846. Fur. s.c. 25 Nov. 1845 till 3 Dec. 1847. Second Sikh War; operations in Jullundur Doab 1848-9; Capt. 28th N.I. (? Medal).

MARTIN, William (1739/40-1766). Ensign, Infantry. *b.* Plymouth 1739/40. Cadet 1764. Ensign 18 Aug. 1765. *d.* Calcutta 1 Aug. 1766.
(*Probably* son of William Martin, of Shadwell.)
Services : (? Permitted to proceed to India as a free merchant 30 Nov. 1763.) Sailed for India as a Cadet in the *Vansittart* 4 Mar. 1764, aged 24.

*MARTIN, William (1774-1842 ?). Lieutenant. 7th N.I. *bapt.* ptely. Silton, Dorset, 25 July 1774. Cadet 1795. Arrived in India 4 Mar. 1797. Ensign 20 Oct. 1796. Lieut. 30 Oct. 1797. Retired 7 Apr. 1802. (? *d.* 1842.) [1]
Son of Albinus Martin and Mary his wife.
Services : Fur. 17 Dec. 1798 till retirement. N.F.P.
Refs. : *Philippart MS.*
[1] *Note :* Pension not drawn after 31 Oct. 1842, but his name continues in *E.I.R.* till Jan. 1851.

MARTIN, William (1789-1882). Colonel. 24th N.I. *b.* St. Nicholas, Aberdeen, 2 Apr. 1789. Cadet 1805. Arrived in India 11 July 1806. Ensign 12 Aug. 1806. Lieut. 1 July 1808. Capt. 11 July 1823. Major 13 Jan. 1834. Lt. Col. 1840. Retired

8 Feb. 1841. Hon. Col. 28 Nov. 1854. *d.* Upton Bishop, co. Hereford, 19 Jan. 1882.

Son of James Martin, of Aberdeen. Brother of James Martin, *q.v.*, and cousin-german of the wife of Richard Charles Lawrence, *q.v.* (? *m.* 1st, ——.) His dau. *m.* Radclyffe Haldane, *q.v. m.* Patna 7 Jan. 1832, Isabel, youngest dau. of Samuel Burnett, of London.

Services : Barasat C.C. Posted Ensign to 10th N.I. in 1807. Transfd. to newly-raised 2/29th N.I. in 1815. Operations against the Bhattis of Hariana 1818 ; Lieut. 2/29th N.I. Third Mahratta War ; Asirgarh ; Lieut. 2/29th N.I. Intr. & Qmr. 1/29th N.I. 18 Sept. 1822 till 16 Oct. 1823. Transfd. to 57th N.I. (late 1/29th) May 1824. First Burma War ; Assam 1824-5 ; occupation of Rangpur (*Lond. Gaz.* 19 July 1825) ; Capt. comdg. 57th N.I., with force under Lt.-Col. Alfred Richards, *q.v.* (India medal). Offg. Bde. Major to Col. Richards' force 15 Mar. 1825 till 9 Oct. 1826. Fur. s.c. 12 July 1827 till 26 Oct. 1829. Comdd. 57th N.I. from 30 Aug. 1836. Posted Lt. Col. to 24th N.I. 14 Jan. 1841.

Refs. : The Times, 10 Feb. 1882. *Guardian,* xxxvii. 229c.

MARTIN, William (1807-1888). Major. 52nd N.I. *b.* Warsop, Notts., 23 Dec. 1807. Cadet 1824. Arrived in India 25 Nov. 1825. Ensign 18 Apr. 1825. Lieut. 13 Sept. 1827. Capt. 16 Sept. 1840. Retired 5 Aug. 1848. Hon. Major 28 Nov. 1854. *d.* 51 Brompton Cresc., London, 16 Mar. 1888.

bapt. Warsop 2 Feb. 1808. 5th son of Rev. Samuel Martin, rector of Warsop, and Selina his wife, youngest dau. of Francis Beresford, of Ashbourne and Osmaston. Brother of Rev. Francis Martin, senior Fellow of Trin. Coll., Camb. *m.* Akyab, Arakan, 26 Mar. 1828, Jane Ryan, dau. of Charles Paton, Junior Comr. in Arakan, *q.v.* (She died 1864.) Ed. Rugby ; admitted 1820.

Services : Posted Ensign to 52nd N.I. Adjt. Arakan Provl. Bn. 30 Jan. 1829 ; do. Magh Levy 5 Oct. 1829 ; do. 52nd N.I. 3 Apr. 1830 till 1836. Fur. p.a. 6 Mar. 1836 till 16 Nov. 1838. Adjt. 52nd N.I. 9 Apr. 1839 till 19 Oct. 1840. Offg. D.J.A.G. Cawnpore Div. 22 Feb. 1840 ; do. Saugor Div. 3 Feb. 1841. Actg. D.J.A.G. Cawnpore Div. 29 Sept. 1842 ; permanent do. 23 Dec. 1842 ; do. Presdy. Div. 1846 till retirement. No record of active service. Author of " Who shall regenerate India ? " London, 1859.

Refs. : Burke's *Landed Gentry,* 15th edn., p. 1542, *s.n.* Martin, of Norton, Worcs. Phillimore's *Notts. Co. Peds.* i. 335, *s.n.* Martin, of Gotham and Warsop. *Howard & Crisp,* xiv. 69, *s.n.* Atlay.

Rugby School Register. A.J. xxvi. 486 ; N.S. xvi. 265-6 ; N.S. xx. 101. The Times, 20 Mar. 1888.

MARTIN, William Joseph (1808-1886). Lieut. Colonel. 9th N.I. b. Keston, Kent, 1 May 1808. Cadet 1823. Arrived in India 2 Nov. 1824. Ensign 20 June 1824. Lieut. 13 May 1825. Capt. 22 Dec. 1843. Bt. Major 11 Nov. 1852. Retired 1 June 1854. Hon. Col. 28 Nov. 1854. d. 2 Lansdown Villas, Torquay, 19 Mar. 1886.
bapt. Keston 7 July 1808. Eldest son of Rev. Joseph William Martin, rector of Keston, and Anne his wife. Brother of Robert Martin, q.v. Addiscombe Cadet 1822-4.
Services : Posted Ensign to 9th N.I. 31 Mar. 1825. Fur. p.a. 19 Feb. 1835 till 21 May 1838. Attached to 3rd L.I. Bn. at Cawnpore and Meerut Oct. 1840 till 1 Nov. 1842, when it was broken up. Fur. s.c. 31 Jan. 1848 till 1850. No record of active service. A lay missionary in Punjab mission of C.M.S. 1854-60.
Refs. : Boase. The Times, 26 Mar. 1886.

***MARTINDALE, John** (d. 1769). Ensign, Infantry. Cadet (?) Ensign (?) d. in India 1769.
m. Lettice. Father of John and Gabriel. (*Probably* father or brother of Sir Gabriel Martindell, K.C.B., q.v.)
Services : N.F.P.
Refs. : Will dated 19 Apr. 1769 ; proved 4 July 1769.

MARTINDELL, Sir Gabriel (c. 1759-1831). Lieut. General, K.C.B. Colonel 14th N.I. b. c. 1759. Country Cadet 1772. Admitted 6 Mar. 1772. Ensign 4 Aug. 1776. Lieut. 21 July 1778. Capt. 6 Aug. 1793. Major 1 Nov. 1798. Lt. Col. 21 Feb. 1801. Col. (25 July 1810) 25 Aug. 1811. Maj. Gen. 4 June 1813. Lt. Gen. 27 May 1825. d. Buxar 2 Jan. 1831, aged 76 (*sic*).
(*Probably* son of John Martindale, q.v.) Father of William Martindell (see Appendix A). His daus. m. John Horatio Clarkson, Henry Finch, John Stuart Rotton, and William Sivright, qq.v.
Services : See D.N.B. Apptd. Cadet 6 Mar. 1772, aged about 13. Being considered too young to join the Select Picket, he remained at school at Calcutta till 1776, when he joined the Army. Lieut. 1/3rd Bengal Eur. Regt. in Oct. 1779 ; Lieut. 31st Bn. in July 1787. Posted Capt. to 4th Bengal Eur. Bn. Aug. 1793 ; as Major to newly-raised 2/13th N.I. Nov. 1798. This Bn. was called after him " *Martdeel-ki-Paltan.*" Second Mahratta War 1804-5 ; Lt. Col. 2/13th N.I., comdg. a detached force in Bundelkhand. Operations

in Bundelkhand 1809 ; Ajaigarh ; Lt. Col. comdg. the force.
Posted Col. to 12th N.I. 25 Aug. 1811. Reduction of Kalinjar
1812 ; Col. comdg. the force. Nepal War 1814-15 ; Jaithak ;
Maj. Gen. comdg. 2nd Div. after Gillespie's death. Apptd. Mily.
Comr. and to comd. troops in Cuttack 28 Apr. 1817. Third
Mahratta War ; Maj. Gen. comdg. a column. Transfd. to 21st N.I.
in 1818. Comdd. 1st Div. of field army, with H.Q. at Cawnpore,
Apr. 1820 till July 1822. Transfd. to 14th N.I. May 1824. To
comd. Cawnpore Div. 31 May 1824 ; Comdt. of fortress of Buxar
26 Jan. 1827 till death. K.C.B. 7 Apr. 1815.
Refs. : D.N.B. E.I.M.C. i. 406-8. *D.I.B. A.J.* N.S. v. 206.
M.I. at Buxar.

MASON, Charles Ord (1790-1828). Captain, 10th L.C. *b.*
London 20 May 1790. Cadet 1808. Arrived in India 19 July
1809. Cornet 9 Nov. 1811. Lieut. 1 Sept. 1818. Capt. 16 Jan.
1824. *d.* London 19 July 1828.

bapt. Marylebone, London, 13 June 1790. Son of Robert Mason
and Eleanor his wife. Brother of David Mason, *q.v. m.* Cawnpore
17 Mar. 1815, Emily Betsy, 3rd dau. of J. B. Fortier, of Tirhut,
B. & O., indigo planter.

Services : Barasat C.C. Cadet d.d. 3rd N.C. 1810 ; posted
Cornet to 5th N.C. in 1811. Third Mahratta War ; Lieut. 5th N.C.
Second in comd. 6th Local Horse 1824 ; transfd. to newly-raised
10th L.C. in 1825. Siege and capture of Bhurtpore ; Capt. 10th
L.C. Fur. 1827 till death.

Refs. : Will dated 6 Oct. 1827 ; proved 9 Feb. 1829.

MASON, David (1787-1855). Captain. 49th N.I. *b.* Westminster, London, 9 Jan. 1787. Cadet 1805. Arrived in India
2 July 1807. Ensign 5 July 1807. Lieut. 13 Nov. 1812. Capt.
1 May 1824. Retired 26 Apr. 1833. *d.* 9 Nov. 1855.

bapt. St. James's, Westminster, 4 Feb. 1787. Son of Robert
Mason and Eleanor his wife. Brother of Charles Ord Mason,
q.v. m. Calcutta 15 Apr. 1809, Miss Jane Forster, natural dau.
of Henry Pitts Forster, B.C.S. (*D.N.B.*), and sister of Henry Forster
(Appendix A). (She died 19 May 1827.)

Services : Barasat C.C. 8½ mos. Posted Ensign to 25th N.I. in
1808 ; Lieut. 1/25th N.I. With Java Inf. Vols. in 1812 ; 3rd Vol.
Bn. 1815-16. Siege and capture of Hathras 1817 ; Lieut. 1/25th
N.I. Third Mahratta War ; Lieut. 1/25th N.I. Actg. Intr. &
Qmr. 1/25th N.I. 1818. Fur. s.c. 27 Dec. 1820 till 1 Nov. 1823.
Transfd. to 49th N.I. (late 1/25th) May 1824. First Burma War ;

Arakan 1825 (*Lond. Gaz.* 1 Oct. 1825); Capt. 49th N.I. (? India medal¹). Actg. Fort Adjt. Arakan 21 Sept. 1825. Fur. s.c. 26 Dec. 1830 till retirement. Placed on retired list on h.p. with effect from 26 Apr. 1833 owing to ill health. (M.C. 18 Feb. 1835.)
¹ *Note:* His name is not included in the India medal roll.

MASON, George (1765/66-1821). Lieut. Colonel, C.B., Artillery. (260) *b.* 1765/66. Cadet 1783. Arrived in India 3 July 1784. Fireworker 9 Apr. 1785. Lieut. 20 Aug. 1792. Capt. Lt. 20 Feb. 1802. Capt. 21 Sept. 1804. Major 11 Dec. 1810. Lt. Col. 6 May 1817. *d.* at sea on board a pilot schooner at Saugor I., Bengal, 7 Aug. 1821, aged 55.

m. (?) His dau. Catharine *m.* Nov. 1829, Lieut. W. C. Webber, R.N.

Services: Apptd. Cadet 5 Sept. 1783. Lieut. F. 1st Bn. Art. in July 1787. On service to Madras Aug. 1793 for siege of Pondicherry; Lieut. 2nd Coy. 1st Bn., transfd. tempy. from 5th Coy. 2nd Bn. Fur. 3 Apr. 1797 till 24 Sept. 1799. Second Mahratta War; Capt. Lt. 3rd Coy. 3rd Bn. Settlement of Hariana 1809; Bhawani; Capt. comdg. the Art. Fur. 8 June 1811 till 1813. Nepal War 1814-15; Major 2nd Bn., comdg. Art. with 4th Div. Siege and capture of Hathras; Major Foot Art. Third Mahratta War; Lt. Col. 2nd Bn., actg. Bdr. comdg. Art. of Centre Div. Fur. s.c. Aug. 1821. C.B. 3 Feb. 1817.

Refs.: Will dated 14 Sept. 1818; proved 10 Sept. 1821. M.I. Dum-Dum cemetery.

MASON, Kender (1790-1821). Lieutenant, Invalid Est. Artillery. (404) *b.* Epsom 18 June 1790. Cadet 1807. Arrived in India 21 Mar. 1809. Fireworker 31 Mar. 1809. Lieut. 29 Aug. 1813. Invalided 18 Dec. 1819. *d.* Calcutta 13 May 1821.

bapt. Epsom 6 July 1790. Son of Kender Mason, of Beel House, Amersham, and Elizabeth his wife, elder dau. of Langford Lovell, of Antigua. Woolwich Cadet.

Services: (? Nepal War 1815; Lieut. 4th Coy. 3rd Bn., with 1st Div.¹)

Refs.: Oliver's *Hist. of Antigua*, ii. 196, *s.n.* Lovell.
¹ *Note:* He may have been absent, sick: he had not joined the force by 1 Jan. 1815.

MASON, William (1739-1766). Lieutenant, Artillery. (42) *bapt.* St. Chad's, Shrewsbury, 6 Feb. 1739. Cadet (?) Fireworker 2 Aug. 1763. 2nd Lieut. 28 Mar. 1764. Lieut. 1 Aug. 1765. *d. unm.* in India 3 Nov. 1766.

Son of William Mason, of Shrewsbury, and Mary his wife.
Services: Lieut. 4th Coy. Art. Resigned his Commission 1 May 1766 during the " Batta mutiny " ; readmitted later.
Refs.: Will dated 19 Sept. 1766 ; proved 1766.

MASSIE, Frederick Lloyd (1789-1813). Lieutenant, 22nd N.I. *b.* Wrexham, co. Denbigh, 20 May 1789. Cadet 1804. Arrived in India 6 Apr. 1806. Ensign 2 Feb. 1806. Lieut. 1 Feb. 1807. *d.* Agra 11 June 1813.
bapt. Wrexham 1 Sept. 1789. Son of Charles Massie, surgeon, and Benedicta his wife.
Services: Nominated for R.M.A., Woolwich, 21 Dec. 1803, but was never admitted. Apptd. Inf. Cadet 15 Mar. 1805. Posted Lieut. to 22nd N.I. in 1807. Settlement of Hariana 1809 ; Bhawani ; Lieut. 1/22nd N.I. Reduction of Kalinjar 1812 ; Lieut. 1/22nd N.I.
Refs.: M.I. Agra Cantt. cemetery.

MASSIE, William Henry (1806-1856). Ensign. 39th N.I. Subsequently rector of St. Mary's, Chester. *b.* Chester 12 Nov. 1806. Cadet 1825. Arrived in India 27 Oct. 1826. Ensign 23 May 1826. Resigned 16 July 1832. *d.* Chester 5 Jan. 1856.
4th son of Rev. Richard Massie, of Coddington, co. Chester, rector of Eccleston, nr. Chester, and Hester Lee his wife, eldest dau. of Edward V. Townshend, of Wincham Hall, co. Chester. Cousin-german of Edward Du Pré Townshend, *q.v.* T.C.D. ; Fellow Commoner 12 Feb. 1831 ; B.A. 1834.
Services: Posted Ensign to 39th N.I. 9 Nov. 1826. Fur. s.c. 1 Mar. 1830 till Feb. 1833, when he resigned with effect from 16 July 1832 (M.C. 6 Feb. 1833). No record of active service. Took holy orders. P.C. of Goostrey, nr. Sandbach, co. Chester, 1833 ; rector of St. Mary-on-the-Hill, Chester, 1847 ; minor canon of Chester cathedral.
Refs.: Burke's *Landed Gentry*, 13th edn., p. 1219, *s.n.* Massie, of Coddington, co. Chester. *Alumni Dub. G.M.* 1856, i. 543.

*MASSON, James (1811-1879). Captain, Invalid Est. 57th N.I. *b.* Walsall, Staffs., 14 Mar. 1811. Cadet 1828. Was already in India when apptd. Cadet. Ensign (4 Dec. 1828) 10 Apr. 1829. Lieut. 8 July 1836. Capt. 11 Aug. 1847. Invalided 31 Dec. 1847. *d.* (? in the Nilgiris, Madras) 20 Oct. 1879.
Son of Thomas Masson and Isabella his wife. *m.* Mhow 8 Nov. 1832, Ann Blake (*probably* dau. of George Blake, *q.v.*).

THE BENGAL ARMY, 1758-1834

Services: Ensign d.d. 57th N.I. 10 June 1829. Posted Ensign to 57th N.I., and served throughout with that Regt. Fur. p.a. 20 Jan. 1840 till 1842; s.c. 17 Jan. 1845 till 1846. No record of active service.

MASTER, Edward Pelham (1806-1857). Bt. Major, Invalid Est. Artillery. (569) *b.* Walcot, Somerset, 16 Apr. 1806. Cadet 1824. Arrived in India 15 Oct. 1825. 2nd Lieut. 16 Dec. 1824. Lieut. 24 May 1829. Capt. 20 Feb. 1844. Bt. Major 7 June 1849. Invalided 1 July 1851. *d.* Cawnpore 1857 (? massacred during June).

3rd son of James Master, Adm. R.N., and Jeanetta his wife, dau. of Rev. Henry Heathcote, rector of Walton-on-the-Hill, Lancs. Brother of Robert Samuel Master, *q.v.*, and cousin-german of Gilbert Coventry Streynsham Master, *q.v.* Addiscombe Cadet 1822-4.

Services: First Sikh War; Sobraon; Capt. comdg. 3rd Coy. 3rd Bn. Foot Art. (Medal). Second Sikh War; Multan; Gujerat; Capt. comdg. 3rd Coy. 3rd Bn. (Medal with clasp).

Refs.: Burke's *Landed Gentry*, 13th edn., p. 1221, *s.n.* Master, of Barrow Green House, Surrey.

MASTER, Gilbert Coventry Streynsham (1805-1839). Bt. Captain, 4th L.C. *b.* Chapra, Bihar, 16 Jan. 1805. Cadet 1821. Arrived in India 20 Aug. 1822. Cornet 17 Mar. 1822. Lieut. 1 May 1824. Bt. Capt. 17 Mar. 1837. *d.* Karnal 24 Oct. 1839.

Elder son of Gilbert Coventry Master, judge of the provl. court of appeal for the Div. of Calcutta, and Augusta his wife, 5th dau. of Sir James Campbell, Kt., of Inverneill. Brother of Robert Augustus Master, *q.v.*, and cousin-german of Robert Samuel Master, *q.v.*, and of Archibald Lorne Campbell, *q.v.* Ed. Rugby; entered the school midsummer 1819.

Services: Posted Cornet to 4th L.C. Oct. 1822. Adjt. 4th L.C. 2 Nov. 1825 till 12 Mar. 1835. Siege and capture of Bhurtpore; Lieut. 4th L.C. Shekhawat expedn. 1834; Lieut. 4th L.C. Fur. p.a. 5 Apr. 1836 till 17 Feb. 1839. Offg. Adjt. 4th L.C. Sept. 1839 till death.

Refs.: Burke's *Landed Gentry*, 13th edn., p. 1221, *s.n.* Master, of Barrow Green House, Surrey. *De Rhé-Philipe. Rugby School Register.* M.I. at Karnal.

MASTER, Gilbert William (1807-1848). Captain, 4th L.C. *b.* Croston, Lancs., 16 Jan. 1807. Cadet 1824. Arrived in

India 15 Oct. 1825. Cornet (?) Lieut. 13 May 1825. Capt. 1 Jan. 1848. *d. unm.* Mussoorie, U.P., 20 Apr. 1848. *bapt.* Croston 9 Feb. 1807. 6th and youngest son of Rev. Streynsham Master, rector of Croston, and Elizabeth his wife, dau. of Sir John Parker Mosley, Bart., of Ancoats. Cousin-german of Robert Augustus Master, *q.v.*, and of William Bayley Mosley, *q.v.* Haileybury 1824.

Services : Posted Lieut. to 4th L.C. in 1825. Siege and capture of Bhurtpore ; Lieut. 4th L.C. Shekhawat expedn. 1834 ; Lieut. 4th L.C. Fur. p.a. 6 Mar. 1836 till 11 Feb. 1839. Actg. Adjt. 4th L.C. 25 Oct. 1839. Gwalior campaign ; Maharajpur ; Bt. Capt. 4th L.C. (Bronze star). First Sikh War ; Mudki ; Ferozshahr ; Bt. Capt. 4th L.C. (Medal with clasp).

Refs. : Burke's *Landed Gentry*, 13th edn., p. 1221, *s.n.* Master, of Barrow Green House, Surrey. *Howard & Crisp*, vi. 143, *s.n.* Master. *I.M.* 22 June 1848, p. 360. M.I. Landour.

MASTER, Robert Augustus (1806-1865). Major General, C.B. 2nd Bengal Eur. L.C. *b.* Dacca 9 Nov. 1806. Cadet 1824. Arrived in India 15 Oct. 1825. Cornet 12 May 1825. Lieut. 13 May 1825. Capt. 10 Mar. 1841. Major 20 Dec. 1851. Lt. Col. 13 Apr. 1855. Bt. Col. 28 Nov. 1857. Retired 31 Dec. 1861. Hon. Maj. Gen. 31 Dec. 1861. *d.* Belbrook House, Cheltenham, 27 Jan. 1865.

Younger son of Gilbert Coventry Master, B.C.S., and Augusta his wife. Brother of Gilbert Coventry Streynsham Master, *q.v.*, and cousin-german of Whalley Master, *q.v. m.* 1st, Kaitha, U.P., 30 Mar. 1830, Isabella, dau. of Mathias Hennessy, late Capt. H.M. 67th Regt. (She died Meerut 9 Oct. 1832.) *m.* 2nd, Mhow 26 June 1834, Marian, 4th dau. of James Kennedy, *q.v.* (*See also* William Alexander.) (She died 11 Jan. 1884, aged 70.) Ed. Rugby ; admitted midsummer 1819.

Services : Posted Lieut. to 7th L.C. Siege and capture of Bhurtpore ; Lieut. d.d. 4th L.C. (India medal). d.d. 4th L.C. 6 June till 1 Oct. 1826. Actg. A.D.C. to Maj.-Gen. Thomas Shuldham, *q.v.*, 23 July 1827. Actg. Adjt. 7th L.C. 24 Mar. 1828 ; permanent do. 28 Jan. 1830 till 28 Nov. 1835. Shekhawat expedn. 1834 ; Staff Ofr. under Col. Kenny. Comdt. 11th Irreg. Cav. 5 Oct. 1847 till Oct. 1855. Second Sikh War ; Multan ; Gujerat ; pursuit of Sikhs and Afghans to Peshawar ; Capt. comdg. 11th Irreg. Cav. (Medal with 2 clasps). Posted Lt. Col. to 7th L.C. Oct. 1855. Mutiny campaign ; siege and defence of Lucknow 30 June till 22 Nov. 1857 (Medal with clasp). Fur. 1858 till 14 Nov.

THE BENGAL ARMY, 1758-1834 251

1859. Transfd. to 2nd Eur. L.C. 28 Dec. 1859. C.B. 24 Mar. 1858.
Refs.: Burke's Landed Gentry, 13th edn., p. 1221, s.n. Master, of Barrow Green House, Surrey. Rugby School Register. Boase. G.M. 1865, i. 394. The Times, 1 Feb. 1865. M.I. in new cemetery, Cheltenham.

MASTER, Robert Samuel (1810-1836). Lieutenant, Engineers. b. Walcot, Somerset, 3 July 1810. Cadet 1828. Arrived in India 28 Oct. 1828. 2nd Lieut. (?) Lieut. 28 Sept. 1827. d. Kyaukpyu, Arakan, 7 June 1836.
5th son of James Master, Adm. R.N., and Jeanetta his wife. Brother of Whalley Master, q.v. Addiscombe Cadet 1826-7.
Services: Asst. to Executive Engr. Agra Div., P.W.D., 28 Dec. 1833. Employed in surveying. Asst. to Supt. of roads, Bankura to Benares, 16 June 1835. Executive Engr. Arakan 11 Aug. 1835; in charge of mily. buildings at Kyaukpyu and civil bldgs. in Arakan 20 Jan. 1836.
Refs.: Burke's Landed Gentry, 13th edn., p. 1221, s.n. Master, of Barrow Green House, Surrey. Bath Chron. 1 Dec. 1836. M.I. at Kyaukpyu.

MASTER, Whalley (1808-1862). Major. 7th L.C. bapt. Walcot, Somerset, 25 Nov. 1808. Cadet 1825. Arrived in India 22 Oct. 1826. Cornet (27 June 1826) 8 May 1827. Lieut. 26 Aug. 1831. Capt. 28 Sept. 1841. Invalided 11 Dec. 1848. Retired 17 Sept. 1856. Hon. Major 17 Sept. 1856. d. 17 York St., Portman Sq., London, 12 Oct. 1862.
4th son of James Master, Adm. R.N., and Jeanetta his wife. Brother of Edward Pelham Master, q.v. m. Almora, U.P., 25 Sept. 1851, Eliza Jane, dau. of William Marcus Carew, Major H.M. 63rd Regt.
Services: Cornet d.d. 1st L.C. 9 Nov. 1826. Posted to 10th L.C. 1827; transfd. to 7th L.C. 8 May 1827. Shekhawat expedn. 1834; Lieut. 7th L.C. Fur. p.a. 8 Mar. 1838 till 22 Feb. 1841. With Army of Reserve (for Afghanistan) Oct. 1842 till Jan. 1843. With Sind F.F. 1846. Fur. s.c. 23 Feb. 1854 till retirement.
Refs.: Burke's Landed Gentry, 13th edn., p. 1221, s.n. Master, of Barrow Green House, Surrey. G.M. 1862, ii. 654. The Times, 14 Oct. 1862.

MATHER, Benjamin (1781-1819). Captain, 2nd N.C. bapt. Charlton, Kent, 29 Oct. 1781. Cadet 1798. Arrived in India

26 Aug. 1799. Cornet 4 June 1800. Lieut. 1 May 1804. Capt. 30 June 1818. *d. unm.* Rajputana 14 July 1819.

Son of James Mather and Ann his wife.

Services: Posted Cornet to 2nd N.C. and served throughout with that Regt. Operations in Jumna Doab 1803. Second Mahratta War; battle of Delhi (w.); (? Laswari; battle of Deig). Nepal War 1814-15; in 1st Div. Capt. Lt. 2nd N.C. 21 Nov. 1815. Third Mahratta War; in Reserve Div.

Refs.: Will dated camp, Masonda, 4 Mar. 1819; proved 30 Aug. 1819.

MATHESON, Patrick Grant (1789-1834). Captain, Artillery. (394) *b.* 28 July 1789. Cadet 1808. Arrived in India 16 Nov. 1808. Fireworker 24 Sept. 1808. Lieut. 23 Oct. 1811. Capt. 12 Dec. 1821. *d.* Delhi 15 Oct. 1834.

bapt. Knockbain, co. Ross, 8 Aug. 1789. 2nd son of Colin Matheson, of Bennetsfield, Lieut. Gordon Fenc., and Grace his wife, 4th dau. of Patrick Grant, of Glenmoriston. *m.* Dinapore 10 July 1813, Hannah Mills Butler, dau. of Alexander Aird, Conductor of Ord., and sister of Robert Abercrombie Aird (see Appendix A). Woolwich Cadet; nominated to R.M.A. 18 July 1804.

Services: Nepal War 1814-15; Pursa; Lieut. 6th Coy. 2nd Bn. Foot Art., with 4th Div. Third Mahratta War; Jawad (blew open the gate); Lieut. 2nd Troop H.A. Apptd. to charge of Ord. Comst. at P.W.I. 27 Feb. 1819; Comy. Ord. 25 Sept. 1819; returned to India Feb. 1821. Apptd. to charge of Delhi magazine 2 Mar. 1821; do. at Allahabad 5 Nov. 1823; do. Delhi 1833.

Refs.: History of the Mathesons, by Alexander Mackenzie, p. 30. Burke's *Landed Gentry, s.n.* Grant, of Glenmoriston. *Stubbs,* ii. 27-8. *A.J.* N.S. xvi. 272. Will dated 9 May 1816; proved 10 Jan. 1835.

MATHEW, William (1789-1862). Captain. 34th N.I. *b.* Thurles, co. Tipperary, 7 Mar. 1789. Cadet 1805. Arrived in India 11 July 1806. Ensign 25 Aug. 1806. Lieut. 8 Jan. 1808. Capt. 11 July 1823. Retired 29 Apr. 1822. *d.* 17 Prince's St., Hanover Sq., London, 23 Nov. 1862.

(*Probably* of the family of Mathew, of Llandaff. ? Son of Francis Mathew, 1st Earl of Llandaff, and half-brother of Arnold Nesbit Mathews, *q.v.*[1])

Services: Barasat C.C. Posted Ensign to 17th N.I. in 1807. Nepal War 1814-15; Jitpur; Lieut. 2/17th N.I., in 3rd Div. Adjt. 1/17th N.I. 24 Nov. 1817 till Jan. 1820. Fur. 13 Dec. 1819

THE BENGAL ARMY, 1758-1834 253

till retirement. Transfd. to 34th N.I. (late 1/17th) May 1824. Retired in 1824 with effect from 29 Apr. 1822, but was permitted to retain his rank of Capt.

Refs.: *The Times,* 26 Nov. 1862 (where his name is given as William F. Mathew).

[1] *Note:* His birth certificate is certified by Robert Cormac (? Richard Carmac), "at the Earl of Landaff's, 13 Grafton St., London, 5 Feb. 1806." Richard Carmac was a farm-bailiff who had been in Lord Llandaff's employ from the year 1785.

MATHEWS, Arnold Nesbit (1765-1820). Major, Invalid Est. Artillery. (281) *b. c.* 1765. Cadet 1782. Admitted 27 Jan. 1784. Ensign (Inf.) 17 Mar. 1785. Fireworker (Art.) 16 Mar. 1789. Lieut. 10 Sept. 1795. Capt. Lt. 27 June 1803. Capt. 5 Sept. 1806. Major 6 May 1817. Invalided 25 Sept. 1817. *d.* Chandernagore, Bengal, 5 Oct. 1820, aged about 54.

Son of Richard Matthews (Mathews), of Cromhall, Gloucs., and Ann his wife. Grand-nephew of William Mathews, *q.v. m.* Fatehgarh 20 Nov. 1806, "Countess Elizabeth Francesca Povoleri, spinster," elder dau. of Marchese Domenico Povoleri by his wife the Contessa Piovene di Vicenza. (She died 1835.) Ed. Sedbergh.

Services: Apptd. Cadet 11 Dec. 1782; sailed for India in the *Lord Macartney* 11 Mar. 1783. Second Mysore War; Cadet. Supy. Ensign, unposted, in July 1787. Transfd. from Inf. to Art. in 1790. Third Mysore War; Bangalore; Lieut. 4th Coy. 2nd Bn. Foot Art. To Madras in Aug. 1793 for siege of Pondicherry; Lieut. F. 4th Coy. 3rd Bn., transfd. tempy. from 4th Coy. 2nd Bn. Operations in Jumna Doab 1803; Sasni; Lieut. 4th Coy. 2nd Bn. Second Mahratta War; Aligarh; battle of Delhi (s.w.—lost a leg); Capt. Lt. 4th Coy. 2nd Bn. Apptd. Fort Adjt. at Agra 1804. Dy. Comy. of Ord. at Fatehgarh 8 Nov. 1804 till 1815. Capt. 3rd Coy. 2nd Bn. After being invalided he retired to an estate which he had purchased at Chittagong. Pub. 1809, a translation in 2 vols. of the "*Mishkat-ul-Masa Bih.*"

Refs.: G.E.C. (1929 edn.) vii. 421, footnote (b). *Sedbergh School Register.* *The Genealogical Mag.* ii. 343, 347-8; iv. 74-6. *The Times,* 31 Mar. 1804. *A.J.* xi. 511. Will dated Chandernagore, 20 June 1820; proved 20 May 1821. M.I. at Chinsura.

Note: The dormant earldom of Llandaff (Landaff) was claimed by his grandson, Arnold Harris Mathew, a priest of Trowbridge and Bath, from 1898 till his death in 1919. The claimant alleged that A. N. M. was eldest son of Francis Mathew, M.P. for Tipperary, afterwards 1st Earl of Llandaff, by Ellis or Elisha his 1st wife, 2nd dau. of James Smyth, of Tinney Park, co. Wicklow, and sister of Sir Skeffington Edward Smyth, 1st Bart.; that he was b. in Paris 16 Feb. 1765 (5 mos. after marriage), and *bapt.* two days later by Bp. Orchard Challoner, and brought up by his father's maternal uncle, Joseph Matthews, solicitor, of Woodend House, Cromhall. According to *Faulkner's Journal*, a dau. was b. to the wife of Francis Mathew of Thomastown on 2 Aug. 1765; and *G.M.* 1839, i. 442, has the following:—" Feb. 26. At Camdentown, aged 66, Mary, dau. of the late R. Matthews, esq. of Cromhall, co. Glouc., sister to the late Major A. N. Matthews, Bengal Art." *Sedbergh School Register* states that he was *bapt.* a Roman Catholic, but is said to have embraced Mohammedanism subsequently. " He refused to hold any communication with his parents, or to return to succeed his father as Earl of Llandaff (30 July 1806). The earldom accordingly passed to his brother, and then became dormant." (Cf. *The Nobilities of Europe*, by the Marquis de Ruvigny (1910), p. 346.)

MATHEWS, Henry Edward (*d.* 1787). Ensign, 4th Bengal Eur.. Bn. Cadet 1782. Ensign 15 Feb. 1783. *d.* Dinapore 9 Aug. 1787.

Son of Bdr.-Gen. Richard Mathews, C.-in-C. of Bombay Army. Nephew of William Mathews, *q.v.*

Services: Apptd. Cadet 12 Oct. 1781; sailed for India with his father in the *Nassau* 8 Feb. 1782. First Mahratta War 1782-5; Cadet. Arrived in Bengal Aug. 1785.

MATHEWS, John (*d.* 1762). Captain, 7th Bn. Sepoys. Cadet (?) Ensign 10 Nov. 1757. Lieut. 8 Apr. 1759. Capt. 11 Dec. 1761. *d. unm.* Calcutta 4 Dec. 1762.

Son of Mary Mathews, of Duke St., Grosvenor Sq., London, widow. Brother of Mary Candell and Eleanor Wade, and nephew of Nicholas Mathews, of Dublin.

Services: Raised at Chittagong in 1761 the 7th Bn. Sepoys (called after him " *Mathews-ki-Paltan* "), which was disbanded Jan. 1784 for its mutinous conduct when ordered on service in Mar. 1782.

Refs.: Will dated 1 Nov. 1762; proved 16 Dec. 1762.

MATHEWS, William (*d.* 1784). Lieutenant, Infantry. Country Cadet 1779. Cornet 16 Sept. 1779. Lieut. 1 May 1781. *d.* Bednore, Madras, Mar. 1784: taken out into the jungle at night whilst a prisoner of war and cut to pieces by order of Tippoo Sultan.

2nd son of Richard Matthews,[1] of Charfield, who owned property at Usher's Quay, Dublin, and at Charfield and Tortworth, Gloucs., and Phyllis Stiles his wife. Elder brother of Bdr.-Gen. Richard Mathews, C.-in-C. of Bombay Army, who was poisoned by Tippoo 7 Sept. 1783. Uncle of Henry Edward Mathews, q.v., maternal uncle of Francis, 1st Earl of Llandaff, and grand-uncle of Arnold Nesbit Mathews, q.v. m. St. Andrew's, Holborn, 1765, Sarah Williams.[2] Father of William Joseph Mathews, q.v.

Services: Apptd. Cadet for the Cav. 19 Aug. 1779. Served with the detachment of Bombay Army under his brother for the invasion of Canara 1782; surrender of Bednore Apr. 1783; taken prisoner with the whole garr. of 600 Europeans, including nearly 100 officers, and 1,500 sepoys, and confined in Bednore. Some 17 of the officers, including his brother, were put to death by poison or otherwise by order of Tippoo.

Refs.: *The Genealogical Mag.* ii. 290. Will dated 2 Dec. 1782; admon. 21 Sept. 1784. Urquhart's *Oriental Obit.*, i. 58.

[1] *Note*: Both he and his brother Richard spelt their name with only one ' t.'

[2] *Note*: She was pensioned on Lord Clive's fund in Dec. 1792.

MATHEWS, William Joseph (1778-1864). Major. 9th N.I. *bapt.* Laugharne, co. Carmarthen, 17 July 1778. Cadet 1794. Arrived in India 30 Oct. 1795. Ensign 6 Dec. 1795. Lieut. 30 Oct. 1797. Capt. 31 Oct. 1806. Major 4 June 1817. Pensioned 5 Feb. 1820. Retired 31 Oct. 1821. *d.* 9 Oct. 1864.

Son of William Mathews, *q.v.*, and Sarah his wife. *m.* St. Clears, Carmarthen, Mar. 1811, his cousin, dau. of Alexander Murray, of Hatton Gdn., London. Ed. St. Paul's; adm. 5 Oct. 1790.

Services: Apptd. Minor Cadet 29 Aug. 1782; apptd. Cadet 13 May 1795; sailed for India in the *Woodcot* 18 June 1795. Lieut. 9th N.I. in 1798; Capt. Lt. 9th N.I. 21 Sept. 1804. Second Mahratta War; pursuit of Holkar 1805-6; Capt. Lt. 1/9th N.I. Operations against Dhundia Khan 1807; Komona (w.); Ganauri; Capt. 1/9th N.I. Settlement of Hariana 1809; Bhawani; Capt. 1/9th N.I. Fur. 22 Jan. 1810 till 1813. A.D.C. to Lord Moira, the G.G., 11 Sept. 1813. Comdd. Bhagulpur Hill Rangers 12 July 1813 till 1820.

Note: The 48th N.I., which mutinied at Lucknow in 1857, was called "*Mutees-ki-Paltan*" after him, having been formed as 2/24th N.I. at Cawnpore in Oct. 1804 from Levies raised by him.

MATHIAS, John (1806-1842). Captain, 33rd N.I. b. Mundham, Norfolk, 3 Aug. 1806. Cadet 1824. Arrived in India 16 Sept. 1825. Ensign 18 Apr. 1825. Lieut. 25 May 1827. Capt. 5 Oct. 1835. d. in camp nr. Khota, Afghanistan (? Jalalabad), 14 July 1842.

bapt. Mundham 10 Aug. 1806. Son of James Vincent Mathias, of Stanhoe Hall, Norfolk, sometime Capt. 62nd Ft., and Sarah his wife, formerly Miss Carter, of Thorpe.

Services : Posted Ensign to 33rd N.I. Leave p.a. 6 mos. to Masulipatam 1 Feb. 1834. Fur. p.a. 6 Mar. 1836 till 9 Feb. 1839. Offg. Paymr. of native pensioners at Meerut and Hapur 13 May 1840. Actg. Bde. Major at Meerut 7 Feb. till 13 Dec. 1841 ; do. Ferozepore 12 Jan. 1842 ; permanent do. 21 Jan. till 9 Mar. 1842. First Afghan War 1842 ; forcing of Khyber ; advance on Kabul ; Capt. 33rd N.I., with Pollock's force.

Refs.: G.M. 1843, i. 554. M.I. Afghan Memorial Church, Bombay.

MATHISON, Robert (1807-1887). Lieut. Colonel. 3rd Bengal Eur. Regt. *bapt.* Lambeth, Surrey, 7 Dec. 1807. Cadet 1827. Arrived in India 31 May 1828. Ensign 19 Jan. 1828. Lieut. 15 Feb. 1836. Capt. 1 June 1851. Bt. Major 20 June 1854. Bt. Lt. Col. 28 Nov. 1854. Retired 9 Dec. 1854. d. at his residence, St. Mary's Terr., Colchester, 1 Apr. 1887.

Eldest son of John Mathison, of the Sec.'s office, East-India House (who was joint-editor of the *E.I.R.* 1803-14), and Lydia his wife, youngest dau. of Frederick Cobbe Pitman, *q.v.* m. Calcutta 15 May 1841, Laura Elizabeth, dau. of Samuel Thomas Carter, Comdr. R.N. (She died 19 Sept. 1887.)

Services : Posted Ensign to 6th N.I. 4 Nov. 1828. Revenue Surveyor in Cuttack 20 Apr. 1838. Rejoined 6th N.I. at Ferozepore Feb. 1842. First Afghan War ; on lines of communication ; Lieut. 6th N.I. Transfd. to 54th N.I. 14 Dec. 1842. Revenue Surveyor and D.C. at Midnapore. Fur. s.c. 15 Sept. 1844 till 23 Nov. 1847. Transfd. to newly-raised 3rd Bengal Eur. Regt. 15 Nov. 1853.

Refs. : Family information. *The Times*, 5 Apr. 1887.

MATTHEWS, Henry William (1806-1884). General. 6th N.I. (now 1st Royal Bn. (L.I.) 9th Jat Regt.). b. London 21 Feb. 1806. Cadet 1823. Arrived in India 27 July 1824. Ensign 3 Mar. 1824. Lieut. 9 Nov. 1826. Capt. 17 Nov. 1842. Major 9 Mar. 1855. Lt. Col. 26 Apr. 1859. Col. 1 Jan. 1862. Maj. Gen. 6 Mar. 1868. Lt. Gen. 19 Dec. 1876. Retired 22 Dec.

1877. Hon. Gen. 22 Dec. 1877. *d.* at his residence, 8 Sydney Pl., Bath, 15 July 1884.

bapt. St. George the Martyr, London, 26 Feb. 1806. Son of Henry William Matthews, H.M.S., and Louisa Ann his wife. *m.* 1st, (before 1841) ? *m.* 2nd, Barrackpore 23 May 1859, Emma, dau. of George Hunter, *q.v.*, and widow of Edward Touchet Milner, *q.v.*

Services : Posted Ensign to 43rd N.I. in 1824. Adjt. Assam Sebundy Corps 19 May 1835 till 27 Sept. 1838, when he rejoined his Regt. for active service. A detachment under his comd. defeated on 8 Mar. 1836 a body of 800 Bhutias under the Dewangiri Rajah at Subankhata on the Bhutan frontier. First Afghan War 1839-40 ; Bt. Capt. 43rd N.I. 2nd in comd. 1st Assam Sebundy Corps 17 Feb. 1840 till 8 Mar. 1841. First Afghan War 1841-2 ; Nott's advance from Kandahar to Kabul ; Ghazni ; Istalif ; rear-guard action in Jagdalak Pass 19 Oct. 1842 (w.) (*Lond. Gaz.* 17 Mar. 1843) ; Bt. Capt. 43rd N.I. (Medal). Gwalior campaign ; Maharajpur ; Capt. 43rd N.I. (Bronze star). First Sikh War ; Sobraon ; Capt. 43rd N.I. (Medal). Comdt. 6th Bengal Native (Light) Inf. (late 43rd N.I.) May 1861 till Apr. 1866. Fur. 17 Jan. 1868 till death.

Refs. : *The Times*, 18 July 1884.

MATTHIE, James (1805-1865). Major General. Colonel 2nd Eur. Bengal Fus. *b.* London 1 Aug. 1805. Cadet 1821. Arrived in India 14 Apr. 1822. Ensign 24 Oct. 1821. Lieut. 1 Jan. 1824. Capt. 8 Sept. 1835. Major 22 Nov. 1843. Lt. Col. 1 Mar. 1850. Col. 19 Aug. 1859. Maj. Gen. 1 Jan. 1862. *d.* at his residence, Gothic House, Upper Hamilton Terr., London, 28 Mar. 1865.

bapt. St. James's, Westminster, 10 Nov. 1807. Son of John Matthie, clerk in the accounts office, East India House, and Elizabeth his wife.

Services : Posted Ensign to 25th N.I. in 1822. Transfd. to Bengal Eur. Regt. in 1823 ; to 1st Bengal Eur. Regt. May 1824. Siege and capture of Bhurtpore ; Lieut. 1st Bengal Eur. Regt. (India medal). Adjt. Rangpur L.I. 5 Dec. 1827 ; do. Assam L.I. 1829 till Aug. 1831. Civil Asst. to A.G.G., N.E. frontier, 31 Aug. till 1 Oct. 1831 ; Principal Asst. at Gauhati 3 Apr. 1833 ; Principal Asst. to Comr. of Assam at Gauhati 20 May 1837 ; D.C. Assam at Gauhati 1 Apr. 1839 till 1852. Fur. p.a. 1846 till 9 Oct. 1847. Posted Lt. Col. to 33rd N.I. 12 June 1850 ; transfd. to 30th N.I. July 1852 ; to 1st Eur. Bengal Fus. Feb. 1853. Second Burma War 1853 ; Lt. Col. comdg. 1st Eur. Bengal Fus. (Medal). Transfd.

258 LIST OF THE OFFICERS OF

to 17th N.I. 13 Jan. 1854. Fur. p.a. 10 Mar. 1854 till 1 Apr. 1859. Transfd. to 21st N.I. July 1856. Col. 2nd Eur. Bengal Fus. 7 Nov. 1859 till death. Fur. p.a. 3 yrs. 13 Dec. 1859.
Refs.: Boase. The Times, 31 Mar. 1865.

MATTOCKS, John (1741/42-1791). Lieut. Colonel, Invalid Est. Infantry. *b.* 1741/42. Cadet 1764. Ensign 5 Mar. 1765. Lieut. 10 Mar. 1772. Capt. Oct. 1779. Major 1 Jan. 1781. Lt. Col. 2 Dec. 1786. Invalided before July 1787. Resigned 11 June 1790. *d.* Calcutta 4 Feb. 1791.

A native of London. *m.* Sarah ——, a descendant of John Hampden (*D.N.B.*). (She died Murshidabad 4 Oct. 1778, aged 27.)
Services: Sailed for India in the *Devonshire* 20 Feb. 1764, aged 22. Posted to 1st Bengal Eur. Regt. 13 Aug. 1765. (Lieut. 14 Dec. 1766.) Dismissed Jan. 1767 for signing an Address to Sir Robert Fletcher, *q.v.*, and sent home; restored by C.D. in England 5 Apr. 1771, to rank as junior Lieut. on his arrival in India; sailed in the *Britannia* 22 June 1771. First Rohilla War; battle of St. George; Lieut. 18th Bn. Sepoys. Resigned Mar. 1775; fur. to Europe; readmitted Apr. 1781. Lt. Col. comdg. Invalids at Moradbagh in July 1787.
Refs.: N. & Q. 1S. iv. 423. Will dated 4 Feb. 1791; proved 18 Feb. 1791.

MAUDE, John Dearden (1751/52-1783). Lieutenant, Artillery. (148) *b.* Lincs. 1751/52. Cadet 1777. Fireworker (?) Lieut. 28 Sept. 1778. *d.* Madras 7 Aug. 1783.

Son of John Maude, of Halifax, and Ann his wife, dau. of —— Kirke, of Lincs.
Services: Apptd. Cadet 13 Nov. 1776; sailed for India in the *Houghton* 9 Feb. 1777, aged 25. Second Mysore War 1781-3; Lieut. 5th Coy. 1st Bn. Art.
Refs.: Hunter's *Familiæ Minorum Gentium* (Harleian Soc. xxxviii), ii. 624.

MAULE, Richard (1811-1841). Lieutenant, Artillery. (618) *b.* 2 July 1811. Cadet 1828. Arrived in India 21 May 1829. 2nd Lieut. 12 Dec. 1828. Lieut. 27 Jan. 1837. *d.* Kahdarrah, Afghanistan, 3 (or 15) Nov. 1841: kld. during the revolt by mutineers of the Kohistan Regt.

bapt. Sheerness, Kent, 2 Aug. 1811. 3rd son of William Henry Maule, of Farm Hall, Godmanchester, Hunts., wages cashier at the Navy pay office, and Alice Ordidge his wife (*née* Sheppard), of Copnor, Portsmouth. Ed. Merchant Taylors' Mar. 1820-Oct. 1826. Addiscombe Cadet 1827-8.

Services : Leave s.c. 6 mos. to Singapore 23 Jan. 1835. Posted to 3rd Coy. 7th Bn. 14 June 1837 ; Actg. Adjt. & Qmr. 4th Bn. 14 Nov. 1837. Placed under the orders of Capt. C. M. Wade, *q.v.*, P.A. Ludhiana, to superintend Art. at Peshawar 3 Nov. 1838 ; comdd. 3rd (or Kohistan) Regt., Shah Shuja's Contingent, 16 Sept. 1839 till death ; placed at disposal of Envoy and Minister at Court of Shah Shuja 15 Oct. 1839. First Afghan War 1840-1 ; operations in Kohistan under Bdr. Sir Robert Sale 1840 ; Tutam-dara (*Lond. Gaz.* 9 Jan. 1841).

Refs. : Robinson. Lady Sale's Journal, pp. 55-6, 105. M.I. Afghan Memorial Church, Bombay.

MAULE, Hon. William Maule (1809-1859). Ensign. 11th N.I. *b.* Brechin, co. Forfar, 30 Mar. 1809. Cadet 1826. Arrived in India 14 Aug. 1827. Ensign 17 Mar. 1827. Resigned 12 July 1830. *d.* 17 Feb. 1859.

Of Fearn. 3rd son of Hon. William Maule, formerly Ramsay, afterwards 1st Baron Panmure, and Patricia Heron his 1st wife, dau. of Gilbert Gordon, of Halleaths. Cousin-german of Andrew Ramsay, *q.v. m.* 16 Apr. 1844, Elizabeth, eldest dau. of William Binney. (She died 11 Feb. 1905.)

Services : Posted Ensign to 11th N.I. 11 Oct. 1827. Fur. s.c. 1 Feb. 1828 till resignation. No record of active service.

Refs. : Burke's *Peerage*, 1923, p. 653, *s.n.* Dalhousie, E.

MAULEVERER, formerly GOWAN, William (1787-1857). Captain. 33rd N.I. *b.* Fetherston, Yorks., 13 Oct. 1787. Cadet 1804. Arrived in India 10 Aug. 1805. Ensign 25 Aug. 1805. Lieut. 25 Aug. 1805. Capt. 26 Sept. 1820. Retired 10 Sept. 1824. *d.* 27 Mar. 1857.

Of Arncliffe, Yorks. ; J.P. and D.L. *bapt.* 12 Apr. 1788. Youngest son of Clotworthy Gowan, *q.v. s.* his aunt, Mary Mauleverer, in 1833, when he became of Arncliffe ; changed his patronymic Gowan for the surname of Mauleverer by Act of Parliament 13 May 1834 (*Lond. Gaz.* p. 898). *m.* Forglen House 30 Apr. 1811, Helen, 2nd dau. of Sir George Abercromby, Bart., of Birkenbog, co. Banff. (She died 6 Sept. 1859.)

Services : Posted Lieut. to 2/16th N.I. in 1806. Fur. 16 Oct. 1808 till 1811. (? Reduction of Kalinjar 1812 ; Lieut. 2/16th N.I.) Bde. Major at Muttra 1813. Fort Adjt. and Bk.Mr. at Delhi 2 Apr. 1814 ; Bk.Mr. 11th (Meerut) Div. 1819-22. Capt. 2/16th

260 LIST OF THE OFFICERS OF

N.I. Fur. 1822 till 1826, when he retired with effect from 10 Sept. 1824. Transfd. to 33rd N.I. (late 2/16th) May 1824.
Refs.: Burke's *Landed Gentry*, 6th edn., p. 1081, *s.n.* Mauleverer, of Arncliffe, Yorks. *Genealogist*, N.S. x. 50.

MAUNSELL, John (1788-1812). Lieutenant, 23rd N.I. *b.* psh. of St. Peter, Dublin, 28 Apr. 1788. Cadet 1803. Arrived in India 2 Sept. 1804. Ensign 17 Aug. 1804. Lieut. 21 Sept. 1804. *d.* between Agra and Etawah 22 Oct. 1812: kld. by bandits.

4th son of Daniel Maunsell, of Ballywilliam, co. Limerick, and Sarah his wife, 2nd dau. of George Meares, of Lion Hill, co. Dublin.
Services: Posted Lieut. to newly-raised 23rd N.I. in 1804. Operations against Dhundia Khan 1807; Komona; Ganauri; Lieut. 1/23rd N.I.
Refs.: Burke's *Landed Gentry of Ireland*, p. 468, *s.n.* Maunsell, of Ballywilliam, co. Limerick.

MAURICE, Richard (1762-1795). Lieutenant, Infantry. *b.* in America 1762. Cadet 1779. Admitted 9 Oct. 1779. Ensign 1780. Lieut. 10 June 1781. *d.* at sea 28 Sept. 1795.

Son of Theodore Maurice, of Marylebone, Middlesex. Brother of James Maurice, of Norfolk, Virginia.
Services: Apptd. Cadet 17 May 1780, aged 17; sailed for India in the *Deptford* 26 June 1781, aged 19, and was captured by the enemy on the voyage out. Lieut. 19th Bn. Sepoys in July 1787 and in 1792.
Refs.: Will dated 29 Aug. 1795; proved 24 Dec. 1795.

MAUVE, John (*d.* 1781). Bt. Major, Infantry. Cadet (?) Ensign 1 May 1759. Lieut. 3 Sept. 1761. Capt. 18 Oct. 1763. Bt. Major Mar. 1781. *d.* Berhampore 18 Oct. 1781.

Probably either French or Swiss. (Desires to be buried at the Kalkapur Dutch factory, Murshidabad.)
Services: Was stationed at Moradbag, Bengal, a "superannuated" Ofr. (*probably* in comd. of Mil. or Invalids), 1773-81. Was proceeding on sick leave when his death occurred.
Refs.: *India Gazette*, 27 Oct. 1781. Will dated 29 May 1781; proved 6 Apr. 1782.

MAVER, George (1792-1834). Captain, 19th N.I. *b.* Dundee 11 Mar. 1792. Cadet 1808. Arrived in India 27 Oct. 1809. Ensign 2 Oct. 1810. Lieut. 30 Apr. 1814. Capt. 13 May 1825. *d.* Barrackpore 24 Sept. 1834.

THE BENGAL ARMY, 1758-1834

Son of Thomas Maver, writer in Dundee.
Services: Barasat C.C. Posted Ensign to 3rd N.I. in 1810; Lieut. 1/3rd N.I. With 1st Ceylon Vol. Bn. Oct. 1818 till 1 Mar. 1820. Transfd. to 19th N.I. (late 2/3rd) May 1824; with 1st L.I. Bn. 1825-6. First Burma War; Arakan 1825; Capt. 1st L.I. Bn. Actg. Bde. Major to Light Bde. in Arakan 8 July 1825.
Refs.: A\J. N.S. xvi. 213.

MAVERLEY, Charles (1738/39-1773). Captain, Infantry. *b.* London 1738/39. Cadet 1764. Ensign 27 Dec. 1764. Lieut. 7 Dec. 1766. Capt. 17 Apr. 1769. *d.* Bankipore 13 Feb. 1773.

Nephew of Mrs. Sarah Gibbons, of Banbury; of Susannah, widow of John Bagot; and of Joanna, wife of Samuel Wotton.
Services: Sailed for India in the *Devonshire* 20 Feb. 1764, aged 25. Storm of Chunar fort Dec. 1764 (shot through body and arm and s.w. by sabre cut on arm); Cadet. Posted Ensign to Bengal Eur. Bn. 5 Dec. 1764. Resigned during the "Batta mutiny" and was ordered down to Calcutta; reinstated later. Fur. s.c. Jan. 1769 till 1772. Granted £500 from Lord Clive's fund Apr. 1771. Bk.Mr. at Dinapore May 1772 till death.
Refs.: *Caraccioli,* iii. 195. Will dated 9 May 1771; codicils dated 3 Mar. 1772 and 10 Feb. 1773; proved 30 Mar. 1773.

MAW, Thomas (1789-1819). Ensign. 14th N.I. Subsequently Lieut. H.M. 17th Ft. *bapt.* Wakefield, Yorks., 9 Apr. 1789. Cadet 1805. Arrived in India 20 July 1807. Ensign (1 July 1807). Struck off 12 May 1809. Restored as Cadet of 1809. Resigned 8 Oct. 1811. *d.* Bengal 11 June 1819.

Son of John Henry Maw and Margaret his wife. *m.* a dau. of H. Bullock, of Colnbrook, Bucks. (She died 14 May 1809.)
Services: Barasat C.C. Posted Ensign to 14th N.I. Struck off the list of the Army by order of C.D., having obtained his appt. by improper means; reapptd. junior Cadet of 1809. Ensign H.M. 17th Ft. 1 Jan. 1810; Lieut. do. 2 Feb. 1813.

MAWBEY, John (1748-1794). Captain, 2nd Bengal Eur. Bn. *bapt.* S. Kilworth, Leics., 19 Sept. 1748. Cadet 1771. Ensign 29 Jan. 1773. Lieut. 6 Apr. 1777. Capt. 31 Mar. 1781. *d. unm.* 26 Oct. 1794: kld. in action at the battle of Bitaurah.

Son of William Mawbey and Martha his wife. Brother of Thomas Mawbey, of Vauxhall Walk, brewer, and kinsman to Sir Joseph Mawbey, of Botleys, Bart.
Services: Lieut. 2/3rd Bengal Eur. Regt. in Oct. 1779; Qmr.

do. 31 May 1780. Capt. 3rd Eur. Regt. in 1782 ; 36th Bn. Sepoys in July 1787 ; 2nd Eur. Bn. in Dec. 1788. Second Rohilla War ; battle of Bitaurah (kld.) ; Capt. 2nd Eur. Bn.

Refs.: Betham's *Baronetage,* iii. (1803), p. 327. Will dated Barrackpore 24 Aug. 1786 ; proved 24 Apr. 1795. M.I. in St. John's churchyard, Calcutta.

MAXTONE, Anthony (1773-1846). Captain. 27th N.I. *b.* 9 July 1773.[1] Cadet 1798. Admitted 26 Nov. 1799. Ensign 4 Sept. 1799. Lieut. 28 Oct. 1799. Capt. 2 Apr. 1811. Retired 22 Feb. 1814. *d.* Cultoquhey, co. Perth, 30 Oct. 1846.

Of Cultoquhey. *bapt.* Fowlis 19 July 1775. 4th son of James Maxtone, 11th laird of Cultoquhey, and Marjory his wife, dau. of Patrick Graeme, of Murrayshall. Cousin-german of Thomas Murray (1794-1806), *q.v.,* and uncle of William Murray Stewart, *q.v. m.* 17 Dec. 1816, Alexina, his 2nd cousin, dau. of John Graeme, of Eskbank, and sister of Robert Graham, of Balgowan, co. Perth. (She died Crieff 1868, aged 81.)

Services : In an office in Edinburgh till 1796, when he joined Thomas Graham, of Balgowan (afterwards Baron Lynedoch), and saw service with the Austrian forces in Italy until the spring of 1797. Ensign 9th (Perthshire) Regt. Mil. of Scotland 1797 ; Lieut. do. 24 June 1798 till 1799. Sailed for India in the *Asia* July 1799. Posted Lieut. to 1st Bengal Eur. Regt. 15 Apr. 1801. Expedn. to Egypt 1801 ; Lieut. Bengal Vols. Second Mahratta War ; Gwalior ; battle of Deig (w.) [2] ; Lieut. Bengal Eur. Regt. Transfd. to newly-raised 27th N.I. in 1805 ; Adjt. & Qmr. do. 1805-10. Operations against Dhundia Khan 1807 ; Komona ; Ganauri. Capt. Lt. 27th N.I. 29 Aug. 1810. Operations in Oudh 1810 ; Capt. Lt. 2/27th N.I. Fur. 8 Jan. 1811 till retirement.

Refs.: Burke's *Landed Gentry,* 13th edn., p. 768, *s.n.* Maxtone-Graham, of Cultoquhey, co. Perth. *The Maxtones of Cultoquhey,* by E. Maxtone Graham, Edin., 1935. Portrait by Sir J. Watson Gordon at Cultoquhey.

[1] *Note:* Qy. 1775.

[2] *Note:* Received a bullet wound in the head and was left on the battlefield as dead.

MAXWELL, Acheson (*d.* 1823). Lieut. Colonel, Invalid Est. 21st N.I. Cadet 1783. Admitted 25 Nov. 1784. Ensign 3 Apr. 1785. Lieut. 11 Aug. 1793. Capt. 2 Nov. 1803. Major 12 May 1811. Lt. Col. 1 Oct. 1815. Invalided 5 May 1821. *d.* Chittagong 27 May 1823.

Services: Apptd. Cadet 28 Mar. 1783; sailed for India in the *Earl Cornwallis* 31 Mar. 1784. Posted to 6th Bengal Eur. Bn. 15 Feb. 1790; transfd. from 4th to 6th do. 11 Nov. 1794; Lieut. 6th Eur. Bn. in Feb. 1796; 10th N.I. in 1798. Adjt. & Qmr. 6th N.I. 29 May 1800 till Jan. 1804. Disturbances in Ganjam, Madras, 1801; Lieut. 6th N.I. Nepal War 1814-15; Major 2/6th N.I., in 1st Div. Posted Lt. Col. to 2/6th N.I. in 1815; to 26th N.I. in 1816; to 2/21st N.I. in 1817. Regulating Ofr. of Invalid Tannah Ests. at Chittagong 1821 till death.

Refs.: Will dated Chittagong 7 Apr. 1823; proved 6 June 1823.

Note: One Acheson Maxwell (1760-1851) was sent home from India with despatches in 1783, and afterwards accompanied Lord Macartney to the Cape in 1796 as Controller of Customs.

MAXWELL, George (1778-1821). Captain. 24th N.I. *bapt.* Dumfries 31 May 1778. Cadet 1794. Arrived in India 8 Jan. 1796. Ensign 12 Nov. 1795. Lieut. 25 July 1797. Capt. 26 Oct. 1805. Retired 25 Nov. 1807. *d.* in France 2 Oct. 1821.

Of Carruchan, Galloway. Youngest son of George Maxwell, of Carruchan, and Henrietta Carruthers his wife. *m.* S. Shields July 1804, Jane, elder dau. of John Clark, of Nunland, D.L. for co. Kirkcudbright. (She died 1839.)

Services: Apptd. Cadet 22 Apr. 1795; sailed for India in the *Prince William Henry* 24 May 1795. Ensign 1st Bengal Eur. Regt. in 1796. Lieut. 12th N.I. Fur. 26 Jan. 1802 till retirement. Transfd. to newly-raised 24th N.I. in 1805. Struck off from 26 Jan. 1807, being 5 yrs. from the date he went on fur. (M.C. 20 Feb. 1809). His retirement from the Service with effect from 25 Nov. 1807, notified in M.C. of 24 July and 1 Dec. 1809. Lt. Col. Galloway Mil. 17 June 1812.

Refs.: Burke's *Landed Gentry*, 9th edn., p. 835, *s.n.* Clark-Kennedy, of Knockgray. Burke's *Heraldic Illustrations* (1853), ii. plate xciii.

MAXWELL, George (1784-1810). Lieutenant, 3rd N.I. *bapt.* Caerlaverock, co. Dumfries, 5 Nov. 1784. Cadet 1800. Arrived in India 22 Aug. 1801. Ensign 14 Sept. 1801. Lieut. 13 July 1803. *d.* Cawnpore 1 Oct. 1810.

b. E. Blackshaw, Caerlaverock. 2nd son of William Maxwell, late of E. Blackshaw. Nephew of A. Maxwell.

Services: Posted Ensign to 3rd N.I. Operations in Bundelkhand against Lachman Dawa 1809; Rajaoli; Ajaigarh; Lieut. 1/3rd N.I.

Refs.: S.M. 1811, p. 317.

MAXWELL, Hamilton George (1787-1829). Major, Invalid Est. 43rd N.I. *b.* in Canada 27 July 1787. Cadet 1803. Arrived in India 18 Mar. 1805. Ensign 3 May 1805. Lieut. 4 May 1805. Capt. 1 Aug. 1818. Major 24 Feb. 1827. Invalided 24 Jan. 1829. *d.* Chunar 17 June 1829.

Of Ardwell, Stonykirk, co. Wigtown. Brother of William Henry Maxwell, Capt. 3rd Ft. Gds. (*Probably* son of Hamilton Maxwell, Lt. Col. 74th Ft., the 2nd son of Sir William Maxwell, 3rd Bart. of Monreith, who died Cuddalore 8 June 1794, aged 39.) *m.* Clifton Aug. 1826, Isabella, youngest dau. of Capt. Abraham Bunbury, of Kilfeacle, co. Tipperary, 62nd Regt., and sister of Matthew Alexander Bunbury, *q.v.* (She *re-m.* 2 Aug. 1830, Sir Abraham Roberts, *q.v.*)

Services: Posted Lieut. to 22nd N.I. in 1806. (? Settlement of Hariana 1809; Bhawani; Lieut. 1/22nd N.I. Reduction of Kalinjar 1812; Lieut. 1/22nd N.I.) Adjt. Champaran L.I. 18 Sept. 1813 till 1819. Nepal War 1814-15; Lieut. Champaran L.I., in 4th Div. Nepal War 1816; Lieut. Champaran L.I., in 1st Bde. Rt. Column. Transfd. to 2/22nd N.I. in 1816; Capt. 1/22nd N.I. Comdg. Resdt.'s Guard in Bundelkhand 1819; do. escort to A.G.G., Saugor & Narbada territories, 1821; do. Resdt.'s escort at Katmandu 1823-5. Transfd. to 43rd N.I. (late 1/22nd) May 1824. Fur. 1825-7. To comd. 2nd Bn. Native Invalids 14 Feb. 1829.

Refs.: Burke's *Landed Gentry*, 13th edn., p. 1597, *s.n.* Sherston, of Evercreech, Somerset. *Howard & Crisp*, xi. 10, *s.n.* Roberts, E. *Bath Chron.* 10 Aug. 1826. *G.M.* 1830, i. 94. Will dated Ghazipur 9 Feb. 1829; proved 29 Sept. 1829. M.I. at Chunar.

MAXWELL, James (1764-1822). Lieut. Colonel, Invalid Est. 21st N.I. *b.* Broomholm, co. Dumfries, 3 Sept. 1764. Cadet 1781. Admitted 28 Aug. 1783. Ensign 6 May 1781. Lieut. 23 Aug. 1782. Capt. 29 May 1800. Major 4 June 1807. Lt. Col. 5 Dec. 1812. Invalided 4 Dec. 1815. *d. unm.* Buxar 12 Oct. 1822.

bapt. Langholm, co. Dumfries, 16 Sept. 1764. 7th and youngest son of John Maxwell, of Broomholm, and Wilhelmina Malcolm his wife. Brother of George Maxwell, of Broomholm, Capt. R.N., and of Robert Maxwell (1752-1792), *q.v.*

Services: Apptd. Cadet 16 Jan. 1781; sailed for India in the *Latham* 13 Mar. 1781. First Mahratta War (from Mar. 1782). Lieut. 35th Bn. Sepoys in July 1787 and Dec. 1792. Capt. Lt. 9th N.I. 4 Mar. 1800. Capt. 2/9th N.I. Fort Adjt. at Buxar 1803-7. Posted Lt. Col. to 5th N.I. in 1813; to 21st N.I. in 1815. Regulating Ofr. at Shahabad 12 Jan. 1816 till death.

THE BENGAL ARMY, 1758-1834   265

Refs.: *S.M.* 1823, ii. 255. Will dated 15 Mar. 1822; proved 12 Mar. 1823. M.I. at Buxar.

MAXWELL, Patrick (*d.* 1779). Captain, Artillery. (106) Cadet (?) Fireworker 30 Mar. 1770. Lieut. 6 Dec. 1771. Capt. 10 Nov. 1778. *d.* Chittagong 3 May 1779.
Services: N.F.P.

MAXWELL, Robert (1752-1792). Captain, Comdt. 35th Bn. Sepoys. *b.* Broomholm, co. Dumfries, 26 July 1752. Cadet 1768. Ensign 11 Feb. 1769. Lieut. 10 June 1770. Capt. 20 Aug. 1779. *d.* Dacca 28 Oct. 1792.
bapt. Langholm, co. Dumfries, 30 July 1752. Eldest son of John Maxwell, of Broomholm, and Wilhelmina Malcolm his wife. Brother of Walter Maxwell, *q.v.* *m.* Berhampore 26 May 1792, Aurora Catherine Smith. (She *re-m.* John Clerkson, *q.v.*)
Services: Sailed for India in the *Kent* 20 Dec. 1767. With Nawab-Wazir's troops in Nov. 1777; Capt. 1/3rd Bengal Eur. Regt. in Oct. 1779. First Mahratta War. Capture of Bijaigarh 1781. Comdd. 35th Bn. Sepoys 31 May 1786 till death.
Refs.: Will dated 10 Feb. 1791; proved 13 Oct. 1797. M.I. at Dacca.

MAXWELL, Robert (*d.* 1776). Fireworker, Artillery. (126) Cadet 1771. Fireworker 17 May 1772. *bur.* Calcutta 18 Dec. 1776.
Son of William Maxwell, of Bristol, merchant, later of New York, and Marion his wife. Cousin-german of Lt.-Gen. Sir Charles William Maxwell, K.C.H., Kt., sometime govr. of Dominica.
Services: Removed as Cadet from Inf. to Art. 11 Jan. 1772.
Refs.: *The Genealogical Mag.* i. 266. Admon. of his estate granted 26 Jan. 1779 to his father, then residing in New York.

MAXWELL, Walter (1759-1793). Lieutenant, 35th Bn. Sepoys.
bapt. Langholm, co. Dumfries, 19 Oct. 1759. Country Cadet 1778. Ensign 22 Apr. 1779. Lieut. 3 Jan. 1781. *bur.* Calcutta 28 Mar. 1793.
4th son of John Maxwell, of Broomholm, and Wilhelmina Malcolm his wife. Brother of James Maxwell, *q.v.*
Services: Apptd. Cadet 9 July 1778. Lieut. 35th Bn. Sepoys in July 1787; Adjt. do. at death.

MAXWELL, William (*d.* 1768). Lieutenant, Infantry. Ensign 9 Dec. 1766. Lieut. 3 Apr. 1768. *d.* in India 1768.

Services: Permitted to proceed to India as a Free Merchant 19 Feb. 1766; commissioned in India owing to shortage of officers after the "Batta mutiny."

MAXWELL, William (1814-1882). Major General. Artillery. (655) *b.* Birdstown, co. Donegal, 9 July 1814. Cadet 1831. Arrived in India 26 Oct. 1832. 2nd Lieut. 8 Dec. 1831. Lieut. 9 June 1840. Capt. 20 June 1849. Bt. Major 24 Mar. 1858. Lt. Col. 18 Feb. 1861. Col. 30 Sept. 1865. Retired 1 Aug. 1872. Hon. Maj. Gen. 1 Aug. 1872. *d.* Worthing 30 Jan. 1882.

Son of Rev. Peter Benson Maxwell, of Birdstown, and Hester his wife, dau. of Robert O'Hara, of Raheen. Brother of Peter Benson Maxwell (*D.N.B.*), and cousin-german (or nephew) of Charles O'Hara (1800-1874), *q.v. m.* 1st, Ghazipur 1 Oct. 1840, Mary Isabella, 2nd dau. of John Henry Matthews, Paymr. H.M. 31st Regt. (She died Naini Tal, U.P., 29 Mar. 1855, aged 33.) *m.* 2nd, Aligarh 16 Jan. 1857, Augusta Anne Susan, eldest dau. of Henry Doveton, *q.v.* (She died Hove, Sussex, 27 May 1926, aged 91.) Addiscombe Cadet 5 Feb. 1830 till 8 Dec. 1831.

Services: d.d. 3rd Coy. 5th Bn. Foot Art. 16 Sept. 1834; d.d. 4th Coy. 5th Bn. 24 June 1835. Asst. Revenue Surveyor in Gorakhpur 29 Oct. 1838. Assumed charge of survey in Agra district 25 Sept. 1839. Transfd. from 4th Troop 3rd Bde. H.A. to 3rd Coy. 4th Bn. 10 Nov. 1840. Apptd. Revenue Surveyor 9 Aug. 1841. With Army of Reserve (for Afghanistan) Oct. 1842 till Jan. 1843. Offg. Executive Ofr., P.W.D., Barisal; do. Bareilly 19 Apr. 1850 till Dec. 1854. Supt. Canals Bareilly 23 Dec. 1854 till 1859. Mutiny campaign; minor services; comdd. troops at Naini Tal and at action at Chinpura 1858 (Medal). Suptg. Engr., P.W.D., Bihar Circle, 26 Jan. 1860. Chief Engr., and Sec. to Chief Comr. C.P., 23 Feb. 1865; subsequently till retirement Chief Engr. Oudh.

Refs.: Guardian, xxxvii. 197c. *The Times,* 1 Feb. 1882, p. 9*f.*

MAXWELL, William George (*d.* 1830). Colonel, C.B., 2nd N.I. Bdr. comdg. in Bundelkhand. Cadet 1782. Admitted 9 July 1783. Ensign 5 Jan. 1783. Lieut. 27 Feb. 1788. Capt. 28 Oct. 1801. Major 1 Sept. 1809. Lt. Col. 16 Dec. 1814. Lt. Col. Comdt. 15 Feb. 1824. Col. 5 June 1829. *d.* Kaitha 13 Dec. 1830.

Of Dalswinton, co. Dumfries. (*Presumably* son of William Maxwell, IV of Dalswinton, which he sold 1785.) *m.* 1st, (?) His 2nd dau. *m.* George Freer Holland, *q.v. m.* 2nd, (? —— Gardner). (She died Kaitha 9 Dec. 1830.) His daus. *m.* Charles Henry Bois-

THE BENGAL ARMY, 1758-1834 267

ragon, Charles Ekins, John Craigie-Halkett, Peter La Touche, Charles George Ross, and William Henry Ryves, *qq.v.* (Said to have been ed. at Eton 1776-9.)

Services : Ensign H.M. 38th Ft. 2 Aug. 1780. Apptd. Cadet 24 Apr. 1782 ; sailed for India in the *Duke of Athol* 11 Sept. 1782. Ensign 6th Bengal Eur. Bn. in July 1787 ; transfd. to 28th Bn. Sepoys 1790. Third Mysore War ; Lieut. 28th Bn. Lieut. 13th N.I. and Bde. Major in 1798. Capt. Lt. 5th N.I. 6 Aug. 1801. Transfd. to 13th N.I. Bde. Major at Chunar 1803-6. Fur. 19 Feb. 1806 till 17 Mar. 1808. D.J.A.G. in the field May 1808. Posted Lt. Col. to 2/13th N.I. in 1815 ; to 22nd N.I. in 1816 ; to 2/6th N.I. in 1817. Comdg. at Moradabad in 1819. Operations in Kotah 1821 ; Mangrol ; Lt. Col. 2/6th N.I. Transfd. to 18th N.I. (late 2/6th) May 1824 ; to 20th N.I. 12 Feb. 1825 ; to 2nd N.I. in 1826. Bdr. comdg. in Oudh 22 Jan. 1825 ; comdg. Bundelkhand district 12 Jan. 1828 ; Saugor Div. 25 Nov. 1830 ; Bundelkhand 30 Nov. 1830. C.B. 23 July 1823.

Refs. : Family information. (? *Eton Coll. Register.*)

MAY, John Frederick (1800-1836). Captain, 72nd N.I. *bapt.* Plymouth 26 Mar. 1800. Cadet 1816. Admitted 4 July 1817. Ensign (?) Lieut. 1 Aug. 1818. Capt. 11 June 1832. *d.* Calcutta 23 Feb. 1836, aged 36.

Son of John May, shipowner and merchant, and Jane his wife. Addiscombe Cadet 1816-17.

Services : Cadet d.d. Bengal Eur. Regt. 1817 ; posted Lieut. to 2/14th N.I. 1818. Actg. Intr. & Qmr. 2/14th N.I. 21 Oct. 1823. Transfd. to 28th N.I. (late 1/14th) May 1824 ; Adjt. do. 13 July 1824. Transfd. to newly-raised 4th Extra Regt. (became 72nd N.I.) May 1825 ; Adjt. do. 13 July 1825 till 11 July 1832. S.S.O. at Berhampore 3 Jan. 1832. Leave s.c. 2 yrs. to Cape 16 Feb. 1836, but did not live to embark. No record of active service.

Refs. : A.J. N.S. xx. 178. Will dated Calcutta 2 Jan. 1836 ; proved 3 Mar. 1836. M.I. in S. Park St. cemetery, Calcutta.

MAYAFFRE, James (*d.* 1781). Captain, Artillery. (88) Fireworker 1 Sept. 1768. Lieut. 11 Mar. 1770. Capt. Lt. 29 Jan. 1774. Capt. 30 Mar. 1778. *d.* 20 Aug. 1781 : kld. in action in the attack on Ramnagar, nr. Benares.[1]

Brother of Andrew and Jane.

Services : Cadet at R.M.A., Woolwich, 1767 ; apptd. Lt. F. in England 24 Dec. 1767. Dy. Comy. of Ord. at Patna in Jan. 1774 ; apptd. Comy. do. 26 Sept. 1777. First Mahratta War 1780-1 ;

with Popham's detachment; Lahar; Gwalior; Capt. comdg. 2nd Coy. 1st Bn. Art. Benares insurrection 1781; Ramnagar (kld.).
Refs.: Naval & Mily. Mag. ii. (Dec. 1827), p. 400. Will dated Burdwan 22 Jan. 1779; proved 9 Feb. 1782.

[1] *Note:* His head was cut off, placed on a spike, and exposed on the walls of Ramnagar.

MAYBERY, Edward (1808-1872). Lieutenant. 37th N.I. *bapt.* St. Mary's, Brecon, 6 May 1808. Cadet 1824. Arrived in India 3 Sept. 1825. Ensign 6 Apr. 1825. Lieut. 14 Dec. 1826. Pensioned 27 Feb. 1833. Retired 5 Oct. 1836. *d.* the Struet, Brecon, 27 Apr. 1872; *bur.* Penderyn churchyard, Brecon.

Son of Thomas Maybery, of Brecon, solicitor and pronothary in the Welsh Court of Gt. Sessions, and Elizabeth his wife. Brother of Walter Maybery and nephew of Walter Maybery, *q.v.*

Services: Posted Ensign to 37th N.I. and served throughout with that Regt. Actg. Adjt. 16 July 1829. Fur. s.c. 7 Sept. 1833. Granted the h.p. of Lieut., viz. 4/- *p.d.* (M.C. 5 Oct. 1836). No record of active service.

Refs.: Theo. Jones's *Hist. of Brecknockshire* (Glanusk edn., 1909), iii. 475. *The Times*, 2 May 1872.

MAYBERY, Walter (1761-1798). Bt. Captain, Infantry. *bapt.* St. John's, Brecon, 7 Sept. 1761. Cadet 1780. Admitted 27 Apr. 1781. Ensign 1780. Lieut. 24 July 1781. Bt. Capt. 7 Jan. 1796. *d.* at sea 21 Jan. 1798, on board the *Gen. Goddard*.

2nd son of John Maybery, of Brecon, ironmaster, and Anne his wife, eldest dau. of John Wilkins, of Maesllwch Castle, co. Radnor, dy. pronothary. Uncle of Edward Maybery, *q.v.*

Services: Sailed for India in the *Grosvenor* 3 June 1780. Lieut. 19th Bn. Sepoys in July 1787 and in 1792. On fur. in 1795; fur. s.c. 20 Jan. 1798.

Refs.: Burke's *Commoners*, ii. 218, *s.n.* Wilkins, of Maeslough Castle. Will dated Dacca 9 Nov. 1797; proved 7 Mar. 1798.

MAYHEW, William Augustin John (1808-1874). Colonel. 6th Bengal Eur. Inf. A.G. Bengal Army. *bapt.* St. Mary's, Lambeth, 21 Jan. 1808. Cadet 1825. Arrived in India 25 June 1826. Ensign 16 Feb. 1826. Lieut. 8 Oct. 1839. Capt. 24 Jan. 1845. Major 6 May 1856. Lt. Col. 10 Oct. 1859. Retired 31 Dec. 1861. Hon. Col. 31 Dec. 1861. *d.* 2 Sandringham Gdns., Ealing, 19 June 1874, aged 66.

Son of Henry Mayhew and Elizabeth Golding his wife. Stepson

of Joseph Martin. *m.* Calcutta 3 Apr. 1854, Maria E., dau. of G. G. Macpherson, Surg. Bengal Est. (*See also* Sir H. E. L. Thuillier.)

Services: Ensign d.d. 49th N.I. 8 July 1826; posted to 8th N.I. 26 Sept. 1826. Actg. Intr. & Qmr. 8th N.I. 20 Sept. 1831; actg. Adjt. do. 2 July 1832. Fur. u.p.a. 15 Jan. till 4 Nov. 1833. Actg. Adjt. 2nd Local Horse 5 Sept. 1838. Adjt. 4th Recruit Depot Bn. 7 Sept. 1839. Adjt. 8th N.I. 20 Nov. 1839 till 29 May 1845. Fur. p.a. 9 Oct. 1847 till 1849. 2nd A.A.G. of the Army 6 May 1850; 1st do., and actg. D.A.G., 18 Nov. 1850. To be. A.A.G. of Burma Force (with official rank of Major) 24 Mar. 1852; D.A.G. do. 2 Sept. 1852. Second Burma War 1852; taking of Martaban and Rangoon; Pegu; D.A.G. (Medal with clasp). Actg. D.A.G. of the Army 7 Nov. 1854; D.A.G. 6 May 1856; A.G. (with official rank of Col.) 10 Dec. 1857 till retirement. Transfd. to newly-raised 6th Eur. Inf. in 1858. Fur. s.c. 29 Mar. till 28 Nov. 1859.

Refs.: *A.J.* N.S. ii. 217. *I.M.* 19 May 1854, p. 260. *The Times*, 23 June 1874.

MAYNARD, Foster (1767-1844). Captain. Artillery. (283) b. 1767. Cadet 1783. Admitted 7 Oct. 1783. Ensign (Inf.) 23 Jan. 1785. Fireworker (Art.) 27 Nov. 1790. Lieut. 23 Jan. 1796. Bt. Capt. 8 Jan. 1798. Capt. (?) Retired on h.p. 11 Feb. 1801 (? 29 Oct. 1800). *d.* Monmouth 27 Dec. 1844, aged 76.

Of Scarborough House, Crewkerne, Somerset. Son of Jonas Maynard and Christian Mercy Clark his wife. *m.* Charlton, Dorset, 9 Mar. 1800, Newland, dau. of W. Martin. (She died 14 Dec. 1857, aged 77.)

Services: Apptd. Cadet 23 Jan. 1783; sailed for India in the *Bellmont* 11 Mar. 1783. Posted to 5th Bengal Eur. Bn. 5 Feb. 1790; transfd. to Art. Nov. 1790. (? Second Rohilla War; battle of Bitaurah; Lieut. 3rd Coy. 3rd Bn. Art.) Fur. 11 Mar. 1798 till retirement.

Refs.: *G.M.* 1800, i. 282; 1845, i. 218.

MAYNARD, Herbert (1807-1840). Lieutenant. 24th N.I. *b.* London 17 Nov. 1807. Cadet 1824. Arrived in India 5 Apr. 1825. Ensign 13 Oct. 1824. Lieut. 8 Aug. 1825. Retired 8 May 1837. *d.* Frognal Rise, Hampstead, 9 June 1840.

bapt. St. James's, Clerkenwell, 9 Mar. 1808. 6th son of Thomas Maynard, of Rodney St., Pentonville, later of Wokingham, Berks., and Dorothea Mary his wife, dau. of Joseph Nourse, of Buckingham. *m.* Lewisham 21 May 1835, Jane Mary Consett, eldest dau. of William Bell, of Chingford, Essex, and grand-dau. of Matthew Consett, of Guildford St. (She died Fellows Rd., Hampstead, 6 Apr. 1880, aged 72.) Ed. St. Paul's; admitted 2 July 1818.

Services: Ensign d.d. 28th N.I. 12 Apr. 1825. Posted Lieut. to 24th N.I. Aug. 1825. Operations against the Kols and Chuars 1832; Lieut. 24th N.I. Fur. s.c. 9 May 1833 till 21 May 1836. Retired on h.p. owing to ill health.

Refs.: Family information. *Gardiner. John Bull,* 31 May 1835. *A.J.* N.S. xxxii. 291. *The Times,* 10 June 1840, p. 6.

MAYNARD, Walter (1739-1804). Lieutenant. Infantry. *bapt.* St. George, Nevis, 24 Mar. 1739. Transfd. as Lieut. from H.M.S. Lieut. 10 Sept. 1768. Resigned 5 July 1769. d. 1804.

Of Gingerland, St. George, Nevis. Son of William Maynard and Frances his wife. *m.* St. John's, Fig Tree, Nevis 17 Dec. 1772, Frances, eldest dau. of William Pemberton.

Services: Ensign 2nd Div. Independent Coys. in N. America 19 Feb. 1760; regimented into 95th Ft. in 1761; Lieut. 95th Ft. 22 Apr. 1762; h.p. Lieut. 1763 till death. Transfd. as Lieut. to Bengal Army (M.C. 1 Sept. 1768).

Refs.: Caribbeana, i. ii. Will dated 28 Feb. 1804; proved (P.C.C.) 16 July 1804.

MAYNE, George (1808-1830). 2nd Lieutenant, Artillery. (579) *b.* Limpsfield, Surrey, 29 Dec. 1808. Cadet 1825. 2nd Lieut. 25 Oct. 1825. *d.* Meerut 9 Feb. 1830.

bapt. Limpsfield 21 Feb. 1809. 2nd son of Rev. Robert Mayne, rector of Limpsfield, D.L. co. Surrey, and Charlotte Cunningham his wife, youngest dau. of Col. Graham, of St. Lawrence House, nr. Canterbury. Brother of Bdr. William Mayne (*D.N.B.*), and grand-nephew of William, last Baron Newhaven. Addiscombe Cadet 1823-5.

Services: Served with 3rd Troop 3rd Bde. H.A. 1826-7. No record of active service.

Refs.: Burke's *Landed Gentry,* 3rd edn., p. 795, *s.n.* Mayne, formerly of Powis, co. Clackmannan. *G.M.* 1830, ii. 190.

WYNELL-MAYOW, John Harding (1808-1876). Lieut. Colonel. 2nd Eur. Bengal Fus. *b.* Colerne, Wilts., 20 June 1808. Cadet 1825. Arrived in India 22 Oct. 1826. Ensign 21 June 1826. Lieut. 19 Oct. 1828. Capt. 23 Oct. 1845. Major 13 Nov. 1854. Retired 10 Aug. 1856. Hon. Lt. Col. 10 Aug. 1856. *d.* 96 Sydney Pl., Bath, 5 Nov. 1876.

Elder son of Rev. Robert Wynell-Mayow and Elizabeth his wife, dau. of William Harding, of Liverpool. His sister *m.* Edward Salusbury Lloyd, *q.v.* *m.* 1st, St. Helens, Lancs., 1 July 1840, Mary Jane, eldest dau. of James Willasey, of Allerton Hall, Lancs. (She died 15 Jan. 1858, aged 46.) *m.* 2nd, Whitchurch, Salop, 1 June 1859, Theodosea, dau. of John Lee, of Whitchurch.
Services: Ensign d.d. 14th N.I. 9 Nov. 1826. Posted to 14th N.I. 8 Jan. 1827. Actg. Adjt. Left Wing 14th N.I. 5 Nov. 1832. Fur. p.a. 27 Jan. 1837 till 28 Dec. 1840. Transfd. to newly-formed 2nd Bengal Eur. Regt. 8 Oct. 1839. With Army of Reserve (for Afghanistan) Oct. 1842 till Jan. 1843. Second Sikh War; Capt. 2nd Eur. Regt. (Medal). A.D.C. to Dy. Govr. of Bengal 7 Feb. and 15 Apr. 1850. Fur. s.c. 24 Feb. 1852 till Oct. 1855.
Refs.: Burke's *Landed Gentry*, 13th edn., p. 1232, *s.n.* Wynell-Mayow, of Bray and Saltash, Cornwall. *The Times*, 10 Nov. 1876.

MEADE, Edward (Richard) (1805-1890). Lieutenant. 55th N.I. *b.* 30 Nov. 1805. Cadet 1822. Arrived in India 23 Oct. 1823. Ensign 11 July 1823. Lieut. 29 Aug. 1824. Resigned 4 Aug. 1836. *d.* 19 Jan. 1890.
bapt. Dromore, co. Down, 20 Dec. 1805. 3rd son of Hon. and Ven. Pierce Meade, archdeacon of Dromore, and Elizabeth his wife, dau. of Rt. Rev. Thomas Percy, bishop of Dromore. *m.* 9 Apr. 1850, Eleanor Eliza, eldest dau. of William George Ives Bosanquet, H.E.I.C.S. (She died Mentone 4 Apr. 1880.) Ed. Eton 1817-20.
Services: Posted Ensign to 28th N.I. in 1823; transfd. to 55th N.I. (late 1/28th) May 1824. Attached to 1st Nassiri Bn. 19 Oct. 1824. Extra A.D.C. to Maj.-Gen. Thomas Reynell, C.B., comdg. 1st Div. of Bhurtpore force, 1 Dec. 1825. Siege and capture of Bhurtpore; A.D.C. (India medal). Rejoined 55th N.I. Sept. 1827. Adjt. 3rd Local Horse 16 May 1828; actg. 2nd in comd. do. 10 Feb. 1829; permanent do. 1 June 1830 till 23 Sept. 1833. Fur. p.a. 4 Feb. 1834 till resignation.
Refs.: Burke's *Peerage*, 1923, p. 519, *s.n.* Clanwilliam, E. *Eton School Lists.*

*****MEADE, Henry.** Ensign. Infantry. Cadet 1765. Ensign 2 Nov. 1765.
Services: Posted to 2nd Bde. in 1766. N.F.P.

MEADE, John Fulton (1802-1820). Ensign. Infantry. *bapt.* Lisburn, co. Down, 24 Nov. 1802. Cadet 1818. Ensign (?) Resigned 9 Oct. 1819. *d.* Calcutta 29 Aug. 1820, aged 17.

Son of Christopher Henry Barry Meade, Lieut. 64th Regt., of Limerick, and Ann his wife, eldest dau. of Joseph Fulton, of Lisburn. Cousin-german of Thomas Fulton, *q.v.*

Services: Was never posted to any Regt. After resigning the Service he joined the firm of Messrs. Mackintosh & Co., Calcutta, as an Asst.

Refs.: Burke's *Landed Gentry of Ireland,* p. 252, *s.n.* Fulton, of Braidujle, co. Antrim. Burke's *Colonial Gentry,* p. 339, *s.n.* Fulton. M.I. in S. Park St. cemetery, Calcutta.

MEADE, Joshua (*d.* 1789). Lieutenant, 20th Bn. Sepoys. Cadet 1781. Ensign 26 Aug. 1781. Lieut. 10 June 1783. *d.* 9 Sept. 1789: drowned between Midnapore and Calcutta.

Services: N.F.P.

Refs.: *G.M.* 1790, i. 474.

MEARES, George Richard James (1814-1867). Ensign. 12th N.I. Subsequently an indigo planter. *b.* Clifton 26 May 1814. Cadet 1833. Arrived in India 20 May 1835. Ensign 19 Feb. 1835. Resigned 4 Dec. 1837. *d.* 8 Aug. 1867.

Of Sinduri factory, Kishunnagar, B. & O. 3rd son of George Galbraith Meares, of Millgrove, co. Roscommon, and Lady Mary Elizabeth King his wife, 3rd dau. of Robert, 2nd Earl of Kingston. Brother of Robert King Meares, *q.v. m.* Calcutta 2 June 1837, Caroline Alicia, 3rd dau. of James Nicholson, solicitor. *(See also* John Richard Abbott.)

Services: Ensign d.d. 10th N.I. 26 May 1835; d.d. 30th N.I. 25 June 1835; posted to 19th N.I. 24 Sept. 1835; to 12th N.I. 6 Nov. 1835. No record of active service.

Refs.: Burke's *Landed Gentry of Ireland,* p. 475, *s.n.* Meares, of Meares Court, co. Westmeath. Burke's *Peerage,* 1923, p. 1297, *s.n.* Kingston, E.

MEARS, Robert King (1807-1825). Ensign, 21st N.I. *bapt.* Bristol 2 Aug. 1807. Cadet 1824. Arrived in India 25 May 1825. Ensign 14 Nov. 1824. *d.s.p.* Penang 19 Aug. 1825.

Eldest son of George Galbraith Meares and Lady Mary Elizabeth King his wife. Brother of William Piers Meares, *q.v.*

Services: Ensign d.d. 2nd Bengal Eur. Regt. 11 June 1825; posted Ensign to 21st N.I.

Refs.: Burke's *Landed Gentry of Ireland,* p. 475, *s.n.* Meares, of Meares Court, co. Westmeath.

THE BENGAL ARMY, 1758-1834

MEARES, William Piers (1808-1869). Lieut. Colonel. 42nd N.I. *b.* Bristol 3 Nov. 1808. Cadet 1825. Arrived in India 18 Mar. 1826. Ensign 28 Sept. 1825. Lieut. 18 June 1833. Capt. 24 Jan. 1845. Bt. Major 11 Nov. 1852. Retired Nov. 1855. Hon. Lt. Col. Dec. 1855. *d.* Clifton 20 Dec. 1869.

2nd son of George Galbraith Meares and Lady Mary Elizabeth King his wife. Brother of George Richard James Meares, *q.v.* *m.* Mary Ada Montrilli.

Services: Posted Ensign to 42nd N.I. Fur. s.c. 21 Feb. 1837 till 19 July 1841. First Afghan War 1841-2; operations in vicinity of Kandahar; advance on Kabul; Bt. Capt. 42nd N.I., with Nott's force (Medal). Fur. s.c. 2 yrs. to Cape and Aust. 24 Sept. 1845. Fur. p.a. 17 Sept. 1851 till 13 Sept. 1854. (? Santhal revolt 1855; Bt. Major 42nd N.I.)

Refs.: Burke's *Landed Gentry of Ireland*, p. 475, *s.n.* Meares, of Meares Court, co. Westmeath. Burke's *Peerage*, 1923, p. 1297, *s.n.* Kingston, E. *The Times*, 24 Dec. 1869.

MEDLAND, Henry (1795-?). Cadet. Infantry. *b.* London 15 Apr. 1795. Cadet 1811. Dismissed in India 29 Nov. 1813.

bapt. St. John the Evangelist, Westminster, 14 May 1795. Son of Thomas Medland, artist and engraver, sometime drawing-master at Haileybury Coll. (*D.N.B.*), and Susannah his wife. Ed. Christ's Hospital, Hertford. Addiscombe Cadet 23 May 1810 till Dec. 1811, when removed.

MEDOWS or MEADOWS, John. Ensign. Infantry. Cadet 1763. Ensign 17 July 1763. Resigned 9 Nov. 1763.

Services: Returned to England in the *Royal George* and arrived 15 Apr. 1764.

MEDWIN, Henry Clough (1790-1815). Lieutenant, 25th N.I. *b.* Horsham, Sussex, 10 Feb. 1790. Cadet 1805. Arrived in India 19 Sept. 1806. Ensign 6 Oct. 1806. Lieut. 10 Dec. 1811. *d.* Bhagwanpur, Nepal, 3 June 1815.

bapt. Horsham 26 Mar. 1790. Son of Thomas Charles Medwin, of Horsham, and Mary his wife, dau. of John Pinfold. Brother of Thomas Medwin, Lieut. 24th Light Dgns., and of Mary Catherine.

Services: Barasat C.C. Posted Ensign to 25th N.I. 1807. Expedn. to Mauritius 1810; Lieut. 1st Bengal Vol. Bn. Nepal War 1814-15; Lieut. 2/25th N.I., in 4th Div.

Refs.: Will dated Calcutta, 3 Sept. 1810; codicil dated 24 Dec. 1814; proved 28 Aug. 1815.

*MEE, Benjamin (*d.* 1796). Cadet. Infantry. Subsequently a banker in Calcutta. Cadet 1785. Arrived in India Apr. 1786. Resigned 1786. *d.* Pyrmont (? Montpelier) 2 Aug. 1796. Only son of Benjamin Thomas Mee, a Dir. of the Bank of England, and Sarah his wife, dau. of Benjamin Hooper. Brother of Mary, wife of Henry, 2nd Viscount Palmerston. Ed. Harrow; winner of the Silver Arrow 1764.

Services: "He accepted the appt. of a Cadet for Bengal, not with any intention of continuing in the army, but merely to get to the East Indies with the sanction of the Coy." (*Hickey.*) [1] After resigning the Service he became a merchant in Calcutta and proprietor of the Bank of Bengal. After leaving India he was a merchant in Fenchurch St., London. Dir. of the Bank of England, 1777-83.

Refs.: Herald & Genealogist, iii. 410. Hickey, iii. 275. *N. & Q.* clxxix. 131. *G.M.* 1796, ii. 706, 787.

[1] *Note:* He is included here solely on the authority of William Hickey. The statement, however, is of doubtful accuracy, no Cadets for Bengal having been apptd. during the years 1784-9, both inclusive.

MEE, George Augustus (Percival) (1804-1850). Lieut. Colonel, 65th N.I. *b.* London 5 Sept. 1804. Cadet 1820. Arrived in India Sept. 1821. Ensign 5 May 1821. Lieut. 1 May 1824. Capt. 17 Sept. 1836. Major 3 Feb. 1843. Lt. Col. 16 July 1849. *d.* Lahore 21 June 1850.

bapt. Marylebone 29 Oct. 1815. Son of Joseph Mee, of Allsop's Terr., London, barr.-at-law, formerly B.C.S., and Anne his wife, the miniaturist (*D.N.B.*), dau. of John Foldsone, painter. Brother of John Edmund Mee, *q.v.*, and of Mrs. Ynyr Burges. His paternal grandmother was Elizabeth, dau. of Rev. Dr. David Burges, vicar of St. Mark's, Dublin. (*See also* William Lamb (1779-1826).)

Services: Posted Ensign to 2/16th N.I. in 1822; transfd. to 29th N.I. in 1823; to 58th N.I. (late 2/29th) May 1824. Siege and capture of Bhurtpore; Lieut. 58th N.I. Adjt. 58th N.I. 7 Feb. 1828; Intr. & Qmr. do. 11 June 1828 till 1836. Intr. & Qmr. Vol. Regt. for China 12 Feb. 1840. First China War 1840-2; capture of I. of Wantong, in Boca Tigris R., Jan. 1841 (*Lond. Gaz.* 11 June 1842); Canton (*ib.* 8 Oct. 1841); Bt. Major Vol. Regt. (Medal). Remained in China with a detachment of 1st Vol. Regt. which he brought back to India in Mar. 1842. Rejoined 58th N.I. Apr. 1842. Comdd. 3rd Inf. Levy 7 Oct. 1842 till 1 Mar. 1843, when it was broken up. Fur. s.c. 5 Mar. 1844 till 1846, and 1 May

THE BENGAL ARMY, 1758-1834   275

1847 till 1849. Posted Lt. Col. to 41st N.I. in 1849 ; transfd. to 65th N.I. Jan. 1850.
Refs.: G.M. 1850, ii. 565. *The Times,* 9 Oct. 1850.

MEE, John Edmund (1807-1839). Ensign, 38th N.I. *b.* London 7 Oct. 1807. Cadet 1828. Arrived in India 14 Oct. 1828. Ensign 20 May 1828. *d.* Delhi 10 June 1839.
Son of Joseph Mee, of 77 Upper Berkeley St., London, barr.-at-law, and Anne his wife. Brother of George Augustus Mee, *q.v.* T.C.D. ; Pensioner 18 Oct. 1824.
Services: Ensign d.d. 58th N.I. 20 Nov. 1828 ; posted to 72nd N.I. 4 Mar. 1829 ; transfd. to 14th N.I. 22 Apr. 1829 ; as senior Ensign to 38th N.I. Nov. 1837. No record of active service.
Refs.: Alumni Dub. De Rhé-Philipe. M.I. in Rajpura cemetery, Delhi.

MEIK, Patrick (1809-1839). Captain, 31st N.I. *b.* Easter Duddingston, Midlothian, 14 Sept. 1809. Cadet 1825. Arrived in India 10 Mar. 1826. Ensign 12 Oct. 1825. Lieut. 13 Apr. 1827. Capt. 20 Dec. 1838. *d.* Quetta, Baluchistan, 17 Aug. 1839.
bapt. Duddingston 2 Oct. 1809. Son of Patrick Meik and Barbara Scott his wife. *m.* Calcutta 1 Nov. 1836, Miss Mary Ann Francis. Ed. Edin. High School.
Services: Posted Ensign to 30th N.I. in 1826 ; transfd. to 31st N.I. 7 July 1830. Operations against the Chuars 1832 ; against the Kols 1837-8 ; Lieut. 31st N.I. Adjt. 31st N.I. 14 Aug. 1835 till 21 Feb. 1839. First Afghan War 1839 ; capture of Ghazni ; Capt. 31st N.I.
Refs.: M.I. Afghan Memorial Church, Bombay.

MEIN, Nicholas George (1809-1828). Ensign, 15th N.I. *bapt.* St. Bridget's, Dublin, 19 Oct. 1809. Cadet 1825. Ensign 26 Apr. 1826. *d.* Aligarh 12 (? 7) Aug. 1828.
Son of John Alexander Mein, Lt. Col. 74th Regt., and Ellen Magdalene his wife.
Services: Posted Ensign to 15th N.I. 5 Oct. 1826. No record of active service.
Refs.: A.J. xxvii. 358.

MEIN, Thomas Alexander (1788-1835). Captain. 37th N.I. *bapt.* Fowey, Cornwall, 15 June 1788. Cadet 1806. Arrived in India 1 Aug. 1807. Ensign 21 Aug. 1807. Lieut. 23 Mar. 1811. Capt. 1 May 1824. Retired 10 Dec. 1831. *d.* 29 Mar. 1835.

Eldest son of Thomas Mein, M.D., R.N., of Eildon Hall, nr. Melrose, and Margaret Ellis his wife, of Orchard and Grove, Cornwall. *m.* Stoke July 1833, Rosamond, 3rd dau. of William Archer, of Lymington, Hants, Capt. 16th Light Dgns. (She *re-m.* 22 Nov. 1836, John Smith, of Devonport.)
Services: Barasat C.C. for 12 mos. Posted Ensign to 18th N.I. in 1809. Lieut. 2/18th N.I. S.A.C.G. 3 Apr. 1813. Third Mahratta War; S.A.C.G. in 3rd Div. A.C.G. 2 cl. 23 June 1818; do. 1 cl. 3 Oct. 1825. Transfd. to 37th N.I. (late 2/18th) May 1824. Fur. p.a. 4 Jan. 1830 till retirement.
Refs.: Memoirs of Susan Sibbald, by F. P. Hett, London, 1926. *A.J.* N.S. xii. 63.

MELLER,[1] **John** (1747/48-1822). Major, Invalid Est. 16th N.I. *b.* 1747/48. Bt. Ensign 1 Aug. 1782. Country Cadet 1785. Admitted 23 Jan. 1785. Ensign 2 June 1785. Lieut. 17 Oct. 1793. Capt. 21 Sept. 1804. Major 25 July 1810. Invalided 15 Mar. 1810. *d.* Calcutta 3 Feb. 1822, aged 74.

m. 1st, Calcutta 20 Mar. 1792, Elizabeth, widow of John Marshall, of Dacca, merchant, and formerly widow of — — Taylor. Father of Eliza, wife of Samuel Mitchelson Horsbrugh, *q.v. m.* 2nd, St. John's, Calcutta, 21 Jan. 1822, Miss Maria Rozento.

Services: Apptd. Bt. Ensign from Condr. of Ord. Recommended by C.-in-C. in Dec. 1784 for promotion to rank of Ensign. Asst. in A.G.'s office in Dec. 1788. Posted to 8th Bn. Sepoys 15 Feb. 1790. Transfd. from 2nd Eur. Bn. to 6th do. 22 Oct. 1792; to 1st do. 20 Oct. 1793. Capt. Lt. 16th N.I. 30 Sept. 1803. Asst. D.A.G. at Presdy. 1804 till invalided.

Refs.: *A.J.* xiv. 195. Will dated 9 Jan. 1822; proved 6 Feb. 1822.

[1] *Note:* His name often appears as Miller.

MELLIS, William (1794-1822). Ensign. Infantry. Subsequently Lieut. H.M. 24th Ft. *b.* Fetteresso, co. Kincardine, 7 Feb. 1794. Cadet 1810. Ensign (?) Resigned 7 Feb. 1814. *d.* on board the *Barossa;* bur. Madras 21 Mar. 1822.

Son of James Mellis, of Newhall, Fetteresso, and Janet his wife. Ed. Aberdeen Grammar School 1804-9.
Services: Cadet d.d. 12th N.I. 1811-13. Ensign H.M. 24th Ft. 7 June 1812; Lieut. do. 26 June 1818.

MELLISH (*recte* **von MELLISCH**), **Dietrich George Alexander Frederick Henry** (1803-1844). Captain, 10th L.C. *b.* Royal

THE BENGAL ARMY, 1758-1834 277

Bavarian Rectory, Völkershausen, Moschenbach, 9 June 1803. Cadet 1823. Arrived in India 5 Oct. 1824. Cornet 21 Feb. 1824. Lieut. 13 May 1825. Capt. 17 Feb. 1836. d. Meerut 14 Oct. 1844.

Son of Joseph Charles von Mellisch. His Godparents were, amongst others, H.S.H. Duke George of Saxe-Meiningen and Lady Elloga von Mellisch. m. Emilie Marie Louise Wilhelmina, dau. of the Baron de Baumbach, of Hesse. (She re-m. Major Arthur William FitzRoy Somerset, elder son of F.M. Lord FitzRoy James Henry Somerset, 1st Baron Raglan, and died 1865, after marrying a third time.)

Services: Posted Cornet to 2nd L.C. 31 Mar. 1825; transfd. as Lieut. to newly-raised 2nd Extra Regt. (became 10th L.C.) May 1825. Siege and capture of Bhurtpore; Lieut. 10th L.C. Adjt. 10th L.C. 21 May 1827 till 8 Apr. 1834. Fur. p.a. 25 Dec. 1835 till 16 Jan. 1839. Suspended by sentence of G.C.M. from rank, pay and allowances for 6 mos. 18 June 1841. First Afghan War 1842; reoccupation of Kabul; Capt. 10th L.C., with Gen. Pollock's force (Medal). Gwalior campaign; Maharajpur (w.); Capt. 10th L.C. (Bronze star).

Refs.: G.M. 1845, i. 222. I.M. 6 Dec. 1844, p. 626.

*MELLISH, Francis (1727/28-?). b. 1727/28. Cadet 1758. d. (?)

Services: Sailed for India in the Bombay Castle in 1758, aged 30. N.F.P.

MELVILLE, David (d. 1784). Ensign; Infantry. Country Cadet 1781. Ensign 4 June 1782. d. Chunar 20 Dec. 1784.

Services: Apptd. Cadet July 1781. N.F.P.

*MELVILLE, Montagu Robert (1798-?). Cadet. Infantry. b. 23 Apr. 1798. Cadet 1816. Never arrived in India. Relinquished his appt. 12 July 1820, owing to ill health.

bapt. Marylebone 24 May 1798. Son of Thomas Melville and Elizabeth his wife, dau. of Robert Anderson.

MENCE, Charles. Cadet. Infantry. Cadet 1772. Resigned 8 Feb. 1773.

Services: Sailed for India in the Nassau 15 Feb. 1772. N.F.P.

MENCE, George (1753-?). Lieut. Colonel. 14th N.I. b. 8 Feb. 1753. Cadet 1768. Admitted 28 Aug. 1768. Ensign 5 Feb.

1769. Lieut. 4 June 1770. Capt. 4 Jan. 1779. Major 7 Feb. 1784. Lt. Col. 1 Mar. 1794. Retired 20 Aug. 1799. (*d.* before 1812.)

Son of Rev. Joseph Mence, rector of All Hallows, London Wall, and a minor canon of St. Paul's. *m.* 1st, Moradbag, nr. Berhampore, 17 June 1786, Miss Elizabeth Donaldson. (*See also* Hon. David Anstruther.) (She died Sept./Dec. 1787.) *m.* 2nd, Kennington Sept. 1805, Mrs. Jane Watson, of Bergies, Scotland. Ed. Merchant Taylors' Jan.-May 1762.

Services: Comdg. one of the Nawab-Wazir of Oudh's Bns. in 1776. Capt. 1/3rd Bengal Eur. Regt. in Oct. 1779 ; 27th N.I. in Oct. 1783. Fur. s.c. 23 Nov. 1783 till Sept. 1785. To comd. 31st Bn. Sepoys 31 May 1786, and was still comdg. in 1792. Lt. Col. 2nd Bengal Eur. Regt. in 1796. Fur. Jan. 1797 till retirement.

Refs.: Robinson. *Forrest,* ii. 520. *Hickey,* iii. 278. *M.M.* 1805, p. 269.

STUART-MENTETH, William (1805-1857). Bt. Lieut. Colonel, 69th N.I. *b.* Closeburn, co. Dumfries, 30 July 1805. Cadet 1821. Arrived in India 25 Dec. 1822. Ensign 18 Dec. 1822. Lieut. (26 Oct. 1824) 13 May 1825. Capt. 2 Feb. 1842. Major 28 Nov. 1854. Bt. Lt. Col. 8 June 1856. *d.* Simla 11 July 1857.

4th son of Sir Charles Granville Stuart Menteath, 1st Bart., of Closeburn, and Ludivina his wife, dau. of Thomas Loughnan. *m.* Calcutta 26 Sept. 1826, Sarah Breviter, eldest dau. of George Hamilton, of Hamilton Lodge, Staffs., Lieut. 16th Lancers, Bk. Mr. at Gibraltar, afterwards at Malta. (*See also* Alister Stewart.) (She *re-m.* Capt. Alexander Bishop Chalmers, Bengal N.I., and died Simla 29 Apr. 1900, aged 88.) Ed. Edin. High School.

Services: Ensign d.d. 1/23rd N.I. 7 Jan. 1823. Posted to 2/9th N.I. 25 Mar. 1823. Transfd. to 1/9th N.I. 17 Oct. 1823 ; to 8th N.I. (late 1/9th) May 1824 ; to 52nd N.I. Aug. 1824 ; to newly-raised 1st Extra Regt. (became 69th N.I.) July 1825. Fur. p.a. 23 Jan. 1835 till 10 Dec. 1837. Offg. Fort Adjt. at Ft. Wm. 12 Feb. 1838 till Feb. 1840. With 1st Vol. Bn. 15 Feb. 1840 till May 1841. First China War 1840 ; Chusan ; Lieut. 1st Vol. Bn. (Medal). Offg. Fort Adjt. and Supt. Gentlemen Cadets at Ft. Wm. 9 June till Sept. 1841. Offg. Dy. Paymr. at Benares 21 Nov. 1841 till Nov. 1843. Offg. Bde. Major at Sukkur 6 May till 6 Sept. 1844. Bde. Major Ambala 13 Sept. 1844 till Aug. 1846 ; do. Delhi Aug. 1846 till June 1854. Fur. p.a. Aug. 1855 till 29 Nov. 1856. Leave s.c. to Simla May 1857 till death.

Refs.: Burke's *Peerage,* 1923, p. 1541, *s.n.* Stuart-Menteth, Bart., of Closeburn, co. Dumfries. *Anderson*, iii. 150. *The House of Hamilton*, by Lt.-Col. George Hamilton (Edin., 1933), p. 997. *De Rhé-Philipe*. *G.M.* 1857, ii. 566. Will dated 8 Oct. 1855; proved 3 Mar. 1858. M.I. in new cemetery, Simla.

MENZIES, Charles (*d.* 1765). Lieutenant, Infantry. Cadet 1763. Ensign 7 Sept. 1763. Lieut. 14 July 1764. *d.* Patna June 1765.

Brother of James Menzies.

Services: Posted to Pioneer Coy. with field army under Major Hector Munro 5 Dec. 1764.

Refs.: Will dated Patna, 23 June 1765; proved 10 Sept. 1765.

MENZIES, Robert (1805-1836). Captain, Invalid Est. 31st N.I. *b.* Fortingal, co. Perth, 12 Apr. 1805. Cadet 1821. Arrived in India 24 Nov. 1822. Ensign 26 Sept. 1822. Lieut. 1 May 1824. Capt. 8 May 1834. Invalided 1 June 1834. *d.* Chunar 22 Aug. 1836.

Son of Capt. James Menzies, of Perth, and Isabella Stewart his wife. *m.* (?)

Services: Posted Ensign to 2/14th N.I. Nov. 1822. d.d. 2/5th N.I. 6 Dec. 1822. Transfd. to 15th N.I. in 1823; to 31st N.I. (late 2/15th) May 1824. Siege and capture of Bhurtpore; Lieut. 31st N.I. (? Operations against the Bhils 1827-8; Lieut. 31st N.I.) Fur. s.c. 9 Feb. 1829 till 24 Feb. 1834.

Refs.: (? Burke's *Landed Gentry*, *s.n.* Stewart-Menzies.) *A.J. N.S.* xxii. 129. Will dated 21 Aug. 1836; proved 28 July 1838. M.I. at Chunar.

MENZIES, William (1778-1861). Captain. 21st N.I. *b.* Edinburgh 20 June 1778. Cadet 1798. Arrived in India 24 Feb. 1800. Ensign 24 Jan. 1800. Lieut. 23 June 1800. Capt. 17 May 1815. Retired 10 June 1818. *d.* 3 Jan. 1861.

bapt. Leith 29 June 1778. Son of William Menzies, of the custom house, Edinburgh, writer, and Elizabeth his wife, dau. of Parker Medcalf, of London. *m.* Edinburgh 13 Aug. 1811, Harriet Fordyce, eldest dau. of Dr. Callander, younger, of Craigforth.

Services: Posted Lieut. to 2/6th N.I. 15 Apr. 1801. Second Mahratta War; operations in Baghelkhand 1803; reduction of Chaukandi; Lieut. 2/6th N.I. Transfd. to newly-raised 21st N.I. in 1804. Fur. 22 Jan. 1810 till 7 Jan. 1814. Capt. Lt. 2/21st N.I. 16 Dec. 1814. Fur. 1815 till retirement.

Refs.: S.M. 1811, p. 716.

MERCER, Alexander (1800-1852). Lieut. Colonel, C.B., 63rd N.I. *bapt.* St. Mary's, Lambeth, 3 Sept. 1800. Cadet 1817. Admitted 7 July 1818. Ensign (?) Lieut. 1 Aug. 1818. Capt. 10 Apr. 1836. Major 6 Mar. 1841. Lt. Col. 18 Mar. 1847. *d.* York St., Portman Sq., London, 12 Nov. 1852. Son of William Mercer and Margaret his wife. Uncle of William Remington Mercer, *q.v.* *m.* 1st, Cawnpore 25 Sept. 1826, Mrs. Mary Smith. (She died Banda 24 Aug. 1833.) *m.* 2nd, Dinapore 8 Aug. 1839, Augusta, dau. of Charles Corfield, of Knowle Lodge, Taunton, and sister of Charles Corfield, *q.v.* (*See also* John Assey Fairhead.) (She died Nimach 16 Dec. 1846, aged 28.)
Services: Posted Supy. Lieut. to 1/27th N.I. in 1818. Transfd. to 53rd N.I. (late 1/27th) May 1824 ; to 2nd Extra Regt. (became 70th N.I.) May 1825. Actg. Intr. & Qmr. 53rd N.I. 1 Oct. 1824 ; do. 2nd Extra Regt. 26 Oct. 1825 ; permanent do. 6 Jan. 1826 till 21 Sept. 1833. Fur. s.c. 8 Jan. 1834 till 25 Nov. 1837. Actg. D.A.A.G. Dinapore 6 Oct. 1838 till 10 Mar. 1841. Tempy. comd. 2nd Oudh Local Inf. Jan. 1842. Succeeded to comd. of 70th N.I. Oct. 1842. (? Gwalior campaign ; Maharajpur ; Major comdg. Rt. Wing 70th N.I.—Bronze star.) Posted Lt. Col. to 70th N.I. Mar. 1847 ; transfd. to 69th N.I. 1848. Second Sikh War ; Chilianwala ; Gujerat ; Lt. Col. 69th N.I. (Medal with clasp). Transfd. to 1st Eur. Fus. 1849 ; to 63rd N.I. Nov. 1849. Fur. p.a. 14 Feb. 1850 till death. C.B. 9 June 1849.
Refs.: Boase. *G.M.* 1852, ii. 662. Will dated 21 Oct. 1848 ; proved 28 Oct. 1854.

*MERCER, George (*d.* 1801). Captain, 7th N.I. Country Cadet 1780. Admitted 26 Feb. 1781. Ensign 17 Aug. 1781. Lieut. 24 Oct. 1781. Bt. Capt. 7 Jan. 1796. Capt. (?) *d.* Kedgeree 20 Dec. 1801, on board the *Milford.*
Services: A Vol. in 1780 ; Lieut. 18th N.I. in Nov. 1783. Fur. 31 Aug. 1785 till 25 June 1787. Lieut. 33rd Bn. Sepoys in Dec. 1788 ; transfd. from 32nd Bn. to 6th Eur. Bn. 10 Nov. 1794. Capt. 1/7th N.I.
Refs.: *A.A.R.* iv. 120.

MERCER, George Duncan (1814-1884). Lieutenant. 45th N.I. Subsequently Major R. Perthshire Rifles. *b.* Calcutta 27 Dec. 1814. Cadet 1832. Arrived in India 4 Oct. 1833. Ensign 21 June 1833. Lieut. 30 Oct. 1838. Resigned 20 Dec. 1838. *d. unm.* Aberdeen 25 July 1884.
bapt. Calcutta 13 Feb. 1815. 2nd son of George Mercer, of

Gorthy, Dryden, and Mavisbank, sometime H.E.I.C. Marine, later a merchant in Calcutta, J.P. & D.L. co. Perth, and Frances Charlotte his wife, dau. of John Reid, Bengal Medical Est., and sister of Henry Solomon Reid, *q.v.* Nephew of William Mercer, *q.v.* Ed. Edin. Acad. 1824-9; Addiscombe Cadet 1 Feb. 1831 till 14 Dec. 1832.
Services: Ensign d.d. 24th N.I. 16 Nov. 1833; posted to 45th N.I. 24 May 1834. Leave p.a. 1 yr. without pay to Tasmania 30 Oct. 1837. No record of active service. Settled in N.S.W. Retired from R. Perth Rifles as Major 21 Feb. 1874.
Refs.: Burke's Landed Gentry, 13th edn., p. 1234, *s.n.* Mercer, of Huntingtower, co. Perth. Anderson, iii. 728. *The Times*, 29 July 1884.

MERCER, Henry (1759/60-1839). Major. 17th N.I. *b.* 1759/60. Country Cadet 1778. Admitted 9 Mar. 1778. Ensign 4 June 1778. Lieut. 12 Sept. 1779. Capt. 3 Oct. 1796. Major 5 July 1801. Pensioned 1804. Retired 1 Jan. 1808. *d.* at his residence, Argyll Pl., Regent St., London, 18 Dec. 1839, aged 79.
m. Margaret, dau. of Charles Weston, of Calcutta, merchant and philanthropist. (She died in Bengal 30 June 1804.)
Services: Lieut. 2/3rd Bengal Eur. Regt. in Oct. 1779; Lieut. 16th Bn. Sepoys in July 1787 and in 1792; Capt. 17th N.I. in 1798.
Refs.: A.J. N.S. xxxi. 91.

MERCER, Stephen (1789-1827). Captain, 35th N.I. *b.* E. Farleigh, Kent, 17 Mar. 1789. Cadet 1804. Arrived in India 13 May 1806. Ensign 22 Apr. 1806. Lieut. 27 Feb. 1807. Capt. 11 July 1823. *d.* Bankura, Bengal, 20 Nov. 1827, of fever.
bapt. E. Farleigh 19 Mar. 1789. Son of Samuel Mercer, of E. Farleigh, and Sarah his wife.
Services: Barasat C.C. Posted to 17th N.I. in 1807. Nepal War 1814-15; Jitpur; Lieut. 2/17th N.I., in 3rd Div. Transfd. to 35th N.I. (late 2/17th) May 1824. Siege and capture of Bhurtpore; Capt. 35th N.I.
Refs.: Burke's Landed Gentry, 13th edn., p. 1235, *s.n.* Mercer, of Toddington Park, Beds. A.J. xxv. 683.

MERCER, William (1755-1801). Captain, 5th N.C. *b.* 8 Jan. 1755. Cadet 1781. Admitted 15 Nov. 1782. Ensign 1781. Lieut. 10 July 1782. Capt. 29 May 1800. *d.* Ghazipur, U.P., 3 Aug. 1801: kld. in a duel by the Hon. Andrew Ramsay, younger brother of 9th Earl of Dalhousie, Commercial Resdt. at Ghazipur.

Of Potterhill, co. Perth (which he sold). 3rd son of William Mercer, of Pitteuchar and Potterhill, sheriff substitute of co. Perth, and Elizabeth his wife, dau. of George Swan. Uncle of George Duncan Mercer, q.v. m. Calcutta 6 Nov. 1788, Barbara, dau. of Robert Forbes, of Corse, co. Banff, and sister of Sir John Forbes, of Hawthornden (who took the name of Drummond).
Services: Ensign H.M. 19th Ft. 26 Dec. 1770, and joined that Regt. at Gibraltar in 1771; Lieut. do. 28 Aug. 1775. Lieut. 72nd Ft. (R. Manchester Vols.) 28 Mar. 1778. Apptd. Cadet 11 May 1780; sailed for India in the *Mount Stewart* 27 June 1780, captured on the voyage, taken to Spain and exchanged. Sailed in the *Ganges* 6 Feb. 1782. Adjt. G.G.B.G. 28 Feb. 1783 till 1796. Third Mysore War 1791; Adjt. G.G.B.G. Qmr. 2nd N.C. June 1796; do. 1st N.C. till May 1800. Transfd. as Capt. to newly-raised 5th N.C. May 1800.
Refs.: Burke's *Landed Gentry*, 13th edn., p. 1234, *s.n.* Mercer, of Huntingtower, co. Perth. *Anderson*, iii. 728. Family information. *Officers of the Green Howards*, by Major M. L. Ferrar. *V.B.G.* (portrait). M.I. Ghazipur cemetery.

MERCER, William Remington (1816-1840). Lieutenant, 70th N.I. *b.* London 26 May 1816. Cadet 1834. Arrived in India 7 June 1835. Ensign 10 Feb. 1835. Lieut. 30 Apr. 1839. *d.* at his brother's house, Edgware Rd., London, 19 Jan. 1840.
bapt. St. Olave, Jewry, 27 Jan. 1817. Son of William Mercer, of Walworth, distiller, and of Canterbury Pl., Kent, and Fanny his wife. Nephew of Alexander Mercer, q.v. Ed. St. Paul's School; admitted 13 May 1825.
Services: Ensign d.d. 30th N.I. 15 June 1835; posted to 58th N.I. 24 Sept. 1835; to 70th N.I. 2 Dec. 1835. Fur. s.c. 10 June 1839 till death. No record of active service.
Refs.: Gardiner. *G.M.* 1840, i. 217.

MEREDITH, John (*d.* 1786). Captain, Infantry. Cadet 1769. Ensign 1769. Lieut. 10 Mar. 1773. Capt. 7 Jan. 1781. *d.* Cawnpore 3 Aug. 1786.
Brother of William and Edward Meredith.
Services: Capt. 1st Bengal Eur. Regt. in 1782.
Refs.: Will dated 25 July 1786; proved 22 Aug. 1786.

MEREDYTH, Arthur Tisdall (1783-1818). Captain, Invalid Est. 9th N.I. *b.* in Ireland 17 Mar. 1783. Cadet 1798. Arrived

THE BENGAL ARMY, 1758-1834   283

in India 20 Sept. 1799. Ensign 24 Oct. 1799. Lieut. 17 Nov. 1799. Capt. 13 June 1812. Invalided 1 Oct. 1814. *d.* Serampore, Bengal, 25 Jan. 1818.

3rd and youngest son of Sir John Meredyth, 1st Bart., of Carlandstown, Meath, and Helen his wife, dau. of William English, of Springfield, co. Tipperary. Uncle of Humphrey Jervis-White, *q.v.* His sister *m.* John Canning, *q.v. m.* 5 July 1816, Elizabeth Ann, dau. of —— Lennon and widow of James William Emerson, indigo planter.

Services : Ensign Loyal Durham Fenc. Inf. 31 July 1798. Posted Lieut. to 2/9th N.I. 15 Apr. 1801. Second Mahratta War ; Agra ; Laswari ; Gwalior ; Monson's retreat ; Bhurtpore ; Lieut. 2/9th N.I. Capt. Lt. 9th N.I. 5 June 1811 ; Capt. 1/9th N.I.

Refs. : Burke's *Peerage,* 1923, p. 1544, *s.n.* Meredyth, Bart., of Carlandstown, co. Meath. *A.J.* vi. 536.

MERRIMAN, James (1780-1809). Lieutenant, 26th N.I. *b.* Marlborough 19 Sept. 1780. Cadet 1799. Arrived in India 10 Dec. 1800. Ensign 25 Aug. 1800. Lieut. 13 Jan. 1801. *d.* Terrowa, nr. Datia, C.I., 22 Mar. 1809.

5th and youngest son of Nathaniel Merriman, of Marlborough, cheese factor, and Elizabeth his wife, dau. of Thomas Baverstock, of Alton, Hants.

Services : Posted Lieut. to 1st Bengal Eur. Regt. 17 Apr. 1801. Second Mahratta War ; battle of Deig (w.) ; capture of Deig (s.w.—12·sabre cuts and lost left arm) ; Lieut. Bengal Eur. Regt. Transfd. to newly-raised 26th N.I. 1805 ; Adjt. & Qmr. do. 1805 till death. Operations in Bundelkhand 1807 ; Sehlehuganj ; Lieut. 26th N.I.

Refs. : Pedigree *of Family of Merriman,* by G. F. M. Merriman (London, 1918), p. 46. Burke's *Visitation of Seats and Arms,* 1S. ii. 34. Burke's *Landed Gentry,* 15th edn., p. 1581, *s.n.* Merriman, formerly of Mildenhall. *G.M.* 1810, i. 282. Will dated 9 Mar. 1809 ; proved 17 May 1809.

MESHAM, Thomas George (1808-1832). Lieutenant, 38th N.I. *b.* Bromham, nr. Bedford, 5 Nov. 1808. Cadet 1824. Arrived in India 9 Aug. 1825. Ensign 11 Apr. 1825. Lieut. 1 Dec. 1830. *d.* camp Jhangi, nr. Midnapore, 1 June 1832, " of fever, whilst engaged in the arduous duty of quelling an insurrection created by a rebellious zemindar." *(A.J.)*

bapt. Bromham 19 Apr. 1809. Son of Rev. Robert Mesham, rector of Ripple, Kent, and Rosamond his wife, dau. of Rev. William

Hayward Roberts, vice-provost of Eton Coll. Cousin-german of Ralph Gore Roberts, *q.v.*
Services: Posted Ensign to 38th N.I. and served throughout with that Regt.; actg. Intr. & Qmr. 28 May 1829, 18 Jan. and 6 Oct. 1830; permanent do. 6 June 1831 till death.
Refs.: Burke's *Landed Gentry*, 13th edn., p. 1236, *s.n.* Mesham (*now* Birchenough), of Pontruffydd, co. Flint. *A.J.* N.S. ix. 186. Will dated Midnapore 3 Feb. 1832; proved 12 Oct. 1832. M.I. Midnapore cemetery.

*MESSMAN, Samuel (*d.* 1767). Lieutenant, Infantry. Cadet 1765. Ensign 9 Nov. 1765. Lieut. June 1767. *d.* Calcutta 23 July 1767.
Services: Apptd. Cadet 18 Feb. 1765. N.F.P.

MESTAYER, Lewis (1741/42-1791). Lieut. Colonel. Engineers. Chief Engr. Bengal. *b.* 1741/42. Cadet 1764. Ensign 23 Nov. 1764. Lieut. 23 Oct. 1766. Major 25 Jan. 1779. Lt. Col. 16 Jan. 1786. Resigned 13 Feb. 1786. *d.* at his house in Upper Gower St., London, 28 Aug. 1791.

Son of Charles Mestayer, of Dublin, merchant, and Jeanne his wife, *née* Trouille.[1] *m.* Walthamstow 5 Aug. 1786, Mary, eldest dau. of Robert Briscoe, of Walthamstow, apothecary, formerly Surg. to 100th Ft. in India.
Services: Apptd. originally a Cadet for Madras; sailed for India in the *Vansittart* 4 Mar. 1764, aged 22. Surveyor of roads in 1765. Dismissed as Lieut. 27 Nov. 1770 (*Court Minutes*, 21 Feb. 1770), and returned to Ireland in Jan. 1772; restored 8 Jan. 1777, to rank as Capt. next below James Rennell, *q.v.*; arrived in India Nov. 1777. Comdg. at Budge-Budge Nov. 1781 till 1784. Chief Engr. Bengal 16 Jan. 1786.
Refs.: *Hickey*, ii. 103. *Caraccioli*, iv. 468. *G.M.* 1791, ii. 1065.

[1] *Note:* She died 5 July 1789, aged 76, and was *bur.* in the French cemetery, Peter St., Dublin.

METCALFE, Sir Thomas Theophilus, first baronet (1745-1813). Major. Infantry. Subsequently a Director, E.I.Co. *b.* 8 Jan. 1745. Cadet 1767. Ensign 31 July 1767. Lieut. 23 Sept. 1769. Capt. 10 May 1777. Major 28 July 1781. Struck off 1793. *d.* Portland Pl., London, 17 Nov. 1813.

1st Bart., of Fern Hill, Berks. *cr.* 21 Dec. 1802. Son of Thomas Metcalfe, an officer in the army, and Margaret his wife, dau. of Rev. John Williams. *m.* Calcutta 18 Apr. 1782, Susannah Sophia

Selina, dau. of John Debonnaire, of Madras, merchant, mayor of Madras 1763, and widow of John Smith (1731/32-1777), *q.v.* (*See also* John Richardson.) (She died nr. Sherborne 10 Sept. 1815.)

Services : Sailed for India in the *Lord Holland* 16 Dec. 1766. First Rohilla War 1774 ; battle of St. George. To comd. 18th Regt. Sepoys 29 Mar. 1782 ; Agent for Mily. Stores in Calcutta 1782 till 6 Dec. 1785. Fur. 1786 till struck off. Dir. E.I. Co. Apr. 1789 till death.

Refs. : Burke's *Peerage*, 1923, p. 1546, *s.n.* Metcalfe, Bart., of Fern Hill, Berks. *G.M.* 1813, ii. 510, 630.

METHOLD, Henry (1793-1855). Lieutenant. 22nd N.I. *bapt.* Tanfield, co. Durham, 27 June 1793. Cadet 1807. Arrived in India 21 Mar. 1809. Ensign 18 Feb. 1809. Lieut. 16 Dec. 1814. Resigned 12 Dec. 1815. *d.* Worthing, Sussex, 28 Nov. 1855, aged 62.

Of Worthing. Eldest son of Henry Methold, of Beamish, Capt. Durham Fenc. Cav., and Dorothea his wife, eldest dau. of Sir John Eden, 4th Bart., of Windlestone Hall, co. Durham, and cousin-german of John Eden, *q.v.* (? His dau. *m.* Joseph Charles Sage, *q.v.*)

Services : Barasat C.C. Posted Ensign to 22nd N.I. (? Reduction of Kalinjar 1812 ; Ensign 1/22nd N.I.)

Refs. : Burke's *Peerage*, 1923, p. 809, *s.n.* Eden, Bart., of W. Auckland, co. Durham. Ruvigny's *Plantagenet Roll of the Blood Royal*, Mortimer-Percy Vol., p. 269. *G.M.* 1856, i. 100.

METHVEN, Alexander (1806-1833). Lieutenant, 65th N.I. *b.* 23 Jan. 1806. Cadet 1825. Arrived in India 20 June 1826. Ensign 5 Feb. 1826. Lieut. 20 Sept. 1827. *d.* Mhow 24 July 1833.

bapt. Queenstown, co. Cork, 30 Jan. 1806. Son of Thomas Methven, Capt. R.N., Comdr. of Revenue Cruisers and Coastgds., Northumberland, and Eleanor his wife. Ed. St. Andrews School and Univ.

Services : Ensign d.d. 41st N.I. 8 July 1826. Posted to 65th N.I. 26 Sept. 1826, and served throughout with that Regt. Adjt. 22 Oct. 1831 till death. No record of active service.

Refs. : A.J. N.S. xiii. 205. M.I. Mhow old cemetery.

METHVEN, Cathcart (1787-1823). Captain, 20th N.I. *b.* St. Andrews 26 Nov. 1787. Cadet 1804. Arrived in India 10 Aug. 1805. Ensign 18 Aug. 1805. Lieut. 19 Aug. 1805. Capt.

1 Jan. 1819. *d. unm.* Calcutta 26 Nov. 1823, from the effects of a fall from his horse, which he survived only a few hours.

bapt. 7 Dec. 1787. Son of Robert Methven, mgte. of St. Andrews, and Euphemia Meldrum his wife. Brother of Robert, writer in Cupar, Thomas, Helen Jane, Euphemia, and Agnes Gray. St. Andrews Univ.; matric. 19 Feb. 1801.

Services: Posted Lieut. to 20th N.I. Capture of Java 1811; Lieut. 1/20th N.I. Asst. to Resdt. at Bantam 1815-16.

Refs.: S.M. 1824, i. 638. Will dated 12 Dec. 1822; proved 3 Dec. 1823. M.I. in S. Park St. cemetery, Calcutta.

MEYRICK, James (1782-1808). Lieutenant, 22nd N.I. *bapt.* Hungerford, Berks., 18 Oct. 1782. Cadet 1801. Arrived in India 6 Aug. 1802. Ensign 7 Aug. 1802. Lieut. 30 June 1804. *d.* Meerut 19 Sept. 1808.

Son of Rev. Edward Meyrick and Ann his wife.

Services: Barasat C.C. Ensign d.d. 16th N.I. 1803; posted to 22nd N.I. in 1804. (? Second Mahratta War; battle and capture of Deig; Bhurtpore; Lieut. 2/22nd N.I.)

Refs.: A.A.R. x. 299. M.I. Meerut old cemetery.

MIARS, Thomas. (*See* **MYERS, Thomas.**)

MICHAEL, Thomas (1793-1829). Bt. Captain, 17th N.I. *bapt.* Claines, Worcs., 11 Mar. 1793. Cadet 1808. Arrived in India 6 Nov. 1809. Ensign 11 Mar. 1811. Lieut. 15 May 1815. Bt. Capt. 11 Mar. 1826. *d.* Delhi 7 Oct. 1829.

Son of James Michael and Ann his wife. *m.* Kempsey, Worcs., May 1823, Mary (? Ann Maria), widow of R. Smith, of Warwick. (She died Lymington, Hants, 8 Mar. 1856.)

Services: Barasat C.C. Posted Ensign to 11th N.I. in 1811. Reduction of Kalinjar 1812; Ensign 2/11th N.I. Siege and capture of Hathras 1817; Lieut. 2/11th N.I. Third Mahratta War 1817-19; Lieut. 2/11th N.I. Fur. 17 Aug. 1821 till 1823. Transfd. to 17th N.I. (late 2/11th) May 1824.

MICHELL, Eardley Wilmot (1813-1885). 2nd Lieutenant. Artillery. (650) Subsequently vicar of Martin, Wilts. *b.* 14 July 1813. Cadet 1830. Arrived in India 3 Oct. 1831. 2nd Lieut. 13 Apr. 1831. Resigned 3 Feb. 1834. *d.* 13 Nov. 1885.

bapt. Hurstmonceaux, Sussex, 9 Sept. 1813. Son of Eardley Wilmot Michell, of Brighton, banker, and of Hurstmonceaux, and Mary his wife. Brother of John Woolmore Michell, *q.v. m.* Hordle,

Hants, 8 Feb. 1841, Catherine Spencer Alicia Beresford, younger dau. of Lt.-Col. Spencer Thomas Vassall (*D.N.B.*), and widow of Hon. Thomas Le Marchant Saumarez. (She died 28 Feb. 1877.) Ed. Eton 1826. Addiscombe Cadet 1828-30. Queens' Coll., Camb.; LL.B. 1840.

Services: Fur. s.c. 24 Jan. 1832 till resignation. No record of active service. Took holy orders. Deacon 1837; Priest 1838. Vicar of Shirley, nr. Derby, 1847-72; vicar of Martin, Wilts. Author of several religious pamphlets.

Refs.: Burke's *Landed Gentry*, 2nd edn., p. 1463, *s.n.* Vassall, of Milford. Burke's *Peerage*, 1923, p. 708, *s.n.* De Saumarez, B. *Eton School Lists. Crockford.*

MICHELL, George Bruce (1805-1866). Major General. 28th N.I. *b.* W. Teignmouth, Devon, 13 Sept. 1805. Cadet 1822. Arrived in India 7 July 1823. Ensign 11 July 1823. Lieut. 31 Jan. 1825. Capt. 1 Jan. 1843. Major 8 Mar. 1849. Lt. Col. 13 Nov. 1854. Bt. Col. 13 Nov. 1857. Retired 26 Apr. 1858. Hon. Maj. Gen. 26 Apr. 1858. *d.* Nice 11 Feb. 1866.

Younger son of Capt. John Taylor Michell, R.N., of Exeter, and Sapphira Seymour his wife, only dau. of John Baily, of Sutton Montagu, Somerset, and Ramridge House in Weyhill, I.W. *m.* Brit. Consulate, Nice, 22 Apr. 1862, Lady Frances Elizabeth Legge, eldest dau. of William, 4th Earl of Dartmouth. (She died 13 Mar. 1922, aged 92.)

Services: Posted Ensign to 8th N.I. in 1823. Transfd. to 9th N.I. (late 1/8th) May 1824. First Burma War; Arakan 1825; Lieut. 1st L.I. Bn. (India medal). Actg. Intr. & Qmr. 9th N.I. 23 Sept. 1830; Adjt. do. 23 Dec. 1832 till 15 Mar. 1836. Actg. Bde. Major at Agra 4 Sept. 1833. Placed under orders of Resdt. at Gwalior 2 Mar. 1836. Comdg. Inf. Regt. of Gwalior Contingent; employed in reduction of Kairoora, Bundelkhand, May 1841. Transfd. to newly-formed 2nd Bengal Eur. Regt. 8 Oct. 1839. Gwalior campaign; Paniar (Bronze star). Comdt. 1st Inf., Gwalior Contingent, 13 Jan. 1844 till 1849. Comdt. Sind Camel Corps Nov. 1849 till 25 Nov. 1850. Fur. s.c. 3 Jan. 1851 till Nov. 1855. Posted Lt. Col. to 59th N.I. Jan. 1855; to 2nd Eur. Fus. Feb. 1855; to 32nd N.I. 5 Aug. 1855; to 40th N.I. Oct. 1855; to 28th N.I. May 1856. Fur. 17 Mar. 1856 till 1857. Mutiny campaign; operations Feb.-Mar. 1858; taking of Rotasgarh (Medal).

Refs.: Ruvigny's *Plantagenet Roll of the Blood Royal*, Essex Vol., p. 193. Burke's *Peerage*, 1923, p. 666, *s.n.* Dartmouth, E. *G.M.* 1866, i. 455. *The Times*, 17 Feb. 1866.

MICHELL, Henry James (1813-?). Lieutenant. 72nd N.I.
b. Rathasbuck, Queen's Co., 14 May 1813. Cadet 1830. Arrived in India 2 July 1831. Ensign 11 May 1831. Lieut. 1 Dec. 1836. Cashiered by G.C.M. 1 Feb. 1843. (*d.* before Aug. 1848.)

bapt. Rathasbuck 21 May 1813. Son of James Michell, of Carter Hill, Queen's Co., and Charlotte Grace his wife. Stepson of —— Connor. *m.* Mussoorie 20 May 1837, Sophia Matilda, dau. of Local Major Henry Forster, comdg. in Shekhawat (see Appendix A). (She *re-m.* 17 Aug. 1848, Lieut. Edward Fraser, Engrs.) Addiscombe Cadet 1829-30.

Services: Cadet d.d. 38th N.I. 12 July 1831; d.d. 13th N.I. 13 Oct. 1831; d.d. 1st N.I. 16 Oct. 1832; d.d. 17th N.I. 23 Feb. 1833. Posted Ensign to 22nd N.I. 19 Oct. 1833. Shekhawat expedn. 1834; Ensign 22nd N.I. Transfd. to 72nd N.I. 24 Sept. 1835. Suspended from rank, pay and allowances for 6 mos. by G.C.M. (G.O. 28 May 1839).

MICHELL, John Woolmore (1806-1891). Major. 49th N.I.
b. Hurstmonceaux, Sussex, 3 Apr. 1806. Cadet 1821. Arrived in India 24 Sept. 1822. Ensign 27 Aug. 1822. Lieut. 10 Aug. 1824. Capt. 27 May 1830. Retired 7 June 1845. Hon. Major 28 Nov. 1854. *d.* Lisburn, Torquay, 27 June 1891.

bapt. Hurstmonceaux 29 July 1806. Son of Eardley Wilmot Michell, of Brighton, banker, and Mary his wife. Brother of William Mitchell, *q.v. m.* Seaford, Sussex, 20 Jan. 1835, Sarah Jane, dau. of H. Harrison. (She died Nimach 1 Apr. 1836.)

Services: Posted Ensign to 22nd N.I. in 1822; transfd. to 25th N.I. in 1823; to 49th N.I. (late 1/23rd) May 1824. Operations against the Bhils 1824. First Burma War; Arakan 1825; Lieut. 49th N.I. Intr. & Qmr. 49th N.I. 25 Sept. 1826 till 10 Apr. 1830. Fur. p.a. 11 Oct. 1832 till 24 July 1835.

Refs.: A.J. N.S. xvi. 151. *The Times*, 30 June 1891.

*MICHELL, William (1808-1825). Ensign, 22nd N.I. *b.* Hurstmonceaux, Sussex, 14 Aug. 1808. Cadet 1824. Arrived in India 9 Feb. 1825. Ensign (12 Sept. 1824). *d.* Calcutta 27 July 1825.

bapt. Hurstmonceaux 21 Oct. 1808. Son of Eardley Wilmot Michell, of Wargroves, Sussex, and of Brighton, banker, and Mary his wife. Brother of Eardley Wilmot Michell, *q.v.*

Services: Ensign d.d. 20th N.I. 18 Feb. 1825; d.d. 28th N.I. 12 Apr. 1825; posted to 22nd N.I.

Refs.: M.I. in Bhowanipore mily. cemetery, Calcutta.

MICHIE, John Donald [1] (*d.* 1801). Captain, 2nd N.I. Country Cadet 1780. Admitted 4 Jan. 1780. Ensign 14 Sept. 1780. Lieut. 31 May 1781. Capt. 10 Sept. 1798. *d. unm.* in Egypt 19 Sept. 1801 : kld. by a fall from his horse.

(*Probably* son of John Michie, of Moffats, N. Mimms, Herts., Dir. E.I. Co., or of his brother Jonathan, merchant, Craven St., Strand, London.) Brother of Jonathan Michie, Capt. Bo. Marine, uncle of John Leys, *q.v.*, and of James Ross, and related to Jonathan Duncan, Govr. of Bombay (*D.N.B.*).

Services : Was Adjt. Ramgarh L.I. Bn. in Mar. 1786 ; do. 31st Bn. Sepoys in July 1787 and in 1793. Lieut. 2/10th N.I. With force employed in Hyderabad, Oct. 1798, in disarming Nizam's troops officered by Frenchmen under M. Raymond ; Lieut. 2/10th N.I. Posted Capt. to 2/2nd N.I. Oct. 1798, but was directed to remain with 2/10th till further orders and to officiate as Adjt. & Qmr. Fourth Mysore War 1799 ; capture of Seringapatam ; Capt. 2/10th N.I. Expedn. to Egypt 1801 ; sailed in the Transport *Eliza* ; Capt. Bengal Vols.

Refs. : Aberdeen Journal N. *& Q.* i. 166. Will dated 24 Mar. 1801 ; proved 3 Nov. 1802.

[1] *Note :* " *Alias* John Michie." (Will.)

MIDDLEDITCH, John Richard (*d.* 1799). Lieutenant. Infantry. Cadet 1782. Arrived in India 22 Jan. 1783. Ensign 4 Apr. 1783. Lieut. 7 Mar. 1790. Struck off 1791. *d.* Bath 17 Feb. 1799.

Of Pickwell House, Georgeham, Devon. *m.* (?) (She *re-m.* Gen. Mackenzie.)

Services : Apptd. Cadet 10 Oct. 1781 ; sailed for India in the *Royal Henry* 6 Feb. 1782. Posted Ensign to 2nd Eur. Regt. 28 Feb. 1783 ; on fur. in Dec. 1788. Subsequently a grocer in London.[1] Apptd. Capt. of the Georgeham Vols. (*Lond. Gaz.* 1 Sept. 1798).

Refs. : G.M. 1799, i. 174.

[1] *Note : Perhaps* son of Joseph Middleditch, grocer in Budge Row, London, who *d.* 1788.

MIDDLETON, Charles (1762/63-1803). Major, 3rd N.C. *b.* Bengal 1762/63. Cadet 1779. Admitted 12 Sept. 1780. Ensign 28 June 1779. Lieut. 19 Feb. 1781. Capt. 1 Nov. 1798. Major 13 Nov. 1800. *d.* 11 Sept. 1803, from fatigue and sun-stroke during the battle of Delhi.

Brother of Samuel Middleton. (*Probably* son of Samuel Middleton, B.C.S., Presdt. of the Board of Trade, and Ann his wife, whose son Samuel was *bapt.* Calcutta 9 Jan. 1763. *Probably* uncle of William Middleton (1783-1822), *q.v.*)

Services : Sailed for India in the *True Briton* 16 June 1779, aged 16. Lieut. 15th Bn. Sepoys in July 1787 and Dec. 1792. To comd. Capt. William Kirkpatrick's escort 6 Nov. 1794 ; comdg. at Jellasore in Aug. 1795 ; Capt. 3rd N.C. in 1798. Operations in Jumna Doab 1803 ; Sasni ; Bijaigarh ; Kachaura ; Major comdg. 3rd N.C. Second Mahratta War ; Battle of Delhi ; Major comdg. 3rd N.C.

Refs. : Pester, *passim. A.J.* v. 325. Will dated camp nr. Ugowly, 9 Dec. 1802 ; proved 29 Sept. 1803.

MIDDLETON, Edmund Pytts (1760/61-1810). Lieutenant. Infantry. Subsequently a Senior Merchant, B.C.S. *b.* 1760/61. Cadet 1779. Ensign 12 Feb. 1780. Lieut. 26 Feb. 1781. Resigned 13 Aug. 1782. *d.* Calcutta 7 June 1810.

Son of Mrs. Hansard. Half-brother of Capt. John Hansard and cousin of Adm. Sir Graham Eden Hamond, G.C.B., 2nd Bart. (*D.N.B.*)

Services : Ensign H.M. 48th Ft. 12 Sept. 1776. Apptd. Cadet 19 May 1779. Apptd a Writer, B.C.S., 1 Aug. 1780. Salt Agent to the 24-Parganas 28 Feb. 1801.

Refs. : Will dated Barripore, 2 June 1809 ; proved 12 June 1810. M.I. in N. Park St. cemetery, Calcutta.

MIDDLETON, George (*d.* 1771). Lieutenant, Infantry. Cadet 1766. Ensign 4 Sept. 1766. Lieut. 15 Sept. 1767. *d.* Sept. 1771.

Services : N.F.P.

MIDDLETON, George (1765/66-1789). Ensign, Infantry. *b.* 1765/66. Cadet 1782. Ensign 30 Mar. 1783. *d.* Dacca 17 Oct. 1789, aged 23.

Services : Apptd. Cadet 7 Nov. 1781 ; sailed for India in the *Rodney* 11 Sept. 1782 ; arrived in India 10 Sept. 1783.

Refs. : M.I. at Dacca.

MIDDLETON, John Forbes (1809-1857). Captain, Invalid Est. 32nd N.I. *b.* Madras 8 Apr. 1809. Cadet 1824. Arrived in India 28 Dec. 1825. Ensign 13 May 1825. Lieut. 30 Jan. 1828. Capt. 19 Dec. 1842. Invalided 30 Nov. 1844. *d.* Dacca 6 Dec. 1857.

bapt. Cannanore, Madras, 10 Dec. 1809. Son of John Middleton and Amelia his wife. Nephew of Maj.-Gen. Charles Middleton, Col. 2nd D.G. *m.* Dacca 2 Apr. 1839, Maria Agnes, only dau. of Robert Doucett, of Dacca. (She died Serampore 27 Jan. 1876, aged 61.)

Services : Posted Ensign to 32nd N.I. Actg. Adjt. to a detachment of Rajputana F.F. under Capt. R. Hawkes, *q.v.,* 12 Nov. 1832. Shekhawat expedn. 1834 ; Lieut. 32nd N.I. Actg. Adjt. 32nd N.I. 14 Mar. 1839.

Refs. : I.M. 28 Jan. 1858, p. 58. Will dated 1 Aug. 1856 ; proved 25 May 1858.

MIDDLETON, John Henry (1796-1831). Bt. Captain, Artillery. (445) *b.* 11 Aug. 1796. Cadet 1812. Admitted 14 Aug. 1813. Fireworker 23 Aug. 1813. Lieut. 1 Sept. 1818. Bt. Capt. 23 Aug. 1828. *d.* Cawnpore 4 Mar. 1831.

bapt. Hinton Ampner, Hants, 19 Nov. 1796. Eldest son of John Charles Middleton, of Chawton (of Twyford), Hants, formerly B.C.S., and Charlotte his wife. Brother of Rev. Frederick Graeme Middleton and of Mrs. Susan Barwell, and cousin-german of William Middleton (1783-1822), *q.v. m.* Matilda. (She died Nasirabad 22 Oct. 1824, aged 19.) Ed. Winchester. Addiscombe Cadet 1811-12.

Services : Third Mahratta War ; Lieut. 1st Coy. 1st Bn. Foot Art. Adjt. & Qmr. Rajputana Div. Art. 2 Apr. 1822 till 25 Sept. 1826. Fur. s.c. 19 Sept. 1826 till 13 May 1830.

Refs. : A.J. N.S. vi. 79. Will dated 14 Aug. 1830 ; proved 10 June 1831.

***MIDDLETON, Peter** (*d.* 1823). Lieutenant, 22nd N.I. Cadet 1818. Was already in India when apptd. Cadet. Ensign 8 Sept. 1819. Lieut. 20 Jan. 1822. *d.* Karnal 9 Oct. 1823.

Services : Posted Ensign to 1/22nd N.I. No record of active service.

***MIDDLETON, Ralph.** Lieutenant. Infantry. Cadet 1765. Ensign 14 Aug. 1765. Lieut. 30 Dec. 1766.

Services : Ensign 3rd Bengal Eur. Regt. in 1766 ; resigned during the " Batta mutiny " ; subsequently readmitted.

Refs. : B.M. Add. MS. 6050, pp. 67, 90.

MIDDLETON, William (*d.* 1783). Ensign, Infantry. Cadet 1782. Ensign 1783. *d.* Madras harbour 19 Apr. 1783 : blown up in the *Duke of Athol.* (See note to James Barnes.)

Services : Apptd. Cadet 17 May 1782 ; sailed for India in the *Duke of Athol* 11 Sept. 1782.

MIDDLETON, William (1783-1822). Major, 16th N.I. *bapt.* Calcutta 15 Dec. 1783. Cadet 1798. Admitted 23 Oct. 1800. Ensign 12 Oct. 1799. Lieut. 28 Oct. 1799. Capt. 16 Oct. 1810. Dismissed by G.C.M. 4 Aug. 1811. Restored in England 14 Apr. 1813. Major 5 Oct. 1821. *d.* Kamptee, C.P., 25 Dec. 1822. Son of Nathaniel Middleton ("Memory Middleton"), B.C.S., sometime Resdt. at Lucknow, and Anna Frances his wife, sister of Robert Morse, of the Calcutta Bar, sheriff of Calcutta 1784. Nephew of William Cator, *q.v.* (? and of Charles Middleton, *q.v.*), and cousin-german of John Henry Middleton, *q.v.* Brother of Mrs. Louisa Herbert and of the wife of Charles Tucker, B.C.S.

Services : Posted Lieut. to 1/16th N.I. 15 Apr. 1801. Operations in Jumna Doab 1803 ; attack on Thathia fort ; Lieut. 1/16th N.I. With 2nd Vol. Bn. 1804-5. Adjt. & Qmr. 16th N.I. 1805 till Oct. 1810. Operations in Bundelkhand 1809-11 ; Capt. 16th N.I. Posted to 2/16th N.I. on his return to India. With 7th Gren. Bn. 1815-16. Transfd. as Major to 1/16th N.I. Served with Narbada F.F.

Refs. Burke's *Landed Gentry*, 13th edn., p. 1242, *s.n.* Middleton, of Bradford Peverell, Dorset. Will dated Calpee 5 Sept. 1821 ; proved 17 Jan. 1823.

MIDFORD, William Herbert Wood (1807-?). Lieutenant. 2nd Bengal Eur. Regt. *b.* Sevenoaks, Kent, 1 Nov. 1807. Cadet 1824. Arrived in India 15 May 1825. Ensign 14 Nov. 1824. Lieut. 20 Apr. 1826. Cashiered by G.C.M. 4 Jan. 1829.

bapt. Sevenoaks 16 Dec. 1807. Posthumous son of William Herbert Midford and Ann his wife, dau. of Thomas Mortimer Kelson, of Sevenoaks, surgeon. Stepson of John Down, of Noah's Ark, Herts.

Services : Ensign d.d. 2nd Bengal Eur. Regt. 3 June 1825 ; posted Ensign to 37th N.I. in 1825. Siege and capture of Bhurtpore ; Ensign 37th N.I. Transfd. to 46th N.I. in 1826 ; exchanged to 2nd Bengal Eur. Regt. 12 Mar. 1827.

Refs. : *A.J.* xxvii. 468, 740.

MIDWINTER, William (1777-1818). Major, 1st N.I. *b.* Kingston, Jamaica, 11 June 1777. Cadet 1795. Arrived in India 15 Mar. 1797. Ensign 3 Nov. 1796. Lieut. 30 Oct. 1797. Capt. 19 Oct. 1805. Major 16 Dec. 1814. *d.* nr. Saugor 16 Oct. 1818.

Son of Dr. William Midwinter and Elizabeth his wife. *m.* 1st, Calcutta 11 Apr. 1798, Elizabeth, dau. of Shearman Bird, senr., B.C.S. *m.* 2nd, London, June 1811, Ann, youngest dau. of M. Thomas, of Pinner Green, Middlesex. (She *re-m.* Richard Newton, *q.v.*)

Services: Lieut. 1st N.I. in 1798. Operations in Bundelkhand 1806-7; Chamir; Sehlehuganj; Capt. 2/1st N.I. Bundelkhand 1809; Rajaoli; Ajaigarh; Capt. 2/1st N.I. Fur. 1810-12. Nepal War 1814-15; Major 2/1st N.I., in 1st Div. Capture of Hathras 1817; Major 2/1st N.I. Third Mahratta War 1817-18; Dhamoni; Major 2/1st N.I.

Refs.: M.M. 1811, i. 562. *Lady Nugent's Journal* (1934 edn.).

MILES, Frederick Alexander (1807-1852). Bt. Major. Artillery. (561) *b.* London 22 Apr. 1807. Cadet 1824. Arrived in India 8 May 1825. 2nd Lieut. 13 Oct. 1824. Lieut. 28 Sept. 1827. Capt. 20 Feb. 1843. Bt. Major 11 Nov. 1851. Retired 16 May 1852. *d.* New England, nr. Hitchin, Herts., 28 Aug. 1852.

3rd son of William Augustus Miles, pol. writer (*D.N.B.*), and Harriet Watkinson, of Bristol, his 2nd wife. Brother of Rawdon Muir Miles, *q.v. m.* St. Pancras, Middlesex, 13 Jan. 1842, Ellen, youngest dau. of Brown Collison, of Guildford St., London, and of New England. (She *re-m.* 20 Feb. 1856, Col. William Tod Brown, C.B., Bengal Art.) Ed. Westminster 12 Jan. till 28 July 1818. Addiscombe Cadet 1822-4.

Services: Intr. & Qmr. 7th Bn. Foot Art. 9 Feb. 1833; do. 6th Bn. 18 Nov. 1838 till 4 Dec. 1840. Fur. p.a. 8 Mar. 1841 till 15 Mar. 1844. Second Sikh War; no actions; Capt. comdg. 2nd Coy. 7th Bn. (No. 6 Field Battery).

Refs.: *Westminster School Register*. *I.M.* 1 Sept. 1852, p. 499. *G.M.* 1852, ii. 436.

MILES, Rawdon Muir (1808-1842). Bt. Captain, 5th N.I. *b.* London 29 Oct. 1808. Cadet 1824. Arrived in India 8 May 1825. Ensign 9 Jan. 1825. Lieut. 25 Apr. 1826. Capt. 23 Nov. 1841. *d.* Tangi Tariki, nr. Kabul, 10 Jan. 1842; kld. in action during the retreat.

bapt. Marylebone 25 Aug. 1817. 4th son of William Augustus Miles, of Marylebone Lane, and Harriet his wife. Brother of Robert Henry Miles, *q.v.* Ed. Repton Priory, co. Derby.

Services: Ensign d.d. 16th N.I. 23 May 1825; posted Ensign to 5th N.I. in 1825. Actg. Intr. & Qmr. 29th N.I. 20 Dec. 1827; do. 72nd N.I. 22 Sept. 1829; Intr. & Qmr. 5th N.I. 18 Feb. 1831

till death. First Afghan War 1840-2 ; outbreak at Kabul ; retreat from Kabul (kld.) ; Capt. 5th N.I.
Refs.: G.M. 1843, i. 554. *The Times,* 21 Jan. 1843. M.I. in St. Peter's, Fort William, Bengal.

MILES, Robert Henry (1805-1867). Lieut. Colonel. 1st N.I. *b.* London 30 Mar. 1805. Cadet 1820. Arrived in India Sept. 1821. Ensign 5 May 1821. Lieut. 2 Apr. 1824. Capt. 20 June 1833. Bt. Major 9 Nov. 1846. Invalided 1 Feb. 1850. Retired 6 May 1861. Hon. Lt. Col. 6 May 1861. *d.* Valetta, Malta, 18 Apr. 1867.

Son of William Augustus Miles, of Branksea I., Poole, Dorset, and Harriet his 2nd wife. Brother of Frederick Alexander Miles, *q.v.* Ed. Westminster 12 Jan. till 28 July 1818.

Services : Posted Ensign to 1/28th N.I. Transfd. to 12th N.I. in 1823 ; to 12th N.I. (late 1/12th) May 1824 ; to 1st N.I. (late 2/12th) 7 Aug. 1824 (? 13 Aug. 1825). Actg. Post Adjt. at Hoshangabad 7 Nov. 1825. Leave s.c. 6 mos. to Penang and Singapore 13 May 1826. Fur. s.c. 8 Dec. 1827 till 5 Oct. 1830, and 15 Aug. 1834 till 12 June 1837. Fur. p.a. 13 Sept. 1843 till Mar. 1848. Second Sikh War ; in garr. at fort Govindgarh, Amritsar ; Bt. Major 1st N.I. (Medal). Fur. s.c. 2 yrs. to Cape and Aust. Dec. 1850 ; fur. s.c. 9 Sept. 1853 till 3 Feb. 1857, and 2 Sept. 1859 till retirement.

Refs. : Westminster School Register. G.M. 1867, i. 822.

MILFORD, Richard. Ensign. Infantry. Cadet 1783. Never arrived in India. Ensign 1783. Struck off 1788.

Services : Apptd. Cadet 19 Mar. 1783 ; was to have sailed for India in the *Earl of Mansfield* 10 Feb. 1784. Shown as on fur. in 1787.

MILLAR, John (1811-1842). Bt. Captain, 26th N.I. *b.* Agra 1 Aug. 1811. Cadet 1827. Arrived in India 20 June 1828. Ensign 10 Jan. 1828. Lieut. 23 Apr. 1834. Bt. Capt. 1842. *d.* at sea 17 Sept. 1842, on board the *Conqueror.*

bapt. Agra 29 Oct. 1811. Son of Archibald Millar, Surg. H.M. 47th Foot, and Margaret his wife.

Services : Ensign d.d. 7th N.I. 17 July 1828. Posted Ensign to 26th N.I. 4 Nov. 1828. Apptd. to d.d. Assam L.I. 6 Feb. 1835 ; and joined July 1835. Operations against the Singphos Aug. 1835 ; against Duffa Gaum, a rebel chief ; action before Beesa stockade Nov. 1835 (s.w. in shoulder) ; against the Singphos in Meriabhum

Hills, Assam, 17 Nov. 1835, in charge of a mortar (s.w.). Actg.
2nd in comd. Assam L.I. 6 Feb. 1836. Rejoined 26th N.I. 14 Jan.
1839. Granted a wound pension June 1839. Fur. s.c. 17 May
1839 till 28 June 1842, and 12 Sept. 1842 till death.
Refs.: *The Times*, 20 Jan. 1843.

MILLCARD, John (*d*. 1772). Cadet, Infantry. Cadet 1771.
d. 15 Jan. 1772; drowned.
Services: N.F.P.

MILLER, Alexander George (1808-1847). Captain. 39th N.I.
b. Glasgow 18 June 1808. Cadet 1824. Arrived in India 9 Aug.
1825. Ensign 11 Apr. 1825. Lieut. 30 Sept. 1827. Capt.
24 Jan. 1845. Retired 15 Aug. 1845. *d*. Largs, co. Ayr, 19 Feb.
1847.
4th son of Robert Miller, of Glasgow, spirit dealer, and Katharine
his wife. Ed. Glasgow High School and Univ.; matric. 1823.
Services: Posted Ensign to 39th N.I. in 1825. Offg. Adjt.
39th N.I. 19 May 1835. Adjt. 2nd Inf. Levy at Jaunpur 22 Feb.
till 21 June 1842. With Army of Reserve (for Afghanistan) Oct.
1842 till Jan. 1843; Bt. Capt. 39th N.I. Fur. s.c. 2 yrs. to Cape
and Aust. 27 Aug. 1843 till retirement. No record of active service.

MILLER, George (1806-1862). Major. 25th N.I. *b*. London
27 June 1806. Cadet 1823. Arrived in India 19 May 1824.
Ensign 17 Jan. 1824. Lieut. 27 Mar. 1826. Capt. 23 Aug.
1834. Retired 15 Aug. 1844. Hon. Major 28 Nov. 1854. *d*.
18 New Ormond St., London, 11 May 1862.
bapt. St. Margaret's, Westminster, 10 Mar. 1809. Son of Major
George Miller, C.B., H.M. 14th Regt., and Mary his wife. *m*. Titalia,
Bengal, 22 Aug. 1828, Miss Catherine Eliza Adams.
Services: Posted Ensign to 1st Bengal Eur. Regt. in 1824.
Transfd. to newly-raised 5th Extra Regt. May 1825; as Lieut. to
40th N.I. 1826; to 25th N.I. 2 Mar. 1827. Actg. Intr. & Qmr.
25th N.I. 3 Mar. 1829; actg. Adjt. do. 30 June 1832; permanent
do. 29 Apr. till 16 Sept. 1834. Comdd. 25th N.I. 31 Aug. 1834
till 19 Aug. 1835. Crimean war; Local Major in Turkey 23 Mar.
1855.
Refs.: *The Times*, 17 May 1862.

MILLER, Robert (1782-1804). Ensign, Infantry. Unposted.
b. Sligo Nov. 1782. Cadet 1802. Never arrived in India.
Ensign 13 Dec. 1803. *d*. at sea 16 Feb. 1804, on board the
Lord Melville, on his passage to India.

*MILLIGAN, Robert (1709-1759). Lieutenant. Infantry. *bapt.*
Newton Longville, Bucks., 16 Feb. 1709. Lieut. 3 Mar. 1758.
Discharged Mar. 1759. *d.* Calcutta 25 Nov. 1759.
Son of David Milligan and Ann Tompkins his wife. *m.* Newton
Longville 29 Nov. 1742, Ann Goodman, of Leckhamstead.
Services: Apptd. in England 11 Feb. 1756, agent for raising
recruits in any part of Gt. Britain for the service of E.I. Co.; apptd.
a Lieut. on the Bengal Est. Mar. 1758; sailed as a Lieut. in the
Pitt in 1758, when he gave his age as 42. In Mar. 1759, the Council
at Ft. Wm. decided that he was not to have a Commission, " for
behaving unlike an officer and a gentleman in his passage from
Europe," but was to return to Europe in the *Bombay Castle.*

MILLS, Charles Ernest[1] (1809-1846). Bt. Major, Artillery.
(582) *bapt.* Handley, Dorset, 22 Oct. 1809. Cadet 1825.
Arrived in India 22 Oct. 1826. 2nd Lieut. 21 May 1826.
Lieut. 17 May 1833. Capt. 3 July 1845. Bt. Major 3 Apr.
1846. *d.* Ambala 29 Dec. 1846.

Son of Andrew Moffatt Mills, of Knoyle, Capt. 1st Ft. Gds., and
Penelope his wife. Brother of John Andrew Moffatt Mills, of
Tortington House, Arundel, Sussex, and grandson of Sir Thomas
Mills, Kt., Town Major of Quebec. *m.* Simla 12 Sept. 1844,
Susannah, dau. of William Chadwick, of the Octagon, Plymouth,
late H.M. 66th Regt., and niece of Thomas Chadwick, *q.v.* (She
re-m. London 28 Oct. 1848, R. T. Hopkins.) Addiscombe Cadet
6 Aug. 1824 till 16 Dec. 1825.

Services: Posted to 12th Coy. 6th Bn. Foot Art. Dec. 1826.
Transfd. to 2nd Troop 2nd Bde. H.A. Dec. 1828; to 1st Troop
1st Bde. Sept. 1834; to 1st Troop 3rd Bde. Nov. 1836. Asst. in
Thagi Dept. 12 Jan. 1836. Transfd. to 2nd Troop 3rd Bde. H.A.
May 1839. Offg. Asst. to A.G.G., N.W.F. Jan. 1842. Transfd. to
1st Troop 2nd Bde. Aug. 1842; to 2nd Troop 3rd Bde. Dec. 1843.
Gwalior campaign; Maharajpur; Lieut. 2nd Troop 3rd Bde.
(Bronze star). Reapptd. Asst. to A.G.G., N.W.F., 18 Jan. 1844.
Posted Capt. to 3rd Coy. 5th Bn. Foot Art. July 1845. First Sikh
War; Mudki, on Staff of G.G.; Ferozshahr, Capt. comdg. 1st
Troop 1st Bde. H.A.; Sobraon, Hon. A.D.C. to G.G. (Medal with
2 clasps). Apptd. Supt. of Ambala Jan. 1846. D.C. and P.A.
cis-Sutlej territory 16 Mar. 1846 till death.

Refs.: Burke's *Colonial Gentry,* ii. 587, *s.n.* Chadwick. *De
Rhé-Philipe.* *G.M.* 1847, ii. 557. Will dated 23 Dec. 1846; proved
4 Feb. 1847. M.I. at Ambala.

[1] *Note:* He signs himself Charles Earnest Mills.

THE BENGAL ARMY, 1758-1834   297

MILLS, James (d. 1789). Ensign, Infantry. Cadet 1783. Ensign 28 Mar. 1785. d. Calcutta 26 Sept. 1789.
Services: Was abroad when apptd. Cadet 16 Jan. 1783. Fur. on h.p. 2 Oct. 1786.

*MILLS, John. Lieutenant. Infantry. Cadet (?) Ensign (?) Lieut. 1 Nov. 1765.
Services: N.F.P. Probably transfd. from H.M.S.
Refs.: B.M. Addl. MS. 6050.

MILLS, William (d. 1773). Ensign, Infantry. Cadet 1770. Ensign 6 Dec. 1771. d. Berhampore 24 Nov. 1773.
Services: N.F.P.

MILNE, Alexander. Ensign. Infantry. Cadet 1765. Ensign 9 Aug. 1765. Dismissed 1766.
Services: Probably dismissed as one of the ringleaders of the "Batta mutiny" in May 1766.

MILNE, Henry (1812-1879). Lieut. General. 1st N.I. (recently 1st Brahmins, now 4th Bn. 1st Punjab Regt.). b. London 15 Feb. 1812. Cadet 1828. Arrived in India 27 Aug. 1829. Ensign (7 Mar. 1829) 5 June 1829. Lieut. 8 Oct. 1839. Capt. 1 May 1846. Major 28 Feb. 1856. Lt. Col. 25 Aug. 1859. Col. 25 Aug. 1864. Maj. Gen. 11 Jan. 1870. Lt. Gen. 1 Oct. 1877. d. 10 Lansdown Rd., Notting Hill, London, 16 Oct. 1879.
Son of John Deas Thompson Milne and Ann Maria Darke his wife. Ward of John Deas Thompson, Comr. of H.M. Navy. m. Hansi 9 Mar. 1835, Marian, dau. of Major Robert Skinner, 1st Local Horse (see Appendix A). (She was massacred at Hansi May 1857.) m. 2nd, ——
Services: Posted Ensign to 21st N I. 7 Jan. 1830. Actg. Adjt. Left Wing 21st N.I. 17 June 1834 and 19 Apr. 1836. Apptd. to Comst. Dept. of Shah Shuja's Contingent 18 Sept. 1838. First Afghan War 1839-42; capture of Ghazni 1839 (Medal); Bamian 1840; defence of Kalat-i-Ghilzai Aug. 1841 till June 1842 (Medal); Goaine; Ghazni; Kabul; Comst. Dept., with Gen. Nott's force. In charge of Abkari Dept. at Ghazipur 14 Aug. 1843. Operations on N.W.F. under Sir Sydney Cotton in Apr. 1858; Major 21st N.I. (Medal with clasp). Posted Lt. Col. to 21st N.I. (became 1st B.N.I. in 1861) in 1859; Comdt. do. 1 Jan. 1864 till 10 Mar. 1867. Fur. p.a. 10 Mar. 1867 till death.
Refs.: The Times, 21 Oct. 1879.

MILNER, Edward Touchet (1804-1843). Captain, 30th N.I.
b. London 9 May 1804. Cadet 1823. Arrived in India 26 July 1824. Ensign 3 Mar. 1824. Lieut. 25 Jan. 1825. Capt. 4 Oct. 1832. *d.* Sunninghill, Berks., 3 Nov. 1843.

bapt. Marylebone 5 July 1804. Son of Thomas Wheeler Milner, of Manchester Sq., London, and of Wheelerfield, Jamaica, and Barbara his wife, 3rd dau. of Gill Slater, of Liverpool, merchant. Brother of Ferdinand Charles Milner, *q.v.*, and related to Alexander Nowell, *q.v. m.* Calcutta 17 Nov. 1835, Emma, dau. of George Hunter (1785-1819), *q.v.* (*See also* Ferdinand Charles Milner and John Scott (1801-1848).) (She *re-m.* Henry William Matthews, *q.v.*)

Services : Posted Ensign to 31st N.I. in 1824. Siege and capture of Bhurtpore ; Lieut. 31st N.I. Operations against the Bhils 1827-8 ; Lieut. 31st N.I. Actg. Intr. & Qmr. 31st N.I. 21 Feb. 1829 ; permanent do. 28 Sept. 1829. Transfd. to 30th N.I. 7 July 1830 ; Intr. & Qmr. do. 14 July 1830 till 23 Dec. 1832. Actg. Bde. Major at Meerut 23 Mar. 1836. Offg. 2nd Asst. Mily. Auditor Gen. 20 May 1839 ; offg. 1st do. 11 Mar. 1840 ; apptd. 2nd Asst. do. 13 May 1840. Leave s.c. to N.S.W. 28 July 1840 till 11 July 1842. Fur. s.c. 11 Oct. 1842 till death.

Refs. : Burke's *Landed Gentry*, 4th edn., p. 1386, *s.n.* Slater, of Chesterfield. *G.M.* 1843, ii. 664. *The Times*, 8 Nov. 1843, p. 7.

MILNER, Ferdinand Charles (1802-1845). Captain, 36th N.I.
b. London 17 May 1802. Cadet 1821. Arrived in India 12 July 1822. Ensign 18 Jan. 1822. Lieut. 11 Sept. 1823. Capt. 1 Feb. 1840. *d.* Meerut 17 July 1845.

bapt. Marylebone 28 June 1802. 4th son of Thomas Wheeler Milner and Barbara his wife. Brother of William Peel Milner, *q.v. m.* Calcutta 3 Feb. 1837, Louisa, 2nd dau. of George Hunter, *q.v.* (*See also* Edward Touchet Milner.) (She died Calcutta 22 June 1840, aged 26.)

Services : Posted Ensign to 26th N.I. in 1822 ; transfd. to 18th N.I. in 1823 ; to 37th N.I. (late 2/18th) May 1824 ; to 36th N.I. 13 May 1825. Adjt. newly-raised 12th Extra Regt. 21 May 1825 till its reduction in 1826. Shekhawat expedn. 1834 ; Lieut. 36th N.I. Leave s.c. to Cape 8 Mar. 1837 till 4 Jan. 1839. Employed with a detachment of his Regt. in Upper Assam in June 1840. Actg. Bde. Major to Bdr. J. H. Littler's force on E. frontier 7 Jan. 1841. Offg. Executive Ofr., P.W.D., Dinapore 15 Apr. 1843.

Refs. : *G.M.* 1845, ii. 550. *I.M.* 4 Oct. 1845, p. 585. Will dated 22 Sept. 1840 ; proved 1 May 1846.

THE BENGAL ARMY, 1758-1834   299

MILNER, John (1804-1846). Captain. 9th L.C. *b.* Preston Hall 4 Feb. 1804. Cadet 1823. Cornet 1 May 1824. Lieut. 13 Jan. 1825. Capt. 29 Nov. 1831. Invalided 23 July 1832. Retired 25 Apr. 1835. *d.* 6 Oct. 1846.

bapt. Aylesford, Kent, 2 Apr. 1804. 2nd son of Charles Milner (formerly Cottam), of Preston Hall, nr. Maidstone, and Harriet his wife, youngest dau. of Sir John Dixon Dyke, Bart. Cousin-german of Augustus Hart Dyke, *q.v.*

Services: Posted Cornet to 8th L.C. in 1824. Siege and capture of Bhurtpore; Lieut. 8th L.C., d.d. 9th L.C. Transfd. to 9th L.C. in 1826. Fur. s.c. 1827 till 21 Oct. 1831, and 1 Oct. 1832 till retirement.

Refs.: Berry's *Kent Genealogies*, p. 82.

MILNER, William Peel (1806-1847). Captain, 31st N.I. *b.* London 22 Nov. 1806. Cadet 1824. Arrived in India 5 Sept. 1825. Ensign 6 Apr. 1825. Lieut. 28 Mar. 1826. Capt. 27 Mar. 1837. *d.* Calcutta 25 Dec. 1847.

bapt. Marylebone 29 Dec. 1806. 7th son of Thomas Wheeler Milner and Barbara his wife. Brother of Edward Touchet Milner, *q.v.* His maternal aunt *m.* John Peel, brother of Sir Robert Peel, 1st Bart.

Services: Posted Ensign to 31st N.I. in 1825. Operations against the Chuars 1832; Lieut. 31st N.I. Intr. & Qmr. 31st N.I. 8 July 1833 till 1837. Actg. detachment Staff Ofr. to troops assembled for service in Singhbhum against the Kols 22 Dec. 1836. Fur. p.a. 28 Mar. 1837 till 10 Jan. 1840. Offg. A.A.G. of the Army 4 Mar. 1840 and 3 Mar. 1841. Offg. A.A.G. Dinapore Div. 13 Oct. 1841 till May 1843, when he rejoined 31st N.I. Comdt. 2nd Oudh Local Inf. 21 July till 26 Dec. 1843. D.A.A.G. Presdy. Div. 9 Sept. 1843; A.A.G. do. at Barrackpore 19 Mar. 1846 till death.

Refs.: *I.M.* 22 Feb. 1848, p. 103. Will dated 1 June 1846; proved 31 Dec. 1847. Hunter's *Familiæ Minorum Gentium*, i. 215.

MINCHIN, Frederick Calder (1808-1871). Lieut. Colonel. 67th N.I. *b.* Bottley Grange, Hants, 3 Dec. 1808. Cadet 1825. Arrived in India 3 Feb. 1827. Ensign 12 Sept. 1826. Lieut. 8 Dec. 1828. Capt. 9 Nov. 1840. Bt. Major 11 Nov. 1851. Retired 17 May 1854. Hon. Lt. Col. 28 Nov. 1854. *d.s.p.* 23 Hanover Sq., London, 10 Dec. 1871.

bapt. Soberton, Hants, 28 Oct. 1809. 3rd son of Henry Minchin, of Holywell, and Elizabeth his 1st wife, elder dau. of John Guitton, of Little Park, Hants.

Services : Ensign d.d. 67th N.I. 16 Feb. 1827. Posted to 30th N.I. 10 May 1827 ; to 67th N.I. 31 May 1827. Actg. Intr. & Qmr. 67th N.I. 2 May 1832. Fur. s.c. 25 Nov. 1835 till 7 Feb. 1839. A.D.C. on personal staff of Lt. Govr. of N.W.P. 15 Sept. 1841 ; offg. Pte. Sec. do. 2 Dec. 1842. A.D.C. and Pte. Sec. to James Thomason, Lt. Govr. N.W.P., 12 Dec. 1843 till Mar. 1852. Rejoined his Regt. for service in Burma 9 Mar. 1852. Second Burma War 1852-3 ; operations in vicinity and capture of Rangoon Apr. 1852, with 40th N.I. ; Pegu ; comdd. a detachment of 67th N.I. in a combined naval and mily. expedn. against the rebel chief Myat Toon, of Donabyu, in co-operation with Capt. Loch, R.N., Feb. 1853 ; Bt. Major 67th N.I. (Medal with clasp).

Refs.: Burke's *Landed Gentry of Ireland, p.* 480, *s.n.* Minchin, of Annagh, co. Tipperary. *Fortescue,* xii. 492. *The Times,* 13 Dec. 1871.

Note: The *I.M.* of 16 Mar. 1853 erroneously reports his death as having occurred at Rangoon.

MINIFIE, Burnet (*d.* 1768). Captain, Infantry. Capt. 27 July 1765. *d.* in India May 1768.

N.B.—The following is conjectural only : (*Probably* son of Rev. James Minifie, of Staplegrove, Somerset. If so, matric. Wadham Coll., Oxon., 16 Dec. 1755, aged 18.)

Services : Ensign H.M. 32nd Ft. 22 Apr. 1757 ; Lieut. do. 26 June 1758 ; Capt. 122nd Ft. (in Ireland) 31 Dec. 1762 ; Irish h.p. 1763. Apptd. in England 10 Apr. 1764, Capt. on the Bengal Est. ; sailed for India in the *Prince of Wales* 16 May 1764. Posted to 2nd Bengal Eur. Regt. 5 Aug. 1765.

Refs.: (? *Alumni Oxon.*) Will dated 1 Sept. 1767 ; proved 22 Jan. 1771.

MINTO, William (1797-1857). Lieut. Colonel. 18th N.I. *b.* Stoke, Hants, 17 Apr. 1797. Cadet 1817. Admitted 4 Aug. 1818. Ensign 13 Mar. 1818. Lieut. 1 Aug. 1818. Capt. 15 Nov. 1828. Major 1 Apr. 1846. Invalided 1 Aug. 1846. Retired 15 Jan. 1847. Hon. Lt. Col. 28 Nov. 1854. *d.* London 16 Oct. 1857.

Son of William Minto, Lt. Col. R.M. Art., by his 1st wife. *m.* Cawnpore 14 Aug. 1823, Miss Eliza Anne Gale Kennedy, nat. dau. of Lieut. John Kennedy, H.M. 76th Ft.

Services : Posted Lieut. to 1/6th N.I. in 1819 ; transfd. to 18th N.I. (late 2/6th) May 1824. Adjt. 18th N.I. 5 Oct. 1824 till 6 Jan. 1826. Siege and capture of Bhurtpore ; Lieut. 18th N.I. (India

THE BENGAL ARMY, 1758-1834   301

medal). Adjt. Dinajpur Local Bn. 8 May 1826. Intr. & Qmr. 18th N.I. 18 Oct. 1826 till 21 Jan. 1828. Attached to Sindhia's Contingent 23 Nov. 1833 ; 2nd in comd. Gwalior Contingent 19 Mar. 1835 ; Capt. Comdt. Cav. do. ; offg. Comdt. Gwalior Contingent 21 Dec. 1839 ; permanent do., retaining also comd. of Cav., 1 Feb. 1840. Capture of fort Khairooa (Kerwa), 12 m. E. of Narwar, C.I., 4 Apr. 1841 ; comdg. the force. Operations against Bundela insurgents in Saugor district Jan. 1842. Comdt. 1st Cav., Gwalior Contingent, 13 Jan. 1844 till invalided.
Refs. : *I.M.* 16 Nov. 1857, p. 807. *I.N.* No. 16, p. 357.

MISSING, John (1759/60-1811). Captain. 20th N.I. *b.* Hants 1759/60. Cadet 1781. Arrived in India 15 Sept. 1782. Ensign 1782. Lieut. 10 July 1782. Capt. 4 Mar. 1800. Retired 8 May 1805. *d.* 2 Dec. 1811.

(*Perhaps* son of Thomas Missing, of Stubbington, Major Hants Mil.) Related to Edward Clarke (*d.* 1812), *q.v.* *m.* Midnapore 26 Jan. 1788, Ann Palmer Chambers.

Services : Lieut. S. Hants Mil. 24 Jan. 1780. Apptd. Cadet 28 Sept. 1781, aged 21 ; sailed for India in the *Ceres* 6 Feb. 1782. On arrival at Bombay as a Cadet in Sept. 1782, was apptd. by Col. Charles Morgan, *q.v.*, an Ensign in the detachment of the Bengal Army serving at that Presdy. during the First Mahratta War. Adjt. 6th Bn. Sepoys 1786-90 ; do. 1st Eur. Bn. in 1792 ; Fort Adjt. at Buxar 1797-1802. Posted to 1/9th N.I. 15 Nov. 1799 ; Capt. 9th N.I. ; transfd. to Marine Regt. (became 20th N.I.). Fur. 1802 till retirement.

MITCHELL, Alexander (*d.* 1794). Lieutenant, Infantry. Cadet 1782. Ensign 11 Mar. 1783. Lieut. 22 Feb. 1790. *d.* Barrackpore 13 Oct. 1794.

Son of John Mitchell, of Monaghan.

Services : Madras Cadet 1782 ; exchanged to Bengal with Henry Hamilton, *q.v.*, 2 Oct. 1783. Ensign 6th Bengal Eur. Bn. in Dec. 1788 ; reposted to do. 5 Feb. 1790 ; transfd. to 4th Bn. Sepoys.
Refs. : *Walker's Hibernian Mag.*, Sept. 1795.

MITCHELL, Godfrey (1757/58-1787). Ensign, 1st Bengal Eur. Bn. *b.* in Ireland 1757/58. Cadet 1782. Ensign 2 Feb. 1783. *d.* Cawnpore 24 July 1787.

5th son of Thomas Mitchell, of Castlestrange, co. Roscommon, and Elizabeth his wife, eldest dau. of Godfrey Wills, of Willsgrove, co. Roscommon.

Services: Sailed for India in the *Earl Talbot* 6 Feb. 1782, aged 24.
Refs.: Burke's *Landed Gentry*, 7th edn., p. 1274, *s.n.* Mitchell, of Castlestrange, co. Roscommon.

MITCHELL, James Campbell (*d*. 1817). Lieut. Colonel. 16th N.I. Country Cadet 1778. Admitted 27 Aug. 1778. Ensign 29 May 1779. Lieut. 29 Jan. 1781. Capt. 30 Oct. 1797. Major 10 May 1804. Lt. Col. 17 Sept. 1807. Retired 19 Feb. 1814. *d*. 24 Dec. 1817.

Brother of Elizabeth, wife of Thomas Harvey, of Cambridge, solicitor. *m*. London 17 Nov. 1796, Harriet, 2nd dau. of Thomas Vaughan, of Woodstone, Hunts.
Services: Lieut. Bombay Marine 27 Aug. 1778. Apptd. Cadet 10 Sept. 1778. Lieut. 6th Bn. Sepoys in Mar. 1784, when granted leave s.c. to sea; 11th Bn. Sepoys in July 1787. Fur. 10 Feb. 1796 till 10 Nov. 1797. Capt. 14th N.I. Comdd. Sebundy Corps in ceded districts of Rohilkhand 1803-5; comdd. Bareilly Provl. Bn. 1805-6; do. Murshidabad Provl. Bn. 1806-7. Posted Lt. Col. to 24th N.I. in 1807. Fur. 18 Feb. 1808 till 13 Dec. 1810. Transfd. to 2/26th N.I. in 1810; to 16th N.I. in 1813.
Refs.: Burke's *Landed Gentry*, 2nd edn., p. 1469, *s.n.* Vaughan, of Woodstone, Hunts. *Pester*, p. 90. *S.M.* 1796, p. 792. Will dated 28 Dec. 1815; proved 8 July 1820.

MITCHELL, Robert (1763/64-1790). Lieutenant, 25th Bn. Sepoys. *b*. in Scotland 1763/64. Cadet 1780. Ensign 1780. Lieut. 9 June 1781. *bur*. Madras 2 Aug. 1790.
Services: Apptd. Cadet 8 Dec. 1779; sailed for India in the *Grosvenor* 3 June 1780, aged 16. Posted to 3rd Bengal Eur. Regt. May 1781; Lieut. 25th Bn. Sepoys in July 1787. Third Mysore War.

*MITCHELL, William (1771/72-1817). Bt. Major, Artillery. (309) *b*. 1771/72. Cadet 1794. Arrived in India 26 Sept. 1795. Fireworker 5 Oct. 1795. Lieut. 18 Feb. 1802. Capt. Lt. 21 Sept. 1804. Capt. 15 Sept. 1809. Bt. Major 4 June 1814. *d*. Calcutta 6 Oct. 1817, aged 45.

Owned house property in William St. and Anne St., Dublin. *m*. St. Helena 1 June 1802, Miss Susan Carruthers. Father of William St. Leger Mitchell, *q.v.*, and of Mary, wife of Peter Nicolson, *q.v.*
Services: Ensign Warwickshire Mil. 1 Mar. 1794; Lieut. do. 25 June 1794. Apptd. Cadet 13 Mar. 1795; sailed for India in the *Minerva* 24 May 1795. Fur. 5 Mar. 1802 till 8 Oct. 1805.

THE BENGAL ARMY, 1758-1834

Capt. 1st Coy. 2nd Bn. Foot Art. Comy. of Ord., in charge of expense mag., 30 June 1810 till death. No record of active service.
Refs.: Will dated Edinburgh 22 Mar. 1805; proved 11 Oct. 1817. M.I. in S. Park St. cemetery, Calcutta.

MITCHELL, William (1806-1888). Lieut. Colonel. 32nd N.I. *b.* I. of Tobago 17 June 1806. Cadet 1821. Arrived in India 6 Jan. 1823. Ensign 30 Jan. 1823. Lieut. 12 July 1824. Capt. 19 Sept. 1836. Bt. Major 9 Nov. 1846. Retired 3 Apr. 1850. Hon. Lt. Col. 28 Nov. 1854. *d.* 3 Jermyn St., London, 22 Mar. 1888.

bapt. St. John's, Hampstead, 9 Oct. 1807. Son of Robert Mitchell, landed proprietor in the W.I., and Isabella his wife. Nephew of M. Fergusson.

Services: Posted Ensign to 16th N.I. in 1823. Transfd. to 32nd N.I. (late 1/16th) May 1824. Siege and capture of Bhurtpore; Lieut. 32nd N.I. (India medal). Actg. Adjt. 32nd N.I. 7 Jan. till 2 May 1832. Shekhawat expedn. 1834; Lieut. 32nd N.I. In charge of a detachment of Irreg. Cav. on the Nepal frontier Nov. 1842 till June 1843. Fur. p.a. 19 Sept. 1844 till 14 Dec. 1847.

Refs.: *The Times*, 27 Mar. 1888.

MITCHELL, William St. Leger (1808-1869). Major General. 56th N.I. *bapt.* Calcutta 4 Apr. 1808. Cadet 1825. Arrived in India 25 June 1826. Ensign 5 Feb. 1826. Lieut. 6 May 1829. Capt. 5 Nov. 1842. Major 15 June 1849. Lt. Col. 28 Nov. 1854. Bt. Col. 6 July 1860. Retired 31 Dec. 1861. Hon. Maj. Gen. 31 Dec. 1861. *d.* 18 Dec. 1869.

Son of William Mitchell, *q.v.*, and Susannah his wife. *m.* (before 1848) Margaret.

Services: Ensign d.d. 42nd N.I. 8 July 1826. Posted to 13th N.I. 26 Sept. 1826. Fur. p.a. 6 July 1836 till 20 Mar. 1839. Actg. Adjt. Left Wing 13th N.I. 11 Nov. 1840. Insurrection in Bundelkhand 1841-2; Chirgaon; Capt. 13th N.I. Fur. 1 yr. without pay 19 Nov. 1844; leave s.c. 1 yr. to Naini Tal 15 Jan. 1848. Second Sikh War; passage of Chenab; Gujerat; Capt. 13th N.I. (Medal with clasp). Posted Lt. Col. to 56th N.I. Feb. 1855; to 61st N.I. Mar. 1855; to 19th N.I. Sept. 1855; to 1st Eur. Bengal Fus. 24 June 1857; to 5th N.I. 1858; to 56th N.I. 1859. To do general duty in Benares Div. 22 June 1860.

MITFORD, William Reveley (1802-1824). Ensign, 31st N.I. *b.* London 24 Nov. 1802. Cadet 1821. Ensign 9 Dec. 1821. *d. unm.* Hazaribagh, B. & O., 27 Apr. 1824.

bapt. St. James's, Westminster, 1 Mar. 1804. Eldest son of John Mitford, barr.-at-law, comr. of bankruptcy, and Sarah Woodward his 1st wife. Cousin-german of William Vernon Mitford, *q.v.* Ed. Westminster; admitted 13 Jan. 1815; left Bartholomewtide 1818.

Services: Posted Ensign to 3rd N.I. in 1822; transfd. to newly-formed 31st N.I. July 1823. No record of active service.

Refs.: Foster's *Peerage*, p. 558, *s.n.* Redesdale, B. *Westminster School Register.* M.I. Hazaribagh.

MITFORD, William Vernon (1809-1861). Lieut. Colonel. 9th L.C. *b.* Dublin 27 Jan. 1809. Cadet 1828. Arrived in India 7 Aug. 1828. Cornet (22 Feb. 1828) 9 Sept. 1829. Lieut. 23 July 1832. Capt. 16 Oct. 1846. Bt. Major 20 June 1854. Retired 9 Oct. 1856. Hon. Lt. Col. 9 Oct. 1856. *d.* 8 June 1861.

Eldest son of Bertram Mitford, of Clontarf, co. Dublin, barr.-at-law, and Frances his wife, 2nd dau. of John Vernon, of Clontarf Castle. Cousin-german of William Reveley Mitford, *q.v. m.* Nasirabad 13 Feb. 1837, Anne Martha, 2nd dau. of C. Wiltshire, of Calcutta. (*See also* William Counsell.) (She died Nasirabad 1 July 1839.) Ed. Shrewsbury 1823-4.

Services: Cornet d.d. 9th L.C. 8 Sept. 1828; posted to do. 3 June 1829 and served throughout with that Regt. Campaign in Sind 1843; Miani; Hyderabad; Lieut. 9th L.C. (Medal).

Refs.: Burke's *Peerage*, 1923, p. 1860, *s.n.* Redesdale, B. Burke's *Landed Gentry of Ireland*, p. 723, *s.n.* Vernon, of Clontarf Castle, co. Dublin. *G.M.* 1861, ii. 97. *The Times*, 12 June 1861.

MOCKLER, James Richard (1779-1810). Captain, 7th L.C. *b.* Trim, co. Meath, 7 Nov. 1779. Cadet 1796. Arrived in India 28 Aug. 1798. Cornet 1 Nov. 1798. Lieut. 29 May 1800. Capt. 1 May 1809. *d.* Calcutta 3 Nov. 1810.

Son of John Mockler, of Trim. *m.* Calcutta 24 Jan. 1809, Miss Frances Georgina Smith, youngest sister of Joseph Barnard Smith, *q.v.* (*See also* William McQuhae.) (She *re-m.* Arthur Smelt, *q.v.*)

Services: Cornet 2nd N.C. Operations in Jumna Doab 1803; Lieut. 2nd N.C. Second Mahratta War 1803-5; battle of Delhi; Laswari; battle of Deig; Lieut. 2nd N.C. Transfd. as Capt. Lt. to newly-raised 7th N.C. 24 Oct. 1805. (? Operations in Oudh 1808. Settlement of Hariana 1809-10; Capt. 7th N.C.)

Refs.: Will dated 31 May 1810; proved 22 Dec. 1810. M.I. in S. Park St. cemetery, Calcutta.

THE BENGAL ARMY, 1758-1834   305

MOCKLER, Robert Henry (1812-1890). Captain. 44th N.I. *bapt.* Litter, co. Cork, 28 Oct. 1812. Cadet 1828. Arrived in India 4 May 1829. Ensign 8 Jan. 1829. Lieut. 21 Jan. 1835. Capt. 15 Nov. 1841. Invalided 19 May 1843. Retired 6 Dec. 1848. *d.* 6 Dec. 1890.
Son of Rev. James Mockler, of Castle Hyde, co. Cork.
Services: Ensign d.d. 50th N.I. 10 June 1829; posted Ensign to 44th N.I. Fur. s.c. 3 July 1829 till 18 July 1832. Operations against marauders in Jhabua, C.I., under Lt.-Col. John Holbrow, *q.v.*, Feb.-Mar. 1836. Fur. 26 Feb. 1837 till 25 Jan. 1841, and 5 June 1846 till retirement.

*MOFFAT, George (*d.* 1788). Bt. Ensign, Infantry. Bt. Ensign 17 Aug. 1781. *d.* Chittagong 7 June 1788.
Services: Commissioned from the ranks when Sergt. Major and apptd. Bt. Ensign of Militia.

MOFFAT, Henry (1804-1832). Lieutenant. 7th L.C. *b.* London 3 Feb. 1804. Cadet 1823. Arrived in India 19 May 1824. Cornet 17 Jan. 1824. Lieut. 13 May 1825. Resigned 25 June 1830. *d.* Burleston, Dorset, 22 Aug. 1832.
bapt. St. Pancras, Middlesex, 6 Mar. 1804. 3rd and youngest son of William Moffat, of Thurscoe Hall, Yorks. (of Mortlake, Surrey, afterwards of Burleston), and Ann Palmer his wife. 2nd cousin of James Douglas Moffat, *q.v.* Ed. Eton 1820-2.
Services: Posted Cornet to 7th L.C. Leave s.c. 18 Mar. 1825; fur. s.c. 21 Mar. 1826 till 10 June 1828. No record of active service.
Refs.: Zetland Family Histories, by F. J. Grant, pp. 60, 64. *G.M.* 1832, ii. 285. Eton School Lists.

MOFFAT, James Douglas (1812-1864). Major. 2nd L.C. *b.* Sapcote, Leics., 16 Sept. 1812. Cadet 1828. Arrived in India 9 Apr. 1829. Cornet (26 Sept. 1828) 22 Mar. 1829. Lieut. 2 Nov. 1840. Capt. 3 May 1849. Retired 7 Feb. 1851. Hon. Major 28 Nov. 1854. *d.* 36 Craven Hill Gdns., London, 11 May 1864.
V of Harperton and Highridge Hall, co. Roxburgh. *bapt.* Sapcote 11 July 1813. Elder son of William Moffat, of Harperton, sometime of Leamington, late Capt. E.I.C.N.S., Comdr. of the *Winchelsea*, and Sarah his wife. *m.* Melcombe Regis 9 Mar. 1842, his 2nd cousin, Jeanette Jane, youngest sister of Henry Moffat, *q.v.* Addiscombe Cadet 1826.
Services: d.d. 3rd L.C. 10 June 1829. Actg. Cornet (having been

2 yrs. in India) 14 Oct. 1831. d.d. 3rd L.C. 14 Oct. 1831. Posted to 2nd L.C. 20 Sept. 1832. Adjt. Shah Shuja's 2nd Cav. 17 Aug. 1838 till 6 Aug. 1839. First Afghan War; capture of Ghazni 1839 (Medal); Parwandara; Lieut. 2nd L.C. On disbandment of 2nd L.C. was posted to newly-raised 11th L.C. (became 2nd L.C. in May 1850). Fur. p.a. 1 Apr. 1841 till 26 Dec. 1842, and 1845-6. Second Sikh War; Multan; Bt. Capt. 11th L.C. (Medal).
Refs.: Zetland Family Histories, pp. 58-9. *A.J.* N.S. xxxvii. 380. *G.M.* 1864, i. 813. *The Times*, 14 May 1864.

MOIR, John De Winter Charles James (1805-1871). Colonel. 28th N.I. *b.* London 9 June 1805. Cadet 1823. Arrived in India 8 Nov. 1824. Ensign 21 June 1824. Lieut. 28 Aug. 1826. Capt. 24 Jan. 1845. Major 27 June 1857. Bt. Lt. Col. 27 Aug. 1858. Retired 31 Dec. 1861. Hon. Col. 31 Dec. 1861. *d.* 18 Jan. 1871.

bapt. St. George's, Hanover Sq., 12 Sept. 1805. 3rd son of William Moir, of Newgrange, co. Forfar, merchant, and Cornelia Isabella his wife. *m.* 1st, Susannah. *m.* 2nd, Manchester cathedral 19 Mar. 1849, Helen, 4th dau. of John Dicas, of London, solicitor.

Services: Posted Ensign to 28th N.I. 31 Mar. 1825. Fur. s.c. 19 Sept. 1826 till 4 Dec. 1829. Adjt. 1st Depot Bn. 18 June 1842 till 1 Mar. 1843, when it was broken up. Fur. p.a. 10 Nov. 1847 till 1849. Expedn. on N.W.F. against Mohmands 1851-2; against Swatis 1852; Bt. Major 28th N.I., with force under Sir Colin Campbell (Medal). A.D.C. to Maj.-Gen. G. W. A. Lloyd, *q.v.*, comdg. Dinapore Div., Jan. 1855 till 1857. Santhal revolt 1855; A.D.C.

MOISES, William (*d.* 1805). Captain, 7th N.I. Cadet 1783. Admitted 20 Sept. 1783. Ensign 14 Feb. 1785. Lieut. 23 Feb. 1792. Capt. 5 Nov. 1802. *d.* Chandernagore (? Barrackpore) 19 July 1805.

Services: Apptd. Cadet 20 Nov. 1782; sailed for India in the *Barwell* 11 Mar. 1783. Posted to 30th Bn. Sepoys 15 Feb. 1790; to 2nd Eur. Bn. 15 Mar. 1790; Lieut. 7th N.I. in 1798.

*MOLITOR, John Wolfgang (*d.* 1759). Captain, Infantry. 2nd Lieut. (Bombay Art.) Nov. 1753. Lieut. Dec. 1755. Capt. Lt. Oct. 1757. Capt. (Bengal Inf.) 6 Nov. 1757. *d.* 7 Apr. 1759: kld. in action at the storm of Masulipatam.

(*Perhaps* of the Swiss family of Molitor, settled at Schuls.)
Services: Was serving at Madras in 1755. Embarked for

THE BENGAL ARMY, 1758-1834

Calcutta 29 Oct. 1756 and joined Clive's camp on 5 Mar. 1757 with 8 Sergts., 8 Corporals, 2 Drums, 53 Privates and 43 *Topasses*. (? Siege and capture of Chandernagore.) Battle of Plassey, having previously voted at the council of war against coming to an immediate action.

Refs. : *Spring*, No. 8. *Hill*, iii. 54, 62, 321.

MOLONY, James (1805-1824). Ensign. 28th N.I. Afterwards Ensign Bo. Est. *bapt.* St. George's chapel, Dublin, 16 Sept. 1805. Cadet 1822. Ensign (?) Resigned in India 14 Feb. 1823. *d. unm.* Bombay 23 Oct. 1824.

3rd and youngest son of Walter Weldon Molony and Mary his wife, dau. of John Spelissy, M.D., and sister of George Spelissy, *q.v.*

Services : Passed as Cadet for Bengal 17 Apr. 1822. Posted Ensign to 28th N.I. Bombay Cadet 1823 ; Ensign 10th Bo. N.I. 21 Feb. 1824. Cashiered in India 8 Sept. 1824.

Refs. : Burke's *Landed Gentry of Ireland*, p. 483, *s.n.* Molony, of Kiltanon, co. Clare. Intest. ; admon. (Bombay) 3 Feb. 1825.

MOLYNEUX, Thomas More (1801-1824). Lieutenant, 1st N.I. *b.* 1 Mar. 1801. Cadet 1817. Ensign (?) Lieut. 1 Aug. 1818. *d.* Nagpur 22 Apr. 1824.

bapt. St. Nicholas, Guildford, 17 July 1812. Son of James More Molyneux, of Loseley Park, nr. Guildford, J.P. and D.L., Capt. 43rd Ft. and Major Guildford Yeomanry Cav. His sister *m.* Arthur Wight, *q.v.*

Services : Posted Lieut. to 1/1st N.I. No record of active service.

Refs. : Burke's *Landed Gentry*, 13th edn., p. 1155, *s.n.* More-Molyneux-McCowen (*now* Longbourne), of Loseley Park, Surrey.

MONCK, George Paul (1789-1806). Cadet, Infantry. *b.* Castle Inch (Inchyolaghan), co. Kilkenny, 2 Oct. 1789. Cadet 1805. Never arrived in India. *d.* at sea 20 Apr. 1806 : lost in the wreck of the *Lady Burges* off Bonavista I. (Tinian I., Ladrones).

bapt. 10 Oct. 1789. Son of Rev. Marcus Monck, chaplain to the Prince of Wales, rector of Rathdowney, Queen's Co., and Anne his wife, dau. of Richard Keily, of Lismore, co. Waterford. Nephew of the wife of Sir John Hamilton, Bart., *q.v.*

Refs. : Berry's *Berkshire Peds.* p. 18.

MONCK, Henry Percy (1758-1787). Lieutenant, Bengal Eur. Regt. J.A.G. Bengal. *b.* in Ireland 1758. Cadet 1778. Ensign 1778. Lieut. 16 Nov. 1778. *d.* Barrackpore 31 July 1787.

Son of Henry Percy Monck and Jane his wife (*m.* 24 Dec. 1757), dau. of John McDonnell, of Castlebar, co. Mayo.

Services: Ensign H.M. 20th Ft. 7 July 1775. Sailed for India in the *Nassau* 1 Mar. 1778, aged 20. Lieut. 1/1st Bengal Eur. Regt. in Oct. 1779. Dy. Judge Advocate, 2nd Bde., Nov. 1781; actg. J.A.G. 21 Nov. 1785; permanent do. 28 Mar. 1786 till death.

Refs.: Archdall's *Lodge's Peerage*, v. 140 *n.*, *s.n.* Monck, V. Berry's *Berks. Peds.* p. 19.

*MONCKTON, George Pakenham (1816-1894). Cadet. Subsequently Madras C.S. *b.* 5 Oct. 1816. Cadet 1833. Resigned Dec. 1834. *d.s.p.* 12 Apr. 1894.

2nd son of Philip Monckton, B.C.S., judge at Gorakhpur, and Henrietta his wife, 4th dau. of Michael Carter, of Inch, and sister of Henry Carter (1793-1844), *q.v. m.* 7 Dec. 1843, Emily Mary, dau. of Sir Timothy Vansittart Stonhouse, Bart. (She died 18 Dec. 1911.) Ed. Westminster; admitted 1 Oct. 1827; K.S. 1830; left 1833. Addiscombe Cadet Feb.-Dec. 1834.

Services: Apptd. Writer, M.C.S., 1837; Asst. to Collector of N. Div. of Arcot 1844; retired 30 Aug. 1848.

Refs.: Burke's *Peerage*, 1923, p. 961, *s.n.* Galway, V.; p. 2100, *s.n.* Stonhouse, Bart. Burke's *Landed Gentry*, 13th edn., p. 1257, *s.n.* Monckton, of Fineshade Abbey, Northants. *Westminster School Register. The Times,* 17 Apr. 1894.

MONCREIFF, William (1757-1794). Lieutenant, 5th Bn. Sepoys. *b.* 18 June 1757. Cadet 1780. Ensign 6 Oct. 1780. Lieut. 12 June 1781. *d.* Benares 9 Oct. 1794.

5th son of Rev. Sir William Moncreiff, 7th Bart., minister of Blackford, co. Perth, and Katherine his wife, eldest dau. of Robert Wellwood, of Garvock. *m.* Edinburgh 10 Jan. 1789, Janet, dau. of James Drummond, of Croftnappick.

Services: Sailed for India in the *Ponsborne* 3 Apr. 1780. Fur. on h.p. 20 Oct. 1786 till 1790. Transfd. from 3rd Bengal Eur. Bn. to 10th Bn. Sepoys 9 Sept. 1791; to 5th Bn. Sepoys 21 Jan. 1794.

Refs.: Burke's *Peerage*, 1923, p. 1585, *s.n.* Moncreiff, B. Scott's *Fasti*, iv. 262.

MONEY, Edward Kyrle (1810-1841). Lieutenant, 2nd L.C. *b.* Friern Barnet, Middlesex, 29 Jan. 1810. Cadet 1826. Arrived in India 24 May 1827. Cornet (19 Nov. 1826) 13 June 1827. Lieut. 11 Nov. 1840. *d. unm.* Ludhiana 17 Nov. 1841.

2nd son of Rev. William Money Kyrle, of Homme House,

Whetham, and Pitsford, rector of Yatesbury (who assumed by R.L. 1844 the name of Kyrle), and Emma his wife, dau. of Richard Down, of Halliwick Manor House, Middlesex. Cousin-german of Ernle Kyrle Money and Spencer Wellington Buller, qq.v. Ed. Winchester. Addiscombe Cadet; nominated 3 Aug. 1825; renominated 9 Mar. 1826.

Services: Cadet d.d. 1st L.C. 2 June 1827; posted Cornet to 2nd L.C. 13 June 1827; actg. Intr. & Qmr. do. 7 Apr. 1831, 8 Nov. 1831, 28 Mar. 1832; permanent do. 5 Apr. 1832 till 2 Mar. 1834. Transfd. to 7th L.C. 13 July 1835; actg. Intr. & Qmr. do. 29 Nov. 1835; retransfd. to 2nd L.C. 9 Jan. 1836; actg. Intr. & Qmr. do. 8 Apr. 1836; permanent do. 19 June 1838. First Afghan War 1838-40; Ghazni (Medal); Kohistan 1840; Parwandara; Lieut. 2nd L.C. On disbandment of 2nd L.C. was attached to 10th L.C. as actg. Intr. & Qmr. Adjt. 4th Irreg. Cav. 1 June 1841.

Refs.: Burke's *Landed Gentry*, 13th edn., p. 1043, *s.n.* Money-Kyrle, of Homme House, co. Hereford. *G.M.* 1842, i. 341.

MONEY, Ernle Kyrle (1814-1883). Major General. Artillery. (654) *b.* Shirehampton, Gloucs., 18 Feb. 1814. Cadet 1831. Arrived in India 16 Oct. 1832. 2nd Lieut. 8 Dec. 1831. Lieut. 29 Apr. 1840. Capt. 5 May 1849. Bt. Major 19 Jan. 1858. Lt. Col. 6 Feb. 1861. Col. 24 Jan. 1865. Retired 1 Aug. 1872. Hon. Maj. Gen. 1 Aug. 1872. *d.* Bromley, Kent, 21 Jan. 1883. 2nd son of Rowland Money, C.B., Vice Adm. R.N., and Maria his wife, 5th dau. of William Money, of Walthamstow, Essex, Dir. E.I. Co. Brother of Rowland Money, *q.v.* *m.* 1st, Abbots Langley, Herts., 26 Sept. 1850, Mary Emma Weller, eldest dau. of Fawcett James Lewin, of Watford, Herts. (She died 20 Apr. 1879). *m.* 2nd, 8 May 1880, Martha, dau. of J. J. Wall. Addiscombe Cadet 5 Feb. 1830 till 8 Dec. 1831.

Services: Posted to 3rd Troop 1st Bde. H.A. 29 Sept. 1838. First Afghan War 1842; reoccupation of Kabul; Lieut. 3rd Troop 1st Bde., with Gen. Pollock's force (Medal). Capt. 6th Bn. Foot Art. Offg. Adjt. Art. Div. 15 Apr. 1848. Fur. p.a. 10 Aug. 1849 till 1851. Transfd. to 2nd Troop 3rd Bde. 1854. Mutiny campaign; siege of Delhi (s.w. 23 July 1857); Major 2nd Troop 3rd Bde. (Medal with clasp). Lt. Col. 5th Bde. H.A.; Col. "F" Bde. R.H.A.

Refs.: Burke's *Landed Gentry*, 13th edn., p. 1043, *s.n.* Money-Kyrle, of Homme House, co. Hereford. *The Times*, 24 Jan. 1883.

MONEY, George (1777-1873). Lieutenant. 16th N.I. (? Subsequently Lieut. H.M. 12th Foot.) *bapt.* St. Kilda's chapel,

S. Shields, co. Durham, 16 Dec. 1777. Cadet 1795. Arrived in India 11 Mar. 1797. Ensign 30 Oct. 1796. Lieut. 30 Oct. 1797. Resigned 1 May 1805. *d.* 26 Mar. 1873.
Son of William Money and Mary his wife.
Services : Lieut. 16th N.I. in 1798. Fur. 1803 till resignation. No record of active service. (? Ensign 12th Ft. 1 Jan. 1812 ; Lieut. do. 15 July 1813 ; h.p. do. 25 Mar. 1817.)

*MONEY, Richard. Cadet. Infantry. Cadet 1767. Never arrived in India.
Services : Sailed for India in the *Norfolk* 9 Mar. 1767 ; went on shore at Madeira to purchase some necessaries and missed his ship. N.F.P.

*MONEY, Rowland (1812–1869). 2nd Lieutenant. Engineers. Afterwards B.C.S. *b.* 30 Mar. 1812. Cadet 1828. 2nd Lieut. 12 June 1828. Resigned 1829. *d.* Les Guimerais, St. Servan, France, 2 May 1869.
bapt. Westbury-on-Trym 27 Apr. 1812. Eldest son of Vice-Adm. Rowland Money and Maria his wife. Brother of Ernle Kyrle Money, *q.v. m.* 18 June 1846, Mary Ann, only dau. of John Tombs, *q.v.* (She died 16 Oct. 1865.) Addiscombe Cadet 1827 ; Haileybury 1829-30.
Services : Writer, B.C.S., 30 Apr. 1831. Member of Board of Revenue, N.W.P. Retired 1866.
Refs. : Burke's *Landed Gentry*, 13th edn., p. 1043, *s.n.* Money-Kyrle, of Homme House, co. Hereford. *The Times*, 10 May 1869.

MONKE, Henry (1795-1838). Bt. Major, 39th N.I. *b.* London 14 Sept. 1795. Cadet 1811. Ensign (?) Lieut. 14 July 1815. Capt. 30 Oct. 1825. Bt. Major 28 June 1838. *d.* at sea 17 Oct. 1838 : lost in the wreck of the *Protector* off the Sandheads, Bengal.
bapt. St. James's, Westminster, 9 May 1796. Son of George Paris Monke, Post Capt. R.N., and Hannah Rebecca his 2nd wife.
Services : Bengal Inf. Cadet 1811 ; Madras Cav. Cadet Oct. 1813 ; retransfd. to Bengal Inf. 1815 ; posted Lieut. to 2/19th N.I. July 1815. Third Mahratta War ; Lieut. 2/19th N.I. Second in comd. Mhairwara Local Bn. 15 July 1822 ; do. 2nd (Gardner's) Local Horse 24 Dec. 1822 till 21 Sept. 1827. Actg. Adjt. of two Regts. of Local Cav. 3 Oct. 1823. Transfd. to 39th N.I. (late 2/19th) May 1824. Tempy. charge of 2nd Local Horse Apr. 1825, and retained comd. during employment of that Corps on active service. First Burma War ; Arakan 1825 ; tempy. comdg. 2nd (Gardner's) Local

THE BENGAL ARMY, 1758-1834   311

Horse. Rejoined 39th N.I. Sept. 1827. Fur. p.a. 28 Feb. 1836;
sailed for India in the *Protector* 6 June 1838, on his return from fur.
Refs.: *The Times*, 23 Jan. 1839, p. 5.

MONKHOUSE, Nicholas Hall (1804-?). 2nd Lieutenant. Artillery. (517) *b.* Newcastle-upon-Tyne 25 Jan. 1804. Cadet 1820. Arrived in India Nov. 1821. 2nd Lieut. 18 Apr. 1821. Resigned 16 Sept. 1823.

bapt. All Sts., Newcastle-upon-Tyne, 5 Apr. 1804. 4th son of Miles Monkhouse, of Newcastle-upon-Tyne, wine merchant, and Lucy his wife, dau. of George Hounsom, of Huntington, Sussex. Addiscombe Cadet 1819-21.
Services: Posted 2nd Lieut. to 3rd Coy. 2nd Bn. Foot Art. No record of active service.

MONRO, Edmund Augustus (1808-1852). Captain. 39th N.I. *b.* Edmondsham, Dorset, 10 Mar. 1808. Cadet 1824. Arrived in India 15 May 1825. Ensign 24 Nov. 1824. Lieut. 24 Feb. 1826. Capt. 25 July 1839. Invalided 22 Apr. 1840. Retired 1 Oct. 1847. *d.* Sion Pl., Bath, 2 Oct. 1852.

bapt. Edmondsham 17 Apr. 1808. 2nd son of Lt.-Gen. William Hector Monro, of Edmondsham House, govr. of Trinidad 1811-13, and Philadelphia his wife, eldest dau. of Edmond Bower, of Prospect Hill, nr. Reading, Capt. R.N. Grandson of Dr. George Monro, VII of Bearcrofts. *m.* Agra 18 Nov. 1830, Margaret, 2nd dau. of Tasker Keys, of Broomfield, nr. Londonderry. (She died Sabathu 7 Jan. 1843.) Addiscombe Cadet 1824.
Services: Ensign d.d. 2nd Bengal Eur. Regt. 3 June 1825. Posted Ensign to 39th N.I. Actg. Cantt. Adjt. at Hoshangabad 4 Nov. 1828; actg. S.S.O. do. 16 June 1829. Leave s.c. to Simla 7 Nov. 1838 till 7 Nov. 1839. No record of active service. d.d. Chunar 12 Feb. 1841. Postmr. at Simla 23 Mar. 1842. Fur. 1 Apr. 1845 till retirement.
Refs.: Burke's *Landed Gentry*, 12th edn., p. 1338, *s.n.* Monro, of Edmondsham, Dorset. Mackenzie's *Monroes of Fowlis*, p. 332. Hutchins' *Dorset*, iii. *I.M.* 16 Oct. 1852, p. 595. *Bath Chron.* 7 Oct. 1852. M.I. at Edmondsham.

MONSELL, Richard (1774-1799). Fireworker, Artillery. (305) *bapt.* St. Mary's, Limerick, 20 Nov. 1774. Cadet 1793. Arrived in India 21 Sept. 1795. Fireworker 16 Sept. 1794. *bur.* Fort Marlbro' 20 Nov. 1799.
Son of Ven. Archdeacon (? Daniel) Monsell.

Services: Apptd. Inf. Cadet 2 June 1794 ; sailed for India in the *Royal Admiral* 14 Aug. 1794. Transfd. to Art. 1795. Actg. Engr. at Bencoolen 1797 till death.

MONSELL, Thomas (1745/46-?). Lieutenant. 2nd Bengal Eur. Regt. *b.* in Ireland 1745/46. Cadet 1764. Ensign 3 Apr. 1764. Lieut. 12 Aug. 1765. Resigned 23 Mar. 1767.

Services: Sailed for India in the *British King* 30 Apr. 1763, aged 17. Posted to 1st Bengal Eur. Regt. 13 Aug. 1765. Was implicated in the "Batta mutiny," but actually resigned his Commission owing to ill health.

Refs.: Broome, p. 601. Proc. of 26 Mar. 1767.

MONSELL, William Devaynes (1792-1819). Lieutenant, 29th N.I. *b.* Terryglass, co. Tipperary, 4 Oct. 1792. Cadet 1808. Arrived in India 27 Oct. 1809. Suspended and ordered to Europe 13 Feb. 1810. Ensign 12 Dec. 1812. Lieut. 25 Nov. 1817. *d.* Multai, C.P., 28 Sept. 1819.

Eldest son of Thomas Monsell, of Belleisle, co. Tipperary, barr.-at-law, chairman of co. Fermanagh (who was son of Ven. Ephraim Monsell, archdeacon of Elphin), and Harriott Augusta his wife, dau. of William Devaynes, of Dover St., London, Dir. E.I. Co.

Services: Posted Ensign to 23rd N.I. in 1813. Transfd. to newly-raised 1/29th N.I. in 1815. Siege and capture of Hathras 1817 ; Ensign 1/29th N.I. Third Mahratta War ; Lieut. 1/29th N.I.

Refs.: A.J. ix. 626. *Genealogist,* N.S. xxi. 202.

MONTAGU, Edward (1755-1799). Bt. Colonel, Artillery. (125) *b.* 20 Feb. 1755. Inf. Cadet 1770. Admitted 26 Sept. 1771. Fireworker 16 May 1772. Lieut. 28 Sept. 1777. Capt. Lt. 20 Mar. 1780. Capt. 13 Oct. 1784. Major 14 Sept. 1790. Lt. Col. 5 Nov. 1796. Bt. Col. 1 Jan. 1798. *d.* 8 May 1799, of wounds received in action at the siege of Seringapatam on 2 May.

4th son of John Montagu, Adm. R.N., kinsman of the Duke of Manchester, and Sophia his wife, dau. of James Wroughton, of Wilcot. *m.* Masulipatam 17 May 1792, Barbara, dau. of John Fleetwood. (She died 3 June 1848, aged 77.) Woolwich Cadet.

Services: Cadet in the Select Picket 1771 ; removed as Cadet from Inf. to Art. 12 Apr. 1772. Operations in Rohilkhand under Goddard 1773 (w. by an arrow in the face). Second Mysore War 1782-4 ; Cuddalore ; comdg. Art. with Col. T. D. Pearse's detach-

THE BENGAL ARMY, 1758-1834

ment. 2nd Bn. Art. in July 1787. Third Mysore War; comdd. Art. at sieges of Nandidrug and Savandrug; siege of Seringapatam; comdd. Art. with centre column; Major 2nd Coy. 2nd Bn. Fourth Mysore War; siege of Seringapatam (s.w.—arm amputated); Bt. Col. comdg. Bengal Art.

Refs.: Burke's *Peerage*, 1923, p. 1499, *s.n.* Manchester, D. Burke's *Commoners*, ii. 54, *s.n.* Montagu, of Lackham, Wilts. *D.N.B. E.I.M.C.* ii. 265-8. *D.I.B. A.A.R.* i. 64. *Stubbs*, ii. 232. Intest.; admon. (Madras) 20 Aug. 1799. M.I. nr. junction of the Cauvery, Mysore State, and in Lacock church, Wilts.

MONTAGU, Henry Seymour (1785-1859). Captain. 20th N.I. *b.* 2 Aug. 1785. Cadet 1800. Arrived in India 15 Oct. 1801. Ensign 28 Oct. 1801. Lieut. 30 Sept. 1803. Capt. 1 Oct. 1815. Resigned 9 Apr. 1822. *d.* at his house, Thurlow Lodge, Clapham, Surrey, 23 Mar. 1859.

Of Westleton Grange, Suffolk, and Thurlow Lodge, Clapham. Eldest son of Montagu Montagu and Anne Catherine his wife, 2nd dau. of Hon. Henry Hobart, M.P. for Norwich, and niece of George, 3rd Earl of Buckinghamshire. *m.* Marylebone, London, 9 Sept. 1823, Maria, youngest dau. of Beeston Long, of Coombe House, Surrey, and niece of Charles Long, 1st Baron Farnborough, of Bromley Hill Place. (She died Clapham 23 Oct. 1832.) His dau. *m.* Sir Frederick Montagu-Pollock, *q.v.*

Services: Ensign d.d. 18th N.I. in 1802. Operations in Jumna Doab 1803; Sasni; Ensign 8th N.I. Second Mahratta War; battle of Delhi; Ensign 8th N.I., d.d. 15th N.I. (India medal). Transfd. to 20th N.I. in 1804; Adjt. & Qmr. do. 25 Mar. 1804 till 1813. Dy. Paymr. to troops on foreign service 1810-11; Asst. Paymr. Gen. in Mauritius 1812. Capt. 1/20th N.I. Fort Adjt. at Ft. Wm. 13 Mar. 1813 till Mar. 1819. Fur. 7 Mar. 1819 till resignation.

Refs.: Burke's *Landed Gentry*, 13th edn., p. 1120, *s.n.* Long, of Hunts Hall, Suffolk. Foster's *Peerage*, p. 102, *s.n.* Earl of Buckinghamshire. *A.J.* xvi. 520. *G.M.* 1859, i. 548. M.I. Petersham, Surrey.

MONTAGU, Robert Copley Rainier (1793-1826). Cadet. Infantry. Subsequently Cornet 22nd Light Dgns. *b.* London 3 Aug. 1793. Cadet 1812. Resigned 13 Nov. 1813. *d.* Plumstead, Kent, 1 Sept. 1826.

bapt. St. George's, Hanover Sq., 31 Aug. 1793. Son of Robert Montagu, of Lower Tooting, Surrey, Adm. of the Blue (who was

son of John, 4th Earl of Sandwich), and Mary Elizabeth his wife, dau. of Thomas Copley, of Bath.
Services: Cornet 22nd Light Dgns. 3 Sept. 1813 ; h.p. do. 25 June 1817.
Refs.: *G.M.* 1826, ii. 285.

MONTAGUE, John Duncan (1807-1825). Ensign, Infantry. Unposted. *b.* Cookham, Berks., 26 Apr. 1807. Cadet 1824. Ensign (?) *d.* Calcutta 25 Aug. 1825.
bapt. Cookham 29 June 1807. Son of John Montague, of Maidenhead, and Elizabeth his wife. Ed. Blundell's 15 Apr. 1818 to 16 Dec. 1819.
Services: N.F.P.
Refs.: *Blundell's School Register.*

MONTEATH, Archibald Douglas (*d.* 1802). Bt. Captain, 5th N.I. Cadet 1783. Arrived in India Oct. 1784. Ensign 5 Jan. 1785. Lieut. 9 Nov. 1790. Bt. Capt. 8 Jan. 1798. *d.* at sea 10 Aug. 1802, on board the *Jehangir* at Kedgeree.
(*Probably* brother of Colin Monteath, *q.v.*, and cousin of Walter Monteath, *q.v.*)
Services: Ensign H.M. 49th Ft. 4 June 1779 ; Lieut. do. 16 July 1781. Posted to 5th Eur. Bn. Feb. 1790 ; transfd. to 6th Bn. Sepoys 9 Sept. 1791 ; to 28th Bn. Sepoys. Third Mysore War 1791-2 ; Adjt. & Qmr. Bengal Vols. 5th N.I. in 1798. Qmr. 2nd Bengal Vol. Bn. 1801 till death.

MONTEATH, Colin (1750/51-1789). Lieutenant, 19th Bn. Sepoys. *b.* 1750/51. Cadet 1772. Ensign 22 July 1776. Lieut. 8 July 1778. *d.* Chunar 25 Jan. 1789, aged 38.
Son of Walter Monteath, of Kepp, and Jean his wife. Brother of Beckie and Jean Monteath. (*Probably* brother of Archibald Douglas Monteath, *q.v.*, and cousin of Walter Monteath, *q.v.*)
Services: Apptd. Chaplain to 3rd Bde. 14 May 1777 ; Lieut. 2/3rd Bengal Eur. Regt. in Oct. 1779 ; 19th Bn. Sepoys in July 1787.
Refs.: *S.M.* 1789, p. 412. *G.M.* 1789, ii. 763. Will dated 12 June 1786 ; proved 17 Feb. 1789. M.I. Chunar.

MONTEATH, Thomas. (*See* **Sir Thomas Monteath DOUGLAS**, K.C.B.)

MONTEATH, Walter (1764-1799). Lieutenant. Infantry. Subsequently Capt. 19th Light Dgns. *b.* Kippen, co. Stirling,

THE BENGAL ARMY, 1758-1834 315

30 Oct. 1764. Cadet 1781. Ensign (?) Lieut. 18 July 1782. Resigned 21 Mar. 1787. *d.* in camp nr. Seringapatam 22 June 1799.

Of Kepp and Arnmore. Eldest son of Walter Monteath, of Kepp, co. Perth, merchant in Glasgow, and Janet (Jean) his wife, 2nd dau. of John Douglas, of Mains. Brother of Major Archibald Douglas Monteath, Madras Cav., and Lieut. William Monteath, 12th Madras N.I. Maternal nephew of Robert and Campbell Douglas; nephew by marriage of Archibald, Duke of Douglas; and uncle of Sir Thomas Monteath Douglas, *q.v.* (*Probably* cousin of Archibald Douglas Monteath, *q.v.*) Glasgow Univ.; matric. 1776.

Services : Apptd. Cadet 23 Jan. 1781; sailed for India in the *Southampton* 13 Mar. 1781. Cornet 19th Light Dgns. 9 May 1784; Lieut. do. 1 Oct. 1789; Capt. do. 25 Dec. 1795.

Refs. : Burke's *Landed Gentry*, 9th edn., p. 418, *s.n.* Douglas, of Douglas-Support. Will dated camp nr. Bangalore, 15 Mar. 1799; proved (Madras) 7 Oct. 1799.

MONTGOMERIE, Archibald (1784-1826). Captain, Pension Est. 34th N.I. *bapt.* Calcutta 29 Dec. 1784. Cadet 1800. Arrived in India 25 Oct. 1801. Ensign 6 Nov. 1801. Lieut. 30 Sept. 1803. Capt. 10 Aug. 1817. Pensioned 18 Feb. 1825. *d.* Serampore, Bengal, 31 Jan. 1826.

Son of Archibald Montgomerie, B.C.S., and Maria Chantrey his wife. Nephew of Hugh (Montgomerie), 12th Earl of Eglinton, and cousin-german of Thomas Montgomerie, *q.v.*

Services: Posted Ensign to 17th N.I. Qmr. 5th Bengal Vol. Bn. 10 Mar. 1811 till 1816. Capture of Java 1811; Lieut. 1/17th N.I., 5th Vol. Bn. Capt. Lt. 17th N.I. 23 Jan. 1817. Third Mahratta War; Capt. 1/17th N.I., Bde. Major 2nd Inf. Bde., Centre Div. of Grand Army. Comdt. Bhagulpur Hill Rangers 1819-24. Transfd. to 34th N.I. (late 1/17th) May 1824.

Refs. : Foster's *Peerage*, p. 244, *s.n.* Eglinton, E. *Seaton*, i. 29-32. Bishop Heber's *Journal*, 2nd edn., i. 272. *G.M.* 1826, ii. 286.

MONTGOMERIE, Hamilton Anne (1788-1851). Major. 53rd N.I. *b.* Ayr 6 July 1788. Cadet 1804. Arrived in India 16 May 1806. Ensign 21 Mar. 1806. Lieut. 11 July 1807. Capt. 11 July 1823. Major 12 Feb. 1830. Retired 10 Apr. 1831. *d.* 1851.

bapt. Ayr 8 July 1788. Son of John Montgomerie, of Boreland, co. Dumfries, and Jacobina Smith his wife. Nephew of William Montgomerie, Major 37th Regt. *m.* Nagpur 8 Sept. 1821, Hannah, 4th dau. of Rev. Dr. Andrew Duncan, minister of Ratho. (*See also* David Bruce.)

Services : Barasat C.C. Posted Ensign to 1/27th N.I. Actg. Adjt. 1/27th N.I. in the field 26 Oct. 1807. Operations against Dhundia Khan 1807 ; Komona ; Ganauri ; Lieut. 1/27th N.I. Intr. & Qmr. 1/27th N.I. 1 July 1814 till Dec. 1816. Transfd. to 2/27th N.I. in 1817. Offg. S.A.C.G. 12 July 1816 ; S.A.C.G. 27 Dec. 1816 till Nov. 1820. Third Mahratta War ; S.A.C.G. with Div. under Lt.-Col. J. W. Adams, *q.v.* Pol. employ at Nagpur 14 Nov. 1820 ; Civil Comr. S. Narbada ; with Resdt. at Nagpur. Transfd. to 53rd N.I. (late 1/27th) May 1824. Asst. to Resdt. at Nagpur. Principal Asst. to A.G.G. Saugor & Narbada territories 23 Apr. 1830. Fur. s.c. via China 23 June 1830 till retirement. Retired on pension of 16/- *p.d.*

Refs. : Scott's *Fasti,* i. 183. *S.M.* N.S. x. 558.

MONTGOMERIE, Thomas (1796-1819). Lieutenant, Artillery. (462) *b.* Dreghorn, co. Ayr, 23 July 1796. Cadet 1814. Fireworker 14 Aug. 1817. Lieut. 1 Sept. 1818. *d.* Calcutta 18 Apr. 1819.

bapt. Dreghorn 27 July 1796. Son of Alexander Montgomerie, of Annick Lodge, co. Ayr (who was brother of Hugh, 12th Earl of Eglinton), Comdr. of the *Bombay Castle* Indiaman, formerly R.N., and Elizabeth his wife, dau. of Dr. John Taylor, Head Surg. Bengal Est., of Townhead, Lancs., and Abbot Hall, Kendal. Cousin-german of Archibald Montgomerie, *q.v.*, and related to John Taylor (1802-1822), *q.v.* Addiscombe Cadet 1813-14.

Services : Third Mahratta War 1817-18 ; Lieut. 3rd Troop H.A. Was A.D.C. to G.G. at the date of his death.

Refs. : Burke's *Landed Gentry,* 4th edn., p. 1026, *s.n.* Montgomerie, of Annick Lodge, co. Ayr. Foster's *Peerage,* p. 244, *s.n.* Eglinton, E. M.I. in S. Park St. cemetery, Calcutta.

MONTGOMERY, George James (1810-1860). Bt. Lieut. Colonel, 15th N.I. *b.* Ceylon 8 June 1810. Cadet 1828. Arrived in India 1 June 1829. Ensign 6 Jan. 1829. Lieut. 26 Feb. 1835. Capt. 24 Jan. 1845. Major 9 Oct. 1858. Bt. Lt. Col. 24 Mar. 1858. *d.* Calcutta 29 Sept. 1860.

Son of William Richard Montgomery, Ceylon C.S., and Catherine Imlach his wife, widow of Surgeon Thomas Anthony Reeder, H.M.

THE BENGAL ARMY, 1758-1834

51st Regt. His sister m. Sir James Anbury Mouat, Bart., q.v. m. Port Stewart, co. Londonderry, 20 July 1848, Julia Mary, 3rd dau. of Hon. and Rev. Charles Douglas, and niece of George Sholto Douglas, 17th Earl of Morton.

Services: Ensign d.d. 2nd N.I. 13 July 1829. Posted Ensign to 15th N.I. 14 Sept. 1829. Comdd. 2 Coys. Sebundy Sappers at Darjeeling 16 Sept. 1839 till 29 July 1840. Adjt. 15th N.I. 7 Jan. 1841 till Feb. 1845. First Sikh War; Ferozshahr; Capt. 15th N.I., with 33rd N.I. (Medal). Fur. p.a. 10 Sept. 1847 till 21 Nov. 1849. Bde. Major at Barrackpore 28 May 1852. Second Burma War 1852-3; Capt. 15th N.I., with H.M. 18th Ft. (Medal). Second in comd. Nassiri Bn. 10 Dec. 1853 till 15 Dec. 1854. Bde. Major, Meerut 28 Sept. 1855; do. Agra Oct. 1855 till 1858. Mutiny campaign, with Agra Bde.; attack on Nimach mutineers nr. Agra 5 July 1857 (horse shot); comdd. force at taking of Agra 23 Aug. 1857; battle of Agra 10 Oct. 1857 (Medal).

Refs.: Burke's *Peerage,* 1923, p. 1610, *s.n.* Morton, E.

*MONTGOMERY, John. Ensign. Infantry. Country Cadet 1782. Ensign (24 Feb. 1783) 10 May 1783.

Services: Apptd. Vol. by Sir Eyre Coote 25 July 1782, to serve with Bengal detachment during Second Mysore War; apptd. Cadet 27 Sept. 1782; posted Ensign to 1st Bengal Eur. Regt. 28 Feb. 1783, whilst still in Madras.

MOODIE, Thomas (1790-1824). Lieutenant, 34th N.I. *b.* Walls and Flotta, Orkney, 1 June 1790. Cadet 1810. Ensign 21 Aug. 1813. Lieut. 12 July 1815. *d. unm.* Kalpi, U.P., 27 Apr. 1824.

2nd son of Major James Moodie, IX of Melsetter, Orkney, J.P., and Elizabeth his wife, eldest dau. of Capt. Thomas Dunbar, of Grange Hill. Brother of Janet Dunbar, wife of his cousin Malcolm Nicolson (1792-1850), *q.v.* Ed. Edinburgh Univ.

Services: Cadet d.d. 16th N.I. 1811-13. Posted Ensign to 14th N.I. in 1813; transfd. as Lieut. to 2/1st N.I. July 1815. Siege and capture of Hathras 1817; Lieut. 2/1st N.I. Third Mahratta War; Dhamoni; Asirgarh; Lieut. 2/1st N.I. Intr. & Qmr. 2/1st N.I. 15 Jan. 1819 till 3 May 1822. Asst. to A.G.G. Saugor 1821; on pol. duty in Bundelkhand 1822 till death. Transfd. to newly-raised 34th N.I. July 1823.

Refs.: The Moodie Book, by the Marquis Ruvigny, p. 52. Will dated Calpee, 25 Apr. 1824; proved 12 June 1824. M.I. Kalpi cemetery.

MOODY, Hugh. Ensign. Infantry. Cadet 1770. Ensign 6 Dec. 1771. Resigned 4 Jan. 1774.
Services : N.F.P.

MOODY, Samuel (1781-?). Captain. 23rd N.I. *b.* Queen's Sq., Bloomsbury, Middlesex, 24 Apr. 1781. Cadet 1799. Arrived in India 11 Dec. 1800. Ensign 29 Aug. 1800. Lieut. 21 Feb. 1801. Capt. 18 Oct. 1812. Dismissed in England 22 Oct. 1815.

bapt. St. George the Martyr, Bloomsbury, 4 June 1781. Son of Samuel Moody, of Queen's Sq., and Elizabeth his wife, dau. of Thomas Johnson.

Services : Posted Lieut. to 1st Bengal Eur. Regt. 17 Apr. 1801. Second Mahratta War ; Gwalior ; battle and capture of Deig ; siege of Bhurtpore ; Lieut. Bengal Eur. Regt. Transfd. to newly-raised 23rd N.I. in 1805. Capt. Lt. 23rd N.I. 4 May 1812. Capt. 1/23rd N.I. Fur. 12 Feb. 1812 till dismissed.

MOODY, Stephen (1790-1856). Major General. Colonel 17th N.I. *bapt.* Newton St. Loe, Somerset, 25 Apr. 1790. Cadet 1805. Arrived in India 13 Dec. 1806. Ensign 24 Dec. 1806. Lieut. 16 Dec. 1814. Capt. 1 May 1824. Major 9 July 1835. Lt. Col. 14 June 1842. Col. 27 Oct. 1852. Maj. Gen. 28 Nov. 1854. *d.* 42 Porchester Sq., Hyde Pk., London, 28 Nov. 1856.

Son of Robert Moody, of Bath, and Catherine his wife. *m.* 1st, Meerut 5 Oct. 1818, Miss Elizabeth Lamborne (*probably* dau. of Charles Wale Lamborne, *q.v.*). (*See also* Joseph L. Revell.) (She died Cawnpore 15 Dec. 1838, aged 37.) *m.* 2nd, Cawnpore 11 June 1839, Mary Faithfull, eldest dau. of Griffiths Holmes, *q.v.* (She died 29 Sept. 1900, aged 80.)

Services : Barasat C.C. 8 mos. Posted Ensign to 4th N.I. in 1807. Nepal War 1816 ; Lieut. 2/4th N.I., in 4th Bde. Centre Column (India medal). Transfd. to 1/4th N.I. 1817 ; Intr. & Qmr. do. 10 May 1823 till 17 June 1824. Transfd. to 7th N.I. (late 1/4th) May 1824. First Burma War ; Cachar 1825 ; Capt. 7th N.I. (clasp to India medal). Fur. p.a. 5 Jan. 1829 till 14 Oct. 1831. Comdd. 7th N.I. Nov. 1837 till Jan. 1838 ; succeeded to comd. of do. 3 Oct. 1838. Posted Lt. Col. to 7th N.I. 21 July 1842 ; to 59th N.I. 13 Feb. 1844 ; to 20th N.I. 16 Nov. 1844. Fur. s.c. 7 Apr. 1845 till 1847. Transfd. to 32nd N.I. Dec. 1847 ; to 70th N.I. Aug. 1850 ; to 11th N.I. 20 May 1851. Fur. s.c. 21 Sept. 1851 till death. Transfd. to 18th N.I. 6 Dec. 1851 ; to 72nd N.I. June 1852. Col. 17th N.I. Jan. 1853 till death.

THE BENGAL ARMY, 1758-1834   319

Refs.: Boase. *G.M.* 1857, i. 122. Will dated Nimach, 6 Jan. 1842; admon. 11 Mar. 1857.

MOORE, Augustus (1790-1809). Ensign, 17th N.I. *b.* 1790. Cadet 1805. Arrived in India 13 Dec. 1806. Ensign 15 Dec. 1806. *d. unm.* Muttra 5 Aug. 1809.

bapt. St. Mary's, Lambeth, 20 June 1790. 8th and youngest son of Edward Moore, of Stockwell House, Surrey, barr. of the Inner Temple, lord of the manor of Leigh Priors, Westbury, Wilts., and Sarah Gray his 2nd wife, dau. of Joseph Saunders, of Ealing. Brother of George Moore (1789-1848), cousin-german of Thomas Perring Moore, and related to Farquharson Tweedale, *qq.v.*
Services: Barasat C.C. Posted Ensign to 2/17th N.I. in 1807. No record of active service.
Refs.: Burke's *Landed Gentry*, 13th edn., p. 1264, *s.n.* Moore, of Frampton Hall, Lincs. Foster's *Peds. of W.R. Yorks.*, *s.n.* More, of Barnborough Hall. Will dated 23 May 1809; proved 15 Dec. 1809. M.I. Muttra Cantt. cemetery.

MOORE, Charles (1754-1781). Captain, Infantry. *bapt.* St. Augustine's, Bristol, 23 June 1754. Cadet 1771. Ensign 13 Jan. 1773. Lieut. 7 Apr. 1777. Capt. 1 Apr. 1781. *d.* Bombay 12 May 1781, of wounds received on service with the Bombay detachment.

Son of Thomas Moore, of Bristol, apothecary, and Anne his wife. Brother of James Moore (1751-1785), *q.v.*, and of Henry Moore, Member of Bombay Council.
Services: First Mahratta War; retreat down the Bhor Ghaut 24 Apr. 1781 (s.w.).
Refs.: *India Gazette*, 9 June 1781. Will dated 16 Feb. 1781; proved at Bombay 5 June 1781.

MOORE, Francis (*d.* 1773). Lieutenant, Artillery. (89) Fireworker 1 Sept. 1768. Lieut. 12 Mar. 1770. *d. unm.* Calcutta 30 Oct. 1773, of liver complaint.

Son of —— Moore and Frances his wife. Brother of Frances Moore.
Services: Cadet at R.M.A., Woolwich, 1767; apptd. Lt. F. in England 24 Dec. 1767. (M.C. 1 Sept. 1768.)
Refs.: Will dated Benares 6 Sept. 1773; proved 16 Nov. 1773.

MOORE, Frederick Russell (1801-1875). Major. 52nd N.I. *b.* Kenton, Devon, 24 Sept. 1801. Cadet 1820. Arrived in India 23 Mar. 1822. Ensign 29 Sept. 1821. Lieut. 16 Mar. 1824.

Capt. 24 Nov. 1836. Invalided 16 Sept. 1840. Retired 24 July 1849. Hon. Major 28 Nov. 1854. *d.* 28 Apr. 1875.
Son of John Hartnoll Moore, of Cadeleigh Court, Devon. *m.* Chittagong 4 Apr. 1827, Jane, eldest dau. of Henry Jacques, *q.v.*, and widow of John Swinton, *q.v.*
Services: Posted Ensign to 2nd N.I. in 1822; transfd. to 26th N.I. 1823; to 52nd N.I. (late 2/26th) May 1824. (? First Burma War; Cachar 1825; Lieut. 52nd N.I.) Actg. Adjt. Tempy. Pioneers 12 Feb. 1827. d.d. Rt. Wing 6th N.I. May-Oct. 1832. d.d. at Chunar 12 Feb. 1841 till 1844. Fur. p.a. 24 Jan. 1847 till retirement.

MOORE, George (1777-1805). Lieutenant, Bengal Eur. Regt. *b.* 20 Aug. 1777. Cadet 1798. Arrived in India 1 Sept. 1800. Ensign 29 Aug. 1799. Lieut. 28 Oct. 1799. *d. unm.* 20 Feb. 1805: kld. in action at the assault of Bhurtpore.
bapt. Rothesay 22 Aug. 1777. 3rd son of Archibald Muir (who spelt his name Moore), mgte. for Rothesay, and Jean his wife, dau. of George Robertson, factor on the Bute estates.
Services: Posted Lieut. to 1st Bengal Eur. Regt. 15 Apr. 1801. Second Mahratta War; capture of Gwalior; battle and capture of Deig; siege of Bhurtpore (mortally w. in 3rd assault); Lieut. Bengal Eur. Regt.
Refs.: J. E. Reid's *Hist. of co. Bute*, p. 243. *Innes*, p. 305. Will dated camp before Dig, 11 Dec. 1804; proved 12 July 1805.

MOORE, George (1789-1848). Colonel, 59th N.I. Bdr. comdg. Rajputana F.F. *b.* 12 Apr. 1789. Cadet 1804. Arrived in India 16 May 1806. Ensign 5 Mar. 1806. Lieut. 1 Feb. 1807. Capt. 11 July 1823. Major 10 June 1826. Lt. Col. 18 June 1831. Col. 26 May 1843. *d.* at sea 29 July 1848, on board the *Earl of Hardwicke.*
bapt. St. Mary, Lambeth, 11 May 1789. 7th son of Edward Moore and Sarah Gray his 2nd wife. Brother of Augustus Moore, *q.v. m.* 1st, Kaitha 20 Apr. 1808, Miss Sarah Munt, of Clapham (*perhaps* sister of George McIntosh Munt, *q.v.*). (*See also* James Templer Parlby.) (She died 9 Mar. 1821.) His daus. *m.* William Blackwood, *q.v.*, and Joseph Towgood, *q.v. m.* 2nd, St. John's, Calcutta, 4 Nov. 1826, Sarah, dau. of John Cattell, of Knowle Hall, co. Warwick. (She died Lucknow 23 Dec. 1835, aged 31.) *m.* 3rd, Simla 15 Nov. 1843, Constance Mary Ophelia, eldest dau. of John Oliver, *q.v.* (*See also* Robert Campbell (1800-1889).) (She died Simla 8 Nov. 1856.)

THE BENGAL ARMY, 1758-1834

Services : Present at capture of Cape in Jan. 1806 as a Cadet. Barasat C.C. Posted Lieut. to 1st N.I. in 1807. Transfd. to newly-raised 1/30th N.I. in 1815. Nepal War 1816 ; Makwanpur ; Lieut. 1/30th N.I., in 4th Bde. Centre Column. In telegraph dept. 1 Apr. 1822 till 20 Sept. 1824. Transfd. to 59th N.I. (late 1/30th) May 1824. Posted to 2nd Gren. Bn. 23 Dec. 1824. First Burma War ; Arakan 1825 ; Capt. 2nd Gren. Bn. Posted Lt. Col. to 59th N.I. 7 Jan. 1832. Bdr. 2 cl. comdg. 3rd Bde. 2nd Div. Army of Reserve (for Afghanistan) 6 June 1842 till 10 Jan. 1843. Transfd. to 7th N.I. 2 Feb. 1843. Posted Col. to 35th N.I. 30 Oct. 1843. Bdr. 2 cl. comdg. 3rd Bde. 2nd Div. Army of Exercise 21 Oct. 1843 ; do. 5th Bde. 12 Dec. 1843. To comd. garr. of Agra 29 Jan. 1844. Bdr. 1 cl. comdg. Rajputana F.F. 30 May 1845 till Mar. 1848. Transfd. to 59th N.I. 1846. Fur. s.c. 3 Mar. 1848 (the first fur. for 44 yrs.) till death.

Refs. : Burke's *Landed Gentry,* 13th edn., p. 1264, *s.n.* Moore, of Frampton Hall, Lincs. Burke's *Royal Families,* ped. lxii. *Patrician,* vi. 310. *I.N.* 1848, p. 405. Will dated Nasirabad, 8 Sept. 1847 ; proved 8 Nov. 1849.

MOORE, Henry (1804-1881). Lieut. Colonel, C.B. 34th N.I. *b.* 25 Oct. 1804. Cadet 1821. Arrived in India 25 June 1822. Ensign 19 Jan. 1822. Lieut. 27 Mar. 1824. Capt. 14 Aug. 1839. Bt. Major 26 May 1841. Retired 24 June 1847. Hon. Lt. Col. 28 Nov. 1854. *d.* Promenade Terr., Cheltenham, 7 Dec. 1881.

bapt. Maryborough, Queen's Co., 31 Oct. 1804. 2nd son of Henry Moore, of Cremorgan, Queen's Co., high sheriff 1784, and Anne his wife, dau. of Mark Scott, elder brother of John, 1st Earl of Clonmell. Brother of Thomas Moore, *q.v.* Ed. Charterhouse Sept. 1817-May 1819.

Services : Posted Ensign to 29th N.I. in 1822 ; transfd. to 17th N.I. in 1823 ; to 35th N.I. (late 2/17th) May 1824 ; to 34th N.I. 13 May 1825. Actg. Intr. & Qmr. 34th N.I. 25 June 1828 ; actg. Adjt. 3rd Local Horse 3 Nov. 1828 ; actg. 2nd in comd. do. 10 Feb. 1829. Fur. s.c. 5 Feb. 1832 till 9 Feb. 1835. Offg. tempy. A.A.G. Meerut Div. Oct. 1838. D.J.A.G. Dinapore and Benares Div. 25 June 1839 ; do. Saugor Div. 16 Mar. 1841 ; do. Sirhind Div. 27 Feb. 1843 till Aug. 1845. Apptd. D.J.A.G. to force proceeding to China 11 Mar. 1840 till 7 Dec. 1843. First China War 1840-2 ; capture of Canton (*Lond. Gaz.* 8 Oct. 1841); sally from Ningpo Mar. 1842 (ib. 6 Sept. 1842) ; D.J.A.G. (Medal). Fur. 10 Aug. 1845 till retirement. C.B. 24 Dec. 1842.

Refs. : Burke's *Landed Gentry of Ireland,* p. 495, *s.n.* Moore, of

Cremorgan, Queen's Co. *Charterhouse School List.* *The Times,*
9 Dec. 1881.

MOORE, James ($17\frac{50}{51}$-1785). Major, 24th N.I. *b.* 24 Feb.
$17\frac{50}{51}$. Cadet 1768. Ensign 8 Jan. 1769. Lieut. 5 Dec. 1770.
Capt. 14 July 1778. Major 1 Feb. 1784. *d.* Ghireti, nr. Palta,
Bengal, 26 Jan. 1785 : committed suicide by discharging the
contents of a fowling-piece into his mouth.[1]
bapt. St. Augustine's, Bristol, 23 June 1754. Son of Thomas
Moore, of Bristol, apothecary, and Anne his wife. Brother of
William Moore, *q.v.*, of Anne Collins, of Bath, and of Mary, wife
of Benjamin Ashe, *q.v.*
Services : Capt. 1/1st Bengal Eur. Regt. in Oct. 1779. Second
Mysore War 1781-5 ; battle of Virakandalur [2] ; Capt. Bengal Eur.
Regt. Transfd. as Major to 24th N.I.
Refs. : Innes, p. 266. Will dated 26 July 1784 ; proved 14 Feb.
1785. M.I. in the compound of a babu's villa at Champdani, close
to the Hooghly R., opposite Palta.

[1] *Note :* "A violent depression of spirits, almost bordering on
insanity, caused the fatal act."—Opinion of the Court of Inquiry.

[2] *Note :* "The brave and seasonable exertion of the Coy. of
Bengal Grenadiers, under the command of Capt. Moore, is worthy
of the highest applause and should be ever held in remembrance
as a proof of the merit of the Coy. in particular and honourable
to the corps they belong to." (Order issued by Sir Eyre Coote
immediately after this action.)

MOORE, James (*d.* 1788). Ensign, Infantry. Country Cadet
1782. Ensign (24 Feb. 1783) 6 May 1783. *d.* Berhampore
12 July 1788.
"The son of a gentleman, is of good character, and was badly
wronged on board ship on his way out to India." (*Orig. Cons.*
18 Mar. 1782, No. 8.)
Services : Sailed for India as a Vol. in Art. in the *True Briton*
16 June 1779. Apptd. Cadet from Corpl. in Art. 18 Mar. 1782 ;
posted Ensign to 2nd Bengal Eur. Regt. 28 Feb. 1783.

*MOORE, John (1807/08-1843). Bt. Captain, 1st L.C. *b.*
1807/08. Cadet 1826. Admitted 26 Aug. 1826. Cornet (13 Feb.
1826) 25 Aug. 1826. Lieut. 24 Oct. 1828. Bt. Capt. 13 Feb.
1841. *d.* in Europe 17 Apr. 1843.
Son of Joseph Moore, Lieut. H.M. 89th Regt.

THE BENGAL ARMY, 1758-1834

Services: Went out to Madras in charge of King's recruits on board the *Marquis of Huntly.* Was Lieut. H.M. 89th at Madras when nominated Cadet in Feb. 1826. Cornet d.d. 2nd L.C. 29 Aug. 1826. Posted to 1st L.C. 25 Sept. 1826. Actg. Adjt. 1st L.C. 27 June 1836; permanent do. 23 Jan. 1839 till Sept. 1840. Leave s.c. in India 1 Feb. 1839 till 31 Jan. 1840. Fur. s.c. 27 Sept. 1840 till 10 Sept. 1842, and 12 Dec. 1842 till death. No record of active service.

MOORE, Nathaniel (1789-1823). Lieutenant. 17th N.I. *b.* Achnacloy, co. Tyrone, 3 Nov. 1789. Cadet 1806. Arrived in India 17 Mar. 1808. Ensign 1 Apr. 1808. Lieut. 28 June 1813. Resigned 31 Aug. 1816. *d.s.p.* 1823.

3rd son of Nathaniel Montgomery (who assumed, in right of his mother, the surname and arms of Moore), of Garvey, Revella, and Fassaroe, high sheriff 1786, M.P. for Strabane and afterwards co. Tyrone, Col. Tyrone Mil., and Mary Anne his wife, dau. of Alexander Boyd, of Ballycastle. *m.* Agnes Cox, of Exeter.

Services: Barasat C.C. Cadet d.d. 12th N.I. 1810; Ensign d.d. 3rd N.I. 1811; posted Ensign to 17th N.I. 1812. Nepal War 1814-15; Lieut. 1/17th N.I., in 2nd Div.

Refs.: Burke's *Landed Gentry of Ireland,* p. 494, *s.n.* Montgomery-Moore, *late* of Garvey, co. Limerick.

MOORE, Thomas (1808-1886). Major General. 5th Bengal Eur. L.C. *b.* Cremorgan, Queen's Co., 23 Sept. 1808. Cadet 1824. Arrived in India 1 June 1825. Cornet 11 Dec. 1824. Lieut. 13 May 1825. Capt. 21 Jan. 1839. Major 1 Apr. 1854. Lt. Col. 16 Aug. 1859. Bt. Col. 27 Sept. 1859. Retired 31 Dec. 1861. Hon. Maj. Gen. 31 Dec. 1861. *d.* 1 Lypiatt Terr., Cheltenham, 1 Oct. 1886.

Of Highthorn, co. Dublin. 3rd son of Henry Moore, of Cremorgan, and Anne his wife. Brother of Henry Moore, *q.v. m.* Sultanpur, Benares, 28 Nov. 1836, Isabella Maria, 3rd dau. of Jonah John Hogg, of Calcutta, and sister of Robert William Hogg, *q.v.* (She died 21 Dec. 1890, aged 71.)

Services: Cornet d.d. 4th L.C. 11 June 1825. Posted Cornet to 1st L.C. in 1825. Transfd. to 8th L.C. 5 Mar. 1826. Adjt. 8th L.C. 18 Jan. 1836 till 8 June 1838. Leave s.c. in India 1 Feb. 1839 till 10 Nov. 1840. Insurrection in Bundelkhand 1842; led a Sqdn. of 8th L.C. and 2 Coys. 13th N.I. against a body of 3,000 Bundela insurgents at Panwari 9 June 1842, killing upwards of 80, including their leader (w. in left knee); Capt. 8th L.C. Granted a gratuity and pension for wound equal to loss of limb. Supt. family money, and Paymr. of native pensioners at Barrackpore, 19 Dec. 1842. Fur. s.c. 12 Feb. 1844 till 16 Oct. 1846. Second Sikh War; Ramnagar; Sadulapur; Chilianwala; Gujerat; Capt. 8th L.C. (Medal with 2 clasps). Paymr. of native pensioners at Hapur Mar. 1850 till 1855. Leave s.c. 2 yrs. to Cape 18 Dec. 1855 till 1857. Transfd. to newly-raised 5th Eur. L.C. in 1858.

Refs.: Burke's *Landed Gentry of Ireland*, p. 495, *s.n.* Moore, of Cremorgan, Queen's Co. *The Times*, 4 Oct. 1886.

MOORE, Thomas Perring (1789-1809). Cornet. Cavalry. Subsequently Writer, M.C.S. *b.* Hadley, Herts., 10 July 1789. Cadet 1804. Arrived in India 16 May 1806. Cornet 29 Mar. 1806. Resigned 20 Feb. 1807. *d.s.p.* at sea 14 Mar. 1809 : lost in the *Jane, Duchess of Gordon.*

6th and youngest son of Peter Moore, lord of the manor of Hadley, M.P. for Coventry, and Sarah his wife, 2nd dau. of Lt.-Col. Richmond Webb. Cousin-german of Augustus Moore, *q.v.*, and 1st cousin once removed of Sir Richmond Cambell Shakespear, *q.v.*, and of William Makepeace Thackeray, the novelist (*D.N.B.*). Ed. Westminster; in school list 1801. Woolwich Cadet; nominated for R.M.A. 25 Jan. 1805 ; resigned in June 1805.

Services: Apptd. Cadet 9 Jan. 1805. Apptd. a Writer on the Madras Est.; Asst. to Sec., Board of Revenue, 1808.

Refs.: Burke's *Landed Gentry*, 11th edn., p. 1184, *s.n.* Moore, of Frampton Hall, Lincs. *Monken Hadley*, by F. C. Cass, p. 75. *Westminster School Register*.

MOORE, William (1752/53-?). Lieutenant. Infantry. *b.* in Ireland 1752/53. Cadet 1776. Ensign 18 Mar. 1777. Lieut. 14 Aug. 1778. Resigned 3 Apr. 1782.[1]

Services: Sailed for India in the *Latham* 10 Apr. 1776, aged 23. Apptd. a Writer for Fort Marlbro' Mar. 1777, but did not take up the appt. Lieut. 2/2nd Bengal Eur. Regt. in Oct. 1779.

[1] *Note:* Resigned owing to ill health due to active service in the field. (? Capt. 18 Mar. 1782.)

MOORE, William. Lieutenant, Pension Est. Infantry. Country Cadet 1778. Ensign 1778. Lieut. 13 Feb. 1779. Pensioned (after 1790).

Son of Thomas Moore, of Bristol, apothecary, and Anne his wife. Brother of Charles Moore, *q.v.*

Services: Apptd. Cadet 27 Feb. 1778. Lieut. 2/1st Bengal

Eur. Regt. in Oct. 1779. On fur. in Dec. 1788. Shown in a MS. *A.L.* of 29 Jan. 1791 as, "Absent by leave—said to have got a Commission in the King's Navy." (One of this name became a Comdr. 24 Dec. 1798.)

MOORE, William. Lieutenant. Infantry. Cadet 1780. Ensign 1780. Lieut. 28 July 1781.
Struck off 1788, never having arrived in India.

MOORE, William White (1789-1861). Colonel. 16th N.I. *b.* 2 Nov. 1789. Cadet 1805. Arrived in India 11 July 1806. Ensign 11 Aug. 1806. Lieut. 2 June 1808. Capt. 14 July 1819. Major 8 Sept. 1828. Lt. Col. 19 Oct. 1833. Retired 4 May 1837. Hon. Col. 28 Nov. 1854. *d.* at his residence, 31 Grove End Rd., St. John's Wood, London, 19 Sept. 1861.

bapt. St. Vedast Foster 27 Dec. 1789. Son of Isaac Moore and Ann his wife. *m.* Berhampore 30 May 1811, Johanna Elizabeth, 2nd dau. of John Pieter Baumgardt, sister of Francis Robert Baumgardt, *q.v.*, and aunt of John Laughton, *q.v.*

Services : Barasat C.C. 11 mos. Posted Ensign to 12th N.I. in 1807. Operations in Oudh 1808 ; Lieut. 2/12th N.I. Suspended from rank and pay for 3 mos. by G.C.M. 11 July 1810. Nepal War 1816 ; Lieut. 2/12th N.I., in 3rd Bde. Centre Column (India medal). Siege and capture of Hathras.; Lieut. 2/12th N.I. Actg. Adjt. 2/12th N.I. 7 Oct. 1817. Third Mahratta War ; Dhamoni ; Lieut. 2/12th N.I. Operations against the Bhattis of Hariana 1818 ; Lieut. 2/12th N.I. Capt. 2/12th N.I. Leave s.c. to Cape 8 Oct. 1822 till 29 Oct. 1825. Transfd. to 12th N.I. (late 1/12th) May 1824. Posted Lt. Col. to 12th N.I. 16 May 1834 ; to 41st N.I. 29 Oct. 1834 ; to 16th N.I. 12 Jan. 1836. Fur. s.c. 7 Jan. 1835 till retirement.

Refs. : De La Ferté. *G.M.* 1861, ii. 458. *The Times,* 20 Sept. 1861.

*MOORHOUSE, Henry (1805-?). Cadet. Infantry. *b.* Chelsea, Middlesex, 5 Jan. 1805. Cadet 1824.

bapt. St. Luke's, Chelsea, 25 Oct. 1805. Son of John Moorhouse and Eliza Ann his wife. Brother of Thomas Mould Edgar Moorhouse, *q.v.*

Services : Was already in Bengal when apptd. Cadet, having accompanied Sir Christopher Puller, the late C.J., from England. (Gen. Letter from C.D., dated 15 Dec. 1824 ; G.O. 139 of 6 May 1825.) N.F.P.

MOORHOUSE, Thomas Mould Edgar (1807-1857). Bt. Major, 35th N.I. *b*. Chelsea 29 Dec. 1807. Cadet 1824. Arrived in India 26 Nov. 1825. Ensign 18 Apr. 1825. Lieut. 30 Dec. 1827. Capt. 29 Oct. 1841. Bt. Major 11 Nov. 1851. *d*. Allahabad 4 June 1857, of heat stroke and fatigue. *bapt*. St. Luke's, Chelsea, 21 May 1811. Son of John Moorhouse, of Clarges St., London, merchant, and Eliza Ann his wife. Brother of Henry Moorhouse, *q.v*. *m*. 1st, Meerut 11 Oct. 1844, Mary Anne, dau. of Alexander Davidson, Surgeon 10th L.C. (She died Allahabad 29 Nov. 1848, aged 24.) *m*. 2nd, Allahabad 24 Aug. 1852, Fanny Sarah, dau. of William Robert Fitzgerald, *q.v*.

Services : Posted Ensign to 35th N.I. Leave s.c. to Cape 6 Nov. 1829 till 25 Nov. 1831. Apptd. to Shah Shuja's army 6 Aug. 1839. First Afghan War 1839-42 ; capture of Ghazni 1839, 2nd in comd. Shah's 4th Inf. (Medal) ; operations in Kohistan 1840 ; Parwandara ; forcing of Khurd Kabul and Jagdalak passes 1841 ; defence of Jalalabad (Medal) ; action of 7 Apr. 1842 (s.w.) ; all engagements leading to reoccupation of Kabul (*Lond. Gaz*. 7 June and 9 Aug. 1842) ; Capt. 35th N.I., with Sir R. Sale's force. Actg. Intr. & Qmr. 37th N.I. July 1840 ; Intr. & Qmr. 35th N.I. 27 Nov. 1841. Actg. Paymr. and Supt. of native pensioners at Meerut and Hapur 8 Sept. 1843 ; do. Allahabad, Jubbulpore and Saugor 23 Nov. 1843 ; permanent do. at Allahabad 15 Jan. 1845 till death.

Refs. : *G.M*. 1857, ii. 466. *I.M*. 17 Sept. 1857, p. 591.

MORAN, John. Lieutenant, Infantry. Cadet 1771. Ensign 5 Mar. 1773. Lieut. 25 Mar. 1778. (*d*. before 1780.)

Services : Apptd. Cadet 1770, but was unable to sail until 1771 owing to illness.

*MORAN, Patrick (*d*. 1769). Captain. Bengal Eur. Regt. Ensign 6 June 1757. Lieut. 1758. Capt. 20 Sept. 1759. Resigned July 1765. *d*. in England 24 Mar. 1769.

Services : Was a civilian in Calcutta at the time of the siege in 1756, and one of the few survivors of the Black Hole. Was subsequently given a Commission as Ensign in Bengal Eur. Regt. Battle of Plassey ; Ensign Bengal Eur. Regt. Expedn. to N. Circars 1758-9 ; battle of Condore (w.) ; storm of Masulipatam ; Lieut. Bengal Eur. Regt. War with Mir Muhammad Kasim 1763 ; battle of Udhua Nullah ; Capt. Bengal Eur. Regt. Battle of Buxar.

Refs. : *Hill, passim*. *Forde*, pp. 64, 66. *Innes*, p. 157. *Broome*, p. 73. *Orme MSS.—India*, xiii. 3639. *G.M*. 1769, p. 215.

THE BENGAL ARMY, 1758-1834

MORDAUNT, Henry (d. 1791). Captain, Infantry. Cadet 1772. Ensign 3 Jan. 1773. Lieut. 29 Mar. 1777. Capt. 25 Mar. 1781. d. in his budgerow nr. Chunar 8 Feb. 1791.

Eldest natural son of Charles, 4th Earl of Peterborough. Brother of Lewis Mordaunt, q.v., and half-brother of Charles Henry, 5th Earl.

Services: Lieut. in H.M.S. Adjt. & Qmr. 1st Regt. Cav. in June 1776; apptd. to Body-Guard of Nawab-Wazir of Oudh 12 Nov. 1778. Fur. 19 Nov. 1779 till 1782. Comdt. of Buxar fort and garr. 21 Nov. 1785 till death.

Refs.: Hickey, ii. passim; iv. 22. M.M. 1808, i. 138, 144-5. S.M. 1791, p. 203. M.I. Benares.

MORDAUNT, Henry (1784-1820). Captain, 7th N.I. b. London 23 Sept. 1784. Cadet 1799. Admitted 30 Oct. 1800. Ensign 10 Sept. 1800. Lieut. 9 Sept. 1801. Capt. 15 June 1814. d. 14 Aug. 1820.

bapt. St. Andrew's Undershaft, London, 21 Oct. 1784. Son of George Mordaunt and Dorothy his wife. (Perhaps nephew of John Mordaunt, q.v.) Ed. Tonbridge School 1793-4; Merchant Taylors' 1794-5.

Services: Posted Ensign to 1/7th N.I. 17 Apr. 1801. Reduction of Kalinjar 1812; Lieut. 1/7th N.I. Capt. Lt. 7th N.I. 1 Feb. 1814. Nepal War 1814-15; Capt. 1/7th N.I., in 2nd Div. Third Mahratta War 1817-18; Capt. 1/7th N.I. With 2nd Ceylon Vol. Bn. 1818-19.

Refs.: Tonbridge School Register, 1553-1820. Robinson.

MORDAUNT, John (d. 1794). Captain, Artillery. (133) Cadet 1772. Fireworker 23 Feb. 1773. Lieut. 8 Mar. 1778. Capt. Lt. 1 July 1782. Capt. 24 May 1786. d. unm. 26 Oct. 1794: kld. in action at the battle of Bitaurah.

Brother of George Mordaunt.

Services: Apptd. Adjt. of Art., Tempy. Bde., 14 Sept. 1778. Capt. 3rd Bn. Art. in July 1787. Second Rohilla War; battle of Bitaurah (kld.); Capt. 2nd Coy. 3rd Bn., comdg. the Art.

Refs.: Hickey, iv. 121-2. Will dated Cawnpore 1 Oct. 1794; proved 16 Dec. 1794. M.I. in St. John's churchyard, Calcutta.

MORDAUNT, Lewis (1759/60-1781). Lieutenant, Infantry. b. 1759/60? Cadet 1776. Ensign 31 Mar. 1777. Lieut. 27 Aug. 1778. d. Calcutta 19 Sept. 1781, of liver complaint, aged 21.

Natural son of Charles, 4th Earl of Peterborough. Brother of Henry Mordaunt (d. 1791), q.v.

Services: Apptd. Cadet 13 Dec. 1775; sailed for India in the *Shrewsbury* 14 Mar. 1776. Lieut. 1/3rd Bengal Eur. Regt. in Oct. 1779. Second Mysore War; apptd. Dy. Baggage Mr. and Dy. Comy. of provisions to Col. Pearse's detachment in May 1781, but returned sick to Calcutta the following month.
Refs.: M.I. in S. Park St. cemetery, Calcutta.

MORE, John Forbes (1783-1815). Capt. Lieutenant, 1st N.I.
b. College kirk psh., Edinburgh, 7 Jan. 1783. Cadet 1800. Admitted 28 Sept. 1801. Ensign 10 Nov. 1801. Lieut. 13 July 1803. Capt. Lt. 16 Dec. 1814. *d.* Calcutta 11 July 1815.
bapt. Edinburgh 25 Jan. 1783. Son of John More, "painter" (? artist), and Christian Forbes his wife. *m.* Lucknow Jan. 1806, Jane Eden, dau. of Richard Grueber, *q.v.* (She died Monghyr 8 Aug. 1860, aged 66.)
Services: Ensign d.d. 19th N.I. in 1802; posted Ensign to 1st N.I. Adjt. 2/1st N.I. 5 June 1805 till death. Operations in Bundelkhand 1806-7; Chamir; Sehlehuganj. Bundelkhand 1809; Rajaoli; Ajaigarh. Nepal War 1814-15; Capt. Lt. 2/1st N.I., in 1st Div.
Refs.: M.I. in N. Park St. cemetery, Calcutta.

MORGAN, Charles (1742/43-1819). Lieut. General. 11th N.I.
b. 1742/43. Capt. 13 May 1765. Major 29 Sept. 1769. Lt. Col. 14 Sept. 1770.[1] Col. 28 May 1786. Maj. Gen. 20 Dec. 1793. Lt. Gen. 26 June 1799. Retired on the Off-reckoning fund 1 Jan. 1803. *d.* Portland Pl., London, 21 Mar. 1819, aged 76.
Uncle of Thomas Morgan (1762/63-1792), *q.v.* (*Probably* brother of James Morgan, *q.v.*) *m.* Calcutta 19 Dec. 1777, Hannah, eldest dau. of William Wagstaff, of Manchester, apothecary, and sister of Thomas Wagstaff, *q.v.* (*See also* Alexander Kyd.) His dau. *m.* Valentine Brown, 2nd Baron Cloncurry.
Services: Ensign 53rd Ft. 7 Mar. 1759. Ensign 5th Ft. 20 Dec. 1759; Lieut. do. 17 May 1762; h.p. do. 1763 till death.[2] Transfd. as Capt. to Bengal Army in 1765; apptd. A.D.C. to Lord Clive 15 May 1765. Dismissed by the Board in Calcutta Mar. 1772, and sailed for England 12 May 1772. Readmitted and arrived in India 15 Aug. 1774. Q.M.G. and contractor for boats Sept. 1778 till Dec. 1781. First Mahratta War; sent to comd. the Bengal detachment; took over comd. from Goddard in Sept. 1782, and brought it back to Cawnpore in Apr. 1784. Fur. 29 May 1784 till Oct. 1788, and 7 Apr. 1790 till 1791. Provl. C.-in-C. Bengal 23 Jan. till 16 Mar. 1797. Comdd. the force assembled in 1797 to

resist the advance of Shah Zaman, of Kabul, into the Punjab. Fur. 5 Dec. 1797 till retirement.
Refs.: *G.M.* 1819, i. 378. *S.M.* 1819, i. 480. M.I. in St. John's church, St. John's Wood Rd., London.

[1] *Note*: Granted, as Q.M.G., tempy. rank of Lt. Col. 11 Jan. 1779, to date from Sept. 1778 ; substantive rank later antedated to Sept. 1770.

[2] *Note*: "Mr. Charles Morgan may proceed to Bengal in a seafaring way."—1 Dec. 1762.

MORGAN, James (1739/40-1808). Colonel. Infantry. *b.* 1739/40. Cadet (?) Ensign 1 Mar. 1759. Lieut. 19 Sept. 1759. Capt. 15 Oct. 1763. Major 2 May 1766. Lt. Col. 3 Apr. 1768. Col. 10 Nov. 1774. Resigned 10 Oct. 1785. *d.* at his house, Above-Bar, Winchester, 29 Oct. 1808, aged 68.

Sometime of Southampton. (*Probably* brother of Charles Morgan, *q.v.*) *m.* in England 19 Dec. 1774, Mary, eldest dau. of Rev. Joseph Warton, D.D., headmaster of Winchester (*D.N.B.*). (She died 18 Nov. 1846, aged 84.)

Services: Apptd. Qmr., vice Francis Cozens, *q.v.*, 15 Sept. 1763. Raised at Patna in Mar. 1764 the 21st Bn. Sepoys, called after him "*Morgan-ki-Paltan.*" This Bn. was incorporated in the two Bns. of 10th N.I. in 1796, becoming eventually 14th and 16th N.I. Battle of Buxar; Capt. comdg. 11th Bn. (late 21st). Posted as Lt. Col. to Inf. Bde. in May 1772. Fur. Feb. 1773 till Nov. 1775. Col. comdg. 1st Div. 2nd Bengal Eur. Regt. in Sept. 1777, when he was apptd. to comd. troops at Berhampore ; comdd. 2nd Bde. 1780-5. Was comdg. 2nd Eur. Regt., and comdg. field station of Cawnpore in Aug. 1781.

Refs.: *Williams*, p. 149. *Cardew*, pp. 22, 23. *G.M.* 1774, p. 598 ; 1808, ii. 1043. M.I. in Winchester cathedral.

MORGAN, James John M'Clary (1809-1836). Ensign, 63rd N.I. *b.* Bengal 11 Oct. 1809. Cadet 1826. Arrived in India 20 May 1827. Ensign 17 Jan. 1827. *d.* Sultanpur, U.P., 20 Sept. 1836.

Son of Thomas Morgan (1760/61-1814), *q.v.* Brother of Thomas William Morgan, *q.v.*, and cousin-german of Sulivan Harington Steer, *q.v. m.* Calcutta 26 Apr. 1834, Miss Arabella Black.

Services: Ensign d.d. 14th N.I. 28 May 1827. Posted to 14th N.I. 17 June 1827 ; transfd. to 55th N.I. 1 July 1828 ; to 63rd N.I. 4 Nov. 1834. No record of active service.

Refs.: *A.J.* N.S. xxii. 191.

MORGAN, Patrick Peter [1] (1783-1836). Captain. 26th N.I. *b.* Ardrahan, co. Galway, 26 Sept. 1783. Cadet 1804. Arrived in India 10 Sept. 1805. Ensign 16 Nov. 1805. Lieut. 23 Aug. 1806. Capt. 12 May 1821. Struck off by sentence of G.C.M. 6 Mar. 1824. *d.s.p.* 1836.

Of Monksfield, co. Galway. 2nd son of Charles Morgan, of Monksfield, and Margaret his wife, dau. of Peter Blake, of Corbally, co. Galway. T.C.D.; Fellow Commoner 6 July 1802.

Services: Posted to 26th N.I. in 1806. Operations in Bundelkhand 1807; Sehlehuganj; Lieut. 26th N.I. Bundelkhand 1809; Ajaigarh; Lieut. 26th N.I. (? Capture of Java 1811; Lieut. 5th Bengal Vol. Bn.) Served with 5th Vol. Bn. till 1816. Operations against Bhattis of Hariana Sept.-Oct. 1818; Lieut. 2/26th N.I.

Refs.: Alumni Dub.

[1] *Note:* Officially, but incorrectly, Peter Patrick Morgan.

MORGAN, Thomas (1760/61-1814). Lieut. Colonel, 15th N.I. *b.* Stafford 1760/61. Cadet 1780. Arrived in India 27 Apr. 1781. Ensign 1780. Lieut. 30 July 1781. Capt. 3 Jan. 1799. Major 21 Sept. 1804. Lt. Col. 2 Jan. 1810. *d.* Banda 14 June 1814.

His daus. *m.* Nathaniel Barrett Bromley and Henry Edwin Page, *qq.v. m.* Calcutta 16 Feb. 1805, Charlotte Macleod Stewart, dau. of Samuel Watson (1748/49-1814), *q.v.* Father of James John M'Clary Morgan and Thomas William Morgan, *qq.v.* (? His sister Jane *m.* Capt. John McClary, the privateering Bengal merchant, brother of William MacClary, *q.v.*)

Services: Sailed for India in the *Grosvenor* 3 June 1780, aged 19. Adjt. 19th Bn. Sepoys in July 1787 and in 1793. Second Mahratta War; Cuttack 1803-4; Capt. 2/7th N.I. Ordered to raise the Cuttack Provl. Bn. in Sept. 1804, and comdd. till 1807. Posted Lt. Col. to 15th N.I. in 1810.

Refs.: Will dated 29 Oct. 1808; proved 25 Aug. 1814.

MORGAN, Thomas (1763/64-1792). Lieutenant, 28th Bn. Sepoys. *b.* in Wales 1763/64. Cadet 1781. Ensign 11 May 1781. Lieut. 28 Aug. 1782. *d.* Calcutta 19 Aug. 1792.

Son of Thomas Morgan, of co. Glamorgan. Brother of Benjamin and John Morgan, and nephew of Charles Morgan, *q.v.*

Services: Apptd. Cadet 23 Jan. 1781, aged 17. Sailed for India in the *Valentine* 13 Mar. 1781. Was Adjt. 9th Bn. Sepoys in Mar. 1786; Lieut. 28th Bn. in July 1787. Third Mysore War

1790-2 ; battle of Arikera ; operations before Savandrug ; Ramgiri ; Shivanagiri ; Seringapatam ; Lieut. 28th Bn.
Refs.: Will dated 15 Aug. 1792 ; proved 23 Aug. 1792.

MORGAN, Thomas William (1807-1844). Bt. Captain. 14th N.I. *b.* Calcutta 10 Oct. 1807. Cadet 1825. Arrived in India 22 Oct. 1826. Ensign 23 May 1826. Lieut. 27 Sept. 1828. Bt. Capt. 23 May 1841. Resigned 1 May 1844. *d.* at sea, on board the *Hindostan*, 21 May 1844, between Madras and Point de Galle.
bapt. Calcutta 22 Oct. 1807. Son of Thomas Morgan (1760/61-1814), *q.v.* Brother of James John M'Clary Morgan, *q.v.*
Services: Posted Ensign to 14th N.I. 9 Nov. 1826. Fur. p.a. 9 Feb. 1837 till 22 Jan. 1840. Gwalior campaign ; Maharajpur ; Bt. Capt. 14th N.I. (Bronze star).
Refs.: I.M. 3 Aug. 1844, p. 497. Will dated 13 May 1844 ; proved 11 June 1844.

MORLAND, Richard Scrope Bernard (1793-1833). Captain, Artillery. (435) *b.* London 13 Aug. 1793. Cadet 1810. Admitted 3 Dec. 1811. Fireworker 20 Nov. 1811. Lieut. 25 Sept. 1817. Capt. 28 Sept. 1827. *d. unm.* Dum-Dum 15 Oct. 1833.
bapt. St. George's, Hanover Sq., 11 Sept. 1793. 5th son of Sir Scrope Bernard, 4th Bart. (who assumed the additional surname of Morland by R.L. 15 Feb. 1811), M.P. for St. Mawes, and Harriet his wife, only dau. of William Morland, M.P. for Taunton. Ed. Westminster School till Feb. 1805. Woolwich Cadet.
Services: Entered R.N., but left the Service after his first voyage. Posted to 1st Troop H.A. in 1813. Nepal War 1814-15 ; Kalanga ; Lieut. F. 1st Troop, with 2nd Div. Siege and capture of Hathras 1817 ; Lieut. F. 1st Troop. Third Mahratta War ; Lieut. 2nd Troop. Fur. p.a. 23 Feb. 1822 till 4 Apr. 1825. Posted to newly-formed 2nd Troop 1st Bde. H.A. in 1825. Siege and capture of Bhurtpore ; Lieut. 2nd Troop 1st Bde.
Refs.: Burke's *Peerage*, 1859, p. 705, *s.n.* Bernard-Morland, Bart., of Nettleham, Lincs. *Westminster School Register. A.J.* N.S. xiii. 270. *N.& Q.* 8S. xii. 172, 272. M.I. in Dum-Dum cemetery.

MORLEY, Henry (1789-1806). Cadet, Infantry. *bapt.* Hampton Lucy, co. Warwick, 5 Apr. 1789. Cadet 1805. Never arrived in India. *d.* Dec. 1806, on his passage to India, in the wreck of the *Skelton Castle*. Struck off with effect from 5 Nov. 1806. (See note to David Allan.)

Son of Rev. John Morley and Mary his wife.

MORRELL, Robert (1767/68-1830). Lieut. Colonel, Invalid Est. 27th N.I. Comdg. Murshidabad Provl. Bn. *b.* 1767/68. Cadet 1781. Admitted 1781. Ensign 28 Aug. 1781. Lieut. 12 June 1783. Capt. 16 Nov. 1802. Major 1 Jan. 1810. Lt. Col. 16 Dec. 1814. Invalided 18 May 1815. *d.* Berhampore 23 May 1830, aged 62.

m. Calcutta 10 Aug. 1801, Miss Frances Hogan, sister of Thomas Cockerell Hogan. (*See also* John Stewart Schnell.) (She died Calcutta 1 July 1859.)

Services : Lieut. 3rd Bn. Sepoys in July 1787. Third Mysore War 1790-2 ; siege and capture of Bangalore. Transfd. from 35th Bn. Sepoys to 3rd do. 16 Apr. 1793. Capt. 5th N.I. Transfd. to newly-raised 27th N.I. in 1804. Operations against Dhundia Khan 1807 ; Komona ; Capt. 27th N.I. Major 1/27th N.I. Comdd. Cawnpore Provl. Bn. 1815-19 ; do. Murshidabad 1819 till death.

Refs. : *E.I.M.C.* ii. 238-9. *A.J.* N.S. iii. 158. *G.M.* 1831, i. 285. Will dated 21 Dec. 1829 ; proved 28 Dec. 1830.

MORRIESON, David (*d.* 1809). Major. Infantry. Cadet 1763. Ensign 11 Jan. 1764. Lieut. 27 Feb. 1765. Capt. 6 June 1767. Major 12 Sept. 1779. Resigned 26 Oct. 1780. *d.* Edinburgh 11 Dec. 1809.

m. 1 Oct. 1782, Rachel Ann, younger dau. of John Wightman (formerly Inglis), and aunt of William Ker, *q.v.* (She died Edinburgh 28 Aug. 1820.) Father of Hugh Morrieson, *q.v.*, and William Elliot Morrieson, *q.v.* Grandfather of Henry Augustus Morrieson, John Morrieson, Robert Morrieson, and William Morrieson, *qq.v.*

Services : Was comdg. at Cawnpore in July 1773, and was passed over for comd. of a Bn. that year as being an invalid. Comdg. a Coy. of Eur. Invalids in Sept. 1777 ; reported as medically fit in June 1778, when he was apptd. to comd. 26th Bn. Sepoys. Major in 2nd Bde. on resignation.

Refs. : Betham's *Baronetage*, v. (1805), p. 448, *s.n.* Inglis, of Milton Bryant, Beds. *Forrest*, i. 84. *S.M.* 1810, p. 78.

MORRIESON, Henry Augustus (1809-1870). Lieut. Colonel. 63rd N.I. *b* Benares 2 Apr. 1809. Cadet 1828. Arrived in India 5 May 1829. Ensign 8 Jan. 1829. Lieut. 25 Sept. 1834.

THE BENGAL ARMY, 1758-1834 333

Capt. 2 Dec. 1849. Bt. Major 28 Nov. 1854. Retired 15 Jan. 1857. Hon. Lt. Col. 1857. *d.* 2 Clarendon Villas, Tunbridge Wells, 24 Jan. 1870.

Son of David Morrieson, B.C.S. (who was eldest son of David Morrieson, *q.v.*), 3rd judge of provl. court of appeal at Murshidabad, and Sophia his wife. Brother of John Morrieson, *q.v.*, and nephew of Hugh Morrieson, *q.v. m.* Wazirabad 8 Aug. 1850, Sarah, dau. of Charles William Brooke, *q.v.* (*See also* Richmond Houghton.) (She died 22 Sept. 1893, aged 71.)

Services: d.d. 50th N.I. 27 May 1829. Posted to 52nd N.I., 14 Sept. 1829. Transfd. to 63rd N.I. 7 July 1831. Actg. Intr. & Qmr. 6th L.C. 21 Dec. 1838. Fur. s.c. 18 Nov. 1840 till 8 Jan. 1844. First Sikh War; Sobraon (w.); Bt. Capt. 63rd N.I. (Medal). Offg. Intr. & Qmr. 41st N.I. May 1848; do. 63rd N.I. 11 Oct. 1852. Offg. Bde. Major at Cawnpore June 1854. Leave s.c. 1855-6.

Refs.: *The Times,* 28 Jan. 1870.

MORRIESON, Hugh (1788-1859). Colonel. 20th N.I. *b.* Edinburgh 1 Dec. 1788. Cadet 1803. Arrived in India 14 Aug. 1804. Ensign 28 Aug. 1804. Lieut. 21 Sept. 1804. Capt. 9 June 1818. Major 21 Sept. 1828. Lt. Col. 13 Jan. 1834. Retired 11 Aug. 1841. Hon. Col. 28 Nov. 1854. *d.* 27 Heriot Row, Edinburgh, 27 May 1859.

bapt. St. Andrew's, Edinburgh, 12 Nov. 1789. 4th son of David Morrieson, *q.v.*, and Rachel Ann his wife. Brother of William Elliot Morrieson, *q.v. m.* 11 June 1844, Elizabeth Constantia, eldest dau. of Richard Pryce, of Gunley, J.P. and D.L., high sheriff co. Montgomery, and widow of Capt. Robert Campbell, R.N.

Services: Posted Lieut. to 4th N.I. in 1805. Employed on survey work 1812-14. Transfd. to newly-raised 2/29th N.I. in 1815. Offg. Asst. Surveyor Gen. 17 Oct. 1815. D.A.Q.M.G. 1 cl. 1 Jan. 1817, to survey Sundarbans. Leave s.c. to sea 28 Oct. 1818 till 7 Oct. 1820. Capt. 2/29th N.I. A.Q.M.G. 13 Feb. 1819 till 1829. Employed on survey and construction of new road from Barrackpore to Berhampore 1821 till 6 Aug. 1824. Attached to E. Div. of Army 6 Aug. 1824. Transfd. to 57th N.I. (late 1/29th) May 1824. Fur. p.a. 15 Jan. 1829 till 1 Nov. 1832. Posted Lt. Col. to 57th N.I. 27 May 1834. Fur. s.c. 11 Feb. 1838 till retirement. Transfd. to 20th N.I. in 1841.

Refs.: G.M. 1859, ii. 91. *The Times,* 31 May 1859.

MORRIESON, John (1813-1877). Lieut. Colonel. 30th N.I. *b.* Calcutta 14 Feb. 1813. Cadet 1829. Arrived in India 30 May

1830. Ensign 30 May 1830. Lieut. 2 Dec. 1838. Capt. 19 Jan. 1846. Bt. Major 28 Nov. 1854. Retired 31 Dec. 1861. d. Medwyn Villa, Queen's Rd., Tunbridge Wells, 12 Nov. 1877.

bapt. Calcutta 20 Dec. 1814. Son of David Morrieson, B.C.S., and Sophia his wife, *née* Brooke. Brother of Robert Morrieson, *q.v.* Ed. Edin. Acad. 1824-6.

Services: Cadet d.d. 52nd N.I. 7 June 1830; d.d. 54th N.I. 7 Apr. 1831. Actg. Ensign (having been 2 yrs. in India) 16 July 1832. d.d. 73rd N.I. 18 Feb. 1833. Posted Ensign to 30th N.I. 20 Aug. 1833. Actg. Intr. & Qmr. 1st L.C. 19 Feb. 1838 and 30 Aug. 1839. Intr. & Qmr. 30th N.I. 10 Jan. 1840 till Apr. 1846. First Afghan War 1842; actions in Khyber Pass on 19, 23 and 24 Jan.; forcing of Khyber in Apr.; advance on Kabul; Lieut. 30th N.I., with Gen. Pollock's force (Medal). First Sikh War; Aliwal; Bt. Capt. 30th N.I. (Medal). Second Sikh War; passage of Chenab; Chilianwala (w.); Gujerat; pursuit of Sikhs and Afghans to Peshawar; Capt. 30th N.I. (Medal with 2 clasps). Fur. p.a. 17 Mar. 1850 till Feb. 1853.

Refs.: The Times, 17 Nov. 1877.

MORRIESON, Robert (1810-1885). Colonel. 52nd N.I. *b.* Calcutta 13 Apr. 1810. Cadet 1826. Arrived in India 13 Aug. 1827. Ensign 17 Mar. 1827. Lieut. 6 May 1829. Capt. 24 Jan. 1845. Major 10 May 1857. Lt. Col. 4 Feb. 1861. Retired 31 Dec. 1861. Hon. Col. 31 Dec. 1861. *d.* Great Malvern 4 June 1885.

bapt. Calcutta 14 Jan. 1811. Son of David Morrieson, B.C.S., and Sophia his wife. Brother of William Morrieson, *q.v.* Edin. Coll.

Services: Posted Ensign to 52nd N.I. 1 Oct. 1827. Actg. Adjt. 52nd N.I. 1 Aug. 1834. Comdg. escort to A.G.G. Rajputana Nov. 1836. Offg. Asst. to A.G.G. Rajputana States 14 Feb. 1837; to take charge of Sambhur lake 1 Sept. 1837; Asst. to A.G.G. Rajputana 4 Jan. 1838; Asst. in charge of Haraoti Pol. Agency 1 July 1847; P.A. Jaipur 25 Dec. 1847. Rejoined 52nd N.I. 4 Oct. 1848. Second Sikh War; Multan; Gujerat; Capt. 52nd N.I. (Medal with clasp). Asst. to A.G.G. Rajputana 30 Jan. 1850; P.A. at Bhurtpore. Placed at disposal of C.-in-C. 26 May 1857. Offg. P.A. at Haraoti 15 Apr. 1858; permanent do. 30 Apr. 1859. Fur. 1860 till retirement.

Refs.: The Times, 6 June 1885.

MORRIESON, William (1816-1842). Lieutenant, 54th N.I. *b.* 13 May 1816. Cadet 1832. Arrived in India 30 June 1834.

Ensign 20 May 1834. Lieut. 14 May 1837. *d.* Gandamak, Afghanistan, 13 Jan. 1842 : kld. in action during the retreat from Kabul.

bapt. Calcutta 30 Nov. 1817. Son of David Morrieson, B.C.S., and Sophia his wife. Brother of Henry Augustus Morrieson, *q.v.* Ed. Edin. Acad. 1826-32. Addiscombe Cadet 3 Aug. 1832 till 13 Dec. 1833.

Services : Ensign d.d. 38th N.I. 7 July 1834. Posted to 25th N.I. 5 Nov. 1834 ; to 54th N.I. 5 Feb. 1835. Actg. Adjt. 54th N.I. 20 Sept. 1838 ; permanent do. 9 Feb. 1839 till death. First Afghan War 1840-2 ; outbreak at Kabul ; retreat from Kabul (kld.) ; Lieut. 54th N.I.

Refs. : M.I. Afghan Memorial Church, Bombay.

MORRIESON, William Elliot (1791-1815). Lieutenant, Engineers. *b.* Edinburgh 5 Apr. 1791. Cadet 1806. Arrived in India 17 Mar. 1808. Ensign 13 June 1807. Lieut. 9 Feb. 1810. *d.* 6 Jan. 1815, of wounds received in action at Jitpur on 3 Jan.

bapt. St. Andrew's, Edinburgh, 14 Sept. 1791. 5th son of David Morrieson, *q.v.,* and Rachel Ann his wife. Brother of Hugh Morrieson and cousin-german of William Ker, *qq.v.* Woolwich Cadet; nominated for R.M.A. 24 May 1805.

Services : Surveyor with Lt.-Col. G. Martindell's detachment in Bundelkhand Jan.-May 1810 ; on survey duty in the Sundarbans 1812-13. Nepal War 1814-15 ; Jitpur (s.w.) ; Field Engr. 3rd Div.

Refs. : Betham's *Baronetage,* v. (1805), p. 448, *s.n.* Inglis, of Milton Bryant, Beds. Will dated 24 Dec. 1814 ; proved 7 Feb. 1815.

MORRIS, Augustus Burke (1811-1849). Bt. Captain, 20th N.I. *b.* Cawnpore 29 July 1811. Cadet 1827. Arrived in India 29 June 1828. Ensign 5 Jan. 1828. Lieut. 11 Oct. 1834. Bt. Capt. 5 Jan. 1843. *d.* Srinagar, Kashmir, 20 Sept. 1849.

Son of Lawrence Burke Morris, *q.v.*

Services : Ensign d.d. 46th N.I. 25 July 1828 ; posted to 20th N.I. 4 Nov. 1828. Intr. & Qmr. 20th N.I. 25 Dec. 1837 till death. Offg. Bde. Major at Barrackpore June 1846 till May 1847, and 17 Sept. till Dec. 1847. Offg. D.A.A.G. Presdy. Div. Dec. 1847 till Mar. 1848. Second Sikh War ; Chilianwala (w.), offg. Bde. Major 6th Bde. ; Gujerat ; pursuit of Sikhs and Afghans to Peshawar, D.A.A.G. 1st Div. of force under Sir W. R. Gilbert, *q.v.* (Medal with 2 clasps). Apptd. Bde. Major to troops in Sind-Sagar district,

Rawal Pindi, May 1849. Leave s.c. to Kashmir 1 Sept. 1849 till death.
Refs.: De Rhé-Philipe. M.I. at Srinagar.

MORRIS, Charles Arthur (1811-1886). Bt. Captain. 29th N.I. *b.* London 2 May 1811. Cadet 1828. Arrived in India 14 Oct. 1828. Ensign 16 Apr. 1828. Lieut. 4 July 1836. Bt. Capt. 16 Apr. 1843. Retired 7 Apr. 1846. *d.* 13 July 1886.
bapt. Marylebone 15 May 1811. Eldest son of Arthur Morris, of Brockham Lodge, Surrey, Col. 14th Foot, and Georgina his wife. *m.* Calcutta 17 Sept. 1834, Lucy Nice, youngest dau. of Richard Humphreys, Comst. Dept. (*See also* John Shipp and J.P. Maillard —Appendix A.) Sandhurst Cadet.
Services: Ensign d.d. 13th N.I. 20 Nov. 1828; posted Ensign to 26th N.I. 4 Mar. 1829. Fur. p.a. 30 May 1830 till 22 Oct. 1831. Transfd. to 29th N.I. 4 Dec. 1831. Fur. s.c. 30 Oct. 1835 till 21 Sept. 1838. Actg. Adjt. newly-raised 1st L.I. Bn. 13 Jan. 1841; permanent do. 27 Mar. 1841 till 2 Dec. 1842, when it was broken up. Fur. s.c. 7 Oct. 1843 till retirement. No record of active service.
Refs.: A.J. N.S. xvi. 213. *The Times,* 24 Jan. 1833.

MORRIS, Edmond (1783-1813). Captain, Bengal Eur. Regt. *b.* Galway 20 July 1783. Cadet 1798. Admitted 12 Nov. 1799. Ensign 14 Oct. 1799. Lieut. 28 Oct. 1799. Capt. 15 Dec. 1808. *d.* 1 July 1813, from fatigue, during the expedn. against Sambas, Borneo.
Son of George Morris (who was elder son of Andrew Morris, of Spiddal and Galway) and his wife, *née* Kelly. Uncle of Charles James Oldfield, *q.v.*
Services: Posted Lieut. to 1st Bengal Eur. Regt. 15 Apr. 1801. Second Mahratta War; Gwalior; battle and capture of Deig; siege of Bhurtpore (w. in 2nd assault on 21 Jan. 1805 [1]); Lieut. Bengal Eur. Regt. Adjt. Native Invalids at Chunar 1807-8. At Amboyna with his Regt. 1811 till death. Expedn. against Sambas, Borneo, June 1813; Capt. Bengal Eur. Regt.
Refs.: Burke's *Peerage,* 1923, p. 1282, *s.n.* Killanin, B. *Innes,* p. 302. Will dated 20 Jan. 1811; proved 25 July 1814.

[1] *Note:* He led the party which volunteered to swim the ditch on this occasion and succeeded in mounting the breach, where he was wounded.

MORRIS, James (1750-1823). Lieut. General. Colonel 17th N.I. *b.* Nov. 1750. Cadet 1770. Ensign 16 Nov. 1771. Lieut.

THE BENGAL ARMY, 1758-1834 337

30 July 1776. Capt. 21 Feb. 1781. Major 1 Mar. 1794. Lt. Col. 1 Nov. 1798. Col. 21 Apr. 1803. Maj. Gen. 25 July 1810. Lt. Gen. 4 June 1814. Transfd. to Senior List 20 Feb. 1821. *d. unm.* Berhampore 4 Sept. 1823.

Brother of Mary and Elizabeth, half-brother of John Horsley, and 2nd cousin of Charlotte, wife of Mr. Wightman, in the Law Dept.
Services: Posted to Cav. 7 Aug. 1777 ; Adjt. 3rd Regt. Cav. 5 Aug. 1778 ; Bde. Maj. Cav. 17 Mar. 1779. Capt. in the Cav. in Feb. 1781 ; 2nd Eur. Bn. in July 1787 ; Persian Intr. to Col. Alexander Mackenzie, *q.v.*, in 1792. Transfd. from 4th Eur. Bn. to 3rd do. 16 Apr. 1793 ; apptd. to comd. 18th Bn. Sepoys 14 Nov. 1794. Major 7th N.I. Posted Col. to 7th N.I. in 1803 ; to 20th N.I. in 1807 ; to 4th N.I. in 1819 ; to 17th N.I. in 1820. Maj. Gen. comdg. at Berhampore 1811 till 28 Jan. 1815.
Refs.: Will dated 31 Aug. 1823 ; proved 11 Sept. 1823.

MORRIS, John (1784-1814). Lieutenant, 5th N.I. *b.* Duneane, co. Antrim, 26 Apr. 1784. Cadet 1804. Arrived in India 6 Apr. 1806. Ensign 20 Feb. 1806. Lieut. 1 Feb. 1807. *d.* Muttra 12 Aug. 1814.

Son of Anne Morris.
Services: Served in Antrim Mil. Barasat C.C. Posted to 5th N.I. in 1807. Operations in Bundelkhand against Gopal Singh 1810 ; Tirowa ; Lieut. 1/5th N.I.
Refs.: M.I. Muttra Cantt. cemetery.

MORRIS, Lawrence Burke (1749-1838). Lieut. Colonel. 3rd N.I. *b.* 1749/50. Cadet 1783. Admitted 21 Aug. 1783. Ensign 7 Feb. 1785. Lieut. 6 Dec. 1791. Capt. 8 Sept. 1803. Major 25 July 1810.· Lt. Col. 1819. Retired 9 June 1819. *d.* Laura Pl., Clapton, 8 Feb. 1838, aged 88.

Of Dalston, Middlesex. *m.* Sarah Dealtry. Father of Augustus Burke Morris, *q.v.*, and of Mary, wife of Samuel Tickell, *q.v.*
Services: Apptd. Cadet 21 Nov. 1782 ; sailed for India in the *Barwell* 11 Mar. 1783. Posted to 6th Eur. Bn. 5 Feb. 1790 ; transfd. from 4th do. to 5th do. 17 Oct. 1792 ; to 1st Bengal Eur. Regt. June 1796. Capt. 3rd N.I. Fur. 22 Jan. 1807 till 1 Dec. 1809. Major 1/3rd N.I. Fur. 1817 till retirement.
Refs.: A.J. N.S. xxv. 199. *G.M.* 1838, i. 330. Will dated 15 July 1836 ; admon. 2 Apr. 1839.

*MORRIS, Robert. Lieutenant. Infantry. Country Cadet 1779. Ensign 7 Sept. 1779. Lieut. 25 Apr. 1781. Resigned 3 Feb. 1783.

Of Nursling, Hants.
Services: Apptd. Cadet 19 Aug. 1779. Posted Lieut. to 17th N.I. (late 24th Bn.).

MORRIS, Robert (*d.* 1802). Captain, 14th N.I. Country Cadet 1779. Admitted 20 Mar. 1779. Ensign 9 Oct. 1779. Lieut. 19 May 1781. Capt. 31 Aug. 1798. *d.* Sultanpur 16 May 1802. Nephew of Moses Crawfurd, *q.v.*
Services: Went out to India in a private capacity in 1777 with Sir T. Rumbold, *q.v.*, going out as Govr. of Madras, and was employed as an Asst. in his office till posted to Bengal Army. Apptd. Cadet 19 Aug. 1779. Capture of Bijaigarh 1781; Lieut. 8th N.I. Lieut. 24th Bn. Sepoys in July 1787 and Dec. 1792.
Refs.: Writers' Petitions, Vol. viii, No. 1 of 1779.

MORRIS, Robert (1777-1804). Lieutenant, Artillery. (306) *bapt.* St. Paul's, Dublin, Dec. 1777. Cadet 1793. Arrived in India 8 Dec. 1794. Fireworker 24 Sept. 1794. Lieut. 15 Feb. 1802. *d.* 22 May 1804 : kld. in action at siege of fort Bela.
Son of Mrs. Mary Morris, of Paradise Row, Dublin.
Services: Apptd. Inf. Cadet 12 Mar. 1794; sailed for India in the *Thetis* 20 June 1794. Transfd. to Art. in 1795. Second Mahratta War; Aligarh; battle of Delhi; Agra; siege of Gwalior; siege of fort Bela (kld.); Lieut. 1st Coy. 1st Bn. Art.
Refs.: Pester, pp. 273, 296. M.I. Kunch cemetery.

MORRISON,[1] **Alexander** (1757/58-1827). Major. 21st N.I. *b.* 1757/58. Country Cadet 1780. Admitted 6 Oct. 1780. Ensign 10 Mar. 1781. Lieut. 24 Oct. 1781. Capt. 1 Jan. 1800. Major 17 Oct. 1805. Retired 1 Feb. 1809. *d.* Gunnersbury Pk., Middlesex, 22 May 1827, aged 69.
Of Gunnersbury Pk. Son of Robert Morrison, barber and wigmaker in Edinburgh. Brother of James, merchant in Memel, and Robert, architect in Edinburgh. *m.* St. George's, Hanover Sq., 15 Sept. 1808, Jane, youngest dau. of John Carnell, of Corendon, and Hazell Hall, Kent. (She *re-m.* 11 Aug. 1838, 9th Earl of Carnwath and died 14 May 1863.)
Services: Apptd. a Gent. Vol. in the Coy. of Bengal Art. 3 Apr. 1780. Lieut. 26th Bn. Sepoys in July 1787. Third Mysore War; Bangalore; Arikera; Seringapatam; Lieut. 26th Bn. Dy. Judge Advocate at Chunar 5 Apr. 1793 till 18 Feb. 1794. Qmr. 1st Bengal Eur. Regt. in 1796. A.D.C. to Maj.-Gen. Robert Stuart, *q.v.*, 2 Oct. 1800 till 1803. Capt. 6th N.I.; transfd. to newly-raised 21st N.I.

THE BENGAL ARMY, 1758-1834

in 1804. Second Mahratta War; Capt. 21st N.I., Comr. of bazars and supplies. Fur. 18 Feb. 1806 till retirement.
Refs.: S.M. 1808, p. 797. G.M. 1827, i. 573.
[1] *Note:* Received a grant of arms (as Morison) in 1806.

MORRISON, Charles (*d.* 1767). Ensign, 3rd Bengal Eur. Regt. Cadet 1766. Ensign 2 Dec. 1766. *d.* Allahabad 10 June 1767.
Services: N.F.P.
Refs.: Williams, pp. 156-7.

MORRISON, Dennis (*d.* 1776). Captain. Infantry. Cadet (?) Ensign 1 May 1764. Lieut. 16 Aug. 1765. Capt. 1 Dec. 1767. Dismissed by C.M. 7 Oct. 1771. *d.* Calcutta 5 Mar. 1776. Brother of Mary and Susanna Morrison.
Services: Midshipman in H.M.S. *Medway.* Comdd. a small detachment of sepoys sent against the Saniyasis in Rangpur early in 1766. Capt. 17th Bn. Sepoys in Nov. 1770. Killed John Campbell (*c.* 1745-1770), *q.v.*, in a duel at Monghyr 12 Nov. 1770; tried by G.C.M. 20 Dec. 1770, and acquitted. After dismissal became Capt. of a Country ship.
Refs.: B: P.P. No. 53, pp. 5-6. Macpherson, pp. 51-2, 54. Will dated 26 Nov. 1766; proved 15 July 1776.

MORRISON, George (*d.* 1764). Captain, Infantry. Cadet 1758. Ensign (?) Lieut. 8 Sept. 1759. Capt. 12 Oct. 1763. *d.* Calcutta 20 June 1764.
Son of —— Morrison and Jane his wife. Brother of Isabella and Margaret Morrison.
Services: N.F.P.
Refs.: Will dated 15 June 1764; proved 22 June 1764.

MORRISON, John. Major. Infantry. Major 1 Sept. 1768. Resigned 17 Dec. 1771. (Living in Nov. 1809.)
Services: Ensign 2nd Bn. 34th Ft. 9 May 1757; Lieut. 34th Ft. 22 July 1758; Capt. 113th Ft. 18 Oct. 1761; h.p. 1763.[1] Sometime a Commissary with the Southern Army in America. Transfd. as Major to Bengal Army (M.C. 1 Sept. 1768) through the patronage of Lord North. Comdd. a Sepoy Bn.; Major in 3rd Bde. on resignation. After resigning his Commission he entered the service of Shah Alam, Emperor of Delhi, and became " General and C.-in-C. of the Great Mogul's forces," and " Ambassador Extraordinary and Plenipotentiary " to George III. " He went to England (in 1773) empowered by the Great Mogul to lay before Government his

proposal to invest the King of England with the absolute sovereignty of the Kingdom of Bengal, and the provinces of Bihar and Orissa, in exchange for a body of British troops to defend his throne at Delhi." (*D.I.B.*) He set out for Delhi in Aug. 1785 by way of Constantinople, Bagdad and Ispahan ; but from Ispahan he went to Shiraz, where he met Jaffier Khan, a claimant to the throne of Persia, and started a new scheme for an alliance with Persia. He did not proceed to Delhi, but returned to Europe by way of Basra in Jan. 1787. Pub. in 1774 a tract on "The Advantages of an Alliance with the Great Mogul."

Refs. : *D.I.B. Macpherson*, pp. 89, 92.

[1] *Note :* Not in Brit. *A.L.* of 1778.

MORRISON, John (*d.* 1803). Captain, 12th N.I. Country Cadet 1779. Admitted 20 Mar. 1779. Ensign 4 Oct. 1779. Lieut. 15 May 1781. Capt. 31 Aug. 1798. *d.* 15 Jan. 1803 : kld. in action at the assault of Sasni.

Only son of Alexander Morrison, supervisor of excise at Dunbar, and Marion his wife, sister of Thomas Fergusson, of Calcutta, merchant. Brother of Marion, wife of Thomas Brown.

Services : Apptd. Cadet 19 Aug. 1779. Campaign against the Rajah of Benares 1781 ; Bijaigarh. Lieut. 24th Bn. Sepoys in July 1787 and Dec. 1792. Capt. 2/13th N.I. in Aug. 1798 ; transfd. to 12th N.I. 1798. Operations in Jumna Doab 1803 ; Sasni (kld. by a musket shot near the ditch) ; Capt. 2/12th N.I.

Refs. : *N. & Q.* cxlviii. 442. *Pester*, pp. 36-7, 41. Will dated Comillah, Tipperah, 20 Apr. 1795 ; proved 12 Feb. 1803.

MORSE, John (1777-1801). Lieutenant, 8th N.I. *b.* Marylebone, Middlesex, 26 Sept. 1777. Cadet 1793. Admitted 8 Dec. 1794. Ensign 14 Oct. 1794. Lieut. 7 Sept. 1796. *d.* Bareilly 9 Apr. 1801.

bapt. Marylebone 24 Oct. 1777. Only son of John Morse, of Weymouth St., Marylebone, and Jane his wife.

Services : Apptd. Cadet 19 Mar. 1794 ; sailed for India in the *Sir Edward Hughes* 20 June 1794. Lieut. 1st Bengal Eur. Regt. 1796 ; transfd. to 8th N.I. 1798.

Refs. : *G.M.* 1802, i. 272.

MORSHEAD, Edward (1801-1879). Captain. 60th N.I. *b.* Calstock, Cornwall, 27 Dec. 1801. Cadet 1818. Admitted 11 Sept. 1819. Ensign (?) Lieut. 1 Jan. 1821. Capt. 31 May 1830. Resigned 30 Apr. 1833. *d.* N.Z. 19 Jan. 1879.

Of New Plymouth, N.Z. *bapt.* publicly Calstock 2 Mar. 1803. Eldest son of Rev. Edward Morshead, rector of Calstock, and of Kelly, Devon, and Mary his wife, eldest dau. of Arthur Kelly, Col. S. Devon Mil. *m.* 1832, Penelope, youngest dau. of Col. John Dillon, of Johnstown, co. Roscommon. (She died Apr. 1875.) Ed. Blundell's 17 Aug. 1812 till 16 Dec. 1815.

Services: Ensign d.d. Bengal Eur. Regt. 1819-20; posted Lieut. to 2/30th N.I. in 1821. Leave s.c. 31 May 1823 till 18 May 1824. Transfd. to 60th N.I. (late 2/30th) May 1824. Adjt. Hill Rangers 31 May 1824 till 1825. Siege and capture of Bhurtpore; Lieut. 60th N.I. (India medal). Actg. Intr. & Qmr. 60th N.I. 1 Sept. 1826. Fur. p.a. 11 Feb. 1831 till 3 Mar. 1833. Emigrated to New Plymouth in 1857.

Refs.: Foster's *Baronetage,* p. 446, *s.n.* Morshead, Bart. Burke's *Landed Gentry,* 15th edn., p. 1636, s.n. Morshead, of Tregaddick, Cornwall; 11th edn., p. 937, *s.n.* Kelly, of Kelly, Devon. Vivian's *Visitations of Cornwall,* p. 600, *s.n.* Morshead. *Blundell's School Register.*

MORTLOCK, John Frederick (1809-?). Ensign. 24th N.I. *b.* St. Edward's, Cambridge, 8 Aug. 1809. Cadet 1828. Ensign 4 Nov. 1828. Resigned 27 Nov. 1829.

Son of —— Mortlock, of Aldeburgh, Suffolk.[1] Ed. Charterhouse, Sept. 1820-June 1821.

Services: Ensign d.d. 24th N.I. 25 July 1828; posted to 24th N.I. 4 Nov. 1828. No record of active service.

[1] *Note:* Probably Frederick Mortlock and Sarah his wife, 2nd dau. of Charles Finch, of Gt. Shelford, Cambs.

MORTON, Joseph (1810-1828). Ensign, 43rd N.I. *b.* Newcastle-on-Tyne 8 Aug. 1810. Cadet 1826. Ensign 9 Sept. 1826. *d.* Benares 1 Aug. 1828, of cholera.

Son of Joseph Morton, of Newcastle-on-Tyne, master mariner. *Services:* Ensign d.d. 58th N.I. 12 Mar. 1827; posted to 43rd N.I. 10 May 1827. No record of active service.

Refs.: A.J. xxvii. 221, 249. M.I. Benares.

MOR(E)TON, Richard Tayce (1762/63-1779). Ensign, Infantry. *b.* London 1762/63. Cadet 1778. Ensign 12 Oct. 1778. *bur.* Calcutta 31 Jan. 1779.

Services: Sailed for India in the *Calcutta* 24 Apr. 1778, aged 15. N.F.P.

MORTON, William [1] (1788-?). Captain, Engineers. *b.* London 14 Mar. 1788. Cadet 1803. Arrived in India 2 Dec. 1804. Fireworker (Art.) (355) 15 May 1805. Ensign (Engrs.) 15 Apr. 1806. Lieut. 23 Jan. 1808. Capt. 4 July 1818. Resigned 1 Mar. 1821. (*d.* before Feb. 1832.)

bapt. St. Martin-in-the-Fields, London, May 1788. Son of Thomas Morton. *m.* Cawnpore 24 Aug. 1811, Miss Juliana Gowan. His dau. *m.* Edward Harvey, *q.v.* Ed. Westminster; K.S. 1801; left Dec. 1802.

Services: Transfd. from Art. to Engrs. Apr. 1806. Stationed at Ft. Wm. 1807-10; at Karnal 1811-12; at Aligarh 1813-16, and 1819-20. Suptg. construction of works at Bareilly 1817-19. No record of active service.

Refs.: Westminster School Register. Will dated Bareilly, 17 Mar. 1819; proved 5 May 1829.

[1] *Note:* His name is given in *Westminster School Register* as William Heppell Morton.

MOSELEY, George Wayland [1] (1789-1850). Lieut. Colonel, C.B. 64th N.I. *b.* Thorley, Herts., 7 June 1789. Cadet 1805. Arrived in India 13 Dec. 1806. Ensign 21 Dec. 1806. Lieut. 7 Dec. 1808. Capt. 1 May 1824. Major 31 Dec. 1830. Lt. Col. 17 Sept. 1836. Cashiered by G.C.M. 22 Dec. 1844. *d.* Boulogne-sur-Mer 14 Jan. 1850.

bapt. Thorley 10 July 1789. Son of Litchfield Moseley, of Somersham Park, and Betsey his wife. *m.* St. John's, Calcutta, 24 July 1822, Sophia, dau. of Col. Johan Frederick Meiselbach, *q.v.* (Appendix A). (*See also* George Byron.) (She died 17 Mar. 1893, aged 89.) His daus. *m.* Charles Farmer, *q.v.*, Hugh Johnson, *q.v.*, and William Ramsey, *q.v.*

Services: Barasat C.C. 11 mos. Posted Ensign to 19th N.I. in 1807. Nepal War 1814-15; Lieut. 1/19th N.I., Intr. & Qmr. L.I. Bn. Apptd. Qmr. to Reserve Bde., Nagpur Subsdy. Force, 14 Nov. 1817. Third Mahratta War; Bde. Qmr. to Col. Adams's Div. Agent for purchase of remount horses N. Narbada Sept. 1818. Second in comd. Baddeley's Local Horse 12 Jan. 1822 till June 1825. Transfd. to 38th N.I. (late 1/19th) May 1824. S.A.G.G. 4 June 1825. In charge of timber agency at Natpur 3 Oct. 1825 till its abolition on 12 June 1829. Operations against the Kols 1832; Major 38th N.I. Posted Lt. Col. to 38th N.I. 28 Dec. 1836; transfd. to 64th N.I. in 1839. First Afghan War 1842; retreat from Ali Masjid to Jamrud in Jan.; Lt. Col. comdg. force of 53rd and 64th N.I.; forcing of the Khyber in Apr. (*Lond. Gaz.* 7 June 1842);

THE BENGAL ARMY, 1758-1834 343

action on march to Ali Masjid 3 Nov., under Wild ; Lt. Col. comdg.
64th N.I. (Medal). Cashiered for "having concealed from the
C.-in-C. the existence of a mutiny which occurred in 64th N.I. . . .
on or about 13 and 14 May 1844." Transfd. to 2nd Bengal Eur.
Regt. 9 July 1844. C.B. 24 Dec. 1842.
Refs.: *I.M.* 8 Feb. 1845, p. 45. *G.M.* 1850, i. 340.
¹ *Note :* His second christian name appears in *A.L.* throughout
his service as Weyland. His birth certificate and the marriage
register, however, give it as Wayland.

MOSEL(E)Y, John (*d.* 1768). Cadet, Infantry. Cadet 1768.
d. 1768.
Services : Lieut. in H.M.S. Sailed for India as a Cadet in the
Salisbury 21 Mar. 1768.

*MOSELY, William Izod. Lieutenant. Infantry. Cadet 1781.
Never arrived in India. Ensign 18 June 1781. Lieut. 24 Sept.
1782. Struck off (?)
Services : Apptd. Cadet 16 Nov. 1781 ; sailed for India in the
Norfolk 6 Feb. 1782.

MOSLEY, William Bayley (1806-1848). Bt. Captain, 10th L.C.
b. 19 Aug. 1806. Cadet 1828. Arrived in India 28 July 1828.
Cornet (4 Mar. 1828) 10 Jan. 1829. Lieut. 9 June 1838. Bt.
Capt. 4 Mar. 1843. *d.* Landour, U.P., 12 Aug. 1848.
bapt. ptely. 21 Aug. 1806 ; *bapt.* Rolleston, Staffs., 7 Oct. 1806.
3rd son of Rev. John Peploe Mosley, rector of Rolleston (who was
2nd son of Sir John Parker Mosley, 1st Bart.), and Sarah Maria
his 1st wife, dau. of William Paget, of Shepton Mallet, Somerset.
Cousin-german of Gilbert William Master, *q.v.* *m.* Sephton, Lancs.,
5 Jan. 1836, Maria Sarah, 2nd dau. of Samuel Lowe, of Whitchurch, Salop, and the Abbey, Burton-on-Trent. (She died 21
Oct. 1878.)
Services : Cornet d.d. 9th L.C. 8 Sept. 1828 ; d.d. 4th L.C.
18 Nov. 1828 ; posted Cornet to 10th L.C. 4 June 1829. Fur. p.a.
without pay 1 Feb. 1835 till 13 Aug. 1836. First Afghan War
1842 ; reoccupation of Kabul ; Lieut. 10th L.C., with Gen. Pollock's
force (Medal).
Refs.: Burke's *Peerage*, 1923, p. 1611, *s.n.* Mosley, Bart., of
Ancoats, Lancs. *Family Memoirs*, by Sir Oswald Mosley, Bart.
(p.p., 1849). *Howard & Crisp*, vi. 142, *s.n.* Master. *I.M.* 4
Oct. 1848, p. 588. Will dated 16 Jan. 1845 ; proved 15 May
1849. M.I. Landour.

MOSTYN, John Salusbury (1798-1827). Lieutenant, 5th Extra N.I. *b.* London 31 Aug. 1798. Cadet 1817. Ensign (?) Lieut. 24 Oct. 1819. *d. unm.* Worthing Aug. 1827.

bapt. Marylebone 24 Apr. 1802. Eldest son of John Meredith Mostyn, of Segrwyd, co. Denbigh, and Cecilia Margaretta his wife, youngest dau. of Henry Thrale, of Streatham Park, Surrey. Ed. Westminster; admitted 18 June 1810; left 1813.

Services: Ensign d.d. 25th N.I. 1819; posted Lieut. to 2/2nd N.I. in 1819. Leave to Cape 1821-2. Transfd. to 22nd N.I. (late 2/2nd) May 1824; to newly-raised 5th Extra Regt. May 1825. Adjt. Burdwan Provl. Bn. 1824-6. Granted fur. p.a. 10 Jan. 1827.

Refs.: Burke's *Landed Gentry*, 5th edn., p. 954, *s.n.* Mostyn, of Llewesog, co. Denbigh. *Peds. of Anglesey and Carnarvonshire Families*, by J. E. Griffith, p. 206. *Westminster School Register.*

MOUAT,[1] **Charles** (1761/62-1830). Colonel, Engineers. Chief Engr. Bengal. *b.* 1761/62. Cadet 1780. Arrived in India 12 Mar. 1781. Ensign 1780. Lieut. 3 Sept. 1781. Capt. 25 Apr. 1797. Major 15 Apr. 1806. Lt. Col. (4 June 1813) 4 July 1818. Lt. Col. Comdt. 1 May 1824. Col. 5 June 1829. *d.* Calcutta 25 June 1830, aged 68.

Grandson of James Mowat, I of Stennis, twin brother of Frederick Mouat, and cousin of Sir James Mouat, Bart., *q.v.* Ed. Westminster; admitted 29 Mar. 1773; in school lists 1775.

Services: Admitted as Practitioner Engr. 8 May 1781. Dy. Draughtsman at Ft. Wm. in July 1787. Stationed at Dinapore 1803-5; at Chunar 1805-12. Suptg. Engr. and comdg. troops at Fort Marlbro' 13 Nov. 1813 till 1818. Actg. Chief Engr. 1820; Chief Engr. 1822 till death.

Refs.: *Zetland Family Histories*, by F. J. Grant, p. 191, *s.n.* Mowat of Stennis. *Westminster School Register. A.J.* N.S. iii. 210. *G.M.* 1831, i. 285. M.I. S. Park St. cemetery, Calcutta.

[1] *Note:* He and the two following spelt their name thus: Mowat is the more usual form of the family name.

MOUAT, Sir James, baronet (*c.* 1765/66-1829). Lieut. Colonel, Engineers. *b. c.* 1765/66. Cadet 1782. Admitted 2 Sept. 1783. Ensign 19 July 1782. Lieut. 19 Aug. 1793. Capt. 1 Jan. 1806. Major (25 July 1810) 1 Sept. 1818. Lt. Col. 29 May 1824. *d.* at sea 9 May 1829, on board the *Prince Regent* on the voyage to England, aged about 63.

Bart., of Inglistoun.[1] Representative of the house of Mowat, of Balquholly. Of York Terr., Regent's Pk., London. Younger son

THE BENGAL ARMY, 1758-1834

of George Mowat (or Mouat). *m.* Edinburgh 5 Sept. 1809, Wilhelmina, 4th dau. of George Mouat, Capt. R.N. Father of Sir James Anbury Mouat, Bart., *q.v.*

Services: Apptd. Practitioner Engr. 16 Aug. 1782. Asst. Engr. at Chunar in July 1787. Second Rohilla War; battle of Bitaurah; actg. A.D.C. to Sir Robert Abercromby, the C.-in-C. Apptd. Surveyor in the field 19 Nov. 1794. Fur. 27 Mar. 1797 till 16 Dec. 1800. Apptd. in May 1803, 1st Asst. in Hindustani at Coll. of Ft. Wm. with effect from 1 Feb. 1803; Professor do. Jan. 1806 till 3 Feb. 1808. Fur. 18 Feb. 1808 till 1810. At P.W.I. 1812-13. Suspended 30 Sept. 1813.[2] Fur. 1813-16. Garr. Engr. at Saharanpur 11 Oct. 1816; do. at Almora, and Executive Ofr. in Kumaon, 1820-5. Fur. s.c. 11 Feb. 1825 till 1827; p.a. 17 Jan. 1829 till death.

Refs.: G.E.C. *Complete Baronetage,* iii. 345, *s.n.* Mowat, of Inglistoun. *Zetland Family Histories,* p. 191. *M.M.* 1809. Will dated 29 Jan. 1828; proved 7 Jan. 1830. M.I. in S. Park St. cemetery, Calcutta.

[1] *Note:* He appears to have assumed the title for the first time in 1825. His elder brother, Sir George Mouat Keith, Bart., Capt. R.N. (who was the first to assume without authority the baronetcy conferred upon Sir George Mowat, of Inglistoun, on 2 June 1664), *d.* Calcutta 9 Aug. 1816.

[2] *Note:* Suspended for "having attempted to dispose of an English horse to H.H. the Nabob of Bengal, for the exorbitant sum of a Lack of Rupees . . ." (*Cal. Gaz.* 30 Sept. 1813.)

MOUAT, Sir James Anbury, baronet (1811-1837). 2nd Lieutenant, Engineers. *b.* Calcutta 21 Apr. 1811. Cadet 1829. Arrived in India 27 Mar. 1830. 2nd Lieut. 12 June 1828. *d.* Saugor 15 Sept. 1837.

Bart., of Inglistoun. *s.* 9 May 1829. *bapt.* Calcutta 24 Apr. 1812. Elder son of Sir James Mouat, Bart., *q.v.,* and Wilhelmina his wife. *m.* Calcutta 29 Feb. 1836, Louisa Caroline, youngest dau. of W. R. Montgomery, Ceylon C.S., and sister of George James Montgomery, *q.v.* Addiscombe Cadet 1827-8.

Services: Attached to P.W.D. 7 Apr. 1830. Actg. Adjt. Corps of Engrs., and Garr. Engr. and Civil Architect at the Presdy., 19 May 1835 till 16 Feb. 1836. Asst. Executive Engr. 8th Div. P.W.D. 1 Aug. 1836; actg. Executive Engr. Kumaon Div. 28 Sept. 1836 till 1 Feb. 1837; Executive Engr. 14th (Saugor) Div. 20 Mar. 1837.

Refs.: G.E.C. *Complete Baronetage,* iii. 345, *s.n.* Mowat, Bart., of Inglistoun. *A.J.* N.S. xxv. 180.

MOUGGACH, John (d. 1800). Captain, 4th N.I. Country Cadet 1778. Admitted 11 Aug. 1778. Ensign 18 May 1779. Lieut. 21 Jan. 1781. Capt. 26 July 1797. d. at sea 26 Feb. (? Mar.) 1800, off the Malabar coast.

Brother of David Mouggach, and uncle of John Mouggach, of Botriphnie, co. Banff.

Services: Asst. to Agent for clothing, 3rd Bde. Fort Adjt. Adjt. of Invalids 1781-7. Adjt. of Calcutta Town Guard 8 July 1788 till 1793. Lieut. 3rd Bengal Eur. Regt. in 1796. Purchased at auction in July 1790 the Coy.'s factory at Fort Gloucester for Rs. 2,450. Capt. 13th N.I., comdg. Sebundy Guards in 1799. *Refs.: A.A.R.* iii. 103. *Cal. Gaz.* 8 July 1790. *B: P.P.* xiv. 218. Will dated 26 June 1799; proved 1 May 1800.

MOULE, John (1794-1867). Major General. Colonel 4th N.I. (now 2nd Bn. 7th Rajput Regt.). *b.* Melksham, Wilts., 9 Mar. 1794. Cadet 1809. Admitted 24 Nov. 1810. Ensign (Nov. 1810) 1 June 1812. Lieut. 19 Jan. 1816. Capt. 29 Apr. 1826. Major 30 June 1840. Lt. Col. 1 Apr. 1846. Col. 9 Apr. 1856. Maj. Gen. 27 Jan. 1858. *d.* Belmont, Melksham, 4 Apr. 1867.

bapt. Melksham 28 Apr. 1794. 3rd son of George Moule, of Bank House, Melksham, atty., and Sarah Hayward his wife. His sister *m.* Christopher Sullivan Fagan and his niece *m.* Gerald Augustus Frederick Hervey, *qq.v. m.* Ludhiana 28 Mar. 1830, Anne Sophia, 3rd dau. of William Conrad Faithfull, *q.v.* (*See also* John Dickson Dyke Bean.) (She died 4 Apr. 1856, aged 46.) Ed. Devizes Grammar School.

Services: Cadet d.d. 15th N.I. 1811-12; posted Ensign to 2/4th N.I. in 1812. Nepal War 1816; Lieut. 2/4th N.I., in 4th Bde. Centre Column (India medal). Fur. p.a. 15 Nov. 1820 till 13 Apr. 1824. Transfd. to 23rd N.I. (late 2/4th) May 1824; Adjt. do. 17 June 1824 till 29 May 1826. Actg. Adjt. 1st Extra Regt. 22 June 1825; actg. Intr. & Qmr. do. 16 Aug. 1825. Siege and capture of Bhurtpore; Lieut. 23rd N.I. (clasp to India medal). Jodhpur demonstration 1834; Capt. 23rd N.I. Actg. Bde. Major at Agra 6 Oct. 1837 till 5 May 1840. Fur. 1846-8. Posted Lt. Col. to 52nd N.I. 1846; to 46th N.I. 1846; to 27th N.I. 1848; to 5th N.I. 1850; to 10th N.I. 19 July 1851; to 11th N.I. July 1852; to 48th N.I. Oct. 1854; to 67th N.I. May 1855; to 2nd Bengal Eur. Regt. Mar. 1856. Bdr. 2 cl. comdg. at Sialkot 11 May 1855. Apptd. to Bde. Staff Jan. 1856; Bdr. 1 cl. comdg. at Ferozepore 2 July 1856, and was comdg. when the Mutiny broke out. Posted

THE BENGAL ARMY, 1758-1834 347

Col. to 33rd N.I. July 1856. Fur. p.a. 28 Dec. 1858 till death.
Col. 4th N.I. (late 33rd) 1861 till death.
Refs.: *The Family of Moule of Melksham, etc.*, by Rev. R. W. M.
Lewis, 1938. *Boase. G.M.* 1867, i. 689. *The Times*, 6 Apr.
1867.

MOULTON, John (1748-1783). Captain, Infantry. *b.* 27 Sept.
1748. Cadet 1770. Ensign 26 Sept. 1770. Lieut. 10 July
1776. Capt. 6 Feb. 1781. *d.* Barrackpore 16 June 1783.

Of the city of London. Son of —— Moulton and Rachel his
wife. Brother of Stephen Moulton, of Chancery Lane, and of
Maria Rachel, wife of Thomas Walker, of Ongar, Essex, surgeon.
Ed. Merchant Taylors' Oct. 1756 till Mar. 1760.

Services: First Rohilla War 1774. Transfd. from 3rd Eur. Regt.
to comd. a Bn. of Sepoys 28 Apr. 1781. Capture of Chinsura from
the Dutch 4 July 1781; Capt. comdg. 2/2nd N.I., 2nd in comd.
to Capt. Charles Chatfield, *q.v.*, comdg. the force.

Refs.: Robinson. Will dated Barrackpore, 20 May 1783; proved
24 Sept. 1783.

MOULTRIE, William (1808-1845). Captain, 57th N.I. *bapt.*
Cleobury Mortimer, Salop, 22 July 1808. Cadet 1824. Arrived
in India 8 May 1825. Ensign 9 Jan. 1825. Lieut. 24 Sept.
1825. Capt. 11 Nov. 1840. *d.* Saugor 12 Apr. 1845.

3rd son of Rev. George Moultrie, of Shrewsbury, vicar of Cleobury
Mortimer (who was 3rd son of John Moultrie, Lt. Govr. of Florida),
and Harriet his wife, elder dau. of John Fendall and sister of John
Fendall, B.C.S. Ed. Shrewsbury School 1819-24.

Services: Ensign d.d. 28th N.I. 23 May 1825; posted Lieut. to
57th N.I. 1825; actg. Intr. & Qmr. 57th N.I. 22 Apr. 1828. Fur.
p.a. 14 Feb. 1837 till 9 Feb. 1841; s.c. 5 July 1841 till 14 June 1844.
No record of active service.

Refs.: Burke's *Landed Gentry*, 5th edn., p. 955, *s.n.* Moultrie,
of Aston Hall, Salop. *Genealogical Mag.* vi. 341. *Shrewsbury
School Register. I.M.* 20 June 1845, p. 346. *M.I.* Saugor.

MOUNSEY, George Stevenson (1759-1838). Major. 6th N.C.
Subsequently H.E.I.C. Recruiting Ofr. for the Carlisle district.
b. Carlisle 1759. Cadet 1781. Admitted 31 Mar. 1782. Ensign
7 Apr. 1781. Lieut. 29 July 1782. Capt. 29 May 1800. Major
13 Mar. 1803. Retired 1 Oct. 1806. *d. unm.* Gilsland, Cumberland, 17 May 1838, aged 78.

J.P. Cumberland. Eldest son of George Mounsey, of Carlisle,

and Margaret his wife, dau. of John Stevenson (or Stephenson), of Carlisle. Ed. Carlisle Grammar School; admitted 30 July 1765. *Services:* Apptd. Cadet 14 Feb. 1781, aged 22. Sailed for India in the *Latham* 16 Mar. 1781; arrived at Bombay Mar. 1782, and was posted to 5th N.I. then serving with Col. Goddard's detachment employed in the First Mahratta War. Transfd. to 2/1st N.I. in 1784; to 32nd Bn. Sepoys in 1787. Third Mysore War; Lieut. 2nd Bengal Vol. Bn. Second Rohilla War; battle of Bitaurah; Lieut. 32nd Bn. Posted to 1st N.C. in 1798; to 2nd N.C.; to 6th N.C. 29 May 1800. Operations in Jumna Doab 1803; Sasni; Bijaigarh; Kachaura; Capt. 6th N.C. Second Mahratta War; Laswari; Major comdg. 6th N.C. Fur. s.c. 27 Mar. 1804 till retirement. H.E.I.C. Recruiting Ofr. in the Carlisle district 1810-13.

Refs.: Burke's *Landed Gentry*, 12th edn., p. 936, *s.n.* Mounsey-Heysham, of Castletown, co. Cumberland. Whellan's *History of Cumberland and Westmorland*, p. 177. *E.I.M.C.* i. 423-4. *Carlisle Grammar School Register. A.J.* N.S. xxvi. 127.

MOWATT, John Lealand (1804-1857). Bt. Colonel, Artillery. (512) *bapt.* Eastbourne 18 Nov. 1804. Cadet 1820. Admitted 19 June 1821. 2nd Lieut. 16 June 1820. Lieut. 1 May 1824. Capt. 20 Apr. 1838. Major 7 Jan. 1848. Lt. Col. 20 Feb. 1855. Bt. Col. 28 Nov. 1854. *d.* of cholera, camp Pipli, on the march to Delhi, 30 May 1857, aged 52.

Son of James Ryder Mowatt, of Eastbourne, Capt. 28th Regt., formerly Bk. Mr. at Romford, and Jane Fulton his wife, of Pittenweem. His sister *m.* Roderick Roberts, *q.v. m.* Residency, Lucknow, 13 Dec. 1826, Anna Maria, 2nd sister of John Tierney Fergusson, *q.v.* (*See also* Hugh Augustus Boscawen (1805-1881) and George Newton Prole.) (She *re-m.* 31 Aug. 1865, Vice-Adm. John Lyons, brother of Theodore Lyons, *q.v.*) Addiscombe Cadet 1819-20.

Services: Actg. Intr. & Qmr. 6th Bn. Foot Art. 10 June 1828; permanent do. 14 Jan. 1830 till 26 May 1838. Offg. Comy. Ord. at Cawnpore 20 Mar. 1837; Dy. Comy. Ord. at Cawnpore 11 Sept. 1838; do. at Delhi 31 Mar. 1839. Fur. p.a. 14 Jan. 1840 till 15 Oct. 1842. Operations against Hill tribes in Sind 1843-5; Capt. 1st Coy. 2nd Bn. Transfd. to 4th Troop 1st Bde. H.A. 24 July 1845. Second Sikh War; Ramnagar; Chilianwala; Gujerat; Major 1st Bde. H.A. (Medal with 2 clasps). Bt. Lt. Col. 4th Bn. Foot Art. Aug. 1853. Transfd. to 5th Bn. 15 Oct. 1854; to 3rd Bde. H.A. 19 Nov. 1856.

Refs.: *Records of Clan Ferguson*, ii. 127. *Scottish N. & Q.*

THE BENGAL ARMY, 1758-1834

1S. xii. 103. *G.M.* 1857, ii. 466. Will dated 1 July 1856 ; admon. 9 Apr. 1858.

MOXON, William (1780-1858). Colonel. 60th N.I. *b.* London 6 Oct. 1780. Cadet 1799. Admitted 4 Dec. 1800. Ensign 10 Oct. 1800. Lieut. 1 Jan. 1803. Capt. 16 Dec. 1814. Major 25 Dec. 1822. Lt. Col. 1 May 1824. Retired 7 Mar. 1826. Hon. Col. 28 Nov. 1854. *d.* Torquay 15 Nov. 1858.
bapt. St. Clement's, Eastcheap, London, 5 Nov. 1780. Son of George Moxon and Deborah his wife. *m.* Calcutta 26 Aug. 1812, Miss Phoebe Hobson.
Services : Posted Ensign to 1/16th N.I. 17 Apr. 1801. Operations in Jumna Doab 1803 ; Thathia ; Ensign 1/16th N.I. With 2nd Vol. Bn. 1804-5. Served with escort to Resdt. at Nagpur 1806-23. (? Third Mahratta War ; Sitabaldi.) Posted Lt. Col. to 60th N.I. May 1824. Fur. 1824 till retirement.
Refs. : *I.M.* 19 Nov. 1858, p. 937. *The Times,* 18 Nov. 1858.

MOXON, Charles (*d.* 1768). Cadet, Infantry. Cadet 1768. *d.* 1768.
Services : N.F.P.

MUDGE, John (1801-1872). Ensign. Engineers. *b.* Freyston, co. Pembroke, 25 Nov. 1801. Cadet 1819. Ensign 1 Mar. 1821. Struck off in England 10 Aug. 1822. *d.* 1872.
bapt. Freyston 18 Jan. 1802. 6th and youngest son of Thomas Mudge, barr.-at-law and horologist (*D.N.B.*), and Elizabeth Kingdon his wife. Cousin of Zachary Mudge Mallock, *q.v.* Addiscombe Cadet 1817-19.
Services : Fur. s.c. 19 Feb. 1821 till struck off.
Refs. : *Mudge Memoirs,* by S. R. Flint (1883).

MUIR, Grainger (1733/34-1786). Colonel. Infantry. *b.* 1733/34. Ensign 1754. Lieut. 18 July 1754. Capt. 12 Sept. 1756. Resigned 31 Aug. 1758. Capt. 27 July 1764. Major 13 Aug. 1768. Lt. Col. 3 Oct. 1769. Col. 11 June 1779. Resigned 1 Dec. 1784. *d.* London 3 Aug. 1786, aged 52.
Son of Major William Muir, H.M.S., and Ann Thompson his wife.
Services : Went out to India in 1747, at the age of 14, and served under his father at the first siege of Pondicherry in 1748. Apptd. a Writer on Bengal Est. 1752 ; resigned his appt. and obtained an Ensign's Commission in 1754. Was in comd. of a party of 20 sepoys at the Jagdea factory in 1756, during the siege of Calcutta, and was

ordered to withdraw to Fulta. Served at recapture of Calcutta; battle of Kasipur; reduction of Chandernagore. Voted at the Council of War before Plassey for immediate action. " Led the advanc'd Guard at the battle of Plassey." (M.I.) Resigned his Commission owing to supercession by John Gowen, *q.v.*, and returned to England. Lieut. H.M. 94th Regt. 7 Mar. 1760; Lieut. 1st Div. Independent Coys. in N. America in 1761. Served in America during the Seven Years' War; expedn. to S. Carolina under Col. James Grant; reduction of Dominica and Martinique under Gen. Monckton. On the disbandment of 94th in 1763, he raised a Coy. of 125 men for E.I.Co., with whom he sailed for India in June 1764. Arrived in Bengal Jan. 1765, when he was given a Capt.'s Commission to date from 27 July 1764. (G.O. 17 Feb. 1765.) Posted to 2nd Bengal Eur. Regt. 5 Aug. 1765. Posted Lt. Col. to Inf. Bde. in May 1772. First Mahratta War; despatched in 1781 from Bengal in comd. of reinforcements for Lt.-Col. Jacob Camac, *q.v.*; succeeded Camac in comd. of the Bengal force Aug. 1781, and in Oct. of the same year he concluded a separate treaty with Sindhia. Comdd. 1st Bde. 1782 till Dec. 1784. Returned to England in 1785.

Refs.: E.I.M.C. iii. 212-14. *Hill's Calcutta,* p. 68. *G.M.* 1786, ii. 715. *Misc. Gen. et Her.* 3S. i. 130. M.I. in Marylebone psh. church. Will dated 15 Dec. 1784, and 26 Nov. 1785.

MULLER, Frederick Rodolphus (1767-1815). Lieut. Colonel, 4th N.I. *b.* Amsoldingen, Switzerland, 11 Feb. 1767. Cadet 1783. Admitted 18 Mar. 1784. Ensign 1 Jan. 1785. Lieut. 21 June 1790. Capt. 25 Aug. 1804. Major 2 Oct. 1808. Lt. Col. 4 June 1814. *d.* Barrackpore 13 July 1815.

Eldest son of Johann Rudolf von Muller (1737-1793), Col. in the service of Frederick the Great. Naturalized 12 July 1806. *m.* 1806, his cousin-german, Maria Albertina Charlotte, dau. of Francis Samuel von Wild, of Bern, and sister of Charles Frederick Wild, *q.v.*

Services: Capt. in a Swiss Regt. of Chasseurs comdd. by Col. James Francis Erskine. Apptd. Cadet 9 Oct. 1782 (Order of Court 20 June 1783; Minute of Committee 17 Sept. 1783). Fur. 6 Nov. 1786 till 1 Sept. 1790. Lieut. 5th Bn. Sepoys in 1792; transfd. from 31st Bn. to 27th Bn. 18 Oct. 1793; Lieut. 2/3rd N.I. in June 1798; 2nd N.I. in Dec. 1798. Operations in Jumna Doab 1803; Sasni; Bijaigarh; Kachaura; Capt. 2/2nd N.I. Fur. 22 Dec. 1803 till 7 Apr. 1807. Capture of Serampore from the Dutch 1808. Expedn. to Macao 1808; Capt. Vol. Bn. Transfd. as Major

to 1/2nd N.I. Comdg. at Ajaigarh in 1813. Transfd. as Lt. Col. to 4th N.I. in 1814.
Refs.: Almanach Généal. Suisse, ii. 381, *s.n.* von Muller, of Uri. Pester, pp. 61, 63. M.I. in Barrackpore cemetery.

MULLINS, Frederick (*d.* 1842). Captain, 12th N.I. Cadet 1818. Was already in India when apptd. Cadet. Admitted 21 Feb. 1820. Ensign 7 July 1819. Lieut. 1 Dec. 1821. Capt. 3 June 1829. *d.* Motihari, B. & O., 30 Apr. 1842.

(*Perhaps* son of Edward Mullins, trader at Chandernagore, who died Calcutta 26 Mar. 1807, aged 56.) His sisters *m.* Thomas Alexander Hepworth, John Oakes, and Arthur Wortham, *qq.v.*

Services: Ensign d.d. Bengal Eur. Regt. 1820. Posted to 2/12th N.I. in 1821. Transfd. to 12 N.I. (late 1/12th) May 1824. Intr. & Qmr. 12th N.I. 11 Aug. 1824 till 9 Feb. 1829. Comdd. 12th N.I. from 28 Nov. 1840. No record of active service.

Refs.: G.M. 1842, ii. 446.

MULOCK, John Lawless Augustus (*d.* 1793). Lieutenant, 4th Bengal Eur. Bn. Country Cadet 1779. Ensign 23 Aug. 1779. Lieut. 11 Apr. 1781. *d.* Calcutta 1 Oct. 1793.

(*b.* before 1755.) 2nd son of Thomas Mulock, of Dublin, and afterwards of Kilnagarna, King's Co., and Mary his wife, dau. of James Lawless, of Shankill, co. Dublin.

Services: Apptd. Cadet 19 Aug. 1779. Lieut. 12th Bn. Sepoys in July 1787 and in 1790.

Refs.: Burke's *Landed Gentry of Ireland,* p. 501, *s.n.* Mulock, of Kilnagarna, King's Co.

MUNDY, Charles Fitzroy Miller (1815-1888). Lieut. General. 34th N.I. Presdy. Paymr. at Calcutta. *b.* 31 Mar. 1815. Cadet 1834. Arrived in India 27 July 1835. Ensign 23 Mar. 1835. Lieut. 1 July 1840. Capt. 21 Nov. 1848. Major 18 Feb. 1861. Lt. Col. 18 Feb. 1863. Col. 23 Mar. 1866. Maj. Gen. 1 Oct. 1877. Lt. Gen. 1 July 1881. *d.* Norris's hotel, W. Kensington, 12 July 1888.

bapt. Walton-on-Trent 2 Apr. 1815. 5th son of Edward Miller Mundy, of Shipley Hall, co. Derby, and Nelly his wife, dau. of F. Barton. Cousin-german of Francis William Mundy, *q.v. m.* St. Martin-in-the-Fields, London, 5 Oct. 1844, Louisa Orth, eldest dau. of J. N. Orth Waldener, of Suffolk St., Pall Mall. (She died 15 Mar. 1884, aged 59.) Ed. Shrewsbury 1829-34.

Services: Ensign d.d. 34th N.I. 8 Aug. 1835; posted to 1st N.I. 24 Sept. 1835; to 34th N.I. 13 Jan. 1836. Leave s.c. to N.S.W.

5 Mar. 1838 till 21 July 1840. Actg. Adjt. 34th N.I. 30 Oct. 1841 till 20 Aug. 1842. Fur. s.c. 5 Mar. 1843 till 9 May 1845. On disbandment of 34th N.I. for mutiny in Mar. 1844, d.d. 21st N.I. May 1845; d.d. 35th N.I. 1845. Posted to new 34th N.I. (late Inf. of Bundelkhand Legion) 1846; Adjt. do. 11 Aug. 1846 till Feb. 1849. Postmr. at Wazirabad Jan. 1850. Bde. Major Multan 25 Feb. 1853; do. Jullundur 3 Aug. 1853 till Feb. 1856. Comdd. Regt. of Kalat-i-Ghilzai 6 Feb. 1856 till 22 Feb. 1858. Dy. Paymr. Benares 3 Feb. 1858; do. Sirhind circle 3 July 1858; Presdy. Paymr. 26 Feb. 1861 till 1871. Admitted to Col.'s allowances 23 Mar. 1873. No record of active service.

Refs.: Burke's *Landed Gentry*, 13th edn., p. 1283, *s.n.* Mundy, of Shipley Hall, co. Derby. Boase. *The Times*, 17 July 1888.

MUNDY, Francis William (1810-1840). Ensign. 69th N.I. *b.* Guildford, Surrey, 21 July 1810. Cadet 1828. Ensign (22 May 1828) 4 Mar. 1829. Resigned 2 Oct. 1829. *d.* Calcutta 23 May 1840.

4th son of Maj.-Gen. Godfrey Basil Mundy, of Upper George St., late 3rd Dgns., and the Hon. Sarah Brydges Rodney his wife, dau. of Adm. Lord Rodney, K.B. Cousin-german of Charles Fitzroy Miller Mundy, *q.v.* Sandhurst Cadet.

Services: Ensign d.d. 13th N.I. 28 Oct. 1828; posted to 69th N.I. 4 Mar. 1829. (? Became a coffee planter in India.)

Refs.: Burke's *Landed Gentry*, 13th edn., p. 1283, *s.n.* Mundy, of Shipley Hall, co. Derby. *G.M.* 1840, ii. 445.

MUNRO, Alexander (*d.* 1778). Captain, Infantry. Lieut. 14 Sept. 1768. Capt. 31 Mar. 1777. *d.* nr. Kalpi 4 July 1778: kld. by banditti.[1]

Son of Sir Alexander Munro, Kt., sometime consul gen. at Madrid, and Margaret Penelope his wife, sister of Gen. Johnstone, of Corehead, co. Dumfries. Brother of Margaret Murray, of co. Ross, cousin of Robert Munro, Comdr. of an East Indiaman, and nephew of Gen. Sir Hector Munro, K.B. (*D.N.B.*), of Novar, co. Ross.

Services: (? Ensign H.M. 89th Ft.) Transfd. as Lieut. from H.M.S. (M.C. 1 Sept. 1768); 1st Bn. Sepoys in May 1772; was serving with troops of Nawab-Wazir of Oudh in Apr. 1778.

Refs.: Burke's *Landed Gentry*, 4th edn., p. 1054, *s.n.* Munro, of Novar. Will dated Calcutta 26 May 1778; proved 15 Oct. 1778.

[1] *Note:* He was proceeding with an escort of 22 sepoys from Kalpi to join Col. Matthew Leslie's camp when he was cut off by a large body of horse and foot. Most of his party fell with him.

THE BENGAL ARMY, 1758-1834

MUNRO, Alexander (1763/64-?). Lieutenant. 29th Bn. Sepoys. *b.* in Scotland 1763/64. Cadet 1780. Ensign 1780. Lieut. 7 July 1781. Resigned 25 Oct. 1793.

Services: Apptd. Cadet 3 May 1780, aged 16; sailed for India in the *Mount Stewart* 27 June 1780, and was captured by the combined French and Spanish fleets; sailed again in the *Hinchinbrooke* 13 Mar. 1781. Adjt. 29th Bn. Sepoys in July 1787 till Oct. 1793.

MUNRO, Charles. Lieutenant. 19th Bn. Sepoys. Country Cadet 1781. Ensign 24 Sept. 1781. Lieut. 28 June 1783. Dismissed by a G.C.M. at Cawnpore 7 Mar. 1785.

Services: Apptd. Cadet 24 May 1781. Dismissed with infamy for perjury before a C.M. on 10 Oct. 1784. (? Became a merchant at Calcutta, where he *d.* May 1793.)

MUNRO, Charles Adolphus (1784-1859). Lieut. Colonel. 74th N.I. *b.* Calcutta 17 Jan. 1784. Cadet 1804. Arrived in India 13 May 1806. Ensign 12 Apr. 1806. Lieut. 22 Sept. 1808. Capt. 11 July 1823. Major 23 June 1835. Retired 15 Dec. 1835. Hon. Lt. Col. 28 Nov. 1854. *d.* Newport, Barnstaple, 16 June 1859.

Son of Catherine Campbell. *m.* West Lodge, Elgin, 15 June 1826, Lucy Eliza, dau. of Major John Lloyd Jones, Madras Est. (She died Pilton, Barnstaple, 4 Feb. 1882, aged 74.)

Services: Barasat C.C. Posted Ensign to 7th N.I. in 1807. Nepal War 1814-15; Lieut. 7th N.I. (India medal). Third Mahratta War; Lieut. 2/7th N.I. With 2nd Ceylon Vol. Bn. 1818-19. Actg. Bk.Mr. 8th (Rohilkhand) Div. 1822. d.d. 1/23rd N.I. 12 Apr. 1823. Fur. p.a. 1 Mar. 1824 till 1 Feb. 1827. Transfd. to 13th N.I. (late 1/7th) May 1824; to newly-raised 6th Extra Regt. (became 74th N.I.) May 1825.

Refs.: *A.J.* xxii. 126. *G.M.* 1859, ii. 94. *The Times*, 20 June 1859.

MUNRO, James (1753/54-1786). Lieutenant, Infantry. *b.* in Scotland 1753/54. Cadet 1777. Ensign 30 Dec. 1777. Lieut. 8 Sept. 1778. *d.* Dacca 25 Sept. 1786.

Brother of Duncan, William, and Archibald Munro.

Services: Sailed for India in the *Duke of Kingston* 24 Mar. 1777, aged 23. N.F.P.

Refs.: *S.M.* 1787, p. 206. Will dated Dacca, 13 Sept. 1786; proved 20 Oct. 1786.

MUNRO, James (1807-1831). Lieutenant, 21st N.I. *b.* Old Monkland, Lanark, 14 May 1807. Cadet 1825. Arrived in India 18 Mar. 1826. Ensign 28 Sept. 1825. Lieut. 16 May 1829. *d.* Nasirabad, Rajputana, 21 Dec. 1831.

Son of George Munro, of Calderbank, and Lilias Murdoch his wife.

Services : Served throughout with 21st N.I. ; Adjt. 8 Mar. 1830 till death. No record of active service.

Refs. : Will undated (written in pencil) ; admon. 1 May 1832.

MUNRO, John (1763/64-1827). Lieut. Colonel. 19th N.I. *b.* in Scotland 1763/64. Cadet 1781. Admitted 4 June 1782. Ensign 17 June 1781. Lieut. 23 Sept. 1782. Capt. 2 Oct. 1800. Major 11 Sept. 1806. Lt. Col. 4 May 1812. Retired 25 Jan. 1815. *d.* Wooden, co. Roxburgh, 3 Sept. 1827. *m.* Edinburgh 25 Jan. 1814, Miss Margaret Scott.

Services : Apptd. Cadet 29 May 1781, aged 17 ; sailed for India in the *Deptford* 26 June 1781. Lieut. 21st Bn. Sepoys in July 1787 ; Lieut. 2nd Bengal Eur. Regt. ; Capt. Lt. do. 29 May 1800 ; transfd. to 8th N.I. Oct. 1801. Operations in Jumna Doab 1803 ; Sasni ; Capt. 8th N.I. Transfd. to newly-raised 23rd N.I.[1] 9 Nov. 1803. Settlement of Hariana 1809 ; Bhawani ; Major 2/23rd N.I. Posted Lt. Col. to 19th N.I. Fur. 1812 till retirement.

Refs. : S.M. 1814, p. 156. *A.J.* xxiv. 529.

[1] *Note :* Called after him "*Murreeroo-ki-Paltan.*"

MUNRO, Robert. Ensign, Infantry. Cadet 1772. Ensign 21 July 1776. *d.* in India (date not known) before 1780.

Services : N.F.P.

MUNRO, Robert (1806-1857). Bt. Major, 10th N.I. *b.* St. Thomas', Jamaica, 24 Oct. 1806. Cadet 1828. Arrived in India 21 Sept. 1828. Ensign 26 Mar. 1828. Lieut. 5 Mar. 1835. Capt. 10 Sept. 1845. Bt. Major 20 June 1854. *d.* Bithur, nr. Cawnpore, 11 July 1857 : kld. by a round shot after escaping from Fatehgarh, where his Regt. had mutinied.

Nephew of James Munro, of Inverness. His nomination was procured for him by Anna Magdalen Munro, of Inverness. *m.* Jane. (She died St. Leonards-on-Sea, 28 Aug. 1857.)

Services : Posted Ensign to 10th N.I. 4 Nov. 1828. Rising in Cuttack 1836 ; Lieut. 10th N.I. Actg. Adjt. 10th N.I. 22 Apr. 1840 ; do. Rt. Wing 10th N.I. 10 June 1843. Fur. s.c. 17 June 1845 till 6 Sept. 1848. Second Burma War 1852-4 ; Pegu, comdg.

THE BENGAL ARMY, 1758-1834   355

detachment 10th N.I.; Capt. 10th N.I. (Medal with clasp). Fur. s.c. 18 mos. June 1855.
Refs.: *I.M.* 1 Oct. 1857, p. 637. M.I. All Sts. Memorial Church, Cawnpore.

MUNT, George McIntosh (1785-1814). Lieutenant, 1st N.I. *bapt.* Morden, Surrey, 12 Aug. 1785. Cadet 1803. Arrived in India 3 Dec. 1804. Ensign 27 Oct. 1804. Lieut. 27 Oct. 1804. *d.* Jampta, nr. Nahan, Sirmoor, 27 Dec. 1814: kld. in action at the assault of Jaithak fort.
Son of John Munt and Sarah his wife. (? His sisters *m.* George Moore (1789-1848), and James Templer Parlby, *qq.v.*)
Services : Posted Ensign to 2/1st N.I. 14 Apr. 1805. Operations in Bundelkhand 1806-7; Chamir; Sehlehuganj; Lieut. 2/1st N.I. Operations against Lachman Dawa 1809; Rajaoli; Ajaigarh; Lieut. 2/1st N.I. Assisted in quelling the insurrection in the palace at Delhi on 24 July 1809. Transfd. to 1/1st N.I. in 1813. Nepal War 1814; Kalanga; Jaithak (kld.); Lieut. L.I. Bn.
Refs.: *De Rhé-Philipe.* M.I. at Nahan.

MURCHISON, Kenneth Archibald John (1780-1813). Captain, 20th N.I. *b.* Bengal Apr. 1780. Cadet 1795. Arrived in India 6 Mar. 1797. Ensign 27 Nov. 1796. Lieut. 30 Oct. 1797. Capt. 30 Mar. 1805. *d.* in England 3 Jan. 1813.
bapt. Calcutta 5 May 1783. Natural son of Kenneth Murchison, of Tarradale, late Surg. Bengal Est. Brother of Robert Murchison, Capt. 43rd Ft., and of Frances Mellish, wife of Martin White (1766/67-1856), *q.v.* Half-brother of Sir Roderick Impey Murchison, 1st Bart. (*D.N.B.*).
Services: Lieut. 2/6th N.I. in July 1798. Expedn. to Egypt 1801; Lieut. Bengal Vols. Lieut. Marine Regt. (became 20th N.I.); Capt. 20th N.I. Fur. 1810 till death.
Refs.: Will dated Calcutta 28 Nov. 1810; proved 1 Feb. 1814.

MURDOCH, John (*b.* 1781). Lieutenant, Infantry. Country Cadet 1778. Ensign 1778. Lieut. 30 Aug. 1779. *d.* Sept. 1781.
Services: Apptd. Cadet 27 Feb. 1778. N.F.P.

MURPHY, Thomas Turner (1782-1808). Lieutenant, 26th N.I. *b.* St. Mary's, Dublin, 7 June 1782. Cadet 1803. Arrived in India 7 Dec. 1804. Ensign 26 Sept. 1804. Lieut. 26 Sept. 1804. *d.* in Bundelkhand 30 Oct. 1808.
(*Perhaps* son of Matthew Murphy, solicitor.) Nephew of William

Bushby, of Gt. Cumberland Pl., London, formerly B.C.S. (? T.C.D.; Pensioner 3 June 1799, aged 17.)
Services: Posted Lieut. to newly-raised 26th N.I. in 1805. Operations in Bundelkhand 1807; capture of Sehlehuganj; Lieut. 26th N.I.
Refs.: (? *Alumni Dub.*)

MURRALL, Thomas William (1788-1811). Lieutenant, 24th N.I. *bapt.* Overton Waterville (*alias* Cherry Orton) 21 June 1788. Cadet 1803. Arrived in India 27 Sept. 1804. Ensign 24 Sept. 1804. Lieut. 24 Sept. 1804. *d.* Java 23 Sept. 1811, of wounds received in action.
Son of Thomas Murrall and Elizabeth his wife.
Services: Posted Lieut. to newly-raised 2/24th N.I. in 1805. Operations in Hariana 1809; capture of Bhawani; Lieut. 2/24th N.I. Capture of Java 1811; Cornelis 26 Aug. (s.w.); Lieut. 6th Bengal Vol. Bn.
Refs.: Name on cenotaph "To the Memory of the Brave" in Barrackpore park.

MURRAY, Æneas (1787-1811). Lieutenant, 26th N.I. *bapt.* St. Columb's, Templemore, Londonderry, 15 June 1787. Cadet 1803. Arrived in India 29 Apr. 1805. Ensign 13 May 1805. Lieut. 14 May 1805. *d.* Java 3 Nov. 1811.
Son of Roger Murray, of the city of Londonderry, and Anne his wife.
Services: Posted Lieut. to 26th N.I. in 1806. Operations in Bundelkhand 1807; capture of Sehlehuganj; Lieut. 26th N.I. Capture of Java 1811; Lieut. Bengal Vols.

MURRAY, Alexander (1746-1822). Captain. Infantry. Afterwards Col. R. Clan Alpine Fenc. *b.* 25 Aug. 1746. Cadet 1772. Ensign 30 Mar. 1773. Lieut. 28 May 1778. Bt. Capt. 7 Sept. 1782. Capt. 22 Jan. 1784. Resigned 1793. *d.* Stockton, Yorks., 18 July 1822.
Of Napier Ruskie, co. Perth. 2nd son of Evan Murray and Janet his wife, youngest dau. of John MacDonald, of Balcony. Brother of Sir John Murray Macgregor, Bart., and Peter Murray, *qq.v.* Grandfather of Alexander Nugent Murray Macgregor and cousin of John Macdonald (1759-1831), *qq.v. m.* 1st, Madras 23 May 1773, Frances, dau. of Major Pascal.[1] (She died 1786.) *m.* 2nd, Edinburgh 25 Mar. 1790, Grace, dau. of James Hay, of co. Banff, and widow of John Macpherson, *q.v.*

THE BENGAL ARMY, 1758-1834 357

Services: Served as a Vol. in Keith's Highlrs. (87th Ft.) in Germany; battle of Wilhelmsthal 24 June 1762; Bruckmühle 21 Sept. 1762. Ensign 77th Regt.; 50th Ft. 1762-72. Being on leave at Madras, he volunteered and served in the Madras Engrs. at siege and capture of Tanjore Aug.-Sept. 1773. First Rohilla War; battle of St. George; Asst. Field Engr., A.D.C. to Col. A. Champion, *q.v.* Comdd. Nawab Nazim's bodyguard at Murshidabad till Dec. 1780. Campaign against the Rajah of Benares 1781; capture of Bijaigarh. C.-in-C. and Member of Council at Bencoolen, Sumatra, Sept. 1782 till 1785. Local Major Sept. 1782; local Lt. Col. Aug. 1783; local Col. 1785. Fur. 1786 till resignation. Raised and comdd. R. Highland Regt. of Edin. Vols. 1797; obtained comd. of R. Clan Alpine Fenc. 1798.

Refs.: Burke's *Peerage*, 1923, p. 1467, *s.n.* Macgregor, Bart., of Lanrick. Foster's *Families of Royal Descent*, i. 64. *E.I.M.C.* ii. 464-6. *Macpherson*, p. 349. *G.M.* 1822, ii. 190, 277.

¹ *Note:* Probably Edmund Pascal, Town Major of Madras in Nov. 1763.

MURRAY, Alexander (1757-1796). Captain, Infantry. *b.* Duffus, co. Moray, 10 June 1757. Cadet 1779. Admitted 12 Sept. 1780. Ensign 5 Aug. 1779. Lieut. 28 Mar. 1781. Capt. 7 Jan. 1796. *d.* Calcutta 6 Dec. 1796.

3rd and youngest son of Rev. Alexander Murray, minister of Duffus 1748-80, and Isobel (*or* Elizabeth) his wife, dau. of Robert Gordon, of Haughs. John Murray, bookseller in Fleet St., London, was exor. of his Will.

Services: Sailed for India in the *Ceres* 16 June 1779. Lieut. 7th Bn. Sepoys in July 1787. Third Mysore War; Bangalore; Arikera; Penagra; Krishnagiri; Seringapatam; Lieut. 7th Bn. Apptd. Adjt. 35th Bn. 23 Apr. 1793. Fort Adjt. at Chunar in Dec. 1795.

Refs.: Scott's *Fasti*, vi. 386. Will dated 5 Feb. 1790; proved 20 Dec. 1796. M.I. in S. Park St. cemetery, Calcutta.

MURRAY, Charles (*d.* 1785). Captain, Infantry. Cadet 1771. Ensign 11 Mar. 1773. Lieut. 28 Mar. 1778. Capt. 7 Jan. 1784. *d.* Berhampore 24 Feb. 1785.

Brother of Margaret Lilias Saunders.

Services: Was Lieut. 28th Bn. Sepoys in Mar. 1780, when he was granted fur. s.c.; returned from fur. Aug. 1783.

Refs.: Will dated Rajmahal, 20 Feb. 1785; proved 12 Mar. 1785.

MURRAY, Charles William (1784-1804). Lieutenant, 18th N.I. *b.* Fatehgarh 25 Mar. 1784. Cadet 1798. Arrived in India 6 Sept. 1799. Ensign 13 Dec. 1799 (? 13 Jan. 1800). Lieut. 29 May 1800. *d.* Calcutta 11 Dec. 1804.
(*Probably* son of Charles Murray, *q.v.*)
Services: Posted Lieut. to 1/8th N.I. 15 Apr. 1801. Second Mahratta War; Bundelkhand 1803; Narnaul; Kanun; defeat of Rajah Ràm Singh 2 July 1804; capture of Jaitpur; Lieut. 1/18th N.I.

MURRAY, George (1777-1798). Lieutenant, 9th N.I. *bapt.* Tain, co. Ross, 8 June 1777. Cadet 1794. Arrived in India 3 Mar. 1797. Ensign 8 Oct. 1796. Lieut. 6 Dec. 1797. *d.* at sea 9 Sept. 1798, on board the *Busbridge* on his passage to England.
Son of George Murray, of Tain, merchant, Capt. Royal Tain Vols., and Mary his wife, dau. of Bailie Nicholas Ross, of Tain, merchant.
Services: N.F.P.
Refs.: *S.M.* 1799, p. 652.

MURRAY, George (1807-1856). Bt. Major, 8th L.C. *b.* Murraythwaite, co. Dumfries, 4 July 1807. Cadet 1825. Arrived in India 20 Mar. 1826. Cornet 25 Oct. 1825. Lieut. 21 July 1835. Capt. 29 Jan. 1847. Bt. Major 11 Nov. 1851. *d.* Mian Mir, Lahore, 12 Sept. 1856.
5th son of John Murray and Catherine his wife, dau. of Thomas Arthington, of Arthington, Yorks. Brother of William Murray (1801-1842), *q.v.* *m.* 1834, Henrietta Sarah, dau. of Rev. S. Goodenough. (She died Mian Mir 6 Sept. 1856, aged 50.) Ed. Edin. High School.
Services: Cornet d.d. 9th L.C. Apr.-Oct. 1826. Posted to 8th L.C. May 1826, and joined in Nov. Fur. s.c. 3 Mar. 1832 till 10 Nov. 1834. Actg. Adjt. 8th L.C. Aug. 1835 till Jan. 1836; permanent do. 8 June 1838 till Nov. 1841. Fur. s.c. 24 Apr. 1842 till Nov. 1845. Second Sikh War; Ramnagar; passage of Chenab; Sadulapur; Chilianwala; Gujerat; Capt. 8th L.C. (Medal with 2 clasps).
Refs.: Burke's *Landed Gentry*, 13th edn., p. 1290, *s.n.* Murray, of Murraythwaite, co. Dumfries. *De Rhé-Philipe.* Will dated Mian Mir 11 Aug. 1856; codicil dated 12 Sept. 1856; proved 26 Feb. 1857. M.I. in R.A. cemetery, Lahore.

MURRAY, Hugh (1797-1819). Ensign, Infantry. *b.* Tain, co. Ross, 24 Sept. 1797. Cadet 1818. Ensign (?) *d.* Calcutta 17 Aug. 1819.

THE BENGAL ARMY, 1758-1834

" Hugh Murray, Esq., younger, of Rosemount, co. Ross." (*S.M.*) *bapt.* Tain 9 Oct. 1797. Son of William Murray, of Tain, merchant, and Christian Rose his wife.

Services: Died within a few weeks of his arrival in India whilst still an unposted Ensign.

Refs.: *S.M.* 1820, i. 292.

MURRAY, Hugh Robertson (1789-1877). Lieut. Colonel. 73rd N.I. *b.* Tain, co. Ross, 1 Aug. 1789. Cadet 1806. Arrived in India 21 July 1807. Ensign 1 Aug. 1807. Lieut. 29 Aug. 1810. Capt. 13 May 1825. Bt. Major 10 Jan. 1837. Retired 2 Aug. 1839. Hon. Lt. Col. 28 Nov. 1854. *d.* at his residence, Lodge Hill, Nairn, 24 Jan. 1877.

bapt. Tain 3 Aug. 1789. Son of Robert Murray.

Services: Barasat C.C. for 10 mos. Posted Ensign to 13th N.I. in 1808. Lieut. 2/13th N.I. To conduct researches in Kumaon on the manufacture of paper for Ordnance purposes Oct. 1816. These came to an end in Mar. 1817 owing to illness, and he was granted a reward of Rs. 1,000. Third Mahratta War; Lieut. 2/13th N.I. (? With 3rd Ceylon Vol. Bn. 1818-19.) Adjt. 1/13th N.I. 17 Aug. 1819 till 1824; actg. Intr. & Qmr. do. 30 Dec. 1823. Transfd. to 27th N.I. (late 2/13th) May 1824; to 5th Extra Regt. (became 73rd N.I.) 1825. Asst. Executive Ofr. P.W.D., Backergunge and Barisal, 28 Apr. 1825 till 31 Dec. 1832, and 13 June 1833 till 1 Nov. 1836, with Arakan and Chittagong in addition. Leave s.c. to Cape 20 Jan. 1837 till 22 Jan. 1839.

Refs.: *The Times*, 27 Jan. 1877.

MURRAY, James (*d.* 1804). Captain, 15th N.I. Cadet 1782. Admitted 4 Feb. 1783. Ensign 17 Feb. 1783. Lieut. 7 Feb. 1790. Capt. 13 July 1803. *d.* in Bundelkhand 27 June 1804. Brother of Helen and Mary, of Queen's Ferry, nr. Edinburgh.

Services: Apptd. Cadet 19 Dec. 1781; sailed for India in the *Royal Henry* 6 Feb. 1782. Posted Ensign to 1st Bengal Eur. Regt. 28 Feb. 1783; 2nd Eur. Bn. in Dec. 1788; reposted to do. 5 Feb. 1790; transfd. to 25th Bn. Sepoys. Operations in Jumna Doab 1803; Sasni; Bijaigarh; Kachaura; Capt. Lt. 15th N.I. Second Mahratta War 1803-4; battle of Delhi; Agra; Laswari; Capt. 15th N.I.

Refs.: Will dated Cawnpore 28 Dec. 1803; proved 20 Mar. 1805.

MURRAY, James (1779-1847). Captain. 19th N.I. Subsequently H.E.I.C. Recruiting Ofr. for London district. *bapt.*

St. James's, Westminster, 5 Nov. 1779. Cadet 1798. Arrived in India 7 Mar. 1800. Ensign 25 Dec. 1799. Lieut. 29 May 1800. Capt. 22 Feb. 1811. Retired 7 Oct. 1814. *d.* Quatre Bras, nr. Dorchester, 22 June 1847.

Son of James Murray [1] and Ann. *m.* 1st, Berhampore 6 Feb. 1802, Elizabeth, 2nd dau. of Henry Wedderburn, *q.v.*, and niece of James Tetley, *q.v.* (*See also* Sir John Cumming.) (She died in England 10 Sept. 1814.) *m.* 2nd, St. Pancras, Middlesex, Sept. 1818, Elizabeth Ann, dau. of Joseph Brewer Palmer Smyth, of New Jersey, and sister of Adm. William Henry Smyth, R.N. (*D.N.B.*). *m.* 3rd (before 1841), Catherine, dau. of John Wood.

Services: Posted Lieut. to 2/19th N.I. 15 Apr. 1801. Fur. 18 Feb. 1806 till 23 Aug. 1808, and 1812 till retirement. No record of active service. Supt. for the London district of the recruiting staff of H.E.I.C. 1819 till death.

Refs.: The Wedderburn Book, i. 385 *n. Howard & Crisp,* xxi. 65, *s.n.* Binny. *A.J.* vi. 557. *Patrician,* iv. 194.

[1] *Note:* Said to have been a nephew of John, Duke of Atholl: if so, he was a son of Maj.-Gen. James Murray, of Strowan.

MURRAY, James (1810-1850). Bt. Captain, 9th N.I. *b.* Kells, co. Kirkcudbright, 11 July 1810. Cadet 1831. Arrived in India 19 May 1832. Ensign 19 May 1832. Lieut. 3 Oct. 1840. Bt. Capt. 9 Feb. 1847. *d.* on board the river steamer *Meteor* at Rajghat, U.P., 5 Jan. 1850.

Brother of Peter Murray, of New Galloway. Ed. Ayr Acad.

Services: Cadet d.d. 2nd N.I. 16 July 1832. Posted Ensign to 36th N.I. 19 Dec. 1833. Shekhawat expedn. 1834; Ensign 36th N.I. Transfd. to 9th N.I. 24 Sept. 1835. Intr. & Qmr. 9th N.I. 16 Aug. 1838 till Dec. 1844. With Army of Reserve (for Afghanistan) Oct. 1842 till Jan. 1843. Fur. s.c. 24 Jan. 1845 till 21 Sept. 1847. Intr. & Qmr. 9th N.I. 12 Oct. 1847 till death.

Refs.: I.M. 9 Mar. 1850, p. 132.

MURRAY, James (1819-1892). Lieutenant. 28th N.I. *bapt.* Cheshunt, Herts., 1 Feb. 1819. Cadet 1834. Arrived in India 28 July 1835. Ensign 23 Mar. 1835. Lieut. 8 Oct. 1839. Retired 15 Aug. 1843. *d.* 7 Nov. 1892.

2nd son of James Murray, of Philiphaugh, co. Selkirk (of Wood Green House, Cheshunt), late Comdr. of the *Devonshire* East Indiaman, and Mary Dale his wife, dau. of Henry Hughes, of Worcester. Ed. Edinburgh Acad.

Services: Posted Ensign to 28th N.I. 24 Sept. 1835; apptd. to Vol.

THE BENGAL ARMY, 1758-1834   361

Regt. for service in China 15 Feb. 1840. First China War 1840;
Lieut. 1st. Vol. Regt. (Medal). Returned to India at the end of
1840 owing to sunstroke. Fur. s.c. 15 Feb. 1841 till retirement.
Refs.: Burke's *Landed Gentry*, 13th edn., p. 1291, *s.n.* Murray,
late of Philiphaugh, co. Selkirk. Burke's *R. Families*, i. 22.

MURRAY, James Charles (*d.* 1790). Lieutenant, 6th Bengal
Eur. Bn. Cadet 1782. Ensign 24 Mar. 1783. Lieut. 1 Mar. 1790.
d. Dinapore 24 Dec. 1790.
Services: Apptd. Cadet 28 Dec. 1781; sailed for India in the
Calcutta 6 Feb. 1782. Posted to 3rd Bengal Eur. Regt. 1783;
to 6th Eur. Bn. 5 Feb. 1790.

MURRAY, James Lumsdaine (1803-1826). Ensign, 1st Extra
Inf. Regt. *b.* The Manse, Kilmadock, co. Perth, 15 May 1803.
Cadet 1823. Ensign 13 Apr. 1824. *d.* Chittagong 5 Jan. 1826.
bapt. 20 May 1803. 2nd son of Rev. Patrick Murray, D.D.,
of Doune, minister of Kilmadock 1791-1837, and Mary Rolland his
2nd wife. Ed. St. Andrews Univ.
Services: Posted Ensign to 49th N.I. First Burma War;
Arakan 1825; Ensign 49th N.I. Transfd. to newly-raised 1st
Extra Regt. in 1825, but never joined that Corps.
Refs.: Scott's *Fasti*, iv. 347. Will dated Mymoo, 8 Mar. 1825;
proved 20 Sept. 1826.

MURRAY, John (1781-1802). Ensign, 10th N.I. *b.* Abernethy,
co. Moray, 12 Mar. 1781. Cadet 1800. Arrived in India 22 Aug.
1801. Ensign 30 Dec. 1801. *d.* Cawnpore 25 Apr. 1802.
Son of Andrew Murray and Jean Grant his wife. Brother of
Charles and Ann Murray.
Services: Ensign d.d. 12th N.I. 1801-2; posted Ensign to
2/10th N.I. No record of active service.
Refs.: *A.A.R.* iii. 121.

MURRAY, John (1796-1830). Lieutenant. 19th N.I. *b.* Crail,
co. Fife, 19 Mar. 1796. Cadet 1811. Ensign 30 Sept. 1814.
Lieut. 1 Aug. 1818. Struck off in India 3 Sept. 1825. *d.* Crail
18 May 1830.
bapt. Crail 20 Mar. 1796. Son of Robert Murray, principal mgte.
of Crail, and Catharine Bell his wife.
Services: Posted Ensign to 2/3rd N.I. in 1814. (? Nepal War
1814-15; Ensign 2/3rd N.I., in 1st Div.) Transfd. to 19th N.I.
(late 2/3rd) May 1824. Fur. 1823 till struck off.
Refs.: *A.J.* N.S. ii. 185.

MURRAY, Hon. John Oliphant (1808-1865). Lieutenant. 47th N.I. Subsequently Chamberlain to H.M. the King of Bavaria. Kt. Grand Cross of the Order of St. Michael of Merit. *b.* Eddleston, co. Peebles, 3 July 1808. Cadet 1825. Arrived in India 25 Oct. 1826. Ensign 23 May 1826. Lieut. 6 July 1828. Resigned 28 Feb. 1832. *d.* Dresden 11 Dec. 1865.

2nd son of Alexander Murray, 8th Baron Elibank, and Janet his wife, dau. of John Oliphant, of Bachilton, co. Perth, styled Lord Oliphant.

Services: Posted Ensign to 44th N.I. 9 Nov. 1826. Exchanged to 69th N.I. 25 Nov. 1826. (? Operations against the Bhils 1827; Ensign 69th N.I.) Transfd. to 47th N.I. in 1828. Leave u.p.a. 12 mos. to Cape 25 Feb. 1831.

Refs.: Burke's *Peerage*, 1923, p. 832, *s.n.* Elibank, B.

MURRAY, Patrick (*d.* 1783). Lieutenant, Infantry. Cadet 1781. Ensign 8 Sept. 1781. Lieut. 19 June 1783. *d.* 26 July 1783, on service with the Bombay detachment.

Services: Was already in India when apptd. Cadet 10 Apr. 1781. First Mahratta War 1782-3; Lieut. with Bengal detachment under Goddard.

MURRAY, Peter (*d.* 1803). Lieut. Colonel, 1st N.I. A.G. Bengal. Country Cadet 1771. Admitted 11 Jan. 1771. Ensign 9 Mar. 1773. Lieut. 27 Mar. 1778. Capt. 18 Oct. 1781. Major 30 Oct. 1797. Lt. Col. 21 Apr. 1800. *d.* at sea off Ferrol 14 Aug. 1803; kld. on board the *Lord Nelson* in action with the French frigate *Bellona.*

3rd son of Evan Murray. Brother of Robert Murray Macgregor and Alexander Murray (1746-1822), *qq.v. m.* Eliza Tuting.[1] (*See also* Edward Rowland Jackson.) (She *re-m.* Mar. 1808, Lt.-Col. Wilkinson Lister Kaye, late 21st Light Dgns.)

Services: Is said to have gone out to India originally as a Surgeon's Mate.[2] "On his passage he was insulted by one of the officers of the ship, to whom, after his arrival in India, he sent a challenge, which the other did not think proper to accept. The Government, however, seeing that he was a young man of spirit, offered him a commission in their service, which he accepted, ..." (*M.M.*) First Rohilla War; battle of St. George. A.D.C. to Bdr.-Gen. Giles Stibbert, *q.v.*, 1780-3. Acting A.G. Bengal 1781-5; A.G. (with official rank of Lt. Col.) 27 Sept. 1785 till 1797. Capt. 3rd Bengal Eur. Regt. in 1796. Fur. 18 Jan. 1797 till 8 Jan. 1801. Major 12th N.I. Posted Lt. Col. to 2/1st N.I. 21 Apr. 1800. Fur.

7 Mar. 1803 till death. "He is supposed to have accumulated a fortune of not less than £200,000." (*M.M.*)

Refs.: Burke's *Peerage*, 1923, p. 1467, *s.n.* Macgregor, Bart. *E.I.M.C.* ii. 461 *n.* *Crawford*, i. 242. *M.M.* 1804, p. 309. *G.M.* 1803, ii. 884.

¹ *Note*: According to Mrs. Eliza Fay they were married at the house of Dr. Rowland Jackson in Calcutta, 27 Mar. 1782.

² *Note*: Col. Crawford (op. cit) is inclined to doubt the correctness of this statement in *G.M.*

MURRAY, Thomas (1781-1846). Major General. Colonel 50th N.I. *b.* Edinburgh 4 Oct. 1781. Cadet 1799. Arrived in India 12 Jan. 1801. Ensign 28 Oct. 1800. Lieut. 22 Oct. 1801. Capt. 16 Dec. 1814. Major 11 July 1823. Lt. Col. 13 May 1825. Col. 18 June 1831. Maj. Gen. 23 Nov. 1841. *d.* Edinburgh 30 Jan. 1846.

Son of Henry Murray, of Old Kirk psh., Edinburgh, hairdresser, and Ann his wife, dau. of John Gray, wigmaker. *m.* Edinburgh 2 Nov. 1819, Martha, dau. of Joseph Furvis (? Purvis), of Liverpool.

Services: Posted Ensign to 2nd Bengal Eur. Regt. 17 Apr. 1801. Transfd. to Marine Regt. (became 20th N.I.) in 1803. Adjt. 2/20th N.I. 28 Dec. 1808 till 26 Aug. 1813. Actg. A.C.G. at Penang 1812-13. Agent for Comst. at Calcuttta 1814 till 27 May 1815. Fur. s.c. 2 Aug. 1818 till 1 June 1821. Transfd. to 40th N.I. (late 2/20th) May 1824. First Burma War; unsuccessful attack on Ramri I. Feb. 1825 (*Lond. Gaz.* 9 Aug. 1825); Major 40th N.I. Posted Lt. Col. to 40th N.I. May 1825; transfd. to 69th N.I. Fur. p.a. 6 June 1826 till 4 May 1829. Transfd. to 61st N.I., 2nd Bengal Eur. Regt., 9th N.I. in 1826; to 53rd, 41st N.I. in 1828; to 69th, 55th, 30th N.I. in 1829; to 23rd, 22nd, 12th N.I. in 1833. Fur. s.c. 20 Feb. 1834 till death. Transfd. to 53rd, 65th, 53rd N.I. Col. 50th N.I. 29 Apr. 1836 till death.

Refs.: *S.M.* N.S. v. 580.

MURRAY, Thomas (1784-1806). Lieutenant, 2nd N.I. *b.* Kinnoul, co. Perth, 15 Feb. 1784. Cadet 1800. Arrived in India 24 Aug. 1801. Ensign 13 Sept. 1801. Lieut. 13 July 1803. *d.* Agra 12 Mar. 1806.

bapt. 27 Feb. 1784. 2nd son of John Graeme Murray (afterwards John Murray), of Murrayshall, co. Perth, and Janet his wife, eldest dau. of Thomas Anderson, of Newburgh, co. Fife. Cousin-german of Anthony Maxtone, *q.v.*

Services: Ensign d.d. 12th N.I. 1801-2. Operations in Jumna

Doab 1803; Sasni; Ensign 1/2nd N.I. Second Mahratta War; battle of Delhi; battle of Deig (w.); Lieut. 1/2nd N.I.

Refs.: Burke's *Landed Gentry*, 13th edn., p. 768, *s.n.* Murray-Graham, of Murrayshall and Bertha Park, co. Perth. *Pester, passim. S.M.* 1807, p. 77. Will dated Agra, 27 Jan. 1806; proved 22 Aug. 1806.

MURRAY, William (*d.* 1770). Ensign, Infantry. Cadet 1769. Ensign 21 Jan. 1770. *d.* Ghireti, Bengal, 30 June 1770.

Services: N.F.P.

MURRAY, William (1768-1787). Lieut. Fireworker, Artillery. (263) *b.* 28 Feb. 1768. Cadet 1783. Arrived in India 25 Nov. 1784. Fireworker 24 Apr. 1785. *d.* P.W.I. 22 Dec. 1787.

Youngest son of Sir Archibald Murray, 7th Bart. of Blackbarony, co. Peebles, and Mary Moorhead his 1st wife.

Services: Apptd. Cadet 5 Nov. 1783; sailed for India in the *Earl Cornwallis* 31 Mar. 1784. Posted to 2nd Coy. Art. at P.W.I. 23 Dec. 1786.

Refs.: Burke's *Peerage*, 1923, p. 1636, *s.n.* Murray, Bart., of Blackbarony, co. Peebles. *G.M.* 1788, ii. 751.

MURRAY, William (1791-1831). Captain, 2nd N.I. P.A. at Ambala. *b.* Monivard, co. Perth, 7 June 1791. Cadet 1809. Arrived in India Oct. 1810. Ensign 7 Mar. 1812. Lieut. 16 Dec. 1814. Capt. 28 May 1829. *d.s.p.* Sabathu, Punjab, 28 June 1831, of inflammation of the bowels.

bapt. 1 July 1791. 3rd and youngest son of Sir William Murray, 5th Bart., of Ochtertyre, co. Perth, and Augusta his wife, youngest dau. of George, 3rd Earl of Cromartie. Brother of Sir Patrick Murray, 6th Bart., Sec. to the Board of Comrs. for affairs of India.

Services: Barasat C.C. till 22 July 1811. Ensign d.d. 2/15th N.I. July 1811; posted to 2/1st N.I. 14 Apr. 1812. Mily. Student at Coll. of Ft. Wm. Oct.-Dec. 1814. Nepal War 1815; Ramgarh; Lieut. 2/1st N.I. in 1st Div.; capture of Malaun; comdg. a body of Irreg. troops—" Hindoouahs " (*Lond. Gaz.* 16 Nov. 1815). Intr. & Qmr. 1/1st N.I. 4 May 1815; do. 2/1st N.I. 1816; do. 1/1st N.I. Feb. 1819 till 25 June 1822. Pol. employ 1816 till death; Asst. P.A. at Ludhiana; Dy. Supt. of Sikh and Hill Affairs 15 Mar. 1823; P.A. at Ambala May 1827 till death. Transfd. to 2nd N.I. (late 1/1st) May 1824. His account of " Manners and customs of the Sikhs " pub. in *A.J.* N.S. xvii (May 1835), pp. 35-43.

Refs.: Burke's *Peerage*, 1923, p. 1638, *s.n.* Keith-Murray, Bart.,

of Ochtertyre, co. Perth. *De Rhé-Philipe. A.J.* N.S. vii. 42.
Will undated; proved 15 July 1831. M.I. at Sabathu.

MURRAY, William (1801-1842). Captain, 22nd N.I. *bapt.*
Dumfries 21 Dec. 1801. Cadet 1818. Admitted 27 Mar. 1820.
Ensign 20 Sept. 1819. Lieut. 11 July 1823. Capt. 12 Nov.
1830. *d.* Jubbulpore 27 June 1842.
2nd son of John Murray and Catherine his wife. Brother of
George Murray (1807-1856), *q.v. m.* All Souls, Marylebone, 20 May
1834, Sophia Ann, eldest dau. of Rev. James Lynn, vicar of Keswick,
Cumberland, and grand-dau. of the bishop of Carlisle. (*See also*
Zachary Mudge Mallock.) (She *re-m.* 16 June 1849, James Stanger,
of Lairthwaite, Keswick, and died 2 Dec. 1879.) Ed. Edin. High
School and Coll.
Services: Posted Ensign to 2/18th N.I. in 1820. Transfd. as
Lieut. to 2nd N.I. July 1823 ; to 22nd N.I. (late 2/2nd) May 1824.
Adjt. 22nd N.I. 29 May 1826 till 1 Mar. 1830. Fur. p.a. 1 Feb. 1831
till 10 Nov. 1834. Actg. A.D.C. to Govr. of Agra 13 May 1835 ;
Dy. Postmaster at Benares 21 Aug. 1835. Asst. to Comr., Saugor
& Narbada territories, 3 Oct. 1835 ; 1st Junior Asst. Comr. Saugor
Div. 22 Nov. 1839 ; offg. Principal Asst. at Jubbulpore 23 June
1842. No record of active service.
Refs.: Burke's *Landed Gentry*, 13th edn., p. 1290, *s.n.* Murray,
of Murraythwaite, co. Dumfries. *A.J.* N.S. xiv. 226. *G.M.* 1843,
i. 554. *M.I.* Jubbulpore.

MURRAY, William (1805-1826). Lieutenant, 28th N.I. *b.*
Bradda, I. of Man, 4 July 1805. Cadet 1823. Ensign 17 Jan.
1824. Lieut. 13 May 1825. *d.* Barrackpore 20 Sept. 1826.
bapt. ptely. Bradda 23 Jan. 1806. Son of Capt. Mungo Murray
and Isabella Heywood his wife.
Services: Posted Ensign to 28th N.I. No record of active service.
Refs.: A.J. xxiii. 529.

MURRELL, John Benjamin (1806-1828). Ensign, Infantry.
b. All Saints, Evesham, Worcs., 26 July 1806. Cadet 1826.
Ensign (?) *d.* nr. Monghyr 8 Jan. 1828, on his way to the Upper
Provinces ; *bur.* at Monghyr.
Son of B. Murrell, of Evesham, banker.
Refs.: A.J. xxvi. 76.

MUSCUTT, James. Lieutenant. Infantry. Cadet 1764. Ensign 2 Oct. 1764. Lieut. 21 Oct. 1765. Resigned 30 Nov. 1767.

Services: Campaign against the Nawabs of Bengal and Oudh 1764-5. Posted to 1st Bengal Eur. Regt. 13 Aug. 1765.
Refs.: *Caraccioli,* ii. 481.

*MUSHARD or MUSKARD, Philip. Lieut. Fireworker. Artillery.

Services: Was a Sergt. on 1 Sept. 1765, when he was apptd. a Condr. of Art. stores. On 14 May 1766, Sir Robert Fletcher, *q.v.*, sent for him and offered to appoint him to act as an Officer owing to the wholesale resignations of their Commissions by Officers during the "Batta mutiny." In Oct. 1766 he gave evidence at the trial by G.C.M. of Sir R. Fletcher, being then a Lieut. F. in the 1st Coy. Art. In the MS. *A.L.* of 1 Feb. 1767 he is shown as Lieut. F., but no date is assigned to him. Stubbs omits him from his *List.*

Refs.: *Broome,* p. 615; appendix, P. lxxiii. *B.M. Add. MSS.* 6050.

MUSTELL, Peter John (*d.* 1773). Lieutenant,[1] 7th Bn. Sepoys. Cadet (?) Ensign 9 Nov. 1764. Lieut. 2 July 1770. *d.* Chittagong July 1773.

m. Mary, dau. of Samuel and Mary Scott, of York. (She died Chittagong 1776.)

Services: Was serving (? in the ranks) at Patna under Col. Eyre Coote in June 1761. To d.d. with Bengal Eur. Bn. 4 Mar. 1765; posted to 1st Bengal Eur. Regt. 13 Aug. 1765.

[1] *Note:* Probably a Brevet Lieut.

MYERS, Thomas (1764-?). Cadet. Artillery. (III.-13). Afterwards B.C.S.; Accountant Gen. Bengal. *b.* 1764. Country Cadet 1781. Resigned in India 5 Aug. 1782.

Elder son of Rev. Thomas Myers, LL.B., of The Brow, Barton, Westmorland, vicar of Lazonby, Cumberland, and Anne his wife, only dau. of Richard Wordsworth. *m.* 2 Jan. 1802, his second-cousin, Lady Mary Catherine, elder dau. of Henry (Nevill), 2nd Earl of Abergavenny. (She died 12 July 1807, aged 24.)

Services: Apptd. Cadet Nov. 1781. Transfd. to B.C.S.; Writer 1 Oct. 1781; Clerk to Court of Requests 20 Nov. 1784; Accountant Gen. 30 Jan. 1796. Left India 1798, and quitted the Service 1805.

Refs.: Burke's *Landed Gentry,* 5th edn., p. 1551, *s.n.* Wordsworth, of Sockbridge, Westmorland. Burke's *Peerage,* 1923, p. 63, *s.n.* M. of Abergavenny. Foster's *Families of Royal Descent,* p. 10.

MYLNE, William (*d.* 1791). Fireworker, Artillery. (250)
Cadet 1783. Arrived in India 20 Sept. 1783. Fireworker
8 Jan. 1785. *d.* P.W.I. 17 Sept. 1791.
Services: Apptd. Cadet 8 Jan. 1783; sailed for India in the *Duke of Kingston* 11 Mar. 1783. Lieut. F. 3rd Bn. Art. in July 1787. Served at P.W.I. 1788 till death.
Refs.: S.M. 1792, p. 258.

N

NAIL, George (*d.* 1785). Ensign, Infantry. Cadet 1783. Arrived in India Aug. 1784. Ensign 19 Mar. 1785. *d.* Cawnpore 13 Apr. 1785.

(*Probably* the George Nail who is acknowledged as a natural son in the Will of Matthew Nail, *q.v.*)
Services: Apptd. Cadet 25 Mar. and 12 Nov. 1783; sailed for India in the *Hillsborough* 28 Jan. 1784.

NAIL, Matthew (or Matthias) (*d.* 1769). Lieutenant, Artillery. (52) Cadet 1763. Fireworker 2 Dec. 1763. 2nd Lieut. 20 Oct. 1765. Lieut. Jan. 1767. *d. unm.* 13 May 1769.
Services: 2nd Lieut. 2nd Coy. Art. Resigned 6 May 1766, during the " Batta mutiny "; readmitted 30 June 1766.
Refs.: Will dated 11 May 1769; proved 6 June 1769.

NAIRNE, Charles (*d.* 1771). Lieutenant, Infantry. Cadet 1767. Ensign 16 Feb. 1767. Lieut. 2 Apr. 1769. *d. unm.* (? Berhampore) 13 Jan. 1771.

Younger son of Sir Thomas Nairne, 3rd Bart., of Dunsinane, co. Perth. Younger brother of Sir William Graham Nairne, 4th Bart.
Services: N.F.P.
Refs.: G.E.C. *Complete Baronetage,* iv. 426. Burke's *Landed Gentry,* 10th edn., p. 1157, *s.n.* Nairne, of Dunsinane, co. Perth. *S.M.* 1771, p. 614. Will dated 21 Oct. 1770; proved 12 Apr. 1771.

NAIRNE, George (*d.* 1771). Lieutenant, Infantry. Ensign 20 Oct. 1766. Lieut. 1 Dec. 1767. *d.* Moradabad, U.P., 26 May 1771.

m. Mary. (She died 29 Mar. 1786.)
Services: Permitted to proceed to India as a Free Mariner 17 Jan. 1766. Commissioned as Ensign in India owing to the shortage of officers caused by the " Batta mutiny."

NAIRNE, Robert (1763/64-1803). Major, 6th N.C. *b.* Bencoolen 1763/64. Cadet 1780. Admitted 10 Nov. 1781. Cornet 1780. Lieut. 12 July 1781. Capt. 29 May 1800. Major 17 July 1801. *d.* 12 Mar. 1803: kld. in action at the reduction of Kachaura fort.

Reputed son of Robert Nairne, sometime 2nd in council at

LIST OF OFFICERS OF THE BENGAL ARMY 369

Bencoolen. m. Cawnpore 19 Feb. 1798, Miss Anne Mercer.[1] (She re-m. 25 Apr. 1817, S. Usher, of Bristol.) His dau. m. Frederick Brooke Corfield, q.v.

Services: Apptd. Cadet 17 May 1780, aged 16. Sailed for India in the Southampton 13 Mar. 1781, aged 17, and was captured by the enemy on the voyage out. Lieut. 28th Bn. Sepoys in July 1787. Third Mysore War 1790-2 ; Arikera ; operations before Savandrug ; Seringapatam ; Lieut. 28th Bn. Bt. Capt. 2nd N.C. in June 1798. Capt. Lt. and Adjt. 4th N.C. Transfd. as Capt. to newly-raised 6th N.C. May 1800. Operations in Jumna Doab 1803 ; Sasni ; Bijaigarh ; Kachaura (kld.) ; Major comdg. 6th N.C.

Refs.: Pester. G.M. 1803, ii. 1035. Will dated 31 Aug. 1802 ; proved 23 Aug. 1803. M.I. Rathbanpur.

[1] Note: She was a natural dau. of Laurence Mercer, B.C.S., brother of William Mercer, q.v., at whose house the marriage was celebrated.

NANGREAVE, Samuel Wareing (1757-1815). Lieut. Colonel. 13th N.I. b. 1757. Cadet 1781. Admitted 15 Sept. 1781. Ensign 1781. Lieut. 15 Oct. 1782. Capt. 21 Feb. 1801. Major 10 Apr. 1805. Lt. Col. 29 Aug. 1810. Retired 30 Oct. 1811. d. unm. at his lodgings, Old Bond St., Bath, 27 Oct. 1815, aged 59 ; bur. Bath Abbey 1 Nov.

3rd and youngest son of Richard Nangreave, of Netherton, co. Chester, barr.-at-law ("Counsellor Nangreave, of Manchester"), and Anne his wife, eldest dau. of Samuel Wareing, of Bury and Walmersley, merchant. Ed. Manchester Grammar School.

Services: Apptd. Cadet 22 Dec. 1780, aged 23 ; sailed for India in the Chapman 13 Mar. 1781. Lieut. 22nd Bn. Sepoys in July 1787 ; 4th Eur. Bn. in Dec. 1788 ; transfd. to 7th Bn. Sepoys 5 Feb. 1790. Third Mysore War ; Lieut. 7th Bn. Apptd. Qmr. 4th Eur. Bn. 21 Jan. 1794 ; Qmr. 3rd Bengal Eur. Regt. in 1796. Lieut. 13th N.I. ; Capt. Lt. 13th N.I. 29 May 1800 ; Capt. 2/13th N.I. Fur. 1 Feb. 1802 till 9 July 1806, and 28 Apr. 1809 till retirement.

Refs.: Burke's Landed Gentry, 2nd edn., iii. 85, s.n. Crompton, of Hacking, Lancs. Ormerod's Cheshire, ii. 61. Manchester Grammar School Register. G.M. 1816, i. 284. M.I. in Bath Abbey.

NAPIER, Alexander (1805-1828). Ensign, 58th N.I. b. Molance, nr. Castle Douglas, co. Kirkcudbright, 21 Sept. 1805. Cadet 1825. Ensign 15 Mar. 1826. d. at sea (between Mar. and July) 1828, on board the Ripley.

bapt. 5 Oct. 1805. Son of John Napier, banker, and Elizabeth McWhinnie his wife.

Services: Ensign d.d. 36th N.I. 2 Aug. 1826; posted Ensign to 42nd N.I. 1826; exchanged to 8th N.I. in 1826; to 58th N.I. 3 Jan. 1827. Fur. s.c. 22 Feb. 1828. No record of active service.

Refs.: A.J. xxvi. 389.

NAPIER, John George (1790-1806). Ensign, Infantry. Unposted. *b.* St. Cuthbert's psh., Edinburgh, 28 Apr. 1790. Cadet 1805. Arrived in India 4 Aug. 1806. Ensign 11 July 1806. *d. unm.* Barasat 23 Sept. 1806.

Youngest son of Maj.-Gen. the Hon. Mark Napier (who was 5th son of Francis Scott, 6th Baron Napier, of Merchiston) and Margaret his 2nd wife, dau. of Alexander Simpson, of Concraig. Uncle of Mark Napier Ogilvy, *q.v.* His sister *m.* Charles Maitland, *q.v.*

Services: Was undergoing instruction at Barasat C.C. when his death occurred.

Refs.: Burke's *Peerage*, 1923, p. 1644, *s.n.* Napier and Ettrick, B. *S.M.* 1807, p. 317. M.I. in Barrackpore cemetery.

NAPIER, Robert Cornelis, first Baron Napier of Magdala (1810-1890). Field Marshal, G.C.B., G.C.S.I. Col. Comdt. Royal (Bengal) Engineers. Constable of the Tower of London. *b.* Colombo, Ceylon, 6 Dec. 1810. Cadet 1827. Arrived in India 8 Nov. 1828. 2nd Lieut. 15 Dec. 1826. Lieut. 28 Sept. 1827. Capt. 25 Jan. 1841. Major 1 Aug. 1854. Lt. Col. 15 Apr. 1856. Col. 18 Feb. 1861. Col. Comdt. 1 Apr. 1874. Maj. Gen. 15 Feb. 1861. Lt. Gen. 1 Mar. 1867. Gen. 1 Apr. 1874. F.M. 1 Jan. 1883. *d.* 63 Eaton Sq., London, 14 Jan. 1890, of influenza.

1st Baron Napier, of Magdala. *cr.* 17 July 1868. Younger son of Bt. Major Charles Frederick Napier, R.A., and Catherine his wife, dau. of Codrington Carrington, of The Chapel, and Carrington, Barbados. *m.* 1st, Madras 3 Sept. 1840, Anne Sarah, eldest dau. of George Pearse, M.D., E.I.C.S. (She died Ferozepore 30 Dec. 1849, aged 29.) *m.* 2nd, Calcutta 2 Apr. 1861, Mary Cecilia, dau. of Edward William Smyth Scott, *q.v.* (She died Hampton Court Palace 18 Dec. 1930, aged 89.) Addiscombe Cadet 4 Feb. 1825 till 15 Dec. 1826. Chatham.

Services: See *D.N.B.* Fur. s.c. 11 Apr. 1836 till 16 Mar. 1839. First Sikh War; Mudki; Ferozshahr; Sobraon; Bde. Major (Medal with 2 clasps). Second Sikh War; both sieges of Multan (s.w.); actg. Chief Engr.; Gujerat (Medal with 2 clasps). Chief

Engr. Punjab 30 July 1849 till 1856. Black Mountain expedn. Nov. 1852 ; against Jowaki Afridis Nov. 1853 (Medal with clasp). Fur. s.c. 4 Apr. 1856 till 1857. Mutiny campaign ; Mily. Sec. and Chief of Staff with Gen. Outram's force ; 1st relief of Lucknow (w.) ; Chief Engr. at capture of Lucknow ; comdd. a Bde. at capture of Gwalior ; comdd. Gwalior Div., and was present at numerous affairs in 1858 (Medal with clasps). Second China War 1860 ; comdd. 2nd Div. of force (Medal with clasps). C.-in-C. Bombay 1865-9. Comdd. Abyssinian expedn. 1867-8. C.-in-C. in India Apr. 1870 till Apr. 1876. Govr. of Gibraltar 1876-83. Constable of the Tower 6 Jan. 1887. C.B. 24 Mar. 1858. K.C.B. 26 July 1858. G.C.B. 27 Apr. 1868. G.C.S.I. 16 Sept. 1867. D.C.L. Oxon. 26 June 1878. F.R.S. 16 Dec. 1869.

Refs. : Burke's *Peerage*, 1923, p. 1646, *s.n.* Baron Napier, of Magdala. *D.N.B. Life* by Lt.-Col. Hon. H. D. Napier, London, 1927. Boase. *D.I.B.* Portrait, Sir F. Grant—C. Mottram, pub. by Graves & Co. 1870. Portrait engraved by C. J. Tomkins from a portrait by Capt. Chas. Mercier, painted for Junior Carlton Club, is in India Office.

NAPLETON, Thomas Edward Augustus (1803-1852). Lieut. Colonel, 13th N.I. *b.* Powderham, Devon, 23 Sept. 1803. Cadet 1819. Admitted 22 Apr. 1820. Ensign 13 Nov. 1819. Lieut. 11 July 1823. Capt. 30 Apr. 1833. Major 5 Feb. 1843. Lt. Col. 10 Aug. 1849. *d.* nr. Ghazipur 6 Jan. 1852.

Eldest son of Rev. Timothy Napleton, rector of Powderham, and of N. Bovey, Devon, and Decima his wife, dau. of Rev. Jonathan Green, D.D., of Ashford Hall, Salop. *m.* Calcutta 26 July 1841, Isabella Margaret, dau. of Robert Davidson, of the firm of Mackintyre & Co., Calcutta, afterwards of Highbury Pk., London. (She died Kensington 27 Aug. 1893, aged 70.) Ed. Blundell's 3 Feb. 1814 till 29 June 1816.

Services : Posted Ensign to 1/1st N.I. Transfd. as Lieut. to 30th N.I. July 1823 ; to 60th N.I. (late 2/30th) May 1824. Actg. Adjt. 60th N.I. 18 Sept. 1824 ; Intr. & Qmr. do. 7 June 1825 till 25 Nov. 1831. Siege and capture of Bhurtpore ; Lieut. 60th N.I. (India medal). Fur. p.a. 1 Mar. 1833 till 20 Mar. 1836. Comdt. Recruit Depot at Meerut 8 Sept. 1838 ; tempy. comdg. Ramgarh L.I. 19 Feb. 1839 ; offg. A.A.G. of the Army 23 Mar. 1839. A.D.C. to C.-in-C. 7 Dec. 1839 till 7 Sept. 1841. Comdt. Bhagulpur Hill Rangers 22 Sept. 1841 till Nov. 1849. First Afghan War 1842 ; reoccupation of Kabul ; comdd. 60th N.I. in attack on Mamu Khel and Kuli Khel (*Lond. Gaz.* 8 Nov. 1842) ; Tazin (*Lond. Gaz.* 24 Nov.

1842); Capt. 60th N.I. (Medal). Posted Lt. Col. to 13th N.I. Nov. 1849.

Refs.: Howard & Crisp, iv. 39, *s.n.* Napleton. Blundell's School Register. I.M. 9 Mar. 1852, p. 130.

NARES, George Walter Adams (1806-1841). Lieutenant. 53rd N.I. *b.* Biddenden, Kent, 10 Feb. 1806. Cadet 1823. Arrived in India 3 May 1824. Ensign 9 Jan. 1824. Lieut. 13 May 1825. Discharged by G.C.M. 13 Nov. 1834. *d.* Lymington, Hants, 24 Aug. 1841.

bapt. Biddenden 2 Aug. 1806. Youngest son of Rev. Edward Nares, D.D., rector of Biddenden (*D.N.B.*), and Cordelia his 2nd wife, dau. of Thomas Adams, of Osborne Lodge, Kent. Cousin-german of D'Arcy Preston, *q.v. m.* Barrackpore 28 July 1831, Mary Isabella, eldest dau. of Darcy Lever, of Alkrington, Lancs., and divorced wife of Major Austen, of Goudhurst, Kent. Ed. Westminster 19 Sept. 1817 till 14 Feb. 1818; Charterhouse Apr. 1820-July 1821.

Services: Posted Ensign to 19th N.I. Exchanged to 53rd N.I. 5 Sept. 1825. Fur. s.c. 25 Jan. 1827 till 17 Feb. 1829. No record of active service.

Refs.: N. & Q. 8S. ii. 91. *Westminster School Register. Charterhouse School List. A.J.* xxvi. 386; N.S. iv. 70; N.S. xvi. 262-3. *G.M.* 1841, ii. 443.

*NASH, Edmund. Cadet. Infantry. Apptd. Cadet 17 Oct. 1783. Declined the appt.

NASH, Henry (1760/61-1789). Lieutenant, 1st Bn. Sepoys.[1] *b.* 1760/61. Cadet 1779. Ensign 8 Aug. 1779. Lieut. 31 Mar. 1781.. *d.* Calcutta 3 July 1789.

A native of Worcs. (*Probably* uncle of Richard Nash, *q.v.*)

Services: Apptd. Cadet 4 Nov. 1778; sailed for India in the *Norfolk* 7 Mar. 1779, aged 18. Lieut. 1st Bn. Sepoys in July 1787.

[1] *Note:* In the burial register he is incorrectly described as Lieut. of Art.

NASH, Henry Gardiner (1791-1830). Captain, 62nd N.I. *bapt.* St. Anne's, Manchester, 5 Oct. 1791. Cadet 1808. Arrived in India 24 July 1809. Ensign 24 July 1809. Lieut. 15 June 1814. Capt. 22 Apr. 1826. *d.* Sitapur, U.P., 20 Oct. 1830.

Son of John Nash, of Manchester, calico printer, later of Newnham, Gloucs., and Mary his wife. Brother of Joseph Nash, *q.v.*, and

THE BENGAL ARMY, 1758-1834 373

uncle of John Dixon Nash, *q.v.* *m.* St. John's, Calcutta, 10 July 1826, Mary Anne, dau. of William Robert Clayton Costley, *q.v.*
Services: Barasat C.C. Posted Ensign to 7th N.I. in 1810. Nepal War 1814-15; Malaun; Lieut. 2/7th N.I., in 1st Div. Third Mahratta War; Lieut. 2/7th N.I. Fur. 19 Jan. 1819 till 1822. Transfd. to newly-formed 31st N.I. July 1823; to 62nd N.I. (late 2/31st) May 1824. First Burma War; Arakan 1825; Lieut. 62nd N.I. Intr. & Qmr. 62nd N.I. 8 May 1826 till 14 June 1827. Promoted Capt. 8 Aug. 1828, subsequently antedated to 22 Apr. 1826.

NASH, James (1796-1826). Lieutenant, 26th N.I. *b.* Calcutta 17 Mar. 1796. Cadet 1819. Ensign 13 Nov. 1819. Lieut. 23 Sept. 1821. *d.* Benares 26 Dec. 1826.
bapt. Calcutta 26 Sept. 1796. Son of James Nash, of Oak Hill, nr. Dawlish, Devon, master mariner, and Maria his wife. Brother of William Duppa Nash, *q.v.*
Services: Ensign R. East Middlesex Mil. 7 June 1813; Lieut. do. 10 Jan. 1814. Posted Ensign to 13th N.I. in 1820; Lieut. 2/13th N.I. Fur. 1822-5. Transfd. to 27th N.I. (late 2/13th) May 1824; to 26th N.I. in 1825, but apparently was still with 27th N.I. at date of death. No record of active service.

NASH, John Dixon (1807-1864). Captain, Invalid Est. 33rd N.I. *b.* Manchester 3 Jan. 1807. Cadet 1823. Arrived in India 19 May 1824. Ensign 16 Jan. 1824. Lieut. 13 May 1825. Capt. 30 May 1834. Invalided 11 Dec. 1837. *d.* Calcutta 26 Feb. 1864.
bapt. Manchester 26 Sept. 1810. Younger son of Sebastian Nash, of Clayton Mills, nr. Manchester, calico printer, and Sarah his 1st wife, widow of Capt. Richards, R.N. Brother of Sebastian Nash (1802-1849) and nephew of Joseph Nash, *qq.v.* *m.* St. John's, Calcutta, 5 Dec. 1826, Miss Ellen Urmston.
Services: Posted Ensign to 33rd N.I. Siege and capture of Bhurtpore; Lieut. 33rd N.I. (India medal). Fur. s.c. 14 Oct. 1834 till 9 June 1837. Leave p.a. 12 mos. to Moulmein 1 Mar. 1839. Apptd. Postmr. at Barrackpore 11 Aug. 1841.
Refs.: A.J. N.S. xvi. 261.

NASH, Joseph (1795-1870). Lieut. General, C.B. Colonel 46th N.I. *b.* Failsworth, Lancs., 22 July 1795. Cadet 1812. Admitted 11 Sept. 1813. Ensign (July 1813) 1 Nov. 1814. Lieut. 25 Dec. 1817. Capt. 24 Jan. 1829. Major 26 Sept. 1841.

Lt. Col. 11 Nov. 1847. Col. 15 July 1857. Maj. Gen. 9 Apr.
1856. Lt. Gen. 23 Mar. 1869. *d.* Dehra Dun, U.P., 1 Jan. 1870.
bapt. Newton Heath chapel, Manchester, 15 Mar. 1805. Son
of John Nash, of Newnham, Gloucs., and Mary his wife. Brother
of Henry Gardiner Nash, *q.v.*, and uncle of Sebastian Nash (1802-
1849), *q.v. m.* Lutheran church, C.G.H., 5 May 1820, Diana
Margaretha Leibbrandt, of the Cape. Ed. Manchester Grammar
School; admitted 7 Feb. 1810.
Services: Posted Ensign to 2/7th N.I. Nepal War 1814-15;
Malaun; Ensign 2/7th N.I., in 1st Div. (India medal). Transfd.
to 1/22nd N.I. 24 May 1816. Third Mahratta War; Nagpur
1817; Ensign 1/22nd N.I. (clasp to India medal); Asirgarh 1819
(*Lond. Gaz.* 30 Aug. 1820); comdg. a Coy. of Pioneers. Leave s.c.
10 mos. to Cape 31 July 1819. Operations in Jodhpur 1823;
capture of Lamba. Transfd. to 43rd N.I. (late 1/22nd) May 1824.
Actg. Adjt. 43rd N.I. 18 Sept. 1826. Leave s.c. 12 mos. to Cape
10 Mar. 1827. First Afghan War 1839-42; Baggage Mr. to Bengal
Column 1838-9; Ghazni 1839 (Medal); Comdt. of Shah Shuja's
Guard at Kabul; operations of Kandahar force under Nott (w.
29 May 1842); capture of Istalif (*Lond. Gaz.* 6 Dec. 1842); Major
comdg. 43rd N.I. (Medal). Gwalior campaign; Maharajpur (*Lond.
Gaz.* 8 Mar. 1844); Major comdg. 43rd N.I. (Bronze star). First
Sikh War; Sobraon (horse kld. under him); Bt. Lt. Col. 43rd N.I.
(Medal). Posted Lt. Col. to 49th N.I. 28 Jan. 1848; to 72nd N.I.
18 July 1848. Second Sikh War; Multan, comdd. Left Centre
Column of attack on 27 Dec. 1848 (s.w.); Lt. Col. comdg. 72nd N.I.
from 30 Nov. (Medal). Transfd. to 18th N.I. June 1852; to 47th
N.I. 1 Dec. 1854. Apptd. Bdr. 7 Nov. 1854; posted to Thayetmyo
1 Dec. 1854; to Delhi Jan. 1855; to Agra 15 Mar. 1856. Col.
46th N.I. July 1857 till death. C.B. 27 June 1846.
Refs.: Manchester School Register, iii. 51. *Boase.*

NASH, Michael. Ensign. Infantry. Cadet 1769. Ensign
16 Sept. 1770. Resigned 3 Feb. 1771.
Services: Was an Ensign in 1st Bde. on resignation.
Note: The Will of Michael Nash, of the city of Dublin, gent.,
was proved P.C. Dublin, 1804.

NASH, Richard (1776-1801). Lieutenant, 12th N.I. *bapt.* St.
Helen's, Worcester, 24 June 1776. Cadet 1799. Arrived in
India 1 Dec. 1800. Ensign 15 Sept. 1800. Lieut. 7 Oct. 1801.
d. unm. Cawnpore (? Dinajpur) 17 Oct. 1801.
3rd son of Richard Nash, alderman of the city of Worcester,

THE BENGAL ARMY, 1758-1834 375

and Sarah his 1st wife, dau. of —— Wilson, and widow of Edward Winsmore, of Woodsfield, nr. Malvern.

Services: Posted Ensign to 1/12th N.I. 17 Apr. 1801. No record of active service.

Refs.: Burke's *Landed Gentry*, 2nd edn., iii. 242, *s.n.* Nash, of Worcestershire.

NASH, Sebastian (*d.* 1790). Lieutenant, Artillery. (180) Country Cadet 1778. Fireworker 6 Oct. 1778. Lieut. 7 July 1782. *d. unm.* Karur, Madras, 14 Dec. 1790.

Brother of John Nash, of Shepley Hall, Lancs. (*Probably* uncle of Joseph Nash, *q.v.*)

Services: Apptd. Cadet 11 Aug. 1778. Second Mysore War 1781-5; Lieut. F. 5th Coy. 1st Bn. Art. Third Mysore War; Lieut. 2nd Coy. 2nd Bn.

Refs.: Will dated Cawnpore 22 Oct. 1788; proved 26 Mar. 1792

NASH, Sebastian (1802-1849). Bt. Major. 4th L.C. *bapt.* Manchester 30 Oct. 1802. Cadet 1819. Admitted 13 June 1820. Cornet 2 Feb. 1820. Lieut. 1 Oct. 1821. Capt. 9 Apr. 1833. Bt. Major 3 Apr. 1846. Retired 1 Aug. 1849. *d.* 1 Aug. 1849.

Elder son of Sebastian Nash, calico printer, and Sarah his 1st wife. Brother of John Dixon Nash and nephew of Henry Gardiner Nash, *qq.v. m.* Meerut 20 Oct. 1825, Miss Ellen Young.

Services: Posted Cornet to 4th L.C.; actg. Adjt. do. 20 May 1822, 12 July 1825, 25 Apr. 1827, 29 Apr. 1829. Leave s.c. 14 mos. to Mauritius 26 Jan. 1824. Siege and capture of Bhurtpore; Lieut. 4th L.C. Leave s.c. 1 yr. to Hills 14 Dec. 1827. Actg. Intr. & Qmr. 4th L.C. 11 May 1830. Shekhawat expedn. 1834; Capt. 4th L.C., Bde. Major. Leave s.c. to Dehra Dun 16 Oct. 1838 till 1 Mar. 1839. Comdd. 4th L.C. June till 20 Nov. 1841. Gwalior campaign; Maharajpur; Capt. 4th L.C. (Bronze star). First Sikh War; Mudki; Ferozshahr; Capt. 4th L.C. (Medal with clasp).

NASH, William Duppa (1808-?). Lieutenant. 46th N.I. *b.* 15 Nov. 1808. Cadet 1824. Arrived in India 29 June 1825. Ensign 8 Jan. 1825. Lieut. 17 Jan. 1826. Resigned 26 Feb. 1830.

bapt. Holy Trinity, Exeter, 20 Dec. 1808. Son of James Nash, of Dawlish, Comdr. E.I.C.N.S., and Maria his wife. Brother of James Nash, *q.v. m.* Calcutta 26 Jan. 1830, Maria Louisa, eldest dau. of John Grimsdick, asst. in the import warehouse-keeper's office, Calcutta, afterwards an indigo planter. (*See also* William Edwards.)

Services : Posted Ensign to 46th N.I. in 1825. No record of active service.

NATION, Henry Matthew (1810-1881). Lieut. Colonel. 3rd Bengal Eur. Regt. *b.* Calcutta 1 Nov. 1810. Cadet 1827. Arrived in India 5 July 1828. Ensign 19 Jan. 1828. Lieut. 8 Oct. 1839. Capt. 7 June 1853. Major 13 July 1858. Retired 31 Dec. 1861. Hon. Lt. Col. 31 Dec. 1861. *d.* New Zealand 12 Mar. 1881.

bapt. Berhampore 29 Nov. 1810. Eldest son of Stephen Nation, *q.v.*, and Mary Anne his wife. Brother of Stephen Nation, *q.v. m.* Calcutta 11 Mar. 1845, Jane Catherine, eldest dau. of Thomas Bruce Swinhoe, of Garden Reach, Calcutta, atty. (She died 3 Mar. 1890.)

Services : Ensign d.d. 65th N.I. 31 July 1828 ; d.d. 23rd N.I. 30 Aug. 1828 ; posted to 23rd N.I. 4 Nov. 1828 ; Adjt. do. 18 Oct. 1833 till 27 Oct. 1840. Apptd. Asst. in Dept. for suppression of *Thagi* 30 Sept. 1840, and served in that Dept. till 1858. Rejoined 23rd N.I. 4 Oct. 1848 for a short time. Transfd. to newly-raised 3rd Bengal Eur. Regt. 15 Nov. 1853. Comdg. 2nd Bengal Police Corps in 1858. No record of active service.

NATION, Stephen (1780-1828). Lieut. Colonel, C.B., 5th N.I. *b* Dulverton, Somerset, 11 Apr. 1780. Cadet 1796. Arrived in India 29 May 1798. Ensign 27 Sept. 1797. Lieut. 10 Sept. 1798. Capt. 25 Dec. 1804. Major 4 June 1814. Lt. Col. 5 Mar. 1823. *d.* Cawnpore 2 Aug. 1828, of cholera.

Son of Matthew Nation, of Dulverton, and Anne his wife. *m.* Calcutta 6 Feb. 1810, Mary Ann, dau. of Philip Brady, marshal of the vice-admiralty court in Calcutta. (*See also* M. A. Bunbury.) (She died 21 Dec. 1867, aged 73.) Father of Henry Matthew Nation and Stephen Nation, *qq.v.* Ed. Blundell's 28 Jan. 1789 till 21 Dec. 1795.

Services : Ensign d.d. Bengal Eur. Regt. 1798 ; posted to 1/8th N.I. in 1799. Operations in Jumna Doab 1803 ; Sasni ; Bijaigarh ; Lieut. 1/8th N.I. Second Mahratta War ; operations to S.W. of Delhi 1803 ; Kanun ; battle and capture of Deig ; Bhurtpore ; Capt. 1/8th N.I. Nepal War 1814-15 ; Major 1/8th N.I., in 4th Div. Nepal War 1816 ; Makwanpur ; Major 2/8th N.I., in 4th Bde. Centre Column. Rejoined 1/8th N.I. in 1817. Third

Mahratta War ; Major comdg. 1/8th N.I., with Centre Div. Comdg. at Kaitha 1821-3'. Posted Lt. Col. to 33rd N.I. July 1823 ; transfd. to 66th N.I. (late 2/33rd) May 1824 ; to 23rd N.I. in 1825. Siege and capture of Bhurtpore (w. 18 Jan. 1826); Lt. Col. 23rd N.I. Transfd. to 9th N.I. 7 Dec. 1826 ; to 5th N.I. 26 May 1828. C.B. 26 Dec. 1826.

Refs.: E.I.M.C. ii. 366-8. *Blundell's School Register. A.J.* xxvii. 476. M.I. at Cawnpore.

NATION, Stephen (1811-?). Lieutenant. 68th N.I. Subsequently D.C. of Barisal, Bengal. *b.* Midnapore 24 Dec. 1811. Cadet 1828. Arrived in India 3 Apr. 1829. Ensign 21 Oct. 1828. Lieut. 13 May 1834. Dismissed by G.C.M. 5 Sept. 1842.[1] (Living in 1860.)

bapt. Calcutta 3 Nov. 1812. Son of Stephen Nation, *q.v.*, and Mary Ann his wife. Brother of Henry Matthew Nation, *q.v. m.* Calcutta 19 June 1850, Miss Amelia Christiana.

Services : Posted Ensign to 23rd N.I. 3 June 1829 ; transfd. to 24th N.I. 18 Dec. 1829 ; to 68th N.I. 2 Aug. 1832. Expulsion of marauders from Jhabua, C.I., Feb.-Mar. 1836 ; Lieut. 68th N.I. Was for many years Agent at Rampur-Boalia, Bengal, of the India Gen. Steam Navigation Co. He subsequently joined the Uncovenanted B.C.S., and in 1860 was D.C. of Barisal.

[1] *Note :* Dismissed for fighting a duel with Lieut. George Perry. Brooke, *q.v.*, at Kyaukpyu on 20 Mar. 1842.

NAYLOR, Christopher Henry (1804-1854). Bt. Major. 2nd Bengal Eur. Regt. *b.* Chigwell, Essex, 16 June 1804. Cadet 1819. Arrived in India Dec. 1820. Ensign 13 July 1820. Lieut. 11 July 1823. Capt. 8 Oct. 1839. Bt. Major 9 Nov. 1846. Retired 30 July 1848. *d.* Sabathu, Punjab, 25 Aug. 1854.

bapt. 28 Feb. 1806. Son of Robert Naylor and Sarah his wife. Nephew of Gen. Tredway Clarke, Madras Art. *m.* Delhi 23 Aug. 1830, Miss Maria Gowan. Ed. Guernsey Grammar School.

Services : Ensign d.d. Bengal Eur. Regt. Posted to 1/22nd N.I. Apr. 1821. Transfd. as Lieut. to 2/9th N.I. Sept. 1823 ; to 8th N.I. (late 1/9th) May 1824. Intr. & Qmr. 8th N.I. 12 Aug. 1828 till 3 Oct. 1831. Jodhpur demonstration Oct. 1834 ; Lieut. 8th N.I. Offg. Intr. & Qmr. 8th N.I. 18 Oct. 1835 ; permanent do. 27 Feb. 1836 till 20 Nov. 1839. Transfd. to newly-formed 2nd Bengal Eur. Regt. 21 Oct. 1839. Against Hill tribes in Sind 1845 ; Capt. 2nd Bengal Eur. Regt. After retirement he settled at Sabathu, where he spent the remainder of his life.

Refs.: De Rhé-Philipe. *A.J.* N.S. viii. 155. *G.M.* 1855, i. 103. M.I. at Sabathu.

NAYLOR, Thomas (*d.* 1782). Major, 23rd N.I. Country Cadet 1764. Ensign 28 Aug. 1765. Lieut. 12 Jan. 1767. Capt. 16 Sept. 1770. Major 13 Jan. 1781. *d. unm.* Lucknow 20 June 1782.

Brother of John Naylor and of Hannah, wife of William Savage. Cousin of Robert Butler. His ancestors formerly owned an estate near Kirklees, Yorks., afterwards in the possession of the family of Armytage, Barts.

Services: Sailed for India as Purser of the *Success* Indiaman 17 May 1764. Apptd. Cadet 26 Dec. 1764. Operations against Shuja-ud-Daulah 1765; sieges of Allahabad and Chunar; Cadet. Posted to 1st Bengal Eur. Regt. 21 Aug. 1765. Bk. Mr. at Monghyr till 5 Jan. 1774. Operations in the Doab against Mahbub Khan 1776; battle of Korah. Bde. Major 2nd Bde. till Sept. 1777. Apptd. 26 Sept. 1777 to comd. one of the Bns. raised for the Nawab-Wazir of Oudh on its transfer to the Coy.'s service. This Bn., which was numbered 30th, was called after him "*Neehwar-ki-Paltan.*"[1] He was still comdg. this Corps (which had now become 23rd Regt. of Sepoys) in Aug. 1781, and on 8 Oct. of that year he attacked with his Regt. and totally defeated a body of 10,000 rebels in the Nawab-Wazir's dominions.

Refs.: Williams, p. 141. *Cardew,* p. 40. *Forrest,* iii. 807-8. Will dated 12 Mar. 1781; proved 6 Aug. 1782.

[1] *Note:* By the reorganization of 1824 it became 21st N.I., subsequently 1st Brahmins, and is now (1928) 4th Bn. 1st Punjab Regt.

NEALE, Pendock (1790-1806). Cadet, Infantry. *bapt.* Camberwell, London, 1 Aug. 1790. Cadet 1805. Never arrived in India. *d.* Dec. 1806, on his passage to India, in the wreck of the *Skelton Castle.* Struck off with effect from 5 Nov. 1806. (See note to David Allan.)

Son of John Mason Neale, of the East India House, and Sarah Mellor his wife, of Soho. Cousin-german of Francis Denty, *q.v.*

Refs.: Burke's *Landed Gentry,* 3rd edn., p. 52, *s.n.* Barry, of Roclaveston Manor, Notts.

NEALE, William. Lieutenant. 1st Bengal Eur. Regt. Country Cadet 1780. Ensign 28 Feb. 1781. Lieut. 21 Oct. 1781. Dismissed by C.M. 13 Mar. 1783.

THE BENGAL ARMY, 1758-1834   379

Services: Apptd. a Gent. Vol. in the Coy. of Art. 3 Apr. 1780. Adjt. 2/1st Eur. Regt. Dismissed for neglect of duty on board the *Warren Hastings.* Granted a charter party passage home 1 Dec. 1786.

NEDRICH, Paal. (*See* **NIEDRICK, Paul.**)

NEILD,[1] **Charles Bridgeman** (1787-1823). Captain, 4th L.C. *bapt.* All Saints, Hertford, 7 June 1787. Cadet 1803. Arrived in India 3 Sept. 1804. Cornet 11 Mar. 1805. Lieut. 31 July 1816. Capt. 14 May 1819. *d.* Hamirpur 6 Mar. 1823. Son of John Neild and Sarah his wife.
Services: Posted Cornet to 4th N.C. in 1805, and served throughout with that Regt. Actg. Adjt. 19 Oct. 1817. Third Mahratta War; Jawad.
[1] *Note:* The name usually appears in contemporary *A.L.* as Nield.

NEILSON, John (*d.* 1767). Captain, Infantry. Capt. 11 Nov. 1763. *d.* 7 July 1767.
Services: Ensign H.M. 37th Ft. 18 Jan. 1757. Ensign 84th Ft. 25 Dec. 1758; Lieut. do. 11 Jan. 1760; h.p. 84th Ft. 24 Nov. 1763. War with Mir Muhammad Kasim 1763; Lieut. 84th Ft., under Major Adams. Transfd. as Capt. to Bengal Army Nov. 1763. Battle of Buxar; comdg. a Coy. of Bengal Eur. Bn. Posted to 2nd Bengal Eur. Regt. 5 Aug. 1765. A survivor of the wreck of the *Fateh Islam* in Aug. 1761.

NEISH, John (*d.* 1786). Lieutenant, Artillery. (170) Country Cadet 1778. Fireworker 26 Sept. 1778. Lieut. 1 Oct. 1781. *d.* Fatehgarh 18 May 1786.
His dau. *m.* William Horatio Green, *q.v.*
Services: Apptd. Cadet from Condr. of Ord. 11 Aug. 1778. Second Mysore War 1781-5; Lieut. 4th Coy. 2nd Bn., in Col. Pearse's detachment.
Refs.: Will dated 12 Apr. 1786; proved 23 Nov. 1786.

NELLEY,[1] **John** (1753/54-1830). Lieut. Colonel. Artillery. (228) *b.* 1753/54. Country Cadet 1781. Admitted 5 Nov. 1781. Fireworker 29 July 1782. Lieut. 28 Dec. 1788. Capt. Lt. 8 Jan. 1796. Capt. 18 June 1802. Major 5 Sept. 1806. Lt. Col. 8 Dec. 1810. Retired 26 Aug. 1813. *d.* Lower Gardiner St., Dublin, 10 Sept. 1830, aged 76.
Of Tubber, Rivilladonne, East and West Liddare, Ballybone and

Ballysheeda, co. Galway, all of which he purchased for the sum of £10,000. Brother of Mrs. Honora Macnamara, and nephew of James Nelley. *m.* 27 Sept. 1792, Charlotte, dau. of Charles Lindsay. (She died Dublin 22 May 1831, aged 52.) His dau. *m.* Frederick Mackenzie, *q.v.*

Services: Apptd. Adjt. to Art. Div. in 1784. (? Second Mysore War; Lieut. F. 5th Coy. 2nd Bn.) Fireworker 2nd Bn. in July 1787. Third Mysore War; Bangalore; Seringapatam; Lieut. 3rd Coy. 2nd Bn. On service to Madras June 1794; Lieut. 3rd Coy. 2nd Bn. (? Fur. 11 Jan. 1801.) Second Mahratta War; Koil; Aligarh; battle of Delhi; Agra; Laswari; capture of Deig; Bhurtpore (w. 20 Feb. 1805 in rt. eye); Capt. comdg. 3rd Coy. 1st Bn. Apptd. Prize Agent for Art. in 1804. Comy. Ord. at Allahabad 4 July 1805 till Aug. 1809. Fur. 1809 till retirement.

Refs.: Burke's *Peerage*, 1923, p. 1700, *s.n.* Ochterlony, Bart., of Ochterlony, co. Forfar. *E.I.M.C.* i. 127-8. *A.J.* N.S. iii. 120. Will dated 28 May 1830; proved 28 June 1831.

¹ *Note:* His surname is usually spelt with only one 'e' in contemporary documents, but he signs himself 'Nelley' in his Will.

NELSON, Richard (1801-1826). Lieutenant, 56th N.I. *bapt.* St. Nicholas, Deptford, 22 Oct. 1801. Cadet 1821. Ensign 26 July 1822. Lieut. 29 June 1824. *d.* Nasirabad 19 Oct. 1826.

Son of Robert John Nelson, of Deptford, builder's assistant, and Catherine Hythe his wife. Brother of George and Catherine Anna Maria. Ed. Tonbridge School 1811-14.

Services: Posted Ensign to 22nd N.I. in 1822. Transfd. to 28th N.I. in 1823; to 55th N.I. (late 1/28th) May 1824; to 56th N.I. in 1824. First Burma War; Arakan 1825; Adjt. 1st L.I. Bn.

Refs.: *A.J.* xxiii. 674. Will dated Nasirabad 5 Oct. 1826; proved 17 Aug. 1827. M.I. Nasirabad.

NEPEAN, Thomas (*d.* 1769). Lieut. Fireworker, Artillery. (90) Fireworker Sept. 1768. *d.* in India 1769.

Services: Cadet at R.M.A., Woolwich, in 1767; apptd. Lt. F. in England 24 Dec. 1767.

NESBITT, Andrew Bell (1806-?). Lieutenant. 10th N.I. *bapt.* Kilmore, co. Cavan, Nov. 1806. Cadet 1824. Arrived in India 15 May 1824. Ensign 14 Nov. 1824. Lieut. 1 May 1827. Invalided 27 Feb. 1832. Struck off 28 May 1837.

Son of Thomas Nesbitt, of Lismore, co. Cavan, Col. in the army, M.P. for Cavan, and Louisa his wife, youngest dau. of Col. John

THE BENGAL ARMY, 1758-1834 381

Daniel De Gennes, of Portarlington. Half-brother of John Nesbitt, of Token House Yard, London, wine merchant (? and of Nathaniel Sneyd Nesbitt, *q.v.*).

Services: Ensign d.d. 2nd Bengal Eur. Regt. 3 June 1825; posted to 50th N.I. in 1825. Siege and capture of Bhurtpore; Ensign 15th N.I. Transfd. to 10th N.I. in 1826. Fur. s.c. 23 Apr. 1830 till 21 Oct. 1831, and 28 May 1832 till struck off. Name removed from the *A.L.* (M.C. 22 Jan. 1840).

Refs.: Burke's *Landed Gentry*, 8th edn., p. 1467, *s.n.* Nesbitt, of Lismore, Cavan. *Nisbet of that Ilk*, by R. C. Nesbitt (London, John Murray, 1941), p. 201.

NESBITT, George Queiros (1816-1848). Captain, 49th N.I. *b.* Lucknow 13 Nov. 1816. Cadet 1834. Arrived in India 14 Aug. 1835. Ensign 12 Dec. 1834. Lieut. 16 Jan. 1840. Capt. 24 Apr. 1847. *d.* at sea 13 Mar. 1848, on board the *Southampton*.

3rd son of Joseph Nesbitt, *q.v.*, and Theresa his 1st wife. Nephew of Joseph Queiros, *q.v.*

Addiscombe Cadet 8 Feb. 1833 till 12 Dec. 1834.

Services: Ensign d.d. 50th N.I. 25 Aug. 1835; posted Ensign to 49th N.I. 24 Sept. 1835. Offg. Intr. & Qmr. 8th L.C. 13 May 1841; actg. Adjt. Left Wing 49th N.I. 21 Jan. 1842; actg. Intr. & Qmr. 58th N.I. 19 Sept. 1842; do. 71st N.I. 6 Feb. till 13 Nov. 1843. Offg. D.C. 3 cl., Saugor & Narbada territories, in 1846. Fur. Dec. 1847 till death. No record of active service.

Refs.: I.N. 25 May 1848.

NESBITT, Joseph (1778-1844). Major General, C.B. Colonel 43rd N.I. *b.* St. Pancras, Middlesex, 18 Dec. 1778. Cadet 1798. Arrived in India 6 Nov. 1799. Ensign 22 Dec. 1799. Lieut. 29 May 1800. Capt. 2 Sept. 1812. Major 20 July 1823. Lt. Col. 13 May 1825. Col. 30 May 1836. Maj. Gen. 3 Nov. 1841. *d.* London 21 Dec. 1844.

Son of George Nesbitt and Mary his wife, dau. of Thomas Orange. (*Probably* related to John Edward Orange, *q.v.*) *m.* 1st, Cawnpore 21 Dec. 1811, Theresa, dau. of Joseph Queiros, of Lucknow, merchant, and sister of Joseph Queiros, *q.v.* Father of George Queiros Nesbitt, *q.v. m.* 2nd, Elizabeth. (She *re-m.* 14 Apr. 1846, Col. Sir Robert Nickle, Kt., K.H.)

Services: Posted Lieut. to 1/3rd N.I. 15 Apr. 1801. Operations in Bundelkhand against Lachman Dawa 1809; Rajaoli; Ajaigarh; Lieut. 1/3rd N.I. Adjt. 1/3rd N.I. 6 Mar. 1809 till 1812. Transfd.

as Capt. to 2/3rd N.I. Nepal War 1814-15; Capt. 2/3rd N.I., in 1st Div. Did duty with 2/9th N.I. 28 Dec. 1821 till 22 Oct. 1822. Operations in Oudh against Kasim Ali Khan 1822; Bardgaon; Capt. d.d. 2/9th N.I. Transfd. to 6th N.I. (late 1/3rd) May 1824. Posted Lt. Col. to 8th N.I. 1825; to 32nd N.I. 1828; to 9th N.I. 10 Dec. 1828. Fur. s.c. 9 Aug. 1829 till 7 July 1834. Transfd. to 8th N.I. 8 Feb. 1834. Fur. p.a. 4 Dec. 1834 till death. Posted Col. to 43rd N.I. 21 Oct. 1836.

Refs.: G.M. 1845, i. 213.

NESBITT, Nathaniel Sneyd (1804-1876). Lieut. Colonel. 22nd N.I. b. Kilmore, co. Cavan, 15 Sept. 1804. Cadet 1821. Arrived in India 3 Aug. 1822. Ensign 23 Feb. 1822. Lieut. 13 May 1825. Capt. 21 Sept. 1837. Major 29 July 1853. Retired 15 Sept. 1854. Hon. Lt. Col. 28 Nov. 1854. d. Algiers 18 June 1876.

Brother of John Nesbitt, of London, merchant. (*Probably* son of Col. Thomas Nesbitt, 53rd Regt., by his wife, dau. of Jeremy Sneyd, of Tutwood House. ? Half-brother of Andrew Bell Nesbitt, q.v.) m. Louisa Adèle Elizabeth. (She died Naples 7 May 1886, aged 69.)

Services: Posted Ensign to 2nd N.I. in 1822. Transfd. to 22nd N.I. (late 2/2nd) May 1824. Actg. Adjt. 22nd N.I. 3 Sept. 1824. First Burma War; Lieut. 22nd N.I. (India medal). Offg. Intr. & Qmr. 22nd N.I. 5 Nov. 1828; permanent do. 28 Sept. 1829 till 20 Sept. 1833. Fur. s.c. 13 Dec. 1833 till 27 Oct. 1837. Comdt. escort of A.G.G. Jaipur 14 Mar. 1839. Postmr. at Jaipur 5 Aug. 1839. Tempy. comdg. Jaipur troops in Shekhawat Nov. 1839. Fur. s.c. 22 Apr. 1841 till 23 Oct. 1844. Second Sikh War; no actions; Capt. 22nd N.I. (Medal). Fur. p.a. 10 Apr. 1850 till 27 Dec. 1852.

Refs.: *The Times*, 12 July 1876.

NESBITT, Samuel (1776-1808). Captain, Invalid Est. 1st N.I. b. Lichfield, Staffs., 20 Feb. 1776. Cadet 1795. Arrived in India 16 Feb. 1797. Ensign 3 Dec. 1796. Lieut. 30 Oct. 1797. Capt. 19 Feb. 1806. Invalided 31 Dec. 1806. d. Calcutta 29 Apr. 1808.

Services: Lieut. 5th N.I. in 1798; transfd. as Lieut to 1st N.I.; Capt. Lt. do. 19 Oct. 1805.

NEUFVILLE, John Bryan (1795-1830). Captain, 42nd N.I. P.A. in Upper Assam, and Comdt. Assam L.I. b. Lymington, Hants, 26 Jan. 1795. Cadet 1810. Ensign 25 Sept. 1813.

Lieut. 3 June 1815. Capt. 16 June 1826. *d.* Jorhat, Assam, 26 July 1830.

bapt. Lymington 21 Mar. 1795. Only son of Jacob Neufville, of Grove House, Lymington, an adherent of the French Royal Family, and Sybella Phoebe his wife. Ed. Eton; Lower School in 1805.

Services: Cadet d.d. 21st N.I. 1811-13; posted Ensign to 2/21st N.I. in 1813. Fur. 2 Jan. 1815 till 1817. D.A.Q.M.G. 3 cl. 1820-3; do. 1 cl. 1823-8. Transfd. to 42nd N.I. (late 2/21st) May 1824. First Burma War; Arakan 1825; Lieut. 42nd N.I. P.A. in Upper Assam, and Comdt. 1st Assam L.I. Bn. (late Rangpur Local Bn.), 10 Mar. 1828 till death.

Refs.: Eton School Lists. A.J. N.S. iv. 38. *G.M.* 1830, ii. 648. M.I. in Gauhati church.

NEWBERY, Charles (1805-1843). Major, Invalid Est. 9th L.C. *b.* Exeter 5 Feb. 1805. Cadet 1820. Admitted 22 Oct. 1821. Cornet 21 Mar. 1821. Lieut. 1 May 1824. Capt. 9 Sept. 1829. Major 23 Dec. 1839. Invalided 28 Oct. 1842. *d.* Mussoorie, U.P., 4 Sept. 1843.

bapt. St. Sidwell's, Exeter, 28 July 1808. Only son of Lt.-Gen. Francis Newbery, of Heathfield Park, Sussex, Col. 3rd D.G., and Amelia his wife, *née* Wooldridge, of Londonderry. Addiscombe Cadet 1819-20.

Services: Posted Cornet to 7th L.C.; transfd. to newly-raised 1st Extra Regt. (became 9th L.C.) 17 June 1825; actg. Adjt. do. 23 Dec. 1825; permanent do. 6 Jan. 1826 till 7 Dec. 1829. Siege and capture of Bhurtpore; Lieut. 9th L.C. Fur. p.a. 1 Feb. 1834 till 15 May 1837. Comdt. 1st Cav., Oudh Auxy. Force,[1] 29 Jan. 1838 till 14 Jan. 1840.

Refs.: The Times, 13 Aug. 1840; 8 Nov. 1843, p. 7. *I.N.* No. 4, p. 79. *I.M.* 6 Dec. 1843, p. 240. M.I. Landour.

[1] *Note:* Raised by him; now 2nd Lancers (Gardner's Horse).

NEWBOLT, George (1811-1889). Lieut. Colonel. 31st N.I. *b.* 26 May 1811. Cadet 1828. Arrived in India 25 June 1829. Ensign 7 Jan. 1829. Lieut. 13 Feb. 1836. Capt. 10 Feb. 1847. Bt. Major 28 Nov. 1854. Retired 31 Dec. 1861. Hon. Lt. Col. 31 Dec. 1861. *d.* 11 Richmond Pk. Rd., Clifton, Gloucs., 3 Aug. 1889.

bapt. Wokingham 28 June 1811. Son of John Thomas Newbolt, M.D., of Brussels, and Catherine his wife. *m.* 1st, Barrackpore 27 Feb. 1832, Frances Anna Maria, eldest dau. of Robert Arding

Thomas, q.v. (*See also* Henry Davis Van Homrigh.) (She died Eton 5 July 1843.) *m.* 2nd, Ghazipur 10 July 1844, Caroline, 4th dau. of John Montgomery Hill. (*See also* Walter Stanhope Sherwill.) (She died Jullundur 18 Jan. 1852, aged 26.) *m.* 3rd, Calcutta 23 Feb. 1853, Georgiana Agnes Joselyn, dau. of J. Chapman. *m.* 4th, Mary Charlotte. (She died Bristol 28 Mar. 1919.)
Services: Ensign d.d. 50th N.I. 21 Aug. 1829; posted Ensign to 31st N.I. Intr. & Qmr. 31st N.I. 8 Oct. 1832 till 8 June 1833. S.A.C.G. 4 June 1833. In charge of Natpur timber agency 1835-7. Apptd. Comst. Ofr. to Art., Army of Indus, 13 Sept. 1838. First Afghan War 1838-40; capture of Ghazni; Lieut. 31st N.I., Comst. Dept. (Medal). D.A.C.G. 2 cl. 9 Mar. 1840; 1 cl. 8 Feb. 1843. Leave to Cape and Tasmania 9 Jan. 1842 till 22 Dec. 1843. A.C.G., 2 cl. 2 May 1845; 1 cl. 24 Dec. 1847. Second Sikh War; passage of Chenab; Chilianwala; (? Gujerat); A.C.G. (Medal with clasp). Joint Dy. Comy. Gen. 19 Jan. 1853; Auditor of Comst. accounts 1 May 1853 till retirement. Fur. 1860 till retirement.
Refs.: *The Times*, 8 Aug. 1889. M.I. Redland Green churchyard, Bristol.

NEWCOMEN, Robert (1789-1819). Lieutenant, 27th N.I. *b.* Drogheda 29 July 1789. Cadet 1808. Admitted 25 Jan. 1810. Ensign 2 Apr. 1811. Lieut. 16 Dec. 1814. *d.* Gadarwara, C.P., 21 Oct. 1819.

Youngest brother of Thomas Newcomen, of Drogheda.
Services: Barasat C.C. Posted Ensign to 27th N.I. in 1811. Fur. 1812 till 10 Nov. 1815. Lieut. 2/27th N.I. With 3rd Ceylon Vol. Bn. 1818-19.

NEWHOUSE, Thomas Henry (1799-1850). Major, Invalid Est. 19th N.I. *bapt.* St. Andrew's, Holborn, 25 July 1799. Cadet 1819. Admitted 24 Mar. 1821. Ensign 20 June 1820. Lieut. 11 July 1823. Capt. 24 Sept. 1834. Major 9 Aug. 1843. Invalided 22 Nov. 1843. *d.* Mussoorie 7 Aug. 1850.

Son of Thomas Postlethwaite Newhouse, of Gray's Inn Sq., and Lucy his wife, dau. of Benjamin Smith, of Lys, Hants, and sister of Lt.-Gen. Sir Lionel Smith, 1st Bart., G.C.B. (*D.N.B.*). *m.* Rajpore, U.P., 4 Apr. 1843, Matilda Henrietta, only dau. of Capt. Turner.
Services: Was already at Bombay when apptd. Cadet. Posted Ensign to 2/14th N.I. 16 Nov. 1820; transfd. as Lieut. to 3rd N.I. July 1823; to 19th N.I. (late 2/3rd) May 1824. d.d. Bengal Eur. Regt. 15 Aug. 1832. No record of active service.

Refs.: Burke's *Peerage*, 1923, p. 997, *s.n.* Smith-Gordon, Bart. *I.M.* 5 Oct. 1850, p. 581.

NEWLAND, Andrew. Cadet 1774. Removed to the Madras Est. (?)
Services: Not in Madras A.L. of 1776, 1778, 1782 or 1787.

NEWLAND, Andrew. Cadet. Infantry. Country Cadet 1778. Dismissed by order of Govt. 16 Feb. 1779.
Services: Apptd. Cadet 11 Aug. 1778. (*Perhaps* identical with the last.) Cadet in 2nd Bde: at Berhampore.

NEWNHAM, Nathaniel (1773-1862). Lieutenant. Infantry. *bapt.* St. Andrew's, Holborn, 7 May 1773. Cadet 1795. Arrived in India 11 Mar. 1797. Ensign 8 Oct. 1796. Lieut. 30 Oct. 1797. Resigned 2 Dec. 1797. *d.* Regent's Pk., London, 15 Feb. 1862, aged 88.

Eldest son of Thomas Newnham, of Southborough, Bromley, Kent, and Mary Bannister his wife, dau. of Francis Johnson, M.D. Ed. Harrow 1785-91. St. John's Coll., Camb., 7 May 1791 ; B.A. 1795. Admitted Lincoln's Inn 24 Apr. 1795.
Services: N.F.P. He subsequently became a banker and underwriter at Lloyd's. Surveyor-accountant of St. Paul's School 1826-7.
Refs.: *Memoirs of the Newnham Family*, by Ellen H. Sealy (1912). *The Times*, 19 Feb. 1862. Portrait as a boy, by Millar, with his uncle, Alderman Nathaniel Newnham, Lord Mayor of London, in Guildhall, City of London.

NEWPORT, Coecilius (1756/57-1792). Lieutenant, 25th Bn. Sepoys. *b.* London 1756/57. Cadet 1779. Ensign 9 July 1779. Lieut. 1 Mar. 1781. *d.* Barrackpore 30 Sept. 1792. ·
Services: Apptd. Cadet 28 Apr. 1779 ; sailed for India in the *Duke of Kingston* 17 Nov. 1779, aged 22. Commenced the march with Col. Pearse's detachment to Madras in Jan. 1781, but went sick at the end of March. Lieut. 25th Bn. Sepoys in July 1787.

NEWTON, Henry Augustus (1793-1830). Captain, 66th N.I. *b.* London 12 Feb. 1793. Cadet 1809. Admitted 2 Aug. 1810. Ensign 1 Nov. 1811. Lieut. 30 Sept. 1814. Capt. 24 Dec. 1825. *d.* Karra, B. & O. (? Cuttack), 27 June 1830.
bapt. Marylebone 26 July 1798. Son of Edward Newton, merchant, and Ann his wife.
Services: Barasat C.C. Posted Ensign to 3rd N.I. in 1811.

Nepal War 1814-15; Lieut. 2/3rd N.I., in 1st Div. Transfd. to newly-raised 33rd N.I. July 1823 ; to 66th N.I. (late 2/33rd) May 1824. Fur. 1824-5. d.d. 1st Nassiri Bn. 4 Aug. 1826 ; 2nd in comd. do. 20 Oct. 1826 ; do. 2nd Nassiri Bn. 9 Mar. 1828 till 1829.

*NEWTON, John Clifton (1759/60-?). Cadet. Infantry. *b.* 1759/60. Cadet 1779. Never arrived in India. Resigned at Madeira 1779, on the voyage out to India.
A native of co. Notts.
Services: Apptd. Cadet 28 Jan. 1779 ; sailed for India in the *True Briton* 16 June 1779, aged 19.

NEWTON, Richard (1787-1835). Captain, 44th N.I. *b.* London 5 Jan. 1787. Cadet 1804. Arrived in India 13 May 1806. Ensign 26 Mar. 1806. Lieut. 22 Nov. 1807. Capt. 20 Jan. 1822. *d.* at sea 23 Jan. 1835, on board the *Albion* off Saugor I.
bapt. St. Bene't Finck, London, 28 Jan. 1787. Son of William Newton and Mary his wife. *m.* Secrora, U.P., 17 Apr. 1821, Ann, widow of William Midwinter, *q.v.* (She died 3 Mar. 1859, aged 64.)
Services: Present as a Cadet at capture of C.G.H. by Sir David Baird in Jan. 1806. Barasat C.C. Posted Ensign to 22nd N.I. in 1807. Actg. Adjt. 2/22nd N.I. 1811-14. Transfd. to 1/22nd N.I. 1814. Intr. & Qmr. 1/22nd N.I. 1 July 1814 till 25 Feb. 1822. Third Mahratta War ; Nagpur. Transfd. to 44th N.I. (late 2/22nd) May 1824. Offg. A.D.C. to Bdr.-Gen. Thomas Shuldham, *q.v.*, 11 Sept. till 3 Dec. 1824. First Burma War ; Cachar 1825 ; Capt. 44th N.I. Offg. S.A.C.G., E. Div. of the Army, 2 Jan. till 4 June 1825 ; actg. S.A.C.G. with force on Sylhet frontier 24 Oct. 1825 till Feb. 1826 ; actg. Bde. Major on E. frontier 31 Oct. 1826. Fur. s.c. 9 Jan. 1835 till death.
Refs.: '*A.J.* N.S. xvii. 132. *G.M.* 1835, ii. 222.

NEWTON, Thomas (1783-1842). Major General. Colonel 40th N.I. *b.* London 22 Oct. 1783. Cadet 1799. Arrived in India 8 Dec. 1800. Ensign 15 Nov. 1799. Lieut. 29 May 1800. Cashiered by G.C.M. 5 Mar. 1812. Reinstated 16 June 1815. Capt. 5 Mar. 1813. Major 29 Apr. 1823. Lt. Col. 22 Sept. 1824. Col. (1 Dec. 1829) 19 Oct. 1833. Maj. Gen. 28 June 1838. *d.* Mussoorie 23 June 1842.
bapt. Trinity Minories, Tower of London, 9 Nov. 1783. Son of Charles Newton [1] and Mary his wife. *m.* 1st, Cawnpore 2 Apr. 1803, Rosamond, dau. of James Powell, *q.v.* (*See also* John Pitt Griffin.) (She died 30 May 1815.) *m.* 2nd, St. John's, Calcutta,

1 Feb. 1821, Anne Catherine, widow of —— Smith. (She divorced him 27 Mar. 1837, and died Calcutta 3 Aug. 1844, aged 44.)
Services: Posted Lieut. to 1/10th N.I. 15 Apr. 1801. Second Mahratta War 1805-6; Lieut. 1/10th N.I., on escort duty. Cashiered by G.C.M. 5 Mar. 1812, but permitted to remain in India pending Court's decision. He then appears to have become an indigo planter. Reinstated with effect from 16 June 1815 (G.O. 15 Mar. 1816). Posted to 2/10th N.I. Third Mahratta War; capture of fort Seoni 21 Jan.; Bainsudder 22 Jan. 1818; Chanda; Capt. 2/10th N.I., with Col. Adams's force. Transfd. to 1/10th N.I. Feb. 1821. First Burma War; operations in Sylhet and Cachar 1824; Bikrampur, comdg. the force (*Lond. Gaz.* 25 Nov. 1824); Dudhpatli; Major 1/10th N.I. Transfd. to 2/10th N.I. 15 Apr. 1824. Posted Lt. Col. to 48th N.I. Sept. 1824; to 66th N.I. 1826; to 59th N.I. 24 Sept. 1828; to 28th N.I. 12 Jan. 1829. Posted Col. to 40th N.I. 16 Apr. 1834; to 25th N.I. 19 Aug. 1835; to 40th N.I. 4 Apr. 1837.
Refs.: *E.I.M.C.* iii. 427-47. *A.J.* N.S. xxiii. 275. *G.M.* 1842, ii. 558. Will dated Mussoorie 7 May 1842; admon. 20 June 1843.
[1] *Note:* Probably Capt. Charles Newton, E.I.C.N.S., and Mary his wife, dau. of Charles Henry Collins, Major of the Tower.

NICHELSON, Harrie (1786-1826). Major, 15th N.I. *bapt.* Chatham 4 Apr. 1786. Cadet 1802. Arrived in India 5 Sept. 1803. Ensign 8 Sept. 1803. Lieut. 17 Sept. 1804. Capt. 5 Aug. 1816. Major 1 May 1824. *d.* Chowringhee, Calcutta, 20 Dec. 1826, aged 41.
Son of William Nichelson and Elizabeth his wife. *m.* Calcutta 13 Dec. 1813, Jane, dau. of Roderick Fraser (1763-1818), *q.v.*, widow of —— Maclean, and sister-in-law of "Sir Lachlan Maclean, of Sudbury, Suffolk." [1] (*See also* John Walker.) (She died 17 Dec. 1828, aged 44).
Services: Cadet d.d. 12th N.I. 1804. Posted Lieut. to 1/11th N.I. in 1804. Second Mahratta War; pursuit of Holkar 1805-6; Lieut. 1/11th N.I. Adjt. 1/11th N.I. 26 Aug. 1811; Intr. & Qmr. do. 1 July 1814 till 1816. Reduction of Kalinjar 1812. Capt. Lt. 11th N.I. 6 Aug. 1816. Fur. 1817-19. Transfd. to 17th N.I. (late 1/11th) May 1824; to 15th N.I. (late 2/11th) in 1826. First Burma War 1824-6; Paymr. at Rangoon to Bengal troops of Sir A. Campbell's force.
Refs.: *A.J.* xxiii. 857. Will dated Calcutta 7 July 1821; proved 10 Jan. 1827. M.I. in S. Park St. cemetery, Calcutta.
[1] *Note:* See James Maclean (1802-1843).

NICHOL, William (*d.* 1781). Lieutenant, 2/1st Bengal Eur. Regt. Cadet 1772. Ensign 6 July 1776. Lieut. 27 June 1778. *d.* Madras Presdy. Feb. 1781.

Services: First Rohilla War 1774; Cadet in the Select Picket. Second Mysore War 1780-1; Lieut. 2/1st Bengal Eur. Regt., with Sir Eyre Coote's detachment.

Refs.: *India Gazette,* 31 Mar. 1781.

NICHOLETTS, Gilbert (1783-1818). Captain, 22nd N.I. *b.* Sodington Tower 1783. Cadet 1799. Arrived in India 9 Dec. 1800. Ensign 18 Oct. 1800. Lieut. 21 Dec. 1801. Capt. 1 Sept. 1814. *d.* Kumarkhali, Bengal, 8 Oct. 1818.

bapt. 5 June 1785. ("He appeared to be 2 yrs. old.") Eldest son of Gilbert Nicholetts, of Hopton Sollers and Brontrees Hall, co. Hereford, and The Hill, Worcs., later of Bishops Tawton, Devon, and Elizabeth his wife. Stepson of Richard Toller, of S. Petherton, Somerset. His sister *m.* John Shapland, *q.v. m.* Calcutta 15 Mar. 1804, Hannah, eldest dau. of Henry Swinhoe, of Calcutta. (*See also* Edward Browne.) (She died 7 Feb. 1858, aged 75.) Father of Gilbert Alfred Nicholetts and William Hamilton Nicholetts, *qq.v.*

Services: Posted Ensign to 1/7th N.I. 17 Apr. 1801. Transfd. to newly-raised 1/22nd N.I. in 1804; Adjt. do. 1805 till 17 Mar. 1810. Settlement of Hariana 1809; Bhawani; Qmr. of Bde. Adjt. & Qmr. Native Invalid Bn. at Allahabad 1810-15. Capt. Lt. 1 Jan. 1814. Capt. 1/22nd N.I. Transfd. to 2/22nd N.I. in 1817. Suptg. construction of bldgs. at Kumarkhali Residency 1817 till death.

Refs.: Robinson's *Mansions of Herefordshire,* p. 17. Will dated 5 Dec. 1808; proved 14 Dec. 1818.

NICHOLETTS, Gilbert Alfred (1811-1841). Lieutenant, 28th N.I. *b.* Allahabad 7 Feb. 1811. Cadet 1827. Arrived in India 29 June 1828. Ensign 12 Dec. 1827. Lieut. 8 Oct. 1839. *d.* at sea 7 Oct. 1841.

2nd son of Gilbert Nicholetts, *q.v.,* and Hannah his wife. Brother of William Hamilton Nicholetts, *q.v.* Sandhurst Cadet.

Services: Ensign d.d. 28th N.I. 25 July 1828; posted to 28th N.I. 4 Nov. 1828. Fur. s.c. 13 Sept. 1841 till death.

Refs.: Robinson's *Mansions of Herefordshire,* p. 17.

NICHOLETTS, William Hamilton (1808-1854). Bt. Major, 28th N.I. *b.* Saharanpur, U.P., 24 Mar. 1808. Cadet 1824. Arrived in India 6 July 1825. Ensign 9 Feb. 1825. Lieut.

THE BENGAL ARMY, 1758-1834 389

20 Sept. 1826. Capt. 10 Aug. 1845. Bt. Major 11 Nov. 1851. *d.* Sitapur, U.P., 19 Oct. 1854.

bapt. Cawnpore 29 Apr. 1810. Eldest son of Gilbert Nicholetts, *q.v.*, and Hannah his wife. Brother of Gilbert Alfred Nicholetts, *q.v. m.* Agra 11 Jan. 1834, Victoria Maria, youngest dau. of Major Thomas Ajax Anderson, H.M. 19th Ft., and widow of W. Russell.
Services: Posted Ensign to 28th N.I.; actg. Adjt. Wing do. 24 Nov. 1831. Actg. Adjt. 1st Inf., Oudh Auxy. Force (became 1st Oudh Local Inf.), 18 Feb. 1839; permanent do. 17 May 1839; 2nd in comd. do. 17 Jan. 1840; Comdt. do. 22 Dec. 1847 till death. No record of active service.
Refs.: Robinson's *Mansions of Herefordshire*, p. 17. *G.M.* 1855, i. 327. M.I. Sitapur.

NICHOLL, Thomas (1796-1842). Captain, Artillery. (453) *bapt.* Watford, Herts., 4 Nov. 1796. Cadet 1813. Admitted 5 Aug. 1814. Fireworker 23 July 1816. Lieut. 1 Sept. 1818. Capt. 20 Aug. 1831. *d.* 12 Jan. 1842: kld. in action in the Jagdalak Pass during the retreat from Kabul.

Son of Thomas Nicholl, of Watford, atty., and Harriot his wife. Bother of William Nicholl, of Watford. *m.* Karnal 30 May 1826, Ann, youngest dau. of J. Satterthwaite, late of Woodside, Devon. (*See also* George Thornton and John Holt White.) (She was pensd. on Lord Clive's fund 26 July 1843; living in 1860.) His dau. *m.* Sir Claude Martine Wade, *q.v.* Addiscombe Cadet 1811-13.
Services: With 6th Troop H.A. 1819; 1st Troop 1820; 6th Troop 1821. Actg. Adjt. & Qmr. Div. Art. with Narbada F.F. 23 Nov. 1820. Siege and capture of Bhurtpore; Lieut. 4th Troop 3rd Bde. H.A. Posted to 2nd Coy. 3rd Bn. Foot Art. 22 Mar. 1832; transfd. to 1st Troop 1st Bde. H.A. 28 May 1832. Leave p.a. to Mussoorie 1 May till 1 Nov. 1839. First Afghan War; Nazian valley under Col. Shelton Feb. 1841; was comdg. Art. at Kabul on 2 Nov. 1842; outbreak at Kabul; retreat from Kabul (kld.); Capt. comdg. 1st Troop 1st Bde. H.A.
Refs.: A.J. xxiii. 86. Will dated Meerut 7 Aug. 1836; codicil dated Karnal 27 Sept. 1838; proved 23 Dec. 1842. Name on Dum-Dum column; M.I. Watford church.

NICHOLL, William (1764-1846). Lieut. Colonel. 5th N.I. *b.* 1764. Cadet 1781. Arrived in India 10 June 1782. Ensign 25 May 1781. Lieut. 8 Sept. 1782. Capt. 29 May 1800. Major 27 Sept. 1807. Lt. Col. 1 June 1813. Retired 21 Oct. 1818. *d.* Beaumont St., Marylebone, London, 15 Apr. 1846, aged 81.

390 LIST OF THE OFFICERS OF

Son of Thomas Nicholl, of Watford, Herts., and Mary Axtell his wife. Cousin of John Shipton, *q.v.* His dau. *m.* James Brook Ridge, *q.v.*

Services: Appt. Cadet 20 Dec. 1780; sailed for India in the *Hinchinbrooke* 13 Mar. 1781, aged 16. Posted to 2nd Bengal Eur. Regt. 1782; transfd. to 29th N.I. 1783; to 3rd Bn. Sepoys 1786. Third Mysore War; siege of Bangalore, d.d. 2nd Vol. Bn.; Savandrug; Seringapatam; Lieut. 3rd Bn. Sepoys, with Col. Cockerell's detachment. Adjt. 2/14th N.I. Transfd. as Capt. to 19th N.I. May 1800; d.d. Marine Regt. 1801. Expedn. to Macao 1801-2; Bde. Major and Paymr. with detachment of Marines. Joined 2/19th N.I. in 1802; transfd. to newly-raised 2/21st N.I. in 1803; apptd. to comd. 2/21st N.I. in 1804. Second Mahratta War; Monson's retreat; Rampura; defence of Khushalgarh with 6 Coys. 2/21st N.I. in Aug. 1804; relief of Delhi; Farrukhabad; siege of Bhurtpore; Capt. 2/21st N.I. In civil and mily. charge of Tonk Rampura 1805-6. Fur. 17 Feb. 1808 till 16 Aug. 1811. Posted Lt. Col. to 2/21st N.I. in 1813; comdg. at Chittagong in 1815. Fur. 29 Jan. 1816 till retirement. Transfd. to 2/5th N.I. in 1816.

Refs.: E.I.M.C. ii. 517-21. Cussan's *Herts.* iii. 212. *G.M.* 1846, i. 664. M.I. at Watford.

NICHOLS, Thomas. (*See* **BROADHURST, Thomas.**)

NICHOLSON, John (1785-1840 ?). Lieutenant. 10th N.I. *b.* Crosby-on-Eden, Cumberland, 16 Nov. 1785. Cadet 1803. Arrived in India 2 Dec. 1804. Ensign 10 Oct. 1804. Lieut. 10 Oct. 1804. Resigned 8 Jan. 1807. (? *d.* Brigg, Lincs., 23 Oct. 1840.)

bapt. 22 Nov. 1785. Son of John Nicholson, of Bunstock, and Jane his wife, *née* Shaw.

Services: Posted Lieut. to 10th N.I. in 1805. (? Second Mahratta War 1805-6.)

Refs.: (? *G.M.* 1840, ii 673.)

NICOL, James (1739/40-1816). Lieut. General. 8th N.I. *b.* Scotland 1739/40. Country Cadet 1761. Admitted 1761. Ensign 14 Nov. 1761. Lieut. 28 Aug. 1763. Capt. 20 Dec. 1764. Major 10 Jan. 1781. Lt. Col. 16 July 1787. Col. 3 May 1796. Maj. Gen. 3 May 1796. Lt. Gen. 25 Sept. 1803. Retired List 1 July 1804. *d.* at the Cape 4 Mar. 1816, aged 76; *bur.* in Dutch church, Cape Town.

Related to Lt.-Col. Charles Nicol, H.M. 66th Ft. Father of James

THE BENGAL ARMY, 1758-1834

Nicol, *q.v.* (*Probably* grandfather of James Douglas (*b.* 1781) and William Douglas (*d.* 1827), *qq.v.*)

Services: Adjt. to Sepoy Bns. (*i.e.* A.A.G.) 2 Aug. 1763 till Jan. 1765. Assault and capture of Patna Nov. 1763. Battle of Buxar 1764; Lieut. 1st Bn. Sepoys. Posted to 12th Coy. Bengal Eur. Bn. 29 Jan. 1765; to take charge of 15th Bn. Sepoys 21 Mar. 1765. Resigned his Commission 8 May 1766, during the " Batta mutiny." On quitting the Service he, together with Thomas Davie, *q.v.*, took service at Benares with Shuja-ud-Daulah, carrying off with them from Calcutta " a quantity of small arms, with which they not only supplied the Country powers, but were actually training up a body of men for their service to our discipline." On application being made by the Board at Calcutta to Shuja-ud-Daulah early in 1767, the latter delivered them up to Sir Robert Barker, *q.v.*, and they were sent under guard to Monghyr. They were kept in confinement in Calcutta, whence they were eventually sent home in the *Norfolk* in Dec. 1767. They brought an action in England for wrongful imprisonment against Mr. Henry Verelst, the Govr. of Bengal, which was not finally settled in the Coy.'s favour till May 1779. Restored by C.D. in July 1780 to the rank he held on his resignation. Arrived in India Aug. 1781. Apptd. to comd. 31st Bn. Sepoys 4 Sept. 1781; to comd. 13th Bn. Mar. 1785; to comd. 36th Bn. 31 May 1786; posted to 2nd Sepoy Bde. 20 Oct. 1786. Major 4th Bengal Eur. Bn. in July 1787; Lt. Col. comdg. 2nd Bde. at Fatehgarh in Dec. 1788. Resided at the Cape after his retirement.

Refs.: Caraccioli, *passim. Broome*, pp. 377, 476. *Proceedings* of 30 Mar. and 12 Dec. 1767. *Genealogist*, N.S. xxxii. 51. *G.M.* 1816, ii. 91. Will dated 1 Mar. 1813; proved 24 May 1816.

NICOL, James (1778-1831). Colonel, 29th N.I. *b.* " in or near London, on or about 23 Mar. 1778." Cadet 1794. Arrived in India 30 Oct. 1795. Ensign 13 Oct. 1795. Lieut. 14 Feb. 1797. Capt. 1 Sept. 1804. Major 16 Jan. 1814. Lt. Col. 6 Apr. 1818. Lt. Col. Comdt. 1 May 1824. Col. 5 June 1829. *d.* London 4 May 1831, aged 52.

Son of James Nicol, *q.v. m.* St. John's, Calcutta, 17 Jan. 1823, Miss Harriet Jeffreys.

Services: Apptd. a Minor Cadet Oct. 1781; struck off 2 May 1786. Apptd. Cadet 29 Apr. 1795; sailed for India in the *Woodcot* 18 June 1795. Second Mahratta War; Aligarh; battle of Deig 13 Nov. 1804 (w.); Capt. 1/4th N.I. Transfd. to newly-raised 26th N.I. in 1805. 1st Asst. in A.A.G.'s office 1807; A.A.G. of the

Army 1809; D.A.G. 22 Feb. 1811; actg. A.G. 1816; A.G. of the Army (with official rank of Lt. Col.) 10 Mar. 1817 till 1825. Major 2/26th N.I. Posted Lt. Col. to 1/8th N.I. in 1818; transfd. as Lt. Col. Comdt. to 9th N.I. (late 1/8th) May 1824. Fur. s.c. 18 Mar. 1825 till death. Transfd. to 29th N.I. 7 Dec. 1826.
Refs.: G.M. 1831, i. 475. A.J. N.S. v. 118.

NICOLAY, Frederick Granville (1805-1833). Lieutenant, Bengal Eur. Regt. *b.* London 27 Sept. 1805. Cadet 1823. Arrived in India 19 May 1824. Ensign 17 Jan. 1824. Lieut. 13 May 1825. *d.* Dinapore 5 Dec. 1833.

bapt. St. James's Palace 18 Oct. 1805. Eldest son of Frederick Nicolay, of Cadogan Pl. (of St. James's Palace), London, of the Treasury, and Maria Georgina his wife, dau. of John Granville. His sister *m.* George Henry Robinson, *q.v. m.* Agra 13 Nov. 1830, Catherine, dau. of —— Bush and widow of Charles Collinson Blackburn.

Services: Posted Ensign to 36th N.I.; actg. Adjt. do. 4 Aug. 1825. Siege and capture of Bhurtpore; Lieut. 36th N.I. Exchanged to 1st Bengal Eur. Regt. 9 Nov. 1826; posted to Rt. Wing Bengal Eur. Regt. on the amalgamation of the two Regts.
Refs.: M.I. at Dinapore.

NICOLL, Henry (1816-1907). General, C.B. 50th N.I. *b.* 4 Nov. 1816. Cadet 1834. Arrived in India 21 July 1835. Ensign (12 Dec. 1834) 8 Jan. 1835. Lieut. 4 Nov. 1838. Capt. 22 Oct. 1849. Major 18 Feb. 1861. Bt. Lt. Col. 18 Feb. 1861. Col. 18 Feb. 1866. Maj. Gen. 1 Oct. 1877. Lt. Gen. 25 May 1880. Gen. 22 Jan. 1889. Transfd. to u.s.l. 1 July 1881. *d.* Lidlington Vicarage, Beds., 5 Feb. 1907.

bapt. Lyndhurst, Hants, 3 Dec. 1816. Son of Samuel John Nicoll, of Alresford, Hants, and Serena his wife. *m.* Agnes, dau. of J. Sim. (She died 1887.) Addiscombe Cadet 1 Feb. 1833 till 12 Dec. 1834.

Services: Ensign d.d. 67th N.I. 8 Aug. 1835; d.d. 38th N.I. 12 Aug. 1835; posted to 50th N.I. 24 Sept. 1835; Intr. & Qmr. do. 5 Jan. 1839 till 1850. Insurrection in Bundelkhand 1842-3. Gwalior campaign; Paniar; Lieut. 50th N.I. (Bronze star). Second Sikh War; in garr. at Lahore; Lieut. 50th N.I. (Medal). Actg. Bde. Major at Cawnpore 1854; Bde. Major on the Est. at Delhi 27 June 1854 till 1860. Santhal revolt 1855. Mutiny campaign; Badli-ki-Serai; siege and capture of Delhi; Bde. Major with Delhi F.F. (Medal with clasp). Fur. 1859-60. Transfd. to

THE BENGAL ARMY, 1758-1834 393

Staff Corps 18 Feb. 1861. Offg. A.A.G. Sirhind 20 Dec. 1862;
A.A.G. Ambala Div. 12 Oct. 1863. Comdg. at Jullundur 1872-3.
Fur. 22 Aug. 1873 till death. Awarded C.B. posthumously in
Lond. Gaz. of 28 June 1907, on the occasion of the 50th anniversary
of mily. operations in India, 1857.
Refs.: *Who Was Who, 1897-1916.*

NICOLSON, James (1788-1835). Captain, Invalid Est. 4th
N.I. b. Kirkwall 16 June 1788. Cadet 1809. Admitted 6 Mar.
1811. Ensign 21 Aug. 1811. Lieut. 16 Dec. 1814. Capt.
21 Aug. 1826. Invalided 9 Apr. 1832. d. Mussoorie, U.P.,
19 Feb. 1835.

bapt. Kirkwall 17 June 1788. Son of Robert Nicolson, atty.,
and Elizabeth his wife, dau. of Thomas Balfour, merchant in
Kirkwall. m. Karnal 20 Apr. 1818, Louisa Ann Maria, dau. of
Edward William Butler, q.v. (See also Isaac Pereira.)

Services: (? Captured on the voyage out in the Ceylon by the
French.) Drew pay from 3 Dec. 1810, the date of surrender of
Mauritius by the French. Posted Ensign to 1st N.I.; Lieut. 1/1st
N.I. (? Nepal War 1814-15; Lieut. 1st N.I.) Adjt. 1st Nassiri
Bn. 27 July 1815 till 28 Dec. 1826; tempy. Comdt. do. 1 Nov. 1820.
Transfd. to 4th N.I. (late 2/1st) May 1824. d.d. 1st Nassiri Bn.
28 May till 26 Sept. 1827. Second in comd. 1st Nassiri Bn. 19 Nov.
1828 till invalided.

Refs.: Will dated Karnal, 3 Dec. 1832; proved 31 July 1835.

NICOLSON, John (1783-1835). Captain, 8th L.C. bapt. Penrith,
Cumberland, 24 Jan. 1783. Cadet 1805. Arrived in India
11 July 1806. Cornet 15 July 1806. Lieut. 1 Mar. 1812. Capt.
26 Feb. 1820. d. Sultanpur, Benares, 31 May 1835.

Son of R. Nicolson, surgeon, and Barbara his wife. m. Cawnpore
13 July 1833, Eleanor Hester Maria, eldest dau. of Francis James
Thomas Johnston, q.v. (See also James Mackenzie.) (She re-m.
Charles Henry Hamilton, q.v.)

Services: Barasat C.C. Posted Cornet to 8th N.C. and served
throughout with that Regt.; Adjt. 8th N.C. 30 Sept. 1812 till 4 Dec.
1820. Third Mahratta War; Jubbulpore; Lieut. 8th N.C., with
Bdr.-Gen. Hardyman's Div. Siege and capture of Bhurtpore.
Actg. A.A.G. Benares Div. 15 Jan. 1835.

Refs.: A.J. N.S. xviii. 243. Will dated Cawnpore 30 June
1834; proved 29 June 1835.

NICOLSON, Malcolm (1792-1850). Major. 30th N.I. b.
Thurso, co. Caithness, 5 Dec. 1792. Cadet 1813. Admitted

5 Aug. 1814. Ensign 28 Nov. 1814. Lieut. 9 Aug. 1816. Capt. 28 Sept. 1825. Major 2 Dec. 1838. Retired 1 Dec. 1839. *d.* Boulogne-sur-Mer 18 Apr. 1850.

3rd and youngest son of Rev. Patrick Nicolson, of Shebster, minister of Thurso 1785-1805, and Mary Maxwell his wife, dau. of Capt. Thomas Dunbar, of Westfield. His sisters *m.* James Nesbitt Jackson and John Samuel Henry Weston, *qq.v.* Nephew of the wife of James Murray MacGregor, and cousin of Charles Seton Guthrie, *qq.v. m.* 1st, Dinapore 12 Aug. 1821, his cousin Janet (Jessie) Dunbar, eldest dau. of Major James Moodie, of Melsetter, Orkney, and sister of Thomas Moodie, *q.v. m.* 2nd, Jubbulpore 11 Mar. 1839, Caroline, 4th dau. of Maj.-Gen. Richard Hassells Yates, Madras Est. (She died 15 Feb. 1906.)

Services : Ensign Ross, Caithness, Sutherland and Cromartie Mil. Posted Ensign to 1/4th N.I. Nepal War 1814-15 ; Ensign d.d. 2/15th N.I., in 4th Div. Transfd. to 2/15th N.I. in 1815. Nepal War 1816 ; Ensign 2/15th N.I., in 4th Bde. Centre Column. Siege and capture of Hathras ; Lieut. 2/15th N.I. Third Mahratta War ; Asirgarh ; Lieut. 2/15th N.I. Comdt. 2nd Narbada Sebundy Corps 21 June 1820 ; do. amalgamated Corps of 1st and 2nd Saugor & Narbada Sebundy Corps 18 Apr. 1828 till retirement. Transfd. to 30th N.I. (late 1/15th) May 1824. Actg. Asst. Supt. roads in Saugor & Narbada territories 5 Oct. 1826 ; in charge of do. 1 Nov. 1831. Executive Ofr. P.W.D., Jubbulpore Div., and in charge of Jubbulpore roads till retirement.

Refs. : *Caithness Family History*, by John Henderson, p. 318. *The Moodie Book*, by the Marquis Ruvigny, p. 53. *The Clan Nicolson*, by J. G. Nicholson (1938), p. 81. Scott's *Fasti*, vii. 137. *A.J.* xiii. 282. *G.M.* 1850, ii. 110.

NICOLSON, Malcolm (1805-1835). Lieutenant, 26th N.I. *b.* Portree, I. of Skye, 12 June 1805. Cadet 1823. Arrived in India 8 Oct. 1824. Ensign 11 May 1825. Lieut. 26 May 1825. *d.* Colgong, B. & O., 7 May 1835 : disappeared from his budgerow on the river ; supposed drowned.

Son of Donald Nicolson, of Scorrabreck, Skye, and Margaret his wife, dau. of Norman MacDonald, of Scalpay. Nephew of Lt.-Gen. Sir John MacDonald, G.C.B. (*D.N.B.*), and cousin-german of James Ranald Burt, *q.v.*

Services : Posted Ensign to 26th N.I. 31 Mar. 1825 ; actg. Adjt. do. 28 Dec. 1826. Leave s.c. to Calcutta 16 Feb. till 16 Aug. 1835. No record of active service.

Refs. : *MacInnes*, p. 165.

NICOLSON, Peter [1] (1808-1845). Bt. Captain, 28th N.I. *b.* Calcutta 24 Sept. 1808. Cadet 1825. Arrived in India 6 July 1826. Ensign 15 Mar. 1826. Lieut. 26 June 1833. Bt. Capt. 15 Mar. 1841. *d.* 21 Dec. 1845: kld. in action at the battle of Ferozshahr.

Son of Simon Nicolson, Surg. Bengal Est., and Mary his wife. Brother of Simon John Nicolson, *q.v. m.* Calcutta 22 Jan. 1835, Mary, youngest dau. of William Mitchell (1771/72-1817), *q.v.* (She died Bankura 3 May 1835.)

Services: Ensign d.d. 28th N.I. 2 Aug. 1826; posted to 28th N.I. 26 Sept. 1826. Actg. Adjt. Ramgarh Bn. 17 Feb. 1832 till Dec. 1833. Against the Kols 1832-3; Lieut. Ramgarh Bn. Principal Asst. to A.G.G., S. W. frontier, 19 Dec. 1833. Leave s.c. to Cape 21 July 1835 till 1 Sept. 1837. A.D.C. to G.G., Lord Auckland, 13 Nov. 1837 till 21 Aug. 1838. Adjt. Shah Shuja's 1st Cav. (Christie's Horse) 17 Aug. 1838. First Afghan War 1838-40; capture of Ghazni (Medal); occupation of Kabul; action nr. Killugu 22 Sept. 1839 (w.); Lieut. Christie's Horse. Apptd. P.A. in Ghilzai country 1840. Returned to India Nov. 1840 in charge of the ex-Amir Dost Mohd. Khan, and had charge of him during his detention in India, finally escorting him as far as the frontier of Afghanistan at the end of 1842. Rejoined 28th N.I. Sept. 1843. Apptd. Extra Asst. to A.G.G., N.W.F., 22 Apr. 1844. Nominated in Nov. 1845 Supt. of Mysore Princes, but never joined this appt. owing to the outbreak of war. First Sikh War; Ferozshahr (kld.); with Sir John Littler's Div. Brought out in Calcutta at the end of 1843, "The New Bengal Army List," only one edn. of which, apparently, ever appeared.

Refs.: De Rhé-Philipe. *Fortescue*, xii. 121, 124. M.I. in Civil cemetery at Ferozepore.

[1] *Note*: His christian name is given as Patrick in his M.I., as "Peter *alias* Patrick" in the marriage register. Elsewhere it appears indifferently as either, the names being interchangeable in Scots use.

NICOLSON, Simon John (1807-1836). Lieutenant, 50th N.I. *b.* at sea 22 May 1807, on the voyage to India. Cadet 1826. Arrived in India 11 May 1827. Ensign 20 Jan. 1827. Lieut. 14 July 1835. *d.* at sea 19 Nov. 1836, on board the *Mary Ann Webb*.

Son of Simon Nicolson, Bengal Medical Est., and Mary his wife. Brother of Peter Nicolson, *q.v.*

Services: Ensign d.d. 20th N.I. 28 May 1827; posted to 50th

N.I. 19 June 1827. Operations against the Kols and Chuars 1832 ; Ensign 50th N.I. Leave s.c. to China 13 Oct. 1834 till 21 Apr. 1835. Fur. s.c. 26 Aug. 1836 till death.

Refs.: The *Clan Nicolson,* by J. G. Nicholson (1938), p. 80.

NIEDRICK, Paul[1] (*c.* 1714/15-1790). Capt. Lieutenant. Artillery. (23) *b. c.* 1714/15. Cadet 1758. Fireworker 7 Jan. 1759. 2nd Lieut. 15 Sept. 1761. Capt. Lt. 5 Dec. 1763. Resigned 13 Mar. 1765. *d.* Musselburgh, Midlothian, 22 (? 29) Jan. 1790, aged 76.

A native of Königsberg, Prussia ; naturalized 20 Dec. 1768. *m.* Edinburgh 14 Jan. 1753, Isobell, dau. of John Turnbull, tailor. (She died Anderstown 24 Jan. 1793.)

Services : Was one of the train of Art. in Edinburgh Castle in Jan. 1753. Corporal in Capt. Robert Hind's Coy. of 1st Bn. R.A. in May 1758, when given a Bengal Cadetship. Sailed for India in the *Bombay Castle* in 1758, aged 42. Battle of Gheria 1763 (s.w.). Pensd. on Lord Clive's fund 29 Sept. 1775.

Refs.: G.M. 1791, i. 182. *Eur. Mag.* 1790, i. 159. *S.M.* 1790, p. 51.

[1] *Note :* His names are given as Paal Nedrich in his licence to marry ; his surname as Nedrick in *Bengal Public Cons.* of 11 Mar. 1765.

NIND, Isaac. Ensign. 1st Bengal Eur. Bn. Cadet 1783. Arrived in India Aug. 1784. Ensign 28 Apr. 1785. Resigned 24 June 1793.

Eldest son of Isaac Nind, of Overbury, Gloucs., and Sarah his wife, dau. of John Pitt, of Gloucs. *m.* Ann, dau. of George Collins. Father of James Nind, and uncle of Philip Pitt Nind, *qq.v.*

Services : Apptd. Cadet 4 Apr. 1783 ; sailed for India in the *Hillsborough* 28 Jan. 1784. Fur. on h.p. 2 Oct. 1786 till resignation. Posted Ensign from Supy. List to 1st Eur. Bn. 12 Sept. 1792.

Refs.: Burke's *Landed Gentry,* 2nd edn., p. 937, *s.n.* Nind, of Elmleigh, Berks.

NIND, James (1790-1824). Captain, 8th N.I. *b.* 9 Sept. 1790. Cadet 1807. Arrived in India 21 Mar. 1809. Ensign (?) Lieut. 31 Jan. 1807. Capt. 15 Feb. 1824. *d. unm.* Betul, C.P., 9 Nov. 1824.

bapt. Bisham, Berks., 3 Oct. 1790. Son of Isaac Nind, *q.v.*, and Ann his wife. Cousin-german of Philip Pitt Nind, *q.v.* Marlow Cadet.

Services: Ensign d.d. 9th N.I. 1809-10; posted Ensign to 9th N.I., but no date of rank as such was assigned till 1813, when he was antedated as Lieut. to 31 Jan. 1807. Nepal War 1816; Makwanpur; Lieut. 2/9th N.I., in 4th Bde. Centre Column. Operations in Oudh against Kasim Ali Khan 1822; capture of Bardgaon; Bt. Capt. 2/9th N.I. Transfd. to 8th N.I. (late 1/9th) May 1824. Served with Nagpur Subsdy. Force in 1824.

Refs.: Burke's Landed Gentry, 2nd edn., p. 937, *s.n.* Nind, of Elmleigh. Will dated Lucknow 1 Jan. 1824; proved 21 Feb. 1825. M.I. Betul.

NIND, Philip Pitt (1793-1824). Bt. Captain, 3rd L.C. *bapt.* Tewkesbury 8 Nov. 1793. Cadet 1808. Arrived in India 21 Oct. 1809. Cornet 31 Dec. 1812. Lieut. 1 Sept. 1818. Bt. Capt. 24 Apr. 1824. *d.* Calcutta 21 Sept. 1824.

2nd son of John Pitt Nind, late of the Tewkesbury Vols., and Charlotte his wife, dau. of John Ireland, of Welland, Worcs. *m.* Springfield 30 Jan. 1824, Caroline, 5th dau. of William Davies, of Winterbourne-Abbas, Dorset. (She *re-m.* 30 Jan. 1838, Capt. William Payne, R.N.)

Services: Barasat C.C. Cadet d.d. 8th N.C. 1811-13; posted Supy. Cornet to 4th N.C. 1813; transfd. to 5th N.C. 1814. Third Mahratta War 1817-18; Cornet 5th N.C. Transfd. as Lieut. to 3rd N.C. Sept. 1818. Fur. 23 Jan. 1821 till 1824.

Refs.: Burke's Landed Gentry, 2nd edn., p. 937, *s.n.* Nind, of Elmleigh. Freeman's Journal, 1824. A.J. xvii. 345. G.M. 1824, i. 456. Will dated 20 Salisbury St., Strand, London, 21 Mar. 1824; proved 25 Sept. 1824.

NISBET, Harry (1794-1890). Ensign. Engineers. Subsequently Senior Mercht., B.C.S. *bapt.* Nevis I. 14 Dec. 1794. Cadet 1810. Ensign 1814. Transfd. to B.C.S. 30 Apr. 1814. *d.* Clifton, Bristol, 6 Dec. 1890, aged 96.

b. Nevis I. 11 Nov. 1794. 4th and youngest son of Walter Nisbet, junr., of Mt. Pleasant, Nevis, and of Grafton St., and Anne his wife, dau. of Robert Parry, of Plas Newydd, Llanrhaiadr, co. Denbigh. *m.* Quedgeley, Gloucs., 19 Feb. 1828, Anne, 2nd sister of F. T. Curtis-Hayward, *q.v.* (She died 10 Oct. 1869, aged 66.) Marlow Cadet; afterwards at Addiscombe 1809-10.

Services: Civil and sessions judge of Saran, B. & O., 29 Dec. 1835. Retired 1840.

Refs.: Oliver's *Hist. of Antigua*, iii. 443. *Nisbet of that Ilk*, p. 187, *s.n.* Nisbet, of Southbroome House, Wilts. *Misc. Gen. et Her.* 5S. ii. 50. *The Times*, 9 Dec. 1890. *Bath Chron.* 11 Dec. 1890.

NISBETT, David (1801-1818). Cadet, Infantry. *b.* Dunbar, co. Haddington, 30 July 1801. Cadet 1817. Never arrived in India. *d.* at sea 24 Aug. 1818, on his passage to India.

bapt. Dunbar 14 Aug. 1801. Son of John Nisbett, of Dunbar, slater, and Johnston Grieve his wife.

NISBETT, David (1809-1857). Lieut. Colonel. 53rd N.I. *b.* Dunbar 5 Apr. 1809. Cadet 1824. Arrived in India 20 Sept. 1825. Ensign 13 May 1825. Lieut. 20 Mar. 1829. Capt. 25 Feb. 1841. Bt. Major 11 Nov. 1851. Invalided 15 Nov. 1852. Retired 5 June 1855. Hon. Lt. Col. 10 Aug. 1855. *d.* 22 Mar. 1857.

bapt. 23 Apr. 1809. Son of Andrew Nisbett, of Dunbar, builder and slater, and Jean Aitchison his wife. Brother of William Nisbett, *q.v.*

Services: Posted Ensign to 53rd N.I.; Intr. & Qmr. do. 13 Nov. 1832 till 10 Sept. 1842. First Afghan War 1842; Bde. Qmr. to Gen. Pollock's force 19 Feb. 1842; do. Bdr. Wild's (3rd) Bde. of Pollock's force 20 Mar. till 10 Sept. 1842; forcing of Khyber; advance to Kabul; march through Khyber to Ali Masjid Nov. 1842; Capt. 53rd N.I. (Medal). Leave s.c. 18 mos. to Cape 9 Jan. 1844. Second Sikh War; in garr. at Lahore; Capt. 53rd N.I. (Medal).

NISBETT, William (1811-1835). Lieutenant, 64th N.I. *b.* Dunbar 22 Feb. 1811. Cadet 1826. Arrived in India 5 Oct. 1827. Ensign 20 May 1827. Lieut. 25 Aug. 1832. *d.* Saugor 28 July 1835.

bapt. 8 Mar. 1811. Son of Andrew Nisbett, of Dunbar, burgess and slater, and Jean Aitchison his wife. Brother of David Nisbett (1809-1857), *q.v. m.* Shahpur, nr. Arrah, B. & O., 12 Mar. 1834, Eliza, 3rd dau. of James Gibbon, indigo planter. (*See also* Ralph Smyth and Sir Frank Turner.) (She *re-m.* 3 Apr. 1838, William Cooke, indigo planter.)

Services: Posted Ensign to 64th N.I. 3 Jan. 1828; actg. Intr. & Qmr. do. 15 Oct. 1834. No record of active service.

Refs.: *Memoir of James Young*, ed. Lt.-Col. W. Johnston, p. 176. *A.J.* N.S. xv. 32; N.S. xix. 54. M.I. at Saugor.

NIXON, Lowther Fletcher (1758/59-1789). Lieutenant, 12th N.I. b. London 1758/59. Cadet 1778. Ensign 13 July 1779. Lieut. 5 Mar. 1781. d. Hazaribagh, B. & O., 10 Sept. 1789.
Services: Sailed for India in the *Earl Talbot* 7 Mar. 1779, aged 20. Operations against the rebel Fateh Shah in the Chapra district, B. & O., Oct. 1781; capture of mud fort at Majurah 17 Oct.; Lieut. 1/32nd N.I. Lieut. 12th Bn. Sepoys in July 1787.
Refs.: India Gazette, 3 Nov. 1781.

NIXON, Peter (d. 1784). Lieutenant, Infantry. Ensign 29 Jan. 1781. Lieut. 5 Oct. 1781. d. Midnapore, Bengal, 12 Apr. 1784.
Services: Apptd. (as Sergt. Major) Adjt. 25th Bn. Sepoys 22 Mar. 1780. Commissioned from the ranks. Leave s.c. to sea 23 Sept. 1782.

NIXON, Walter (1779-1804). Lieutenant, 21st N.I. *bapt.* St. Paul's, Dublin, 13 Sept. 1779. Cadet 1799. Arrived in India 8 Jan. 1801. Ensign 11 Oct. 1800. Lieut. 17 July 1801. d. Sikandra 24 Aug. 1804: kld. in action on the Banas R. during Monson's retreat.

Son of George Nixon and Mary his wife. (Almost certainly son of George Nixon, of Redmills, Chapelizod, co. Dublin, and Mary his wife, dau. of Capt. Theophilus Desbrisay.)
Services: Posted Ensign to 1/17th N.I. 17 Apr. 1801; transfd. to newly-raised 2/21st N.I. in 1803. Second Mahratta War; Rampura; Monson's retreat (kld.); Lieut. 2/21st N.I., A.D.C. to Monson.

NOBLE, Richard (1786-1806). Cadet, Infantry. b. Harborne, Staffs., 2 Oct. 1786. Cadet 1805. Never arrived in India. d. Dec. 1806, on his passage to India, in the wreck of the *Skelton Castle*. Struck off with effect from 5 Nov. 1806. (See note to David Allan.)

7th child of Rev. Mark Noble, F.S.A., rector of Barming, Kent (*D.N.B.*), and Sarah Pratchet his wife.

NOBLE, Samuel (1775/76-1843). Bt. Major. 2nd N.C. b. 1775/76. Cadet (Art.) (287) 1790. Admitted 2 Sept. 1791. Fireworker 9 June 1791. Transfd. to Cav. 1 July 1797. Lieut. 1 Nov. 1798. Capt. 11 Mar. 1805. Bt. Major 4 June 1814. Retired 21 Sept. 1815. d. at his residence, Moyne Hall, co. Cavan, 16 Feb. 1843, aged 67; bur. Aghalurcher churchyard, co. Fermanagh.

Formerly of Ashgrove, Belturbet, later of Moyne Hall. 2nd son of William Noble, of Donagh House, co. Fermanagh, and Elizabeth his wife, dau. of William Black. *m.* (before 1808) his cousin Prudentia, 2nd dau. of Major Jerome Noble, 28th Regt., and widow of John Powell (*d.* 1804), *q.v.* (*See also* Samuel Black.) (She died 12 Feb. 1834, aged 62.)

Services : Apptd. Cadet 16 Mar. 1791 ; sailed for India in the *Northumberland* 16 Apr. 1791. On service to Madras June 1794 ; Lieut. F. 3rd Coy. 2nd Bn. Art. Apptd. Qmr. 2nd N.C. 29 May 1800. Fur. 21 Feb. 1803 till 1 Feb. 1807, and 1811 till retirement.

Refs.: Burke's *Landed Gentry of Ireland*, p. 513, *s.n.* Noble, of Glassdrummond, co. Fermanagh. Will dated 7 Jan. 1840 ; admon. 25 Aug. 1854.

NOKE, James (*d.* 1805). Colonel, 26th N.I. Cadet 1770. Admitted 16 July 1770. Ensign 20 Nov. 1771. Lieut. 2 Aug. 1776. Capt. 24 Feb. 1781. Major 1 Mar. 1794. Lt. Col. 1 Nov. 1798. Col. 30 Sept. 1803. *d. unm.* Cawnpore 13 Nov. 1805.

Brother of Godfrey Noke, of Stratford, Essex, and of Sarah Anne, wife of Thomas Willmott, of Salisbury, atty. (*Perhaps* son of Godfrey Noke, free merchant, who was *bur.* Calcutta 5 May 1769.)

Services : Capture of Bijaigarh 1781. Capt. 4th Bengal Eur. Bn. in July 1787 ; apptd. to comd. 22nd Bn. Sepoys 8 Dec. 1794 ; Major 2/3rd N.I. in June 1798. Posted Lt. Col. to newly-raised 2/17th N.I. Jan. 1799.[1] Operations in Jumna Doab 1803 ; Lt. Col. comdg. 2/17th N.I. Apptd. Col. 17th N.I. in 1803 ; transfd. to newly-raised 26th N.I. Oct. 1804.

Refs. : Will dated 7 Oct. 1805 ; proved 13 Jan. 1806.

[1] *Note :* This Bn., which became 35th N.I. in 1824, was called after him " *Noke-ki-Paltan.*"

NOLLEKENS, John Joseph (1735-1772). Captain, Bengal Eur. Regt. *bapt.* London 29 Jan. 1735. Ensign 1758. Lieut. 8 Dec. 1758. Capt. 10 Dec. 1761. *d. unm.* Chittagong Jan. 1772.

Eldest son of Corneille François (Joseph Francis) Nollekens, " Old Nollekens," originally of Antwerp (*D.N.B.*), and Mary Anne le Sacq his wife. Brother of Joseph Nollekens, the sculptor (*D.N.B.*), and of Mary Edmund.

Services : Sailed for India in the *Ilchester* in Oct. 1753. Transfd. to Bengal Army from H.M. 39th Regt. in 1758. Campaign against the Nawabs of Bengal and Oudh 1764 ; battle of Patna (s.w.) ; Capt. Bengal Eur. Regt., comdg. Eur. Grens. Apptd. shortly after-

wards to comd. 2nd Bn. Sepoys, but was left sick at Patna, thereby missing the battle of Buxar.
Refs.: *Nollekens and his Times.* *Williams,* p. 74. *Broome,* p. 445. Will dated 5 Jan. 1772; proved 21 Feb. 1772.

NORFAR or NORFOR, John (*d.* 1783). Lieutenant, Infantry. Cadet 1772. Ensign 18 July 1776. Lieut. 6 July 1778. *d.* Calcutta 12 Apr. 1783.
Services: Transfd. from 14th Bn. Sepoys to 1/3rd Bengal Eur. Regt. 11 Aug. 1778, and was still serving with this Bn. in Oct. 1779.
Refs.: *Hickey,* iii. 209.
Note: Was one of the leading amateur actors in Calcutta, excelling especially in female parts. Mrs. Eliza Fay writes of him in Mar. 1781 that, "he has rather an effeminate appearance off the stage, yet I am told he is a very brave Officer when on service; and though always dressed as if for a ball, when he makes his appearance, is among the most alert in a moment of danger."

NORGATE, Charles (1805-1864). Lieut. Colonel. 18th N.I. *b.* Hethersett, Norfolk, 3 Dec. 1805. Cadet 1825. Arrived in India 16 May 1826. Ensign 5 Nov. 1825. Lieut. 24 July 1826. Capt. 3 Sept. 1839. Major 3 Apr. 1852. Retired 31 Jan. 1853. Hon. Lt. Col. 28 Nov. 1854. *d.* Hethersett 8 Feb. 1864.
Son of Thomas Starling Norgate and Mary Susan his wife, dau. of Benjamin Randall. *m.* Thetford 6 Jan. 1859, Sophia, 2nd dau. of Rev. William Collett, of Thetford. (She died 7 May 1904, aged 75.)
Services: Posted Ensign to 18th N.I. Actg. Adjt. 18th N.I. 15 Aug. 1827, 15 June 1829, 12 Nov. 1832; permanent do. 22 May 1833 till 29 Nov. 1839. Fur. p.a. 25 Feb. 1840 till 10 Sept. 1842. Second Sikh War; in garr. at Lahore; Capt. 18th N.I. (Medal).
Refs.: *G.M.* 1864, i. 404. *The Times,* 13 Feb. 1864.

NORRIS, Robert (1787-1863). Lieutenant. 9th N.I. *b.* Brushford, Somerset, 27 July 1787. Cadet 1804. Arrived in India 10 Dec. 1805. Ensign 19 Sept. 1805. Lieut. 20 Sept. 1805. Retired 21 Feb. 1816. *d.* at the Belvedere, Malvern Wells, 17 Feb. 1863.
Sometime of 20 Lansdowne Pl., Cheltenham. *bapt.* 31 July 1787. Son of Rev. John Norris and Ann his wife.
Services: Posted Lieut. to 2/9th N.I. in 1806. Capture of Java 1811; Lieut. 3rd Bengal Vol. Bn. (Medal). Fur. 3 Apr. 1813 till retirement.
Refs.: *The Times,* 21 Feb. 1863.

NORTH, William (*d.* 1769). Ensign. 2nd Bengal Eur. Regt. Cadet 1764. Ensign 24 Aug. 1765. Dismissed by C.M. 15 Oct. 1766. *d. unm.*; *bur.* Calcutta 1 Sept. 1769.

Son of —— North and Mary his wife, who *re-m.* —— Whittle. Nephew of John North.

Services : Sailed for India in the *Success* 17 May 1764. Posted to 2nd Bengal Eur. Regt. 21 Aug. 1765. Dismissed as one of the ringleaders of the " Batta mutiny " in May 1766.

Refs. : Broome, p. 601. Will dated 31 Aug. 1769 ; proved 1 Sept. 1769.

NORTON, Henry (1788-1850). Lieut. Colonel, 69th N.I. *b.* St. James's, Westminster, 18 Jan. 1788. Cadet 1804. Arrived in India 10 Sept. 1805. Ensign 17 Sept. 1805. Lieut. 18 Sept. 1805. Capt. 11 July 1823. Major 29 June 1835. Lt. Col. 2 Feb. 1842. *d. unm.* Mussoorie, U.P., 28 June 1850.

Son of Ann Stevens. Brother of Ann, wife of James Penfold, of Worthing.

Services : Posted Lieut. to 12th N.I. in 1806. Operations in Oudh 1808.; Lieut. 12th N.I. Actg. Adjt. 5 Coys. 1/12th N.I. 1 Apr. 1812. Transfd. to newly-raised 1/30th N.I. in 1815. Nepal War 1816 ; Makwanpur ; Lieut. 1/30th N.I., in 4th Bde. Centre Column. Actg. Adjt. Left Wing 1/30th N.I.15 Nov. 1820. Comdg. at Tanghi, B. & O., in 1819. Fur. s.c. 23 Nov. 1821 till 27 Oct. 1824. Transfd. to 60th N.I. (late 2/30th) May 1824 ; to 1st Extra Regt. (became 69th N.I.) 1825. Actg. Agent for army clothing, 1st Div., 3 Oct. 1825. Actg. Bde. Major to troops at Muttra 27 Sept. 1830. Comdg. 69th N.I. from 5 Nov. 1836 ; posted Lt. Col. to 69th N.I. 1 July 1842. Transfd. to 4th N.I. May 1845 ; to 69th N.I. 1846 ; to 20th N.I. Oct. 1848 ; to 69th N.I. Dec. 1849. Leave s.c. 1 yr. to Naini Tal 1 Sept. 1845 ; s.c. to Mussoorie 16 Sept. 1848 till death.

Refs. : I.M. 5 Oct. 1850, p. 581. Will dated Mussoorie 27 July 1850 ; proved 6 Nov. 1850. M.I. Landour.

NORTON, James (Christopher) (1793-1822). Lieutenant, 25th N.I. *b.* Bath Sept. 1793. Cadet 1809. Ensign 13 Aug. 1812. Lieut. 4 June 1815. *d.* Titalia, Bengal, 17 June 1822.

bapt. St. James's, Bath, 9 Oct. 1793. Only son of Christopher Norton, of Penkridge and Congreve, Staffs., and Janet his wife, elder dau. of Rev. Dr. George Moir.

Services : Barasat C.C. Cadet d.d. 15th N.I. 1811 ; posted Ensign to 2/25th N.I. in 1812. Nepal War 1814-15 ; Ensign 2/25th N.I., in 4th Div. Nepal War 1816 ; Chirriaghati ;

THE BENGAL ARMY, 1758-1834

Makwanpur; Lieut. 2/25th N.I., in 3rd Bde. Centre Column. Adjt. Rangpur Local Bn. 13 Dec. 1816 till death.
Refs.: Burke's *Landed Gentry*, 13th edn., p. 258, *s.n.* Moir-Byres, of Tonley, co. Aberdeen. *Families of Moir and Byres*, by A. J. Mitchell Gill (Edin., 1885), p. 33.

NOTON, Thomas (1790-1824). Captain, 45th N.I. *b.* London 30 Apr. 1790. Cadet 1804. Arrived in India 13 May 1806. Ensign 24 Apr. 1806. Lieut. 24 July 1807. Capt. 1 May 1824. *d.* 17 May 1824 : kld. in action at Ramu, Burma.
bapt. St. Bride's, London, 31 May 1790. Son of Benjamin Noton, of Fleet St., grocer, and Margaret his wife.
Services: Barasat C.C. Posted to 1/23rd N.I. in 1807. (? Operations against Dhundia Khan 1807; Lieut. 1/23rd N.I.) Fur. 12 Dec. 1813 till 1816. Third Mahratta War; Lieut. 1/23rd N.I. With 3rd Ceylon Vol. Bn. 1818-19. Actg. Adjt. 1/23rd N.I. in 1822; Intr. & Qmr. do. 1823 till May 1824. Transfd. as Capt. to 45th N.I. (late 1/23rd) May 1824. First Burma War; Chittagong 1824; disaster at Ramu (kld.); Capt. 45th N.I., comdg. the post.

NOTT, Sir William (1782-1845). Major General, G.C.B. Colonel 42nd N.I. *b.* nr. Neath, co. Glamorgan, 20 Jan. 1782. Cadet 1799. Admitted 30 Oct. 1800. Ensign 28 Aug. 1800. Lieut. 21 Feb. 1801. Capt. 16 Dec. 1814. Major 23 May 1823. Lt. Col. 2 Oct. 1824. Col. 1 Dec. 1829. Maj. Gen. 28 June 1838. *d.* Carmarthen 1 Jan. 1845.
bapt. 11 Aug. 1782. 2nd son of Charles Nott, of Shobdon, co. Hereford (of Holt, Gt. Chadfield, Wilts.), and Mary Bailey his wife, of Seething, Norfolk. *m.* 1st, Calcutta 5 Oct. 1805, Letitia, 2nd dau. of Henry Swinhoe, of Calcutta. (*See also* Edward Browne.) (She died Delhi 25 Oct. 1838.) *m.* 2nd, Lucknow 26 June 1843, Rosa Wilson, dau. of Capt. Peter Luke Dore, 3rd Buffs. (She *re-m.* Thomas Twisden Hodges, M.P., of Melbourne, Aust., and of Hempsted Park, Kent, and died 25 Aug. 1901.)
Services: See *D.N.B.* Enrolled in a Vol. Corps formed in Carmarthen shortly after the landing of the French at Fishguard in Feb. 1797. Posted Ensign to 2nd Bengal Eur. Regt. in 1800. Transfd. as Lieut. to Marine Regt. (became 20th N.I.). Served on board the *Lord Castlereagh* in comd. of a detachment serving as Marines on W. coast of Sumatra July 1804. Agent for family money 1 Aug. 1807 till 1823. Capt. 2/20th N.I.; transfd. to 1/20th N.I. 31 May 1823; to 25th N.I. (late 1/20th) May 1824.

Fur. p.a. 10 Mar. 1823 till 25 Nov. 1825. Posted Lt. Col. to 20th
N.I. 1824 ; to 43rd N.I. 1825 ; to 16th N.I. 22 Apr. 1828 ; to 38th
N.I. 7 July 1833. Posted Col. to 38th N.I. 13 Jan. 1834 ; to
42nd N.I. 11 Aug. 1838. Bdr. 2 cl. to comd. 2nd Bde. for
Afghanistan 1 Nov. 1838. First Afghan War 1838-42 ; Maj. Gen.
comdg. at Kandahar (Medal). Apptd. Envoy to King of Oudh at
Lucknow in 1843. Leave s.c. 2 yrs. to Cape 9 Feb. 1844 ; fur.
s.c. 26 July 1844. Presented with the Freedom of the City of
London (*The Times*, 13 Dec. 1844). G.C.B. 2 Dec. 1842.

Refs. : *D.N.B.* *D.I.B.* *G.M.* 1845, i. 203. *I.M.* 4 Jan. 1845,
p. 9. Will dated 9 Sept. 1843 ; admon. 24 Apr. 1845. M.I. St.
Peter's, Carmarthen. Statue at Carmarthen ; painting by B. R.
Faulkner in Council reading-room in I.O. ; portrait, J. D. Francis—
G. T. Payne, pub. by J. W. Welch, 1845.

NOWELL, Alexander (1759/60-1842). Ensign. 6th Bengal Eur.
Bn. *b.* 1759/60. Cadet 1783. Arrived in India 17 Sept. 1783.
Ensign 20 Apr. 1785. Resigned 8 Oct. 1792. *d.s.p.* Netherside,
Yorks., 17 Nov. 1842, aged 82.

Sometime of Tirhut, B. & O., subsequently of 45 Wimpole St.,
London, and Underley Park, Westmorland, which county he
represented in Parliament. 2nd son of Ralph Nowell, of Gawthorp
Hall, Lancs., and Sarah his wife, dau. of Thomas Whitaker, of
Holme, Lancs. Related to Ferdinand Charles Milner, *q.v. m.* 1st,
Dinapore 6 Jan. 1793, Maria Theresa, dau. of Thomas Kearnan, of
the City of London, sister of Thomas Kearnan and widow of Henry
Watson, *qq.v.* (*See also* Richard Humfrays or Humphreys.) (She
died London 21 Mar. 1824.) *m.* 2nd, 5 Apr. 1825, Charlotte, 4th
dau. of James Farington, of Shawe Hall, Lancs. (She died 2 Jan.
1842.)

Services : Apptd. Cadet 8 Jan. 1783 ; sailed for India in the
Pigot 11 Mar. 1783. Posted Ensign to 2nd Eur. Bn. 15 Feb. 1790.
" Quitted the army to engage in making indigo, by which he amassed
a prodigious fortune, . . ." (*Hickey.*) He returned to England
c. 1805.

Refs. : Burke's *Landed Gentry*, 13th edn., p. 1328, *s.n.* Nowell,
of Netherside, Yorks. *Hickey*, iii. 271. *N. & Q.* 6S. xii. 257.

NOWLAN or NOWLAND, James (1739/40-1780). Captain.
Infantry. *b.* in Ireland 1739/40. Cadet 1761. 2/Lieut. (Bo.)
12 Apr. 1763. Lieut. (Bengal) 10 Feb. 1764. Capt. 8 July 1766.
Resigned Sept. 1766. *bur.* Bombay 1 Aug. 1780.

Services : Sailed for India in the *True Briton* 26 May 1761,

aged 21. Transfd. from Bo. Est. 1763. Restored as junr. Capt. on Bo. Est. 17 Mar. 1779, with rank from 21 Mar. 1780. Accompanied Mark Wood, *q.v.*, in a journey overland to India via Helvoet Sluys, Brussels, through Germany, Venice, Alexandria, Cairo, Suez and Fort George, 24 Mar. to July 1779.
Refs.: Intest.; admon. (Bombay) 7 May 1781.

NUGENT, Edmund McIntosh (1810-1831). Ensign, 66th N.I. *bapt.* Chapra 14 Oct. 1810. Cadet 1826. Arrived in India 16 June 1827. Ensign 7 Feb. 1827. *d.* 25 July 1831, aged 22: drowned at sea nr. Ramri I., Lower Burma, by the capsizing of a boat, along with William Counsell, *q.v.*
2nd son of George Nugent, *q.v.*, and Mary his wife. Brother of George Nugent, *q.v.*
Services: Posted Ensign to 66th N.I. 19 June 1827. No record of active service.
Refs.: A.J. N.S. vii. 104.

NUGENT, George (*d.* 1819). Captain, 8th N.I. Fort Adjt. and Bk.Mr. at Chunar. Cadet 1799. Was already in India when apptd. Cadet. Admitted 23 Apr. 1801. Ensign 30 Sept. 1800. Lieut. 1 Jan. 1803. Capt. 16 Dec. 1814. *d.* Chunar 14 June 1819.
m. Monghyr 22 Apr. 1807, Mary, dau. of John Williams (1741/42-1809), *q.v.* (*See also* George Heard.) Father of Edmund McIntosh Nugent and George Nugent, *qq.v.* (His widow *re-m.* —— Campbell.)
Services: Posted Ensign to 2/8th N.I. 17 Apr. 1801. (? Operations in Jumna Doab 1803; Sasni; Bijaigarh; Kachaura; Lieut 2/8th N.I.) Second Mahratta War 1803-5; Laswari; Rampura; operations nr. Tonk Rampura; assault of Dhalra 21 Mar. 1805; Lieut. 2/8th N.I. Fort Adjt. at Monghyr 1807-14; Fort Adjt. and Bk.Mr. at Chunar 11 Sept. 1814 till death.
Refs.: M.I. Chunar.

NUGENT, George (1808-1842). Captain, 66th N.I. *b.* Monghyr 16 Apr. 1808. Cadet 1825. Arrived in India 7 July 1826. Ensign 15 Mar. 1826. Lieut. 27 June 1830. Capt. 7 Nov. 1840. *d.* Afghanistan 8 Sept. 1842: kld. in action at Jagdalak.
Eldest son of George Nugent, *q.v.*
Services: Ensign d.d. Rt. Wing 4th Extra Regt. 2 Aug. 1826; posted to 30th N.I. 26 Sept. 1826; exchanged to 66th N.I. 27 Oct. 1826. Actg. Intr. & Qmr. 66th N.I. 30 Dec. 1832, and 26 July

1834 ; permanent do. 18 Sept. 1834 till 5 Feb. 1841. Actg. S.A.C.G.
17 Feb. 1841. Attached to Gen. Pollock's force 23 Feb. 1842.
First Afghan War 1842 ; Mamu Khel (*Lond. Gaz.* 8 Nov. 1842);
Jagdalak (kld.) ; S.A.C.G. (ib. 24 Nov. 1842).

Refs.: M.I. in Barrackpore Church and in Afghan Memorial Church, Bombay.

*NUGENT, William (*d.* 1767). Captain, 3rd Bengal Eur. Regt. Capt. 2 Aug. 1765. *d.* Allahabad May 1767.

Son of Ignatius Nugent. *m.* (in England before 1764) Mary.

Services: Ensign (Pole's) 62nd Ft. 10 Sept. 1746 ; on the (Irish) h.p. thereof 9. Feb. 1748/9 till posted Lieut. to 20th Ft. 7 Sept. 1756, with which Regt. he served in Germany. Lieut. h.p. 119th Ft. Apptd. in England 2 Nov. 1764, Capt. on Bengal Est. ; sailed in the *Grenville* 4 Mar. 1765. Transfd. as Capt. to Bengal Army (G.O. 1 Aug. 1765) and posted to 3rd Eur. Regt. 5 Aug. 1765.

Refs.: B.M. Add. MS. 6050. Williams, p. 155*n*. Admon. (P.C.C.) 7 July 1770.

NUNN, Ebenezer (*d.* 1781/82 ?). Captain. Infantry. Cadet 1767. Ensign 1 Oct. 1767. Lieut. 24 Sept. 1769. Capt. 11 Mar. 1777. Suspended 3 Aug. 1778. (? *d. c.* 1781/82.)

Younger son of Richard Nunn, of Hill Castle, co. Wexford, and Sarah his wife, dau. of —— Haddock.

Services: Sailed for India in the *Calcutta* 31 Dec. 1766. Was serving with Nawab-Wazir of Oudh's troops in Nov. 1777. Tried by C.M. at Cawnpore Aug. 1778, and suspended till the pleasure of the Hon. Coy. be known. (See note to Alexander Mackintosh.) Sailed for England Jan. 1779.

Refs.: Burke's *Landed Gentry*, 4th edn., p. 1098, *s.n.* Nunn, of St. Margaret's, co. Wexford. Will proved in 1782, P.C. Dublin.

NUNN, James (1803-1832). Lieutenant, 7th N.I. *bapt.* Wexford 24 July 1803. Cadet 1824. Arrived in India 23 July 1825. Ensign 20 Mar. 1825. Lieut. 23 Aug. 1826. *d.* Gorakhpur, U.P., 8 Oct. 1832, aged 29.

Son of Richard Nunn and Hannah his wife. *m.* Cardoness, Paterson's R., Aust., 17 Aug. 1830, Miss Barbara Adair.

Services: Posted Ensign to 21st N.I. Siege and capture of Bhurtpore ; Ensign 21st N.I. (? d.d. 35th N.I.). Leave s.c. 18 mos. to N.S.W. 20 Dec. 1828 till 4 Feb. 1831. Exchanged to 7th N.I. 7 June 1832.

Refs.: (? Burke's *Landed Gentry*, 4th edn., *s.n.* Nunn, of St. Margaret's, co. Wexford.) *A.J.* N.S. v. 153. M.I. at Gorakhpur.

NUNN, William (*d.* 1772). Cadet, Infantry. Cadet 1772. *d.* in India 2 July 1772.

m. Charlotte.

Services : Came out to India as a Midshipman in the *Lord Holland* (Comdr. Fasham Nairn), which sailed 19 Feb. 1771. Was left sick at Calcutta 23 Feb. 1772, and was shortly afterwards apptd. a Cadet. His widow was admitted a Pensioner on Lord Clive's fund with effect from the date of her husband's death. (Court Minutes, 27 Jan. 1774.) " Mr. Nun [*sic*] having been guilty of some high and capital Offence was stolen out of England by Capt. Nairn of the *Lord Holland* Indiaman, who to gloss the matter made him a Midshipman during the passage and on his Arrival at Calcutta obtained his being appointed a Cadet. He died a few days after he had joined the Select Picquet and among his Papers the Court of Enquiry found a letter from Capt. Nairn desiring Mr. Nunn, Gentleman Cadet, to keep up his Spirits for that next year he would procure him the King's Pardon." (Mily. Cons., Ft. Wm., 17 Dec. 1772.)

NUTHALL, John (1773-1829). Lieut. Colonel Comdt., 6th L.C. *b.* Bloomsbury, London, 18 Aug. 1773. Cadet 1793. Arrived in India 25 Sept. 1794. Cornet 22 Sept. 1794. Lieut. 8 Jan. 1796. Capt. 12 Sept. 1803. Major 4 Apr. 1807. Lt. Col. (4 June 1813) 25 May 1816. Lt. Col. Comdt. 1 May 1824. *d.* New Lodge, Reigate, Surrey, 26 Mar. 1829.

bapt. St. George's, Bloomsbury, 25 Aug. 1773. Son of Thomas Nuthall and Mary his wife. *m.* Oct. 1817, Myra, 2nd dau. of Robert Nuthall, of Earlswood, Reigate, and sister of Robert Centlivre Nuthall, *q.v.* (She died 28 May 1885, aged 87.) His dau. *m.* Andrew Macdougall, *q.v.*

Services : Apptd. Cadet 19 Feb. 1794 ; sailed for India in the *Rose* 2 May 1794. Posted Ensign to 6th Eur. Bn. 8 Nov. 1794. Capt. Lt. 3rd N.C. 13 Nov. 1800. Second Mahratta War 1803-6 ; battle of Delhi ; Laswari ; Rampura ; battle of Deig ; pursuit of Holkar ; Capt. 3rd N.C. Operations against Dhundia Khan 1807 ; Komona ; Ganauri ; Capt. comdg. 3rd N.C. Operations in Bundelkhand against Lachman Dawa 1809 ; Rajaoli ; Ajaigarh ; Major 3rd N.C. Posted Lt. Col. to 5th N.C. May 1816. Fur. 31 Dec. 1816 till 1819, and 27 Dec. 1821 till death. Posted as Lt. Col. Comdt. to 6th L.C. May 1824.

Refs. : Pester, *passim.* *A.J.* xxvii. 522. *G.M.* 1829, i. 381.

NUTHALL, Robert Centlivre (1808-1836). Lieutenant, 19th N.I. *b.* Hackney, Middlesex, 4 Apr. 1808. Cadet 1825. Arrived in India 10 Mar. 1826. Ensign 25 Sept. 1825. Lieut. 25 May 1826. *d.* Puri, B. & O., 23 July 1836.

bapt. St. John at Hackney 13 May 1808. 3rd son of Robert Nuthall, of Earlswood, transfer accountant at E.I. House, and Mary Grace Butterworth his wife. Brother of Thomas John Nuthall, *q.v.*, and of the wife of John Nuthall, *q.v. m.* (before 1828) ? His dau. *m.* William Mills Tritton, *q.v.*

Services: Posted Ensign to 19th N.I. Rising in Cuttack July 1836 ; Lieut. 19th N.I.

Refs.: A.J. N.S. xxii. 118. Will dated 20 Oct. 1834 ; proved 24 Oct. 1836. M.I. at Puri.

NUTHALL, Thomas John (1803-1880). Major General. 71st N.I. Dy. Comy. Gen. *b.* Hackney 5 Mar. 1803. Cadet 1823. Arrived in India 12 June 1824. Ensign 7 Jan. 1824. Lieut. 27 Dec. 1824. Capt. 1 Mar. 1835. Major 8 Oct. 1850. Lt. Col. 17 Apr. 1856. Col. 18 Mar. 1859. Retired 21 Jan. 1859. Hon. Maj. Gen. 21 Jan. 1859. *d.* 1 Kent Terr., Torquay, 21 Dec. 1880.

bapt. St. John at Hackney 1 Apr. 1803. 2nd son of Robert Nuthall and Mary Grace his wife. Brother of Robert Centlivre Nuthall, *q.v.*, and grandson of Thomas Nuthall *(D.N.B.). m.* 1st, Calcutta 3 Oct. 1829, Miss Eliza Tate. (She died Cawnpore 4 Sept. 1848.) *m.* 2nd, Lahore 10 May 1852, Margaret Mackenzie, dau. of Henry Brooks. (She died 1870.)

Services: Posted Ensign to 46th N.I. First Burma War ; Assam 1824-5 ; Rangpur ; Lieut. 46th N.I. (India medal). Leave p.a. 12 mos. to Calcutta 20 May 1829. S.A.C.G. 4 June 1833, and passed the remainder of his service in the Comst. Dept. Attached to Staff of Army of the Indus as D.A.C.G. in executive charge of H.Q. 13 Sept. 1838. D.A.C.G. 2 cl. 9 Oct. 1838 ; 1 cl. 20 Dec. 1842 ; A.C.G. 2 cl. 10 Jan. 1845 ; 1 cl. 13 Sept. 1847 ; Dy. Comy. Gen. 9 Nov. 1852 till retirement. Offg. Comy. Gen. 3 Mar. 1857. Posted Lt. Col. to 50th N.I. July 1856 ; transfd. to 71st N.I. in 1858. Fur. p.a. Feb. 1858 till retirement. Employed in 1843 in compiling a Code of Comst. Regulations.

Refs.: The Times, 25 Dec. 1880.

NUTTALL, Adam *(d.* 1787). Fireworker, Artillery. (243) Cadet 1783. Fireworker 1 Jan. 1785. *d.* 22 May 1787 : lost at sea in the *Ganges* in Balasore Roads.

Services: Lieut. E. Regt. Middlesex Mil. 13 Aug. 1779. Apptd. Cadet 25 Feb. 1783 ; sailed for India in the *Atlas* 11 Mar. 1783. Was on sick leave when his death occurred.

www.ingramcontent.com/pod-product-compliance
Lightning Source LLC
Chambersburg PA
CBHW061926220426
4366CB00012B/1819